GOLDEN GATE GARDENING

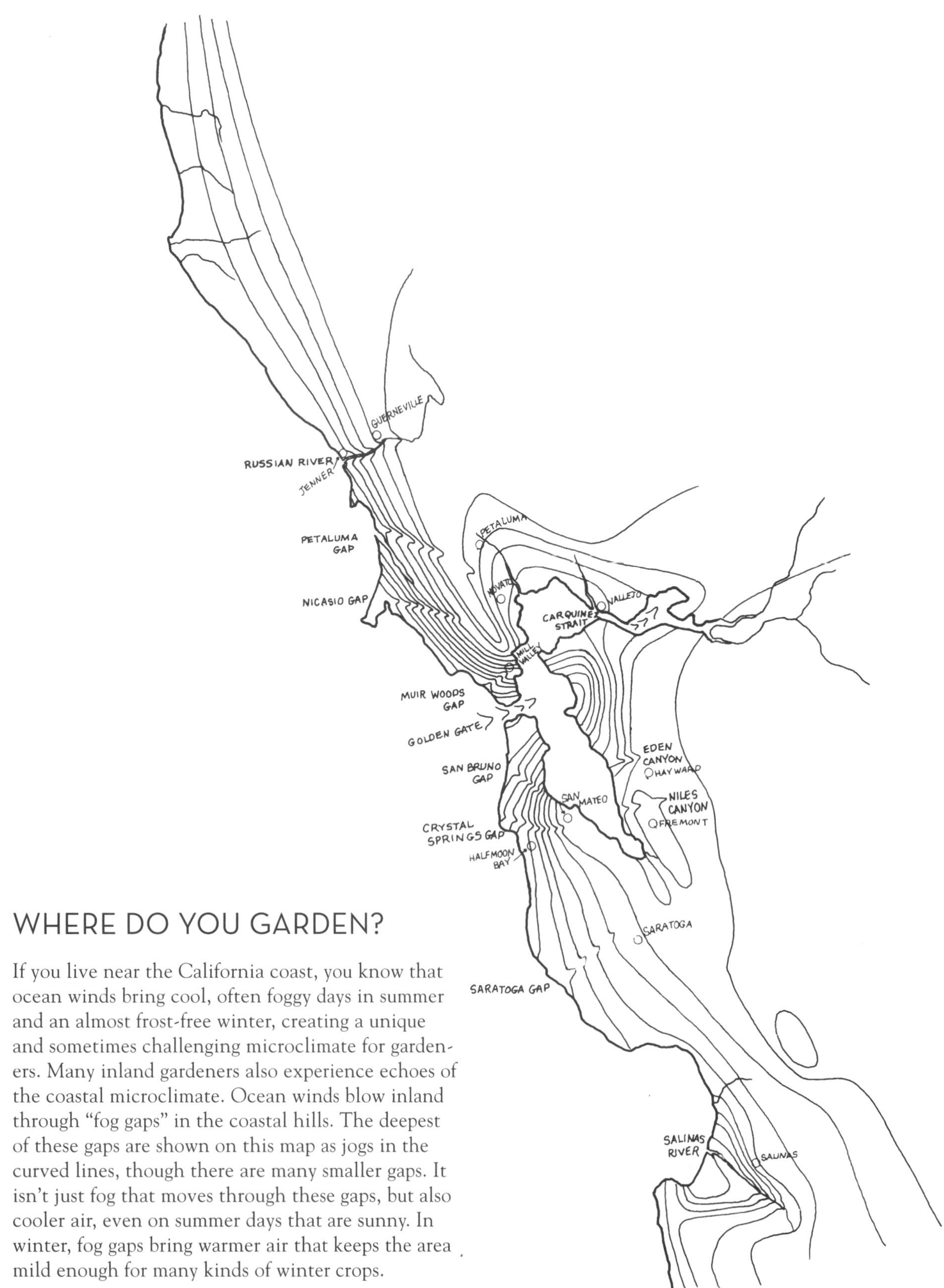

WHERE DO YOU GARDEN?

If you live near the California coast, you know that ocean winds bring cool, often foggy days in summer and an almost frost-free winter, creating a unique and sometimes challenging microclimate for gardeners. Many inland gardeners also experience echoes of the coastal microclimate. Ocean winds blow inland through "fog gaps" in the coastal hills. The deepest of these gaps are shown on this map as jogs in the curved lines, though there are many smaller gaps. It isn't just fog that moves through these gaps, but also cooler air, even on summer days that are sunny. In winter, fog gaps bring warmer air that keeps the area mild enough for many kinds of winter crops.

3RD EDITION

GOLDEN GATE GARDENING

The Complete Guide to Year-Round Food Gardening in the SAN FRANCISCO BAY AREA and COASTAL CALIFORNIA

Pam Peirce

SASQUATCH BOOKS
SEATTLE

For my parents,
Sheldon James Peirce and Lynton Wicks Peirce,
who taught me to think, to garden, and to dream big dreams.

Copyright © 1993, 1998, 2002, 2010 by Pam Peirce
All rights reserved. No portion of this book may be reproduced or utilized in any form, or by any electronic, mechanical, or other means, without the prior written permission of the publisher.

Originally published in 1993 by agAccess, Davis, California, in cooperation with Riverhouse Nursery, Sacramento, California.
Second edition published in 1998 by Sasquatch Books, Seattle.
Revised second edition published in 2002 by Sasquatch Books, Seattle.

Printed in the United States of America
Published by Sasquatch Books

18 17 15 14 13 15 14 13 12 11 10 9 8 7 6 5 4

Cover illustrations: Linda Holt Ayriss / Photodisc ® / Getty Images ®
Cover design: Rosebud Eustace
Interior design revision: Rosebud Eustace
Interior composition: Emily Ford
Interior illustrations and maps: Mimi Osborne

Library of Congress Cataloging-in-Publication Data

Peirce, Pam.
Golden Gate gardening : the complete guide to year-round food gardening in the San Francisco Bay area and coastal California / Pam Peirce. — 3rd ed.
p. cm.
Second ed. published 1998.
Includes index.
ISBN-13: 978-1-57061-617-4
ISBN-10: 1-57061-617-5
1. Vegetable gardening—California—San Francisco Bay Area. 2. Vegetable gardening—California—Pacific Coast. 3. Gardening—California—San Francisco Bay Area. 4. Gardening—California—Pacific Coast. I. Title. II. Title: Complete guide to year-round food gardening in the San Francisco Bay area and coastal California.
SB321.5.C2P45 2010
635.09794'6—dc22
2009047389

Sasquatch Books
1904 Third Avenue, Suite 710
Seattle, WA 98101
(206) 467-4300
www.sasquatchbooks.com
custserv@sasquatchbooks.com

Table of Contents

Acknowledgments

The idea for this book took root after I saw Binda Colebrook's book *Winter Gardening in the Maritime Northwest* (Sasquatch Books). I was able to adapt her planting dates to my winter garden, and doing so made me see how useful a local book could be.

Since that time, many people have inspired and helped me to get this book from idea to paper and print.

Early on, I told Sue Reid, who coordinated the city-sponsored Community Gardening Program in San Francisco, of my plans to write a local book, and her close questioning helped me see what I needed to know and to form a plan of both garden and library research.

Kathy Van Velsor, past director of the San Francisco Ecology Center, first suggested that I teach vegetable gardening. The material I developed for those first four-week classes lies at the core of this book.

Jane Radcliffe and the members of her community college writing workshop listened to my first attempts to put the words for this book on paper, and their advice and encouragement nurtured the seedling.

Leonard Rifas drafted more accessible versions of the climate maps that appeared in *Publications in Geography* and redrew some of my planting charts. This material helped in the drawing of the final versions as they appear in this book.

Doug Brentlinger and Mark Zielenski offered both emergency and (in calmer times) ongoing computer support.

Many experts kindly accepted my requests for information and/or read portions of the manuscript for accuracy. Following are their names and the subjects in which they provided expertise:

Laura Brainin-Rodriguez, nutritionist, Stanford University Student Health Center (nutrition); Larry Costello, Cooperative Extension, San Mateo County (soils); Jeff Cox, writer for *Organic Gardening* magazine (various subjects); Barbara Emerson, weed specialist (weeds); Denise Erickson, Pier 39 (cutting flowers); Nancy Garrison, Cooperative Extension, Santa Clara County (various subjects); Dr. Ken Hagen, Division of Biological Control, U.C. Berkeley (beneficial insects); Dr. Ann King, Cooperative Extension, San Mateo County (various subjects); Gordon Lane, pest control advisor (pesticides and pest control); Dr. Rex Marsh, Department of Wildlife and Fisheries Biology, U.C. Davis (vertebrate pests); Doria Mueller, Pesticide Education and Action Project (pesticides); E. Jan Null, meteorologist, National Weather Service (weather and climate); Chester Prince, U.C. Cooperative Extension, San Francisco (various topics); Dr. Robert Raabe, Department of Plant Pathology, U.C. Berkeley (pest chapter); Dr. Charles Turner, weed specialist (weed list); Dr. Jim Vlamis, U.C. Berkeley (soils); Ron Voss, Department of Vegetable Crops, U.C. Davis (onions); Norm Welch, U.C. Cooperative Extension, Watsonville (strawberries); and Dr. Becky Westerdahl, Department of Nematology, U.C. Davis (nematodes). I am most grateful for the time and information provided by all of these experts, although I, of course, take final responsibility for the accuracy of all of the information in this book.

In addition, I would like to thank Barbara Pitschel, head librarian of the Helen Crocker Russell Library of Horticulture of the San Francisco Botanical Garden Society for her cheerful support and thorough reference work during my years of research.

Many people, gardening in different microclimates within the fog-affected coastal California area, contributed to this book by sharing their experiences with me either through long conversations or by returning questionnaires. They include: Jeff Brown, The Farm; Pat Casio, Dogpatch Community Garden; Diana Colby, Alice Street Garden; Robert Conover; Rosalind Creasy; Ed Dierauf, Argonne Community Garden; Kristina Elmstrom; David Gilden; Bill Grimes, California Rare Fruit Growers; John Hooper, Sonoma Antique Apple Nursery; Wendy Johnson and Peter Rudnick, Green Gulch Farm; Caroline Morrison, Hooker Alley Community Garden; Liz Milazzo, Dearborn Community Garden; Robin Parer, Hooker Alley Community Garden; Mimi Osborne, Fort Mason Community Garden; Jean Scherr, Argonne Community Garden;

Jake Sigg, California Native Plant Society; and Tree, Kaliflower Garden. Thanks also to the community gardeners of Dearborn Garden, to all of my gardening class students, and to everyone who asked so many great gardening questions.

In addition, I would like to thank the many volunteers who helped with the San Francisco tomato trials of 1986–88. These include Anthony Del Nuovocared, Eric Engles, Megan Evart, Eleanor Ewing, Richard Fashbinder, Lotta Garrity, Tanya Harjan, Bernadette McAnulty, Pilar Mejia, Eileen Neustadt, Richard Peltier, Dannette Peltier, Michael Peltier, Amy Peltier, Rosanna Scott, Maya Slocum, John Sanroma, Mary Sullivan, and Pat Wynne.

There are also many people who are unaware of how much they helped with this book, because I learned by watching their gardens grow. Many thanks to all of the community gardeners of San Francisco whose gardens, the unsuccessful as well as the successful ones, taught me more about what doesn't work, and what does, than I could ever learn from my garden alone.

Thanks to Maria-Marta Herrara for many evenings of delightful conversation over the tasting of garden foods. Also thanks for letting me start unruly crops that would take over her tiny backyard, and then for being able to laugh.

Thanks to Iris Goldman for her moral and material support during the too-long process of getting this book published.

Thanks to Mimi Osborne, for patience and precision in translating my requests into the drawings that illustrate this book.

I would like to thank the following people for help in editing the first edition of the book:

Jo Brownold, who read the first finished chapters and called them excellent; David Goldberg, who read it all and gave good advice; Susan Lang, who edited the first eleven chapters with a gardener's eye; and Karen Van Epen of agAccess, who pulled the whole book together. For proofreading the manuscript, thanks to Ellen Zagory. For turning the manuscript into the finished book: Timothy Rice, Clara Maria Okrongly, and Dave Reagan.

Special thanks to Morrie Camhi, who helped the book out of publishing limbo, and to Daniel Reidy, who helped to negotiate its rescue. And thanks to AgAccess, for producing the first edition.

For help with the second edition, thanks to the following experts: Barri Bonapart, Attorney (tree law), Doug Heath of Seminis Seeds (tomatoes), Carolyn Harrison of Sonoma Antique Apple Nursery (fruit), Adam Kushner of Pesticide Action Network of North America (pesticides), Steve Temple of the Cooperative Extension (beans), Mary Risely of Tante Marie's Cooking School in San Francisco, and Matt Sartwell of the bookstore Kitchen Arts and Letters in New York City (choosing recent cookbooks for the Suggested Reading list).

I would also like to thank Christina Faulkenburg for checking all of the websites to make sure the addresses were correct.

Thanks to Gary Luke and Sasquatch Books for publishing the second edition of *Golden Gate Gardening*; to Joan Gregory, who ably saw it through production; and to Patrick Barber, typesetter and gardener, for his skill and enthusiasm.

For this third edition, I would like to thank Christina Johnson for researching current seed and plant sources for recommended varieties, arborist Lisa Gerhard for researching fruit varieties, City College Horticulture Professor Malcolm Hillan for advice on soil and water chapter revisions, and City College Nursery Specialist Pat Morgan for help updating pesticide ingredient information. For help with inland planting calendars, thank you to Santa Clara County Master Gardener Program Coordinator Carol Frost; to Master Gardeners Bracey Tiede, Nancy Garrison, Karen Schaffer, and Susan Zaslaw; and to Contra Costa County independent garden teacher Sue Phalen.

Thank you again to Gary Luke and Sasquatch Books for publishing a third edition, as well as to editor Terence Maikels, copy editor Kathleen Atkins, project editor Rachelle Longé, designer Emily Ford, and production manager Liza Brice-Dahmen for ably bringing the book into being.

And, of course, I continue to be grateful to my husband, David Goldberg, for good advice as well as for his patience and support while I am engrossed in the creation of a book.

About This New Edition

You are holding in your hands a book that has helped many people grow food in our California climates. I wrote the first edition after realizing that we live in a complex of microclimates quite different from anywhere else in the country. National gardening books will tell you how to grow food somewhere in the United States, but you just can't grow food "somewhere"—you grow food in a particular place. So I created this book to tell you what to do in your garden and when to do it, particularly for the mild winter parts of central and northern California.

Though *Golden Gate Gardening* is a regional gardening book, it is also a complete gardening book. It covers soil preparation, composting, watering, starting from seed, management of pests, and attracting beneficial creatures—all the topics you need to understand to make your food garden successful. It also covers culinary herbs, edible flowers, and fruit trees and shrubs; there's even a regional list of flowers for cutting.

As this third edition is published, *Golden Gate Gardening* is seventeen years old. It has served some readers for half a lifetime. One reader told me he used it to learn gardening while he was in college, living with several roommates, and is using it now to hone his gardening skills while he and his wife raise a family in their own home. The book also continues to be popular with both individual gardeners and gardening classes. People tell me it has become a classic. So why change it to prepare a new edition?

Can you improve on a classic? You bet you can. Here are three major reasons why this edition is better than the last. First, I have modified the book to make it as useful to inland gardeners of our region, whose gardens fog rarely reaches, as it is for those who actually hear the foghorns. Second, because the world is constantly changing, I have carefully updated all the information in the book, from vegetable varieties to pest management strategies. Third, I have learned more about how best to do some gardening tasks, and about mistakes I see many gardeners making. Let me tell you more about these updated, new, and expanded features.

If you live anywhere in California affected by the ocean fog, you may have come to depend on *Golden Gate Gardening* for precise gardening directions, and those directions remain intact in this edition. If you live farther inland, you may have thought the book didn't apply to you. However, for this edition, I have expanded the text to include what you need to know to apply the basic gardening information as far inland as central Contra Costa County or Santa Clara County, and in comparable regions. In addition, I've included two new planting calendars, one for Walnut Creek, the other for San Jose (in Appendix III), to guide you through a year-round planting schedule. Finally, I've revised the fruit chapter, adding to it to include instructions and varieties that are appropriate inland as well as in coastal locations.

Who would think so much could change in California gardening in so short a time? Yet since the last edition was released just ten years ago, so much has changed. Starting with vegetables, there are new pest-resistant varieties as well as newly available heirlooms that you will want to know about. I've added information on them, and told you where you can buy them.

Pest management concepts also continue to develop. Live trapping is no longer recommended for dealing with pest mammals, so I have explained new strategies for reducing wildlife damage. Flowers to attract beneficial insects have become the new companion plantings, so I've included a list of such plants—including ones that specifically attract native California bees. And the list of chemicals available for managing snails, slugs, insects, and diseases continues to evolve, with the introduction of several new ones with much lower potential for harm to health and the environment.

Finally, I've updated all of the resources and added many new ones: places to obtain seeds, garden supplies, fruit trees and shrubs, gardening education and experience, and more. Nearly all of these resources are now reachable by their websites, which you will find in Appendices VI and VII. And though you will find much to read on those websites, the Suggested Reading list (Appendix VIII) has also been updated to include many excellent new books that will add immensely to your understanding of gardening and many related issues. I've also included recent books on food in America that have become a particularly welcome addition to my bookshelf.

And what else have I learned recently that I'm passing on to you? I've learned to grow several new crops as well as new ways to use the old ones. A few new weeds have shown up in our area, too, and you will learn to identify and combat them. I also learned since the last edition of this book that gardeners are confused by all the bags of soil-like stuff in the nursery. The labels don't always explain the purpose of what's in the bags, so I've tried to clear up the confusion (see pages 75–77). And I have learned more about cooking from a garden. I've added more recipes, especially for cool-preferring crops that are easier to grow around here than in cold winter regions, and I've completely rewritten Chapter 16 (A Garden-Based Cuisine) to help you enjoy the process of eating what you grow.

It is my wish that this book assist you in successful gardening in any of the particular microclimates of our region. May your gardening efforts give you a wonderful sense of accomplishment, many delicious meals, and a strong, flexible body. May they add to your stock of patience, persistence, and thrift, and to your understanding of our dependence upon the earth and upon each other.

On Writing About Gardening

The way I garden is based on long experience, on familiarity with the fabric of soil and plant. To write about how to garden, I must begin by describing the threads and how they are woven. But describing the warp and weft is not the same as seeing the pattern whole.

I cannot teach the fabric of gardening through writing. Only gardening can teach that. But I can add to my description of the threads a sketch of what the fabric looks like to me. I want those who read to know that there is a fabric to discover: a richness and a sense of wholeness and well-being beyond the textbook list of what to plant where.

Although I use the discoveries of science in the garden, I do not think in the rational and linear way of the scientist all the while I garden. There is a continuity between my garden and that of the earliest gardeners. The Mexican milpa had no tidy rows. It was a tangle of vines climbing trees, of vegetables jumbled together.

And nobody wrote about how to garden at first. How did people learn to garden? From each other. From parents. People gardened in families, next to other families. Someone would try something new to see if it would make more of some food. If it worked, they'd do it again and others would copy.

....

But after a few years we might slip and not do it just the same way. There would be no record. So we might make up songs to help ourselves remember and to teach the children. (It is the same thing.) Then we would go into the garden or the fields and sing together while we worked. Sometimes there would be a different song for each stage of the growing. Besides teaching, it would make us feel happy and close to sing together as we watched our food plants grow.

At first everyone would sing together or, if the women were the gardeners, we the women would sing. But eventually the ways would become old and perfected and not so likely to be lost. Then song leaders might develop, who walked in the gardens and fields and did the singing. We would still love to listen to the old songs, which would remind us of the old magical feeling about how our ancestors discovered the way to grow plants to feed the people.

....

Now writing often takes the place of the community, of sharing knowledge directly with the people whose lives I share. When I cannot sing with my people, I write.

Pam Peirce
San Francisco

ONE

Year-Round Bounty

ES, WE CAN GARDEN ALL YEAR long in San Francisco and the nearby coastal regions of California. In fact, this favored climate often extends thirty or more miles inland. Whereas most other parts of the country have a single growing season from spring to fall, we can enjoy twelve full months of productive and rewarding gardening. There are crops to plant and harvests to enjoy every month of the year.

In much of the continental United States, winter is a time to shovel snow and read seed catalogs while dreaming of the next summer's bounty. But here, winter days are likely to find us out in our gardens, maybe even in shirtsleeves, picking tender salad greens, cutting stately artichoke buds, and making sure our pea vines are finding the trellis. And because our winter chill is so brief, we can begin our "spring" gardens long before the calendar tells us that spring has begun. By April or May, when gardeners in colder climates are just beginning to dig and plant, we are already harvesting crops planted in February—pulling sweet spring carrots and cutting succulent stems of broccoli. As we move into summer, gardeners in cool-summer parts of our region have another advantage. Crops that are impossible to grow in hot summers in most of the nation produce harvests for us throughout the summer. We can pick mild-flavored salad greens and cut creamy heads of cauliflower all summer long. In the areas closest to the coast, summer gardens may even include peas, a crop that must be relegated to early spring and fall in where summers are hotter.

But, of course, our climate is not a perfect one for gardening. In areas near the coast, the biggest challenge is growing crops that require more sunshine and heat than cool, often foggy summers provide. Unfortunately, these crops include some that most gardeners yearn to grow. Every year seed catalogs entice us with photographs of large plump tomatoes, eggplants, melons, and peppers—but when we try to grow these crops, we are often disappointed. Not only is the harvest smaller than promised, but each fruit is often smaller as well. We become aware that, for these crops, our coastal summers do not measure up.

In hottest summer parts of the region, the challenge is the opposite, forcing us to notice that even many heat-loving crops will sulk when the temperature reaches into the 90s F. Strawberries and beans slow down until moderate temperatures return. Here we plant summer crops where afternoon shade will offer some relief and make sure our plants do not lack for water. Water-saving techniques, important throughout California, are particularly so where summers are scorching.

Gardening in the San Francisco Bay Area and along the coastal regions from Mendocino to Monterey Bay is largely rewarding, even though some aspects of it may be frustrating. This book will help you to take advantage of the region's opportunities and minimize its drawbacks. Here, season by season, is what you should expect.

SUMMER AND EARLY FALL

The most salient feature of our Mediterranean-climate summers is the lack of rainfall. When it isn't foggy, we live under clear, blue summer skies. In most places, our region's summers are also windy.

Tomatoes and peas in a cool summer garden. The tomato on the right is warmed by a Wall O' Water.

The wind blows mainly from the west or northwest, coming in from the ocean. Hills and low coastal mountains block some of the wind, but closer to the ocean, gardens are windier and the wind is also colder. In coastal areas, June, July, and August are known for blustery days and brisk nights. Highs are often only in the 60s or 70s F, and lows in the 50s or even the 40s.

The main reason for cool coastal summers is this chill wind, but the wind also often carries fog. The amount of summer fog varies day by day throughout the region, sometimes reaching far inland, other times clearing entirely or just fringing the coast. Fogginess varies from one side of a hill to another, and from neighborhood to neighborhood. Some areas are sunnier, but with a cooling effect from the ocean breeze; in others, foggy days can outnumber sunny ones. There, cottony fog banks billow over the hills, fog fingers slide down the valleys, high fogs blot out the sun, and low fogs shroud gardens.

While hot summers have their drawbacks, coastal summers are unlike any others in the nation. The summers are long, in that they are not bounded by frosts, but the cold and the fog-reduced light play havoc with warm season crops, such as tomatoes, corn, peppers, eggplants, and melons.

Nothing contributes more to the reputation of the coastal microclimates than the poor performance of tomatoes. Actually, among the warm-season crops, tomatoes are among the better adapted, ripening at least some fruit in all but the most severe microclimates. However, the plants often form fruit later than expected and ripen it late. Tomatoes that do ripen tend to be smaller and of poorer quality than those grown in warmer climates. Corn, peppers, eggplants, and melons are progressively less tolerant of cool summers.

That's the bad news.

The good news is that no matter your garden's summer microclimate, you can considerably improve your chances by choosing warm-season crop varieties developed to cope with cool summers and by planting them in protected areas of your garden. You may not find an eggplant variety that will bear in profusion in sight of the ocean, but you can find early corn varieties that will bear in sunnier parts of San Francisco. And inland gardeners who choose early melon varieties and use soil warming techniques in spring report success.

The best news for those of us beset by fog and cold summer nights is that there are many vegetables that do not just tolerate these conditions, but actually thrive in them. These include all of the cool-season crops, such as beets, broccoli, carrots, lettuce, peas, and potatoes. In most other parts of the country, gardeners have to squeeze these crops in during the early spring, before the summer heat hits, or just early enough to miss the first autumn frost. These crops will gladly, even enthusiastically, grow throughout a cool and foggy summer.

If you live where summers are coolest, make cool-season crops the backbone of your summer garden. But even here, you won't be limited entirely to cool-season crops. Some warm-season vegetables, such as scarlet runner beans and zucchini, brave the fog. Pumpkins, winter squash, bush and pole beans, cucumbers, and sunflowers tolerate almost as much fog. If you have any success growing bush beans, zucchini, or short-season corn, you can probably plant these crops more than once during a summer. In one of San Francisco's warmer neighborhoods, I can plant successive crops of corn every month from the middle of April to the middle of July and harvest sweet corn on the cob from the middle of July to the middle of October.

In July or August, as you are sowing your last successive plantings of warm-season crops, you can also plant some of the best crops for fall and winter harvests. Carrots, beets, and kohlrabi should be seeded, and broccoli and celery seedlings transplanted. All of these crops will grow quickly in late summer, then more slowly as the days shorten. In very foggy neighborhoods, midsummer plantings should be in the ground by July 15; in favored locations in Santa Clara county, crops planted in August or even as late as October may still mature before winter.

Even during the foggiest of summers, the sun will occasionally peek through. Fog often spreads and retreats in roughly weekly cycles, separated by one or more days of sunshine. Once in a while, these sunny days heat up as warmer air from the Central Valley temporarily replaces the cold sea breeze. The temperature reaches the high eighties or beyond, and everyone who can do so heads for the coolness of the beach. When this happens our gardens, accustomed to foggy days, may wilt temporarily in the unusual heat. The whole garden, and especially midsummer seedbeds, will need extra water.

At the very end of summer and into early fall, the fog usually relents. September and early October often mark the longest stretch of warm, sunny days. Summer and early fall harvests can be spectacularly large and varied, and the combination of warm- and cool-season crops lets you work wonders in the kitchen. Every time I venture into my garden, I return with a huge basket filled with ripe, richly colored, fragrant vegetables and herbs. I whirl bright green, satiny basil leaves and plump, piquant garlic cloves into a savory pesto sauce or make a colorful pasta primavera sauce with tender green beans and yellow summer squash. I make coleslaw and green salads with all manner of fresh salad vegetables. From my small corn patch, I harvest ears that are sweeter than any in the grocery stores, and I make memorable shortcakes from sweet ever-bearing strawberries. In late summer, I simmer a hearty minestrone made with flavorful homegrown scarlet runner beans, zucchini, potatoes, carrots, and herbs, adding fresh homemade tomato sauce if I have enough tomatoes.

And, if the bounty of vegetables and herbs were not enough, there are the flowers. Summer and early fall offer a profusion of flowers for bouquets. There are blossoms of every hue—yellow, orange, white, and purple cosmos; pink, peach, and red godetias; pink, blue, and purple cornflowers—to decorate the harvest table. Flowers become part of the menu as well. I fry delicate squash blossoms, serve nasturtium hors d'oeuvres, and use violas to accent a fruit salad.

The bounty continues well into fall. One day, as I harvest, I notice that the garden looks unkempt and overgrown, with flowers and vegetables reaching over each other in a lanky tangle. Summer vegetables either look ragged or have begun to die back. The summer garden has given its all, but fortunately the gardening year does not stop then.

FALL AND WINTER

If the first heavy rains of fall are late, you could be harvesting your last summer flowers and vegetables in the middle of November or even later. Sooner or later, however, cold days with heavy rains will kill cucumbers, squash, tomatoes, and other summer sojourners. Now is the time to pull out the decaying plants. Relish the last cucumber of summer; harvest the remaining tomatoes from their blackened vines and let them ripen indoors or use them green. Pick over flowers for the last bouquet of summer, and cover any unused garden areas with a winter mulch.

As early fall turns into a typically wet and chilly winter, your garden will be far from barren. Those beets and carrots you planted in July or August will be nearly mature, and they will wait in the ground until you are ready for them. Summer-planted kohlrabi and radicchio will add interest to your winter meals. As the weather turns cool, brussels sprout plants begin to bear their knobby sprouts. Broccoli may form heads in fall or, in the case of some varieties, in February or March. Your winter harvest can also include leeks, Swiss chard, and sunchokes planted as long ago as the previous January.

Some crops can be planted into late fall. You need only plant on a couple of days in October or November to collect great harvest dividends later. Now is the best time to plant two of the crops best suited to the area: garlic and artichoke. November is also a good time to plant peas and a less familiar winter legume, the fava bean. Onion sets (planted for harvest as green onions) and seedling lettuce plants are also worth growing through the winter months.

Rainfall, like fog, varies from place to place and from one year to the next. Kentfield in Marin County receives 46 inches of rain in a season, whereas nearby San Francisco averages only 23 inches. Within San Francisco, rainfall is heaviest nearest the ocean and on the south and west sides of hills. The entire region experiences many winters of continuously waterlogged soil as well as periodic bouts with drought. But, generally, we rarely need to water our gardens between late October and the end of March.

Although we get our share of soggy winters, heavy frosts are rare. Many San Francisco winters pass with no recorded freezing temperatures at all; other winters may bring one or two light frosts, usually in December or January. Areas farther from the ocean or where high hills stand between your garden and the ocean are more likely to experience frosty nights from November through March. Gardens in low-lying areas and on the shady, north side of hills and mountains are also more likely to receive frost.

Still, these tend to be frosts, not freezes, meaning that the soil is not frozen and tender roots are not killed. Many cool-season vegetables can withstand considerable frost. In fact, inland gardeners will be glad to know that most of the cool-season crops can stand up to typical frosts of the inland part of our region. A few, such as peas, potatoes, and artichokes, may need protection on the coldest nights, but most will survive in style. It would take colder winters than happen in Walnut Creek or Mountain View to kill a leek or a broccoli plant, so inland residents can also enjoy year-round harvests.

During most years, my fall harvest includes the last of summer's treats. I savor the last crisp cucumber in a spicy Indian cucumber salad and the last green beans and zucchini in a cheesy omelet, and I pick the remaining green tomatoes to slice and fry. Soon my attention turns to the gifts of winter.

I steam fresh, sweet brussels sprouts to dip in mayonnaise mixed with soy sauce, stir-fry pungent mustard greens with tofu and noodles, and warm up December evenings with steaming potato leek soup. My winter salads combine lettuce with spinach, chicory, sorrel, grated carrots, and gleanings of wild greens. Sunchokes may add crunch to salads or, seasoned with garden herbs, make a salad by themselves.

There are even flowers for bouquets—not many, but a few—that bloom into the colder months. Sweet-scented stock, colorful pansies, and sunny calendulas are winter standbys; calla lilies and forget-me-nots number among the flowers blooming by January. Often, a few plants of some summer flower will survive and bloom through the winter chill. I take particular joy in culling a small bouquet from the flowers that do appear in winter, often finding enough of them only after a careful search and valuing them more for their rarity.

SPRING

By February, the days become noticeably longer and warmer. Delicate, pink plum blossoms and bright yellow daffodils assure us that winter is ending. The air smells sweet. We are rooting about for the last of winter's sweet carrots and beets. Overwintering broccoli varieties are forming their dark green or vibrant chartreuse heads. Artichokes are responding to the warmth and lengthening days by forming promising buds, nestled deep in pale, lacy leaves. Fall-planted peas are so sweet that they beg to be eaten right from the vine. Greens, from celery to lettuce, are more tender and crisp than at any other time of year. In cold-winter climates, the period from February to April is sometimes called the "hunger gap." Our year-round gardens close that gap, and close it deliciously.

February marks the start of the early spring planting season. Carrots, radishes, onions, broccoli, cabbage, lettuce, Swiss chard, potatoes, and other cool-season vegetables thrive in the cool temperatures, high humidity, and increasing sunlight. The climate will vary from year to year, during dry years allowing you to get a crop or two planted in January and during exceptionally wet years forcing you to delay planting until the end of March. But, generally, you can plant all kinds of cool-season spring crops after the middle of February, whenever the soil is dry enough.

During very warm springs, or with careful protection, tomatoes and zucchini can be planted as early as February. Early plantings of these summer crops are not without risk. If late rains are heavy, darkening the days and keeping the soil from warming, early growth will be slow.

All February plantings are vulnerable to late winter storms, which are especially likely to bring hail. Icy pellets may damage seedlings, and they will leave their mark on older plants. Look for small white dots on the tops of leaves, indicating where hailstones have killed the surface cells.

Gradually you will see more rainbows than rain, with spectacular cloud displays at the edges of passing storms. It is a time to begin noticing how long it has been since your garden received its last good soaking. Your plants will probably need their first deep watering by March or April, although seedbeds will certainly have demanded water earlier. Until next fall, you are your garden's only effective water source. Any rainfall during that period is usually too brief to penetrate very far into the soil. Near the coast, late spring is often warmer and sunnier than midsummer. Gardeners often get a tan while planting squash and beans in May, but they lose the tan to summer fog long before the crops are ready to pick.

My spring harvests combine the last of winter's crops with the first crops of the new year. I bake the last of winter's cabbage into savory stuffed cabbage leaves for Saturday supper, or serve an elegant leek and shrimp quiche at a spring brunch. I shred the last of the beet harvest and pickle it to add a vermilion accent to spring salads. As the days warm in April and May, I pull the first tender spring carrots

and pick the season's first strawberries. Soon there are new potatoes to steam for a delicate potato salad and young cactus pads to serve in a peppery Mexican sauce.

Spring bouquets are colorful and varied, from fragrant sweet peas and freesias to brightly colored ranunculus and elegantly formed columbine. As I pick spring flowers, I admire my garden. The freshly planted seedlings of spring always fill my heart with hope and joy, even in a climate that allows gardeners a never-ending cycle of fresh starts.

TWO

On Learning to Garden

As you survey your backyard you probably have a vision of a beautiful garden—green and thriving all year, either neat and orderly or wild and profuse. You can just see those lettuce leaves sparkling with dew, strawberries glowing like jewels, and lush tomato plants sagging with ripe fruit. In your vision, flowers bloom profusely in every imaginable color, and herbs offer their pungent or sweet flavors from tidy hedges. The branches of fruiting trees and shrubs droop under the weight of their bounty. But there are precious few gardeners, no matter how expert, who haven't experienced failed visions: seeds that never came up, plants that were eaten by pests, even gardens that ended up looking like wastelands. Your goal as a gardener is to bring your gardening reality closer to your gardening vision.

Many of the most difficult tasks facing a gardener come at the beginning: understanding the climate, grasping the basics of what to grow and when to plant, reclaiming the land from rampant pests and weeds, building the soil, and learning to water properly. Once you've mastered these tasks, gardening successes will follow one another quickly. Soon you can begin the fun of fine-tuning—growing more and better vegetables, herbs, fruits, and flowers. I can provide part of what you need to succeed: a knowledge of the problems you are most likely to encounter in this region and how to solve them. I can give you specific advice on the following aspects of gardening in our area.

- Choosing planting times that will produce the strongest plants and the best crops.
- Getting your seeds or seedlings off to a good start.
- Watering successfully, in harmony with our seasons.
- Turning your shifting sand or reluctant clay into a fertile, easy-to-work soil that will let plants thrive.
- Rescuing your garden from the clutches of tenacious weeds, such as fennel, oxalis, bindweed, and blackberry.
- Controlling those consummate garden consumers: snails and slugs.
- Preventing predation by local pest insects.
- Preventing damage by plant diseases.
- Harvesting in ways that will stimulate the plants to bear more food or flowers.

You must provide the rest of the solution, which consists of a can-do attitude and some roll-up-your-sleeves effort!

THE IMPORTANCE OF STARTING SMALL

It is vital not to take on too much garden too fast. If this is your first experience gardening, start with a few crops and a small plot of land. This approach is especially important if you are a beginner dealing with an overgrown garden and uncooperative soil. Once you get one small area under control, you will be carried along by the sweet feeling of success.

Even if you plan to use your whole yard as a garden, divide it into sections and plant only one section at first. With our year-round climate, you can start another section every couple of months if the first ones are going along nicely, or you can reseed them if they are not faring well. This will help keep your garden from getting away from you. If the garden begins to be too much, make your next section smaller and simpler. (See page 22.)

If you start with too much variety or too large an area, you may find that you are missing harvests, overlooking serious pests until too late, or feeling overwhelmed because too many tasks need doing all at once. A garden requires a special kind of attention and patience. Although a plant may require very little care for most of its life cycle, it cannot be ignored when it does need your attention. A more modest beginning will give you time to adjust to the rhythms of just a few crops at first, before adding others.

Harvesting is often a large part of the work of food gardening. What a pity to miss out on the rewards of your efforts! It can happen all too easily. Although harvesting is usually fun, it can take up to two-thirds of your gardening time. Some crops must be picked as often as every couple of days, and they will not always be ready on a schedule that is convenient for you.

The worst consequence of taking on too much at once is that, if your garden is not running smoothly, it becomes a source of bad feelings rather than the positive ones you hoped it would bring. If you are a beginner or a very busy person, rest assured that you can reap the same satisfying feeling from a few square feet of productive, well-maintained space as from a much larger garden.

Think of your garden as a tapestry—the more you study it, the more details you discover.

LOOKING, RECORDING, AND THINKING

Make a conscious effort to look at your garden. Look at plants for the pleasure of watching them unfold. Look to spot problems in time to solve them. Look to decide the best time to harvest. And look to develop a feel for the plants—how they grow and how they react to stress.

Take your morning coffee or tea to the garden, or maybe an apple when you get home from work. Walk around and see how things are going. Turn leaves over. Notice what is flying or crawling about. Sit down. If there is no place to sit, get a little watching stool. Study a plant or a square foot of ground until you've learned something new.

Look at other people's gardens and compare your plants with theirs. Try to find out how their microclimate differs from yours. Ask when they planted, what varieties they chose, and what they added to their soil. This information will help you decide what your plants need and how best to provide it.

No one learns to garden all at once. Often things go right the very first time, but it may take two or more years of adjustments to get some crops right. Sometimes problems pop up after years of success. Talking to other gardeners, reading about gardening, trying new things—these are all ways to increase your successes.

Keeping a record will help you learn faster, as it allows you to repeat successes and encourages you to learn from failures. Record keeping can be as simple or as complex as you like. The simplest method is to record on a calendar or in a date book when you put in seeds and what varieties you planted. You can also record the beginning and end of the harvest. Some gardeners keep a file card on each plant variety, recording planting times, harvest dates, flavor, problems encountered, and how they might grow it differently in the future.

You may want to map your garden. A drawing of the plots marking the different crops you planted will help you identify seedlings when they come up. A new map each season will help you plan crop rotation, a practice that helps control pests and maintain good soil health. (See page 86 for more on rotating crops.) These seasonal maps are a good place to record what you added to the soil in different parts of your garden.

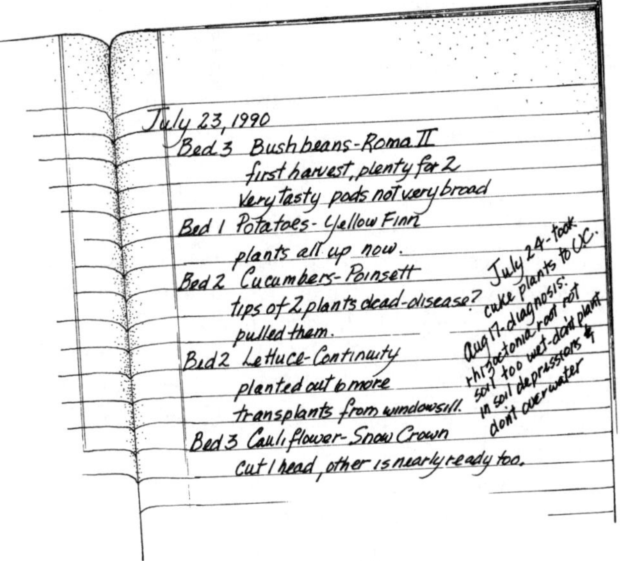

July 23, 1990
Bed 3 Bushbeans-Roma II
first harvest, plenty for 2
Very tasty pods not very broad
Bed 1 Potatoes-Yellow Finn
plants all up now.
Bed 2 Cucumbers-Poinsett
tips of 2 plants dead-disease?
pulled them.
Bed 2 Lettuce-Continuity
planted out to more
transplants from windowsill.
Bed 3 Cauliflower-Snow Crown
Cut 1 head, other is nearly ready too.
July 24-took cuke plants to CE.
Aug 17-diagnosis: rhizoctonia root rot soil too wet-don't plant in soil depressions & don't overwater

Gardening diary entries

You can also keep a gardening diary, in which you record the weather, how the plants are growing, what you did that day, what you ate from the garden, recipes, and so on. Keep in mind that you must organize the information so that you can find it later. I begin by recording the date on a separate line. In the left-hand margin where it will be obvious, I put the most important information: a bed or plot number and the name of the crop and the variety. Underneath I describe the condition of the plant, the amount harvested, and any problems encountered and treatments applied. I leave a little room on the right-hand side for notes, such as identification of pests or the results of treatments I tried.

LEARNING FROM EXPERIMENTS

As you watch your garden grow, read this and other books, review your gardening diary, and talk to your neighbors, questions will come to mind. Will September-planted carrots mature before winter in my garden? Will the pepper variety that the seed catalog lists as "the earliest ever" produce better than the one I grew last year? What if I planted by the moon?

Whenever you aren't sure if something will work, it is a good idea to set up an experiment. This is not hard to do if you remember four principles: (1) test only one factor at a time; (2) have a control so that you will have something to which you can compare your experimental results; (3) use a large enough sample (more than one plant, more than one trial) to be sure that your results aren't a fluke; and (4) make a record of your results, so that you will have a clearer idea of what happened and will be able to compare later tests more precisely.

If you experiment by planting carrots at a later time than usual, create a control by planting some of the same carrot variety at your usual earlier planting time. Plant ten or more carrots in each planting. Give both plantings similar soil conditions and sun exposure; water and fertilize them in the same way. Then measure and record the growth of each planting weekly or monthly.

To test a new variety of any crop, seed it on the same day that you sow a familiar variety. At least four plants of each variety are necessary for the experiment; in that way, you won't accidentally compare individual plants that are atypical of the varieties. Grow both the test and control varieties randomly intermixed (but, of course, carefully labeled) in an area with similar soil, light, and other conditions. Then measure and compare their height, amount of foliage or fruit, or other important information on the same day several times during their growing season.

To test a technique, such as planting by the moon, plant several specimens of the same crop variety under similar conditions. Only vary the factor you are testing, in this case the time you plant in relation to the phase of the moon. Use information in a current-year almanac to pick planting times that are considered exactly right for the moon phases and others that are thought to be exactly wrong. Then record the height or productivity of the plants, at the same age, several times during the season. (You will not be able to draw any conclusions from moon-phase planting tests until you have repeated them several times, since the weather in the few weeks after you plant will exert a big influence on the crops, and this is not what you are testing. Only after you have tested the same crop repeatedly, over several years, will you be able to discern any pattern that occurs despite the weather.)

Throughout this book are ideas for simple experiments to help you gain new, reliable information specific to your garden. If you want further help in setting up an experiment, try contacting the Cooperative Extension office in your area or local community gardening organizations. *Improve Your Gardening with Backyard Research*, listed in Appendix VIII, Suggested Reading, will also be helpful to you.

Gardening is a fairly recent phenomenon in our part of the world. So great was the area's natural bounty that the Native Americans who lived here didn't need to develop agriculture. Spanish friars were the first to till the ground. Then, as the population grew, small farmers began to supply the nearby towns with produce, making our area, including much of San Francisco proper, a major agricultural district. Most of these farmers are gone now, having sold their land for urban use—often because they could not afford the higher property taxes resulting from nearby development. Much of what they knew about growing food in this region went with them. Recently, gardeners and organic truck farmers have been reviving the idea that this is a good place to grow food, and what they learn will help us use our environment more successfully.

Many local gardeners who have experimented and kept records over the years contributed to the information in this book through interviews and questionnaires. Their records and those of other gardeners will continue to expand our knowledge.

If you learn what you can grow in your particular microclimatic corner of the region, you can make valuable contributions to other gardeners who live nearby or in similar microclimates. New information on varieties that prosper here, ways to succeed with borderline crops, or unorthodox times to plant will make it easier for future gardeners to enjoy bountiful harvests. If you make discoveries, share what you learn with local gardening organizations, or write me a letter.

WHEN SOMETHING GOES WRONG

Just as successes, even small ones, build confidence, failures rob us of that can-do, self-assured feeling. Beginners often jump to a too-hasty conclusion about what went wrong or keep themselves from analyzing the problem by denigrating themselves: "I just don't have a green thumb." Not only beginners but also experts have failures. One of the ways they became experts was to take failures as challenges. By setting out to find a solution, you will learn something about your current problem; at the same time, you are bound to discover techniques, skills, or other information to help you solve future problems.

First, carefully observe what went wrong and be prepared to describe the problem clearly. Reread anything you can find that might explain what happened, and if this doesn't set you on the right path, ask gardening friends or experts for advice.

Form a hypothesis: My cucumber plants are growing slowly and are pale green because the soil in which they are growing is short of nitrogen. I think this may be so because I know that cucumbers have a high need for nitrogen (see page 218) and that nitrogen deficiency is common in local soils (see page 73), and I suspect that I haven't adequately fertilized my soil. Also, I have read about the pests cucumbers can get, observed the plants carefully, including with a magnifying glass, and have seen no insects or recognizable disease symptoms.

Then form a plan: I will make chicken manure tea (see page 81) and add it to the soil once a week when I water. If the leaves green up quickly, I will assume my hypothesis was correct. (To be absolutely sure that you are right, you will need a control. So leave a couple of plants unfertilized.)

Finally, apply your new knowledge the next time you grow the crop: Try the same cucumber variety the next year, this time adding more nitrogen fertilizer to the soil from the start. As a double-check, grow a couple of control plants in soil treated the same way but lacking nitrogen fertilizer.

THREE

What Can You Grow?

ALTHOUGH SO MUCH IS possible in mild-climate gardens, many gardeners use only a part of the year and try only a few of the potential crops. Even after limiting themselves, they still often have disappointing results. This happens because most gardening books and seed packets don't provide enough information to help gardeners deal with the local climate. We can't figure out where the climate fits in those charts claiming to give planting dates for the whole nation. We wonder why so many crops don't do what the seed packet says they should do. Why does the patch of corn, planted at the time the packet suggested, take twice as long to bear ears as the packet promised or, in some cases, form no ears at all? Why do the tomatoes, which were supposed to taste as sweet as honey and grow as big across as a hamburger bun, taste bland and make slices no bigger across than a pickle?

Or, perhaps even worse, we may not know that we are missing some of the best planting times and harvests. Seed packets that refer only to last frost dates will not necessarily make it clear that peas planted in November will result in bountiful April harvests. And most seed sources won't even offer the varieties of broccoli that overwinter in this region.

Without proper information, beginning gardeners and gardeners new to the area may quickly get the idea that the local climate is hostile to vegetable crops in general. Actually, it is hostile only to a few inappropriate crops and to inappropriate planting times. True, it affects coastal gardeners right where it hurts, in the glamorous crops such as tomatoes, corn, and melons. However, we can grow many other desirable crops, some of which do not succeed in prime tomato and melon country. The moral is obvious: ignore your unique climate and you will encounter frustration; understand it and you will be on your way to year-round, bountiful harvests.

MICROCLIMATES

Did I say "climate"? I should have said "climates," because even within the region covered by this book, there are a number of distinct microclimates. Newcomers commuting to a job as close as a mile away are often surprised to find that the climate there is very different from the one they left a few minutes earlier. San Francisco is famous for its several microclimates, but the same is true in other parts of the region. The local joke is, "If you don't like the weather, just walk a few blocks." Unfortunately, the plants in our gardens are unable to take this advice. Crops that succeed in one garden may fail in a garden only a few blocks away.

The climate along the coast of our region is far more similar to the climates of other California coastal locations, even those hundreds of miles away, than to places a few miles inland. The average maximum daily temperature for June, July, and August in Point Reyes, on the west coast of Marin County, tends to be within two or three degrees of that at Point Piedras Blancas, nearly two hundred miles south along the coast. During the same period the average maximum daily temperature in Point Reyes is an extraordinary twenty-three to twenty-seven degrees cooler than in Walnut Creek, which is less than thirty miles inland. As a general rule, the maximum daily temperature during these three

Vegetable Crops and the Region's Microclimates

All-Region List: Crops that are likely to flourish in all areas covered by the book. In inland areas, some of these crops are better grown in cooler parts of the year.

Moderate Fog List: Crops that need a bit more warmth and sunlight, so will not thrive in the foggiest areas.

Less Fog List: Crops that will produce a satisfactory harvest only in the warmest parts of the near-coastal region, or in more inland areas away from coastal influence.

Inland Microclimate List: Crops that will thrive only in warm-summer inland microclimates, away from most of the coastal influence.

All-Region List

Artichoke
Arugula
Asparagus
Bean, scarlet runner*
Bean, fava
Beet
Bok choy
Broccoli
Cabbage
Carrot
Cauliflower
Celeriac
Celery
Chayote squash
Chervil
Cilantro
Florence fennel
Garlic
Greens (mustard, chard, collards, kale, etc.)
Ground cherry
Herbs, perennial
Kohlrabi
Leek
Lettuce
Onion
Parsley
Parsnip
Pea (including snap and snow peas)
Potato
Pumpkin*
Radicchio
Radish
Salsify
Spinach
Spinach, New Zealand
Squash, summer*
Squash, winter*
Sunchoke*
Sunflower*
Tomato (cherry) (borderline)
Turnip
Watercress

Moderate Fog List

Amaranth*
Basil*
Bean, snap (bush and pole)*
Corn (short-season varieties)*
Cucumber*
Tomato (cherry and very short-season varieties)*
Tomatillo*

Less Fog List

Bitter melon*
Corn (most varieties)*
Eggplant (early)* (borderline)
Tomato (midseason varieties)*
Pepper (especially cool-tolerant varieties)* (borderline)
Winter melon*

Inland Microclimate List

Bean, asparagus (yard-long bean)* and black-eyed pea*
Cucumber (Asian varieties)*
Eggplant*
Jicama*
Melon*
Okra*
Pepper*
Spinach, Malabar*
Sweet potato*
Tomato (late-season varieties)*

**warm-season crop (the rest are cool-season crops)*

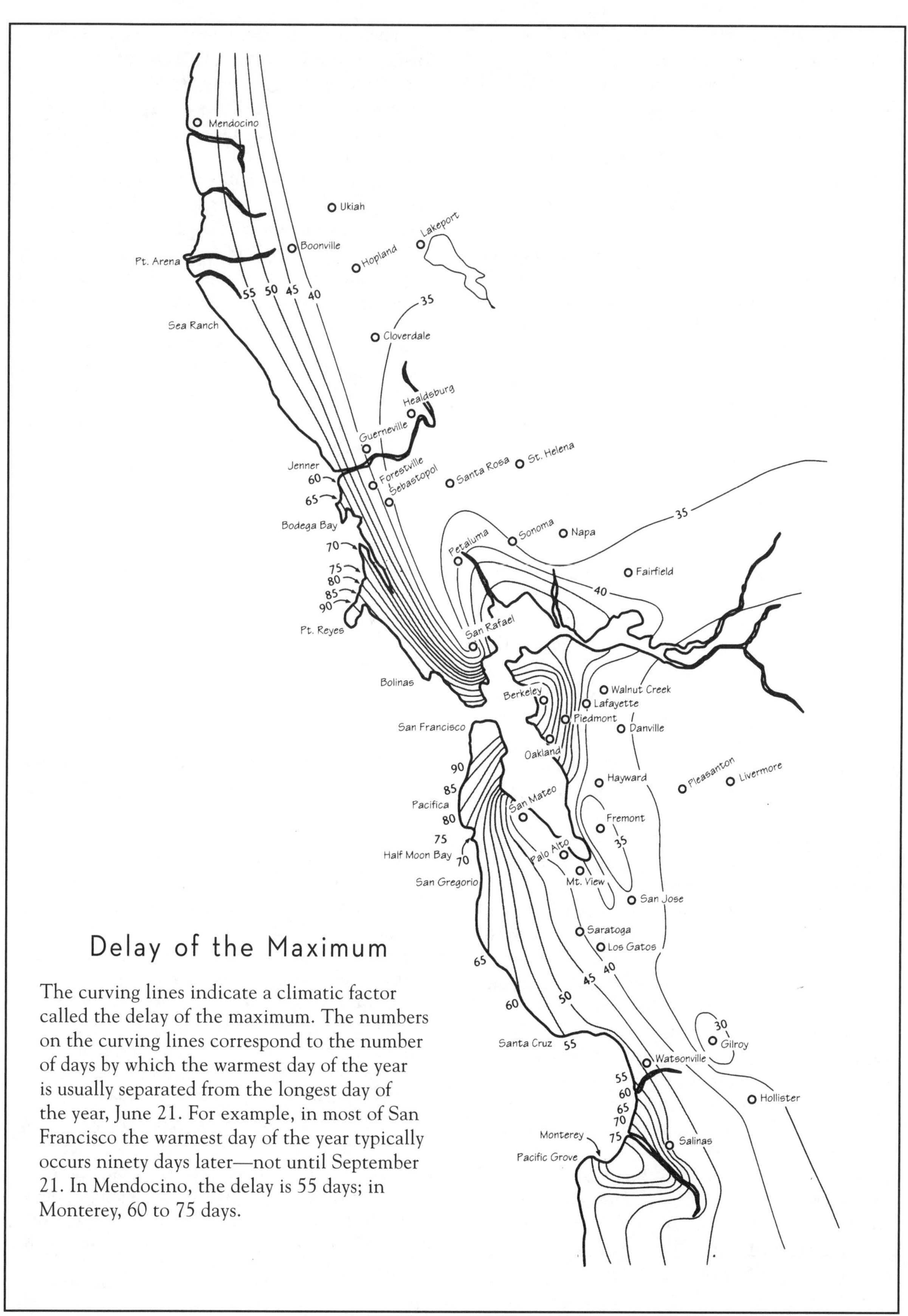

Delay of the Maximum

The curving lines indicate a climatic factor called the delay of the maximum. The numbers on the curving lines correspond to the number of days by which the warmest day of the year is usually separated from the longest day of the year, June 21. For example, in most of San Francisco the warmest day of the year typically occurs ninety days later—not until September 21. In Mendocino, the delay is 55 days; in Monterey, 60 to 75 days.

months increases by four and a half degrees for every ten miles inland from the coast.

In general, the nearer you are to the coast, the foggier and colder the summer, the wetter the fall and spring, and the less likely that there will be winter frost. However, the change of climate is not a steady and easily mapped one. It is modified by hills that block the wind from the ocean and by fog gaps, such as the Golden Gate, through which the cool, foggy ocean breeze can flow inland. (See map on page ii.) The San Francisco Bay and other inland bodies of water also moderate the climate, making the areas around them cooler in summer and warmer in winter.

WHAT WILL GROW HERE

The Vegetable Crops and the Region's Microclimates sidebar (see page 12) lists most of the vegetables in Chapter 11 and some of the herbs in Chapter 12, according to how they adapt to various microclimates of our region. The All-Region List, fortunately lengthy, represents crops that are likely to flourish in all areas covered by this book. In fact, many of them grow *better* near the coast in summer than they do in inland heat. Plants on the Moderate Fog List need more heat and sunlight, so they will not thrive in the foggiest areas. The Less Fog List includes crops that produce a satisfactory harvest only in areas at least as warm and sunny as the warmest parts of San Francisco. Even there, these crops will be slower and possibly smaller than they would be if there were no ocean influence. The Inland Microclimate List contains crops that will thrive only in parts of the region with the warmest summers and the least ocean influence. Warm-season crops from all of the lists will grow progressively faster and bear better where summers are warmer.

How do you adapt this information to your own garden? If you live very near the ocean, with no intervening hills, as in a neighborhood on the west side of San Francisco or very near the coast in other counties, you should start with the All-Region List. If you live a few miles inland, but still to the west of coastal hills, or if your garden is unshaded and protected from the wind, add a couple of crops from the Moderate Fog List and see how they fare. In the path of a fog gap, the cool air and fog will extend farther inland. If you live several miles from the coast and out of the direct path of a fog gap, you can probably grow crops from the Less Fog List.

The map on the previous page shows the area covered by this book; curving lines indicate a climatic factor called the delay of the maximum. The numbers on the curving lines correspond to the number of days by which the warmest day of the year is usually separated from the longest day of the year, June 21. For example, in most of San Francisco the warmest day of the year is typically ninety days after the longest day—not until September 21! Those who live anywhere in the western half of Central and Northern California will find this book a useful guide to year-round gardening. Inland gardeners will find the basic information and winter calendar particularly useful. Within the reach of coastal influence, where the delay of the maximum temperature is 45 days or more, this book will also help you cope with the cooler and foggier summer. Appendix I provides further climatic data to help you predict your microclimate in locations from Mendocino to Monterey and as far inland as the fog and cool ocean breezes ever reach.

The list of crops that will grow in foggier parts of the region was originally developed in the 1970s by the staff of San Francisco's then city-sponsored community gardening program. I have expanded the list and added other lists over the years as I have learned more.

The staff of the City's community garden program also divided the City into three growing zones that coordinate generally with the first three of the current lists. The roster of neighborhoods, including a couple that they omitted, is included with the San Francisco map on the opposite page.

In recent years, a second attempt has been made to map San Francisco's microclimates, this one by the Division of Urban Forestry in the Department of Public Works. It divides San Francisco into seven microclimates (see opposite page) and lists relative amounts of fog, cool temperatures, wind, and salt air in each area.

I wish I could tell by your town and street address whether you can successfully grow cucumbers and eggplants, but there is no magic line east of which a crop will succeed. Minor variations in the terrain make a great deal of difference. In any neighborhood there are pockets of wind and warmth that may create conditions typical of another zone. Also, the weather can vary enough from year to year to affect what you can grow. For example, gardeners in the foggiest areas may be able to grow corn successfully during a particularly sunny summer, but not every year.

San Francisco Microclimates

San Francisco Neighborhoods: Local neighborhoods according to what climate is typical for that area.

Fog Belt

- Diamond Heights
- Ingleside
- Lake Merced
- Richmond
- Sunset/Parkside
- West of Twin Peaks

Transition Zone

- Eureka/Noe Valleys
- Excelsior
- Glen Park
- Haight
- Pacific Heights
- Western Addition

Sun Belt

- Bernal Heights
- Hunters Point/Bayview
- Mission
- Russian/Telegraph Hill
- South of Market

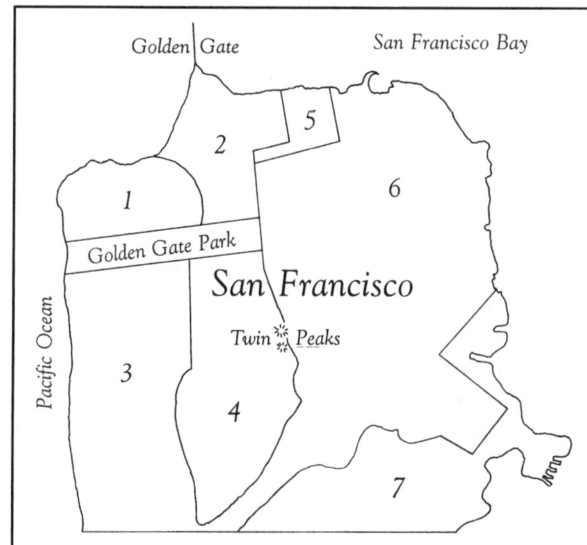

Area 1 Cool temperatures, foggy to clear days, light winds, sandy and loamy soils

Area 2 Cool to moderate temperatures, foggy to clear days, light winds, sandy and loamy soils

Area 3 Cool temperatures, foggy, salt air, heavy winds, sandy soil

Area 4 Cool to moderate temperatures; foggy to clear days; light winds; sandy, clay, loamy, rocky soils

Area 5 Cool to moderate temperatures; clear days with light fog; light winds; sandy, clay, loamy, rocky soils

Area 6 Moderate to hot temperatures; clear days; light winds; sandy, clay, loamy, rocky soils

Area 7 Moderate to hot temperatures; clear days; heavy wind; sandy, clay, loamy, rocky soils

From the Division of Urban Forestry in the Department of Public Works

The best you can do is to use the maps and lists to estimate your microclimate, notice how much fog and wind you actually get, and talk to other gardeners in your area. Then try to grow some crops and see how well they do. Take a few calculated risks, and soon you will be the expert on what you can grow in your particular microclimate. You will learn a great deal by watching your plants. Compare your successes and failures with those of friends gardening in nearby yards or other neighborhoods.

Because the microclimate boundaries are not sharp and because they vary from year to year, you will sometimes succeed against all odds. Although you should concentrate on crops that you know will do well where you live, you may sometimes want to grow crops listed for a warmer zone. If so, start with a very small planting. Consult Chapter 11, inquire at nurseries, and study seed catalogs to choose varieties most likely to succeed in cool, shady climates. Then give the plants the warmest, sunniest location you've got. Inland, you will make some of the same calculations in winter, trying a crop that might not be able to handle your likely winter lows. If you have the option, select a variety said to be particularly cold hardy. Give it a protected location, maybe add hoops over the bed that you can cover with a row cover or clear plastic if hard frost threatens.

If your experimental plants don't even come close to succeeding, you will know that you were too ambitious. But if they almost succeed, try again next year with a different variety, a minigreenhouse (see page 33), or some other trick. You may find a way to succeed every year, or at least during especially favorable years.

WHEN TO GROW IT

To make full use of our mild climate, you must break out of the spring-to-fall gardening pattern and begin to see the year as continuous, overlapping seasons. To use the full year, you need to know the range of times a crop can be planted and the length of time a crop will need to grow before it is harvested.

In this chapter, there are two different planting calendars (pages 18–21), one for foggier areas and another for sunnier (though still ocean-influenced) microclimates. (If you live farther inland, refer to either of two additional planting charts—one for Walnut Creek, the other for San Jose—in Appendix III.) In all of the planting charts, the heavily shaded bars indicate the planting times most likely to bring success. The lightly shaded bars signify that plantings at this time may succeed. Your particular garden may have a particularly warm or cool microclimate. Or one year may allow crops planted early or late to succeed while another may not. Also, some varieties of the crop may be adapted to certain planting times, while another may not be. Some crops have seasonal varieties—for example, you will find lettuce varieties that withstand cold weather and others that are resistant to bitterness or flowering during warm summer weather. (If you garden farther inland, see the Inland Planting Calendars in Appendix III.)

For full details of possible vegetable planting times, see individual listings in Chapter 11. For information on when to plant herbs, refer to Chapter 12. For times to seed vegetables and herbs indoors, see pages 52–53 in Chapter 6. For edible and cut flower planting times, consult Chapters 13 and 14.

When it comes to planting times, there are advantages to gardening in both foggier and sunnier microclimates. For example, in gardens with cooler, foggier summers, carrots for a fall crop should be planted no later than July. More inland, they can be planted through August or even September, since they will grow faster in the heat of late summer. In foggier gardens, however, gardeners have the advantage of being able to plant such cool-season crops as peas or broccoli late in the spring, when weather would turn too warm for them in sunnier areas. You will need to experiment a bit to learn how plants respond in your particular garden. Soon you will be learning about the microclimate of your garden by watching the plants.

To help you figure out how long a crop will occupy space in your garden, seed companies list the number of days required from seeding to the start of the harvest. These figures are frequently quite different for different varieties of a crop, and you will often choose a particular variety partly because of its number of days to harvest. For example, coastal gardeners will often select an early variety of a warm-season crop, since summer cold and fog retard the growth of these crops. 'Early Sunglow' corn, listed in catalogs at fifty-five days, takes ninety days

Fog and Plant Size

You could map the effects of cool summer temperatures and fog by growing bell peppers or other plants that will bear a crop in the warmer and sunnier parts of the region but not in the coolest, foggiest areas. Although there are differences in the responses of different varieties, the following is a typical pattern.

If you planted bell pepper plants from the same nursery six-pack on the same day in the foggiest areas, transitional areas, sunny areas, and just outside the fog-affected region, you would see clearly the effects of cold and fog. In the foggiest, coldest locations, the plant might grow 10 inches high but most likely would set no fruit. The plant in transitional areas might grow 1 or 2 inches higher and make few and small fruit. In sunny areas you might get a plant 15 to 18 inches high, bearing at least five or six good-sized peppers. Just outside the region with significant fog—for example, in Santa Rosa or even a pocket of warmth and sun in Oakland—the plant might reach 2 feet high and be covered with splendid peppers.

Interpreting Seed Packets

To guide a gardener to the right planting time, seed packets often bear the same standard recommendations. I have long thought of these common rhythmic phrases as little poems. One refrain advises planting "as soon as the ground can be worked in the spring." In an area with cold winters, this means planting the seeds when the soil has thawed and the mud from the melted snow has dried a bit. In our climate, the ground is never frozen under snow and, when the storms are not too close together, the soil is often dry enough to be worked in winter, although the soil temperature may be too low for even cool-season seeds to sprout. I usually interpret the seed packet instruction to mean that the crop can be seeded here in the open ground starting in February, when perhaps two-thirds of the winter rain has fallen and the days are significantly longer than they were in December and January. In fact, many such crops can be planted here much of the year.

Another standard phrase advises us to plant "as soon as the ground is thoroughly warm, and all danger of frost is past." This recommendation is more ambiguous in the context of our climate. Even though all danger of frost may be past by the middle of February in your location, the soil is usually not thoroughly warm until the beginning of May. Most crops labeled in this manner should not be planted outdoors until at least the middle of April, although earlier planting is sometimes possible. For example, summer squash may do just fine when planted as early as February—as long as the seeds manage to germinate. On the other hand, corn may be stunted if it sprouts in soil that is too cold for it, and the soil temperature may be too low for corn as late as April. Consult the charts on pages 18–21 and in Chapter 11 for more information on vegetable planting times.

in a sunny San Francisco garden. A late corn, listed at ninety days, may not be able to ripen there at all. Cool-season crops, such as cabbage and broccoli, often take longer than the listed number of days when they are growing during the winter. This is less critical since they will eventually mature if they were planted early enough. Some of the best varieties take the longest to mature, but you will want to grow them anyway because they make up for their tardiness with taste.

When you have learned the best planting times and how long a crop is likely to require to grow, you can choose planting times that make certain sequences of crops possible. For example, peas planted in November will probably be harvested by the end of April. On May 1, you can plant 'Early Sunglow' corn in the same spot. The corn should be finished by July 30, in time to seed carrots for fall and winter harvests. If you had planted the peas in early March instead of November, they might not be finished until June. You could still plant the corn on June 15 and harvest it by September 15, but then it might be too late for carrots. Whatever sequence you choose, there is always *something* you can plant next. If your corn harvest runs into September, you can plant the space to garlic in the middle of October.

You make trade-offs when you choose planting times. For example, you may want to plant garlic, but a lack of space in your garden in October and November may prompt you to wait until December. You may even wait until February, when the days are a bit longer and warmer. The garlic might grow larger if planted in October, but the later planting may work out just as well. If it doesn't, that's a trade-off you won't make next year.

You will not be able to try every crop or every possible planting time in a single year. Although the list of planting times suggests planting corn during four different months, that is something I rarely do. I may plant corn early one year, early and late the next, and in midseason the following year, and then I may skip a year altogether.

HOW MUCH TO PLANT

One of the skills that comes with gardening experience is the ability to grow just as much as you want of a crop, not too much or too little—at least most of the time. I've seen charts that purport to tell you how to do this, listing how much to grow to feed a family of four, assuming that everyone eats a standard (but unspecified) amount. Actually, no prepared list can reflect how much you and your family can or will eat of each crop.

Planting Times for Foggier Microclimates

	January	February	March	April	May	June	July	August	September	October	November	December
Artichoke (bareroot)												
Bean, fava												
Bean, scarlet runner												
Bean, snap (bush)												
Bean, snap (pole)												
Beet												
Broccoli (plants)												
Brussels sprouts (plants)												
*Cabbage (plants)												
Carrot									?			
*Cauliflower (plants)									?			
Celery (plants)								?				
Chayote squash												
*Chinese cabbage							?		?			
Collards									?			
Corn, sweet (early)												
Cucumber												
Eggplant (plants)												
Garlic (sets)												
Kale (plants)									?			
Kohlrabi (plants)									?			
*Leek												
Lettuce												
Melon												
Mustard										?		
*Onion, bulb (seeds)												

	January	February	March	April	May	June	July	August	September	October	November	December
Onion, bulb (sets)												
Parsnip									?			
Pea												
Pepper (plants)												
Potato (tubers)												
Radish (small)												
*Radish (winter)										?		
Rhubarb (bareroot)												
Shallot (sets)												
*Spinach				?							?	
Squash, summer			?									
Squash, winter (and pumpkin)												
Sunflower												
Sunchoke (tubers)												
Swiss chard										?		
Tomato (plants)	?											
Turnip									?			

KEY:

A heavily shaded area means it is okay to plant this crop at these times.

A lightly shaded area means that these times will work for some varieties, in some locations and/or in some years.

? A question mark (?) means that you may sometimes be able to extend planting times even beyond the end of the lightly shaded area, though not commonly.

* An asterisk before the name of a crop (*) means that varieties of the crop have widely differing preferred planting times. For example, most winter radishes should be planted from midsummer into fall, but some varieties can be planted in the spring.

Planting Times for Sunnier Microclimates

	January	February	March	April	May	June	July	August	September	October	November	December
Artichoke (bareroot)												
Bean, fava												
Bean, scarlet runner												
Bean, snap (bush)												
Bean, snap (pole)												
Beet										?		
Broccoli (plants)										?		
Brussels sprouts (plants)												
*Cabbage (plants)												
Carrot												
*Cauliflower (plants)												
Celery (plants)												
Chayote squash												
*Chinese cabbage		?		?								
Collards				?						?		
Corn, sweet (early)												
Cucumber												
Eggplant (plants)												
Garlic (sets)												
Kale (plants)												
Kohlrabi (plants)										?		
*Leek												
Lettuce												
Melon												
Mustard											?	
Okra (plants)												
*Onion, bulb (seeds)												

	January	February	March	April	May	June	July	August	September	October	November	December
Onion, bulb (sets)												
Parsnip										?		
Pea											?	
Pepper (plants)												
Potato (tubers)												
Radish (small)												
*Radish (winter)				?						?		
Rhubarb (bareroot)												
Shallot (sets)		?										
*Spinach				?						?		
Squash, summer												
Squash, winter (and pumpkin)												
Sunflower												
Sunchoke (tubers)												
Swiss chard										?		
Tomato (plants)		?										
Turnip												

KEY:

A heavily shaded area means it is okay to plant this crop at these times.

A lightly shaded area means that these times will work for some varieties, in some locations and/or in some years.

? — A question mark (?) means that you may sometimes be able to extend planting times even beyond the end of the lightly shaded area, though not commonly.

* — An asterisk before the name of a crop (*) means that varieties of the crop have widely differing preferred planting times. For example, most winter radishes should be planted from midsummer into fall, but some varieties can be planted in the spring.

Instead of relying on such charts, think about how well you like a crop, how much each plant will produce, and how long you will be able to harvest the crop. Then plant it, see how well you guessed, give away any extra, and estimate again next year. If you were planting a huge garden, you would probably want to be more accurate, but in a small space little is lost by a wrong guess.

Here is an example of how to estimate. Leeks produce one leek per plant. If you harvest only mature leeks, the leek season will last from September until about the end of February: six months. Decide how many leeks you will use in a month. Perhaps you will have potato and leek soup once a month, quiche once a month, and three quiches during the holidays. You may also want to use leeks occasionally in new ways, one of which may turn out to be a favorite. Assuming two leeks per soup or quiche, that is four leeks each for six months, plus six for the holiday quiches, or thirty leeks altogether. Add another half-dozen for good measure, for a total of thirty-six. This sort of estimate is rough, but it will save you from drastic underplanting or overplanting.

You are more likely to overplant if a crop has a short harvest season. Cauliflower and corn, for example, must be picked within a week or so of maturity. In these cases, you must be careful not to plant too much at one time. You should plant no more than you can eat in two or three weeks (which includes some refrigeration time). If you want to harvest the crop over a longer period, you must plant a successive crop every few weeks during the crop's planting season. In the case of cauliflower, you may decide that your family can eat one head of cauliflower a week, or four a month, from April through July. Accordingly, you would start four plants from seed each month from January through April. You may want to start a few extra to allow for accidents, but this gives you the general idea.

As you read about the different vegetables in Chapter 11, you will learn more about how much each plant produces and how long it can be harvested. You will find it easy to grow enough of some crops and harder to grow enough of others, because either they occupy a lot of space or you eat so much of them.

The per-plant production of many crops is obvious, although size varies somewhat according to the variety and the health of the plant. Root crops such as carrots and beets produce one root per plant. Leafy crops make one plant, although many can be picked leaf by leaf while the plant continues to grow more leaves. In addition to root and leaf crops, there are fruiting crops such as tomatoes and beans. It is harder to guess how much fruit a fruiting crop will bear if you've never grown it before.

USING THE ENTIRE YEAR

My original inspiration for year-round gardening in my own garden was from a small book called *Winter Gardening in the Maritime Northwest*, by Binda Colebrook. As I read it, I realized that if gardeners in Western Washington State could harvest vegetables in winter, I certainly could. From Binda, I learned that most cool-season vegetables can easily shrug off the occasional light frost of a maritime-influenced Northern and Central California winter. And because we are so far south of Washington State, they can mostly survive our inland winters as well. Even in Sacramento, gardeners can garden all year—for example, planting peas in the fall to harvest in March.

At about the same time that I read Binda's book, I discovered that there were seed companies particularly useful to our region's winter vegetable gardeners. Nichols Garden Nursery and Territorial Seed Company, both in Oregon, and West Coast Seeds, in British Vancouver, have particularly useful varieties.

Over the years, I have come to see the gardening year less as a spring to fall event than a late summer to late summer cycle. In late summer, warm-season crops are finishing up, but there is much to plant. In midwinter, I begin starting seedlings to plant early in the calendar year, and then segue into starting seedlings of the warm-season crops. Sometimes I draw up a calendar that runs July to July, so the winter season is in the middle, instead of half at the beginning and half at the end. This makes the fall to late winter part of the planting schedule much easier to see.

A SIMPLIFIED PLANTING SCHEDULE

The best way to get the most from our mild climate is to map out the planting year in advance. You will never be able to use all of your garden all year if you wait to see a bare spot in your garden before deciding what to plant next. If you are a beginner, a good way to learn to think in terms of year-round planting is to divide the year into four main planting seasons: April–May, July–August, October–November, and February–March. Even though some crops don't fit the format, and other planting times are possible for many of the crops, at least this method allows you to get a plan under way; refinements can follow later.

The Simplified Planting Calendar on page 25 lists appropriate crops to plant during these four seasons. Start by dividing your garden space into four equal parts. These could be only a few square feet each; even if your garden space is large, limit the size of your first four beds to no larger than 100 square feet each. Decide which will be used for your first-year garden in which of the four seasons. A primary concern will be that the areas planted in October–November and in February–March will get some winter sun. Next, choose some crops that you would like to grow from each of the four lists. Don't try to grow too many crops, even if you have lots of room and like to eat everything.

Choose a season in which to plant the first bed, aiming for the earliest period in which you think you can have the soil in one bed amended and seeds or other starts ready to put in. Don't rush.

If it is November, for example, try for February–March. If the soil is still too wet in February, you can amend it in March.

Now move through your first year, planting another area in each of the four periods. By the time you plant your third bed, some of the crops from the first bed will be ready to harvest, so you will also have space there for crops from the third planting season list. Then, when you plant your fourth bed, you can also replant some or all of the second bed with crops from the list for the fourth season. After a couple of years, you will probably no longer keep the four areas distinct, but ideally you will still be planting all year.

Beginning gardeners often do not get a fall garden in because in July and August, when they should be planting many fall crops, their whole garden areas is still tied up with the summer crops they planted, all at the same time, in April and May. Using the preceding plan, the area that was planted in February and March is vacant in time to put in late summer crops for fall. Then, February and March of the next year, these late summer crops will be finished, freeing the area for another February and March planting.

As you carry out this plan, you will want to incorporate principles of crop rotation, as described on page 86, so that you won't exhaust your soil or spread diseases among your crops. To do this, just make sure that when you replant a bed, you choose a plant from the appropriate one of the four lists that is from a different rotational group. For example, when replanting a bed that held October–November crops with April–May crops, you would want to follow peas with a crop that was not in the legume or the cabbage family, such as with carrot, to reduce the spread of pea powdery mildew.

Fruiting Crop Production Estimates

Bean, snap, bush: ¼ pound per plant, over a few weeks.

Bean, snap, pole: A bit more than bush snap bean and for a little longer.

Bean, scarlet runner: Even more productive than pole snap bean, and for 2 months or longer.

Corn: 1 or possibly 2 ears per plant, over a couple of weeks.

Cucumber: 10 to 12 per plant, over 2 to 3 months.

Pea, bush: ⅛ pound or less of actual peas per plant, over several weeks.

Pea, pole: A bit more than bush pea and for longer.

Pepper, bell: 3 to 8 per plant, over 2 to 3 months; size varies on the same plant and by variety.

Pumpkin: 1 to 5 per plant, over 1 to 2 months; usually picked and stored for use in winter.

Squash, summer: 10 to 20 per plant, over 2 to 3 months.

Squash, winter: 2 to 5 per plant, over 1 to 2 months; usually picked and stored for use in winter.

Tomato, cherry: 30 to 100 or more per plant, over 2 to 3 months.

Tomato, paste: 50 to 100 or more per plant, over a month or so.

Tomato, standard size: 10 to 50 or more per plant, over 2 to 3 months.

PLANNING FOR A WINTER HARVEST

Even with planting charts, many local gardeners find it a challenge to make full use of our winter gardening season. It is often hard to find time to go into the garden for very long during the short, cold, wet winter days. Night comes so early that we may still be in the middle of our commute when it falls. Happily, winter gardens give back a lot for a small amount of time spent harvesting and weeding. With a little planning, and some preparation earlier in the year, you could be harvesting fresh leeks, chard, arugula, carrots, beets, parsnips, broccoli, cabbage, parsley, cilantro, a number of herbs, and more from winter into spring. Even if you have only one of these crops to harvest in winter, you are gardening year-round—but why not try for a few more?

Most of the planting for winter harvests is done well before the rains start, so the crops are either off to a good start or ready for harvest by the time the unpleasant part of winter sets in. Look over the planting calendars in this book and choose some cool-season crops you would like to eat in winter. Read the entries in Chapter 11, so you are sure you understand the best schedule. Leeks can be planted the previous spring, to mature in a corner of your garden into fat stems for winter soups. Broccoli plants set out in late summer make fall or even late winter crops.

If you want to grow one of the few crops that are usually planted in fall after rains start, such as garlic, peas, fava beans, or artichoke roots, you can prepare the soil well ahead of time. On warm fall days, clear the areas where you will grow these crops; fertilize and dig them. Mulch the bed and keep the soil somewhat moist until the rains are underway. When the time comes to plant, you will need only an hour or two of decent weather to get the seeds or plants into the ground. The same treatment is good for plots where you plan to plant a winter cover crop (see page 87). If there are plots you intend to leave fallow, or unplanted, until spring, you can just weed and mulch them, skipping the fertilizing and digging till time to plant spring crops.

Winter is easier on the gardener in that there is little or no watering to do. Even when there is an occasional dry spell, watering may not be needed, since the soil will dry more slowly during the shorter, colder winter days. (This also means that crops are not using up precious water from reservoirs.) Crops need less thinning, tying, staking, and other types of attention, since they are growing more slowly. And insect pests are fewer. Broccoli and cabbage are free of imported cabbageworm and cabbage root maggots. Leafminers leave the Swiss chard and beets alone.

It is true that weeds grow in winter. In fact, their growth tells you how ideal our winter weather can be for some plants. Many of our crops and common weeds have Mediterranean origins, meaning they evolved in that region's similar climate, growing into its mild, wet winters. Weeds that come up with the fall rains are better dealt with early in the season, before winter fully sets in. If you go out on sunny fall days and get them then, they will be small and easier to remove, and most of them will not yet have made seeds (See more on winter weeds on page 148.)

HOW CROPS ARE AFFECTED BY WINTER COLD

You may be having doubts about whether vegetables are actually going to grow or even stay alive in your garden through the winter. You may have once lived in a place where winter came in fast and hard, killing most of the vegetables in the garden. Even if you grew up in a mild climate, you may have been reading books on gardening from places that get as cold as that. The following information on crop hardiness will help you understand winter gardening in our region.

Warm-season vegetables, such as tomatoes and beans, are killed by temperatures below freezing (32°F or 0°C), so they rarely make it through any of the region's winters. Tomatoes and peppers, being tropical perennials, do make it through the milder winters of San Diego. I have brought a pepper through a San Francisco winter in a year winter was particularly mild, but the cold set it back so badly it didn't bear peppers again.

Most of the cool-season crops survive easily down to 25°F (–4°C), and some can live if the thermometer reads 15°F (–9°C) or even 10°F (–12°C). They may not survive prolonged periods at these temperatures, but if the cold continues for only a few days, they will be fine. It is hard to be exact about hardiness, since there are variables. Sometimes different varieties of the same crop vary in hardiness. Another part of the equation is whether the plants have adapted to cold before freezing temperatures; that is, have they been growing in a garden that has slowly become colder, or did it remain warm and then suddenly experience a frost? Plants also tend to survive cold better if they are healthy and pest free. Growing in moist soil will help as well, since moist soil doesn't get as cold in the same air temperature as dry soil—it's an echo of the tempering effect of the ocean on winter cold on nearby land.

Northwest gardeners tell us that the early, short-season cole crops, such as broccoli and cauliflower, are less hardy than the late ones that are sold as "overwintering" varieties. This makes sense,

Simplified Planting Calendar

February–March

- Asparagus (roots)
- Bean, fava
- Beet
- Broccoli (plants)*
- Carrot
- Cauliflower (plants)*
- Collards
- Kale
- Leek
- Lettuce*
- Mesclun (see page 236)
- Mustard*
- Onion (sets)
- Parsnip
- Pea
- Potato (tubers)
- Radish
- Spinach*
- Sunchoke (tubers)
- Swiss chard
- Turnip

April–May

- Basil
- Bean, scarlet runner
- Bean, snap, bush, or pole
- Carrot
- Cauliflower (plants)*
- Celery
- Corn
- Cucumber
- Eggplant (plants)
- Lettuce, leaf*
- Melon
- Pepper (plants)
- Pumpkin
- Squash, summer
- Squash, winter
- Sunflower
- Swiss chard
- Tomato (plants)

July–August

- Bean, snap, bush (by mid-July)
- Beet
- Broccoli (plants)*
- Brussels sprouts (plants)
- Cabbage (plants)*
- Carrot
- Chicory
- Chinese cabbage
- Collards
- Corn (by mid-July)*
- Endive
- Lettuce*
- Potato (tubers)
- Radish, winter
- Rutabaga
- Spinach*

October–November

- Artichoke (roots)
- Bean, fava
- Cabbage (plants)*
- Garlic (sets)
- Lettuce*
- Onion (seeds)
- Pea (during November)
- Rhubarb (roots)
- Shallot (during November)

**Check seed catalogs to learn about which specific varieties are most likely to do well if planted in this season (see page 40).*

since the early ones were bred for spring and fall cropping where winters are too cold for survival anyway, so they have probably had the hardiness bred out of them.

Some winter crops don't really grow larger in the winter, but will hold at maturity, ready to be eaten, for a long time. These include root crops, such as carrots, beets, leeks, and parsnips. Others, such as cabbage, kale, and overwintering broccoli, will grow slowly but need to get a good start before serious cold sets in. A few, including fava beans and garlic, grow like mad, cold or no. Peas also grow nicely all winter as long as there aren't heavy frosts.

Being Prepared for Frost

In climates with very cold winters, gardeners may protect their crops from the first early frost or two, but after that, they harvest them and store or preserve them, because the temperatures will soon be too low for the crop's survival. Here, we expect the warm-season vegetables to die in winter, but we expect that the cool season ones will not. They may be challenged by the cold, but probably not killed. We try to give them the best care possible so we can get the most from them throughout and after the coldest period; therefore it's wise to have a few tricks up our winter gardening sleeves.

Before the cold days arrive, use this technique to make your winter crops more resistant to cold: avoid adding nitrogen fertilizer during the last few weeks before the rains start. Nitrogen fertilizer will promote rapid, tender growth at the wrong time. Do any fertilizing of overwintering crops a bit earlier in the season. Also, plant the most frost-sensitive plants on the west side of an object that will shade them, as they will recover better from a frosty night if they can begin to thaw before the sun strikes them in the morning.

If you notice on a clear winter evening that the temperature is dropping toward freezing, beware. Frost is most likely when there is no night cloud cover to hold in the scant warmth of the winter sun. On such nights you can cover tender crops with a

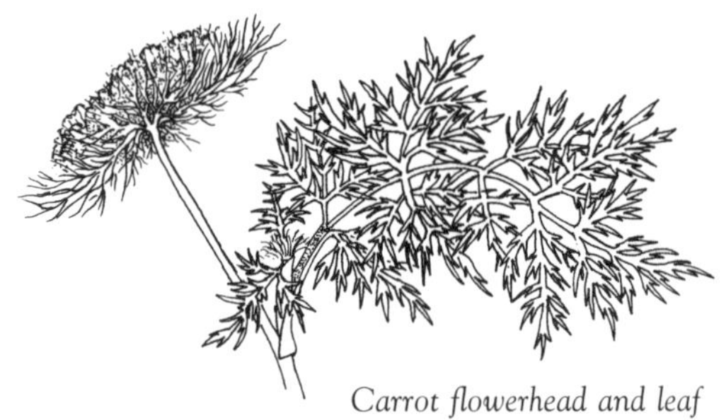

Carrot flowerhead and leaf

floating row cover (see page 50), straw, newspapers, plastic, or even old bed sheets to keep warmer air near the soil from radiating outward into space. Make sure the cover touches the ground all around the plants you wish to protect. If you use plastic, prop it up so that it doesn't rest on the plants.

When the frost is over, observe the plants for a while to assess the damage. In a few days you will be able to tell if plants will recover. During the February 1989 frost, my celery plants were frozen for three nights in a row. When I harvested a few stalks, I heard the ice crunch as the knife cut through, so I thought the plants would surely die. But a couple of days later the plants were almost as good as new, the only damage consisting of dead tips on about one-tenth of the leaves.

Perennials such as chayote and strawberries have the ability to die back and regrow, so even if they look dead, don't give up on them until past the time they would normally grow back in spring.

Cold frames, cloches, and the like are small structures that stop the wind and hold in some heat. They let the sun shine through but keep heat from reradiating into the atmosphere. They can be used over single plants or an entire bed of seedlings. Although these structures can be pressed into action to avoid an occasional frost, they are best used to enable you to plant a bit later in fall, start cool-season crops a little earlier in spring, and seed winter lettuce and greens successfully in the garden. Coverings that are portable are most useful for protecting winter crops, since you may need them only sporadically. For more on cold frames, see page 58.

Dealing with Decay

Often a problem in a winter garden, decay first affects the last of the summer crops. At the beginning of the rainy season, tomatoes as well as winter and summer squash may rot on the bottom where the fruit touches the wet soil. Small boards or a drying mulch such as wood chips can save the last of the crop. In locations closest to the ocean, drying beans on the vine is chancy. If there are several cold, wet days together, the beans may decay before they dry. The best way to save them is to shell them and spread them out in a warm, dry place. (See page 182 for more on harvesting dry beans.)

During very wet winters, decay of the leaves and stems of winter crops may be a problem. It is important to remove damaged and decaying leaves from plants before the decay spreads. When harvesting Swiss chard, tear the stalks sideways from the base instead of leaving stumps that may rot. Even if a plant has some decay on it, the undecayed part is perfectly all right to eat. If the outer leaves of a cabbage head are decayed, just peel them off and eat the rest.

Roots may rot in winter if the soil is very clayey and poorly drained. Any work you do throughout the year to improve clay soil pays dividends in your winter garden. A soil that drains well not only prevents decay but also warms faster in spring.

Remembering to Harvest Biennials

After they overwinter, many vegetables go to seed, often surprising gardeners. Carrots, parsley, beets, Swiss chard, leeks, onions, cabbage, and collards are among the many spring seeders. Maybe you planted your winter carrots so late that they never grew very big but you thought they might grow more in spring. Perhaps you grew a few more leeks than you could eat before March. One day you notice that both are sending up tall stalks. In a few weeks the plants seem to have become nothing but stalk and flower—the carrots sporting little umbrellas and the leeks graceful minarets. Although these flowering plants are interesting to watch, they are not much use in the kitchen, since the carrot roots become pale and woody and the leeks wither around their tough seed stalks.

All of these spring-flowering crops are biennials. They are plants that evolved in Mediterranean or Middle Eastern climates, where they survive a winter much like ours, then bloom, set seed, and die in their second year. Cold-winter gardeners may never see the flowering stage of these crops, since the plants die before spring. You will learn more about managing biennial crops as you read about growing each one later in this book. In general, when a crop is a biennial, you will want to plant it soon enough that the plant has time to get big before the coldest part of winter, and then eat it before the cold stimulates flowering.

YEAR-ROUND GARDENING MEANS . . .

- **You can eat fresh garden produce all year with little need for food preservation.**

  Although many local gardeners may preserve one or two favorites (I make green tomato chutney and freeze some basil in a pesto base), they don't spend much time preserving their produce. Instead, they eat whatever is fresh in the garden each month.

  Here are the reasons I don't preserve much food. First, my garden space is limited. I would rather use valuable space in summer to start a bed of winter broccoli than plant twice as many tomatoes for canning. Second, there are winter substitutes for some summer crops. I prefer to grow winter-producing chayote rather than freeze zucchini. Third, the root cellar, the old standby of the cold-winter gardener, doesn't work well here because our climate is too mild. Carrots and beets store best in the ground and cabbage on the stalk.

- **Your gardening work will be spaced out over the year.**

  True, there is somewhat more work in spring, but even the spring planting season is spread out over several months. Harvesting takes place throughout the year rather than in one late-summer blitz. Cleanup chores are staggered, because crops finish at different times. Since you usually have only small vacant areas at any given time, soil preparation is rarely done all at once.

- **Your soil will need more care because it is in continuous use.**

  When crops are growing all year, they remove nutrients the year around. Also, organic matter in the soil continues to break down throughout our mild winter months. It is probably best if you fertilize your soil and add organic matter not once, but twice a year.

- **You must attend to weeds all year.**

  There are summer weeds and winter weeds. The latter sprout in your garden when the rains start, just as the hills are greening up. It is tempting to ignore them, since they make the garden pretty, but some winter weeds—such as Cape oxalis, onion lily, and many perennial grasses—are among the most invasive and must be controlled. Winter weeds go to seed in March and April, but the clever gardener never lets them get that far, having cut them or dug them in long ago. (See page 148 for tips on winter weed control.)

- **You have more leeway for mistakes.**

  Year-round gardening is more forgiving of failures than a single short growing season. When you see a crop has failed, you often have plenty of time to replant it. If it refuses to succeed, there are usually several other crops to try during the same or the next season.

FOUR

Planning Your Garden

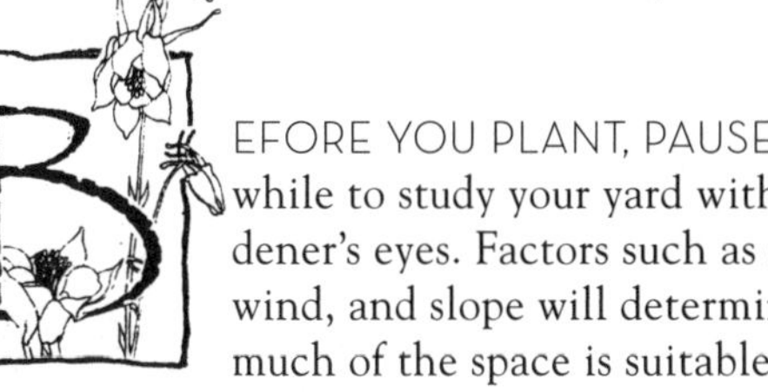

BEFORE YOU PLANT, PAUSE A while to study your yard with a gardener's eyes. Factors such as shade, wind, and slope will determine how much of the space is suitable for an edible or a cut flower garden, as well as which areas are best suited to particular crops. By arranging your garden well, you can make it more attractive and efficient to tend. And by fitting it into other uses of outdoor space, you can get more pleasure from your yard.

FINDING SUNSHINE

The overriding problem of many local gardeners is shade. The inevitable fog and rain clouds, sometimes in combination with shadows cast by buildings and large trees, unfortunately make some yards impossible for vegetables. In our hilly terrain a yard may also sit on a steep and shady north-facing slope.

Leafy vegetables need four hours of full sun each day. Fruiting vegetables, such as beans and tomatoes, need at least six hours of sunlight daily. Since our summer days are so often foggy, it is best to have a site that is unshaded eight to ten hours a day during the summer. Generally, herbs require a fair amount of sunlight, although some, including watercress, chervil, and Japanese parsley, are suited to the shade. Most edible as well as cut flowers need as much sun as fruiting vegetables, but again there are exceptions. Flowers requiring part shade include forget-me-not, foxglove, and columbine. Most fruiting trees and shrubs also need full sun, although deciduous trees can be in shade during the winter, when they are dormant.

What is the minimum sunny area for a vegetable garden? Although more space may be preferable, even 2 square feet receiving four hours of sun a day will grow a couple of dozen carrots or eight leaf lettuce plants. A 4- by 10-foot area is probably plenty to keep one or two people in salads. If you decide that too little of your yard gets enough sun for vegetables and there seems to be no way to let more sun in, first look up—to porches, roofs, and stairways—for sunny space. (See Container Planting and Rooftop Gardening on page 36.) If you can't find any, be content to plant shade-tolerant ornamentals in your garden and look for a sunny yard to borrow or a community garden to join. A community garden can be a satisfying choice, especially for a beginner, since you can watch other gardeners and learn by asking questions. Such gardens often have long waiting lists, but don't be discouraged; sign up right away and the wait will be shorter than if you put it off. (See Appendix VII for community garden resources.)

If a tree in your yard is blocking sunlight from your garden, you can decide to remove it, or consult a licensed arborist about sound ways to prune it that let in more light. If you are planning a new landscape, plant only small trees, or keep them on the north side of your vegetable garden or in an area already shaded much of the time by a building. Some localities have laws that provide you a right to a view through neighbors' trees, and, by implication, sunlight; others do not. Search for such laws by calling city hall, the parks department, or the public works department. In addition, housing associations sometimes have such rules, and your or your neighbor's property title may reveal an easement to allow a view. Research first, then talk to your neighbor; pursue mediation if necessary.

Summer shadows are shorter than those cast during the winter, because the sun climbs higher in the summer sky. The summer sun also reaches around to shine from slightly north of due east in the morning and north of due west in the afternoon, so the north side of a barrier, such as a hill, building, or fence, gets a bit of direct sun in summer.

Once you have determined which parts of your garden get enough sun to grow vegetables in summer, you must figure out where there will be enough sun for a winter vegetable garden. Because of the difference in the angle of the sun, areas of your yard will be unshaded for a part of the day in summer but will spend the winter in deep, cold shade. If you're lucky, there will be an area that is relatively unshaded all or most of the day during the winter.

December 21, the shortest day of the year, is the day of the longest shadows. Look at your garden at noon on or about this day; the area still in sun is the best place to plant winter crops, such as broccoli, peas, and garlic. If you find that your crops are struggling in too much shadow this winter, take note of the sunniest area and plant there next year. Another way to determine the amount of winter sunlight is to observe the shadows cast at midnight during a night of the full moon closest to June 21, the longest day of the year. The part of the garden that is bathed in moonlight will get the most winter sun. For information on finding and using tools that allow you to predict various seasonal shadows, consult *Designing and Maintaining Your Edible Landscape Naturally* by Robert Kourik (see Appendix VIII, Suggested Reading).

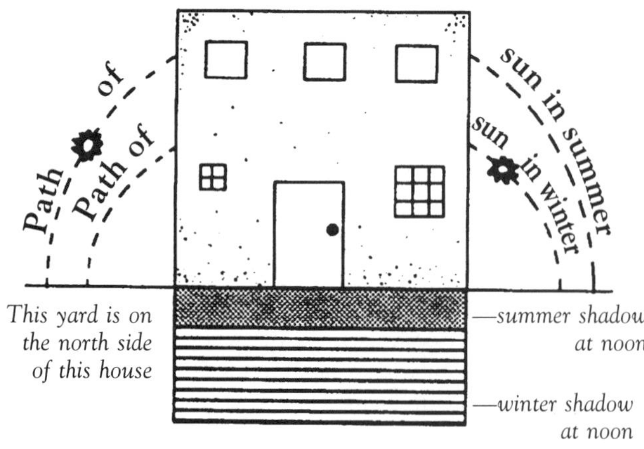

More of your yard will be in shadow in winter than in summer because the winter sun is lower in the sky. To determine the altitude of the sun at noon on the solstice, use the following formulas:

Summer solstice noonday sun angle = $90^\circ + 23.5^\circ$ – *your latitude in degrees*

Winter solstice noonday sun angle = $90^\circ - 23.5^\circ$ – *your latitude in degrees*

(For San Francisco, latitude = 37° 47')

Near the edge of areas too shady to plant are areas that are in shade at ground level longer than they are in shade at a level several feet above the ground. There are ways to use this upper-story sunlight. One is to plant vigorous, tall-growing plants such as sunchokes, sunflowers, and chayote. A second is to raise the soil level 1 to 3 feet; the increase in elevation may be just enough to make a difference for your plants.

FINDING SHELTER FROM THE WIND

The region covered by this book is generally a very windy place. As a gardener, you must take wind into account because it makes a difference in what you can grow and when you can plant it. You will have a windier yard if you are in the path of one of the fog gaps between the mountains or hills. The narrower the gap, the stronger the wind. Although buildings may block the wind in an urban area, the wind is also intensified by being forced to flow around buildings. For example, skyscrapers have created wind tunnels in many downtown streets of San Francisco. Gardens high on the north and west sides of the area's many hills will also be especially windy, since the winds come primarily from the northwest and increase at higher elevations. A gardener high on the north side of one of San Francisco's central hills reports that in the path of cold spring winds not even cabbage will grow before May.

Many urban gardens are edged with a solid fence for privacy. Although a solid fence offers some protection from wind, the air just behind it will be turbulent. Shrubs or open fences that let a little air through do a better job of tempering the wind. Consider replacing a solid fence with either a partially open fence or an open, lightly vine-covered one. If you prefer the privacy of a solid fence, you may want to add a panel of semi-open, wind-baffling material to the top of the fence. Prefabricated redwood latticework or a plastic 50-percent shade cloth will slow the wind while still letting some light through.

Another approach is to use glass in your fencing. It doesn't prevent turbulence, but it does let light and heat through. One local garden has 1½-foot-high glass panels atop the perimeter fence as well as several 4-foot-high glass walls within the garden area. These walls, placed parallel to each other and about 10 feet apart, create a near-greenhouse environment in the spaces between them. For such walls, use tempered glass fixed between 4 by 4 posts securely set in concrete.

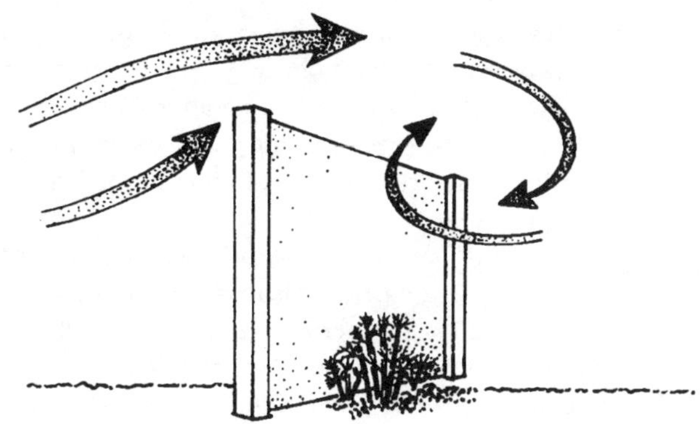

Wind effects with solid fence . . .

IDENTIFYING MICROCLIMATES WITHIN A GARDEN

Because of the desire to grow warm-season crops that may be borderline and to get the greatest variety in winter harvests, gardeners in our region tend to become fanatical about identifying different microclimates within a single yard. We want to find the warmest place in summer, the location least likely to get frost in winter, the spot with the least wind, and so on.

Although the center of your garden away from shadows cast by the house and any fences is probably the sunniest spot overall, the area south of a barrier on the north side of your yard may be warmer and sunnier in winter. A wall, fence, or hedge on the north side of the garden doesn't shade the yard, because the sun shines mostly from the south. The area in front of a northern barrier gets more sun than areas in front of barriers on the other sides of the garden. It also gains some heat and possibly light because the barrier is there. Light-colored barriers reflect light back onto the planting area in front of them; dark barriers absorb and reradiate heat, as do dense materials such as stone, concrete, and bricks.

added panel . . .

You can change the microclimate in front of a fence or wall by changing its color. Either paint it directly or attach a thin sheet of painted plywood. For a wooden fence, mount the plywood on a couple of vertical strips of 1 by 1s so that it won't trap water and cause the fence to decay. Sunlight reflected from a light-colored barrier stimulates fruit production. Here is the perfect place to put tomatoes or citrus trees. A barrier that is painted black or otherwise darkened will absorb heat during the day and radiate it back at night. Such a barrier will not stimulate fruit production, but it will help plants grow bigger and protect them somewhat from winter cold. The area in front of a dark-colored barrier is a good environment for winter greens.

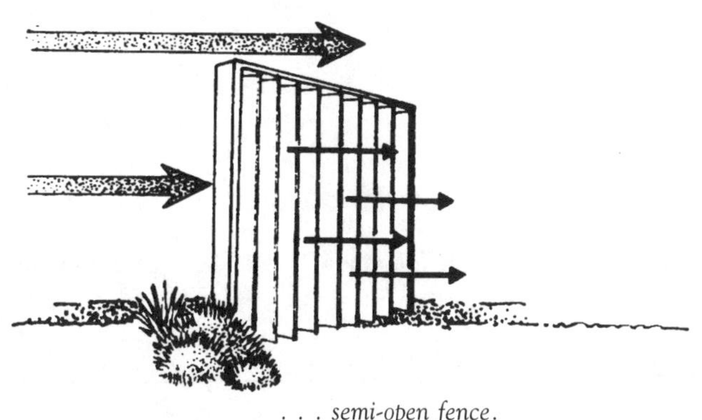

. . . semi-open fence.

A fence or wall on the east side of your yard creates the second warmest and brightest microclimate. Plants growing in front of it will receive morning shade and afternoon sun. Since afternoons are less likely to be foggy and are usually warmer than mornings, the area in front of an eastern barrier will get the best of the day's warmth and light, even if it does not get as much sun as the area in front of the northern barrier. Also, as mentioned in the section on frost protection (see page 56), plants growing in front of a barrier to the east have a better chance of surviving frosts, because the sunlight does not strike them in the morning when they are still frozen.

A barrier on the west side of a garden traps the cooler morning sun and provides protection from the prevailing west winds. Light and dark surfaces on structures located to the east and west will reflect and absorb light as on structures located to the north, but the effect won't be as pronounced, since they will not receive as much total light or heat.

The worst place for a vegetable garden is on the north side of a barrier. For much of the year the barrier blocks the midday sun and makes the area just north of it shady, cold, and damp. The taller the barrier, the larger the affected area. The affected area will be even larger in the winter, when the sun is lower. The shadow from a tall

Salt Spray

Within a few blocks of the ocean, the air contains a significant amount of salt spray. If you live very near the coast, you are probably well aware of the spray because it clouds your windows and makes your locks stick. Salt also settles on your plants and soil. There is less salt deposit and less corrosion on the sides of houses facing away from the ocean, so gardens are probably less affected when the ocean breeze is blocked by a house, fence, or trees.

Most of the salt will be leached by watering and rain, but some will remain. The effect is probably small, but it may be critical for sensitive plants. You can help salt-sensitive plants somewhat by occasionally spraying their leaves with fresh water, although you may have to weigh the benefit of spraying against the possibility of encouraging disease. The following is a list of the relative sensitivity of various crops to salt in the soil.

RELATIVE SALT TOLERANCE OF CROP PLANTS

Vegetable Crops

High Salt Tolerance	Medium Salt Tolerance	Low Salt Tolerance
Beet Kale Asparagus Spinach Swiss chard	Tomato, Broccoli, Cabbage, Bell pepper, Cauliflower, Lettuce, Sweet corn, Potato (White Rose), Carrot, Onion, Pea, Squash, Cucumber, Cantaloupe	Radish Celery Green Bean

Fruit Crops

High Salt Tolerance	Medium Salt Tolerance	Low Salt Tolerance
None	Fig Olive Grape	Pear, Apple, Orange, Plum, Almond, Apricot, Peach, Strawberry, Lemon, Avocado

house on the south side can cover the yard all day for several winter months.

A barrier with an overhang—such as a house with eaves—that faces south, west, or east will create a special environment. In summer, the area under the overhang will be shadier and cooler than the open garden, making it an ideal location for cool-season crops. In winter, it is a good site for tender crops. The sun, lower in the sky during the winter months, will shine under the overhang. In addition, the overhang will block some of the rainfall and keep cold air from sinking onto plants below. Since drier soil tends to be warmer, the soil beneath the overhang will be warmer than soil in open areas of the garden. (Be sure to provide irrigation during winter dry spells.)

In a yard that is not level, consider the location of cold pockets—low areas where cold air collects as it pours downhill. Avoid putting frost-tender plants in these low spots, which can be several degrees colder than the surrounding terrain. Some gardening books suggest that you leave a gate open or build an open fence at the low end of a yard to let the cold air flow out; alas, research has shown that cold air moves more like porridge than water, and the opening would have to be much wider than most yards for appreciable amounts of cold air to depart!

Minigreenhouses

A minigreenhouse is a temporary structure designed to protect one or several plants. By blocking wind, it allows air to warm. It can be used in summer or winter for borderline crops. It must be tall enough to accommodate the growing plants, and it must allow you to reach in to tend the plants or to harvest.

One way to build a minigreenhouse is with polyvinyl chloride (PVC) pipe arched over beds and covered with floating row cover or clear plastic. Or you can place stakes around a plant and wrap row cover or clear plastic around them, leaving the top open. A third option is to construct a large framework of wood or PVC and cover its top and sides. Enter by rolling back the covering. Be careful if you use plastic, as it can mean overheating.

Minigreenhouses are a good place to experiment. Start several plants of the same variety at the same time inside the minigreenhouse and outside in the open garden; check their progress to see if the protected plants produce any faster than the unprotected ones.

MAKING ROOM FOR A VEGETABLE GARDEN

You may find that you have competing needs for the unshaded parts of your yard. Sun-loving ornamentals, picnic and social areas for adults, and play areas for children are likely to compete with vegetable gardening for unshaded space. After you evaluate your yard for sun and shade, think of ways in which special-purpose areas can overlap. Here are some ideas that may work for you.

Intersperse vegetables among ornamental plantings, even in the front yard.

- Plant some ornamentals, especially edible flowers but also cutting flowers, in the vegetable beds.
- Design an attractive pattern of raised planting beds to contribute to the ornamental quality of your garden.
- Plant in hanging pots, containers placed on a stairway, and containers placed at the edge of a deck or play area.
- Place benches or a picnic table in the vegetable garden area. If you have a garden workbench or an outdoor sink in which to clean your harvest, let it double as an outdoor kitchen area during barbecues.
- Construct a bean trellis playhouse for children in their play area.
- Reserve a garden plot for children to use.
- Don't squander valuable sunny space for a compost pile; relegate it to a shady spot.

GARDENING IN BEDS

Where I grew up, gardening was something you did in long rows with 2-foot-wide paths between. You stood or squatted between a row of carrots and one of beans, and you hoed or harvested. Now I plant in garden beds in which the plants grow very close together, and I tend the plants from paths between the beds. Generally, garden beds are 3 to 5 feet wide and 3 to 20 feet long, and the paths between them are 1½ to 3 feet wide. The soil level in garden beds may or may not be raised above that of the paths, and the beds may be framed or unframed.

Production is often greater in beds than in the same area planted in rows. In part, this occurs because more plants will fit into the same space, since some of the path area between rows has been eliminated. Another reason is that you can concentrate soil-building efforts on the soil in the beds, rather than in the whole area. This means you are more likely to go to the expense and take the time to build rich soil. You never have to walk on the soil in beds, so it stays light and fluffy, allowing plant roots to grow better. Another benefit is that gardens planted in beds conserve water, since only the beds and not the paths need to be watered.

Food Among the Flowers

Some vegetables and herbs are attractive enough to plant in ornamental areas of the garden. Such dual-purpose landscaping is especially useful in a small yard. When you use food crops ornamentally, treat annual vegetables as you would annual flowers, replacing them when they become unsightly. Some, such as lettuce, can be harvested and replaced with transplants several times a year. To avoid unsightly, yellowing foliage, you may want to pull others, such as beans, before the harvest is over. Plant annual flowers to screen perennial crops, such as artichoke and garlic, that go through a dormant or less attractive phase.

Vegetable crops grown ornamentally usually must be very healthy in order to be attractive. Well-grown lettuce is quite pretty, whereas lettuce left growing too long or with inadequate fertilizer or water can be downright homely. A level of pest damage that may be acceptable in a food garden may spoil the effect in a flower bed. You may want to practice growing edible crops in a less prominent setting before letting them star in an ambitious decorative scheme. Here are some ideas for growing vegetables decoratively.

- In ornamental beds: Artichoke, cabbage (especially purple cabbage and flowering varieties), garlic, herbs (especially curled parsley and variegated thyme and sage), lettuce, chicory, endive, onion, pepper, and potato.
- In the back of borders: Artichoke, asparagus, tall herbs (especially pineapple sage, anise hyssop, African blue basil, and lemon verbena), scarlet runner bean, pole pea, purple-podded pole bean, sunchoke, sunflower, and tall tomato varieties.
- In decorative containers: Bok choy, African blue basil, cabbage, Swiss chard, herbs, lettuce, pepper, radish, and dwarf tomato varieties.
- In hanging baskets: Herbs and dwarf tomato varieties.
- On arbors: Chayote, hops, pea, pole bean, and scarlet runner bean.

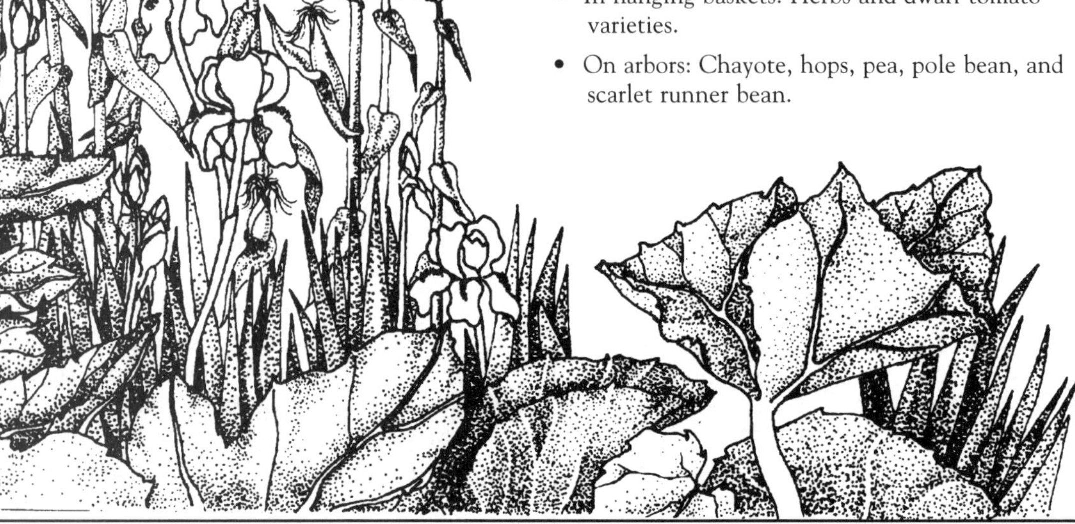

You can discourage weeds on paths between beds with a smothering mulch of sawdust or wood chips over overlapping layers of cardboard from cut-open cardboard boxes. This will reduce weediness and prevent the paths from being muddy in the rainy season. Paths can be made semi-permanent and more handsome with crushed rock, unmortared bricks, or flagstones. Such materials will also collect and reradiate warmth from the sun, possibly improving production in the beds. Be sure any material you use for your paths is permeable, so rain falling on it can seep in to recharge the groundwater.

If you have a relatively sandy or well-amended, deep soil, a frameless bed or one consisting only of 2 by 4s is sufficient. Having a frame here serves mainly to delineate the edges of the beds. If your soil is clayey, a frame 6 to 12 inches tall will help the soil warm faster and drain better. It also leaves room to dig in plenty of organic amendments that will further improve drainage and thus increase the amount of air in the clay.

When gardeners are making framed beds, they usually toss a bit of soil from the paths into the beds as they are making them, raising the soil level in the beds a bit. Double digging (see page 86) does this as well, since the loosened soil take up slightly more room.

If your garden is to be built where you do not have a deep soil, such as where there is bedrock near the surface, in a place that was recently a salt marsh, or on a concrete surface, you have to build a raised bed. To grow plants, such as salad greens, that could be grown in a shallow pot, your bed could be as low as a foot tall. To grow plants that need deeper soil, you would have to build a taller bed. See page 37 for a rough idea of the soil depth needed by plants you might want to grow.

Beds higher than a foot have become a fashion feature in gardens, but are really necessary for only two reasons: (1) to grow deep-rooted plants when there is no usable soil below the bed, or (2) if you have difficulty working at ground level. A bed 2 feet tall can be gardened from a wheelchair. See books in Appendix VIII, Suggested Reading, for many other ideas to make gardening easier for disabled persons.

There has also been a misguided trend toward filling tall garden beds with potting or planting mix, rather than with actual soil. Such materials are appropriate for containers, or for use in a shallow (foot-deep) raised bed that doesn't have usable soil beneath it, but not for a two- or three-foot-deep bed. For deeper beds, use soil. See page 77 in Chapter 8, on soils, for more guidance.

Bed planting, and especially framed-bed planting, has additional bonuses for beginners. Beds help to define the garden space. They demarcate areas where the soil should be improved to support plant growth and areas that can be made into paths. If you start your garden with a framed bed, you will see one neatly planted bed, not a few lonely plants in a corner of your yard. My first garden as an adult was in a neighbor's otherwise untended backyard, and I remember thinking that it looked insignificant, almost accidental—a small island of crops floating in a sea of weeds. In a neatly framed bed, it would at least have looked intentional.

By drawing up a plan before you start to build, you can put the first bed in the right place to begin an attractive pattern of beds. This attention to design will help to inspire you to garden and will make your edible plantings more attractive so that even nongardeners will appreciate them.

Raised beds should be narrow enough so that the shortest person helping with planting and harvesting can reach the center. Length is not important, but don't make them so long that you get tired of walking all the way to the end when you want to get to the other side. Paths should be at least 1½ feet wide; 2 feet is a little less crowded, and 3 feet is spacious. You will come to resent the wasted space if you make them too wide, but remember that from time to time you may need to maneuver a wheelbarrow to each bed. By making every other path wider, you can compromise between space and convenience.

Frames for beds can be built from various materials. The considerations are cost, beauty, durability, bulkiness, and safety for food crops. Wood is a popular choice, although eventually it will rot from being in contact with soil that is alternately wet and dry. Redwood, particularly the red heartwood, and cedar decay more slowly than other woods, so they have been popular for building raised beds, though environmentalists concerned about over-harvesting these woods would prefer you use alternatives. Old railroad ties have sometimes been used, though the creosote used to preserve them is toxic to plants and people. It has been assumed that after decades of use the creosote is not still leaching from them. Word is, in any case, old railroad ties are rather rare these days.

Until recently, wood treated with chromated copper arsenate (CCA), commonly called pressure-treated wood, had been widely used in landscape construction. However, after December 2003, the US Environmental Protection Agency (EPA) withdrew CCA-treated wood from consumer use. The main concern with CCA-treated wood was direct contact with its surface, as when children play on a CCA-treated structure, but there was also evidence of slight leaching of arsenic into nearby soil and plants.

A number of alternative, non-arsenic-containing decay-prevention treatments have been created recently, including ammoniacal copper citrate (CC), copper azole (CBA), and alkaline copper quaternary ammonium (ACQ). In 2009, none of these had been approved by the EPA for use in vegetable gardens, nor had any of them been approved for use by organic farmers. Faced with the environmental and safety concerns, some gardeners just build raised beds from untreated wood, assuming they will decay and need replacement in 5 years. (However, they avoid using painted recycled wood, because the paint may contain lead.)

An alternative to wood is "plastic lumber," made from recycled plastic. Its formulation sometimes includes sawdust or recycled tires. It has a long life and is said not to leach toxins, though I wouldn't want to use one that contained recycled tires, since those do leach toxins. Plastic lumber differs from wood in being more flexible, so it will need stabilizing to keep it from bending if beds are very long.

Other possible raised bed construction materials include plastic, bricks, or concrete. Plastic modular units are available that can be linked together to build a bed. While they are easy to construct, drawbacks include cost and adding more new plastic to our environment. Bricks are expensive new, cheaper or free if used. (The used ones are harder to build with if they are chipped or have clinging mortar.) To build more than one brick high, you need to use mortar, a more ambitious undertaking than hammering some boards together. Concrete blocks can be bulky, but you can find narrower ones. Again, mortar will be required to stack them. Rebar driven into holes in the blocks can help stabilize them. Poured concrete is a possibility, but the alkaline leachate from freshly poured, traditional concrete can raise the pH of nearby soil, creating an unsuitable growing environment. Look for new, alternative concretes that are stronger, recycle waste materials, and emit less CO_2 in their manufacture than traditional concrete.

SLOPING YARDS

In a yard that slopes, even gently, planting rows should be arranged to follow the contour of the slope. If you build framed raised beds, make the downhill side higher and level the soil. A yard with a significant slope should be terraced, with wood, concrete, or stone retaining walls built to hold the soil.

Terracing can be done by the traditional method of cutting steps up the slope, putting in retaining walls, and using the soil removed to fill the area behind the next lower walls. However, modern urban terraced gardens are more often made by the less labor-intensive method of setting up retaining walls and depositing purchased soil behind them. Consult a book on garden construction to be sure you are providing the strength and drainage that retaining walls need. On terraces more than 2 feet high, the walls must be braced and anchored. A steep hillside should probably be left to a contractor, since a poorly constructed retaining wall could slide dangerously.

If you can do only part of the terracing at first, start at the bottom. Make the level areas wide enough so that you can work on them. If the slope is so steep that the terraces must be less than 4 feet wide, you could plan a vertical stairway path every 4 feet and plant in terraced strips between the paths.

As a bonus in a terraced yard, you get a little reflected light and radiant heat from the retaining walls, especially if the terrain slopes to the south.

ARRANGING YOUR CROPS

Although what you will learn later about individual vegetables will help you decide the best way to arrange your crops, here are a few general tips. Plant tall crops, such as corn and pole peas, to the north so that they won't shade smaller plants. Plant perennials, such as herbs and artichoke, away from the areas that you will be turning each season to plant new crops. If you are planting in rows or beds that are longer than wide, orient the planting areas east to west for the greatest exposure to the sun. If your garden is on a slope, orient the rows or beds to follow the contour of the terrain.

CONTAINER PLANTING AND ROOFTOP GARDENING

To avoid shade and to maximize your garden space, you may decide to grow plants in containers on a deck, porch, stairway, or roof. These areas can produce good crops, but there are special considerations. If you are planning an extensive roof garden, you may want to consult a structural engineer to

Gardening in Containers—How Deep Should They Be?

In choosing containers, you'll want to consider the necessary root depth for your crops. The following is a list of depth requirements for many common vegetables, herbs, and flowers.

6–10 inches deep: Arugula, basil, beet, carrot (short or round), chervil, chicory, chive, cilantro, garden cress, lettuce (butterhead, looseleaf), mizuma and other salad mustards, onion (green and pearl), parsley, peppermint, radish, spinach, thyme, tomato (dwarf cherry), watercress.

Larger herbs, such as oregano, sage, and marjoram, will be stunted, but they will still produce a small crop.

Flowers: Small flowers such as alyssum, lobelia, pansy, dwarf marigold, or small types of dianthus.

10–15 inches deep: Carrot (longer), celery, Chinese cabbage, garlic, leek, lettuce (crisphead, romaine), mustard, oregano, potato, strawberry, Swiss chard, tomato (dwarf or patio).

Flowers: Taller flowers such as godetia, calendula, salpiglossis, cornflower or cosmos.

15–18 inches deep: Bean (all kinds), collards, cucumber, eggplant, kale, melon (short-vine varieties), pea, pepper, pumpkin (short-vine varieties), squash (summer and winter), tomato (short vines).

Flowers: Most annual and perennial flowers.

18–24 inches deep: Broccoli, brussels sprouts, cabbage, cauliflower, corn, tomato (any kind).

Flowers: Floribunda roses, small hybrid tea roses, sunflower.

Extra fertilizer and water will allow crops to grow in slightly smaller containers.

find out how much additional weight your roof can bear and whether or not the surface can withstand regular foot traffic without springing leaks.

Containers can consist of wooden planters, clay pots, plastic buckets, or even sturdy plastic bags filled with planting mix. Be sure they are deep enough for the plants you want to grow (see the sidebar above). The containers will need drainage holes. Don't risk rotting your wooden deck or stairs by placing planters directly on them. Use small wooden blocks under the containers or devise other methods to raise them so that the wood underneath stays relatively dry.

A planting medium for use in containers needs to be porous and moisture retentive. On a roof or stairway, it also needs to be as lightweight as possible. Garden soil is too heavy, and it is also too difficult to keep evenly moist in containers. Use a potting or planting mix. The high content of organic matter in these substances will make it weigh less and hold moisture better. The moisture-holding capacity is important because water evaporates more quickly from small volumes. In a mix that holds water well, the moisture level does not fluctuate as much between waterings.

Because container plants require more water, fertilizers must be applied more often. Even if you planted in pure compost, you would probably need to add liquid fertilizers, since the constant watering that containers require will leach nutrients out of the mix. (See Chapter 8 for more information on soils, planting mediums, and fertilizers.)

As you plan your container garden, consider where the water to maintain it is to come from.

Try to get a hose to the planting area, since your willingness to carry water in buckets may not last the season. For a back porch or stairway, a houseplant hose that attaches to a sink faucet may be the answer. Drip irrigation is also a great idea for a container garden; use one drip emitter for each container or one for each plant in larger containers.

As you garden higher up, you are likely to encounter stronger winds. The cooler air and the drying effect of wind will be more serious for container plants, not only because soil in containers dries out faster, but also because it heats up and cools off faster and reaches more extreme temperatures than soil in the ground. The wind can also shred and break plants.

Some plants need protection from the wind only until they are past the seedling stage. One method of protection is to plant several inches below the top of the container, then stretch a piece

of floating row cover (see page 50) over the rim. Or cover the seedbed with any of the protectors mentioned in Chapter 6, anchoring them to keep them from blowing away. A floating row cover can also be used on plants that have grown taller than the edge of the container; be sure to place the cover over a frame so that the wind doesn't cause the plants to rub against the material. Once the plants are established, mulch the soil in the containers to reduce evaporation. You may find that you can't grow vegetables in some sites without installing a windbreak. Plastic 50-percent shade cloth, which lets half of the light through and takes up little space, is a good choice for a deck or roof garden. Put it on the north and west sides to block wind best.

FIVE

Obtaining Seeds and Other Starts

NCE YOU HAVE DECIDED which crops to grow, boost your chances of success by getting the best seeds, transplants, or other starts that you can find. The plant material should be vigorous, well adapted to our climate, and free of diseases and other pests. Since some pests can spread swiftly through a planting or even the whole garden, take sensible precautions. Never plant potatoes, onions, or garlic from grocery stores, as produce doesn't have to be free of plant diseases to be sold as food. Be cautious about accepting plants from someone else's garden. Don't save and grow seeds from a diseased plant, because the disease may be seed borne. Read the individual crop listings to find out about pests that can spread by seed, in the soil, or by other methods.

BUYING SEEDS

Local seed racks are a handy source of garden seeds, but some very desirable varieties are available only by mail. Appendix VI lists seed companies that I have found useful. My favorite seed companies are those that provide the most information about the seeds they carry, include varieties especially suited to our climate, or offer the unusual. Many of the seed companies have a wide selection, but some are specialists. A few concentrate on only one or two crops, offering many varieties, including some that are well adapted to our climate. Others specialize in crops and varieties that grow in areas with climates similar to ours—for example, the Pacific Northwest, areas of Great Britain, or the Mediterranean. A number carry only heirloom, nonhybrid seed, or organically grown seed.

In the chapters on various plants you might like to grow, when there are only a few sources for a crop or a variety, I have given source lists with codes that refer to companies listed in Appendix VI, Seed and Starter Plant Sources. Here you will learn the contact information and web addresses of the companies, as well as more information on reading a seed catalog.

The Web offers a wonderful way to order seeds and other plant starts, but it is also valuable, especially for a beginner, to have several print seed catalogs in which to browse. Having them before you all at once will help you get an overview of what is available and will enable you to compare information on crops and company policies efficiently.

In comparing varieties, you will notice that the catalogs tend to present a rosy picture. If you compare the descriptions of different varieties of the same crop in the same catalog, and then compare the same varieties in different catalogs, you will learn to read between the lines. For example, the description of one variety may focus on appearance, whereas another variety may be described as the best tasting one that the seed company carries. The pretty variety may not taste very good, but you won't be told that.

Beware of novelty items that have little accompanying information. Often the description focuses on one very desirable trait but ignores other important features. It may be a "wonder" variety that is quite productive, but when you taste it you decide the real wonder is that anyone would ever want to eat it. (I immediately become suspicious of any crop that I'm told to "cook like asparagus." Very few steamed vegetables taste anything like asparagus. To me, this is nothing more than name dropping.)

Novelty crops are not necessarily unsuitable, however. For example, the purple-podded bush bean is delicious and very useful in much of our region. Try to find out as much as you can about a novelty crop before ordering it, and consider your planting an experiment, backed up with other crops that have a good chance of success.

When selecting cool-season crops, such as lettuce and broccoli, look for varieties that are suited to planting in certain seasons—for example, a particularly heat-tolerant variety in late spring and an especially cold-tolerant one in late summer. When selecting warm-season crops, such as tomatoes and corn, look for varieties that mature early, tolerate cool weather, or have a proven track record in similar climates. Varieties developed for short, hot, northern summers may or may not thrive, where summers are cooler and many summer days are foggy. In addition, at this latitude, our summer days are shorter. If a crop is susceptible to certain plant diseases that are prevalent here, check for resistance when you are evaluating varieties.

SAVING SEEDS

If you grow an open-pollinated variety (see page 42) that you particularly like and if the plants are free of seed-borne diseases, you may want to save seeds to grow next year. Our mild winter climate makes it easy to grow many crops for seed production, but other conditions complicate the process.

In a garden that is small or lies near other gardens, cross-pollination may cause undesired variability or even crosses between different related plants, such as beets and Swiss chard. You may plant what you thought were beet seeds and end up with something closer to Swiss chard! Also, damp weather may force you to harvest seeds as soon as they have matured and to dry them indoors before they decay. Here are some facts about saving seeds from vegetable crops. (For more information, see various books in Appendix VIII, Suggested Reading, about seed saving.)

Storing and Testing Seeds

At the end of the year, you will probably have leftover seed packets as well as seeds saved from your plants. All of these can be stored for planting next year. Of the common vegetables, only corn and onion seeds lose significant viability after the first year. Most seeds last three to five years.

Make sure that packets and other seed storage containers are labeled with the crop, variety, and current year's date. Store them in a cool, dry place. Keeping seed packets in closed glass jars with a commercial desiccant provides extra protection. A little powdered milk wrapped in a paper towel will also work if you change the milk after opening the jar a few times. (Bean seeds keep best in a less tightly sealed container, such as a yogurt tub.)

A simple test will determine whether or not seeds are still viable. Fold a paper towel in thirds and place a row of 10 or 20 seeds of a single variety along one short side of the rectangle, stopping 1 inch from one end. Beginning at the seeded edge, roll the towel up and fasten the ends with wire twist ties. Set the rolled towel in a drinking glass, placing the end without seeds at the bottom. Keep a little water in the glass so that the towel stays moist. After the normal germination period has passed, check to see how many seeds sprouted. If 90 percent or more germinated, the seeds are healthy. If fewer than 50 percent sprouted, discard the seeds. If the percentage is in between, use the seeds but sow them more thickly than usual.

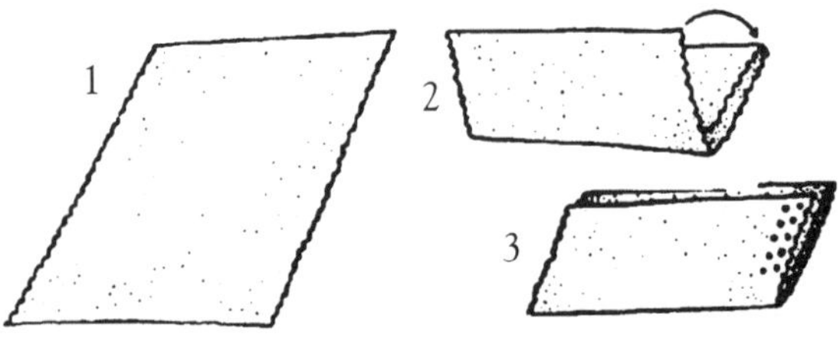

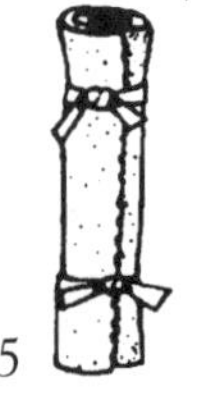

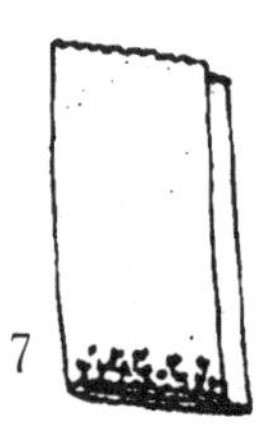

- The best seeds for a beginner to save are bean, pea, lettuce, and tomato, since these are mostly self-pollinating. The seeds of many other plants, such as squash and plants in the cabbage family, must be either pollinated by hand under a protective covering or isolated from other varieties in order to prevent unwanted crosses.
- To collect pea and bean seeds, you need only remove the mature seeds from the dry pods. Tomato seeds need a fermenting to free them from the ripe fruit. Scoop seeds and pulp from ripe tomatoes, and mix them with a little water in a clear drinking glass or jar. Stir two or three times a day. When the seeds sink to the bottom after two to four days, add water and pour off the pulp several times until the seeds are clean, and then spread them on a plate to dry. Lettuce seeds are among many seeds that must be separated from small lightweight dead flower parts, known as chaff. Rub the seeds between your finger and thumb to separate them, then blow gently to make the lightweight chaff fly away. As an alternative, shake the seeds through a screen.
- Bean, pea, lettuce, and tomato plants ripen seeds in a few months, but certain other crops may take a year or more.

BUYING TRANSPLANTS

Growing from nursery starts is easy, fast, and rewarding if you buy plants in good condition. There are times when both beginners and busy experienced gardeners appreciate the shortcut of purchasing transplants. Beginners are especially delighted to be able to create an almost instant garden.

Transplants fulfill an important role by allowing you to plant when the weather is too cold for outdoor seeding. Gardeners in our region must usually wait until May for the soil to become warm enough for tomato seeds to germinate. But if tomatoes aren't seeded until May, very little of the fruit will have time to ripen. Another example is lettuce—gardeners in this area often use lettuce transplants in winter, when the soil is too cold for lettuce seeds to germinate well, but not too cold for the plants to grow.

Transplants are less vulnerable to pests than germinating seedlings are. Tiny basil seedlings can disappear in a blink, but 6-inch-high transplants aren't as much of a pushover. If something does start chewing on them, at least you have a chance to notice the damage and take action before the plants disappear. Snails love to eat squash seedlings until the plants grow three or four leaves—that's when the leaves and stems develop unappetizing prickles.

Transplants save garden space. When you use them, you can grow more plants and produce larger harvests, because you are not taking up space getting crops from seed to the transplant stage.

What to Look For

Buy seedlings that are in the best possible condition. If you don't have much experience shopping for seedlings, get them at a reputable nursery rather than a store that keeps a few seedlings as a sideline. Examine the plants carefully. Vegetables, in particular, grow so quickly that they can't be left in tiny seedling pots for very long. When the roots begin to grow in circles and through drainage holes, the plant is said to be pot bound or root bound. Another result of sitting too long on the nursery shelf is that the seedlings use up all the nutrients in the container mix. The bottom leaves turn yellow and begin to drop, a sign of nitrogen deficiency. The remaining leaves may take on a purplish or reddish tinge, a sign that phosphorus is lacking. New leaves don't develop fully but stay small. Plants in such poor condition may be permanently damaged.

Look for plants with a fresh green color (unless another color is normal) that are at least as wide as tall and do not have roots growing out the bottom of the pot. Reject any seedlings with many leaf scars on the lower stem, indicating where leaves have fallen off. If you aren't sure, ask a nursery employee to show you seedlings that arrived within the past week and you will soon learn to recognize fresh stock.

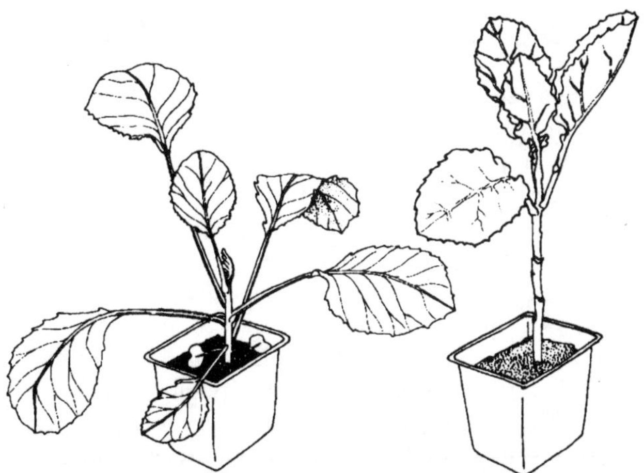

A good nursery plant. *A poor nursery plant.*

Paradoxically, young plants in small containers are often the best buy when it comes to transplants. Young plants are better able to handle the shock of transplanting than older plants are. Plants that have not yet bloomed or formed flower buds have more energy to recover from transplanting, and they will grow larger and produce more generously. Although little marigold or zucchini plants in bloom may look cute, resist the temptation to buy them. Early flowering is often a sign that the plant is stressed for water or nutrients.

There are exceptions. Tomato is such a fast-growing, almost weedy crop that larger plants, even those with flowers, often produce earlier harvests. Try planting a smaller and a larger tomato plant of the same variety on the same day to see if you really are gaining an advantage. Much depends on whether the larger tomato plant was growing in a big enough pot with adequate water and fertilizer.

Look also to see if you have one or several seedlings to a container cell. Several per cell can be a bonus, but only if their roots aren't so tightly enmeshed that some die in separation.

Beware of buying plants that will not do well in your microclimate. You can't always assume that a plant will succeed just because it is available locally. A nursery may carry melon seedlings simply because their customers ask for them, even though the chance of a melon crop in nearby neighborhoods is slight. Likewise, the nursery may stock seedlings of certain crops much earlier than they can thrive without protection in your garden. If in doubt, refer to the growing instructions for each crop in this book, or discuss the crop and its timing with a nursery employee. (See the instructions for handling transplants on page 56.)

RIGHT NAME, RIGHT PLANT

The most common vegetables have become so familiar that you can be pretty sure of getting the right crop without knowing its scientific name. Almost everyone refers only to the common name of the crop and to the variety or cultivar name, such as 'Early Girl' tomato. Knowing the scientific name can be important when you are looking for an unusual crop or an herb, and it is often helpful even when the plant is well known. Scientific names show relationships among plants, and they can help you understand how to grow a plant when you see how similar it is to another, related plant. (For more on scientific names, see Appendix II.)

Common names seem easier, but they are often confusing because they are not subject to any rules. The same common name may be used for several different plants, or one plant may have several common names. For example, the names oregano and marigold are applied to more than one species of plant. You will often read that marigold is an herb used in medieval cooking, but the marigold used was *Calendula*, the pot marigold, not *Tagetes*, the Mexican marigold that brightens so many summer flower gardens. *Tagetes*, which tastes very different from the pot marigold, was unknown in the Old World during the Middle Ages. In the case of oregano, there is a labyrinth of common and scientific names between you and the plant that you want to use to season your pizza. When you know the scientific name of a plant, you know that it will be the plant described by that name in books and that all seed packets and nursery seedlings that are correctly labeled will produce the same kind of plant.

Beginning gardeners are often put off by scientific names, probably because they can't figure out how to pronounce them or remember how to spell them. Rest assured that it isn't important for you, as a gardener, to know how to do either. Just copy the name of the plant that you want and check it against the name on a nursery label or in a seed catalog.

When it comes to vegetables, fruits, and herbs, gardeners usually want to find not only a particular species, such as tomato, but a particular variety of the species tomato. In nature, varieties are commonly formed when a group of plants in a certain species gets isolated from the main species, as they would on an island or in a mountain valley. After a period of time, they become somewhat different from the rest of the species, though they could still interbreed with it if their isolation were to end.

Humans have created many plant varieties through selective seed-saving and plant breeding, and when a variety is selected or bred by humans, it is called a *cultivar* (short for cultivated variety), though the terms *variety* and *cultivar* tend to be used interchangeably. Most of the varieties you find in seed catalogs are cultivars. For example the tomato variety 'Early Girl' is, properly speaking, the tomato cultivar *Solanum lycopersicum* 'Early Girl'.

Open-Pollinated Cultivars

Most of our common food crops have evolved from less desirable wild plants because gardeners and farmers selected seed from the plants that they thought were the best. Over the years, and over the centuries, carrot roots and tomato fruits got bigger, and green beans became more tender with less "string" to remove.

When all this selection resulted in a really good variety, farmers, gardeners, or commercial seed producers gave it a name. Then they kept it from crossing with other varieties to keep it pure, so it could be grown each year and passed down through generations. From then on, instead of trying to improve the crop, they just save seeds from the plants most like the parent plants so that they maintain the cultivar in a more or less steady state. Cultivars that are produced this way—by selecting seed from the plants most like the desired ones—are called open-pollinated cultivars.

These days you often hear the terms *heirloom seed* or *heirloom variety*. An heirloom variety is an open-pollinated one that people have preserved by saving seed each year for a long time. Heirloom is an inexact term, like *antique*. An heirloom may have been grown for hundreds of years but generally dates at least to the first half of the twentieth century. What is certain about it is that many people liked it well enough to keep it, and that it is open-pollinated. (Some heirloom varieties, such as potatoes, may be propagated by tubers, bulbs, or other nonseed means.)

With the introduction of hybrids in the mid-twentieth century, interest in heirlooms diminished for a while, but now new interest and improved worldwide communication has led to rediscovery and distribution of many heirloom varieties. Now we can enjoy treats like 'Nero di Toscana' kale and 'Stupice' tomato.

Hybrid Cultivars

Loosely speaking, a hybrid is a plant or an animal with unlike parents. We have all heard about the mule, which is a "hybrid" of a horse and a donkey—two different species of animals. And we know that a mule is sterile; it generally cannot produce offspring. While there *are* plant hybrids created by crossing different plant species, most hybrid vegetables are created by crossing two different varieties within the same species of vegetable, so the seed they produce will grow.

When you see the word *hybrid* used to describe a plant cultivar, it almost always means that the cultivar is an F_1 hybrid. F_1 means first filial generation. To understand what that means, we have to back up just a bit.

To create an F_1 hybrid, plant breeders start with a number of open-pollinated plants. They select two plants that they think are potentially good parents for their hybrid and breed each of the parents in isolation, selecting for offspring that have only the desired traits. Then, when the genetic material of each of the parent lines is uniform, they cross the parents. The seed from this cross will be the F_1 hybrid seed that they will sell.

Plant breeders use the same parents each time they want to produce more of the same hybrid seed, producing the same combination of desirable traits each time. Because certain genetic traits are more dominant—or stronger—than others, they will be expressed each time the cross is made. For example, if large fruit, mild taste, and disease resistance are dominant traits, and one or the other parent has each of them, all of the F_1 hybrid plants from that cross will have those traits.

Breeders create F_1 hybrids because growers, especially farmers, have found them useful. Hybrid seeds have been custom bred for certain combinations of traits, and the plants they grow will be uniform, all having the same traits. Also, they offer an advantage known as hybrid vigor, a special vigor that often results when plants or animals with very different genetic material are crossed.

Which Is Best?

Some gardeners grow mainly open-pollinated or mainly hybrid seed. I grow more open-pollinated than hybrid seed but will select hybrid seed sometimes to obtain particular traits. Here are some of the advantages and disadvantages of the different types of seed:

On the plus side, a hybrid cultivar is uniform. An 'Early Girl F_1' tomato from one seed company should be genetically the same as from any other. It also means that the plants you plant should all behave in the same way. If the cultivar has disease resistance or an early ripening date, all plants should have these traits. You also benefit from the extensive testing breeders do for hybrids, such as for disease resistance. Finally, hybrid vigor may make it easier to produce a crop if the crop is borderline for our climate.

On the minus side, you can't save seed from a hybrid cultivar. That is, you can certainly collect the seed, and you can plant it, and, unlike the less viable mule, it will probably grow, but the offspring will show every possible recombination of the traits of the parents. Only about a fourth of the plants are likely to resemble the parents. That is, the F_1 hybrid is unstable. If you keep selecting the best plants from each generation and growing them out, year after year, you could eventually create your own open-pollinated cultivar based on the genetic material in the hybrid, but most of us don't have the space and time to do that. So, if we buy hybrid seed, we buy it again each year.

Another minus is that if everyone bought only hybrid seed, some very good open-pollinated seeds would be likely to be lost.

When you buy open-pollinated seed, you contribute to maintaining genetic variability—keeping many old cultivars alive and well. And many of these varieties are very good. They introduce a wider variety of colors, forms, and flavors. They may even have disease resistances, though they have not been formally tested for them. They show more variation among plants grown from the same seed package. This can be good if it means that they don't all ripen at the same time, since home gardeners often prefer, for example, a few weeks to eat up the cauliflower.

Open-pollinated seeds can be saved and replanted, so you don't have to rebuy seed every year. (Though if the crop you are growing can be cross-pollinated, you will have to make sure that no pollen from other cultivars has reached your crop's flowers; for example, you don't want pumpkin pollen to reach your zucchini flowers. For more information see page 40, page 265, and books on seed saving in Appendix VIII, Suggested Reading.)

On the minus side, you may not be able to find an open-pollinated cultivar with just the traits you want. Most of my favorite cucumber cultivars are F_1 hybrid crosses between regular slicers and Asian-type cucumbers. These cultivars have the mild flavor and tender skin of the Asian cukes, but are much better at coping with cool weather.

An interesting aside concerning open-pollinated cultivars is that, because they are not totally uniform genetically, strains may develop among plants of the same cultivar being maintained in different places. Thus the seeds of "Yellow Sweet Spanish" onions that you get from one seed source may be slightly genetically different from the ones you get from another source. This can work to your advantage if one strain is better adapted to your growing conditions. To find out if open-pollinated strains are different and how they differ, talk to an expert, such as a seed company professional or a plant breeder who has worked with them, or try the different strains yourself and compare them.

Compare Cultivars

Whether you grow hybrid or open-pollinated cultivars or both, it is a good idea to keep trying and comparing new ones. This will help you find the very best ones for your growing conditions—and the ones you like best to eat.

To run a simple variety trial, grow a minimum of four plants each of at least two cultivars or two different strains of an open-pollinated cultivar. Plant all of the seeds on the same day and grow them under similar conditions. Compare the time to the first harvest, the size of the plants or the amount of harvestable fruit, the flavor, and other traits. When you find a favorite, grow it each year, but keep trying new alternatives.

SIX

Getting Plants Started

CAN'T BELIEVE EVERYTHING grew!" is an exclamation I often hear from first-time gardeners. Yet why shouldn't crops grow? Countless people have grown our common vegetables and herbs over the centuries, depending on them for food and seasoning. From the beginning, gardeners chose food plants partly for their easy natures. Through selection and breeding they created plants that were even more dependable. Although the history of domesticated flowers is shorter, we can still choose from a rainbow of easy-to-grow flowers.

From the time that growing fields were first cultivated, gardeners have figured out the most efficient ways to get plants started. Some plants grow better when they are direct-seeded—sown where you want them to grow in the garden. These plants include fast, vigorous growers, such as mustard greens, and crops that transplant badly, such as carrots. For crops that can be easily moved, such as cabbage, the use of transplants means earlier starts and better protection from pests. Plants whose growth from seed is impossible, unreliable, or very slow are usually grown in ways that bypass seeding—for example, onions grown from sets or herbs grown from cuttings.

SOWING SEEDS DIRECTLY

Seeds are designed to spring into action as soon as conditions are right for growth. These conditions—warmth, moisture, oxygen, soft soil, and protection from pests—are more difficult to control when you direct-seed in the garden than when you sow indoors in seeding trays. If you follow these planting guidelines, however, you should have little trouble getting outdoor-sown seeds off to a good start.

Making Sure the Soil Is Warm Enough

The seeds of most warm-season plants require a minimum soil temperature of 60°F for germination. The seeds of most cool-season plants need at least 40°F, although a few crops can sprout at 35°F. These include lettuce, onions, spinach, and parsnip. All seeds germinate faster and better in soil that is warmer than the minimum: 80° to 90°F for warm-season crops and 70° to 80°F for cool-season crops. When we start seeds indoors, we commonly aim for these ideal, higher temperatures.

If the temperature of the top 2 inches of soil, where seeds are planted, is going to rise above 60°F in our climate, it will generally do so by May. (You can be pretty sure that the soil is above 60°F when it feels warm to your hand.) The soil temperature begins to drop by October, falling into the forties or even the thirties by December, and then rises slowly as the days lengthen.

Most gardeners don't know the temperature of their soil, instead making rough guesses. This usually is fine, but if you want to become more precise, get a soil thermometer from a garden shop or nursery. To find out how warm the soil is where seeds will germinate, insert the thermometer 2 inches deep.

Preparing the Soil

Work the soil when it is moist, but not soggy. If the soil is too dry or too wet, you will damage its structure by digging—and the seeds may not come up anyhow. Soggy soil packs tightly, cutting off oxygen and suffocating the seeds. Dry soil is difficult to moisten thoroughly without washing away the seeds;

also, seeds that are surrounded by dry pockets won't be able to germinate. To see if your soil has the correct moisture level for digging and planting, pick up a handful and squeeze it in your hand. Soil that is too dry won't form a clump. If it is wet enough to form a clump, prod it lightly with a finger. Soil that is too wet will remain in a clump. Soil that is just right will crumble easily when prodded.

If the soil is bone-dry, as it may be in midsummer, soak the planting area for two hours, then let it dry for a day or more before you plant. Never water the soil on the same day that you plant until after the seeds are in the ground.

If the soil is too soggy, allow it to dry out for a few days. Sometimes in late winter or early spring, soil is still too wet when I am ready to put early crops in the ground. I have often been able to plant sooner at this time of year by tarping a garden plot during rain. Place an overturned bucket or two in the center of the plot, drape with the tarp so that the water will run off, and then weight the edges of the tarp with bricks or rocks. Take the tarp off as soon you have a day or more of dry weather so that the soil can dry faster.

Plan what you will add to improve your soil. Rock fertilizers and well-decayed organic matter, such as compost, rotted (aged) manure, and peat moss, can be mixed into the soil on the day that you dig it. Soluble commercial chemical fertilizers and high-nitrogen organic fertilizers such as blood meal can also be applied the same day that you plant, but they should not be mixed evenly into the soil. To keep the concentrated chemicals from burning plant roots, apply these materials 2 to 3 inches to one side of the seeds. As an alternative, place them 2 to 3 inches below the seeds. The fertilizers will dissolve and move downward when you water, and the roots will grow into the fertilized area without being burned.

Do not turn under a cover crop or any other undecayed organic matter, such as fresh manure, kitchen garbage, or fresh weeds, on the day that you plant. Wait several weeks after you dig in such materials to avoid burning your seeds or the roots of your crops.

When your soil's moisture level is correct for digging and your plot is cleared of weeds, you are ready to prepare your seedbed. If you are going to add soil amendments or fertilizers to the whole area on the day you plant, spread each one over the entire bed. When you have them all on the soil, loosen it by turning the top 6 to 8 inches with a shovel. Walk backward as you dig, to avoid stepping on the freshly turned earth. Lift a shovelful of soil and flip it off the shovel so that it falls on its side—turned one-quarter to three-quarters of the way over. (Mixing doesn't need to be complete, just enough to get your added materials into slots in the soil.) Use your shovel to break up large clods, and reach down to remove any large rocks or perennial weed roots you turn up. Use your shovel to roughly relevel the soil as you dig. As much as possible, avoid walking on the prepared soil.

Use a rake, a hoe, or your hands to form a fine seedbed in the top 3 to 4 inches of soil. Do this by crumbling small clods and removing stones or chunks of organic matter. The seedbed needs to be finer for small seeds than for larger ones; a piece of undecayed bark that a bean seedling can easily push aside will stop a carrot seedling in its tracks. Smooth and level the soil, using your hand in a small area and a garden rake in a larger area. The bed should be level so that water doesn't collect on one side, although a very slight slope will help clay soil to drain.

How Deep? How Far Apart?

Use the information on the seed packet as a general guide to planting depth and spacing, but take into account that the directions may refer to row plantings. For a bed, use the spacing suggested for plants within a single row. For example, if the packet recommends planting 2 to 3 inches apart in rows 18 to 30 inches apart, then space all the seeds 2 to 3 inches apart in a bed. When you switch to seeds of another kind of plant, add together half the proper distance for each, and leave that much space between the two plantings. When you plant in hills, or small groupings, don't put all the seeds in the same spot; leave the suggested space between them.

You can still plant in rows if you like, but rows can be much closer together, maybe 2 to 3 times the distance between plants in a row. You can also plant wide rows instead of a single file of seeds. Do this by preparing a seedbed 6 or 12 inches wide and sowing seeds all across it. This is a particularly useful way to grow small leafy plants, such as cilantro or spinach or root crops like carrots. You can even plant a few square feet of a crop, scattering the seeds at the distance apart suggested on the seed packet.

Large seeds can be planted individually where you want them. It is possible to plant small seeds the same way, but scattering them is easier and just as effective. You may want to sow small seeds more thickly than usual as insurance against seedling loss, but you don't want a solid mat of seedlings.

Making a Seed Glass

If you are new at gardening or are growing an unfamiliar crop, you may have trouble recognizing the tiny seedlings when they emerge. The seed leaves of most plants look very different from the true leaves. To the inexperienced eye, weed seedlings may look like crop seedlings—or worse, the crop seedlings may resemble weed seedlings and get pulled! Here is a method that will help you identify the seedlings that you are growing.

You will need a paper towel and a straight-sided clear drinking glass or wide-mouthed jar, 1½ to 2½ inches in diameter. Fold the towel roughly in thirds, so that it is as wide as the glass is tall. Roll it into a tube that is about the same diameter as the glass. Insert the towel tube and push it against the inside of the glass so that it opens a bit and rests on the glass in several places. Pour an inch or so of water in the bottom of the glass. When the towel has absorbed water to the top, pull it back in several places and drop a seed in, until there are five to ten seeds resting partway down around the glass. Place the glass in a warm room and check it daily to be sure that there is water in the bottom.

You can start a seed glass anytime, but if you start it on the same day that you sow the seeds outdoors, you will get an idea of what is happening beneath the soil. The seeds in the glass will probably germinate ahead of the seeds sown outdoors if your house is warmer than the garden soil. Notice that the roots grow before you see shoots; this tells you that the garden-planted seeds are active before you see them break through the surface. When shoots begin to form on the seedlings in the glass, move the glass close to your brightest window so that the seedlings will develop normally enough to be identified. Seedlings germinated this way will not transplant well and should be discarded.

Fold a paper towel in thirds, then roll it into a tube with about the same diameter as the glass. Moisten the towel and plant seeds between it and the glass—the seedlings will show you what to expect in your garden.

To prevent this, before you scatter small seeds, mix them with sand, sieved compost, damp milled sphagnum (peat) moss, or coir.

Gardeners with limited space often try to squeeze in as many plants as they can. Most plants should be spaced far enough apart so that at maturity their leaves just touch those of the next plant. There should be at least ½ to 1 inch between the mature roots of a root crop. Some crops, such as kohlrabi, are very sensitive to crowding and will not mature properly when spaced closer than the seed packet suggests. Other crops, such as bush beans, don't mind being a little jostled.

Closer spacing will give you more plants in the same area, but generally, each plant will be less productive. If the plants are only moderately crowded, the total harvest will be bigger than if you had used the recommended spacing. However, each crop has a point beyond which crowding will decrease total yield. You can jam in more plants when you are planning to harvest them young—for example, baby beets or mustard greens. Another special case is the seeding bed. Close spacing doesn't matter, since you'll be transplanting the seedlings to another, permanent bed when they are still small.

For planting depth, follow the advice on the seed packet. The rule of thumb is to plant at a depth two to three times the diameter of the seed. In very sandy soil or during one of our uncommonly warm spells, plant a bit deeper to lessen the risk of the seeds drying out. In clay soil or during cold weather, plant a bit shallower. Seeds that must struggle to find the surface, especially in cold soil, may rot before they break through.

Putting the Seeds In

When planting individual seeds, use your finger or a small stick to make each planting hole the recommended depth. When planting seeds in a row, open a furrow with a trowel or other tool, then drop the seeds in and gently firm the soil back on top.

To scatter-sow, skim off a thin layer of soil and pile it on one side of the planting area. Working in 1- to 4-square-foot blocks marked off with stakes will help you keep track of your progress when you are sowing a large area. After scattering the seeds, sprinkle soil from the pile until the seeds are covered to the desired depth.

The soil used to cover seeds should be fine and well pulverized, with no rocks or large pieces of organic matter that may block the emerging seedlings. If your soil is clayey, you will get better results by covering the seeds with dampened sifted compost, potting mix, or milled sphagnum moss.

Use your hands to firm the soil over the seeds, but don't walk on the seedbed. (I remember Dad asking me when I was a small child to walk barefoot down the just-planted rows. It took only one try as an adult to realize why he had asked *me* to do it!) The soil should press against the seeds, but not so tightly that the seeds can't push out.

Use small sticks to mark off the area that you planted. If you are planting several crops at the same time, put in plant labels or draw a map so that you will remember what you planted and where you planted it. Water the seedbed thoroughly, using a sprinkler that lets the water fall like a gentle rain.

Until seedlings are a couple of inches high, you need to water your seedbeds and young seedlings whenever the soil surface has been dry for a half day. You don't need to water very long, since the deeper soil is still moist, but remember that the seeds and the roots of seedlings are near the surface and can die from too little water in only a day or two. Even if you have a drip irrigation system, you still need to keep the surface moist at this time. Some gardeners have rigged a mini sprinkler system on a separate timer, around beds, so it can supplement the drip system while there are seedbeds or seedlings in the bed. But if you can check every day or so, this shouldn't be necessary.

Troubleshooting

What if you wait twice the number of days suggested on the seed packet and still nothing comes up? What could have gone wrong? Consider these possibilities, keeping in mind that there may be more than one cause. Plant again, this time taking precautions and watching more closely.

- The seeds may have dried out in the middle of germination. Did the weather suddenly turn hot, or did you forget to water? Did you neglect to firm the soil in the seedbed?
- The seeds may have rotted. Did you plant much earlier than recommended? Did you plant too deep? Did you water clay soil too much, especially during cold weather?
- The seeds may have been too old to germinate. Did you keep the seeds too long before planting them? Corn and onion seeds last only a year or two; others last up to five years if they are kept cool and dry.

- The seedbed may have been damaged. Cats often ruin seedbeds because they love to dig in freshly turned soil. Sometimes people accidentally tread on unmarked seedbeds, crushing the seedlings before they come up.
- An insect or other animal pest may have eaten the seedlings before you even noticed that the plants were up. Snails, slugs, cutworms, earwigs, pillbugs, sowbugs, birds, and rabbits are among the local pests that eat seedlings. Sometimes they gobble young plants so quickly that you are positive that nothing came up. If you keep close watch, however, you will see the tiny seedling stems, shorn of their leaves, standing for a day or so before they wilt to nothing.

Presprouting Crop Seeds

Sometimes you can improve your success rate by presprouting the seeds—that is, getting them to germinate before you plant them. Carrot, celery, and parsley seeds are sometimes presprouted to shorten their long germination periods. Corn is often presprouted to be sure that the seeds have the warmth they need while germinating. Other seeds can be presprouted, although it will not help beans and peas—in fact, experiments have shown that presprouting lessens their vigor.

Arrange the seeds between two dampened paper towels placed on a plate or tray. Keep the towels moist until the seeds swell and the root tips just begin to push their way out. Large seeds can be uncovered and planted individually. If you were careful to space small seeds the right distance apart, you can plant them, towels and all, at the recommended seeding depth; the roots will grow through the towel, which will soon disintegrate in the seedbed.

Protecting Seedlings

Germinating seeds and small seedlings demand special attention during their first few weeks, when they are especially vulnerable to pests and to competition from weeds and from other crop seedlings growing too close to them.

Clear potential pests from the seeding area before you plant, and consider using barriers to protect your seedlings until they are growing well. If snails are your worst problem, you can reduce the hazard considerably by nailing copper strips around the frame of a planting bed (see page 125). Sprinkling weed leaves on the seedbed may discourage cats. (For more information on protecting seedlings from pests, see the individual pest listings in Chapter 9.)

For severe pest problems, a floating row cover provides maximum protection. Place the cover over a large planting or cut it into pieces to protect individual plants or small groups of plants. Start with a piece larger than the area you wish to protect so that you can gather the material to form a loose center, giving the seedlings a little room to grow. Tuck the edges firmly into the soil all around. For convenience in tending the seedbed without having to remove the row cover and tuck it in each time, stretch the cover over a wooden frame. A rectangle built from 1 by 4s will protect seedlings. To protect taller plants, build an open-sided frame made of 1 by 1s. Let the row cover extend below the frame, and then staple it to the inside of the wood. To prevent entry by pests, press the frame firmly against the soil and push a little soil against it.

Weeds compete with tiny crop seedlings for water, nutrients, and light. See Chapter 10 for information on weed control, including methods of presprouting weeds to clean up a seedbed before you plant.

As damaging as weed competition can be, competition from other crop seedlings is just as serious, because they are vying for the same nutrients in the same tier of soil. The result is smaller, weaker plants. Unless you are growing a crop for harvest when it is very young, thin the plants when they are still small, before they have begun to crowd each other. Use scissors to cut the unwanted seedlings at ground level so that you don't damage the roots of the remaining plants. Seed packets usually provide instructions for thinning if it will be required. Also look for any special instructions for individual vegetables in Chapter 11.

GROWING YOUR OWN TRANSPLANTS

Although raising transplants takes time and care, it is cheaper than buying nursery starts, and it gives you many more options. Homegrown transplants, just like purchased ones, allow earlier planting, withstand pests better than direct-seeded plants, and save garden space. You can start transplants indoors anytime, or you can sow seeds in a special garden bed during warmer weather. For example, in June you can use a square foot of space as a seeding bed for growing beet and broccoli transplants, which you can move to a permanent spot in your

Floating Row Covers

These translucent lightweight materials, similar to nonwoven interfacing used in sewing, offer many benefits to gardeners. Pests can't get through them, but water and most of the light can. The air under them is several degrees warmer than the surrounding air. They also reduce evaporation, keeping the soil beneath them more evenly moist.

Floating row covers have other advantages over clear plastic sheets. When you use a floating row cover in spring or fall, you should never have to rush out and lift it to keep the plants from scorching. In cool, foggy summers, only rare heat waves will necessitate removal of the cover. (Remove it when temperatures exceed 80°F.) A floating row cover can usually rest directly on the plants, without any stakes to hold it up—although in very windy sites it may require support to prevent injury to seedlings.

The covers are available in different weights, and if pest protection is your main goal, use a lightweight material that blocks as little as 5 percent of the light. Floating row covers may make your garden look like a laundry after a windstorm has blown through, but the untidiness is a small price to pay for sneaking tender seedlings past hungry snails and other pests. (Appendix VII includes suppliers of floating row covers.)

vegetable garden in July after you harvest garlic or a spring lettuce crop.

When you produce your own transplants, you have a wider choice of varieties. Nurseries can't possibly carry all the new varieties developed every year. The public expects to find the most common varieties at the nursery, which leaves little room for less familiar varieties that may be better suited to our area. Sometimes the best choices for your microclimate are available only as seeds. The broccoli transplants in nurseries are almost always short-season varieties, not the long-season, overwintering ones that do so well in our mild winters. Pepper seedlings are likely to be 'Yolo Wonder', whereas several other varieties, such as 'Gypsy' and 'Early Cal Wonder', bear more fruit in a borderline microclimate.

Another advantage of growing your own transplants is greater control over timing. I often find that the seedling I want is not available at the nursery when I want to plant it. I want broccoli transplants in July, but they usually don't arrive in nurseries until a month or so later.

Finally, it is fun to grow seedlings because there are almost always some to share. I start more than I need, because who knows how many will grow? Usually, most of them come up and reach transplanting age. After moving as many as I want into the garden, I wait a week for any disasters to happen. Once the cutworms or hailstorms have taken their toll, I fill in with some of the extra seedlings. Any that remain are for friends, to let them try new varieties and to celebrate nature's generosity.

You may choose to grow seedlings indoors because it's easier to keep an eye on them. I always start celery, parsley, leek, and onion seeds indoors, because they take so long to germinate and the plants are so slow in their initial growth that I am afraid I will overlook them in the garden.

It is important to know the best times to sow each kind of seed and how long it should grow before it is ready for transplanting. The seeding chart on pages 52–53 provides information on growing transplants for various vegetable crops.

Notice that there is often a range of times when seeds can be sown for transplants. When crops have a short planting season, as do cucumbers and brussels sprouts, it is a good idea to sow seeds at the beginning of the period suggested in the chart; if the sowing isn't successful, you can try again before it's too late. When the planting season is longer, as it is for beets or lettuce, you can start seeds every few weeks for a series of harvests.

Few crops benefit from being grown indoors longer than the time given in the seeding chart. Peppers and tomatoes may profit, but only if they are moved into large enough containers and given adequate light, water, and fertilizer. To grow them indoors for more than six to eight weeks, you would probably need a greenhouse, a large sunny window, or artificial lighting suitable for growing plants.

To start transplants indoors you will need a sterile potting mix, containers, drip trays, a warm place for germination, and a cooler, well-lighted place where the seedlings can grow.

Choosing a Seeding Mix

There are many recipes for seeding mixes, and no single right choice. The easiest course is to buy a seeding or potting mix. In addition to being sterilized, purchased mixes are formulated to hold air and moisture. Most mixes are adequate for seeding, but at the nursery you can request one with a finer texture. Or, if you already have a coarse mix, just sieve out the large particles before using it for small seeds. Although most commercial mixes work fine, occasionally you will run into a problem. I don't know why, but very few seeds came up in one mix that I tried some years ago. (Currently, potting mix manufacturers aren't required to reveal information such as nutrient analysis, pH, or salt content, but they may have to disclose it in the future.) Try planting a few seeds in a bit of the mix; if they sprout, proceed with the planting.

Many gardeners like to make their own seeding mix. Some start their seeds in pure horticultural vermiculite (the mineral mica treated with heat). Others make mixes using various purchased materials. One common mix consists of equal parts horticultural vermiculite, perlite (a form of volcanic ash), and milled sphagnum moss. Another popular mix calls for equal parts loamy soil, milled sphagnum, and sharp builder's sand (not beach sand, which is too fine as well as too salty).

If you use garden soil in your mix, pasteurize it first. Otherwise, your seedlings will be exposed to diseases—particularly damping-off, probably the most common cause of death of seedlings grown indoors. (For information on damping-off, see Chapter 9.) Also pasteurize any seeding mix that you are reusing.

Soil can be pasteurized in a regular oven, but it will reek unless you take precautions. Keep the odor to a minimum by using a large plastic broiling bag, sold in supermarkets for cooking meat. Place about a gallon of moistened soil in the bag, fasten the bag as directed on the label, and heat at 275°F for 30 to 40 minutes. You don't want the soil temperature to exceed 180°F, because higher temperatures will kill more of the helpful organisms in the soil and will also release dissolved salts, which are toxic to plant roots. To check the temperature, insert a meat thermometer through the bag. Do this toward the end of the heating time, so that the odor escapes only briefly.

Make sure that the medium is moist but not wet when you plant the seeds. Seeding mixes can be moistened right before you plant, since they contain much more organic matter than garden soil and are less likely to compact. If your mix is bone-dry, pour it into a large plastic container or bowl and add barely enough water to moisten it, then stir well with your hands.

A seeding mix needn't contain nutrients, since the newly emerged seedling draws on nutrients stored in the seed. If your homemade mix doesn't contain fertilizer, add it only after the seedling develops its second set of true leaves. Many commercial potting mixes contain fertilizer, but that may not be indicated on the bag, and nursery workers don't always know. I usually watch the seedlings for good healthy color and fertilize if the color fades. A good fertilizer for seedlings is fish emulsion or a liquid houseplant fertilizer, applied at half the recommended strength once a week.

Choosing Seeding Containers

Almost any container 2 to 3 inches deep can be used for seeding. Deeper containers use more planting mix than necessary, since the seedlings will be transplanted before the roots are 3 inches long. Individual containers are the easiest to use, since you won't have to separate the roots at transplanting time. Six-celled nursery containers, paper cups, margarine and yogurt containers, and plastic or clay pots are all suitable for seeding transplants. If a container doesn't have drainage holes, puncture the bottom.

Half-gallon milk cartons are useful for starting transplants. Cut them in half lengthwise and use the halves as flats in which to start small seedlings. Or cut them in half the other way and use the bottoms as 4-inch pots and the tops as square rings for starting fast-growing plants with delicate roots, such as squash and cucumbers.

To use the rings, set them in a drip tray, fill them with potting mix, and plant the seeds. At transplanting time you will be able to lift the cardboard rings.

I rarely use purchased options such as peat pots or peat pellets, because they are expensive and I have observed that plant roots don't always grow through them as they are supposed to. I do use an Accelerated Propagation System (APS) seed starter. Each reusable unit has a tray of open-bottomed cubicles (my favorite has twelve). The cubicles are

Growing Your Own Transplants

When to Seed

These are the months during which it is most useful to start seeds to grow transplants. When there is more than one useful time to start seeds, I have listed it.

Reason

I've given the most important reasons for growing your own transplants of each crop. There are often different reasons to grow transplants of a crop at different times of year. I've used the following codes to describe possible reasons:

EM=easier to monitor than in garden
PP=pest protection
ES=to get an early start
SS=to save garden space
NN=not in nursery at time needed
DV=to get different varieties

When more than one reason is given for planting at a particular time, they are listed in order of importance, with the most important reason first.

Time Required

This is the number of weeks you should allow between seeding the crop and transplanting seedlings into the garden. It includes time for hardening off.

Pot Up?

Here is an indication of whether or not the crop is easily, or usually, or even can be, moved to a larger pot before it is planted out in the garden. Yes means it can be and often is done. Possible means it is possible but not usually done. No means it's not done.

Starred (*) crops are the ones you may find most useful to grow as transplants. These are the crops that transplant best and give you the greatest benefits in terms of an early start and/or protection from pests.

Except for leeks and onions, seedlings that you are about to transplant to the garden should be roughly as wide as they are tall. Be especially careful not to let your bean, pea, squash, cucumber, pumpkin, or corn seedlings get overgrown before you transplant them. It is best in most cases to sow seeds of those crops directly in the garden, but if you do choose to grow seedlings for transplanting, plant them out when they have only 2 or 3 true leaves.

Crop	When to Seed	Reason	Time Required	Pot Up?
Asparagus	Feb–April	EM, SS	8–12 weeks	yes
Basil*	March–May	PP, DV, ES	3–4 weeks	possible
Bean, Snap	Late March to mid-April	ES, PP	3–4 weeks	no
Beet*	Jan–Feb	ES	4 weeks	no
	April–July	SS	4 weeks	no
Broccoli*	Dec–Jan	ES, DV, NN	5–7 weeks	yes
	Feb–July 1	DV, NN, SS	5–7 weeks	yes
Brussels Sprouts*	May–June	DV, NN, SS	5–7 weeks	yes
Cabbage*	Dec–Jan	DV, ES, NN	5–7 weeks	yes
	April–July	DV, SS	5–7 weeks	yes
	Aug–Oct	DV, ES, SS	5–7 weeks	yes

Crop	When to Seed	Reason	Time Required	Pot Up?
Cauliflower	June–Aug	DV, SS	5–7 weeks	yes
	Jan–April	DV, SS	5–7 weeks	yes
Celery*	Jan–Feb	EM, ES	8–12 weeks	possible
	July–Aug	EM, SS	8–12 weeks	possible
Chard	Dec–Jan	ES	4 weeks	yes
Chayote*	Nov–March	EM, ES, PP	4–12 weeks	yes
Chives*	Dec–Feb	EM, ES	4–6 weeks	possible
Collards*	Dec–Jan	ES	5–7 weeks	yes
Corn	Early April	ES	3–4 weeks	no
Cucumber	March–April	ES, PP	3–4 weeks	no
	April–May	PP	3–4 weeks	no
Kale	Dec–Jan	ES	4–6 weeks	yes
	Aug–Sept	SS	4–6 weeks	yes
Kohlrabi	June–July	SS	4–6 weeks	possible
Leek*	Dec–Jan	EM, ES	10–12 weeks	yes
Lettuce*	Feb–Sept	DV, EM, PP, SS	3–6 weeks or more	yes
	Oct–Jan	ES, EM, PP, DV	3–6 weeks or more	yes
New Zealand Spinach*	March	EM, ES	8–12 weeks	possible
Onion seed (for bulb onions)	Sept–Dec	DV, EM, ES	8–10 weeks	yes
Onion seed (for green onions)	Any time	EM	8–10 weeks	no
Parsley	Dec–Feb	EM, ES	6–8 weeks	possible
	March–May	EM, SS	6–8 weeks	possible
Pea	Oct–Nov	PP, SS	3–4 weeks	no
	Jan–Feb	ES, PP	3–4 weeks	no
Pepper*	March–April	DV, ES	6–8 weeks or more	yes
Pumpkin	March–May	ES, PP	3–4 weeks	no
Spinach	Feb–Mar	ES, PP	4–6 weeks	no
Squash (winter)	March–May	ES, PP	3–4 weeks	no
Squash (summer)	Feb–May	ES, PP	3–4 weeks	no
Tomato*	Dec–April	DV, ES	6–10 weeks or more	yes

watered automatically by an absorbent mat that wicks water up from a reservoir. With this gadget, you can sow seeds and then go out of town for a week without losing a single plant. If you grow more than one kind of plant in the same APS unit, be sure their germination times are similar, so you can transplant them all at once. (The APS seed starter is sold by Gardener's Supply; see Resources for Gardeners, Appendix VII.)

Used seeding containers can be a source of damping-off, although I have often simply washed them in plain water and had no problem. If you want to be sure, or if damping-off has been killing your seedlings, run dishwasher-safe containers through a cycle. Scrub other containers thoroughly, then soak them for ten minutes in 9 parts water and 1 part household bleach, and rinse well.

PLANTING THE SEEDS

In each container, plant two or three seeds at the recommended depth. Pat the seeding mix gently but firmly, leaving the surface flat and level. Label the containers and note what you planted in a journal or calendar. You can buy plastic labels at a nursery, cut your own labels from cottage cheese or yogurt cartons, or use popsicle sticks. Write with a waterproof marking pen or a number two pencil. When you use an APS starter, you can draw a map of what you planted in it. (I've found it helpful to put an indelible ink mark on one corner of the tray, so that I can quickly see if it faces the same direction as the map that I have drawn.)

Water well with a gentle trickle or soft spray until the container drips, or set the container in a pan of water and let the seeding mix absorb water, remembering to drain the pan as soon as the mix is thoroughly moist. Although a greenhouse is designed for dripping pots, the rooms in your home are not. Set your seeding containers in shallow baking pans, polystyrene trays from grocery purchases, or cafeteria trays from a restaurant supply store.

Check your seeding containers daily, and water just a little whenever you notice that the surface is dry. Don't keep the mix soggy or let the containers stand in water, since excessive moisture encourages damping-off. Covering the containers with a plastic bag or a sheet of glass will help keep the moisture in, but don't make the cover airtight or let it touch the surface of the mix.

Until the seeds break through the surface, keep the containers in a warm location away from direct sunlight, such as the top of a refrigerator, or water heater, or on a shelf above a radiator. Different kinds of seeds have different optimum soil temperatures for germination, but most perform best when given more heat than the average room temperature (see page 45). They will still germinate if your house is cool, but it may take a few days longer. If your house is often chilly and your seeds are taking a long time to germinate, consider purchasing a seedling heat mat. This relatively inexpensive plug-in appliance is as thin as a piece of cardboard and can be rolled up for storage. I use one that is 12 by 20 inches (I don't use the thermostat, which is sold separately) and it has worked well to hurry up seed germination in the winter months.

Enough Light?

Seedlings should be as wide as they are tall; that is, the height of the plant should be similar to the spread of the seed leaves or, later, the true leaves. If seedlings become tall and narrow, with small leaves, your indoor growing location doesn't have enough light. This is most likely when you are trying to start transplants during the short, dim days of December and January.

If you aren't sure whether you have a window bright enough to grow seedlings, grow a small container of seedlings indoors at the same time that you are starting the crop in your garden. Keep the container in the brightest spot you have. Right up next to a south-facing window is best. After a while, compare the plantings. Lettuce is a good seedling to try, since you can start it outdoors during most of the year. If you have enough light indoors to grow reasonably sturdy lettuce seedlings, then you have enough light to grow most other seedlings for at least a few weeks.

You can make a perfectly good indoor lighting setup inexpensively using an ordinary shop light and two fluorescent bulbs. The bulbs can be cool white or one cool white and one warm white. As the seedlings grow, keep their tops 6 inches from the lights, by either raising the fixture (using hooks on chains) or starting the plants on piled-up bricks or newspapers and removing layers as the plants grow.

Caring for the Seedlings

As soon as the first plants come up, take off any covering and move the containers to a cooler, brighter spot. A window or protected porch, where the temperature is 60° to 65°F during the daytime and cooler (but not below 50°F) at night, is ideal. Check the soil daily, making sure that it doesn't get too dry or too soggy. The seedlings will bend a little to reach for the light, but they won't develop a permanent crook if you turn the containers daily. When you see the first true leaves forming above the seed leaves, thin the seedlings enough so that you will be able to separate them to transplant them. Choose the sturdiest seedlings and use scissors to clip the others at the soil surface, since pulling them out may damage the roots of the remaining plants.

Watch the seedlings closely to be sure that they are continuing to grow. Slowed growth indicates that the plants are becoming root bound—their roots have filled the pot and are beginning to circle it. Seedlings that become root bound may never grow to full size, so it is important to get your little plants into the garden or, if advisable for that crop, into larger pots.

Some plants can or should be potted up—moved to a larger pot to grow a little more before being planted outdoors. If you are going to pot up, you can do it as soon as the seedlings have developed their first true leaves. Be very careful when handling seedlings; they are fragile, and a light touch is essential. Separate and lift plants, keeping as much seeding mix as possible on their roots. With six-packs, push the plants out from the bottom. Move each seedling to a container that is 2 to 4 inches in diameter, such as a small plastic pot or the lower half of a quart or half-gallon milk carton with drainage holes punched in the bottom. Put some fresh potting mix in the container and set the seedling at the same level at which it was growing. Fill potting mix in around the seedling, press down carefully but firmly, and water well. Keep newly potted seedlings out of strong light for a day or two.

If a seedling is potted up twice before it is moved to the garden, add a little sieved compost or composted manure to the potting mix for the final pot. You don't need to pasteurize it, since seedlings become less susceptible to damping-off as they grow older.

Hardening Off the Seedlings

Plants can't be moved directly from your living room or kitchen to the more demanding environment of the garden. While they are still in their containers, they need gradual exposure to outdoor temperatures and light intensities—a process called *hardening off*. Prepare them by withholding fertilizer and keeping the soil on the dry side for about a week.

Every day for a week or more, leave the plants outdoors for gradually longer periods, but bring them in at night. Put them in the shade at first, then in a partly sunny place, and finally in a location as sunny as your garden plot. Don't leave them where they will be whipped around in the wind, and be sure to bring them indoors if frost is expected. If you can't harden off the plants as gradually as you would like, just do the best you can. As an alternative, begin the process in a cold frame in a shady spot; you needn't bring them indoors at night unless the weather is expected to turn very cold. (See page 58 for more on cold frames.)

Transplants from a nursery have already been hardened off before you buy them. Buy nursery starts no more than a few days before you intend to plant them. Keep them outdoors, but pay attention, because the small amount of soil in the container will dry out quickly. Water them lightly to keep the soil moist. Don't add any fertilizer before you plant the seedlings in the garden, since you don't want to encourage rapid growth until the plants have more space for roots.

Moving Transplants into the Garden

The best time to move transplants—either purchased or homegrown—is the afternoon or evening of a foggy or overcast day. I've broken the rules and transplanted seedlings on very hot mornings when I was pressed for time, but that makes the process riskier. Seedlings transplanted in hot weather need extra protection and careful monitoring for the first few days. The garden soil should be moist but not soggy. During late winter and early spring it may be a bit wetter than is ideal for seeding. This is all right for transplanting, if you are careful not to pack it down too much.

The space between transplants, as between seeds, should equal the diameter of a mature plant. Closer spacing is possible but there is a limit to how much a crop can be crowded.

In prepared soil, use a trowel to dig a hole as deep as the mass of the rootball and a bit wider. Use the trowel to mix any compost or powdered rock fertilizer you are adding into the underlying few inches of soil. Dig the hole a bit deeper if you are planning to add a commercial chemical fertilizer or a high-nitrogen organic fertilizer, such as blood meal or worm castings. Mix it in well and place an inch of plain soil above the mixture so that the roots won't come in contact with the fertilizer right away.

Turn the pot over, supporting the plant stem between your first and second fingers, and tap the bottom. If the container is made of flexible plastic, push it enough to bend it and force the soil out. (You may have to run a knife around the inside of the container to release the soil, but usually this is not necessary.) Pull off the pot and set it aside, then use the same hand to cradle the soil ball. If the plant is root bound, gently open circling roots at the bottom of the rootball before planting. Set the plant in the hole at the right depth and use the other hand to fill the soil back in around it.

Most seedlings should be planted at the same depth as they were growing, but there are exceptions. If a seedling falls over despite careful planting, it probably developed with too much of the upper root exposed. Reset the plant deeper so that it stays upright, but be sure the place where leaves join at the bottom of a plant is not buried. Tomatoes and cole crops, such as broccoli, cabbage, and cauliflower, should always be set a little deeper than they were growing (see details in individual crop entries in Chapter 11). Firm the soil around each plant, but avoid touching the stem.

Generally, soil around transplants should be level. Don't plant on a mound, or push soil up around stems, or plant in depressions. (Planting on a wide mound is sometimes useful in clay soil, but not little individual mounds.) If you want to sculpt soil to make watering easier, you may make a raised lip around the seedling, a few inches from the stem. The lip will wash away in a couple of weeks, but won't be needed by then.

Sometimes you will find seedlings bunched together in a container. To separate them, start by using your thumbs at the top of the potting mix, between the plants, to divide it into sections. Then continue to divide it into smaller sections, gently tugging the plants apart. Avoid handling the roots as much as possible. In fact, I try to mostly touch the potting mix rather than the plants. The roots of some may be damaged so much that the plants should be discarded. Still, buying or growing seedlings this way can be economical, as you can usually separate the majority successfully if they aren't too entangled. Examine your planting carefully to make sure you haven't put two or more seedlings in the same hole. This will stunt the plants.

When you finish transplanting, water the plants thoroughly, wetting the leaves (even those of tomatoes) but taking care not to knock over the plants. If any of the leaves stick to the soil, flip them up when you finish watering. If you are going to stake the plants, drive the stakes now, before the roots spread out or the plants sprawl. You can apply mulch now or later, remembering to keep it a couple of inches away from the stems. (See page 79 for information on when and how to mulch.)

Caring for Transplanted Seedlings

Although both nursery and homegrown transplants are usually less delicate than germinating seeds, they are still very vulnerable in the first week or two after transplanting. They can succumb to transplant shock—a combination of root damage and sudden exposure to a harsher environment. Also, the tender young plants are so appetizing that they can be an overnight sensation with certain kinds of pests.

Transplants will always undergo some transplant shock, but it can be minimized by the skill with which you plant them. Treat the roots gently, since damaged roots mean that the plant can't take up as much water and nutrients. The shock will be even more severe if the transplant wasn't properly hardened off or if the weather turns unexpectedly hot, cold, or windy. Experience will tell you when transplants need special help adjusting to their move. You will probably lose a few plants as you learn, but soon you will develop a sense of when and how to protect seedlings.

If the weather is sunny and warm, transplants appreciate some shade during the first day or two to slow the loss of water from their leaves. A board or piece of cardboard stuck in the ground to the southwest of the seedlings and leaning over them may do the trick. Or put a large opaque plastic bag, such as a trash bag, over two stakes, on the southwest side of a few seedlings, leaning it to provide as much afternoon shade as possible. I often put weeds to work for my new transplants. I sprinkle a light covering of seedless and rootless weed clippings, such as dandelion or dock leaves, on the seedlings. The fresh weed clippings will shade the plants at first, letting more light in as they dry out. They will also humidify the air around the plants with the moisture they lose.

If the transplants were hardened off well enough and the root damage was not severe, the young plants won't need shade after the first couple of days. However, if plants weren't properly hardened off or if they were kept in a dimly lighted place too long after coming from the nursery, they may burn on very sunny days for the first week or two. Sunburned leaves either turn white or become brown and crisp. If you put the plants in partial shade when the damage is still minimal, you may save them. In the future, try to better prepare transplants for the outdoors.

Plants that are properly hardened off will have developed some resistance to cold and their growth probably won't be stopped by cold nights. Still, sometimes you may want to provide special cold protection—for example, when you plant warm-season crops extra early in spring. Any warmth that is gained from a protective device will help speed plant growth.

Portable cold frames, plastic jugs with the bottoms cut off, and purchased hot caps (little covers made of translucent paper) are among the common protectors.

Wall O' Water is a commercial product consisting of a ring of upright, water-filled plastic tubes that surrounds a seedling. Sometimes gardeners build low structures of stakes or arches with clear plastic over them. Floating row covers will also protect individual plants or entire rows and planting beds from the cold. Black plastic used as mulch between plants will help warm the soil (see page 79). Tubeless tires or inner tubes filled with water were once used to warm the soil around plants growing within them but are now considered toxic hazards.

The local pests most likely to attack new transplants include birds, cutworms, earwigs, the imported cabbageworm (on cabbage-family plants), slugs, and snails. Among the most vulnerable seedlings are basil, beans, cabbage-family plants, lettuce, and peas. For specific advice, read first about the crop that you are transplanting and then about the pests likely to attack it. However, only experience will teach you the problems of your particular garden. For example, the pea seedlings in some gardens may be eaten to the ground in fall and winter, whereas in other gardens they may grow unscathed. You want neither to spend hours building fortifications against pests that will not strike nor to forget about your seedlings for a week and return to find them gone. Experience gained in your particular garden—and only that—will show you the balance.

If you are just beginning to garden, you won't know which pests will attack. Plastic strawberry baskets placed over the transplants and weighted with a stone are a good light defense. This barrier will stop birds, rabbits, and large snails (after midsummer, baby snails will crawl right through the mesh). An effective cutworm defense is a cardboard, plastic, or metal ring around the plant (see page 117).

Guard against pests when you use protective devices. Beware of devices that have openings big enough only to admit snails; once they get inside, they may be unable to find their way out and thus be forced to live on the only available vegetation—namely, your precious seedling.

Gardeners sometimes cut off the bottoms of plastic jugs or glass bottles so they can be set over seedlings. If you do this, exclude pests by covering the mouth of the container with a piece of cloth or floating row cover attached with a weatherproof plant tie. (You can't just screw the lid on a jar, because the lack of ventilation will cause the plants to fry in the sun.) If you use a floating row cover, be sure to tuck the edges firmly into the soil all around. Check your Wall O' Water every couple of days for snails, which can usually be found on the interior walls and in the water-filled tubes just above the water line.

As long as the transplants look fine, don't worry if they don't seem to grow much for a week or even several weeks. They are working hard to repair roots and toughen up. When you see new growth beginning, you will know that they, and you, have successfully weathered the delicate period.

INSTEAD OF SEEDS: OTHER WAYS TO START PLANTS

Some plants rarely or never produce seeds and must be reproduced by vegetative, or asexual, means—from underground structures, such as bulbs and tubers, or by division, cuttings, or layering. Even when plants can be seeded, they are sometimes reproduced more efficiently when you bypass the seeding process and use a vegetative method.

Although most vegetable crops are best grown from seed, a few are not. Potatoes rarely form seeds and are almost always grown from tubers, called seed potatoes, which are planted either whole or cut into pieces. Onion, garlic, and shallot can be grown from seed, but they mature much faster from small bulbs, known as sets. Artichoke and rhubarb also mature very slowly from seed and so are usually grown from divisions, made by cutting the thickened base of the plant into sections and allowing each to grow into a separate plant. Many common perennial herbs are rarely started from seed, because they grow *very* slowly as seedlings. Also, seedlings of the same type of herb often vary dramatically in scent and flavor; growing a new plant from a cutting, or piece of the parent plant, ensures that the new plant will have the same taste and smell. At least two perennial herbs, French tarragon and lemongrass, never flower and can be reproduced only by vegetative means.

Many perennial flowers and fruit crops are also best propagated by vegetative means. Perennial flowers often grow into a clump that becomes so crowded that fewer blossoms are formed. When the clump is divided into several plants, each blooms more freely. Fruit trees are usually reproduced by cuttings or by grafting the stem of a plant that produces good fruit to the roots of a compatible plant that grows well

Cold Frames

Small covering structures that provide a protected environment in which to start seeds and grow seedlings are known as *cold frames*. You can build a permanent cold frame—a raised wooden frame partially filled with soil—in a sunny corner of the garden, or you can make portable cold frames to place over seedbeds or transplants wherever they are growing.

A cold frame for a small garden typically provides 4 to 6 square feet of growing space. The top covering, which must let in light and hold heat, is usually set at a slight angle, lower on the south side, so that the sun will shine on it more directly. (In a permanent cold frame, you can also slant the soil to catch more sun.) Glass and plastic film are the most commonly used coverings. Since even our winter days are rarely very cold, and occasionally may be quite warm, glass- or plastic-topped cold frames must be ventilated.

You can buy a thermostatically operated cold frame opener, but the open lid can serve as a snail portal, locking snails in as the cold frame automatically closes. As an alternative, build a cold frame covered completely with a porous material such as a floating row cover. A compromise is to make an open cold frame, consisting of just a top and two sides. Snails will get in, but in no greater numbers than in the garden at large, and they won't be trapped inside to devour everything in sight. Neither a porous nor an open-sided cold frame is quite as warm as a glass- or plastic-covered one, but either offers some protection from the cold without inviting snail damage.

Another way to deter pests is to put the cold frame on a sturdy garden worktable. Treating the table legs with a sticky substance such as Tanglefoot, which is available at most nurseries, will discourage insects from climbing up, and wrapping copper strips around the legs will keep snails away.

in local soils. Most gardeners buy fruit trees already grafted, but you may want to try the technique. (For books about vegetative propagation and grafting, see Appendix VIII, Suggested Reading.)

Division, stem cuttings, ground layering, and root cuttings are relatively simple techniques that allow us to make new plants from ones that are already growing. Novice gardeners are often reluctant to cut off part of a plant or plunge a spade into the roots of a plant to divide it. It may seem less natural than growing a plant from seed or too advanced for a beginner, but plants are more than willing to reproduce in these ways. Learning these techniques will reduce the need to purchase new plants when older ones need renewing.

Look up information about each type of plant that you want to propagate, either in this book or another reference, to see which methods are recommended, the best time of year to use them, and other important details. Hedge your bets: try several cuttings or layerings at a time but leave some of the plant, or several plants, intact in case something goes wrong.

Division

This involves cutting a large perennial plant clump into several sections, each with shoots and roots. You can divide clumps of small plants growing close together, such as clumps of chives, or multistemmed plants growing from underground runners, such as sweet woodruff or mint. If a plant grows from a thickened crown with a number of sites bearing smaller roots and shoots—for example, artichoke or rhubarb—you can cut the crown into chunks, each of which will grow into a new plant. Lemongrass is an example of another kind of clump that can be divided. It has many stalks, each of which has actively growing roots or the beginnings of roots.

Often you will want to divide the entire plant or clump of plants into smaller ones, but in some cases you may choose to remove one or more sections, leaving the parent plant to grow where it is. Just tuck the soil back around the base of the parent and keep it well watered for a few weeks while it heals and reestablishes roots.

Generally, divide a plant when it is dormant—when there is the least active growth occurring above the ground. In our mild climate, divisions are most often made in late autumn or late winter before new growth starts, typically in February. Plant the divisions right away in a well-prepared bed and keep them well watered, as you would transplants, for the first few weeks.

Stem Cuttings

This method of reproduction consists of cutting pieces of stem and inserting them in a cutting mix, where they will grow roots and develop into new plants. Cuttings that are taken when the plant is actively growing, but not blooming, are known as softwood cuttings. Chrysanthemum, French tarragon, lemon-verbena, rosemary, sage, scented geranium, and thyme are good subjects.

Snip off 3- to 6-inch stem tips with at least four nodes (places where leaves are attached to the stems). Put them in a plastic bag in your refrigerator if you don't plan to prepare them immediately. To prepare the cuttings, cut the bottom of the stem diagonally ¼ inch below the bottom node. Then strip the leaves from the bottom two or three nodes, allowing leaves to remain on two or three upper ones. Dipping the bottoms of the cuttings into a rooting hormone will increase your chances of success, but it's not always necessary. Bury the nodes from which you removed leaves into a shallow container filled with container mix or cutting mix.

Typically, cutting mixes are very porous, to reduce the possibility of decay and to provide good aeration. They usually have no plant nutrients, or very low levels of nutrients, as these may inhibit initial root growth and encourage decay.

Place a clear plastic bag over the top of the container. Push three short bamboo stakes into the cutting mix to keep the plastic bag from collapsing on the cuttings. Lift the bag briefly every day or two to let in fresh air. Keep stem cuttings out of direct sunlight until roots have formed. Regularly check the cutting mix to be sure that it is moist, but don't keep it soggy. Once rooting begins, add half the recommended number of drops of liquid houseplant fertilizer to the water when you water the cutting mix. A cutting may succeed even if the leaves wilt or if some leaves drop, but if the stem wilts you will know that the cutting was too immature to succeed.

Expect to wait at least three to six weeks, and perhaps several months, for the cutting to develop into a rooted plant. You will know that it has rooted when you see new growth. Let the plant grow a bit longer to make sure that it is well established. Transfer each rooted plant to its own container and water it right away. Keep the plants out of direct sunlight for the first few days, then gradually expose them to conditions similar to those in the garden. When you see that they are growing well, plant them in the garden.

Ground Layering

The process of burying the stem of a growing plant so that roots form along it is known as *ground layering*. The rooted stem, which can be cut from the parent plant, will grow into a new plant. Layering works best in spring or summer, when the plant is actively growing. Any plant that can be grown from cuttings can also be reproduced by layering, which has the advantage of using the energy of the parent plant to nurse the new plant as it begins to grow.

Choose a low branch that can be bent to the ground, and bury a section that is about 6 to 12 inches from the tip. You may improve your chances by preparing the stem: Remove any leaves on the part that will be buried. If the stem is thick enough to do so, notch the underside shallowly just below a leaf attachment point, then dip the notch into rooting hormone and insert a small twig or pebble to keep it open.

Dig a hole 3 to 4 inches deep and wide enough to bury the stem without breaking it. If the stem is too springy to stay buried well, weight the buried part with a rock or use a U-shaped metal irrigation bracket to hold it down.

Leave several inches of the branch tip above the soil. If it lies flat on the ground, tie it to a small stake to hold it more upright.

Keep the soil moist and watch for new growth, which signals that the propagation was successful. The process will take from several months to more than a year. Cut the old stem, then dig up the new plant and move it to a well-prepared garden site.

Root Cuttings

Some plants can be reproduced from root cuttings—pieces of root that sprout shoots and additional roots to become whole plants. Plants that will grow into new plants from root cuttings include comfrey, French tarragon, horseradish, and sea kale. Cut the roots into sections while the plant is dormant. You can either replant the cuttings directly in the ground or store them in containers in a dark place, replanting them during the season when active growth resumes. Either way, they should not be allowed to dry out.

Often the process is more successful if the roots are buried right side up, so conventions have developed for cutting the top and bottom ends of the roots differently. How you handle root cuttings depends on the kind of plant that you are growing; see the individual crop listings.

SEVEN

How to Water

SINCE OUR WEATHER FROM April to October is essentially dry and our winter rains fickle, local gardeners must learn the best way to water a garden. Watering by the calendar—say, once or twice a week—doesn't work well, because the amount of water needed depends not only on rainfall but also on soil type, wind, sunshine, fog, temperature, day length, and the age of the plants. No one can give you a perfect watering schedule for your garden—but with a few guidelines and a season or two of practice, you can become so attuned to your garden's needs that you almost always water just right.

Here's the secret: for mature plants, water until the soil is holding all the moisture it can to a depth of a little more than 2 feet, and then don't water again until the top 1 to 2 inches of soil have dried out.

Two inches of water applied to the surface (picture a 2-inch layer of water on the soil) will soak 2 feet deep in sandy soil; it takes 4 inches of water to penetrate to the same depth in clay loam soil. Water again when the top 1 inch of sandy soil and the top 2 inches of clay soil are dry. (The reason for the difference is that sandy soil is drier to a greater depth when its top layer has dried out.) When remoistening the top, you want to soak only 1 foot deep, so add only half as much water as you did to soak 2 feet deep.

This method may mean watering sandy soil as often as every two or three days during a hot spell and not watering clay soil for two weeks or more during foggy weather. It ensures that there is water deep in the soil where plant roots grow, and it allows air into the soil between waterings so that the roots can breathe.

APPLYING WATER

You can water with a plain hose or one with a sprinkler or special nozzle attached, or you can use a soaker hose, drip irrigation, or various homemade soaking devices. Hand-held sprinklers or other sprinkling methods are good for watering seedbeds from the day you plant until the seedlings are a few inches tall, and for watering just-transplanted seedlings until they recover from transplant shock. When you plant or transplant, your soil should already be moderately moist (see page 86), but you will need to water a bit more as soon as you plant, to make sure the seeds or transplant roots are in contact with water. Then you will need to water briefly whenever the surface has dried for a half day, to make sure the soil near the surface, which is where the seeds and young roots are located, stays moist. You shouldn't water too long at any one time during this period, since you run the risk of washing away seeds or seedlings, and besides, the lower soil should already be moist. In small areas, a hand-held sprinkler is best for this job. In larger areas, where hand watering would take too long, use a sprinkler you can set up on the ground. An oscillating sprinkler, one that turns from side to side, letting water sink in before applying more, is a good choice. Most elegantly (and expensively), you could install a separate micro sprinkler system along with a drip irrigation system.

Once the plants are up and growing, and transplants are not wilting, it is usually better to water at the ground level rather than by sprinkling, for several reasons. First, water on the leaves makes certain plants more susceptible to diseases and encourages snails and slugs. The weight of the water may pull some plants over. Also, sprinklers waste water, which evaporates from leaf surfaces and from droplets flying through the air.

It is also better, once plants are past the seedling or recent transplant stage, not to water with a hand-held hose. As plants mature, you should wait longer between waterings so that air can return to the upper soil. When you do water, you need to do it longer, to moisten the soil more deeply. Because people tend to get bored standing there, hose in hand, before they've watered long enough, it's better to put the hose down and leave it running while you do other things, moving it occasionally. You can use a sprinkler head turned low to spread the water a little, or for a tree or other single plants, use an attachment called a bubbler. Because of the risk that you will forget and leave the hose in one place too long, consider attaching a simple timer to the hose bibb, so it will turn off after a certain amount of time. Or consider a soaker hose to deliver water at ground level over a larger area at once. A soaker hose either has tiny holes punched along its length or is made of a porous material. It can be placed on the surface, running along rows or curving through a bed. If it is plastic or rubber, it can be laid under mulch or buried a couple of inches under the soil and left there all season.

Drip irrigation systems can do a good job of watering vegetables and fruit trees if they are planned well. Such systems consist of plastic tubing that delivers water to the plants at low pressure. There can be emitters (openings that deliver water) at only the ends of tubes, or there can be built-in emitters every few inches. A drip system can just manually screw onto a hose that you turn on when you are ready to water or can be permanently attached and run automatically by a timer. Most commonly, timers deliver water in a weekly schedule selected by the gardener, but some timers actually receive a wireless signal based on current weather data, which causes them to reset the watering times accordingly. If you have a system for a landscaped garden, you will want a separate station for vegetables, so they can have their own schedule. You can also group herbs that need less water and then use fewer emitters for them or put them on a different schedule.

When you are ready to set up a system, it is wise to go to a store that provides not only materials, but advice and directions. At a minimum, you need to learn how to check the water pressure and flow of your faucets before you design a system so that you won't give it more to do at once than the water supply will allow. You will also need to be sure your system is filtered properly and meets legal requirements for materials (San Francisco requires some fittings to be metal) and safety (you need a backflow preventer to avoid contaminating your house water supply).

Making Your Own Custom Watering Devices

Many gardeners use homemade devices to provide an even water supply to individual large plants, such as tomatoes and squash. One of the most common techniques is to sink a porous container—such as an unglazed clay pot with a cork in the drainage hole or a plastic container with small holes punched in the bottom—into the soil next to a plant. Water poured into the container will seep slowly into the soil. These devices are particularly useful in sandy soil, since they get water deep into the soil, where it won't evaporate as quickly. Here are a few practical tips.

- If hammering a nail through a plastic container doesn't work, try heating the nail. Using a pair of pliers, hold the nail over a candle flame, then push the hot nail through the plastic.
- To avoid damaging roots, sink a watering device into the soil when the plant is still young. Locate it at least 3 inches from the plant.
- If you add a little manure or compost to the water, you can fertilize while you water. (See page 81 for directions for making manure or compost tea.)

Choosing Hose-End Watering Devices

Don't make the mistake of choosing a hose-end device that delivers a hard jet of water. This might be good for washing a car, but it's not for a garden, where a hard spray will only wash away soil and knock plants over. Rather than one of those multispray-pattern wonders or one that makes a strong jet when you squeeze a trigger, choose a simple one that will deliver water as if it were gentle rain.

Two popular hose-end watering devices are the fan sprinkler and the water breaker. The fan sprinkler is fan-shaped and delivers a band of droplets. The water breaker delivers a higher volume of water in a circular pattern, like a shower head. Either device can be hand-held or propped on a fence or other support, or just placed on the ground to water a small area. Either of these sprinklers can also be attached to a water wand, a rigid aluminum tube with an angled end. The water wand allows you to reach into hanging plants without a ladder, or under plants in low pots without leaning over.

Two other useful sprinklers are designed to rest on the ground and sprinkle a larger area. My favorite has no moving parts, just two short side wings to stabilize it and a 2-inch wide-domed central area with a rectangular pattern of tiny holes. The rectangular pattern is useful, because it more or less approximates the shape of my rectangular planting beds. You can set it in the bed, using a metal U-shaped "earth staple" to secure it just as you want it. The other kind if the oscillating sprinkler, one about a foot long that turns from side to side. It is particularly good for watering soil that is prone to runoff, such as clay soil that isn't amended well yet, since it gives water a second or two to sink in before swinging back to deliver more.

Design help is advised for larger systems, but you can probably design one for a small bed or container garden without help. You use larger, half-inch tubing to get water to an area and then attach quarter-inch tubes to deliver the water. Tubing with emitters only at their ends can run to an individual container or to a larger plant, like a tomato or a tree. A newly planted fruit tree can start with one line with an emitter at its end, then you can add more as the tree matures. For a rectangular vegetable bed, a half-inch tube across a shorter end, from which you run 3 or 4 tubes with inline emitters, works well. Inline emitters may be spaced either every 12 or 6 inches. Twelve-inch spacing is best if you have clay or clay loam. Use tubing with an emitter every 6 inches if your soil is sandy or well-amended or if you are using potting or planting mix. Use U-shaped metal earth staples to anchor the lines at intervals or to anchor an emitter in a pot. (There are mini-staples for use in pots.)

When you are preparing soil for a new planting, you will probably want to lift any drip lines. Reset them before you plant, so you can see where the water will be delivered before you sow seeds or set transplants.

A drip system doesn't let you forget about watering altogether. Unless your timer adjusts automatically, you will need to change your schedule in rainy or very hot weather. And over time things can go wrong. You need to run the system and watch it periodically, to make sure you don't have leaks or clogged emitters. Timers that aren't on your house's electrical system have batteries, and these run down. Timers eventually stop working and need to be replaced. (Be sure to keep the manual that comes with your timer. Read it to find out how to change the watering schedule, what the system will do to indicate it has a low battery, and how to troubleshoot. If you do lose it, you can find the text online at the website of the manufacturer.)

Vegetable gardeners who water by hand often use their watering time to weed, stake, mulch, harvest, and generally putter in their gardens. Don't let your wonderful, timesaving, drip irrigation system lull you into ignoring your garden's other needs—and your enjoyment of time in your garden.

HOW MUCH IS ENOUGH?

You may wonder how you are supposed to divine what is going on under the ground. Is the soil wet only a few inches deep, or a couple of feet? Have you just added 2 inches of water, or 5 inches?

By late winter, the rains have usually saturated our soils to a depth of 6 feet or more. If you plant in late winter or spring as soon as the soil near the surface is dry enough to work, you can assume that the deeper soil is still moist. At that time of year,

Checking the Soil Moisture

You'll be more confident that you are watering correctly if you check the soil moisture before and after you water. Either dig a hole about 6 inches deep with a trowel or use a moisture meter. You can usually see a difference between the colors of dry and wet soil in the sides of the hole, or you can feel for moisture. When using a moisture meter, slowly push the probe into the soil to get readings at different levels.

Although you can get along fine without a moisture meter, you may want to buy an inexpensive one to use during your learning period. In fact, you may want to use both a trowel and a moisture meter the first couple of times, so you can feel what the meter readings mean. You will find yourself digging or probing a lot at first, but later you will need to do it only once in a while.

There are three times when a test with a trowel or moisture meter is especially useful: (1) to find out if the top 1 to 2 inches of soil are dry, (2) to make sure that you watered long enough so that you didn't leave a dry layer between wet layers (wait until the next morning to probe the soil), and (3) to find out if a light rain has wet the soil deeply enough so that you don't have to water.

you only have to worry about keeping the top layer watered. If you are starting a garden anytime from late spring to early fall in soil that has not been watered since the winter rains, you can assume that the soil has dried out and that you need to water thoroughly before planting. (After you water deeply, don't work the soil until it has dried a couple of days; to know when it is ready, see page 86.)

Whether you are soaking dry soil or just moistening the surface, you will need to know how much water you are adding. Here's a way to find out: Set a sprinkler up on the ground. Use an indelible marker to mark the one-inch level from the bottom of a pint-sized plastic tub. Set the water flow to the sprinkler so that it covers a measured area (four feet square, for example) and place the marked tub under the sprinkles. Time how long it takes for the sprinkler to fill the tub to the one-inch level. This is

Soaker hoses are an effective watering tool.

how long it will take to deliver one inch of water to your soil using that sprinkler when it is set to cover that much area. You might like to use several tubs or retime the process with the tub in different parts of the sprinkler pattern to be sure you weren't in a part of the pattern with particularly high or low flow.

Determining the flow from a soaker hose is trickier. Your best bet is to run the soaker hose in the garden for a set period, such as one or two hours, then check the soil moisture to see how deep the water has penetrated. From that, you can figure out how long to run the water in the future.

MORE WATERING WISDOM

The rate of evaporation from the soil and from leaf surfaces is greater when the weather is dry, windy, warm, or sunny than when it is humid, still, cool, or cloudy. Large plants use and lose more water than small plants, and fast-growing, tender plants, including most vegetables, use more water than slow-growing, tough plants such as an established bougainvillea vine or a cactus. Plants are most harmed by a water shortage when they are growing rapidly—when seeds are germinating or when plants are forming large tender leaves, thickened roots, bulbs, tubers, flowers, or fruit.

Seedbeds are a special case. When the surface of a seedbed has been dry for half a day, water it briefly. Keep the surface moist until the seedlings have been up for a week or so, then gradually water less often as the roots grow deeper into the soil. Transplants also need brief but frequent watering for the first week or two after they are in the ground.

Whenever you water, keep the flow low enough so that the water soaks in as fast as it comes out of the hose. If water runs off the surface when you begin to water, turn the flow down. Runoff is often a problem in clay soil, since the tiny clay particles are so tightly packed that water enters slowly. The best remedy is to dig in plenty of organic matter before you plant. If water soaks in well at first but then begins to run off, you will know that you have watered long enough and no more water can enter until the water already in the soil penetrates deeper. To help the soil absorb water, some gardeners punctuate irrigation: they turn the water on and off in ten- or fifteen-minute cycles.

Since water runs off sloping surfaces, try to keep the beds and rows level or nearly so. If soil is slightly sloped, you can build raised lips around recent transplants to hold water until it can soak in (but don't plant in depressions). On a moderate slope, run planting rows along the contours rather than up and down. On a steep slope, make terraces (see page 36).

Some gardeners sculpt the soil, even when there is no slope, to keep the water where they want it while it soaks in. They are following the lead of California agriculture, which often uses a system of raised rows with irrigation trenches between. Although I sculpt the soil for certain crops that require a lot of water, such as squash, my well-amended soil absorbs water so well that most crops don't need this special help.

THE BEST TIME TO WATER

You may read that the best time to water is the morning. It is true that early watering is appropriate if you are using a sprinkler, because it gives the plants plenty of time to dry before nightfall, when darkness slows drying. (Wet leaves are more susceptible to certain diseases.) Also, there is less evaporation in the cooler, usually calmer early morning.

If you water at ground level and don't wet the leaves, you may do just as well to water a couple of hours before dark. Evaporation is low then because the sun is sinking and the sea breeze has usually died down.

Actually, the best time to water is when the plants need water and you have the time to provide it. Even midday watering (if that is your only available time and the plants are thirsty) is better than no watering. You may have heard that midday watering on a hot day can burn leaves, but this is not so. If plants have wilted before you watered, they may show brown "burned" edges when they recover, but this is from the wilting, not the watering. They will also be more susceptible to edge burn if the water source is saline or if it is unfiltered gray water. Salt spray from the ocean can also burn leaves if you are very near the ocean.

WATERING THROUGH THE YEAR

Your garden needs different amounts of water at different times of the year. With a little practice, you will learn to keep the soil moisture at the right level for your plants the year around.

Spring

You rarely need to water established plants before the end of February, but you may have to water to keep seedbeds moist. By April, most gardens begin to need regular watering. By May, don't count on nature to help water your garden: you're usually on your own until the fall storms begin.

Another Watering Philosophy

Despite what I've said about the benefits of deep, infrequent waterings, you will find that some gardeners believe in watering a vegetable bed a little every day or two so that the surface is constantly moist. This is a central tenet of French-intensive/biodynamic gardening. (See *How to Grow More Vegetables* by John Jeavons, listed in Appendix VIII, Suggested Reading.)

Frequent, light irrigation may be fine if your soil is either sandy or very spongy with lots of organic matter, and it may be beneficial for fast-growing crops such as radishes and lettuce. However, it probably provides too much water for a garden planted in poorly amended clay soil. It is also inappropriate for slow-growing plants, including shrubs and trees, which grow much better when given less frequent, deep waterings.

If you water frequently, you must not miss waterings, because the plants will be more dependent on surface roots and thus more sensitive to a dry soil surface.

Signs of Trouble

Chronically underwatered plants are stunted. Their leaves lack a healthy luster, and any fruit they make is undersized. Strawberries are small and rubbery. Carrots and other fleshy roots are smaller than normal and tough. Underwatered plants may show signs of nutrient deficiency because roots take in nutrients from the soil via water. They are often more vulnerable to some pests, especially mites. Underwatered plants may wilt, and they will die if they've gone past the point where watering will revive them.

Overwatered plants suffer too. Their oxygen-starved roots often fall prey to fungus and other diseases. If rot sets in, the plants may turn yellow, and they eventually wilt and die.

Wilting is a tricky symptom because it may be due to dry soil, root rot caused by wet soil, or other damage to roots caused by pests and unrelated to soil moisture. Plants may wilt on an unusually hot day because the roots can't work fast enough to supply the plant with water. Squash plants often wilt on hot days but perk up in the cool of the night. If your plants are wilting from unaccustomed heat, help them out by sprinkling them lightly to cool the leaf surfaces.

Many vegetables respond badly to alternating periods of very dry and very wet soil. When moisture fluctuates too widely, carrots and cabbage heads split, and tomatoes develop blossom-end rot. Sometimes these problems develop when it rains heavily just before the crops are harvested. Adding plenty of organic matter to the soil and mulching will reduce the effects of fluctuating moisture.

Late spring rains can fool us. We may think that a light rain has watered our plants, when really it only moistened the surface. When you aren't sure, check the soil moisture with a trowel or moisture meter. Your neighbors may raise their eyebrows if they see you watering just after a rain, but you will know you are right to do so. I've even watered *during* a sprinkle! It was the only time I could get to my garden, and I knew the sprinkle would let up before the soil was wet enough.

Hot spells, which often occur as early as March, can also surprise us. Our gardens may suddenly become very thirsty. When those glorious hot spring days come, remember to head to your spring seedbeds before you head to the beach or to the park.

Summer

The summer months are almost always rainless, and the question is not whether to water, but how often. In the most ocean-influenced parts of our region, we typically have cycles of fog and sun, interrupted occasionally by a hot spell. It is often windy as well. Fog decreases the amount of water that your garden needs, and sun, heat, and wind increase it. Getting seeds and transplants started during the summer poses a problem, since the soil can dry out unexpectedly fast during hot, windy days. You can try planting at the beginning of a foggy period, but it is hard to predict how long these periods will last.

Heavy fog does occasionally turn to falling mist. While this doesn't moisten the soil much, it certainly reduces evaporation from soil and plants. Redwood forests depend on fog drip as a major source of moisture. Fog condenses on tree leaves and then falls to the ground. However, if your garden is being dripped on by trees, it is probably in too much shade.

Gardens farther inland will have fewer foggy days and increasingly hot summers, as ocean influence diminishes. In hot summer weather, it is especially important to pay attention to watering, and wise to mulch soil to reduce water loss.

Summer is the vacation season. Before you leave on a trip, invite your garden sitter over to look at your plants. Point out where there are seedlings or recent transplants, or where maturing garlic should be left to dry. Draw a simple map of the garden identifying the plantings. If your sitter is not an experienced gardener, write out a regimen, such as this: "Water all areas except the garlic bed. Let the hose run with a low to medium flow, moving it often, for about one hour. Water on Tuesday and Sunday." Your schedule may not turn out to be perfect, but any schedule is safer than telling an inexperienced gardener to water when he or she thinks the garden looks dry.

As summer draws to a close, you may be tempted to ease off on watering, a typical gardening pattern in cold-winter regions. In those regions, many gardeners plant just once, in spring, and use up their harvest by the end of summer. They don't need to water as often because summer rainfall is common. If a dry spell comes late in the season, they may let it finish off the garden, knowing that the first frost will soon do the same anyway. In our region, summer harvests often continue into

November, sometimes even December, and crops for fall, winter, and spring harvests are actively growing in late summer, so we need to keep watering until the rains take over.

If you run out of energy to water your garden by the end of summer, stop to think why. Was it too hard to keep a poorly amended sandy soil watered? If so, resolve to add more organic matter and to use a moisture-holding mulch. Did you grow vegetables that you didn't particularly like? Make note of the crops that weren't a chore to water and grow only those next year. Did you take on too much? Consider scaling down your vegetable, herb, and flower beds and planting some of the garden with low-maintenance, water-conserving landscape plants.

Fall and Winter

The early fall sprinkles may not be much help in watering your garden. Check the soil moisture, as you did in spring, with a trowel or moisture meter. Once the rains really get going, you may not have to water at all for several months, but then again maybe you will. If you are lulled into thinking that winter watering is unnecessary, one day you may find that your garden doesn't look as good or produce as well as it used to. (If you plan to be away during the winter, have a garden sitter ready to water, but only if little or no rain falls for more than two or three weeks.)

When you do need to water, you will find that there are fewer daylight hours in which to do it. Even during a dry winter, however, you will never have to water very often. The days are shorter and not as bright, since the sun's rays are dimmed by reaching the earth at a lower angle. The days and nights are cooler, evaporation decreases, and plants grow more slowly. Gardeners get to relax a bit.

Actually, in winter you must be careful not to overwater, especially if your soil has a high clay content. If there have been fall rains, even if they were followed by a winter drought, the deep layers of your soil will probably still be quite moist. Water the surface layers if rain fails to happen, but don't overdo it: slowed evaporation in winter could leave your soil waterlogged for days.

Most vegetables that grow in winter, especially the cole crops, don't mind wet leaves. (Watch how rain rolls off cabbage or broccoli leaves.) The combination of cold and dampness can encourage rot, however, so try to keep moisture from collecting in plant crevices. If any part of plants starts to decay, remove it so the decay can't spread. Stubs of Swiss chard leaves are particularly decay-prone—see the Swiss chard entry (page 268) for harvest tips.

Near the coast, if frost occurs at all, it is generally not until December or January, by which time rains have taken over watering. But inland, icy weather could occur before this has happened. Plants are more susceptible to frost if the soil is dry. Therefore, if rain hasn't wet the soil yet, be sure to water ahead of frosty periods. In even colder winters, deeply frozen soil creates a kind of winter drought, but in our region, frozen soil, if any, will be shallow, so deeper roots can still draw water.

TRIAL AND ERROR

You will soon get a feel for watering. You may be sitting in an office looking out a window and realize that it is the second warm day in a row, that you haven't watered for four days, and that your garden probably needs water. At first, you may guess wrong and find that your soil is drier or wetter than you expected. In time, you will become quite accurate.

Fine tuning your sense of how much to water various crops will take more than one season. For example, you may look back on your gardening year and realize that your strawberry plants were small and produced few berries. In reading again about strawberries and noting that ample moisture is needed, you resolve to provide more water next year. If you do and the result is a larger, more fruitful crop, then you will know that you have learned to water strawberries properly.

WHAT IF THERE IS A DROUGHT?

Since central California is at the southern margin of a storm region centered in the Pacific Northwest, our rainfall is inconsistent. Some winters we find ourselves enjoying sunny days and listening to warnings that the snow pack in the Sierra may not be deep enough to fill our reservoirs for the summer. The luck of the draw means that this rarely continues for many years in a row, but it reminds us that it is risky building big cities and developing intensive agriculture in a semiarid region.

Drought or no drought, it is essential that we use water-conserving gardening methods every year: dig in plenty of organic matter, apply mulch, refrain from using sprinklers on windy days, and avoid runoff. When drought does come and water departments set quotas, it takes careful planning to have enough water for dishes, showers, flowers, and vegetables. Although vegetables and many flowers need quite a bit of water, you can still enjoy some fresh garden produce and bright blooms if you carefully plan your household water use and adopt water-wise gardening practices. Your careful gardening practices will enable you to grow vegetables with less water per plant than that used in large agricultural operations.

Conserving Household Water

Inspect your entire water system, indoors and outdoors, for leaks. Check your water meter for movement, over an hour or two, when no water is being used. (A water meter is usually located under a liftable cover in the sidewalk in front of the house.) Any movement at all indicates that water is leaking. If food coloring dripped into the toilet tank colors the water in the bowl without the toilet having been flushed, you have found one leak to repair. Replace washers in any dripping faucets and hose connections, and install low-flow shower heads. Follow your water district's recommendations for reducing household water use.

Gardening to Save Water

Decide on your gardening priorities to make the best use of your water allowance. Get rid of any thirsty ornamentals that you never liked much anyway. Don't grow more vegetables or flowers with high requirements for water than you can handle. If food crops went to waste last summer, plant a smaller area this year. Consider planting much of your nonedible landscape in drought-tolerant plants. Since all plants need extra water when they are first getting established, wait until fall so that the rains will help water the new plantings. (Several water districts in our area publish lists of drought-tolerant ornamentals.)

Concentrate on gardening practices that make efficient use of water. Adding plenty of organic matter to your soil will mean less-frequent watering, since well-amended soil is able to hold more water than soil that is poor in organic matter. Compost or manure will do more to help soil retain moisture than bark products or rice hulls.

Avoid deep turning of the soil; dig only when you are adding organic matter. Apply mulch around vegetables and ornamentals, and pull weeds before they can rob your desirable plants of moisture. You won't be able to stint on fertilizer for edible crops, but you can slow the growth and the water requirement of ornamentals and lawns by providing little or no fertilizer during the summer of a drought year.

Planting beds, raised or not, can save water, since the paths are left dry. Make sure your paths are made of materials that rainfall can percolate through, to help replenish the groundwater. When crops are planted close enough so that their leaves touch when the plants are mature, they form a living mulch that reduces evaporation from the soil. On slopes, form watering basins around plants or make channels between rows of plants to prevent runoff.

Take a good look at how you water. Water districts tell us that most gardeners overwater. Keep your garden moist enough to grow healthy plants, but make sure that you are waiting as long as possible between thorough waterings. Check the soil with a trowel or moisture meter (see page 64), and don't add water until the soil is dry 1 to 2 inches deep. Avoid overhead sprinkling, especially on hot, windy days. As a reminder to move your hose before you lose water to runoff or leaching, set an alarm clock or timer. You can buy a timer that attaches to the hose faucet and automatically turns off the water. Soaker hoses and drip irrigation, properly timed, can provide great water savings.

Using Gray Water

When drought leads to water rationing or penalties for high water use, a gardener's thoughts often turn to the idea of reusing household water. Untreated waste water that comes from bathtubs, showers, bathroom washbasins, and clothes washing machines is known as *gray water*. (It does not include waste water from kitchen sinks, dishwashers, photo lab sinks, water used to wash diapers, or, need I say, flushed toilet water, all of which are known as *black water*.)

Gray water can have a place in watering a garden. The bacteria, skin flakes, and the like that it contains act as fertilizer, and percolating through aerated garden soil sanitizes it. However, there are many important considerations in using it safely for yourself and your plants. I will list the salient cautions here, but I strongly recommend that you do some reading (see Ecology/Ecosystem Complexity in Appendix VIII, Suggested Reading) before you start, and especially before you consider rerigging any plumbing. (Poor plumbing design can destroy appliances and result in almost immediately clogged plumbing.)

First and foremost, consider that gray water can spread disease. It should not be reused at all if anyone in the household has an infectious disease, and even if everyone is healthy, you should avoid any direct contact with the stuff or contact between gray water and edible parts of plants. It should never be stored for more than a few hours before use, since bacteria will multiply in it. It should not be applied by sprinklers, so it won't blow around, nor should you allow it to run off of your property. The lowest-tech method of applying it is to carry buckets of gray water to the plants, but this does run the risk of contact with unclean water. Do wear waterproof gloves. Do be realistic about what you will carry, since gray water mustn't sit around. And, of course, you will need to rinse the buckets with clean water sometimes, to avoid bacterial buildup.

Because of health hazards, it is not wise to use gray water to water a lawn on which people may walk or sit, and current California law says it "shall not be used for vegetable gardens."

A second major consideration is that gray water often contains cleaning products that will harm your plants or soil. If you plan to reuse water, it should not contain products with chlorine, boron, or sodium in them. These will poison your plants and ruin your soil for a long time to come. Are these in your cleaning products? Read labels, though this may not clarify what is in a detergent. Don't use gray water containing water softeners, fabric softeners, bleach, or any product you aren't sure of. Biodegradable products are not necessarily safe for use in gray water systems. The term *biocompatible* has been coined to mean safe for use in gray water, and there are products so labeled, but read labels carefully to make sure a product is in fact formulated for gray water reuse. (If you know your gray water contains toxic substances, you can still conserve by using it to flush the toilet. Pour it into the bowl, not the tank, until it has replaced the water that was in the bowl.)

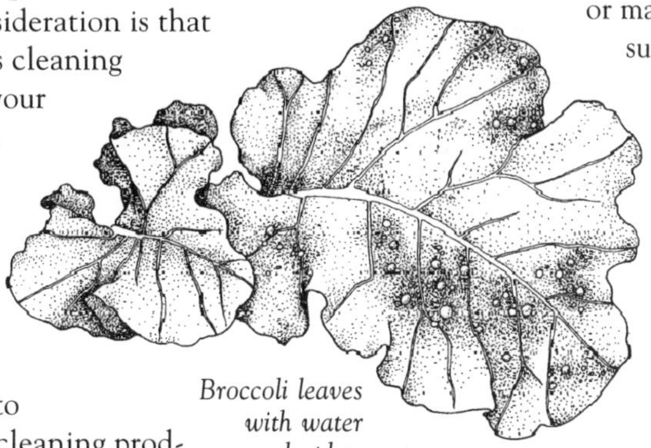

Broccoli leaves with water droplets

A third consideration is that gray water is generally alkaline. Even one of the biocompatible laundry soaps on the market has pH of 7 to 8. Avoid using gray water on plants that prefer acidic soil, such as citrus, rhododendrons, or camellias. (More on soil pH and plants on page 72.)

Finally, gray water is very likely to eventually clog any watering system you devise. It is extremely unwise to run it into a drip irrigation system.

You can rank gray water sources and use them for different purposes. The water that runs out of the tap while you are waiting for it to get hot is clean and safe for all uses. Hold large plastic bottles under the tap or put a bucket or two in the shower. Water used for steaming or boiling vegetables is safe for all plants, and sanitary if you use it immediately.

Other gray water is best used to water ornamentals or fruit trees only, allowing cleaner water to be used for watering vegetables. Even so, when you are using gray water in any part of the garden, you should alternate it with fresh water to flush salts and pH-changing substances from the soil.

Storing Rainwater

Rain catchment systems collect and save roof runoff for later use. Rain barrels can be purchased or made from repurposed containers, such as clean 55-gallon drums. Rainwater is ideal for growing plants, because it has no chlorine, chloramines, or other chemicals used in household water supplies. However, the water that ran over your roof is likely to contain lead, copper, zinc, or other contaminants, so it is not good for drinking or cooking and is probably best used on ornamentals rather than on food crops. As with gray water use, learn local regulations and see publications listed in Ecology/Ecosystem Complexity in Appendix VIII, Suggested Reading, before you proceed with rain catchment plans.

EIGHT

Down to Earth

SOIL . . . EARTH . . . DIRT—whatever we call it, we know what we want from it. We want it to be good and rich, so that the plants rising from it will be large and sturdy. Local soils may not be good or rich, but we can usually make them so even when they don't seem to hold much promise for improvement. Only occasionally is a soil a complete bust, so yours probably is suitable for gardening but needs work. With enough effort, you can transform almost any patch of ground into a rich, crumbly garden soil in three to five years. In the first year alone, you can make a tremendous difference. To know how much work your soil needs you must look at it, feel it, dig into it, and possibly send it to a soil laboratory for analysis.

EVALUATING YOUR SOIL

First you must determine your soil type. When gardeners talk about this, they are referring to the soil *texture*—the ratio of sand, silt, and clay particles in the mineral, or rock, portion of a soil.

Sandy soils, often called light soils, are made up primarily of large mineral particles with large spaces, or pores, between them. As a result, sandy soils are well aerated, but they drain so fast that it is hard to keep them moist in warm weather. Fertilizers wash out easily and must be replaced often. In their favor, sandy soils warm early in spring and are easy to dig.

Clay soils, also known as heavy soils, contain a relatively high proportion of clay, the tiniest of mineral particles. Clay particles actually attract fertilizer molecules, so clay soils hold plant nutrients better than sandy soil, and any fertilizers you add will stay there longer. The tiny pores between clay particles hold water tightly, so clay soil dries out more slowly than a sandy soil. However, if clay soil becomes too dry, it becomes difficult for water to enter, creating the hazard of runoff. And if clay soil is kept too wet, it can contain too little air for plant roots, causing them to drown. Clay soils warm slowly in spring and are difficult to dig. It is especially important not to dig clay soils when they are too wet, as this can make them even less able to hold air (see page 86).

Soils can be made up of any proportion of mineral particle sizes. Northern and central California have some soils that are at the extremes, from the very sandy dune soils near the San Francisco coast to soils high in clay in eastern San Francisco, Marin, much of the peninsula, and the East Bay. However, there are also areas of loamy soils, ones that have a more balanced mixture of particle sizes.

The intermediate-sized particles, between sand and clay, are called *silt*. Loamy soil, which is 40 percent sand, 40 percent silt, and 20 percent clay, is considered an ideal garden soil, because this proportion gives soil a good balance between the ability to hold air and the ability to hold water and nutrients. Slightly different proportions are still called *loams*. Depending on proportion, they could be *sandy loam*, *loamy sand*, *clay loam*, and so on. A band of loam extends from Santa Clara County up through Fremont, and north as far as eastern Berkeley. Another begins in a wide band around Concord and extends south, encompassing part of Walnut Creek and narrowing as you follow it southeast. Another band of loam, this one higher in clay,

Soil pH

The relative alkalinity or acidity of soil is measured on a scale from 0 (completely acid) to 14 (completely alkaline), with 7 the neutral point. Most soils in our region are near the middle of the scale, although there are some that are more acidic or alkaline than is best for a garden. Peat soils in some parts of the Delta are acidic, while those near the edge of the Bay from Alameda around to San Bruno on the Peninsula tend to be alkaline. Most vegetables, herbs, and flowers listed in this book grow best when the soil is between pH 6.5 and 7, although they can tolerate a range from pH 6 to 7.5. Potatoes are unusual because they thrive in soil as acidic as pH 5. When soil pH is incorrect for a plant, it becomes unable to extract the nutrients it needs from that soil.

All soils are slightly more acidic at the end of the rainy season. Sandy soils tend to be more acidic than clay soils. Soils under trees that have acidic debris, such as oaks or redwoods, also tend to have a lower pH. Repeated use of ammonium- or sulfur-based fertilizers will make any soil more acidic. If the site was used for acid-loving plants, such as fuchsias, camellias, or rhododendrons, it may have been acidified on purpose.

If your soil is too acidic, raise the pH by adding ground limestone or dolomitic lime. To raise the pH of 100 square feet of soil by 1 point (for example, from 5 to 6), add 5 pounds of lime to sandy soil, 7 pounds to loam, and 8 pounds to clay soil. (Do not use quicklime and slaked or hydrated lime, which can burn plants and injure soil life.)

If your soil is too alkaline, lower the pH by adding sulfur. To lower the pH of 100 square feet of soil by 1 point (for example, from 7.5 to 6.5), add 1 pound of sulfur to sandy soil, 1½ pounds to loam, and 2 pounds to clay soil.

In general, the addition of organic matter, including compost, will bring any soil closer to the ideal of a slightly acidic 6.5 and keep it there through a buffering action. Peat moss, cottonseed meal, pine needles, and oak leaves have a more acidic action, which is helpful if you are combating alkaline soil or trying to acidify soil for plants that prefer a low pH. Animal manures often contain salts that raise pH, so it's best to alternate them with other amendments. Wood ash raises pH, so it should be avoided in alkaline soils.

extends down the coast from Half Moon Bay to Monterey. This coastal band, known as *clay loam*, has roughly equal amounts of sand, silt, and clay, but feels more claylike than you would expect, since a little clay goes a long way in changing the characteristics of a soil. (A soil map poster for California is available through the University of California, ANR Communication Services. See the listing in Appendix VII, Resources for Gardeners.)

A map cannot always predict what soil you may have. Patterns may be more complex than a map shows, and also your soil may have been disturbed during construction. Surface soil may have been scraped away or replaced with soil from elsewhere.

You can use your hands to get a rough idea of your soil's texture. First, examine your soil when it is dry. Dry sandy soil feels gritty and pours through your fingers. Dry clay soil forms hard clods, but if you pulverize it, it doesn't feel gritty. Sand still feels gritty when it is wet. If you try to roll it into a snake it immediately crumbles. Wet clay soil feels slippery and sticky. When you roll it out, it can form a snake several inches long. Dry loam has softer clods than dry clay, and will form a thick snake, but will break before you roll it thin.

You may also want to learn more about some characteristics of your soil that aren't so easy to see, such as its pH, its fertility, and whether it is polluted. Unless someone has been fertilizing your soil, it is probably not high in the major nutrients plants need. You can assume this, or you can test it. For a rough analysis, you can use a home test kit available from a nursery or garden store. For a more exact and complete analysis and instructions for correcting imbalances, have your soil tested professionally. The state of California does not sponsor soil tests, so you must look for a commercial laboratory. Try finding one through a local nursery, garden store, or gardening organization.

If you have your soil tested professionally, have it checked for heavy metals as well, to set your mind at ease. (See page 75 for more on polluted soils.) Professional soil tests will also reveal your soil's pH—whether it is alkaline or acidic. You could also test this with a home kit that uses litmus paper or a probe-type pH meter. Some professionals

Our Local Soils

The soils in this region vary dramatically. Some areas near the coast have very deep sandy soil. In some gardens, by the coast and elsewhere, sand may be laid over a heavier soil. Lowland areas around San Francisco Bay are often loamy, but with a high percentage of clay. Some of the deepest and richest loams are found near creeks or former creeks. Other areas are covered with very heavy clay called *adobe*. Although rich in minerals, adobe is hard to manage, turning rock-hard when it dries.

Because of the limited rain and mild winters, all local soils have a relatively thin topsoil. Rainier regions with cold winters, such as the Midwest and parts of the Northeast, favor the building of a thick, organic topsoil. There, the warm summer rains encourage lush growth, which is killed in winter and decays slowly. Here, lighter rainfall means sparser natural growth, which decays the year around, due to our mild winters, and quickly dissipates.

Some soils, especially on eroded hillsides, are very shallow. Often they contain large chunks of shale, sandstone, serpentine, or granite. Although you can't garden in pure rocks, a few rocks aren't all bad. They absorb heat well and reradiate it to warm the surrounding soil. As they break down, they release nutrients, although this happens so slowly that it has no great effect on your garden. Avoid planting root crops, such as carrots or beets, in rocky soil as they will be stunted and deformed. If your soil is essentially gravel or if solid bedrock lies within a foot or so of the surface, you will probably have to garden in a raised bed.

Garden plants languish in the excessively magnesium-rich soil that has developed over serpentine rock. Outcrops of this greenish rock occur here and there throughout the area. There are some in Sonoma County. In Marin County, they reach to the top of Mount Tamalpais and to sea level on the Tiburon peninsula. In San Francisco, outcrops occur in the Presidio, under and around the Mint, and elsewhere, and in San Mateo County, they appear in the Crystal Springs hills. In areas of the Oakland-Berkeley hills, serpentine breaks the surface. Improve serpentine soil by adding 5 pounds gypsum (calcium sulfate) per 100 square feet. The calcium in gypsum will chemically displace the magnesium. In addition, fertilize well.

Some local soils may contain excess salts that will harm plants. Salty soils are more likely along the margins of the Bay, where land has been reclaimed from salt marshes. (Salt spray may get into soils very near the ocean, but this is not likely to be a large quantity.) There are different kinds of salt-laden soils, and some are easier to fix than others. In some the salts are soluble and can be leached, but in others sodium is chemically bound to the soil and must be displaced before the soil is leached (gypsum comes to the rescue again, providing calcium to supplant the sodium). If your plants are not growing well and you suspect that salts may be the problem, get a soil test and follow the recommendations. (See the chart about salt tolerance on page 32.)

Many urban areas are no longer covered with the soil they had naturally. Some areas, especially at the edges of San Francisco Bay, are built on landfills. The Bay coast of San Francisco is built on fill that includes the hulks of sailing vessels abandoned during the Gold Rush! Soil in your neighborhood may have been hauled in from construction sites elsewhere. The contractors who built your home may have scraped off the original topsoil and may or may not have poured a layer of presumably better soil over whatever was left in your yard. Transported soil differs from naturally occurring soil in that it has been piled topsy-turvy, usually burying the thin layer of topsoil. Your garden soil may bear little resemblance to your area's predominant soils, leaving you with unique difficulties to overcome.

Even if your yard has original soil, it may have been compacted to make the foundation firmer when your house was being built. If this is the case, you may need to rototill before you can install a garden—one of the few times that a rototiller is useful in a small garden (see page 87).

discount the accuracy of inexpensive probe meters, but they are very useful for rapidly delineating soil areas with a pH problem. To be sure they are accurate, you might want to calibrate one with a litmus paper test first. For more on pH, see the Soil pH sidebar on the opposite page.

Perform any soil tests before you have begun to add anything to your soil; if you have already begun to do so, take the tests at the end of a growing season, several months after your last addition to your soil. A big advantage of a professional test is that you can ask for instructions for correcting or ameliorating any problems your soil may have. Be sure to include with your soil sample a note that you intend to grow vegetables, and say whether you want advice for organic gardening.

Finally, you will want to know the depth of your soil. If it has been growing trees and shrubs, it is probably plenty deep, but some soils are not. They may have bedrock or packed-in rocks near to the surface, or may even have been laid over a slab of concrete. Dig a few holes and see what is under there. Assuming you have soil of reasonable depth, you are now ready to begin improving it.

ADDING ORGANIC MATTER

If you have very sandy or clay soil, you may imagine that the best way to improve it is to add the opposite-sized mineral particles. This is not usually the best plan, since the amount needed is huge, and the risk of doing more harm than good is high. It takes an especially large amount of sandy soil to change the texture of clay soil, and adding just a little could make your soil perform worse. Usually the best way to improve any soil for growing vegetables and flowers is to amend it by adding organic matter to it.

Organic matter will improve your soil no matter what its texture was when you started. If you are lucky enough to start with loam, you are ahead of the game, because organic matter makes loam even better. But if not—and most of us aren't that lucky—you will find that adding organic matter to sandy or clayey soil creates the next best thing: a *made loam*. Much of the rest of this chapter is concerned with what kind of organic matter to add, how to add it, and how best to prepare it to add to your soil. If this is done well, it can not only improve the structure of your soil, but also go a long way toward fertilizing your crops.

Before we continue, I should point out that you do not need to dig organic matter into areas of a garden planted in ornamental trees and shrubs, and especially not in areas growing California native and drought-tolerant Mediterranean plants. It is better to grow those plants in the soil you have, and then apply organic matter as mulch, a layer on the surface. Vegetables and garden flowers, especially annual flowers, are a special case, needing a soil that provides plenty of nutrients, water, and, particularly, air, so they will grow fast. We usually don't want that kind of fast growth from trees and shrubs, and it would actually shorten the lives of many California native plants.

But for our food and flower gardens, adding organic matter is the best thing we can do for our soils. Unless you have inherited soil built up by a vegetable gardener, you can assume that it is low in organic matter. (A notable exception is the organic soil of the Delta, where organic matter deposited over centuries by reeds and grasses has decayed slowly because the soil was waterlogged. Drained, this soil is ideal for agriculture and is the source of local carrot, corn, and asparagus crops.)

Organic matter is useful when you first add it. It pushes tiny clay particles apart, letting in more air, and fills the large pores among sand particles, allowing sandy soils to hold onto more water and nutrients. Organic matter becomes even more useful as it decays. Soil life eventually digests it into humus, a dark earthy substance that acts as a sort of glue holding sand, silt, and clay particles in little bunches, or aggregates. These aggregates give the soil a crumbly property and enable it to hold both air and water well. In other words, organic matter changes the soil's *structure*, which is the term used to describe the way the mineral particles adhere to each other.

Pick up a handful of soil when it is moist and squeeze it. Then prod it gently with your finger. Without organic matter, sandy soil doesn't hold together at all and clay soil forms a solid lump. Soil that has a good crumb structure holds together lightly but will fall apart into fluffy loose aggregates. Because it holds moisture so well, it feels cool and damp whether it is wet or relatively dry. Don't expect to have a crumb structure unless your soil has been amended with organic matter for several seasons. If you need an example, find a longtime gardener in your neighborhood who will let you get the feel of well-amended soil. Holding it once is worth at least a thousand words.

Humus-rich soil is less likely to compact. That's why Dad was confident in asking me as a child to walk down his seed row. Even though I was small and light, I might still have compacted the soil had it not been so fluffy. Humus is colloidal, just like gelatin. If you smack a richly organic soil with your palm, you will see plants growing in it quiver up to a couple of feet away.

When you add organic matter to sandy soil, you won't have to water or fertilize as often. A well-amended sandy soil can hold up to seven times more water than the same soil unamended. Humus also increases the ability of sandy soil to hold nutrients.

A few seasons of adding organic matter will make a clay soil easier to work and will let water soak into it more readily. Plants will grow better because the soil contains more air. Seedlings will break through more easily, plant roots will grow deeper, and root crops will be well formed.

Although adding organic matter to a loam is not as crucial from the viewpoint of soil structure, it provides a nutrient reserve to any kind of soil that cannot be matched by commercial fertilizers, and it encourages healthy soil life.

Types of Organic Matter

A wide variety of organic materials can be used to amend soil. You can buy, scavenge, or produce your own organic amendment. Compost, homemade or purchased, is ideal, but other substances will also serve.

You can purchase organic matter labeled *compost*, *soil amendment*, or *soil conditioner*, or you can look for free sources. Some of the best organic materials are barnyard manure, green plants, and fallen leaves. Straw, rice hulls, shredded bark, and peat moss can be used, but they are less desirable because they decay more slowly.

If the label on a purchased amendment says that the product was *composted*, that means it has sat around and decayed for a while, so that it is partway to becoming humus. Materials commonly composted are barnyard manure, sawdust, and fallen leaves (sold as leaf mold). A product sold as *compost* is usually a mixture of several different organic substances that have decayed together to a relatively stable state. When you dig in a composted material or compost, you can plant right away.

After you dig in fresh material, such as kitchen scraps, fresh barnyard manure, or green manure (see page 76), you must let it decay for a few weeks before planting. Waiting may be worthwhile, since these materials are often free. Look around for organic matter that may be available for the asking, such as stable manure or pulp left over after making apple juice (pomace) or wine (grape pulp).

Kitchen scraps require special care to avoid problems with rodents. Use vegetable matter only; chop large pieces before you bury the scraps. Bury the scraps so that there is 12 inches of soil above them.

Polluted Soils

The soils in urban areas usually contain remnants of the lives of people who have lived there. I have found marbles, blue glass bottles, and bits of crockery. Once, in a new community garden in a vacant lot, we found enough bricks and concrete to make a small patio.

With the exception of broken glass, these findings pose no danger, but there could be a hazard from invisible pollutants. Virtually all homes built before World War II were coated with paint containing lead, which found its way into the soil nearest the house as the paint weathered or was scraped and sanded in preparation for repainting. The lead in the yard could be more widespread if a building burned down on the property. Paint made after 1978 is free of lead.

Lead has also entered the soil from the air, emitted by cars fueled by leaded gasoline; happily, lead has been prohibited in U.S. gasoline since 1995. Because lead is heavy, it doesn't rise into the atmosphere but settles on surfaces near roads. Cadmium, a heavy metal in tires, may also pollute areas near roads. Soils in front and side yards next to busy streets and not screened by a fence or shrubbery are most likely to be polluted. The safest location for a food garden is 75 feet from busy streets, with a building, fence, or hedge to block the wind, but let a soil test be your guide.

Another possible source of lead is lead arsenate, once used as a pesticide in orchards but now banned. Consider this a possibility if your yard was once part of one of the area's many commercial orchards.

If you are new to the property and find that part of the yard is unusually bare, suspect that it may have been treated with a long-lasting herbicide. Test your theory by trying to germinate radish seeds. If several tries fail, have your soil tested professionally.

When your soil is tested professionally, you will get recommendations with your test results. If there turn out to be low levels of pollutants in your soil, good gardening practices can reduce the hazard. The organic matter that you add to the soil will bind pollutants and keep them out of plant roots. If the pollutant levels are high, you will get instructions with your soil test, explaining what is safe to grow and eat. While it isn't probable, it could turn out that pollution levels are too high to garden safely. Then you might have to remove the soil and replace it, build raised beds and fill them with clean soil, garden in containers, or join a nearby community garden.

You can start at one corner of an unplanted area and work your way across and down it. You can garden in the place where you dug in food scraps after about two months. (One San Francisco gardener dug in all her kitchen scraps a couple of years before she planted. When she finally did plant, the crops practically leapt onto her table.)

Instead of tying up garden space while you wait for fresh material to decay, you can make your own compost by one of several different systems. (For more on compost, see page 88.)

Straw and wood products such as sawdust, shredded newspaper, and ground bark are low in nitrogen. Unless you add nitrogen, the soil microorganisms that break down fresh organic matter will devour nitrogen compounds in the soil to fuel their activity. If you buy any of these fresh products, check to see if they have been "nitrogen stabilized." This means that a nitrogen source has been added. If not, you can add it yourself at the rate of a half pound of actual nitrogen per 15 pounds of wood product. For example, that amounts to 10 pounds of a fertilizer that contains 5 percent nitrogen, such as 5-10-10, or 4 pounds of blood meal, which contains 13 percent nitrogen. (To interpret the numbers on a fertilizer label, see page 84.) Wood products that have been composted don't need to be nitrogen stabilized; neither does straw that was used as animal bedding, since the animal wastes contribute nitrogen. (The straw bedding is probably best treated as fresh material and allowed to decay for a while before you plant.)

When you are considering a wood product to use as an amendment, be aware that both hardwood and softwood products are thought to be safe, but do not use shavings or sawdust made from wood containing toxic substances such as a preservative (see page 35). Also avoid plywood sawdust, which contains toxic materials in the glue. Use caution when adding very fine sawdust from sanding, since pockets of it may prevent water from passing through.

Rice hulls are a particularly useful material for use in clay soils because they immediately open the soil, and they break down so slowly that they don't rob the soil of nitrogen. They are a loose, flyaway material, so you have to watch out for winds while you are digging them in, but if you have clay, probably the more rice hulls you can add the better.

Alternate amendments as much as possible to avoid adding too much of any type of material to the soil. Animal manure as commonly sold tends to have a high salt content because it is often from confined animals, so the salts-containing urine is mixed with the manure. This is especially true of manure from feedlots. Some gardeners believe that redwood products inhibit plant growth, whereas others say it isn't so. To be safe, don't depend completely on any one material. One of the advantages of compost is that it consists of many materials.

Green Manure

Growing plants and then digging them into the soil to decay is one of the standard techniques used by organic farmers to improve their soils. Such *green manures* are economical, requiring only a purchase of a little seed. They are dug under while they are still young, at which time they will decay fairly quickly.

Some of the best choices for green manure crops in our area are fava beans planted in fall or winter, red clover planted in spring, and vetch planted in early to late fall. These plants are all legumes, so their roots host special bacteria that fix nitrogen from the soil. When you dig in the plants, extra nitrogen is released in a form other plants can use.

Gardeners often confuse growing fava beans for green manure with growing them for beans. If you harvest a legume's seeds, you will greatly reduce the amount of nitrogen the plants return to the soil. As a green manure crop, you use the fava bean plants when they are about a foot and a half to two feet tall, well before they have formed pods.

If you are gardening in a very small space, you may be loath to use part of it to grow plants, dig them under, and then wait the couple of months it takes for them to decay before you can plant something else. To free up space for other crops faster, you can grow the green manure crop and then pull it, chop it up, and use it in compost.

Weeds are also fine green manure or compost ingredients, as long as they have not yet formed seeds that will regrow and are not perennial weeds that regrow from bulblets or runners still in the soil.

If green manure fits into your planting schedule, it's practically free fertilizer and amendment, but if you find you have access to plenty of organic matter without growing green manure, don't feel that you must grow some anyway. A farmer may have no other option, since there is much land to keep fertile. An urban gardener with a small plot may find other responsible ways to keep the soil in good shape without growing green manure.

How Much? When?

Organic matter is commonly measured by the depth of a layer spread out over the soil and then

Calculating Volumes of Amendments, Compost, and Soil

When you purchase organic soil amendment or compost, it is sold by the cubic foot in bags or by the cubic yard in bulk. To calculate how much material you need, figure out the area of the garden space you wish to cover, then multiply the area by the depth of the layer of amendment. Remember to express length, width, and depth in the same unit of measure.

For example, here's the calculation to cover a bed 9 feet long and 4 feet wide with a layer of material 3 inches (.25 feet) deep:

9 feet × 4 feet =
36 square feet × .25 feet = 9 cubic feet

Nine cubic feet is 4½ bags containing 2 cubic feet each, so you should buy 5 bags and save the extra cubic foot of material for later. To put the same 3-inch layer of material on five beds of the same size, you would need five times as much material, or 45 cubic feet. Since there are 27 cubic feet in 1 cubic yard (3 by 3 by 3 feet), 45 cubic feet is about 1⅔ cubic yards. To help you visualize a cubic yard, it's about 6 cubic feet less than the volume of a typical refrigerator.

When you need more than 1 cubic yard of a material, it may be cheaper to have it delivered in bulk. You can usually order only full or half cubic yards, so to get 1⅔ cubic yards, you'd order 2 cubic yards (54 cubic feet) and save the extra ⅓ cubic yard for later. A contractor's wheelbarrow holds 3½ cubic feet or so when it is filled level with the top, so it would take on the order of sixteen wheelbarrow trips to move 2 cubic yards of material.

dug in. A maintenance amount for soil that is already in good shape is 1 or 2 inches per year. If your soil has not been amended, this is the minimum you should apply, but 3 or even 6 inches a year would be better.

You aren't trying to create a soil that is mostly organic matter. A highly organic soil has about 5 percent organic content. Soil creatures large and small continually digest what you add, turning it to humus, and you want to add a bit more than they need and then stay just ahead of them. They will digest it faster in sandy soil or where summers are warmer. If your soil doesn't seem to improve much over time, try adding more organic matter.

If you garden year-round, it is wise to divide your annual amount in two. You don't have to add organic matter at any particular times or to the whole garden at once. Just add it as part of preparing to grow the next crop. It often works out that you add some in spring, more in late summer or fall.

Potting Mix? Planting Mix? Topsoil?

Gardeners often buy potting mix or planting mix when they need organic amendment or soil. This is unwise not only because it's a waste of money, but because the substance you buy may not serve the purpose for which you intend it.

Potting mix may look like soil, but it is not. It is formulated to hold much more water than soil, and also much more air. However, because it has few or no soil mineral particles (sand, silt, or clay), and because most of the organic matter in it is not nutrient-rich, it does not provide long-term fertility. You are expected to use it in containers and, after the first few weeks, fertilize it quite frequently. Real soil has and holds fertility, so needs much less frequent fertilizing.

Potting mix is ideal for filling shallow containers, up to about a foot deep. In such containers, real soil would behave badly. When it had just been watered, it would not contain enough air, so roots would begin to drown. Then it would dry out too fast and soon be so dry the roots couldn't get moisture. Use potting mix in containers or in a raised bed up to a foot deep you've built on an impermeable surface such as concrete.

Don't put any gravel or pot shards at the bottom of containers of any kind; no matter what you've heard, research shows clearly that they will impede drainage rather than help it. Potting mix will shrink after a year or so, as the organic matter in it decays. Replace it when it shrinks. (You can dig the old potting mix into the garden.)

Planting mix (sometimes called "nursery mix") is potting mix with more sand or even sandy loam added. It works better than potting mix in containers that are a little deeper. It is still not soil, and it is probably going to cost more than buying a material sold as a soil amendment if what you want is something to improve your soil.

If you have soil and want to add organic matter to it, the most economical ways to do that are by growing green manure or making your own compost from free materials. If you want to purchase organic matter, good choices are either single ingredients like composted leaf mold, composted manure, or rice hulls, or ones labeled *soil amendment*, *compost*, or *worm castings*.

What about buying topsoil? The soil science definition of topsoil is soil in the top layer of a naturally occurring soil. It has a relatively high organic content—that is, 3 to 5 percent—from the natural falling of dead plants and animals and their decay by soil microorganisms. The organic matter has been falling to the ground and decaying for eons, so topsoil contains a significant amount of humus. (The designation of *topsoil* has nothing to do with the texture of the soil, so it could be clay, some kind of loam, or sandy.)

Although it may be true that you lack topsoil because your topsoil has been scraped off during construction, or is dune sand or some other natural soil that contains little or no organic matter, you probably can't purchase true topsoil. There is no legal definition of topsoil. Materials sold as topsoil will vary. Some may be a blend of sand and some kind of organic soil amendment such as ground-up bark or rice hulls, others may be unamended soil.

In neither case will they have more humus—the dark, sticky end-product of the decay of the organic matter—than does the soil you already have. So again, if you have soil, amend it with organic matter and let the soil creatures begin to work on it to create topsoil. This will be less expensive, or even free if you find free sources of organic matter that can be used either as is or as raw materials for compost.

If you have soil of any sort, what you need is organic matter to add to it. However, there are times when a gardener does need to obtain soil.

Keeping Your Soil Alive

Soil care is basically a kind of wildlife management. You want a large, active population of creatures, from beneficial bacteria to earthworms. Most of this soil life is invisible, but it works wonders for the health of your plants. Various creatures in turn break down organic matter until the chemical nutrients are released into the soil for plant use.

Evidence is mounting that an active soil life plays a significant role in helping green plants fight diseases and other pests. Some microorganisms produce antibiotics that inhibit diseases, and others are actual predators of pests that damage plant roots. Some bacteria and fungi live in what appears to be a mutually beneficial association with the roots of green plants, using carbohydrates that the plants manufacture while releasing nitrogen in a form that the plants can use.

These helpful soil creatures need adequate moisture and air. They work best in warm soil, but some activity will continue as long as the soil is not frozen. Unlike green plants, which make their own food through photosynthesis, most soil creatures need to break down organic matter to obtain energy and carbon.

When the soil dries completely, the soil life dies, goes into a resting state, or moves to another garden. If you intend to plant but don't get to it in early spring, keep the area watered.

When the soil lacks air, many helpful soil creatures leave or cease activity. Creatures that are tolerant of low-oxygen conditions are likely to be the sort that attack plant roots. When soil gets waterlogged, which is more likely in winter, disease organisms sometimes get the upper hand.

Digging and turning the soil lets in more air, enabling soil creatures to multiply more quickly. Turning clay soil, which is low in air content, is more useful than turning sandy soil, which already has plenty of air. If you dig sandy soil often, the soil microorganisms may digest organic matter faster than you can add it.

Organic matter must be replaced, since soil organisms will eventually digest even the humus. Dig more organic matter in at least once a year, and twice if you are gardening the year around. Dig it into the top 6 to 10 inches of soil, where there is enough air to support the helpful soil organisms. An organic mulch spread on the soil surface will serve as an additional food source for soil life.

Avoid chemicals that are toxic to soil life. Any chemical fungicides or herbicides that work in the soil. Even water-soluble fertilizers can kill helpful soil life. If you must use pesticides that can harm these beneficial creatures, use them in ways that will cause the least damage (see page 111).

One is when there is really no soil, as when the yard is basically a rock outcropping, or if you are replacing polluted or salty soil. The other is if you plan to build tall beds because you don't want to—or cannot—stoop to reach into them. If you are filling a two- or three-foot-tall raised bed, use plain, unamended, clean (that is, weed-seed-free), sandy loam (soil that is up to 50 percent sand, up to 20 percent clay, and the rest silt, or as close as you can get to that). (You will have to ask, to be clear what you are buying. Perfectly good unamended sandy loam is sometimes sold as topsoil.) Fill your bed nearly to the top with the sandy loam, and then dig a few inches of organic soil amendment into the top 6 inches and continue to amend and fertilize it as you would any other garden soil.

If you fill a tall bed with potting mix, you will waste money. Besides that, it will require more water, it will hold fertility poorly, and it will shrink, requiring extensive refilling and remixing every few years. I often see tall beds filled with potting or planting mix that are growing miniature vegetable plants because the gardener doesn't realize how much water and regularly added fertilizer these artificial growing mediums will require. Potting mixes usually have some fertilizer in them to start, but it lasts only a few months, and after that you will need to fertilize often.

Soil in bags may be more difficult to locate than potting mix in bags, but it can be found. It is heavy, about 100 pounds per cubic foot, so you may want to buy it in half-full bags. You may not be able to handle a wheelbarrow if it is full of soil, because of the weight, so you may need to make more trips to move soil than you would to move an equal volume of lighter materials.

If you are adding purchased soil over existing soil, always dig a little of the purchased soil into the first few inches of the existing soil to reduce the abruptness of the interface or the change of soil texture. This is important to allow water to flow between the two distinct layers.

MULCHING

Mulch is a material that a gardener lays on the surface of the soil to conserve water, modify the soil temperature, prevent soil crusting, lessen erosion, keep weeds down, reduce diseases, and keep plant parts from touching the soil and decaying. Mulch can be organic, such as compost or cocoa bean hulls, or inorganic, such as black plastic or crushed stones. An organic mulch acts like leaf litter on the forest floor, decaying slowly into the soil to improve its structure and increase fertility. When you dig it in at the end of the growing season, you are adding organic matter to the soil.

The *no-till method* of gardening calls for covering the garden permanently with an organic mulch, planting through it and never digging it in. This method, which controls weeds and produces a soft, fertile, water-retentive soil, was popularized by Ruth Stout, who gardened that way in Connecticut for some fifty years, many of them from a wheelchair. She planned her garden to save labor, and her book *How to Have a Green Thumb Without an Aching Back* (see Appendix VIII, Suggested Reading), is well worth reading for her gardening wit and wisdom.

I have seen the no-till method work well enough in a sunny garden in the Mission district of San Francisco. The gardener grew many crops, including tomatoes, under a 6-inch layer of straw. However, if spring is long and cool where you garden, warm-season crops will get a faster start if you allow the soil to warm thoroughly before you apply any organic mulch. The foggier the site, the more critical this factor is. An organic mulch can cool the soil by as much as ten degrees—undesirable in a climate barely warm enough for some crops anyway.

Before laying mulch, clear away weeds and water the soil well. Apply an organic mulch around seedlings only when the plants have several true leaves. Lay the mulch between young seedlings, leaving an open circle; later, after they have toughened up, you can draw it up to the stems. If you are using plastic, cut crisscross slits for transplanted seedlings or lay strips between rows. Whenever you use plastic as mulch, tuck the edges into the soil or else snails and slugs will cluster on the underside.

If the mulch you plan to use is sold by the cubic foot or cubic yard, use the method described on page 77 (for organic matter) to determine how much you will need.

Local Mulching Plan

In late winter and early spring, you will be concentrating on gardening techniques that warm the soil. If you use an organic mulch, choose a dark material, such as compost, cocoa hulls, or rotted sawdust, and use only a thin layer to minimize the cooling effect.

Black or clear plastic will warm the soil. In fact, clear plastic may warm it too much in the sunnier parts of our region. Both types of plastic are best reserved for early plantings of warm-season crops.

Help from Earthworms

If earthworms did nothing else, they would serve as an indicator of healthy soil. Their tunneling aerates the soil, improves drainage, and opens channels for plant roots. They eat organic matter and excrete it as castings, which soil bacteria and fungi can digest and break down into plant nutrients more easily than they can the original organic matter.

When you first start to garden, before you've improved the soil, you may not see many earthworms. After you add organic matter and begin to keep your soil moist, earthworms will migrate from neighboring yards and multiply in your soil. In addition to consuming organic matter in the soil, they will pull bits of organic matter from the soil surface down into their tunnels. When you thin vegetable seedlings or pull small weeds, leave some pulled plants on the soil surface for the earthworms. (Make sure the weeds don't have seeds or roots that will regrow.)

Try not to injure earthworms when you are digging. A garden fork will cut fewer earthworms than a shovel or spade, and all hand tools are less damaging than a rotary tiller. (It is not true that an earthworm cut in half can regenerate to form two worms.) When you are digging, move to a safe location any earthworms you see wandering around in search of their lost tunnels. Loosen some moist soil in a shady spot and put them on it.

If you use water-soluble fertilizers in your soil, the earthworms will move deeper for a few days until the chemicals bind to the soil and become harmless. If you use these fertilizers often and over most of your garden, the earthworms will leave your yard.

Sevin bait, sometimes used as an earwig control, is an example of a pesticide that will kill earthworms along with its intended victims, although a small amount used occasionally in a small area probably wouldn't wipe out your entire earthworm population. That said, using a less-toxic alternative, such as Sluggo Plus (iron phosphate bait with spinosin) would be wiser.

You will find earthworms for sale, but if your soil is not a good habitat for them, they will not stay. Most people just improve their soil and wait for earthworms to arrive. If you do choose to buy earthworms, a couple dozen night crawlers should be able to colonize a hundred square feet or so in no time. (The species used for making worm compost are different—see the Earthworm Compost sidebar on page 93.)

You may want to lay the plastic for a week or two to warm the soil before you plant, then leave it on for a while to get the plants off to a good start.

When air and soil temperatures are warm, you may choose to lay an organic mulch to reduce the need for water. If you do, don't lay it on top of plastic. The cooling effect of the mulch will be of less concern once the soil is as warm as it will get and the warm-season crops are well established. In fact, the cooling effect may actually work to your advantage if you are growing cool-season crops in a warm summer microclimate.

Organic mulch will help keep the soil cool during hot weather. Experiment to see which crops will benefit from summertime mulching and which will be hindered where you live.

Straw is a good choice for mulch to cool soil in hot summers. Sometimes you can get free straw bales that were used for Halloween or Thanksgiving decorations, or relatively clean straw from someone who keeps barnyard animals, or you can buy it at a farm supply store. Don't get hay by mistake. Hay contains many seeds, such as wheat or oats. These will grow, quickly creating a field of grain instead of a garden. Avoid using gravel, pebbles, or large chunks of bark as mulch in a vegetable garden. They do not decay and add nutrients to the soil, and you would have to rake them out of the way every time you changed crops.

As you head into the rainy season, your mulching goals will change. The mulch will help cancel the damaging effects of heavy rain pelting bare soil. Mulch any areas that will be vacant for all or part of the winter, including areas between widely spaced plants such as broccoli. You can leave the area under vegetable leaf canopies bare, since the leaves will protect the soil and the bare places will catch and radiate more warmth. (See page 148 for tips on using weeds, either living or pulled, as a winter mulch.) If you have dormant perennial beds, mulch their soil lightly but don't pile up mulch over plants as you would in a cold-winter climate, since that will only encourage decay. At the end of winter, dig the organic mulch into the soil.

FERTILIZING

To grow a healthy garden, you don't have to be an expert in plant nutrition. Usually it's enough to know a few basic facts about the nutrient content of our soils. Of the major nutrients, local soils are generally low in nitrogen. They may be low in phosphorus and available potassium as well. Organic matter contains all three nutrients, but even if you are adding organic matter, you will probably want to pay special attention to these major three, to be sure you have added enough.

Surveys show that most gardeners don't fertilize their gardens at all the first year. This means that crops must mine the soil for nutrients left by decaying vegetation and dissolving minerals. Some crops may get by, but the soil will be depleted and will not support crops as well the second year. A regular fertilization program will return nutrients to your soil.

Nitrogen is the nutrient that must be added most often, not only because local soils are often low in it, but also because it is easily lost from the soil. A lack of nitrogen causes slow growth and yellowed lower leaves. Adding too much nitrogen results in lots of lush growth at the expense of flowering and fruiting—this symptom is often seen on tomato plants that are given too much nitrogen. Add nitrogen in a form that is released slowly or, if it is quick-acting, add it more than once during a growing season. You can supply nitrogen with either organic substances or synthetic fertilizers.

Phosphorus doesn't have to be replaced as often as nitrogen since it doesn't move in the soil. Essential for flowering and fruiting, phosphorus also contributes to early growth and root formation. A deficiency causes stunting and poor fruit and seed development. The leaves turn dark green and there may be some reddening or purpling on the plant. Organic gardeners often add phosphorus in the form of bonemeal, rock phosphate, or soft or colloidal phosphate. Many synthetic fertilizers contain phosphorus as well.

Potassium is usually plentiful in soils, and though little of it is available in a form available to plants at any given time, our regional soils often supply enough of it. When it is lacking, plants don't grow as large, though this could be due to other causes and is difficult to use for diagnosis. Plants may have brown edges on lower leaves, fall over, or have small fruit. An adequate supply aids disease resistance. If you are using decayed plant matter as a fertilizer, you will be adding potassium. Greensand, which is a ground-up granite rock, provides potassium, as do some synthetic fertilizers.

Plants need a number of other nutrients in smaller amounts. There are three *secondary nutrients*: calcium, sulfur, and magnesium. Needed in tiny amounts are boron, chlorine, copper, iron, manganese, molybdenum, nickel, and zinc. Local soils are most often adequately supplied with these secondary and trace nutrients. Those who use synthetic fertilizers sometimes purchase a separate trace mineral fertilizer just to make sure. However, organic substances, used as amendment or fertilizer, return the trace minerals that were in the living creatures they derived from, so no separate trace mineral source is usually required. You are not likely to encounter obscure nutrient deficiencies, but if your plants do not grow well and you can't determine that they have any disease, you can send a soil sample along with a description of the symptoms to a soil laboratory.

If you are growing plants that prefer more acidic soil, such as citrus or blueberries, you may see deficiencies of zinc or iron, not because the soil doesn't contain them, but because these plants can't extract them unless the soil is acidic. A zinc deficiency causes abnormally small leaves that are either mottled or pale between the veins. An iron deficiency causes yellowing between the leaf veins. Both zinc and iron deficiencies can be corrected by using chelates—forms of the minerals that can be absorbed by the plants even when the soil pH is wrong—or by acidifying the soil.

Manure or Compost Tea

Steeping compost or well-composted barnyard manure in water to make a "tea" and using this as a liquid fertilizer is an old practice of organic gardeners. You put some of either material in a large container (a covered plastic bucket is ideal for containing the odor) and fill it with water. Use about 2 cups solid material per 1 gallon water. Let it sit in the garden for three days or more, stirring it a couple of times a day. Every two weeks or so apply the liquid around your plants before you water them. When the liquid is gone, pour the slurry in the garden in an area between plants and start over.

Organic? Biodynamic? Sustainable? Permaculture?

Organic farming is what many farmers did, before the mid-twentieth century. Improvements in organic agriculture were developing in the early twentieth century at the same time that the use of synthetic chemical fertilizers and synthetic pesticides were becoming more widespread. In 1940, British governmental agronomist Sir Albert Howard published *An Agricultural Testament*, explaining his improved methods for making compost. Also at about the same time, American businessman J. I. Rodale became the first to use the term "organic" to refer to farming or gardening. Beginning in 1942, he published *Organic Gardening* magazine, promoting the idea that compost and manures remained better materials to increase soil fertility and promoting methods of pest control other than the new synthetic pesticides.

As time passed and unexpected problems arose with the use of the new agricultural chemicals, more consumers saw organic farming as a way to avoid the new hazards. Soon it became clear that we needed legal definitions of exactly what was meant by organic farming. In 1979, the California Organic Food Act was signed, setting forth very clear and useful guidelines for allowed and prohibited materials and practices. Then, in 1990, in response to a drive for national standards, the federal government passed the Federal Organic Foods Production Act. In 2002, the National Organic Program (NOP) took effect, taking precedence over any state laws. It covers not only what a farmer can use or do but also labeling for foods that contain organically produced ingredients.

To be certified as an organic farm, the land must be certified free of prohibited substances for at least three years. On the website of the USDA, you can read "National List of Approved and Prohibited Substances," delineating what is permitted to organic farmers and what is not. Farmers keep careful records of what they use, and in order to remain certified, they must pay for inspections to ensure that they are following the laws.

The NOP lists materials, not products. That is, it includes ferric phosphate (iron phosphate), the active ingredient in Sluggo brand snail bait, but not Sluggo. Various state agencies and nonprofits review particular products and judge if they can be used under the NOP. The one most often used in California is the Organic Materials Review Institute (OMRI). When you see the "OMRI Listed" logo on a fertilizer or other garden material, you know it has been approved for use by certified organic farmers. But still, to maintain certification, organic farmers must report all materials they use to a certifying agent, including OMRI listed products.

Because many opinions go into a national law, there have been controversies about what is to be included, and there probably will be again. While the National List was being created, there was controversy about the use of bioengineered crops, irradiation, sewer sludge–derived fertilizers, antibiotics, and growth hormones for livestock. Public opinion, in the form of more letters than the USDA had ever received on a single issue, weighed in and led to the prohibition of all of these. Despite the national law, there will probably always remain some questions about what *organic* should mean. For example, various plant extracts, known as botanical pesticides, have traditionally been used by organic farmers. One, nicotine, is no longer permitted due to its extreme toxicity. Another, rotenone, has been implicated, along with some synthetic pesticides, as a possible cause of Parkinson's disease, but it is still permitted.

The organic farming and gardening movement arose from a desire to cope with an economy that often puts short-term monetary goals ahead of long-term goals for human and ecosystem health. Even after long debate and law creation, organic farming principles will probably continue to need refining. And there are also those who wish to use practices taught in other gardening and farming paradigms, either alone or with organic methods.

Some gardeners and farmers are attracted to the ideas of biodynamics. This set of practices, many of them mystical and without support from scientific studies, include planting by the moon and the use of various herbal preparations, some of them buried in cow horns before being added to compost. Its origins are deep in European folk practices, as compiled by the German educator and mystic Rudolph Steiner. These days, biodynamic farming or gardening is most often practiced by those who also follow modern organic practices. There are no legal standards applicable to biodynamic practices.

People who eat organically grown food often do so with the goal of finding "pure" food in an age in which our food suppliers often seem to put profit ahead of safety or nutrition. But beyond our individual benefit, it is also important to protect the earth against practices that degrade its future ability to support life. The term *sustainable agriculture* is often used to describe farming that is working toward the second goal.

Sustainable agriculture reduces the use of nonrenewable resources, or tries to avoid, as Al Gore has put it, treating the earth's resources as if they were being offered in a fire sale. There is much overlap between sustainable and organic practices. A sustainable farmer or gardener might use green manure or manure from nearby sources and reduce use of synthetic fertilizers or pesticides in order to reduce the use of petroleum and reduce environmental pollution. A farmer may practice sustainable agriculture without adhering to NOP rules and becoming certified as an organic farmer, and an organic farmer may add sustainable farming practices beyond those required to be certified as organic.

The concept of a sustainable community is also included in sustainable farming. For example, if working conditions and income levels for farmers and farm labor are decent, the stable workforce will be able to create nearby communities that are better places to live.

It must be said that the organic farming law does not apply to farmers who earn less than $15,000 a year from farming. In addition, some small farmers who earn more than that have chosen not to become certified as organic because they find the laws and the expense burdensome. Such farmers may seek to build trust with customers, saying that they farm organically as they define it. They may sell produce as "not sprayed," a term with no legal standing. There is also a "buy local" movement to stress that support of nearby farmers saves petroleum used for transportation. (The average food item travels 1,500 miles to reach an American kitchen.) A second value of "buying local" is that of keeping local small-scale agriculture healthy in the face of corporate agriculture.

The organic farming law certainly does not apply to home gardeners. I tell you this to encourage you to think for yourself when ambiguities arise. Even if you decide to "go organic," you will never have an organic certifier to ask about a new product for your garden. You can read the NOP list or look for the OMRI logo, but there will be times when a product is not OMRI listed, though it seems to fit the criteria for listing. This could be because the product is too new to be listed or the manufacturer may have chosen not to pay for the required analysis.

Another new approach to how we produce what we need to live from the earth is permaculture. This concept was first imagined by an Australian, Bill Mollison. His initial idea was to design a system that could produce as much as possible of what he needed to feed, shelter, and clothe himself in a relatively small area with a minimum of effort. The concept has developed into a holistic way of thinking about our relationship to the earth, using all the ideas we can assemble to design a living environment that provides energy, water, food, waste recycling, community, and any other needs we can meet. Permaculture will be a powerful tool for helping us to see systems rationally and make intelligent design decisions for a sustainable future. Gardening is only one part of permaculture, and a permaculture certification doesn't provide a full education about gardening or horticulture.

Types of Fertilizers

Fertilizers may be inorganic or organic, dry or liquid, faster or slower to release nutrients. Some contain a single nutrient; others contain many.

There are two types of inorganic fertilizers: rock fertilizers, which are mineral deposits ground to a powder, and synthetic fertilizers. Since rock fertilizers are not water soluble, they do not burn plants and are long lasting. Although these natural substances are inorganic, they are often used in an organic fertilizing program.

Synthetic fertilizers such as superphosphate or ammonium nitrate are manufactured materials. Whether dry or liquid, they are water soluble, washing out of the soil easily. They can burn plant roots if they are used in concentrations that are too high or if the undiluted chemical touches plant roots. Some synthetic fertilizers are encapsulated in materials that cause them to release nutrients more slowly; they are safer to use and last longer than the quick-release types.

Organic fertilizers are natural organic materials. Sometimes, as with barnyard manure, the actual content of nutrients is low, but the fact that the material is applied in large quantities compensates. Most organic fertilizers will not burn plants, although those with a high nitrogen content, such as blood meal, worm castings, or cottonseed meal, can do so if used in large amounts.

Compost definitely provides nutrients to plants, and could, theoretically, provide all they need, if the nutrients were in the original mix. The main issue is whether it provides enough nitrogen.

Fertilizer Formulas

When you have your soil tested by a laboratory, you will get recommendations for fertilizing it along with your written report. This is the only way you can be sure of adding just the right amounts of fertilizer that contain just the amount of nutrients your soil lacks. (If you tell the lab you are planning to grow vegetables organically, you will also get recommendations for organic fertilizers.)

Without a soil test, gardeners often just choose sources of nitrogen, phosphorus, and potassium and add a moderate amount of each. This less exact approach works pretty well. Theoretically, you could add more than you need of one or more nutrients, because the soil might already contain them (see opposite page). The formulas that follow are just two out of many possibilities. Each includes both organic amendment and fertilizer.

Formula 1

Spread at least 2 inches of compost made by the cold method or a purchased amendment. Over each 100 square feet, sprinkle 16 pounds of alfalfa meal (nitrogen source), 5 pounds of bone meal (phosphorus source), and 1 pound of kelp meal (potassium source). In soil that is already in good shape, or in poor soil after the first couple of years of this program, reduce the amounts of fertilizers to 5 to 10 pounds of alfalfa meal and 2 pounds of bone meal; continue to add the 1 pound of kelp meal.

Formula 2

Spread at least 2 inches of an organic soil amendment. Over each 100 square feet of bed, sprinkle 3.5 pounds of blood meal (nitrogen source), 10 pounds of soft or colloidal phosphate (phosphorus source), and 10 pounds of greensand (potassium source). Don't add more soft or colloidal phosphate for two to three years or more greensand for as long as ten years. Do continue to add organic soil amendment and blood meal, but reduce blood meal to 1½ to 2½ pounds after the first couple of years (or if soil is already in good shape when you begin).

In both cases, spread each substance completely over the area, then add another, until all are spread. Then dig them all into the top 6 to 8 inches of soil. All these nutrients, except for soft phosphate and greensand, should be replenished in six months to a year. The soft phosphate will last two or three years and the greensand as long as ten years.

If compost was made by the hot or fast method (see page 91), and did heat up, at some point it had plenty of nitrogen. Cold method or slow compost could also have enough, if attention were paid to the proportions of materials in it, though the pile might have been too small, or inadequately watered, or added to over too long a time for it to heat up. If you purchase compost, read the label and make educated guesses about its fertilizer value. Some bagged compost products are made with relatively low-nitrogen materials and will require additional fertilizer to grow vegetables.

How Are Fertilizers Labeled?

Whenever you buy a packaged product for use as a fertilizer—whether it is an organic material, a rock powder, or a synthetic chemical fertilizer—you will find three numbers on the label: the N-P-K rating. They stand for the percentages by weight of nitrogen (N), phosphorus (P), and potassium (K), listed in that order. For example, a fertilizer labeled 5-10-10 contains 5 percent nitrogen, 10 percent phosphorus, and 10 percent potassium. The rest of what's in the product is necessary for the formulation and could be inert as far as the plants are concerned; sometimes it provides some other nutrients. A fertilizer containing all three major nutrients is called a *complete fertilizer*, although it clearly doesn't provide all of the nutrients plants need to grow. If a fertilizer lacks one or more of the three major nutrients, a 0 appears in the place its amount should be. For example, greensand (0-1-6) contains no nitrogen, 1 percent phosphorus, and 6 percent potassium.

How Much to Add?

Often you will add fertilizer from a box or bottle that's imprinted with instructions about how much to use, but you might find yourself applying purchased fertilizer that isn't so labeled. For example, bags of alfalfa or cottonseed meal are economical sources of nutrients but may come without directions.

Keep in mind that it is worse to add too much fertilizer than too little. If plants get too much fertilizer at once, they can be damaged or killed. Nitrogen is probably the most commonly overused, but other nutrients, especially if they are in soluble form, can be a problem. Also, if you are using very long-lasting materials such as soft or rock phosphate or greensand, pay attention to how long these materials usually last in soil, since adding them too often could result in too high an amount of phosphorus or potassium in the soil.

Remember that plants need very small amounts of even the major soil nutrients. Plants make most of their own food through photosynthesis. Up to 90 percent of a plant is water. Of the remaining solids, most are carbon, hydrogen, and oxygen that the plant has captured through photosynthesis, and turned into sugar, then into more complex biological compounds. Only a small part, about 0.5 percent of the plant's weight, consists of all of the other plant nutrients, from nitrogen to molybdenum. In other words, though plants can't live without fertilizer, they don't need their "three square meals a day" from it.

Here's how to use the numbers on the label as a guide to avoiding adding too much nitrogen. A general rule is not to apply more than a quarter ounce of actual nitrogen per square yard of soil. If you know the percent by weight of nitrogen in the substance you are using, you can calculate how much is enough. For example, if it is a 5-10-10 fertilizer, it is 5 percent nitrogen, or 0.5 ounces of nitrogen per 10 ounces of fertilizer. So you would want to add no more than 5 ounces of fertilizer per square yard.

The N-P-K rating of compost is usually rather low, not because the nutrients aren't there, but because most of the nutrients it contains are not in presently useable form. It's high in complex carbohydrates, which feed soil life, slowly releasing nutrients. This is the very definition of an organic soil amendment and why amendments can also be fertilizers, depending on the organic material used.

Proportion of Nutrients

Another term you will hear is *balanced fertilizer*. This term implies that a fertilizer contains nutrients in a balance best for plants, but it may not be so. The term is sometimes just used as a synonym for "having the same amount of N, P, and K," and plants definitely don't use these nutrients in equal amounts. The term is also used for some other particular balance of these three nutrients. In some cases, as when one is feeding palms or orchids, someone may have actually determined this was a good balance of the three macronutrients for the plants in question, but in most cases it doesn't mean much.

To accurately decide the perfect nutrient balance for your garden, you'd have to know both the needs of the crops and how much of each nutrient is already in the soil. A farmer might have both the soil and the plant tissue from a particular crop tested each year. You aren't going to do that for each crop in your little garden, so you will just be making educated guesses and watching your plants.

One generalization can be made about the proportion of nitrogen (N) to phosphorus (P). A fertilizer or fertilizer mix with more N than P (such as 10-5-5) would be best for producing leafy growth, while a fertilizer with more P than N (such as 5-10-5) would be better for encouraging flowering and fruiting. Tomatoes given more nitrogen than phosphorus show the principle well by producing big leafy plants with few flowers, and therefore few fruits.

Organic Versus Synthetic Fertilizers

Organic gardeners argue that the heavy use of synthetic fertilizers kills soil life through chemical burning and harms the environment by seeping into wells, rivers, and now, even oceans. They point out that the "dead zone" at the mouth of the Mississippi River is growing, as fertilizer runoff from the Midwest pollutes the Gulf of Mexico, and that the fact that so much of the fertilizer is lost shows how wasteful it is to use these substances. They also argue that the manufacture and transport of these fertilizers consumes a large amount of primarily petroleum-sourced energy, whereas organic fertilizers are renewable resources. Further, often organic fertilizers are recycled waste products that can be used near where they were produced rather than transporting them to landfills or incinerators.

On the other hand, potassium is potassium, whether it comes from kelp or potassium sulfate. Synthetic fertilizers can help produce healthy plants in the short run, although I encourage you to rely primarily on organic materials.

One time when synthetic fertilizers often do help plants grow better is during cold weather in early spring, when you are trying to get seedlings off to a rapid start. Organic fertilizers require the action of soil life to release nutrients, and the soil may still be too cold for that to happen.

Besides being dug into the soil, many fertilizers can be banded, or placed in the soil near where the roots of the young plants will grow. This is usually done on the day that you plant. A typical placement is 2 to 3 inches to the side or 2 to 3 inches below the seeds or seedlings.

If you want to give your plants an extra boost, you can use liquid fertilizers, poured into the soil. Fish emulsion and liquid kelp are organic liquid fertilizers commonly used this way, and so are chelated minerals. Use the kelp or fish emulsion about a month after planting and then monthly while the plant is growing. You can use manure or hot compost to make an excellent liquid fertilizer to water into the soil (see the Manure or Compost Tea sidebar on page 81).

DIGGING

Before you dig, be sure that the soil is moist, but not soggy. Pick up some soil and squeeze it in your hand. If it won't form a clump, it is too dry. If it will remain in a clump even when you prod it with your finger, it is too wet. At the right moisture for digging, the soil clump will fall apart easily. (See also page 63.)

Gardeners don't agree about how to dig. Some advocate digging the soil very thoroughly, whereas others think you should dig as little as possible. Most practice something in between these two theories. They dig to the depth of a shovel once or twice a year, mulch at least part of the year, and either dig the mulch in or add other organic matter when they dig. When digging in an amendment, they may turn it under completely or just turn it sideways so that whatever was layered on top is left in roughly vertical layers in the soil.

Spade, digging fork, shovel

Among those who feel that you should dig very well are advocates of double digging, a central practice of French-intensive/biodynamic gardening. Although there are many variations, double digging consists of three basic steps: (1) digging out soil to the depth of a shovel, (2) using a shovel or garden fork to loosen the soil at the bottom of the hole, and (3) replacing the top layer of soil. The digger works across the area, double digging strips about a foot wide. You'll find complete instructions in *How to Grow More Vegetables* by John Jeavons, listed in Appendix VIII, Suggested Reading, and in many other gardening books.

Double digging is most useful in heavy clay soil, since it gets air into the soil and allows roots to grow deeper. If you have a sandy soil that is already loose and airy, double digging won't make much difference. But if you have a thin layer of sand over heavy clay, or any other change in texture in the first 18 inches of soil, double digging will make the interface between the layers less abrupt so that water can pass through.

The no-till theory holds that soil rarely needs to be dug and that doing so disrupts natural cycles and damages the soil structure. Gardeners who subscribe to this theory may dig to the depth of a shovel and amend at the beginning, but from then on they rely on mulch to improve the soil from the surface down. They use a trowel to open up small planting holes or rows, then add fertilizer and plant. This was Ruth Stout's method (see page 79) and it seems particularly suited to sandy soil, which loses nutrients when you dig it, already contains plenty of air, and warms quickly even under mulch.

ROTATING YOUR CROPS

The idea behind crop rotation is that by not planting the same crop in the same place, season after season or year after year, you will use your soil more effectively and be able to avoid a buildup of soil diseases and other pests. Farmers devise rotation plans that help to make the best use of their particular soils and to avoid pests they experience. It is more difficult to rotate crops in a small garden, because there may be areas not suited to a full range of

What About Rototilling?

Gardeners debate the wisdom of using a rotary tiller to turn the soil. In much of the country, the gardening year begins with rototilling. This method is practical in large gardens that stand nearly empty in spring. However, hand digging uses less fossil fuel and is easier on soil structure and soil life. If the soil is sandy or loamy, you can probably easily hand-dig a small garden of less than 2,000 square feet. Expect to accomplish much less in clay soil. Also, if your garden has perennial weeds that grow from cut root pieces, rototilling will help these weeds multiply. If you are gardening the year around, hand digging will be made easier by the fact that you are unlikely to be digging the whole garden at once.

You may choose to rent a rotary tiller to help you deal with compacted soil that you are trying to open up for gardening. Even sandy soil can become compacted and hard to work if it is bare and trampled often. Use the tiller with patience, going over the soil several times, digging a little deeper with each pass. You may be able to dig only an inch or so each time. Before starting, be sure that the soil is the right moisture for digging.

crops—due, for example, to wind exposure or lack of full sunlight. Rotation may be less effective for pest management in a small garden as well, since the distances are so short that soil pests can just wiggle over to the next bed. But still, all gardeners will want to practice rotation to some extent, for whatever benefits it can offer.

There are several different ways to categorize crops for a rotation plan. One is to divide crops into four groups: three depending on the part of the plant harvested—fruit crops, root crops, leafy crops—and the fourth group being the legumes (peas and beans). Another is to divide crops by the botanical plant family to which they belong. In this second method, you'd have solanaceous crops (tomato, potato, eggplant, and so on); cucurbits (squash and cucumber); carrot family (carrot, parsley, parsnip); beet family (beet, chard); onion family (onion, leek, garlic); and, again, the legumes—plus a few crops in other families.

A third way to group crops is by heavy or light feeders, as shown on page 89. In this scheme, legumes used to be grouped as "soil builders." However, it has been shown that when you harvest the beans or peas, legumes don't actually "build" soil, in the sense of adding nitrogen. In fact, they are probably a wash, nitrogen-wise, so I have renamed this group *soil neutrals*.

In practice, most rotation schemes depend on all of these ways of dividing crops and also consider special categories, such as celery and celeriac, which can both get celery late blight and so should be rotated together. However you rotate, follow each crop with something as different as possible from what was there before—such as having a different part harvested or being from a different plant family. Each species uses a slightly different component of micronutrients, and each one has slightly different susceptibility to soil pathogens.

Rotations sometimes include a cover crop that is turned into the soil to become green manure, or even a period of fallow, in which no crops are planted. They may include the sequence of (1) fertilizing, (2) growing a heavy feeder, and then (3) growing a light feeder with minimal or no additional fertilizer.

When the soil contains a serious disease organism or other pest, then pest control becomes an overriding issue in crop rotation. Since there is no chemical cure for many soilborne diseases, rotation plays an important role even in nonorganic agriculture. A rotation plan must leave enough years between plantings of affected crops for the pest to die out. In extreme cases, a garden or sections of a garden are left unplanted every couple of years to halt the buildup of soilborne diseases. Resistant plant varieties and good growing conditions are the best defenses against most diseases, but rotation helps too.

To avoid soil diseases, it is best not to plant tomatoes in the same place more than once every four years, but this is hard to do in a small garden. Actually, my worst tomato disease, tomato late blight, is caused by windblown spores. (See Late Blight of Potato and Tomato on page 135 for more information on fighting this disease.)

A particularly serious problem in small urban gardens is the lack of sunlight. If you have only a certain area that is sunny enough to ripen tomatoes in summer, it is likely to be the same area that is sunny enough to grow cole crops in winter. Both crops are heavy feeders. If you have this problem, pay special attention to soil fertility. If you are leaving part of the garden fallow over winter because it is too shady, be sure to cover it with an organic

Sample Rotations

Here are a couple of rotations for coastal central California gardens. They are meant not as recipes but as practice in thinking through a crop rotation.

Plan A: In April or May, work in compost and fertilizer, then plant tomatoes (heavy feeder). During the summer, lay an organic mulch around the plants. By the middle of October, remove the tomato plants and dig in the mulch. Plant peas (soil neutral) in November, adding a small booster of nitrogen when you plant. In May, pull the spent peas and compost them, but don't add them to a cold pile unless they are free of powdery mildew. Dig in compost, then plant potatoes (light feeder). After harvesting the potatoes in August, add fertilizer and plant broccoli (heavy feeder, cole crop). As winter weeds come up, pull them and make a mulch of the ones that won't reseed or reroot. When you pull the broccoli the following February, dig in the weed mulch and plant carrots (light feeder). Harvest them by May or June, making way for beans (soil neutral).

Plan B: In February, work in compost and fertilizer, then plant mixed lettuces (heavy feeder). In early May, when the lettuces have been harvested, plant bush romano beans (soil neutral) with no additional soil preparation. In October, add compost and plant garlic (light feeder). Early the following August, add fertilizer and plant a fast-growing variety of cabbage (heavy feeder, cole crop). After harvesting the cabbage in November, plant fava beans (soil neutral) and mulch them with pulled weeds in late winter. In April or May, pull out the fava beans, move the stalks to a compost heap, and dig in the weed mulch. As an alternative, chop the stalks and add other organic matter to create a sheet compost (see page 92), then dig it in when it is ready. In May or June, plant summer squash or cucumbers (heavy feeders) and side-dress the plants with fertilizer twice during the summer. After removing the plants in October, sow onion seeds (light feeder).

mulch or grow green manure so that you return some nutrients to the soil.

Rotation may seem complicated if you try to figure it all out ahead of time. Some do write out location cycles, divide the garden into several sections, and rotate crops through in a preset order. But probably most home gardeners who practice rotation do so in a more free-form manner. They may jot down or remember some rotation rules, and then draw a map of their garden two or even three times a year as a reminder of what was growing where, to help carry out their plans.

Crop rotation is a very old practice, and you will come across many schemes, some of them developed to deal with local conditions, such as special soil problems or particular diseases. When you are reading about a rotation scheme, try to find out if the conditions for which it was designed are similar to yours. A fallow period that is part of a particular rotation may be there to avoid a soil pest that you don't have, or a particular rotation may have been planned to avoid having to buy fertilizer. Traditional farm rotations might allow for up to two years before adding any organic matter or fertilizer. In part, this is because the rotations were for places with colder winters, where the soil wasn't used year-round. Here, if we garden all year, we could hardly get away with fertilizing so rarely. Also, on a farm, fertilizer can be a large expense, while in a small garden, the amount of fertilizer you need is so small that it is often easy to provide it at what agriculturists would call "luxury levels."

In areas where the soil needs annual liming to make it less acidic, particularly in the Northeast, gardeners often add lime or wood ash just before they plant a cole crop (broccoli, brussels sprouts, cabbage, cauliflower, collards, kale, or kohlrabi). Cole crops don't mind slightly alkaline soil, and they can use the extra calcium in lime or the extra potassium in wood ash. My soil, like many local soils, doesn't need liming and isn't short of calcium, so I skip this practice.

MAKING COMPOST

I grew up in a composting household. Dad read *Organic Gardening* magazine in its earliest years and learned to compost. He made vast amounts in one end of our vegetable garden, and it seems to me that some of our best chats took place while he was back there adding garbage, turning the piles, and sifting the final product. While he worked he taught me to appreciate the beauty of compost. I love the feel, look, and smell of it. If you have

Categorizing Crops for Rotation

When planning a rotation, refer to the following lists for guidance and also read individual crop listings in Chapters 11 and 12. This is only one way to categorize plants for rotation. Others are by plant family or by groups of crops that attract the same pests.

Heavy Feeders

CROP	FAMILY
Basil	Mint
Beet	Goosefoot
Celery	Carrot
Cole crops	Mustard
Corn	Grass
Cucumber	Gourd
Endive and chicory	Aster
Lettuce	Aster
Parsley	Carrot
Spinach	Goosefoot
Squash	Gourd
Tomato	Nightshade

Light Feeders

CROP	FAMILY
Carrot	Carrot
Leek	Amaryllis
Mustard	Mustard
Onion	Amaryllis
Parsnip	Carrot
Pepper	Nightshade
Potato	Nightshade
Shallot	Amaryllis
Swiss chard	Goosefoot
Turnip	Mustard

Soil Neutrals

CROP	FAMILY
Bean, fava	Legume
Bean, lima	Legume
Bean, scarlet runner	Legume
Bean, snap (pole and bush)	Legume
Pea	Legume
Soybean	Legume

never made compost, you probably think that organic gardeners are a little nutty over the stuff, but I encourage you to try making some and see the results for yourself.

Hot or Cold: What's the Difference?

Composting is done either by the hot, or fast, method or by the cold, or slow, method. Both methods produce an excellent organic soil amendment, but if compost has heated to 140°F or more, you know it has enough nitrogen to satisfy plants. Although both methods recycle garden and household waste, hot composting can handle more kinds of waste. The hot method takes as little as three to six weeks, whereas the cold method requires three months to a year.

Hot compost is a ferment, just as yogurt is, and requires close attention to the needs of the fungi and bacteria carrying out the process. You must mix everything together in the right proportions, then see that conditions remain favorable while the soil organisms partially digest your mixture. Unlike yogurt making, hot composting generates its own heat. The fungi and bacteria in compost raise the temperature in the center of the pile to 140°F to 160°F. This is hot enough to kill weed seeds, disease spores, and insect eggs. Also, unlike yogurt, hot compost must be stirred or turned at least once while it is fermenting. Turning moves the materials that were on the outside of the pile to the inside. When the organisms have done their work, the pile cools down, and the compost is ready to use.

If you don't have the time or energy to attend to a hot compost pile, you can make cold compost. In fact, if you don't build the pile all on the same day, choose ingredients carefully, and turn it regularly, it will be a cold pile. Some or all of the pile will never heat up enough to kill seeds, spores, or eggs, so you should not add any materials that require sterilization. Helpful microorganisms are responsible for the slower cold process, but they are different from those operating at high temperatures.

If you make cold compost with whatever is on hand, not paying attention to a balance of low and high nitrogen materials, chances are the finished product won't have as much nitrogen as that of well-made hot compost. However, if you do happen to add enough high-nitrogen material at the beginning, it could be as high in nitrogen as a hot pile. Cold compost that didn't start with plenty of high-nitrogen materials will still be an excellent soil amendment and will fertilize with other nutrients. Just be sure you add another source of nitrogen when you use it.

A cold compost pile will take longer than a hot one, but you can speed it up by adding at least some high-nitrogen material such as manure, chopping materials as you add them, and keeping the pile moist. A specific kind of cold compost is a sheet compost (see the sidebar on page 92). This is not a way to make soil, since soil would also contain quite a bit of sand, silt, or clay, but it is a very good soil amendment.

While earthworm compost is technically a cold compost, since it doesn't heat, it is really a separate method. It results in compost that is high in nitrogen. (See page 93.)

A good plan for many urban gardeners is to make an earthworm compost using kitchen scraps, and then compost garden green waste separately, either in ongoing cold piles or in periodic hot piles with an added nitrogen source. The nitrogen source could be grass clippings or fresh barnyard manure. Assuming you don't have a huge lawn or some animals on site, you'd find these last ingredients elsewhere and bring them in for the occasion.

To find out more about composting, see the publications listed under Soil and Soil Fertility in Appendix VIII, Suggested Reading, or attend classes taught by gardening organizations listed in Appendix VII, Resources for Gardeners.

Every Compost Pile Is Unique

Just remember that no single type of organic material has to be in compost. A gardener who lives near a cabinetmaker's shop may use lots of hardwood sawdust. Another gardener may collect trash barrels of spent hops from a nearby brewery, and yet another may gather used bedding from a local riding stable. All these materials will produce hot compost if the carbon-nitrogen ratio is correct.

Garden books written for other areas will stress locally available ingredients that may not be easily obtained here. They usually list fallen tree leaves and lawn clippings as main ingredients. Our lawns are not as extensive as those elsewhere in the country, and many of our trees are evergreen. Although evergreens shed some leaves throughout the year, the leaves are tougher and slower to decay than deciduous leaves. Some common evergreens, such as eucalyptus and juniper, contain resins that resist decay, so they should be used in moderation.

Keep your ears and eyes open for local treasures. Check with your local recreation and park department to see if you can have some of their clippings. If there is a rice mill nearby, ask for hulls. If a nongardening friend has a rabbit, request the manure. I once accompanied a San Francisco community gardener on a compost hunt that took us to the waste bins of the wholesale produce terminal, a rice mill, a little-known horse manure dumping ground on the south side of San Francisco, and an industrial park where the gardeners had agreed to leave bags of pesticide-free grass clippings.

The Ins and Outs of Compost

When you are considering compost ingredients, you will want to know how quickly a material breaks down and whether it contains toxic substances or attracts rodents or cats. Certain materials are fine for a hot pile but should be left out of a cold one.

A truly hot pile will kill weed seeds, disease spores, and insect eggs, but a cold pile, or a sort-of-hot pile, will not.

To avoid breeding rats and mice, do not use kitchen scraps unless you have a compost system that has no openings over a quarter-inch in diameter, the size a baby mouse can slip through. You don't want a completely closed bin, since it does need ventilation and drainage, but unless you can keep the openings under a quarter-inch, keep the food scraps out. (Food scraps are much better used in a redworm compost system anyway.)

Sifting finished compost

How to Make Hot Compost

There are several methods for making hot compost; they all share some basic features.

1. Choose a good site.

Pick an out-of-the-way spot at least 3 by 3 feet, on bare ground, in either the sun or the shade. The pile should be a minimum of 3 feet high. Although a frame is not necessary, it makes the pile easier to shape and turn. Two frames side by side make it possible to turn the pile back and forth between them. A ring of hardware cloth (galvanized fencing with quarter-inch openings) makes a good frame. Put a layer of coarse, dry organic matter, such as dry weeds, twigs, or straw, on the ground before you build the pile.

2. Provide the correct carbon-nitrogen ratio.

Build the pile all on the same day. It should contain roughly 30 parts carbon to 1 part nitrogen. You can come close simply by alternating 3- to 5-inch-thick layers of "brown" (low-nitrogen) and green or fresh (high-nitrogen) materials. You will know you added too much high-nitrogen material if the pile starts to smell of ammonia. Sawdust is a very low-nitrogen material—it contains 200 to 500 parts carbon to 1 part nitrogen. Other low-nitrogen materials include paper (170 to 1), straw (80 to 1), and corn stalks (60 to 1). High-nitrogen materials include fresh manure (20 to 1), grass clippings (19 to 1), and table scraps (15 to 1).

3. Don't include big chunks of material.

Avoid large or woody materials.

Chop fresh plant material into pieces no longer than 4 to 6 inches and avoid woody stems over ½ inch in diameter. (You can sift out any undigested chunks and add them to the next pile.)

4. Provide the correct moisture.

The microorganisms that make compost need moisture. Water each layer as you add it, and then keep the pile about as moist as a wrung-out sponge. The pile is too wet if water runs out the bottom.

5. Provide air or, more accurately, oxygen.

If there is not enough oxygen in the pile, a different set of microorganisms will take over the pile, producing a compost that smells terrible and contains much less nitrogen than a well-aerated pile. Avoid too much fine sawdust, since it can compact and exclude air. In rainy weather cover the pile with a waterproof tarp. If you use a bin, makes sure that air can enter through the sides (leave space between the wooden slats or use wire mesh for the sides).

6. Turn the pile frequently.

For the fastest compost, turn the pile after three to four days, when the temperature should have reached 140°F to 160°F, then turn it every two to three days until turning doesn't stimulate more heat. Always turn from top to bottom and from sides to center. A pitchfork or garden fork works better than a shovel or spade. Turning allows the microorganisms to work on all parts of the pile and gives them oxygen.

7. Correct your pile.

There are three main signs of trouble in a hot compost pile: the interior of the pile doesn't begin to heat up within two days, the pile stinks strongly of rot, or the pile gives off a strong smell of ammonia. Since every compost pile is different, it is impossible to be exact about how much corrective material to add, but you will soon be able to judge.

The pile doesn't heat up within two days.

- If the pile seems too wet, add thin layers of sawdust or other dry material while turning.
- If the pile seems too dry, add water while turning.
- If the moisture seems right, sprinkle in a high-nitrogen material, such as fresh horse manure or grass clippings while turning the pile.

The pile stinks strongly of rot.

- The pile is too wet. Add thin layers of dry material while turning.

The pile begins to smell strongly of ammonia.

- The pile contains too much nitrogen. Add thin layers of sawdust while turning it.

Fine in All Piles

- Healthy vegetable or flower plants pulled from the garden.
- Weeds without ripe seeds or roots that will regrow. Freshly pulled green weeds are preferable, but add dried ones if you have them.
- Vegetable or fruit scraps, including citrus peels, from the kitchen.
- Crushed eggshells, nutshells, or shells of shellfish.
- Barnyard manure, or hamster, rabbit, or gerbil manure, fresh or rotted, with or without bedding.
- Human urine from a healthy person. Dilute one part urine with five parts water.
- Fresh or partly rotted straw.
- Coarse sawdust.
- Grass or shrub clippings without pesticide residue.
- Fallen tree leaves, especially from deciduous trees.
- Rice hulls, coffee grounds, or tea leaves.
- Residue from making beer, wine, or apple cider.
- Seaweed, preferably rinsed to remove sea salt.
- Plants that are poisonous, like poison hemlock or oleander. These are OK in a compost pile, since the poisonous compounds will be digested by microorganisms.
- Unbleached paper with nontoxic (soy or water-based) inks. Newsprint is unbleached, which you can tell by leaving it in the sun for a few days and watching it turn yellow. Compost-safe inks are becoming more common, since newspapers often want to be considered environmentally safe. Black ink is probably OK (see Controversial Items).

For Hot Piles Only

By this I mean piles that you are sure will reach 140°F or more; in other words, these ingredients are best not used unless you have perfected the art of the hot compost pile.

- Weeds with ripe seeds that will regrow.
- Vegetable or flower plants that are diseased or contain insect eggs. Again, use caution.
- Feathers or hair. Although very slow to break down, they add considerable nitrogen.

Keep Out of All Compost Piles

- Bermuda grass, quack grass, Cape oxalis bulbs, onion lily (wild onion) bulbs, bindweed runners, false garlic bulbs. These would theoretically be killed in a hot pile, but it isn't a risk I'd like to take.
- Blackberry brambles. Even if they don't reroot, they make prickly compost.
- Fats or cereal products, since they attract rodents.
- Sawdust from plywood, pressure-treated wood, or wood that may have been painted with lead-based paint or treated with poisonous materials (see pages 35–36).
- Sewage sludge, since it may contain heavy metals.
- Manure from humans, dogs, or cats, as these can carry diseases.
- Glossy paper, bleached paper, or paper printed with colored ink if you haven't researched the type of ink used. Bleached paper contains traces of dioxin, a toxin. Toxicologists doubt that plants take up much dioxin from soil, but most composters prefer not to use bleached paper anyway.
- Branches or stems greater than half an inch in diameter or over a few inches long.
- Rocks, glass, plastic, or metal.

Sheet Compost

Here is a style of cold composting you can use the first year that you garden or during a few months between crops on a small part of your garden. Layer different kinds of organic material up to a foot high. Chop large pieces and avoid long, stringy material. As a nitrogen source, include manure or freshly cut or young, nonwoody pulled weeds without seeds or roots that may regrow. Keep the pile moist until it shrinks noticeably.

The composting process may take a month or several months, depending on the type and size of materials. A couple of weeks before you intend to plant, add manure, human urine, blood meal, or another nitrogen source. Dig the partially formed compost into the soil and water the area until it is just moist. If you are preparing the area for a seedbed, move any chunks of organic material that didn't decay to an area that you won't be digging soon.

Earthworm Compost

Earthworms from your garden soil, both the larger "nightcrawler" types and smaller species, will live around the edges of a hot compost pile and can thrive throughout a cold one. Other species called *redworms* can be purchased to help you create rich, high-nitrogen compost from kitchen wastes.

When I was a child in Indiana, we had earthworm compost in the basement all winter long. The compost didn't smell or attract vermin, and I rather liked knowing that the worms were down there working away on the compost that would enrich our spring garden, though I knew better than to talk about it in school!

In recent years, worm composting has become more widely known. And while worms can work outdoors all year in coastal California, some gardeners prefer the convenience of a bin in the basement, under the sink in the kitchen, or doubling as a windowseat.

Use a plastic or plywood container with a lid (plywood is less likely to overheat). The container needs drainage holes, which must be under one-quarter inch in diameter to exclude mice and rats. If the container is used indoors, it must have a drip tray.

Tear newspaper with compost-safe inks into narrow strips and fill the bin almost to the top, and then sprinkle it with water and toss it until it is barely moistened or as wet as a wrung-out sponge. The strips will become more compact when moistened, but don't add so much water that they become a compact mass. There should still be air spaces within the newspaper bedding. Add a handful of soil (to provide digestive grit) and about 1,000 redworms (available at local nurseries or garden stores, or ask friends and neighbors). Then tuck a pound of food scraps just under the surface of a small area of the newspaper bedding, and stand back. Let the worms work on that first pound for a couple of weeks before you add more food scraps. After a few weeks, the redworms will multiply to a population size that can handle a pound of food scraps for each square foot of bin surface per week.

In a worm compost bin, newspaper provides a carbon source, and garbage a nitrogen source. The worms digest both until nothing is left but a dark brown, pleasant-smelling compost that is higher in nitrogen than most hot compost. In fact, it is so rich that you should never dig in more than a one-inch layer of it at a time.

To renew a worm bin, trowel all of the worms and finished compost to one end and remake a newspaper bed in the rest of the bin. While you are renewing the bin, add food scraps only in the end of the bin with the fresh bedding; after a few days, when the worms have moved into the new bed, harvest the compost. You can go to the trouble of saving the worms that stay in the compost, or not, as you choose. To remove them, make small piles and brush off the surface castings. The worms will crawl away from light, so at the end you will have harvested compost and a ball of redworms to put back in the bin.

For much more on composting methods, including plans for making wooden worm bins, troubleshooting tips, and details of the worm life cycle, see the book *Worms Eat My Garbage* (listed in Appendix VIII, Suggested Reading). Call local gardening stores or gardening organizations for information about local sources of wormboxes and redworms.

Controversial Items

- Old compost or soil. Some sprinkle a little of either in every other layer, to introduce composting bacteria. These are present in the environment anyway, and piles will contain soil if there are pulled plants, but adding old compost or a bit of soil won't hurt.
- Pine needles or oak leaves. It is true they have a somewhat acid action at first, but it is OK to use them in moderation.
- Woodchips or leaves from acacia, California bay, eucalyptus, juniper, or pittosporums. Again, use in moderation in case chemicals they contain have some inhibiting effect on plant growth.
- Woodchips from tree work. All kinds are very slow to break down.
- Purchased fertilizers that are high in nitrogen, such as cottonseed meal, blood meal, or fish meal. These can serve as a nitrogen source, but most composters prefer the challenge of building compost from free, waste product materials.
- Purchased bacterial starters or herbal starters. Compost happens perfectly well without complicated herbal formulas or purchased bacteria. Save your time and money.

Buyer Beware

In every area of life, there are products for sale that you probably don't need. This is certainly true of gardening, and in no areas more than that of soil preparation and fertilization and the making of compost. So in the interest of saving you money, a few words to the wise:

- There is nothing magic about organic fertilizer ingredients that are fashionable or from faraway places. The manure from a local stable is as useful as bat guano from faraway islands if used in the right amount and the right proportion to other fertilizers. Compost made from local, free ingredients, or bagged, bulk ingredients chosen by price and nutrient content, are as effective as expensive blends of organic fertilizers sold with impressive brand names.
- Soils already have beneficial microbes. It may be that one day we will be able to buy some that are perfect for improving the ecosystem of the soil we have, but for the most part the microbes for sale now will be a waste of money. A possible exception is inoculants for legume seeds, which ensure the right symbiotic bacteria will be present when they germinate, though even here, if you have leguminous weeds (vetch and burclover) or your soil has grown beans or peas in the past, these bacteria are probably present already.

- Newsprint with colored ink. The *San Francisco Chronicle* printers have assured me that both black and colored inks in the paper are safe for composting, though they can't vouch for colored ink in advertising inserts. To learn about a particular paper, you will probably have to make some phone calls or send some e-mails.
- Lime. Definitely don't use slaked or hydrated lime, since it will kill the very organisms that you are trying to get to digest your composting materials. Dolomitic limestone can help if you are worried that the compost will make your soil too acidic, although this is unlikely.

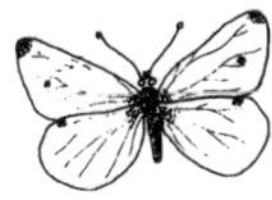

NINE

Managing Bugs and Blights

HERE IS NO DENYING THAT pests can do horrible things to the plants we were hoping would produce food or flowers. Big holes in leaves or fruit, flowers eaten to shreds, ugly creeping gray mold all over the plants. Even faced with these problems, most of us dislike the prospect of using pesticides. Why shouldn't we, since one of the joys of growing our own food is knowing that no dangerous chemicals have been used on or near it? I have decided that most problems can be solved without them, and that I'd rather give up on an occasional crop than use a chemical that could poison me or the environment.

In this chapter, you will learn how to prevent common problems of vegetable crops, identify these problems when they do occur, and take steps to solve them. You will learn how to attract and protect the many creatures that eat your garden pests. You will learn about some new pest management chemicals that have very low environmental impact. And finally, you will get help reading pesticide labels so that you can evaluate pesticides existing now or developed in the future and use them more effectively and safely.

UNDERSTANDING PEST OUTBREAKS

Every garden has some pest problems. The first step in managing them is having an idea of which ones to expect and the factors that increase or reduce them. Why do some pests mentioned in gardening books never appear in your garden? Why are some crops relatively pest-free, while others are almost always attacked by one or more pests? Why are there worse outbreaks in some years than in others? Although experience will teach you the answers, some general principles will help you begin:

- **Geography and climate** If you read gardening books intended for the entire United States, you will come across pests that never or rarely appear here. Some, such as the Colorado potato beetle, have not migrated this far west yet, and careful quarantine methods may prevent them from doing so. Even within our region, some pests are more common either inland or along the coast. Tomato hornworms and cucumber beetles prefer warmer inland areas, while onion root maggots prefer cool coastal microclimates.
- **Weather** Pests are more numerous when the weather of a particular year favors their growth, and less common when it doesn't. Frequently, unusual weather brings unusual levels of pests. A very cold winter can result in fewer pests, if their overwintering stages were killed, or a very wet spring might support a larger population of pests that lived on spring grasses before they moved on to your garden's summer crops.
- **What you grow** Many pests attack only certain crops, leaving other crops entirely unaffected. The powdery mildew of squash and pumpkins will not infect peas, and powdery mildew of peas will not spread to squash, as these are different diseases (although each will attack certain other crops and some kinds of ornamentals). Onion root maggots, frustrating as they are, are limited to plants in the genus *Allium*. Sometimes particular crops of several unrelated crops are affected. In my garden the bean aphid, a

charcoal gray to black insect, attacks only fava beans, artichokes, garlic chives, and nasturtiums.

To have a crop wiped out by a pest is an unnerving experience that calls for regrouping and new tactics. But you can at least keep from becoming discouraged by realizing that the problem is often self-limiting. While you plan a strategy to control the pest the next time you grow the susceptible crop, you can be enjoying harvests from the many other crops you planted that are immune to that pest.

- **How much food there is for pests to eat** If you clear an overgrown garden but ignore the snails, and then put in tender vegetable seedlings, hungry snails will surely wipe you out. Conversely, when your cleared garden of early spring gives way to a lush summer garden, the same number of snails, earwigs, slugs, and other chewing pests may eat the same amount, but less of each plant will be lost to them.

  Another aspect of this factor is how many nearby gardeners are growing a particular crop. Some pests, now rare in an area, could become more common if more gardeners begin to grow the crops they feed on. If new pests appear, gardeners can slow their spread considerably by acting to control them before they become endemic.
- **Health of the plants** Plants that are struggling against poor growing conditions are often more susceptible to pests. Poorly watered beans tend to get spider mites; tomatoes fed too much nitrogen are more likely to get aphids. Some crops are typically attacked by pests late in the season, when they are past their peak. Peas, for example, often fall victim to powdery mildew as they near the end of their bearing period, especially if the weather is also warm at that point. (However, while the health of your plants may make a difference in some cases, many pests are perfectly happy to attack healthy plants.)
- **Natural predators and parasites** Gardeners often notice only the insects that are eating a crop, but the garden is alive with insects, and a good many of them are busy eating the pesky ones. Not only insects, but also salamanders, snakes, spiders, birds, and even raccoons help control pests. In the soil, helpful microorganisms destroy soil pests. If all of these creatures didn't help us with pest control, we would be in big trouble.

  You will have fewer pests if you garden in ways that encourage natural helpers. One of the best ways to do this is to eliminate or drastically reduce your use of environmentally disruptive pesticides. If a pesticide is moderately disruptive, use it only if you can take precautions to protect creatures that might be harmed. This is important, because pesticides are often more lethal to predators than to the pests.
- **Chance** Yes, of course, chance is part of the picture too. The soil around a plant given to you by a friend can carry pests to your garden, or pests and diseases may come to the garden on the wind. Insects can carry disease-producing organisms; the insects become infected while feeding on infected plants, then spread the disease throughout the neighborhood as they feed.

THE PROBLEMS WITH PESTICIDES

Farmers had their first big successes using chemicals to control pests in the last century. Twentieth-century chemists applied themselves to the development of synthetic, petroleum-based pesticides and, beginning with DDT in 1939, introduced a host of new ones. For several decades, many gardeners, as well as farmers, applied these early pesticides on a regular, and even a preventive basis. In so doing, they ran into some peculiar and unexpected difficulties. While pesticides seem to work fine in the short run, if they are overused they don't work as well in the long run. In fact, they sometimes seem to make pest problems worse.

- **Resistance** The first unwelcome surprise was that hundreds of pests developed resistance to chemicals that once were lethal to them. Gardeners, farmers, and professional pest eradicators have had to change chemicals, in some cases several times, to find ways to kill "super insects" or "super mites."
- **Resurgence** Another surprise was that even when a pesticide treatment seemed to have killed off a pest, it soon reappeared in much greater numbers. This effect, called resurgence, occurs because the pesticide has also killed the natural enemies of the pest. As soon as the pesticide wears off a bit, the few pests that either escaped or were resistant are able to multiply freely.
- **Secondary pest outbreaks** Sometimes after a resurgence is brought under control with a second spraying, another pest suddenly appears on the scene, one that was never a problem before. These secondary pest outbreaks occur

because spraying has left the new pest free of both competition and enemies.

- **Residue** Yet another hazard of pesticide use, poisonous pesticide residues can injure your family, your pets, and nonpest wildlife living in or visiting your garden. Pesticide labels will tell you how long to wait after using the chemical before touching or eating the plant, but children, pets, and birds can't read the label. And some kinds of pesticide, especially synthetic ones, stay toxic for a long time. If these get into groundwater or into streams and lakes, they can poison creatures in the world beyond the borders of your garden. Some types remain toxic long after they are ingested. These accumulate in the bodies of the animals at the top of their respective food chains, such as pelicans, eagles, and humans. A prime example is DDT, removed from the U.S. market in 1972 due to this hazard.

One example of a large-scale spray program illustrates some of the preceding principles. From 1980 to 1982 the insecticide malathion was sprayed over a large area in central California, to try to prevent the spread of the Mediterranean fruit fly, a pest of orchard fruits. Although it may have controlled the fly, the spray program had some impressive side effects. One of them was resurgence. There were dramatic outbreaks of whiteflies, aphids, and mites in the treated area, because the spray had killed their predators. A secondary outbreak also occurred, in that a wild shrub, coyote brush, was seriously damaged by a gall midge, previously not a serious problem. And either direct poisoning or residue killed so many honeybees that beekeepers were afraid their hives might not get through the winter.

LOOKING FOR ALTERNATIVES

Largely because of the preceding problems, pesticide use has tended to become more expensive. Farmers may find they are using more, to fight resurgences and secondary outbreaks. Chemical companies find they need to develop new chemicals constantly to stay ahead of pest resistance and the discovery of unwanted side effects. When they have developed them, they find they must spend more and more to test and register the new chemicals.

A combination of cost, environmental awareness, and the willingness of the public to look at alternatives has led to new interest in alternative pest management strategies. Some ideas are quite old but have been neglected during the ascendancy of pesticides. For example, plant scientists have turned their attention to breeding more plant varieties that resist attacks by insects and diseases. And research has revealed not only beneficial creatures that can be bred in captivity and released to help with pests, but also ways to protect and increase the beneficial insects already living in our gardens.

Other pest control ideas are made possible by modern understanding of chemistry and biology. New oil formulations are much less toxic to leaves, so they allow the use of oil sprays in summer as well as on dormant woody trees and shrubs in winter. Some new pesticides based on bacteria or the toxins they produce are specific to the pests they kill.

Forming a Strategy

As the public has become more aware of the consequences of using pesticides, interest in alternative methods of pest control has increased. A new way of thinking and acting, Integrated Pest Management (IPM) has gained in popularity among farmers and other professionals who are combating pests on a large scale. And you can adapt this successful method to protect your own garden from pest infestations.

What Is IPM?

IPM is a decision-making process that treats pest problems not as isolated attacks by the enemies of desirable plants, but rather as disruptions of a garden ecosystem. The solution then is not just to kill the pest, but to modify the ecosystem in ways that reduce pest damage. And because you, your children, pets, the beneficial insects in your garden, the birds, the groundwater, the air, and the soil are also elements of the ecosystem, you will want to choose pest control methods that do not harm or pollute these elements.

The first decision that practitioners of IPM make is whether the pest damage is serious enough to bother with at all. They monitor the number of pests and the extent of damage carefully. Then, if the problem is deemed serious enough, either economically or aesthetically, they choose one or more management techniques, starting with the ones that least disrupt or damage the environment. IPM *does* include the option of using the more toxic pesticides, and pesticide marketers often imply that IPM is just a way to use pesticides wisely. However, the decision whether to use a particular tactic is up to the farmer or gardener—who can, for example, decide to use no chemicals at all or only ones permitted to organic farmers.

Are Any Vegetable Crops Safe from Pests?

Crops that are pest-free, or almost pest-free, in local gardens: Arugula, cilantro, endive, leeks, New Zealand spinach, parsnips, peppers, prickly pear cactus, salsify, sunchokes, Bolivian sunroot, and most perennial herbs.

Crops that rarely see damage other than by snails, slugs, earwigs, or cutworms: Beans, basil, and lettuce.

Crops susceptible to pests that sometimes—but not always—attack: (You may well be able to avoid these pests by means of preventive measures and/or luck, but then again, maybe you won't.) Artichokes, carrots, celery, corn, cucumber, garlic, onions, peas, potatoes, spinach, Swiss chard, and tomatoes.

Crops almost always attacked by certain pests: Squash and pumpkin get powdery mildew almost without fail, although some squash varieties are more resistant than others, and cabbage family crops rarely escape attack by cabbageworms—and probably by one or more other pests as well.

ADAPTING IPM

The approach I use in my garden owes much to IPM, although I do not study each problem with the precision of the IPM farm advisor before I act. I don't need that much accuracy, as my livelihood is not at stake. So I make a decision based on my observations and experience, such as seeing white cabbage butterflies fluttering over my young broccoli plants in the spring, and knowing that if I ignore them, their caterpillars will destroy my crop. Or noticing that snails are particularly fond of basil seedlings, so unless I have controlled snails perfectly, I will need to protect basil while it is young. Most of my pest management methods are measures other than pesticides. I do occasionally use pesticidal chemicals permitted to organic farmers, but I prefer to put up with some damage or grow something else rather than to use more environmentally disruptive chemicals.

Examine Your Plants

Make a habit of examining your plants closely and often, beginning when they are quite small. You want to become aware of a pest when it first arrives, not after it has done serious damage. Look at different parts of the plants: the leaf tops and undersides, the older leaves, the young leaves and buds at the tops of the plants, the stems near the soil line, and the developing fruit.

If you see that your plants aren't thriving, your first question should be: Is a pest causing the problem, or is it just a symptom of poor growing conditions? If plants are smaller than they should be, are wilted, have yellow leaves, or are not setting fruit, but you can't find an insect or clear signs of a disease, carefully read over the entry for that crop in Chapter 11 to see whether you planted it at the right time of year or it might have a nutrient deficiency or be receiving inadequate water. Some physiological problems resemble diseases. Common examples are blossom end rot of tomato and summer squash.

Know Your Enemy

If you find signs that a pest is causing the damage, the next question you should ask is: Which pest is it? If you aren't sure which pest is the culprit, you can hardly take effective action to control it. Often you will see only the damage at first and need to do some sleuthing to find out what caused it. You might see several insects or other creatures in the vicinity, and you don't want to incriminate the wrong one!

For instance, to find out what is chewing holes in leaves, look at both sides of the leaves. Look for feeding pests and also for insect eggs. If you still don't see any pests, try examining the plants after dark, with a flashlight, as many chewing pests, such as slugs, snails and earwigs, are night feeders.

When leaves are puckery and distorted, or stippled with tiny light dots, the cause may be sucking pests, such as aphids, whiteflies, or mites. These pests often prefer to feed in the buds, flowers, the youngest leaves, and developing fruit. Examine distorted plant parts carefully, including leaf undersides. Use a hand lens, as some of these pests are quite small. If you still see nothing, suspect a viral disease—another cause of puckered leaves.

If a plant suddenly wilts, suspect damage to the roots. Pull away the soil at the base of the plant and check the upper part of the root for damage or pests.

Cabbage family plants, carrots, and onions are often infested by root maggots.

Another symptom, spots on the leaves, can be caused by different types of diseases: bacterial, fungal, or viral. For help identifying them, read descriptions of the most common diseases later in this chapter.

I have listed the pests I know often infest vegetable plants in this area, and this will be enough information to help you to identify most of the ones you will see. Look first at the ends of individual crop listings to see what pests commonly attack a crop, then see the pest listings for more information on appearance, damage caused, and control. If you can't identify your problem from the information in this book, use resources listed in the appendices to help you identify it. Master Gardener hotlines and clinics are often able to help (see Appendix VII, Resources for Gardeners, for contact information). Several useful books are listed in Appendix VIII, Suggested Reading. You will also find much useful information on the Internet. Start with the University of California IPM pages, at www.ipm.ucdavis.edu. You will find other State Cooperative Extension sites, such as those of the University of Washington and Cornell University, are also quite helpful.

Decide How to Control the Pest

Once you know which pest you've got, you can make effective decisions about controlling it. The first one you need to make is whether your problem is serious enough to require any method of control. In a farmer's field, this would be done with careful monitoring and record keeping, but in your small yard, you needn't be so formal. For example, I sometimes notice western spotted cucumber beetles in my garden—perhaps about six a summer. When I recognized the very first one, I killed it immediately, and began to examine my cucumber and squash leaves for more beetles or for beetle damage every time I came to the garden. That first summer I was nervous, but now that I know there are never enough beetles to do much harm, I ignore them. On the other hand, I have learned from experience that cabbage root maggots often infest my spring-planted cabbage family crops, so I always take preventive measures against them. You will soon be learning from your own gardening experience when action is needed and when it is not.

When you decide that you do need to control a pest, you sometimes also have to select the right time to control it. To do this, read about the pest you have, or ask someone who knows about its habits. Often, as with imported cabbage moths, the answer is that you need to act as soon as you notice the problem. But your timing may also need to be related to the life cycle of the pest, the plant it attacks, or the natural enemies that feed on it. For example, the right time to add mineral oil to corn ears (to repel corn earworms) is when the silks have wilted and as their tips have just turned brown.

When you read about an IPM program for management of a pest, you will often read a list of different ideas to try. You need to choose among them to create an effective strategy that isn't too expensive, doesn't take too much time, and disrupts the environment as little as possible.

IPM theory divides these control tactics into four categories: (1) cultural (what is grown, when it is planted, and how it is cared for), (2) mechanical (physical removal of the pest, or barriers to prevent it from having access to the plant), (3) biological (use of any living organism to prey on the pest), and (4) chemical (use of a chemical, usually one lethal to the pest).

For example, a list of options for controlling an imaginary pest called a tomato nastybug might read: plant a resistant tomato variety (cultural control), plant later than usual (cultural control), pick the nastybugs off the plants by hand (mechanical control), protect fruit with individual nylon net covers (mechanical control), buy and release nastybug-eating insects (biological control), spray your plants with commercial soap spray (chemical control), or, as a last resort, spray with a more toxic pesticide (chemical control).

In the pest entries later in this chapter, I divide tactics into these categories, but you won't always find them in neat lists. Sometimes you will have to put together lists from several different sources or add a newly discovered idea to a list you already have. Before you make decisions, you need to be able to recognize different categories of tactics. For example, suppose that, halfway through the summer, you come across an entirely new idea for controlling tomato nastybugs: "Nastybugs have been shown to be susceptible to a spray containing the living bacterium *Nastybug getticus*." You would add this to your list as a biological tactic.

To help you place tactics in one of the four categories, here is a list of some common ones:

1. **Cultural.** This category includes a wide variety of basic preventive measures. They are particularly important to pursue if you hope to avoid chemical methods or if there are no chemicals to kill the pest you hope to curb.

- Choosing varieties that have genetic resistance to the pest.
- Avoiding infected seed, sets, plants, soil, and containers. Includes seeking certified disease-free starts.
- Choosing planting depth of seed or space between plants to discourage pests. Or, for indoor seeding, using sterile planting mix and appropriate temperatures and moisture levels.
- Taking better care of your plants by planting at a more favorable time of year, improving the soil, watering more effectively, fertilizing properly, or making sure the plants get enough sunshine.
- Growing plants that will repel the pest (companion planting or intercropping). (This was once considered important, but many of the old recommended plant associations have been studied and shown not to work well. For more on this, see sources in the Companion Planting section of Appendix VIII, Suggested Reading.)
- Eliminating pest breeding and hiding places, cleaning up plant debris.
- Rotating crops and seeding beds to avoid pest buildups.
- Not growing affected crops for a certain amount of time or possibly permanently. This might become necessary if there are no adequate controls or none you are willing to use, but you will rarely need to resort to this extreme.

2. **Mechanical.** Into this category fall many simple, commonsense strategies that involve some degree of direct physical intervention. They may be free, requiring only some effort, or you may need to purchase materials to make barriers or traps.

- Handpicking the pest from the plants. This is the most direct method, and it works well for some pests as long as your garden is small enough to pick over relatively quickly.
- Washing pests from plants with a strong spray of water.
- Removing from the garden individual leaves or whole plants that have a disease or a pest infestation.
- Creating barriers of various kinds, from paper wraps for seedling stems or copper strips to repel snails, to fences to keep out deer or rabbits.
- Using traps to catch pests or to lure them to places where you can gather them quickly. Sometimes traps are baited with food or beverages that appeal to the pest.
- Disturbing the soil to kill insect larvae.
- Hand pulling weeds, presprouting them, or smothering them.

3. **Biological.** Helpful organisms can be as selective as careful handpicking, but they save you work by hunting the pests for you.

- Encouraging all kinds of natural predators in your garden by providing food, water, and shelter, and by avoiding use of the pesticides that harm them. (Attracting beneficial insects by planting the flowers that attract them is often spoken of as the new companion planting.)
- Buying beneficial creatures that eat pests outright, parasitize them, or kill them with a biological toxin. These may be insects, bacteria, helpful nematodes (microscopic worms), or even domestic birds. (Chickens and ducks can reduce insect and snail populations in a garden.)

4. **Chemical.** These range from the quite safe (soap sprays) to the most toxic of pesticides. They include repellents, baits, dusts, and sprays. Pesticide is a general term that includes insecticides, miticides, fungicides, bactericides, and even herbicides (chemicals that kill weeds).

- Soap sprays. Various pesticidal soaps have been developed for use as insecticides, as fungicides, or as herbicides. All are relatively nontoxic to humans.
- Oil sprays (mineral oil or vegetable oil). These have most often been used when deciduous fruit trees are dormant, but new oils are available that are safe to apply to some vegetable crops.
- Chemical elements or simple inorganic compounds, such as those containing sulfur and copper, are often used to treat plant diseases. Iron phosphate bait can be used to kill snails and slugs.
- Synthetic insect hormones used as lures for baits or to disrupt insect reproductive cycles. These are not yet used much in home gardens, but watch for developments.
- Pesticides derived from plant extracts, which are known as botanicals. Examples are pyrethrum and rotenone. In general, plant-derived pesticides break down quickly, leaving no residue in the environment or on the crop, but they can be very poisonous when they are first applied, so must be handled with caution.

- Synthetic pesticides, mainly manufactured organic compounds. These include metaldehyde snail bait, glyphosate herbicide, and pyrethroids, which are synthetics that resemble the botanical pesticide pyrethrum.

Very roughly speaking, cultural tactics are the least likely to harm you or the environment, and chemical tactics the most likely to do so, but there are some ambiguities. If the wrong beneficial creature is released in the wrong place, for example, it might eat something other than the pest, disrupting the environment in unexpected ways. Bacterial pesticides could be considered a biological tactic, but since they are sprayed on and often depend on a toxin the bacterium produces, some would call them a chemical tactic. And some chemical pesticides, such as soap sprays, although chemicals, are virtually nontoxic to humans.

Assuming you have decided to take action, you may find one, a few, or many possible tactics to choose from. Which you choose will depend on considerations such as the time of year, how many plants you have, the severity of the problem, and your environmental concerns. You will, roughly speaking, want to try the least environmentally disruptive tactics first. If a tactic is time consuming or expensive, or if you want to judge its effectiveness alone, you may try one at a time. Or you may try several together.

Here's an example of an IPM decision-making process: "Well, I can't try a resistant tomato variety this year, because my plants are already half-grown, so I will table that idea till next year, and ditto for planting later in the season. Picking nastybugs by hand sounds quite unpleasant, but they are eating my tomatoes so fast that I think I will start picking them off right away. I know I have far too many plants to have time to tie netting on all the fruits, so that's out. Since I would really rather not handpick these creatures, I will place an order for some of those nastybug-eating insects. If any nastybugs are still hanging around after I release those, I will spray my tomato plants with a soap spray. (I might change my plans if, for instance, I learn that the nastybug-eating insects are rather expensive, so I then decide to give the soap spray a try first.) I don't want to use anything more toxic, so if this plan of action doesn't do it, I will pull out this year's crop."

Assess the Results

While your program will probably work well, whatever the results of your efforts, you will enter the next season knowing more than you did earlier, having eliminated some possibilities, and you will no doubt have ideas to try next. Sometimes it takes more than one year to work out a really effective system, but when you have done it, you will feel *so successful*!

What are some reasons for failure of a pest management effort based on IPM principles? Assuming you identified the pest correctly, it could be that you had trouble carrying out a tactic effectively. Maybe there were really too many plants to handpick, and you couldn't keep up. Maybe you didn't really spray with the soap twice a week as the label recommended.

Or, it is possible that you are trying a method that has not proven to be effective but is often repeated in books and magazines. In their eagerness to avoid pesticides, gardeners try many tricks, and sometimes the trick appears to have worked, but didn't really. Then the gardener passes on the idea, by word of mouth or in print, although it has never been properly tested.

To continue the nastybug story, you may read that sprinkling paprika on tomato plants during the night of a full moon is guaranteed to drive the nastybugs away. But when you try it, your nastybugs just go right on feeding. If entomologists had been there to study the origin of this theory, they might have reported that the nastybugs disappeared when the gardener sprinkled paprika because they were all mature and had entered cocoons for the winter.

Or you may read that a gardener in Florida repelled nastybugs by spreading coffee grounds around her plants, but when you try it, your California strain of nastybug is not repelled by, but is actually attracted to plants surrounded by coffee grounds. Or your uncle in Topeka may write to tell you of the perfect solution for tomato nastybugs, but when you ask him to describe his pest, you realize that it is different from your bug despite the fact that it has the same common name.

Unfortunately, sometimes you can even buy products that do not work well, still on the market because folk wisdom says they work and because they are profitable to sell. Yes, watch for new ideas, but use some caution. Try to find an evaluation of a product by someone who isn't trying to sell it to you.

Also be sure to try unproven ideas one at a time and leave part of your crop untreated for comparison, so you can accurately assess the worth of the innovation.

NATURAL REINFORCEMENTS

When we think of biological pest management tactics, we often think mainly about the lady beetles and other helpers we can buy, but we get vastly more help against pests from creatures that occur naturally in our garden. As you spend time in your garden, you will become familiar with its helpful residents. If you encourage them, they will be delighted to help you reduce the numbers of pests. Generally, beneficial insects fall into two groups. Some are predatory, meaning they actually devour pests. These tend to be larger and thus more visible. Large hunting wasps, for example, are easy to see as they cruise from plant to plant in search of prey. Other helpful insects are parasites, meaning they lay their eggs in other insects, or, if the host insect dies, they are more correctly called parasitoids. You may never see the tiny wasps that parasitize aphids, though if you see the mummified aphids they have killed, you will know they are there (see illustration on page 114). Besides insects, many other kinds of creatures help out.

As a beginning gardener, you may mistake some of your helpful creatures for pests. Many gardeners recoil from the large, black, soil-dwelling beetles that lift up their rears threateningly when you disturb them. But these are actually helpful rove beetles that devour pests in the soil. Often the larva of an insect looks entirely different from the adult. For example, the most common lady beetle larvae are small, alligator-shaped charcoal gray and orange creatures. The larvae of beneficial insects generally eat many more pests than the adult insects. You can see that it's a good idea to try to identify all the creatures that live in your garden. Then you will not only recognize your pests, but also appreciate how much help you are getting from the other creatures that also call your garden their home.

HELPFUL CREATURES YOU MAY SEE

Following are descriptions of beneficial creatures you are most likely to see in your garden.

Lacewings

You may see the ⅓-inch, buff-colored brown lacewing or the slightly larger green lacewing, both of which have large, nearly transparent wings. Lacewing larvae are mottled brown and gray alligator-shaped creatures. Some kinds disguise themselves by heaping debris on their bodies. All lacewing larvae are predators that eat aphids, thrips, caterpillar eggs, leafhopper nymphs, mealybugs, and mites. Brown lacewing adults and adults of some species of green lacewings also feed on these pests. All adult lacewings also feed on nectar and pollen. If you live in a cool summer microclimate, you are more likely to see the brown lacewing than the green one. The green lacewing is sold for pest control, but it must only be released when weather is warm.

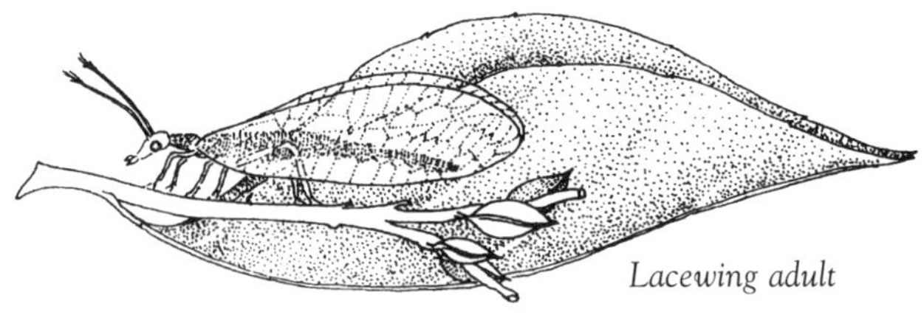

Lacewing adult

Lady Beetles

Lady beetles (or ladybugs), the best-known of the helpful beetles, are represented by a number of local species. In general, the larger reddish-orange ones eat aphids, while the smaller, blackish or gray ones eat such pests as whiteflies, scales, mealybugs, or spider mites. The lesser ashy gray lady beetle, a tiny mottled gray and brown species, eats powdery mildew spores. Many lady beetle species devour pests most actively in the spring, but some are more active in the fall. *Hippodamia convergens*, the convergent lady beetle, is the one collected in the Sierra Nevada and sold to gardeners. It has red, or orange-red, wing covers, marked with 0 to 13 black spots. The name "convergent" comes from the converging white bars forming a V-shaped marking on the top of its thorax (the body part between the head and the wings). The larva is about ⅓ inch long; the adult, ¼ inch. Convergent lady beetle larvae can eat 100 aphids an hour; adults eat 50 to 100 aphids a day. They are fairly common naturally and are also available for purchase. However, they tend to fly away when released, so it is wise to

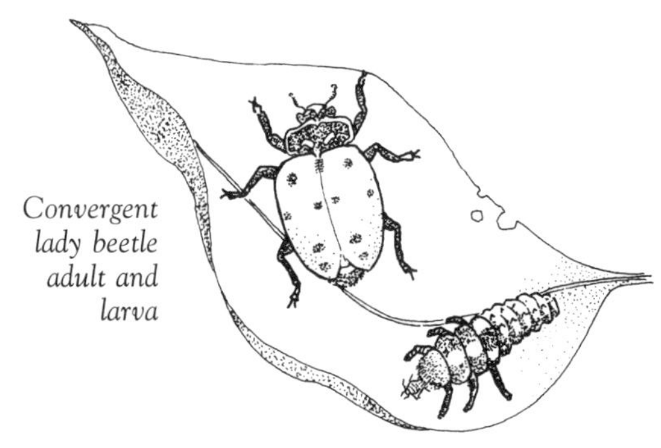

Convergent lady beetle adult and larva

garden to attract them rather than depending on purchased ones.

Ground Beetles

The small, shiny, black or iridescent beetles that scurry about when you disturb debris at the soil surface are ground beetles. Some species eat small snails; others hunt and eat caterpillars. Some eat some plant material as well, and others live mainly on seeds. These beetles are unlikely to seriously damage your crops, and the seed eaters probably help by eating weed seeds.

Rove Beetles

These black beetles, with very short wings that leave their abdomens exposed, live at or near the soil's surface. They often raise their rears in the air as if to sting, though they cannot do so. One tiny local rove beetle eats mites. Other small ones destroy cabbage and onion maggots. You are most likely to notice the large rove beetle *Ocypus olens*, an insect inadvertently introduced to the Northwest in soil ballast brought in on foreign ships in 1931. Although alarming in appearance, it is beneficial, as it relishes snails (even large ones) and slugs. It is black, lustrous (not shiny), over an inch long, and one of those that lift the rear in a threatening manner when disturbed. Protect immature ones as well. They are a dull yellow-grayish.

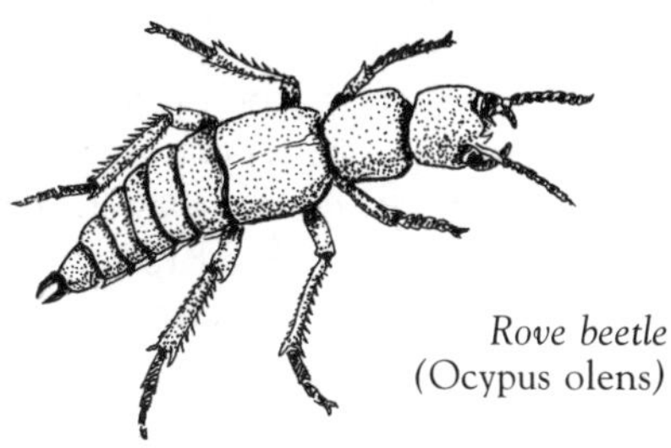

Rove beetle
(Ocypus olens)

Soldier Beetles

If you see narrow beetles with dark wing covers and orangish heads crawling on roses or other aphid-infested plants, chances are they are soldier beetles. The adults, which are about ⅝ inch long, eat aphids and pollen. The larvae eat insects in the soil. The beetles bear a slight resemblance to lightning bugs, to which they are fairly closely related.

Syrphid Flies

These flies are sometimes called hover flies, describing the way they hover in place like little helicopters. They are often brightly marked in black and yellow, so that they look like bees at first glance, but they do not sting. The larvae, which are ⅛ to ¼ inch long, are legless maggots that taper toward their head ends. Most are whitish, but one common one is jade green with a white or red stripe down its back. You may find the larvae feeding among aphids, which they eat at the rate of one a minute, but they may also eat scales, leafhoppers, or mealybugs. Adults, which are under ½ inch long, require pollen from flowers before they can lay eggs. These insects tolerate cooler conditions than most predators, so they are likely to be a big help even in cool summer microclimates.

Tachinid Flies

This group of ⅛- to ½-inch flies resembles houseflies, but these flies are parasitoid, killing other insects by feeding inside them. They lay oval white eggs on an insect or on leaves where pest insects will eat them. The stout, legless maggots eat their hosts from the inside. Prey include caterpillars, adult beetles, and grasshoppers. Among the vegetable pests they may help manage are imported cabbageworms, cabbage loopers, cutworms, corn earworms, tomato hornworms, squash bugs, and cucumber beetles. Although you may never identify a tachinid fly, gardeners sometimes are able to watch them lay eggs on caterpillars, which thrash about, trying to avoid the fly. Adults feed on pollen, nectar, and honeydew, and sometimes eat aphids or leafhoppers.

Parasitic Wasps

Some thirty families of wasps are parasitoids that kill other insects. A number of these wasps are native to our area. Ichneumonid wasps, averaging one and a half inches long, parasitize caterpillars. The smaller brachonid wasps include *Diaeretiella rapae*, which is parasitic on the cabbage aphid and the asparagus aphid. This wasp is the one responsible for creating aphid "mummies," and you are more likely to see this evidence of its presence than the wasp itself. Other braconid wasps feed on caterpillars and on fly larvae. Chalcid wasps are the tiniest wasps. Though you are not likely to see them, particular chalcid wasps control mealybugs, aphids, scale, and the larvae of beetles, moths, and butterflies. Adult parasitoid wasps feed on pollen and nectar. Some are native, and several species are sold to control various insect larvae. Parasitic wasps do not sting humans.

Hunting Wasps

Besides the parasitic wasps, other wasps are predatory, hunting and catching insects that they either eat themselves or feed to their young. Several of these wasps are common in local gardens. They are yellow and black, or a shiny blue-black, and ¾ to 1 inch long. They may build papery nests to house their larvae, or they may dig small burrows in the soil. While you may want to remove wasp nests if they are on your house, do tolerate them in the less often visited parts of your property, as most are insect hunters. Yellow jackets are also hunting wasps. They may be a nuisance at a picnic, and their presence is not welcomed by those unfortunate people who are highly allergic to their sting, but I can testify that they catch insect pests, having once watched one fly away with a large cabbageworm.

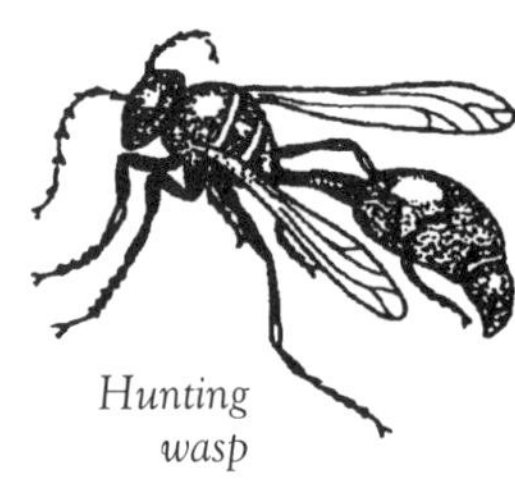
Hunting wasp

Bees

Bees are important beneficial insects because they are necessary to pollinate many kinds of flowers. Without bees, we wouldn't have squash, cucumbers, sunflower seeds, and many kinds of berries, tree fruits, and nuts. The honey bee, a species imported from Europe, is the main commercial pollinator in the United States. Recently, the honey bee has been suffering from a mysterious problem, colony collapse disorder, which causes adult bees to abandon their hives, leaving the young to die. While the problem is still being studied at this writing, it is suspected that there are various reasons, and it is quite likely that pesticide residue is part of the problem.

In addition to honey bees, native bees, including the large bumblebees and hundreds of smaller species, contribute to pollination. Bumblebees, like honey bees, form hives, but most of the other native bees dig individual nests—some in soil, others in wood—and deposit a supply of pollen to feed their young. Recent studies, led by Dr. Gordon Frankie, at U.C. Berkeley have revealed more about their habits and how to attract them. He has found that the soil-nesting types are better able to inhabit unmulched soil, and that many of the same plants that attract other beneficial insects attract native bees as well. See the list of plants to attract native bees on page 108, and see Appendix VII, Resources for Gardeners, for sources of more information on these bees.

Ants

Ants have a mixed effect. They loosen and aerate soil by building nests in it. But ants can also disrupt the activities of various natural enemies of aphids, scales, and mealybugs, preventing them from eating the pests. See the listing for aphids for information on controlling ants.

True Bugs

The insect group known as "true bugs" includes squash bugs and other pests. It also includes a ¼-inch black-and-white insect, called *Orius tristicolor*, also known as minute pirate bug, which eats insect eggs, small insects, and spider mites. Its immature stages mature from yellow, to orange, to brown; the adults feed on pollen and nectar. This is a fairly common predator and one of the first to appear in spring, although it's so small and inconspicuous that few gardeners would notice it.

Earwig

The common local earwig is a European species, *Forficula auricularia*. While it does often damage plants, it also eats some pest insects, notably some kinds of aphids. (More on earwigs as pests on page 117.)

Praying Mantis

These strange-looking insects are well known as devourers of other insects. The species *Tenodeora aridifolia sinensis* was introduced to the United States from Asia to control garden pests, but it hasn't become established here, so you aren't likely to see it unless you or a neighbor released it. You can buy the egg cases, from which will hatch many small mantises. The praying mantis is no longer considered a very efficient means of pest control, as it is an unselective predator, eating anything in sight, including pollinators and other predators. Still, on the average it probably eats more pests than predators, because pests are usually more numerous.

Spiders and Mites

These eight-legged creatures are closely related to insects. All spiders and some mites help control garden pests. Spiders eat all kinds of insects, including some beneficial ones, but on balance they eat more pests, including all kinds of flying insects and earwigs. Spiders make some gardeners nervous, but in my many years of gardening I have never been bitten by a spider. I enjoy watching the wide variety of spiders in my garden, from the tiniest lemon yellow ones to gawky daddy longlegs, which look like spiders on stilts.

While some mites suck the sap from plants, a number of native mite species are predatory. They live on pest mites, small insects, and insect eggs.

Like the pest mites, they are tiny, requiring a magnifying lens to see. Unlike pest mites, which are slow-moving, they run quickly as they hunt their prey.

Amphibians

While salamanders are not usually major contributors to pest control in a small garden, they do help out. My garden has a number of California slender salamanders living under rocks and near the compost pile. They are brown, 2 to 5 inches long, with legs so small you don't notice them at first. They eat slugs, sow bugs, aphids, termites, beetles, and ants. If you uncover a salamander, gently cover it again to keep it from harm.

You may see toads as well, particularly if you live near a creek or pond close to the edges of the San Francisco Bay—areas inhabited by the Western toad. This creature reaches 4 to 5 inches across, and is greenish-brown with a cream-colored stripe down its back. Like other toads, it is an unselective predator, eating just about anything that moves and is smaller than it is. It is best not to try to remove toads from their natural habitat, as they need water to reproduce. It is also illegal to collect them. However, if your garden is near a place where they live, you can encourage them to spend time in it by providing a moist, sheltered place made with coarse mulch materials or old boards.

Reptiles

Some gardens are home to garter snakes and lizards, both harmless and at least some help in controlling garden pests.

Birds

Our region is home to many kinds of birds, most of which we welcome whether they help out with pests or not. At a minimum, they indicate that the environment is reasonably unpolluted, and many birds that eat plant matter at other times of year prey on insects in the spring when they are raising young. Some local birds, among them robins, mockingbirds, and flickers, help significantly against pests. Robins eat many kinds of insects, including wireworms, cutworms and caterpillars. Mockingbirds eat beetles, grasshoppers, and other insects. Flickers eat ants, caterpillars, cockroaches, and ground beetles, and the presence of flickers may drive some of the pest birds from your garden. (For information on birds as pests, see page 126.)

Microorganisms

Pests, like all other creatures, are attacked by agents of disease. Many kinds of naturally occurring fungi, bacteria, and viruses infect and kill pests. Helpful microorganisms in the soil protect plant roots from soil pests.

ENCOURAGING YOUR NATURAL ALLIES

While some beneficial insects, mites, and other creatures are offered for sale, your first goal should always be to keep the ones you have and find natural ways to attract more of them. These are going to provide the most help. Much of the help they provide is background help. That is, you may not realize they are helping, but if they were gone you would notice the difference.

The most important way to encourage beneficial creatures to live in your garden is to avoid using pesticides that kill them. Your natural allies are, unfortunately, often more susceptible to pesticides than your pests are. First, there are fewer of them. Predaceous insects are the lions and tigers of the insect world, living on the great herds of plant-eating pests. The deaths of relatively few predators allow bursts of increase in pest populations. Also, predators tend to be larger than pests, so they are more likely to be hit by spray. Then, of course, both predators and parasites must eat pests that have been sprayed, further poisoning themselves. Finally, pesticides also kill the many relatively harmless creatures that serve as the predators' alternative food and that keep predators in the neighborhood at times when pests are inactive.

An ideal garden, from a predatory creature's point of view, includes an ample supply of insect life. While you hardly want to be raising pests for your predators to eat, you don't want to kill every insect in sight, either.

You can provide the predators with another source of nourishment besides pests. Many beneficial insects, including adult lady beetles, wasps, flies, and lacewings, either require pollen or nectar to lay eggs or will eat these if the pests they eat are scarce. By providing the flowers such insects prefer as pollen and nectar sources, you encourage them to show up before your pests get out of control and to stay after they have reduced pest populations. You may be able to get some beneficial insects to spend their whole lives in your garden.

The flowers that attract beneficial insects best are small and shallow-necked. Such flowers are common in many plant families—carrot, mint, mustard, onion, buckwheat, and daisy, to mention only a few. Some of the best flowers to attract beneficial insects are those of vegetable crops, and for this reason I often let one or two plants of mustard, leek, onion, parsnip, carrot, parsley, or garland chrysanthemum bloom. I have seen many syrphid flies hovering around garland chrysanthemum blooms and hunting wasps at leek and parsnip flowers. Many herbs are good attractants as well. African blue basil seems to be especially attractive to lady beetles. On mine, I have seen all stages in the lady beetle life cycle at once. The attractant plants include ones that are good cut flowers, such as cosmos and scabiosa, as well as California natives such as ceanothus, coyote brush, and native buckwheats. Attractant flowers that bloom in late winter or early spring are especially valuable, since they may bring beneficial insects to your garden before your pests become numerous. While you will find many lists for specific insects, it turns out that many plants reappear as food sources for several of them. The sidebar on page 108 has a list of many of the plants most likely to succeed as attractants. See Appendices VII and VIII, Resources for Gardeners and Suggested Reading, for more sources of information on this topic.

You may notice advertisements for baits you can apply to attract beneficial insects. These can be useful as part of a program to encourage predators, but unless you know what you are doing, they may be no help. They are designed primarily for attracting the green lacewing and stimulating it to lay eggs, but chances are you won't have many green lacewings in your garden unless you've released them yourself. Lady beetles and the more common brown lacewings will eat this bait too, but they will not come to the area because they are attracted to it. Late May or early June are the best times to spray such a bait, because there is usually a lull in aphid populations then.

To make your own bait, mix the following ingredients in a glass or plastic container: ⅔ cup warm water, 4 tablespoons brewer's yeast, 2 teaspoons honey, and ½ cup sugar. Stir well to dissolve solids. Keep this in a sealed jar in the refrigerator for up to 10 days. Mix 2 tablespoons of bait in a quart of water and spray plants when temperatures are under 80°F. If you've released some green lacewings, spray in the evening to supplement their diet and encourage them to stay. Spray in the morning to feed native lady beetles.

Beneficial insects also need water in the form of droplets—called "free water"—from which they can sip. Fog drip and heavy dew can provide enough, but when the air is dry, insects appreciate water sprinkled on plants. Sprinkle only plants, such as the cole crops or parsley, that aren't made susceptible to diseases by having wet leaves. Or you can provide an "insect bath," using a medium-sized terra cotta saucer. Place rough rocks in the water, rising above the surface, to provide landing places and shallows where insects can sip. Change the water twice a week to thwart mosquito larvae. Some insects may use the water that emerges from drip emitters when a drip system is running. I have noticed honey bees sipping at mine.

A healthy soil will encourage helpful creatures that live in the soil or at the soil surface. Limit the use of soil pesticides and soluble synthetic fertilizers. And when you add plenty of well-rotted organic matter, you increase the likelihood that helpful soil creatures will outnumber harmful ones. However, if you are using undecayed organic substances, such as green manure or fresh animal manure, as soil amendments, you should dig them in and then not plant for a couple of months, as some of the organisms that carry out the early stages of decay are also capable of attacking living plants.

Leave some dark, moist places on the surface of the soil to attract salamanders and predatory beetles. While you will be cleaning up your garden to avoid snails, slugs, and the like, it is wise to preserve some easily checked flat rocks, pieces of wood, or mulched areas to offer predators safe harbor.

HIRING HELPERS

The idea of buying a predator or a parasite of a pest and releasing it to save a crop is very appealing, especially when you see the tubes of cute lady beetles on the counter of the nursery. There is definitely a place for introduced enemies of pests in agriculture and floriculture, but at this time only a few have been proven useful in small gardens. Research continues, so more could prove effective. However, at this writing, I recommend for purchase mainly microscopic beneficial creatures, since these less-mobile creatures are more likely to stay put and work on your pests.

A main problem of releasing purchased beneficials into a small garden is that, if they are mobile, they tend to range farther than the boundaries of the garden. In general, predators and parasites will stay long enough to clean up the last pest only if they are in an enclosed space, such as a greenhouse, or in the middle of a big field, in which the same plants extend a long distance in all directions.

Lady beetles have a further reason to fly. They have an instinct to fly from the place they are released in spring before they feed. It is estimated that only 10 percent of them will stay put. When lady beetles are released in the summer, they are more likely to stay, but then they do not feed on pests—or on anything else. Also, these lovely and beneficial insects are being decimated in their overwintering grounds by greedy commercial collectors who are able to quickly and profitably scoop up large masses of the hibernating bugs for sale in garden stores. I know that some suppliers say their lady beetles have been fed a special diet after trapping them to "minimize their migratory behavior," and that lady beetles may come with directions for encouraging them to stay, such as refrigerating them, releasing a few at a time, or releasing in the evening. It is also said that if you sprinkle the pest-ridden plants with water, then drape them with a piece of row cover or a thin sheet, and release the lady beetles under the cover, they may be trapped by it long enough to settle down and feed. This may all be so, but I also know that the beetles fly down from the mountains to feed nearer the coast on their own each spring, and that if a garden is attractive to them, they will show up.

Green lacewings are another often-released beneficial insect. They have proven successful in some commercial situations, not so much in others. Effectiveness depends, in part, on how they are released. Adult lacewings fly before laying eggs. The most effective method of release has been found to be holding purchased eggs until larvae hatch and then releasing the larvae. This should be repeated several times, weekly. As with lady beetles, preserving beneficial insects already present is likely to be more effective and will save money, too.

Predatory mites have succeeded in controlling mites in strawberry and almond plantings and in greenhouses. Still, your best bet in a small garden is probably to conserve naturally occurring mites by avoiding pesticides that harm them. Most carbamates, organophosphates, and pyrethroids are particularly toxic to predatory mites, so their use is often followed by pest mite outbreaks.

Microscopic organisms available for purchase can be very useful in small gardens. *Bacillus thuringiensis* (sold as Bt, Dipel, or Thuricide) is a bacterium that infects many kinds of caterpillars, including cutworms, imported cabbage worms, and cabbage loopers. It doesn't affect their predators, nor does it cause systemic infections in humans. (It can, however, cause minor eye inflammations, so do treat Bt with caution and keep it out of your eyes.) Bt has to be sprayed while pests are actively feeding and usually works best when the feeding larvae are young. Wait for the first signs of damage, then spray both sides of affected leaves thoroughly and repeat as often as the label recommends. Research continues in this direction, with other bacterial organisms being developed for use in pest control. (See Appendix IV, Understanding Pesticide Ingredients, for more details on these.)

Predatory nematodes are microscopic worms that live exclusively on insect larvae, never harming plants. Among the pests they kill are cabbage and onion maggots, wireworms, and carrot rust fly maggots. The nematodes are usually worked into the top few inches of the soil in the spring. To be sure of success, follow directions carefully, applying them when the soil is warm enough for them to survive, and at the time when the pest you hope to control is active. Apply them over only the area of soil suggested; if they are not numerous enough they won't eat all the pests. And note that they must be reapplied each year, as they do not survive our winter temperatures. Predatory nematodes can also be used above ground, to kill insect larvae that live in plant crevices (for example, artichoke plume moth larvae; see page 114).

USING PESTICIDES

Because I have emphasized so strongly limiting the use of pesticides, you may wonder why I am about to spend several pages talking about how to use them. One reason: I think every gardener should have a basic understanding of this subject. Another reason: there are now a number of products classified as pesticides that I can and do recommend. Fortunately, the age in which synthetic, broad-spectrum, highly toxic pesticides were dominant options is passing. A number of new choices—including horticultural oils, soaps, iron phosphate snail baits, and bacterially derived pesticides—are minimally disruptive to the environment or toxic to you.

As I've said, you need to understand some basic information to make intelligent choices among available products. How does a substance work? Is it harmful to bees? How toxic is it to humans? Which one that will kill this pest is the least-toxic choice? You need to know the right questions to ask and where to find the information. You may want to know this before you use a product yourself, and you may find yourself talking to someone else who is trying to make a decision about using a pesticide. You might, for example, be able to help a neighbor

Flowers for Desirable Insects

Flowers That Attract Beneficial Insects and Mites

The plants on the following list, compiled from many sources along with my own personal observations, will attract beneficial insects and mites to your garden. If you watch your garden carefully, you may be able to add more plants to the list.

Vegetables: Amaranth, carrot, garland chrysanthemum, leek, mustard and other mustard family crops, onion, parsnip, sunflower.

Herbs: Carrot family (chervil, cilantro, coriander, dill, fennel, parsley); mint family (anise hyssop), basil (especially African blue basil), lemon balm, rosemary, thyme; herbs in other plant families: chamomile, epazote, garlic chives.

Weeds: Amaranth, chickweed, dandelion, white clover, wild fennel, wild mustards, wild radish.

California native plants: Baby blue eyes (*Nemophila menziesii*), California buckwheat (*Eriogonum* spp.), California lilac (*Ceanothus* varieties), California poppy (*Eschscholzia californica*), coffeeberry (*Rhamnus californica*), coyote brush (*Baccharis pilularis*), deergrass (*Muhlenbergia rigens*), elderberry (*Sambucus* spp.), golden sticky monkey flower (*Mimulus* sp.), goldenrod (*Solidago californica*), hollyleaf cherry (*Prunus ilicifolia*), meadowfoam (*Limnanthes douglasii*), narrowleaf milkweed (*Asclepias fascicularis*), phacelia (various native *Phacelias*), St. Catherine's lace (*Eriogonum giganteum*), toyon (*Heteromeles arbutifolia*), yarrow (*Achillea* spp.).

Non-native flowers: Daisy family (bachelor's buttons [*Centaurea cyanus*], coreopsis, cosmos [especially white and pale yellow], daisies in general, feverfew, marigold, rudbeckia, sunflower, tansy, yarrow); plants in various other plant families: bee balm (*Monarda* spp.), corn cockle (*Agrostemma*), evening primrose (*Oenothera* spp.), perennial candytuft (*Iberis sempervirens*), pincushion flower (*Scabiosa*), rose campion (*Lychnis coronaria*), sweet alyssum (*Lobularia maritima*).

Non-native shrubs: Evergreen euonymus (*Euonymus japonicus*), oleander (*Nerium oleander*).

Flowers That Attract Native Bees

The following list is based on the work of Dr. Gordon Frankie at U.C. Berkeley, who has led a project to observe which plants are utilized by California native bees. He says that plantings of a single species over 3 feet across are most attractive to the bees. (To read about Dr. Frankie's work, including his tips on native bee watching, see Appendix VII, Resources for Gardeners.)

Non-native plants: Bidens (*Bidens ferulifolia*), black-eyed susan (*Rudbeckia hirta*), blanket flower (*Gaillardia × grandiflora*), bluebeard (*Caryopteris incana*), blue mist (*Caryopteris × clandonensis*), calamint (*Calamintha* spp.), calendula, calliopsis (*Calliopsis tinctoria*), catmint, catnip, coreopsis, cosmos (*Cosmos bipinnatus* and *C. sulphureus*), evening primrose (*Oenothera* spp.), globe artichoke, Himalaya blackberry, lavender, marigold, Mexican sunflower (*Tithonia*), oregano, pincushion flower (*Scabiosa*), pumpkin, pride of Madeira (*Echium candicans*), purple coneflower (*Echinacea purpurea*), purple toadflax (*Linaria purpurea*), rosemary, Russian sage (*Perovskia atriplicifolia*), sage (*Salvia brandegeei, S. chamaedryoides, S. greggii, S. uliginosa*), scented geranium (*Pelargonium* spp.), sea holly (*Eryngium amethystinum*), squash, sunflower, thyme, tomato, wild mustards.

California native plants: Bee plant (*Scrophularia californica*), black sage (*Salvia mellifera*), bush sunflower (*Encelia californica*), California buckwheat (*Eriogonum* spp.), California poppy (*Eschscholzia californica*), Ceanothus, coffeeberry (*Rhamnus californica*), elegant clarkia (*Clarkia unguiculata*), gilia (*Gilia achillifolia* or *G. capitata*), goldenrod (*Solidago californica*), gum plant (*Grindelia spp.*), horehound (*Marrubium vulgare*), manzanita (*Arctostaphylos* spp.), penstemon (*Penstemon heterophyllus*), phacelia (various native *Phacelias*), seaside daisy (*Erigeron glaucus* 'Wayne Roderick'), tidytips (*Layia platyglossa*), toyon (*Heteromeles arbutifolia*), yarrow (*Achillea* spp.).

better protect prize plants while also reducing toxic drift into your garden.

Finally, pesticides are designed to kill something, so no matter how low in toxicity, you need to treat them with respect. Start by learning to read the label, which is the law. If you don't follow the directions on the label, you are the one considered at fault.

Reading Pesticide Labels

This next section would best be read with a pesticide label in your hand. Any one will do, since the parts of each label are the same. I know that pesticide labels are not inviting to read, starting with the fact that they use such small print. And it's true you may not find everything you want to know about a pesticide on its label. But everything that is written on the label is, nonetheless, very important. The information on the label must appear there by law, and you are required by law to heed it. But beyond that, the label information will help you to apply the pesticide effectively, with the least hazard.

You should read the label carefully before you purchase a pesticide, and read it again every time you mix, use, store, or dispose of the chemical.

- **Personal Safety** First, look for one of the three signal words—"Caution," "Warning," or "Danger-Poison"—which should appear prominently on the front and also under "Hazards to Humans and Domestic Animals" at the top of the fine print. These summarize the immediate, or acute, toxicity of the product, the amount that in short order killed half of the mammals (usually rats) used to test it. This is expressed as the LD_{50} (lethal dose for 50 percent) showing milligrams of poison per kilogram of body weight (mg/kg). Because toxicity is in proportion to body weight, a lethal amount varies with the size of the animal or person involved. Smaller people, such as children, would be harmed more by a specific amount of a pesticide.

  Most of the products you will be using will probably be labeled "Caution." These have an LD_{50} that translates to a toxic dose of one ounce (two tablespoons) or more for an adult human. There are two classes of pesticides so labeled. Class III pesticides are considered slightly toxic. An example is the bacterial pesticide Bt (*Bacillis thurengiensis*). With its LD_{50} of 2,500 mg/kg, an average-sized human being would need to eat a couple of pounds of Bt to risk death. Class IV pesticides are considered relatively nontoxic. An example is soap spray, which is virtually nontoxic to humans.

  If the product in your hand reads "Warning," the lethal dose for an average human would be between a teaspoon and an ounce. This can also be described as a Class II pesticide.

  The label on the product you are holding should not read "Danger-Poison," since pesticides with this signal word should be in the possession of only professional pesticide applicators. The lethal dose for an average human for a pesticide labeled "Danger-Poison," or Class I pesticides, could be as much as just under a teaspoon, but could be as little as a few drops.

  I decided long ago that I preferred to work only with pesticides labeled "Caution." This is because one of the main benefits of gardening, for me, is peace of mind, and I do not have peace of mind while worrying about whether the sprayer will leak or whether I will breathe something toxic.

  The signal words on labels are good rough guides to toxicity, but they do not detail the toxic effects of the pesticide. They express mainly the immediate danger from eating the chemical (oral toxicity). Sometimes some data on the immediate danger of absorbing the chemical through the skin (dermal toxicity) are folded into the choice of signal word. The dangers from breathing the chemical (inhalation toxicity) are usually not well enough understood to be included.

  Long-term toxicity is not included in the signal word at all. So you won't learn from the label about any ability to cause cancer (oncongenicity), mutation (mutagenicity), or birth defects (teratogenicity). Because I thought you might like to know these facts, I have included as many of them as I could find in Appendix IV, Understanding Pesticide Ingredients.

  Even if you are using chemicals with relatively low toxicity to mammals, you should treat all pesticides as though they are extremely toxic, since this is the surest way to avoid accidents, and since long-term effects might result from repeated exposure to even relatively less-toxic chemicals.

  Besides the signal word, more information on the label that will help you use a pesticide safely is in the "Precautionary Statements." Here you may learn whether the pesticide is absorbed through your skin or is a hazard to breathe. You may be given precautions such as wearing gloves or avoiding spraying it on windy days. Do pay attention to these warnings. (See also general safety precautions within Mixing, Using, Storing, and Disposing with Care on page 112.)

There may also be information on what to do in the event of an accidental poisoning, and a "Note to Physician" on the label. In addition to what's on the label, you should have handy the number of your local poison control center and your physician. Telling someone else which pesticide you are applying and where the container is located is extra insurance.

- **Active Ingredients** Next, find the list of ingredients. These are given as percentages by weight. Listed first will be the common names for the one or more ingredients that make the pesticide effective against a pest. For example, a snail bait may contain the active ingredient iron phosphate or may include that plus the bacterial fermentation product spinosin. Note that the active ingredient is often different from the brand name, the name in big letters at the top of the label. The product brand name may be Sluggo, but the active ingredient is iron phosphate.

  Knowing which active ingredient is in a pesticide lets you find more information, so you can decide whether you want to use a product. For example, pyrethrum, which is the dried, powdered flowers of the pyrethrum daisy (*Tanacetum cinerarifolium*), is permitted to organic farmers and lasts only briefly in the environment. Pyrethroids, on the other hand, are synthetic substances similar to pyrethrum, which are not permitted to organic farmers and are much longer lasting in the environment. I have researched a number of common active ingredients in Appendix IV and made recommendations based on this research.

- **Inert Ingredients** Inert ingredients are the ones that make up the rest of the formulation but are not active as pesticides. The inactive part of a formulation could be water or could include solvents or materials to help the substance stick to a plant. Recently, the EPA reassessed inert ingredients and now requires ones of "highest toxicological concern" to be listed on labels. In addition, the signal word (defined earlier) now takes into account toxicity of inerts. For more on inert ingredients and finding out which ones are in a particular product, see Appendix IV, Understanding Pesticide Ingredients.

- **Environmental Disruption** Information about possible damage to creatures you didn't intend to kill, and ways to minimize that damage, is given in the "Precautionary Statements" under the heading "Environmental Hazards." As with the human toxicity warnings, the information given here is not necessarily complete. You may learn that the material should be kept out of waterways, and you may be told why; for example, that it will kill fish or that it will kill the marine invertebrates on which fish feed. You may be told that the material will kill birds or bees. The information on bees is the closest the label usually gets to telling you that the substance kills beneficial insects. Pesticides that kill honey bees will also kill native bees and the many beneficial wasps, hunting or parasitic, that are closely related to bees. It is also possible that a chemical, especially a synthetic one that didn't previously exist in the environment, will harm the environment in ways not yet known. (When DDT was first released, no one anticipated its accumulation in mother's milk.)

  Other information you might like to know—but won't find on the label—is how long the pesticide will remain toxic in the environment, whether it is an endocrine disrupter, and whether it accumulates in the fat of animals who eat contaminated food. If you know the active ingredient, these are topics you can research, and I have done so for a number of active ingredients. (See Appendix IV.)

- **OMRI Listed** If you are interested in being an organic gardener, you will want see whether the logo "OMRI Listed" is on the label. It means that the Organic Materials Review Institute has approved the particular product for use by organic farmers. OMRI is a national nonprofit organization that determines which input products are allowed for use in organic production and processing. Submission of a product is voluntary, and the analysis is paid for by the company submitting the product. If the logo is on the label, you can be assured that the particular product has been deemed permissible; that is, in agreement with the ingredients list in the list of the National Organic Program.

  There are some reasons, however, that a product could be in accordance with the NOP program but not OMRI Listed. It could be a new product, still under consideration by OMRI. It could be made by a small company that has chosen not to pay for review by OMRI. Or it could be that a product doesn't contain anything considered hazardous enough that it has to be registered as a pesticide; that is, it is EPA exempt.

An example of the latter would be a product whose active ingredient is clove oil.

- **Effectiveness for Intended Purpose** Of course, a main consideration before you buy any pesticide is whether it is effective against the pest you want to eliminate. Check the label to learn the pests for which the product is registered, and be sure that your particular pest is included. If the pest you are combating is not listed on the label, not only is it unlikely the product will kill it, but it is illegal to use it to try to control that pest.

  Next, find out whether the product can be used on the plant the pest is damaging. The label may list plants for which the product can be used, or simply state that it can be used on all plants in a certain group. It may also list plants for which it should not be used. Using a pesticide on nonrecommended plants could cause them serious damage.
- **Use in Food Gardens** In your food garden, be sure to use only pesticides registered for use on food plants. Other chemicals may also kill your pests, but they may leave residues on or inside the plant that would endanger you if you ate it. For example, some types of pesticides, called systemics, enter every cell of the sprayed plants. This means that they can't be washed off, and if they are still in the plant at harvest time it will not be safe to eat. No systemic pesticides are registered for home use on food plants.

  If a product is registered for use on food plants, the label will tell you how many days you must wait between your application and harvest to be sure that the chemical is no longer present in a toxic form. Even when you wait this long, be sure to wash all food harvested from plants exposed to pesticide and also any food picked from nearby plants.
- **Directions for Use** Pay close attention to the correct timing and placement of the chemical. It can make the difference between effective control and failure. For example, spraying your plants with Bt when pest caterpillars are already large is a waste of time. This bacterial pesticide has the most effect when caterpillars are still very small. When they are older, they are eating too little each day to get a toxic amount of the bacterium. Bt is best timed a week or so after you first see caterpillar eggs or when you see the first small caterpillars. As another example, soap spray kills only when it lands on the pest. It does no good to spray plants with soap when pests aren't present, or to spray the tops of the leaves when the insects are feeding on the undersides. And soap sprays must be repeated at several intervals, so that new pests hatching on or flying to the plants will also be killed.

Sparing Friendly Creatures

What a pesticide label doesn't do is give you a plan for minimizing harm to beneficial creatures. IPM practitioners have worked out such a plan, and the following checklist will help you to carry it out:

1. **Avoid using toxic chemicals as much as possible.** Use cultural, mechanical, biological methods or least-toxic chemicals like oil or soaps first and in preference. Use more toxic chemicals only when other methods have proven unsatisfactory. Use chemicals only when there are many pests present, never preventatively "just in case" pests might attack.
2. **Choose chemicals that are as specific as possible for the pests you wish to control, not broad-spectrum pesticides.** When possible, choose active ingredients that affect pests more than predators. For example, *Bacillus thuringiensis kurstaki*, a type of Bt, kills only caterpillars, not other insects, so it spares the wasps that parasitize the caterpillars.
3. **Choose formulations that are least harmful to beneficial insects.** For example, honeybees and wasps are least likely to be poisoned by granules. Sprays are more likely to harm them, and dusts even more so. The most harmful formulation for such insects is microencapsulation. Bees pick up poisons from these time-release capsules while pollinating. Then they eat the poison while cleaning their legs. No microencapsulated pesticides are currently registered for use on food plants, but their use on nearby ornamentals could harm the bees that pollinate your food crops.
4. **Choose chemicals that will not persist in the environment, killing creatures you didn't intend to kill long after your particular problem is solved.** If more than one chemical will kill the pest, choose the one with the shortest half-life. For example, pyrethrum or pyrethrins break down more quickly than the synthetic pyrethroids. (See Appendix IV.)
5. **Time pesticide applications to minimize harm to susceptible beneficial creatures.** For example, apply pyrethrum or pyrethrins in the evening, when honeybees are inactive.

6. **Use pesticides only in the area where the pests are found.** Never apply them to unaffected plants.
7. **Never use a higher concentration than the one recommended on the label for the pest and plant you are treating.** If you do, you won't kill more pests, but you will certainly harm more of the nonpest creatures in your garden.

Mixing, Using, Storing, and Disposing with Care

Buy only the smallest amount of a pesticide that will do the job; don't buy the large economy size and save leftovers for later. If you buy more than you need, you will have more to store, and you are more likely to end up taking leftovers to a toxic dump site later on. When you are treating only a small garden, you will often be buying premixed dilutions with built-in applicators. This gives you maximum protection from mixing accidents.

If you ever do mix your own solutions, do it outdoors, away from areas where anyone might eat. Wear rubber or neoprene gloves—unlined, since cloth linings can absorb pesticides and hold them against your skin. Wear a long-sleeved shirt, long pants, and shoes. Wear safety glasses if they are suggested on the pesticide label. Make sure any measuring utensils are clearly marked with an indelible ink pen "For Pesticides Only." Mix in small amounts, to avoid storing mixed pesticides in containers other than the ones with the labels, and because the mixtures may not be stable.

If you mix herbicides, use separate utensils, clearly labeled "for herbicides only," and use different spraying equipment. This will protect your desirable plants from poisoning by traces of herbicide left in utensils or sprayers.

If a substance must be sprayed, protect yourself while you do it. Spray only when it's cool and not windy—early mornings are most likely to provide such conditions. Wear a long-sleeved shirt, long pants, socks, closed-toe shoes or rubber boots, and a brimmed hat made of nonabsorbent material. Check whether a respirator is required when you are using either a spray or a dust. When you finish, wash your hands thoroughly before you eat or smoke. If there is any danger that any of the chemicals got on you or your clothes, shower immediately. Keep the clothes you wore when spraying separate from other dirty clothes and immediately launder them separately. Line dry the clothes, to spare your dryer possible contamination. Run the washer on empty once before you launder uncontaminated clothing.

Store pesticides in their original containers with labels intact. Never put them in other containers, to avoid their being mistaken for something else. Store pesticides away from human and pet food, out of reach of children, in a cool place, and preferably in a locked cupboard.

Pesticide labels offer advice on how to dispose of the empty or partially filled container. You can dispose of empty containers by wrapping them in several layers of newspaper and then putting them in the garbage. However, be aware that no matter what the label says, it is illegal in California to put unused pesticide in the garbage can. Partially filled containers should be taken to a toxic waste collection site, where they will be isolated from less toxic waste. Each county has its own arrangement for collecting such wastes, from toxic turn-in days to permanent toxic waste collection sites. Many counties have a free toxic waste collection site for county residents. See Appendix VII for information on how to find out what your county provides, as well as how to contact other resources offering advice on pesticide use and disposal.

Compendium of Pests

PESTS AND STRATEGIES AGAINST THEM

I've compiled the following list of pests from my own gardening experience and that of local consultants. These are primarily pests of vegetables, and the list is as complete as I can make it for these plants. I have also mentioned some pests of fruits and flowers, but you should refer to other references for complete lists of the pests affecting those plants. I haven't much to say about herbs here, because herbs have very few pests.

If you need a checklist of pests that might affect a particular vegetable, you should turn to the listing for that vegetable. For cabbage family plants in general, see the Mustard Family sidebar on page 198.

I have divided the pests into categories based on the type of creature that causes the damage: first insects, then other invertebrate animals (such as mites and snails), vertebrate animals (domestic and wild), and diseases (fungal, bacterial, and viral). Individual pest listings are organized in the following way: (1) what you will see, (2) what the pest is like, and (3) what you can do about it.

In general, management tactics are listed in the order in which I've suggested that you try them, earlier in this chapter: cultural, mechanical, biological, and then chemical. In practice, sometimes management tactics work better in a slightly different order; so, if I will arrange them that way.

INSECT PESTS

Insect pests primarily damage your garden in one of the following ways: they chew the stems, leaves, buds, or flowers of the plant; they suck sap from the plants; or they bore into the roots, fruits, or seeds. Typical symptoms of chewing pests are holes in leaves and flowers or pockets in fruits. Leafminers chew out the insides of leaves, but the surface layers remain intact. Seedlings attacked by chewing insects may be eaten completely.

When sucking insects are involved, infested parts of the plant may become distorted, pale, or stippled, due to a loss of chlorophyll. While sucking insects may be found anywhere on the plant, you should especially check rapidly growing parts like stem tips and flower buds.

Root-chewing insects crawl through the soil to invade the roots. The symptoms are wilting (even when the plant is well watered), stunting, and yellowing leaves. Of course, these symptoms could be caused by disease or other problems, but when you pull out an affected plant, you can generally see holes in the roots or the pests themselves. Plants may even be severed from their roots!

When you read about insects you will often encounter the names of different stages of their life cycles. Here is a brief review of how insects develop, and the terms used to describe the various stages. Some insects hatch from their eggs and just grow steadily, shedding skins, until they gradually mature into adults. The immature stages of these insects are called *nymphs*. Two of the many kinds of insects that develop this way are aphids and earwigs.

Other insect eggs hatch into *larvae*, which are wormlike creatures. An insect larva eats and grows, then rests, as a *pupa*. During its resting period (which may or may not be spent in a cocoon) the pupa metamorphoses into a very different looking adult. The larvae of particular kinds of insects are typically referred to by specific names, for example, caterpillars (butterflies and moths), grubs (beetles), and maggots (flies).

Aphids

These are tiny teardrop-shaped, slow-moving creatures, usually feeding in clusters. In fact, what you may notice is not individual insects, but an encrustation of some kind on your plant. You need to look very closely, perhaps with a hand lens, to see individual insects. Most will be wingless, though some will have clear wings. Aphids are most commonly gray, black, or light green, and are about ⅕ inch long. You may find them on the growing tips of the plants, on the flowers, or on leaves, especially on the undersides. When aphids are present, leaves may become twisted or rolled and may turn yellow. On woody plants or on very badly infested herbaceous plants, a sooty black substance may cover leaves and stems. Ants may be crawling about on affected plants.

Aphids are sucking pests that insert a hollow beak and remove plant sap. After the aphid has digested the sap, it excretes a substance, known as honeydew, that still contains some plant sugars. This substance attracts ants and also serves as food for the sooty mold fungus. Controlling aphids will control either of these attendant problems.

Our region is home to a number of aphid species, and they attack many kinds of vegetables, flowers, and woody plants. The cabbage aphid, a gray species, will be found on cabbage family plants, the light green pea aphid on peas, and so on. For details about appearance and control of particular species, see information in the pest sections of various vegetable listings.

Just a few aphids will do little direct damage to your plants, but they do spread plant diseases, so you shouldn't tolerate many of them. And sometimes they multiply until the plant is severely stunted. Aphids reproduce very rapidly, making many generations in a season. Some winters are mild enough that they continue to feed and multiply but, if not, they overwinter as eggs, glued to a plant.

Since there is some evidence that weakened plants are more likely to be attacked, attention to good growing conditions may pay off. Aphids may attack plants whose roots were badly damaged in transplanting, or those that are underwatered or have been given too much nitrogen fertilizer. Some crops, such as tomatoes, do not have a high need for nitrogen, so special care must be taken not to give them too much.

A small percentage of aphids develop wings and fly to infest new plants. A mulch made of aluminum foil repels flying aphids, who become confused by the reflected sky. However, vigilance is called for, as this mulch also repels aphid predators, so any aphids that do land may multiply more rapidly. (The aluminum may also help plants grow larger, by reflecting more sunlight onto them.)

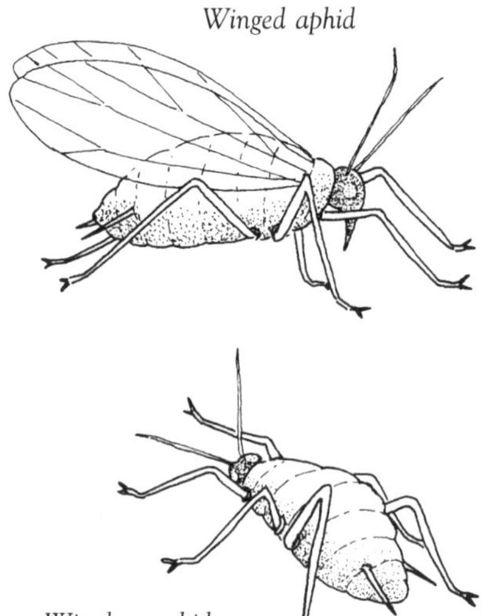

Winged aphid

Wingless aphid

Repelling flying aphids won't stop infestations that have already begun. If possible, crush aphids when you see them. If the aphids are lodged in places where it is difficult to crush them, or if you have many infested plants, wash them off with a strong spray from a garden hose. It won't do just to sprinkle the plants; you need to aim a fairly high-pressure nozzle from many directions to knock aphids from their niches. Support the leaves and flowers with your hand as you spray, to avoid injuring them. The force of the water often fatally injures the pests that have their feeding parts attached to the plants. A few that weren't feeding may survive to climb back onto the plant, requiring a repeat water spray, but it is rare for one treatment of any kind to get rid of aphids completely. If a single leaf or a whole plant seems to be hopelessly coated with aphids, you may choose to remove it rather than fight a losing battle.

Aphids have many natural enemies, so efforts to foster these will pay off. One reason to start with a spray of water is that this is least harmful to those natural enemies, which can then return and help you wipe out the survivors. Lady beetles, lacewings, syrphid flies, and others all eat aphids. You may see aphid "mummies" left by the parasitoid braconid wasp *Diaeretiella rapae*. These are puffed up, pale brown, dead aphids, eventually with a single round hole where the adult wasp emerged.

Ants protect aphids from their natural enemies. This is especially true of the Argentine ant, the small, dark reddish ant that comes into our houses so often. One way to get rid of the ants is to get rid of the aphids. If you have large populations of ants, consider using a boric acid bait, such as Drax. (Under no circumstance should you ever use a product called "ant chalk" that is sometimes available as an import from China. This product is illegal to use and is extremely toxic to humans.)

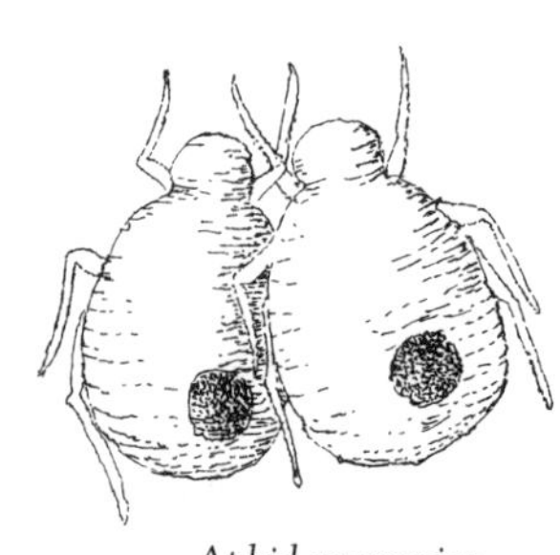

Aphid mummies

You may be able to get rid of aphids by using mechanical means like water sprays and removal of leaves or plants that have been overrun, to keep their populations low enough that natural enemies can do the rest. However, you may want to also use a chemical tactic against them. The least-toxic chemicals that will kill aphids are soap sprays (if you get a direct hit) and summer oils. Oils kill the eggs as well as the adults. Because the insects multiply rapidly, you may need to repeat your efforts on the order of once a week (read the label for exact timing). However, a single spraying with summer oil is sometimes enough. Other moderately toxic pesticides are labeled to control aphids, including neem and pyrethrum.

Artichoke Plume Moths

Often the first you will see of this pest is an unsightly, dark feeding trail in the scales or the heart of a harvested artichoke bud. If you are very observant, you may be warned earlier in the season, when irregular holes appear in the new leaves at the hearts of the plants. Sometimes you may see small light brown larvae in the damaged areas.

The moths responsible for this damage lay single eggs on the undersides of the lower leaves. The larvae feed first on the young shoots at the center of the plant and then move up to the flower buds. They pupate on the underside of the older, lower leaves and in the leaf litter. You may never see this pest, but if it attacks, it can make your artichokes pretty unappetizing.

To prevent artichoke plume moths, begin by cleaning up dying leaves and leaf litter. Divide the plants often enough that they do not become huge thickets, difficult to search for signs of the pest. Remove any nearby thistles, especially bull thistles, as they serve as alternate hosts for the pests.

Encourage native lacewings and parasitic wasps. These offer some help, although they alone can't control a serious plume moth outbreak. If the plume moth shows up, try breaking its life cycle by removing its food source part of the year. One way is to cut back your artichoke plants during the summer, removing or burying the trimmings. The other is to grow a variety, such as 'Imperial Star', that forms buds the first year; dig it under each fall and replant from seed. During an active infestation, you can apply beneficial nematodes, using a pressurized sprayer, once a week for three weeks, starting when the pale yellow or off-white larvae are ¼-inch long.

Cabbage Root Maggots

When a cabbage or other cole crop plant wilts even though it is well-watered, suspect the cabbage root maggot. Eventually, infested plants may actually fall over, since the maggots have bored through the roots just under the soil. Radishes and turnips have thicker roots, so they may not be killed by the pest, but they are ruined by the many wormholes with small white maggots inside.

Cabbage root maggots are the larvae of a small fly that lays its eggs next to plant stems. When the maggots hatch, they enter the soil and begin to feed on roots near the surface. After feeding for several weeks, they pupate, emerge as adults, and breed to begin another cycle. The first larvae appear as early as late March, and there will be several life cycles during the warmer months. In the fall, the year's last pupae rest for the winter in the soil, emerging as adults the following spring.

For years, I read about using tarpaper rings to protect seedlings from this pest. These didn't work, but I developed my own method, which works very well. I wrap the lower stems of the seedlings with paper or plastic tape, and then set the plants so that half of the wrapped part of the stem is above ground, half below. I have used strips of brown grocery bag paper, paper florist's tape (the kind used to wrap flower stems in a corsage), or a soft plastic tape, used in landscaping, known as flagging tape.

To make the wrap, you need at least 1 inch of bare stem—2 inches is even better. Remove the seed leaves and possibly a lower leaf, if you must (and if the seedling has several more). Push a finger gently into the potting mix at the plant base to gain an extra ¼ to ½ inch if you can. Cut the tape 2 to 3½ inches long. Start the wrap at the top, just below the lowest leaf, and turn the plant, wrapping firmly and slowly, diagonally downward. The wrap needs to hold in place, but should not be as tight as you can make it. (Practice on a pencil if you need to.) Plant immediately, holding the bottom of the tape in place, with half of the wrap buried and half above the ground. As the plant grows, it pushes aside the wrap. An occasional maggot finds its way through a wrap, but I lose vastly fewer plants than without it.

This method works fine as long as you are setting out transplants, but if you are sowing seed directly, as you always do radish or turnip, you can hardly wrap each stem. I'd read that wood ash in the soil would discourage root maggots, but when I mixed a large amount of wood ash into the first few inches of the soil where I planted turnips, root maggots still did a lot of damage. Instead, I've had good luck covering seedbeds with floating row covers, well tucked in at the edges. Row covers or row covers on wooden frames can also be used to cover whole beds of the larger cole plants.

Another strategy is to grow susceptible crops when the pest is inactive. If you need to get a cabbage family crop started in mid- or late summer, use one of the kinds of barriers just described until weather cools. Plant radishes unprotected in October through March in areas where winter weather permits. For "spring" cole crops, use short-season cabbage or broccoli, set out as early as possible. Transplant cabbage seedlings into your garden as early as January and broccoli seedlings in February, wrapping the stems as you transplant them for extra insurance. Even without the wraps, early planting can help, as these older cole crop plants are less likely to be killed by the maggots than younger, later planted ones. If you must plant in later spring, wait until late May or June, when there should be a letup of a few weeks' duration while the first spring generation pupates.

Remove any infested plants from the garden, digging into the soil to try to get all the pests that were in or near the root. Don't plant cabbage family crops in the same soil the following year.

Of the native predators, some small rove beetles eat cabbage root maggots, though they are not likely to provide control by themselves. You can help them out considerably by applying purchased predatory nematodes to your soil when you expect the first spring maggot generation. (See page 107 for a discussion of predatory nematodes and Appendix VII for sources.)

Cabbage Loopers and Imported Cabbageworms

When there are irregular holes in the leaves of your cabbage family plants, look for either of these voracious pests. Both are smooth, green caterpillars, from very tiny to over an inch long, depending on their age.

Cabbage loopers, the larvae of a brown moth, move inchworm-fashion, a style of locomotion known as looping. They grow to 1½ inches long, and have several fine, light lines down their sides and back. In addition to cabbage family plants, they may also eat beet, celery, lettuce, parsley, pea, potato, spinach, or tomato leaves.

Imported cabbageworms crawl without looping. They are the larvae of the white cabbage butterfly. This butterfly has opaque white wings with a couple of black dots and a wingspan of a little over an inch and a half. You will often see it fluttering about your garden in the warmer months. Cabbageworms grow to about 1¼ inches, are a velvety, light jade green, and may have faint orange or yellow stripes. They eat mainly plants in the cabbage family, including ornamental and weed species.

Both pests are common in this region, and one or both are almost certain to infest your cole crops. Both complete several generations in the spring and summer, overwintering in the soil as pupae, ready to strike again in the new year.

These caterpillars are most damaging when the plants are small, sometimes eating up whole seedlings. However, because the adult insects are inactive in cold weather, your earliest plantings of cabbage family plants may escape damage until they are quite mature, when the proportion of leaf damage is less significant. Then, midsummer and early fall plantings will need protection only until weather turns cool. It might be practical to use floating row cover on cole crop seedlings that are growing into the fall, removing it when the plants become larger and you no longer see cabbage butterflies in your garden.

In warmer weather, begin to inspect cole crop seedlings when they are quite small. Look for the pale yellow, dome-shaped eggs of the cabbage looper on the tops of leaves, and the pale yellow to orange, rocket-shaped eggs of the imported cabbageworm on the undersides of the leaves. If you crush the tiny eggs about every 5 days, neither of these caterpillars will be able to hatch. Also check for the young caterpillars by inspecting both sides of the leaves and the heart of the plant. The imported cabbageworms are hard to see because they are almost the same color as the leaves and can easily be mistaken for a leaf midrib. If you see deposits of greenish feces, you can surmise there is a caterpillar around somewhere. (While you are searching, you can also remove cutworms, slugs, and snails and crush any incipient aphid colonies.)

Cabbage white butterflies have chalky white wings.

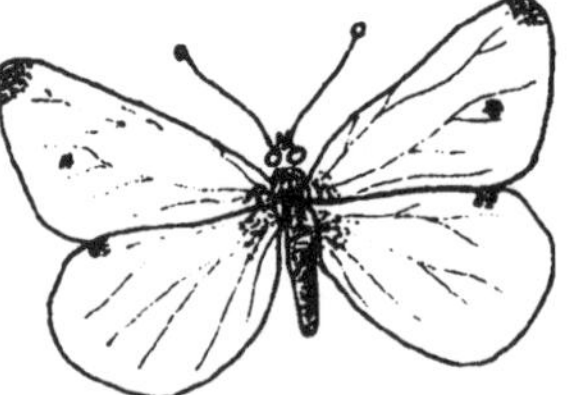

Both cabbage worms have a number of natural enemies, including tachinid flies, spiders, wasps, and yellow jackets, though these will not offer complete control. If you have a serious infestation and too many plants to handpick, you may want to use Bt berliner-kurstake (see page 107). Watch for the eggs on leaf undersides and begin to spray within a week of first spotting them, since Bt works best when the caterpillars are still small. Cover the leaves with spray, including the leaf undersides, and repeat as directed on the label. Both pests are also susceptible to neem and pyrethrum, although these shouldn't be necessary if you use Bt.

Cucumber Beetles

You may see either of two cucumber beetles in your garden. Both are shiny black beetles, about ¼-inch long, with markings on their wingcovers. The wingcovers of the western spotted cucumber beetle are yellow-green with twelve black spots, while those of the less common western striped cucumber beetle are yellowish with three black stripes. The adults do the most damage, chewing holes in leaves and flowers of many plants, but especially those of cucurbit crops, beans, and corn. They may also eat stone fruit, such as peaches or plums. The soil-dwelling cucumber beetle larvae eat roots. The larvae of the western spotted cucumber beetle feed on corn, sweet pea, and grasses. Those of the western striped cucumber beetle feed on cucurbit roots.

In the east, closely related cucumber beetles cause serious damage to cucurbit plants by spreading bacterial wilt disease. Neither western cucumber beetle species spreads wilt, but they can transmit cucumber mosaic virus. The adults can also cause serious damage to young cucurbit plants, though older plants are able to withstand some damage. The larvae of the western spotted cucumber beetle are less damaging to corn roots than are those of the spotted cucumber beetle common in the east. However, the larvae of the western striped cucumber beetle can seriously harm young cucurbit plants.

Both kinds of cucumber beetles overwinter as adults, most often in weeds outside your garden. In the spring they mate, and females lay eggs at the base of host plants. Larvae feed on the roots for a few weeks, then pupate and become adults. There are two or three generations a year.

If you see an occasional cucumber beetle, do handpick and destroy it. Also clean up plant litter and any fruit you don't intend to harvest, to reduce hiding places for the pest. If you only see one now and then, that is probably all you need to do.

Predatory nematodes applied at planting time will help somewhat in control of these pests, by reducing the number of larvae. Adults may be killed by neem or pyrethrum, but you will have to use either one repeatedly, since new adult beetles will continue to fly in from outside your garden. Probably the best protection is to cover young cucurbit plants with floating row cover until they are large enough to withstand some damage, removing them in time for bees to pollinate the flowers.

Cutworms

These pesky caterpillars kill seedlings by chewing through the stems of many kinds of vegetable and flower seedlings at the ground level. The seedlings fall over, and if they are very small, they may wilt so quickly that you think they simply vanished! There are many species of cutworms, including some that climb into older plants to feed. You don't often see them, because they feed at night, but you may turn them up when you are digging the soil. I have also found them living in deep pockets they have eaten into young cabbage heads. These up-to-2-inch-long, fat, puffy, caterpillars roll into a tight "C" shape when they are resting. They may be gray or brown, often with mottled markings, or may be nearly black. Their pupae, which you may find in your soil, are golden-brown, torpedo-shaped, and usually about ¾ inch long. Cutworms are the larvae of several species of drab-colored, night-flying moths. After passing through several generations in the warm part of a year, they overwinter in the soil as eggs, larvae, or pupae, depending on the species.

In truth, while gardening books are full of dire warnings about these pests, they have never been numerous in my gardens. However, if you find they are causing problems, you may want to protect transplanted seedlings with half-buried protective rings made from toilet paper, paper towel tubes, or yogurt cups with their bottoms cut out.

Bacillis thuringiensis kurstake will kill cutworms, but the trick is to get them to eat some before they find your plants. Old books suggested making a bait by mixing one or two parts by weight of Bt into bran or apple pomace (the stuff left over after making apple cider). Perhaps a better solution is to use Sluggo Plus, a new formulation of the original snail bait that now includes the bacteria-derived active ingredient spinosad. Predatory nematodes will also help control cutworms.

Earwigs

The European earwig (*Forficula auricularia*) is a glossy, dark brown insect, up to .6 inches long. Because of the "pincers" on its rear end, it is often called a "pincerbug." We are assured by entomologists that the pincers are not weapons with which to pinch us, though they do look threatening.

Earwigs damage plants by eating leaves and flower petals. They even eat corn silks, sometimes ending a hope for sweet corn. Earwigs eat fallen petals and other plant debris and will also eat other insects. (It is said they eat aphids in apple trees, including woolly apple aphids.) In small numbers, earwigs may not threaten our crops, but if they become numerous, they can cause great damage.

Female earwigs, which you can identify by the fact they have smaller pincers than the males, lay 50 to 90 eggs in winter just under the soil surface. When the nymphs hatch, in late winter or early spring, the females bring them out at night to take them to food. At first, the nymphs look like tiny ants, but by May they are recognizable as small earwigs. Females may lay a second batch of eggs while the first nymphs are still small, and they help them get started finding food too. Last year's earwigs die by midsummer to be replaced by newly maturing adults.

Damage by earwigs is usually worst in spring, as hordes of hungry nymphs mature and find newly cleared gardens planted with tender seedlings. At this time of year, gardeners often attribute to slugs and snails damage that was actually caused by earwigs. The earwigs feed at night, hiding by day under the soil, in garden debris, or deep in plant crevices. You may need a night visit to your garden with a flashlight to confirm that they are to blame.

You will probably always have some earwigs in your garden, but you can reduce populations to levels that will keep damage low, and the best time to do it is from early spring to midsummer.

Start by cleaning up places they love to hide, such as piles of plastic pots or empty soil amendment bags. If you find earwigs, you can shake them from objects held over a bucket of soapy water, or shake them onto pavement and step on them (a bit of energy is required for this, but it can be done). You may also find earwigs living in fruit or ornamental trees, vines, or weedy areas. Thinning too-thick growth in trees will reduce cover for the pests.

Traps made of rolled damp newspaper held with a rubber band, or pieces of bamboo, will attract earwigs, but must be emptied daily or they will serve as earwig houses. Shake them over soapy water or put them in a plastic bag. (Freeze the plastic bag; then you can compost the insects if you like.) To trap earwigs in a way that doesn't require daily attention, you can put a half-inch of beer or oil in a shallow container. Such a trap can catch up to 50 earwigs a night, clearing from approximately a square yard. Either sink a tuna can so that its rim is even with the soil surface or use a cottage cheese-type container with a lid. The lid helps if cats or raccoons are about. Cut two or three ½-inch holes halfway up the sides of the container, sink it to the level of the holes, and put the lid on. Snails and slugs don't seem very interested in beer in my garden, but earwigs walk right in.

European earwig adult

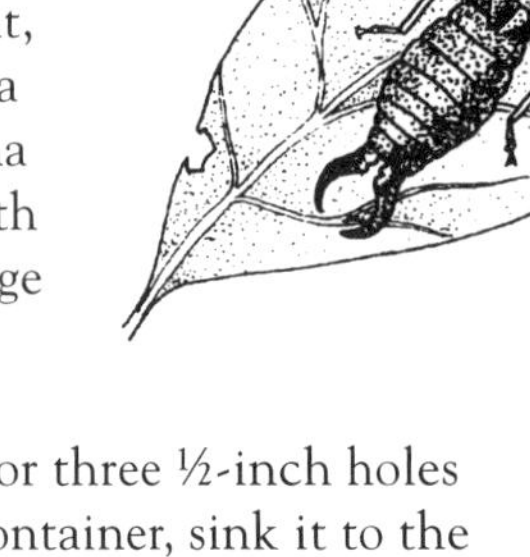

The major predator of European earwigs is said to be a tachinid fly (*Bigonicheta spinipennis*). I haven't see those, but I have seen an earwig in the web of a pale yellow crab spider and have watched one being eaten by a daddy longlegs spider. A friend has observed a cricket eating an earwig.

Earwigs are listed on the label of Sluggo Plus, an iron phosphate formulation with the bacterial insecticide spinosin that also kills snails, slugs, pill bugs and sow bugs, and cutworms.

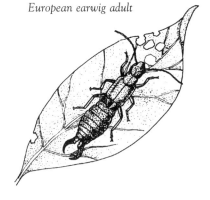

Flea Beetles

If you have flea beetles, numerous tiny holes will appear in the leaves of affected plants. On examination, you will see small insects, reminiscent of fleas, leaping around the leaves. They may be black, dark green, or various other colors. They may be particularly serious on seedlings or may attack older plants as well.

Of the several species of flea beetles, some are highly selective, while others attack a wide variety of plants. Taking all of the common species into account, many garden crops are susceptible, including all nightshade family crops, spinach, beets, sunflower, pumpkin, cabbage, and radish. Flea beetle larvae may feed on leaves or may live in the soil, feeding on the roots of the preferred plants. The adults overwinter in the soil or in garden debris, then lay eggs. The pest may complete more than one generation each summer.

These pests are more common inland; for example, in Berkeley and in the warmer inland areas of San Mateo and Sonoma counties. I have seen only one kind in San Francisco, a black species that feeds on arugula and radish—possibly the western black flea beetle. It appears only in the summer, allowing me to grow unblemished arugula and radish in spring and fall, though I will eat arugula with minor damage. If you have flea beetle damage, clean up garden debris, especially in the winter, so there are fewer hiding places for adults. Control weeds, particularly those in the same plant family as the affected crop plants. If the pests damage transplants, use large, well-hardened-off seedlings, and give plants very adequate supplies of fertilizer and water, for if they are healthy and fast-growing they can often survive the insect's attacks. Cover susceptible transplants or seedbeds with floating row cover until they are large enough to tolerate some damage.

If the flea beetle in your garden has soil-dwelling larvae, cultivate the surface frequently to disturb eggs and larvae. You may also see some improvement if you apply beneficial nematodes to the soil. But you will need to learn when the larvae are in the soil, to be sure you are applying the control in time. For help identifying the species you have, and to learn more about its life cycle, try calling the Cooperative Extension service. Be sure you can report all of the affected crops, and try to study the pest long enough that you can describe it. In the past, flea beetles have been controlled with pyrethrum, rotenone, and various synthetic pesticides. Rotenone is less used these days, as we understand more about its toxicity to humans. Pyrethrum is still an alternative. Several trials of spinosad have shown good results, though in 2009 it was not yet registered for use against flea beetles.

Leafminers

Gray, light green, or brown trails or blotches will appear on the leaves of vegetables or flowers when you have leafminers. If you hold a damaged leaf up to the light, you can often see shadows of the small insects inside the leaves, feeding between the layers. Sometimes the pests have already left the leaves, but you will still see their frass, or feces, as dark shadows.

Leafminers are the larvae of various small flies. The serpentine leafminer eats winding tunnels in the leaves of many vegetables and flowers. Another, the beet leafminer, eats irregular blotches in leaves of beets, chard, spinach and the related weed, lambsquarters. The beet leafminer adult fly lays small clusters of tiny white eggs on the undersides of leaves. After the larvae eat and grow in the leaves, the pupae emerge through holes and fall to the ground to finish maturing. Their life span is highly variable but may take as little as a month, which allows several generations to develop each season. Leafminers are usually only a minor problem, disfiguring a few leaves rather than destroying plants. However, if you ignore them long enough for a reservoir of pupae to build up in the soil, they can become quite serious pests.

As soon as you notice leafminer damage, either pinch the leaves to kill the visible larvae or pick the affected leaves and remove them from the garden. Also remove dead leaves and debris under affected plants. If you are plagued by the beet leafminer, grow susceptible plants in the late summer so that they mature in the fall and winter when this pest is less active. A February planting might also escape damage long enough for a crop to be harvested young. Remove lambsquarters from gardens where beet leafminers are a problem, and till the soil in the fall to kill overwintering pupae. Floating row cover is a good means of avoiding damage to late summer transplants until cool weather kills the flies (in October in San Francisco) or to let an early spring planting mature past late March.

Natural enemies, such as parasitic wasps, often are fairly effective in keeping leafminers from becoming serious pests. In fact, leafminer outbreaks often follow use of chemical pesticides that kill these wasps.

Chemical control of leafminers has been difficult for vegetable gardeners in the past, since the chemicals that could be used on food crops didn't kill the eggs or larvae hidden inside the leaves. There are now a few more options; however, if you have a bad infestation of these pests, spraying to control them is going to be quite time-consuming, so you may prefer to rotate away from susceptible crops in the warm months for a couple of years. Summer oil sprays will smother the eggs if applied before they hatch. A good time to use this method is in late March, when the first spring eggs are laid, to gain a few weeks for a spring crop. The botanical pesticide neem oil kills all stages of the pest and repels them for up to several weeks, but will need reapplying if the leaves get wet or as new leaves form on fast-growing crops. Spinosad is also registered to control leafminers.

Onion Maggots

When onions or shallots are stunted, yellowing, and dying, pull one of the plants and check for onion maggots. These quarter-inch white maggots are the larvae of a small gray fly. The pest is more active in cool coastal climates, where it is relatively common.

In the spring, the first generation of female adult flies lays tiny, elongated white eggs on the soil nearby. As onions mature, the flies may lay eggs in the leaf joints. Each of the year's several generations of maggots matures by eating into onion bulbs, often introducing decay, and then forming dark brown pupae in the soil. The final generation overwinters as pupae.

Shallots are perhaps most susceptible, followed by, in order, white onions, yellow onions, and red onions. Leeks, walking onions, onion lilies, garlic chives, and chives seem not to be affected.

Crop rotation can help prevent damage by this pest. Rotate onions or shallots with crops in other plant families. Make sure there is no manure that has aged less than six months in the soil where you are about to plant susceptible crops. In fact, you should avoid adding any organic matter at this planting, since this seems to help the maggots survive. At the end of the season, remove all onions from the garden, even ones that flowered or were otherwise not harvestable.

Turn the soil in the fall to kill pupae, and turn the soil a couple of weeks before you plant susceptible crops. The insect has some natural enemies, including parasitic wasps, a parasitic fungus, and birds, but these may not be active in this area. Beneficial nematodes, applied to the soil in spring when soil has warmed, have shown some effectiveness against onion maggots. Try the species *Steinernema feltiae*, which has shown greater effectiveness against maggots. (See page 107 for more on predatory nematodes.)

Covering a seeded bed with row cover or screening can prevent early damage. Row covers could be used during the entire period the crop is in the ground, though this might be rather inconvenient.

Spittlebugs

Every spring, gardeners notice small blobs of white foam, like spittle, on their plants. These are caused by the nymphs, or immature stages, of an insect known as a froghopper. A nymph secretes the bubbles in which to hide from predators while it sucks sap from the leaves. The tiny green nymphs—which do look a bit froggy, with their big heads and eyes—mature into insects similar to leafhoppers. These insects don't do serious harm to plants, but they can cause distorted leaves, making edibles such as parsley rather unappetizing. If you wash them off with a hose a couple of times a week, damage will be minimal, and in a month or so they will disappear until the following spring.

Tomato or Tobacco Hornworms

These large caterpillars devour tomato and other nightshade family plants. Once you see one, it is unmistakable: up to four inches long, light green with diagonal white markings on its sides, and an upright curved "horn" at its rear end. However, these very markings camouflage the creature down among the leaves until it has eaten many of them. The caterpillars tend to start eating in the center of the plant, where you won't notice, and work outward, eventually eating whole branches and even green or ripe fruit. They remain so well hidden at first that you might notice their large black droppings under the plant before you actually see an insect.

Tomato hornworms and tobacco hornworms do the same thing in a garden, but you can tell them apart, if you like, by the horn, which is black on a tomato hornworm and red on a tobacco hornworm. (Seems backwards, doesn't it?) Both are larvae of large, mostly brown moths known as sphinx moths.

In areas where they are common, hornworms may descend upon tomato plants in large numbers. However, they are so uncommon near the coast that I have seen only about five of them, and those one at a time, in the years I've gardened in San Francisco. Still, because a hornworm can eat quite a bit in a single night once it puts on any size, you will want to watch for this pest wherever you garden.

Handpicking is often sufficient to control hornworms. When they are present in large numbers, they may be controlled by spraying the plants with the bacterium *Bacillus thuringiensis kurstake* (Bt), although this works best while the caterpillars are still small. A naturally occurring braconid wasp parasitizes hornworms by laying eggs in them. The wasp larvae feed on the hornworm, then pupate in white cocoons, which protrude from the parasitized caterpillar. I have never seen such a parasitized hornworm here, but should you ever see one, do leave it alone so the hatching wasps can attack other hornworms too. Lady beetles, lacewings, and trichogramma wasps will all help with control by eating hornworm eggs.

Whiteflies

You know you have whiteflies when you see tiny, snow-white, winged insects clustering on the underside of leaves and fluttering about when disturbed. The infested leaves may turn yellow or seem dry and slightly curled. On careful inspection you may see small shiny spots on the undersides of the leaves. These are the larvae—flat, immobile discs fastened tightly to the plant. Whitefly adults and their larvae both suck plant juices. Beans, tomatoes, cucumbers, and squash are common host plants, especially when these plants have been given too much nitrogen fertilizer or are growing in otherwise poor conditions. The same whitefly species that feed on vegetables may also feed on ornamental garden plants. There are several other species, including some that infest citrus.

While just a few whiteflies do little harm, they reproduce quickly, and heavy infestations weaken or kill plants. On woody plants or on severely infested herbaceous plants, whiteflies create the conditions that favor development of sooty mold, as do aphids (see the aphid listing).

Whiteflies lay eggs on the undersides of leaves. These hatch into "crawlers," which crawl around for up to two days, then settle down to become immobile larvae. (Larvae lack legs and antennae and are covered by a waxy shield, all traits they share with scale insects.) Whiteflies can complete a life cycle, from egg to adult, in 30 days, and will complete several overlapping cycles in a summer season. The plants are soon infested with a mixture of adults, larvae, crawlers, and egg cases. Most control methods work on only some of these stages, making control difficult. If an annual vegetable plant has become heavily infested, it may be easier to pull it, clean up its debris, and discard all of it. But you can probably bring a light or moderate infestation under control.

Check lower leaves for early signs of whiteflies, and remove the leaves if you see the pest. When infestations are very light, you can hold them down by treating both sides of the plants' leaves with a strong spray of water once a week. You can also use yellow sticky traps to monitor for the presence of this pest and to control light outbreaks, although be aware that this method removes only adults, leaving eggs, crawlers, and larvae. To have any effect, you will need to use one trap for every two large plants.

Some gardeners use a small vacuum cleaner to remove adult whiteflies from plants. While this could be very satisfying, it, like sticky traps, removes adults only, so at best, it would have to be repeated every few days to have any hope of reducing the population. Still, if you have such a tool, you might want to use it in combination with other tactics.

Among natural enemies that feed on whiteflies are several small lady beetles, orius bugs, lacewings, and several parasites. The parasitic wasp *Encarsia formosa* is available commercially for control of whiteflies in greenhouses, but it is not recommended for outdoor use, since it probably won't survive outdoor temperatures.

Among chemical controls that kill whiteflies, soap spray and summer oils are the least disruptive to the environment. Apply either to the undersides of leaves every 4 to 6 days until control is achieved. Use caution in applying soap spray, as a high concentration is suggested for whitefly control and may damage some plants. Try a little at first, wait 48 hours, and if there is no damage, proceed. The botanical pesticide neem is effective against all life stages of whiteflies. It is best to avoid use of other chemical controls, as whiteflies tend to rapidly develop resistance to most pesticides.

Wireworms (Click Beetles)

Wireworms are leathery, pale yellow larvae, ½ to ¾ inches long, that turn up when you are digging the soil. They have a yellow-brown band at each end. They eat roots and tubers, killing young plants or stunting larger ones. They may attack root crops, potatoes, cabbage, corn, beans, lettuce, or onions. You might find one actually tunneling in a root crop or in potatoes, but it is more likely that you will just find them loose in the soil.

Wireworms are the larvae, or grubs, of the click beetle. You may also turn up pupae and adult click beetles. The pupae are pale yellow and you can see their developing beetle-like features—legs, wings, and so on. The adults are narrow brown beetles, up to about ¾ inch long, that snap their bodies, making small clicking sounds when they are on their backs, trying to turn upright again.

If you just see a wireworm or click beetle now and then while you are digging, the damage is probably not severe, but destroy any you find. Also turn the soil anytime between midsummer and fall, whenever you are between crops, to destroy larvae and pupae that would otherwise overwinter. If you have a severe problem, dig the soil once a week for four to six weeks. Also amend your soil well, as the pest may be more severe in poorly drained soil.

Potatoes or carrots have been suggested as a trap for wireworms. I tried putting cut grocery store potatoes an inch or so under the surface, with a stick inserted in the potato to mark the spot. I waited the prescribed two days, and up to a week; however, the wireworms in my garden were not attracted to this bait. Predatory nematodes should reduce the wireworm population (see page 107).

OTHER INVERTEBRATE PESTS

Mites

There are many species of pest mites. They attack a variety of food-bearing plants, from tomatoes to citrus. These spider relatives suck plant juices, eventually causing woody plants to drop their leaves, and often killing herbaceous plants. Typical symptoms are dull-colored leaves, stippled with pale dots. In some cases the leaf undersides, or entire leaves, may be covered with a dirty-looking web. A magnifying lens will reveal tiny yellow, orange, green, black, or red creatures in the webbing. Or if you tap the leaves over a piece of white paper, the mites will fall onto it. You will see tiny specks that start to crawl about.

While mites are most common in hot, dry areas, you may see them in cooler coastal gardens, especially on plants that are underwatered. They are also common on plants grown indoors. In local gardens, I have seen spider mites on tomatoes, beans, squash, eggplants, strawberries, and raspberries.

Pest mites are preyed upon by native predatory mites as well as by the six-spotted thrips, the larvae of certain flies, the orius bug, and lacewings. Another natural enemy of mites is the spider mite destroyer, a 1⁄16-inch-long black lady beetle. Using pesticides that harm these natural enemies can result in increased numbers of pest mites.

Dusty, underwatered plants are more likely to attract pest mites, and underwatering will reduce the plants' resistance to them. If you have an infestation, begin by washing the plants down with water, on both sides of the leaves. Repeat this every 5 to 7 days. If paths are dusty, applying a woodchip mulch to them will reduce blowing dust. Also make sure the plants are growing in adequately watered soil. This may reduce mite numbers enough, but if not, you can apply soap or summer oil spray, following label instructions.

Several species of predatory mites are available for purchase and may be worth getting if you have mites in several fruit trees or other extensive infestation. When you consult a supplier, they will usually try to determine which pest mite you need to control. They may ask you what plant is affected and whether it is growing indoors or out.

Mites are one of the creatures whose infestations have definitely become worse since the advent of pesticides. Pest mites have become resistant to many pesticides, and these chemicals unfortunately do kill mite predators. Sevin (Carbaryl), in particular, kills mite predators while sparing the pest. This stimulates increased reproduction of the mites, so mite outbreaks often follow Sevin applications.

If mites have become a severe problem on annual vegetable crops, as they can in a neglected garden, I strongly suggest you pull all the unhealthy and infested plants, clean up the infected debris, and replant with a less susceptible crop.

I suspect that many local tomato plant deaths blamed on disease are really caused by a mite called the tomato russet mite. Infested plants have a yellowish or bronzed, greasy look. To identify these tiny mites, you need at least a 15× hand lens, and a 30× microscope would be even better. Tomato russet mites are shaped like longish cones, with legs at the wider (front) end. They are yellowish, tan, or pink. If you are using a strong enough hand lens, you can often see larger, faster-moving, predator mites hurrying among the russet mites, devouring them. The predator mites have the more typical spiderlike shape, with four legs on each side.

It's best, in controlling tomato russet mites, to avoid killing the predator mites, since these can keep low populations of pest mites in check. An effective precaution, where russet mites have occurred before, is to apply sulfur dust (or spray) once, when plants are large but have no symptoms yet, and once again in three to four weeks if symptoms appear. Also, remove any tomato debris from your garden at the end of summer and don't let other nightshade family crops or weeds overwinter either. Purchased predatory mites, *Phytoseiulus persimilis*, will help control tomato russet mites, which are also susceptible to the botanical pesticide neem.

Nematodes

Nematodes generally stunt plants, and may also cause lumpy roots, discolored or bumpy leaves, or various other malformations. Nematodes are tiny, primitive worms that either attach themselves to plants and suck sap, or live inside them. They are unrelated to earthworms. While most kinds of nematodes prefer warmer climates, some kinds may live in our area, and could attack your crops.

Root knot nematodes, which are fairly common in this region, attack many kinds of plants, including carrots, tomatoes, and squash. They live on the roots, causing them to develop lumpy swellings and causing carrots to fork. The pest is more common in sandy soils than in other kinds and more common in warm soil.

Another common type, the stem and bulb nematode, attacks all allium crops, miner's lettuce, parsley, celery, salsify, and daffodils. You can identify an infestation by rubbing the leaves with your fingers to feel any rough spots. Affected onion plants will be stunted. If you cut the bulb in half crosswise, there will be dark rings in it. The basal portion of the bulb becomes swollen and spongy and may separate from the bulb.

A third kind, the cyst nematode, attacks cole crops, causing stunted plants. Also, they cause plants that would have ripened all at once to have a staggered harvest.

A number of kinds of nematodes damage roots, but do not leave readily identifiable symptoms. Even root knots, though identifiable as nematode damage, do not tell you which root-knot nematode you have. Stunting, the most common symptom of nematodes, could have several other causes. Before you jump to the conclusion that nematodes did it, consider whether your stunted plants might have lacked water, fertilizer, soil aeration, or sunlight. Try to improve any growing conditions that might not be optimum.

If you still strongly suspect nematodes are causing your problems, ask a Cooperative Extension office for information about having your soil tested in a nematology lab. Once you find out which kind, or kinds, of nematodes you have, you can ask about specific control techniques.

Nematodes often enter a garden in soil surrounding plants from other gardens. While nursery soil is probably pest-free, the soil in your friend's yard may not be, so accept gift plants with caution. When nematodes do enter a garden, they generally appear in one part of it first. Because they move only a few feet a year on their own, it is possible to keep them from spreading to your whole garden. Take care not to move plants or soil from infested to clean areas. On any particular day, work the infested area last. After working where nematodes are active, clean your tools with a forceful jet of water, then with 1 part household bleach in 9 parts water. Don't let the wash water run back into your garden.

If nematodes have become a problem in your garden, you will probably need to combine several methods to keep them at a level that allows you to grow crops. When you know which species of nematodes you have, you can often reduce their numbers by planning a rotation of nonsusceptible crops and resistant crop varieties.

Do keep the level of soil organic matter high, adding 3 to 4 inches a year. This stimulates natural enemies of nematodes, including soil bacteria and fungi.

Plant as early as possible to give crops a chance to grow large before the pest becomes active. When you pull any plant, assume nematodes are feeding on its roots, and remove them as well. Remove infested crop plants from the garden.

If the infestation is severe, you might want to try leaving half of your garden fallow each year. This will reduce root-knot nematode infestation in the fallow half by 80 to 90 percent. If you rotate garden halves each year, you should be able to have a garden that, though half the size, has only minimal damage.

During the fallow, don't let anything grow in the area unless you know it is immune to the nematodes you have. This generally means bare soil, with even weeds hoed out while tiny. You can grow an immune cover crop, but only if you keep weeds out of it.

If you are using a bare soil fallow, keeping it watered will increase its effectiveness, though this will encourage weeds, and so increase the work of hoeing them out. Solarization during all or part of a fallow will also further reduce nematode populations, if you live in a microclimate warm enough for this technique to work (see page 149).

Marigolds can help reduce certain root-knot nematodes, but it will not help at all to just scatter them here and there among your crops. First, you must know which kind of nematode you have. (Marigolds are not effective against the northern root-knot nematode, for example.) If you have a susceptible nematode, plant the entire infested area solidly with French marigolds, *Tagetes patula*, for an entire season, being careful not to let anything else grow there.

Organic gardeners who are trying to combat plant parasitic nematodes without resorting to highly toxic soil chemicals will be interested in new research. The predatory nematode *Steinernema riobravis* (not a commonly sold species) has shown itself to be effective against root-knot nematodes. There are also several products based on various bacteria that show promise. Neem Cake, the material left after extracting the neem pesticide, is sold as a soil supplement but also may have some activity against plant parasitic nematodes. If you have a clear diagnosis, it will be worth your while to seek more information on current research.

Snails and Slugs

These pests should be strong suspects when your seedlings are partly or entirely eaten and your larger plants have holes in the leaves. However, other pests, such as earwigs or birds, could be the culprits. To convict snails or slugs, look for shiny slime trails on the plants or on the soil. Then hunt for snails, which hide on smooth plant leaves or on other flat surfaces, or slugs, which hide in moist crevices in plants, as well as on and in the soil.

Most of the snails that plague our gardens are the brown garden snail (*Helix aspersa*), which was imported to Oakland from France in the 1850s to serve as a food source. It is, indeed, edible, being the smaller of the two French snail species used as escargots. Several other nonnative snails, large and small, are active in our region, but are much less numerous. Snails do not reach large populations in wild, unwatered California habitats, but in our gardens, summer water produces year-round food, and brown garden snails, in particular, often become very numerous. Among our common slugs, there are both native and European species. The non-native species of both snails and slugs are helped in their successful multiplication by the fact that they don't have a full component of natural enemies here in California.

While beginning gardeners are often reluctant to kill snails and slugs, when these mollusks are numerous, they can cause quite a bit of damage. They are particularly damaging to seedlings and so can wipe out a newly planted garden. They are also fond of peas, beans, lettuce, and basil of any age; they will eat cabbage family plants, and cucumber or squash seedlings when they are young enough not to have prickly leaves. A single snail or slug can easily eat a transplanted cucumber or cabbage seedling in one night. (Check individual crop listings for more information about susceptibility to snails and slugs.)

Snails and slugs feed all year and breed in the warm season. Snails are hermaphroditic, each individual animal capable of laying eggs. Slugs are either hermaphroditic or change sex as they mature. Both lay eggs just under the soil surface. Those of snails look like pearly white BBs, while those of slugs are smaller and more transparent. From midsummer to fall, you will find many young snails and slugs in your garden. In spring, you will find midsized and mature individuals. Snails live for several years.

Beginning gardeners often prefer hands-off methods of snail and slug control, such as barriers, traps, or bait. While these methods can help, when you have a lot of these pesky mollusks, a hands-on approach is usually required at the beginning and must usually be repeated periodically to keep the situation under control.

Your first step in controlling both pesky mollusks should be a thorough garden cleanup. Your goal should be to remove as many snails and slugs as you can find and to reduce the areas in which they can hide. You can do this through a combination of nighttime and daytime searches. It is wise to begin your control efforts before summer's warmth begins the mating and egg-laying period.

Visits to your garden after about 10 p.m. will reveal snails and slugs out of their hiding places and actively feeding. If you repeat hunts for several nights in a row, you will make a dramatic difference. You can also find quite a few snails and slugs still out on wet or foggy mornings—good news for the early-to-bed, early-to-rise crowd.

In addition, you will want to do some daytime hunts, to discover the places your snails and slugs are hiding all day.

Snails spend their days glued to smooth, dry surfaces in shady spots. They might choose a broad-leaved plant, a fence, or a flowerpot. They are especially attracted to plants with strap-like leaves, such as lily-of-the-Nile, leeks, and irises. (Their only means of self protection is to draw into their shells and drop into the underbrush when they feel vibrations, so you will learn to reach for them quickly, before they feel the plants move.) They even climb trees in their nightly forays, then cling to the bark in the daytime.

You should be able to eliminate some snail hiding places, such as weedy undergrowth covering the edges of raised bed frames, but you can't expect to eliminate every hiding place. You won't want to pull your leek crop, for example, or take out the vine that makes your fence a shady refuge. But once you know which areas in your garden attract snails, you can hunt for them there. Continue to search snail hiding places, daily if possible, until your catch becomes noticeably smaller. Then continue hunts of their favorite hiding places once a week. Don't stop handpicking; keep it as a part of your ongoing control program even if you use other methods as well. It's your most effective weapon.

Slugs, which are much like snails, but without shells, have similar habits, except that they like moister hiding places. Clean them out as you clean out snails, just looking deeper for them into any moist crevices. While you will find many of your garden's slugs this way, they will be easier to miss than the snails. Some dig several inches into the soil, not even coming up every night to feed, so any hunting or trapping method you use for slugs must be repeated every few days for several weeks. If your garden adjoins a natural area, you may find dramatically large, yellow native banana slugs in your garden. They are rarely numerous, and the best idea is probably to carry them a distance into the natural area and release them.

Beginning gardeners find it difficult to believe that they can control snails and slugs effectively simply by handpicking. One San Francisco gardener found this out by a roundabout route. One day a man I didn't know asked me what to do about his rampant and destructive snails. I suggested he search for and remove them, but he was reluctant and seemed discouraged. So I suggested he pay his small son to collect snails for him. Several years later, when he was hired to edit the SLUG newsletter, David Gilden reported the following story: He hadn't liked my second idea either, but, afraid that he would never have a successful garden, he negotiated to pay his son five cents per snail. His son was so zealous and his garden's snails so numerous that David soon realized the catches were proving too expensive. Driven by a need to economize, he began to hunt snails himself when his son wasn't home. Working together (sort of!), father and son soon brought the snail population down to quite manageable proportions—and his garden thrived.

As for the snails and slugs you collect, think of them as potential fertilizer. Crushed and buried, they add valuable nutrients to your soil. (Tossing them over the fence is not only rude, but doesn't work, since they are capable of crawling back the same night. And throwing them against the fence is likely to only injure them, so that later you will be collecting the same snails, but with healed-over shell cracks.)

In summer, you will probably uncover snail or slug eggs from time to time while you are digging in your garden. To prevent them from hatching, it is sufficient to spread them on a dry surface.

A step beyond searching out sites where snails and slugs hide or lay eggs is creating traps. Black plastic, wooden boards, and either clay or plastic flowerpots all work. Arrange them to provide shady hiding places for snails or moister hiding places for slugs. Empty them daily if possible, but at least every couple of days.

Various barriers can stop snails or slugs. Gardening books often tout substances you spread on the soil surface around plants in hopes that snails and slugs won't climb over them. Wood ash, diatomaceous earth, rice hulls, and cedar sawdust are examples. These may work for a while, but become less effective when you water the plants, wetting the barrier material. Also, even when fresh, they may not stop the pests if the seedling in the middle is a favorite, or if you have not reduced your population by handpicking first.

Snails and slugs do not like to crawl on copper, which does to them something akin to what a metal fork does to us when it touches a metal tooth filling. You can purchase copper strips to fasten around planter boxes, wooden frames of raised beds, or tree trunks. To make the barrier most daunting, get the 4-inch-wide strip with flaps, attach it flaps up, and bend them outward. Be sure all of the pests are out of the enclosed area. Be aware that snails and slugs will take another route to get to your plants if they can find it. For example, they will climb a fence and then an overhanging tree branch, or will climb weeds that are growing over the copper strip. Copper snail strips do not work well as free-standing barriers, simply stuck into the ground around a plant or plants, because plants overgrow them too quickly.

Floating row cover is sometimes the best barrier to protect the most susceptible seedlings. I use bubbles of row cover to protect seedlings of cucumbers until they get a few prickly leaves, as well as peas and basil. I may use a wooden frame covered with row cover to protect basil until it is about 8 inches high, after which it can fend for itself, or even to grow a small planting of bok choy to maturity. See page 49 for more information about using row cover.

Baited traps may help you in your efforts to prevent snail and slug damage. There are commercial traps, with baits based on the fact that yeast or beer may attract the pests. The idea is to drown them rather than use poisonous baits. The traps you set up for earwigs (see page 117) may also trap snails and slugs, though mine usually do not.

We do get some help controlling slugs and snails from resident mammals, birds, and reptiles, including raccoons, opossums, rats, ravens, and garter snakes. The California slender salamander eats small snails and slugs. There is one insect predator in many of our gardens that, like the snail, came from Europe. It is a large black rove beetle, *Ocypus olens*, described on page 103. Though these are alarming in appearance, protecting them will pay off.

Another European predator, the decollate snail, has been introduced into some Southern California orchards to prey on brown garden snails. However, it is illegal to release it outside of certain Southern California counties, and also not in your self-interest to do so, since it also feeds on tender plant leaves and earthworms.

Domestic ducks are a possible biological control, as they are fond of snails and probably will eat slugs as well. But they need to be penned, because they are also fond of vegetables. (When ours nibbled our corn silks, that was the last straw!) And be sure the duck pen can be secured against raccoons at night, as these predators will kill ducks. You can pen ducks in temporary enclosures while they eat pests, or carry snails to them. Children often enjoy feeding snails to ducks, and in fact sometimes need to be given a daily limit to avoid overfeeding them. Chickens can be taught to eat snails too, but you may have to crush the shells of the larger ones for them.

Finally, I must mention human beings as potential snail predators. Should you be fond of escargots, or develop a taste for them, you can eat your garden's snails. If you plan to do so, do not use toxic baits. You will need to keep snails you plan to eat in a cage briefly while their digestive tracts clean out. (See references in Appendix VIII, Suggested Reading, for a source for complete details.)

Salting slugs and snails will kill them; however, it isn't a good strategy because salt is toxic to plants. If you sprinkle it on too many pest mollusks, you might add a lethal amount to your soil.

For many years, the main lethal baits available to combat snails and slugs were based on the active ingredient metaldehyde or on metaldehyde plus carbaryl. The ones with carbaryl would also kill earwigs, sow and pill bugs, and, unfortunately, earthworms. Both active ingredients were hazardous to humans and pets. Now, new baits have been developed that are less toxic to mammals and other nontargeted creatures in the environment.

Recently developed baits consist of iron phosphate in a flour base. This kills snails and slugs, but is relatively nonhazardous to people, pets, or the environment. If it isn't eaten by a mollusk, and so breaks down in the soil, the small amount of iron phosphate becomes a fertilizer. While depending on bait alone is a poor idea, since snails will eat a lot of plants on their way to finding bait, these less-toxic baits can have a place in even an organic gardener's snail management plan.

Remember, though, that this is a bait, so don't put it up around your tender seedlings. Sprinkle it at perimeters of beds or gardens, or in unsearchable areas you don't want to remove, such as groundcover, to intercept snails and slugs. Follow directions on the label carefully.

A new formulation—not yet approved for organic farmers at this writing, but likely to be—contains both iron phosphate and the bacterially derived pesticide Spinosad. The label for this bait includes earwigs, sow and pill bugs, and cutworms.

Pill Bugs or Sow Bugs

These gray, many-legged and many-segmented creatures crawl about on the soil and on decaying debris. They look almost alike and both reach a ½ inch in length, but they are two separate species. The species that can roll into a ball is known as a pill bug, the one that can't is called a sow bug. Both species are also sometimes called wood lice or potato bugs. They are not lice or bugs, but crustaceans, like shrimp.

These two species have very similar habits. They must live in moist places, and they eat mostly decaying plant matter. However, they may eat actively growing parts of plants if there isn't enough of their favorite food around. This is especially likely in two cases. One is in the late summer and fall, since their population has been increasing all summer. When summer's plants are starting to die, pill and sow bugs may climb up into them to eat decaying parts. They may also munch strawberries and young zucchini squash in the fall, when these fruits are maturing slowly. The second case in which pill and sow bugs are likely to eat living plants is in spring just after you have cleared the garden for planting. Because you have removed or dug most of their food into the soil, they are likely to munch hungrily on your tiny seedlings.

If you pay attention to actual damage, rather than just being alarmed by the sight of these creatures, you will rarely feel a need to control them. I usually ignore them, as long as they are just going about their business of eating debris. But if I see a huge population in a sheltered place on the soil surface among my crops, and notice them on my living plants, I act to reduce their population. I read about and tried several kinds of traps, such as half citrus rinds, cut side down, set about the garden, but my pill and sow bugs ignored these. So I usually just scoop some into a plastic bag, seal it, freeze it, and then compost the contents. Often you can avoid the need to take action after you clear your spring garden if you just clear it a couple of weeks before you plant. This allows the hungry pill and sow bugs (and often some of the earwigs, snails, and slugs as well) to move to another location before your seedlings appear. Another way to discourage pill and sow bugs is by letting the surface of your garden's soil dry out between waterings.

Pill and sow bugs are among the creatures that break down organic materials in a cold compost pile and live in the outskirts of a hot one. They also live in redworm compost, where they do no harm. If you have an overpopulation of these creatures in your garden, you could reduce it by moving your compost pile farther from your most susceptible crops or making sure it is a hot pile.

VERTEBRATE PESTS

Birds

You can suspect birds of doing the damage if seedlings are clipped, fruit is pecked, or sunflower seeds stolen before you can harvest them. Birds that are likely to be serious garden pests in this region are house finches, house sparrows, white-crowned sparrows, and rock doves. Blackbirds, starlings, jays, and crows also sometimes cause damage here to garden plants. Some of these birds do eat insects, but usually only in the spring, when they need extra protein for reproducing and raising their young.

In contrast, birds that eat large numbers of insects are welcome in gardens. Although there is no evidence that birds can successfully control any particular pest, robins, mockingbirds, and flickers are likely to make a significant contribution to pest control. (For information on what these helpful birds eat, see page 105.)

Of the common pest birds, house finches are brown birds slightly larger than sparrows. The males have rosy red crowns, breasts, and rumps; a variant form has yellowish markings. They eat mostly seeds, seedlings, fruit, flower buds, berries, and other soft fruits—although they do catch some insects to feed to their young. As with any seed-feeding bird, most of the seeds they eat will be weed seed, simply because there is so much weed seed available.

An occasional house finch will likely do little damage, but if you live near a large house finch population, you can expect some trouble. House finches do not migrate, so they are here all year long. In the winter months, house finches feed in small flocks. In the spring, they pair off and build nests in evergreens or on the ledges of buildings.

House (or English) sparrows are plump birds; females are mostly pale brown, males have a black mask and bib in breeding plumage; both have gray and brown markings on their heads, backs, wings and tails. Like house finches, they are nonmigratory birds that fly and roost in flocks of a dozen or so, when not paired for nesting. They live mainly on seeds, although in the summer they eat some insects as well. They may nest in trees, but instead often use the cavities and ledges of such urban structures as bridges, buildings, and billboards.

In contrast to house finches and house sparrows, white-crowned sparrows are migratory birds, usually here just in fall and winter. They move northward to breed in the spring and summer. White-crowned sparrows have gray breasts and prominent black-and-white stripes on their heads. They may pull up and eat seedlings and may peck at mature plants. They will also eat some insects. They like to feed at the edge of deep brush or dense woods, so gardens in such locations are likely to suffer more.

The pigeon, or rock dove, is a common urban bird. This once-domestic species eats a wide variety of food. When people feed pigeons, the birds increase in numbers and in utilization of an area. They often congregate and nest on buildings, and if your garden is near one of these sites, they may feed on your garden seed and small plants.

You may have little or no bird damage in your garden, or tender lettuce plants may be reduced to ragged nubbins every time you set them out. It all depends on the nearby bird population. If birds are a problem, protect your plants with bird netting, a one-inch plastic mesh. You can just lay it loosely over the top of a bed of seedlings, propping it up only when the seedlings are too delicate for even such light material. The edges should touch the ground or the sides of a raised bed, but do not need to be tucked into the soil. Just weight the netting with a few stones. You can drape plastic netting over fruit trees too, or tie it over ripening sunflowerheads. You can also build frameworks of plastic pipe, cover them with plastic bird netting, and place such structures as needed over beds of vegetables and flowers. These can be as low as 1 foot high for crops such as lettuce or strawberries, or they can be high enough that you can enter and stand inside them.

Floating row cover will keep out birds, along with snails, slugs, and other pests. And pigeons and other large species can also be discouraged by driving numerous small, brushy, leafless woody prunings into the ground around seedlings or even just laying them on the ground in seeded areas. Inflated plastic snakes may scare birds away, or fluttering shiny foil hung on strings along a row, or even recycled CDs, but birds may return when they get used to these objects. Such scare tactics will be most effective if you put them up as soon as birds begin to eat in your garden, rather than after they have been around for a while.

It is against federal law to kill many kinds of birds, and others may be protected by local laws. Also, no pesticides are registered for use on birds by homeowners. Licensed pest eradicators will know the laws concerning bird control.

Cats

If you see your seed beds dug up, cats may have caused the damage. They leave earth piles with scratched-out soil depressions around them. Loose soil is, unfortunately, the original kitty litter. Cats dig up seeds and destroy seedlings with their digging and scratching. I've had only minor cat damage myself, despite gardening in neighborhoods with high cat populations. But gardeners will sometimes report that their particular garden plot seems to have become the favored W.C. of the neighborhood's entire cat population.

If the cat damage is light to moderate, try tactics to make the bare soil surface less obvious or inviting. I have repelled cats successfully by scattering my seedbeds with the green leaves of grass and weeds (avoiding seed heads), renewing these camouflages every few days until the plants are well up. Cayenne pepper, sprinkled on the soil, may discourage some cats, and some gardeners swear by coffee grounds. Floating row cover or chicken wire laid over seedbeds presents a more formidable challenge to more determined cats. For bare areas among maturing plants, use a large-particle mulch such as straw.

If you have been bothered by many cats, or by cats of great determination, you may want to build a permanent structure of netting or wire to exclude them from your plantings. One gardener found that a fishing net of the type used to catch large bass (purchased from a fishing supply shop) was an effective barrier. He built a walk-in structure of this net against his garden fence.

Commercial cat repellents may work briefly, but can become quite expensive for extensive garden use.

Deer

Because their main natural predators—gray wolves, mountain lions, bobcats, and coyotes—are absent or rare, deer have multiplied freely in California suburban and rural areas. They eat a wide variety of plants, devouring leaves as well as woody twigs. To identify deer damage, look also for the tracks of their pointed, cloven hooves, or use a flashlight to find the animals at night.

There are many tactics for repelling deer, including bars of soap or small bags of human hair hung from plants or blood meal sprinkled on the ground among them. Some gardeners report success with a sprayed-on homemade mixture consisting of 2 old eggs mixed in a blender with half a cup of water, then reblended with 2 tablespoons Tabasco sauce or chili powder and two more cups of water. Among commercial repellents, Deer-Away is reportedly one of the best for protecting ornamental trees and shrubs and nonbearing fruit trees. It lasts about two months, and, like most deer repellents, is not for use on plants you intend to eat. Repellents work best if applied before deer begin eating plants. Because deer may simply get used to a repellent or ignore it when they are very hungry, this method is not totally reliable.

Deer will usually stay away from a dog, but unless the dog is unleashed and able to chase them, they may get used to its barking. And, of course, a barking dog may keep you and your neighbors awake.

The only certain way to keep deer out of an area is with a deer-proof fence. This should be 7 to 8 feet high and made of woven wire mesh with 4- or 6-inch openings, supported by sturdy posts. It needs to have a sturdy gate that is kept closed. Alternatively, there are electrified fences designed to keep deer out.

Gardeners have made up many lists of plants deer won't eat, but deer often surprise us by eating plants they aren't "supposed to" like. What they will eat varies, depending in part on the choices available to them and in part how hungry they are. When local numbers are high, or late in the dry summer, deer may be less particular.

Among food crops, deer are reputed to dislike artichoke, asparagus, rhubarb, onions, leeks, garlic, prickly pear cactus, squash, and a number of kinds of culinary herbs. I can report that I once grew corn and squash successfully in an area inhabited by deer. (Alas, gophers ate many of these plants, but the deer left them alone.)

Dogs

When plants are knocked over and flattened, sometimes you need look no farther than a dog, especially if there are also signs of digging and fresh animal feces present.

Gardens open to the street in densely populated areas require some fencing to avoid dog problems, something that all urban community gardeners learn quickly. Whether your home garden is safe from your own dog depends on how well trained it is and on whether its needs are adequately met. Remember that a dog needs adequate exercise and interesting activities. If you take your dog for walks and play with it, it is much less likely to wreak havoc in your garden.

Raised beds provide a pattern that many well-trained dogs can understand. Dogs can be taught to romp on the paths, not on the beds. Some dogs will not respond to such training, however, in which case your dog will need a separate fenced area. If you find that your dog lies down on your plants, it is probably looking for a cool place to sleep. You may be able to redirect the dog by planting something soft but resilient, such as mondo grass, in a shady corner in which it has slept before. Planted in the fall, it should be sturdy enough to take the abuse by the time days are warm enough for the dog to need it.

Gophers and Moles

Raised piles of earth are often the work of the underground-dwelling mammals, gophers and moles. Gophers leave crescent-shaped mounds when they surface, and moles pile up earth like small volcanoes. Moles sometimes also leave ridges of loose earth between their mounds as they channel about near the surface.

Gophers are small, thickset, brown rodents with small ears and big front teeth. They are almost entirely vegetarian, and will eat your garden plants with relish. A single gopher makes extensive underground tunnels. They will eat bulbs, roots, seeds, and whole plants. (Watching a corn stalk tremble, then slowly disappear down a gopher hole, was one of my most maddening gardening experiences!)

Moles are gray to nearly black furry creatures with hand-like forefeet, designed for efficient digging. They have pointy snouts, only sparsely covered with hair, and their eyes and ears are so small they are not easily seen. They are not rodents, but insectivores. They eat very little plant material, preferring earthworms, grubs, and other soil creatures. However, they do disturb plant roots by heaving the soil about, exposing the roots to the drying air. If you have a redworm composting system that isn't enclosed, moles may find it and hunt the redworms.

Many strategies have been tried to repel gophers and moles. Gardeners sometimes still plant gopher spurge (*Euphorbia lathyrus*), with poor results. It's true that gophers don't eat it, but they will pass quite close to it on the way to other plants. You would need to plant a gopher spurge barrier several feet wide all around your garden to keep gophers out. Ultrasonic devices or small wind-turned noisemakers aren't likely to repel gophers and moles for long, as the animals soon become accustomed to the disturbance. And there isn't good evidence that any kind of sharp or smelly material placed in the tunnels will drive these pests away.

A recently arrived gopher, one whose burrow system is relatively incomplete, may be flushed out or drowned with water. However, where gophers have been present for some time, the use of water is ineffective.

You can keep gophers or moles out of your garden beds by installing gopher wire under the beds. While this strategy takes some time to carry out, gopher wire will last for years and is a certain deterrent while it lasts. Dig out your bed to a depth of a foot or more. Cover the bottom and sides of the hole with galvanized wire mesh. A mesh with ½-inch openings, known as hardware cloth, is best, but even galvanized chicken wire, which has about 1 inch openings, will be a big help. Overlap any pieces by a foot. If you have raised bed frames, cut the wire long enough so that it overlaps with the sides of the beds for a few inches. Some garden supply stores sell gopher wire by the yard and also sell prefab gopher wire pockets, suitable for putting under individual perennial plants (See sources in Appendix VII, Resources for Gardeners, under Sources of Gardening Supplies and Books.)

Any efforts to decrease insect larvae in your garden's soil, such as treatment with beneficial nematodes, will discourage moles. Worm bins built to exclude rats and mice, by having no openings over ¼ inch, will also exclude moles.

A cat or a dog will sometimes hunt gophers, filling in for wild predators. The Hungry Owl Project has installed some barn owl nesting boxes, though this works best on a large scale, since the birds don't hunt right under their nest.

Farmers and gardeners have long depended mainly on traps to keep gopher and mole populations in check when damage becomes intolerable—using different types of traps for gophers and moles. A new type of trap, the cinch trap, is easier to use than traditional models and can be used for either animal. For more information on these traps, see Gophers Limited, in Appendix VII, Resources for Gardeners.

Poison baits are sometimes used to control gophers. They are among the most toxic products you will ever handle in your garden, and they must be used with extreme care so that none of them remain above ground where they could poison pets or other animals. Poisoned gophers don't usually emerge from their tunnels, so the chance of another animal being poisoned by the carcass are small, but exclusion or trapping don't introduce toxins at all, so those methods are preferable.

Meadow Voles

These native California rodents, which are larger than mice but smaller than rats, live in wild and semiwild areas. They may cause little damage most of the time, but they occasionally build up large populations and head for gardens, where they feed on lawns, tree and shrub bark, leaves of ornamentals, and vegetables. If you know there are meadow voles nearby, it is wise to keep a cleared area around your vegetable garden, ideally 15 feet wide, removing thick mulch, grassy weeds, and other dense cover.

You can keep meadow voles out of an area with a barrier of ¼-inch wire mesh that is a foot high above ground and extends 6 to 10 inches below ground. This could stand alone or be installed at the bottom of other fencing. It could also be put around a single fruit tree to prevent bark gnawing near and just below the ground level. Cats or dogs are often very good hunters of these small rodents, and voles are a particular favorite of barn owls, but none of these predators will prevent all garden damage when vole populations are very high.

Opossums

These nocturnal animals are still uncommon enough to startle viewers. They are about 12 inches tall and 33 inches long, including a foot-long, naked tale. They have light gray fur and a pointy face. Not native to California, opossums were introduced several times for fur or food and escaped captivity here. In urban and suburban areas, they often live under porches or decks or in other parts of poorly secured buildings. Their diet in the wild includes insects, lizards, snakes, meadow voles, snails, and birds and their eggs, as well as green plants, fruits, and nuts. Given a chance, they will eat pet food, garbage, fallen orchard fruit, and garden vegetables. These relatively slow-moving animals are rarely aggressive, but may fight a dog or cat if they are cornered.

Make your property less attractive to opossums by keeping overgrowth trimmed, sealing up buildings, keeping food scraps out of compost, securing garbage in covered cans, and taking any pet food in at night. Exclude opossums from a garden by building a 4-foot-tall chicken wire fence with the top 12 to 18 inches bent outward and not supported, so when the possum climbs, it falls backward. Alternatively, add an electrified wire atop any fence, 3 inches out from the fence.

Rabbits

If your garden is next to an open field, meadow, or brushy area, even in a city, rabbits (the larger jackrabbits or the smaller cottontails) may be a significant problem. You can exclude them with chicken wire fencing, three feet tall, which can be installed at the bottom of any existing fence. Fencing for rabbits should at least be tight to the ground. Ideally the wire mesh should extend 6 inches below the ground surface and then be bent outward another 6 inches.

Pest Mammals as Community Problems

Gardeners used to be advised that pest mammals such as raccoons, opossums, skunks, and tree squirrels were wild animals, feeding in gardens that happen to be at the edge of their wild habitat. We were offered scare tactics to frighten the animals into returning to the wild. In fact, we were often told we should trap these animals and release them "in the wild." However, these days, these animals generally do not have a wild habitat to return to. Instead, they are living in ecosystems that are thoroughly enmeshed with human habitation. (One pest, the rat, has been enmeshed for centuries.)

In our urban environments, careless humans have created a bounty of new food sources, allowing mammal populations to grow beyond what wild food could support. Instead of a steady state, controlled by predators, the animals may experience population booms followed by starvation. Very hungry animals become aggressive and not so easily discouraged. If they can, raccoons will enter our homes in search of pet food, or even food in our cupboards, and they may not be particularly afraid of humans.

To prevent a determined mammal from eating our garden plants, we have to exclude it with an effective barrier, such as a fence or a net, or apply an effective repellent. It is also wise to start looking at the overall picture.

Animals need shelter, water, and food. Cities offer shelter in poorly sealed homes and sheds, spaces under decks, junk in yards, and thick underbrush. Water is available from garden ponds, birdbaths, and old tires. As to food, there is often plenty of unsecured garbage, pet food left outdoors, fruit abandoned under trees, and seed falling under bird feeders. Bird feeders are a particular bonanza, since some animals eat the grain, and others eat the birds and mammals it attracts. Snakes come for the birds, rats, and mice; raccoons hunt the birds and snakes. As if all of this weren't enough, some soft-hearted people intentionally feed raccoons and tree squirrels, not only helping them overpopulate an area but also reducing their fear of humans, which increases their aggressiveness. (One East Bay raccoon blocked the way until a passing human gave up the food he was eating.)

Experts tell us that the best way to reduce the population of these pest mammals is by modifying their habitat; that is, closing up openings that allow them to shelter in buildings and removing access to water and food that have let them multiply out of proportion to the available natural habitat. This is made difficult by the fact that one needs to address these issues not in a single backyard, but in whole neighborhoods.

Several governmental agencies and nonprofit organizations offer help addressing both specific questions and the larger issues. These include the California Department of Fish and Game, county vector control programs, agricultural commissioners, municipal health departments, the SPCA, and wildlife rescue organizations. Some offer educational programs for neighborhoods, surveys, or inspections, either voluntary or in response to reports of problems. In an ideal world, neighbors would cooperate to manage urban wildlife wisely, perhaps having events to share information and help each other make the neighborhood less inviting. However, I am quite aware how far from ideal this world is.

Another ideal-world idea beginning to get some play is introducing raptors—birds of prey—to help manage wildlife populations in urban and suburban areas. Part of the reason for huge population increases of particular animals is lack of natural enemies. We probably don't want to reintroduce native predators like bobcats and coyotes, but cities have introduced peregrine falcons to hunt pigeons. And barn owls attracted by providing nesting boxes will help with gophers, rats, and voles. For more information, see The Hungry Owl Project in Appendix VII, Resources for Gardeners.

Excellent information about managing pest mammals can be found in the U.C. Davis Publication, *Wildlife Pest Control around Gardens and Homes*, listed in Appendix VIII, Suggested Reading.

Raccoons

Here is an animal that has prospered in civilization. While it is a native species, it has expanded its territory by a quarter and increased its population by 15 to 20 times in the past century. Now, raccoons live even in the hearts of our big cities. I will never forget the night that one awakened me by walking on the roof of the porch outside my bedroom, then peered in at me, its masked eyes at human height! Like opossums, raccoons are nocturnal animals that eat both animals and plants. They can kill larger birds than can opossums, including chickens, ducks, and wild birds, and are notorious for eating pet fish in garden fish ponds. They turn up lawns, looking for grubs in the soil, and occasionally eat vegetable crops, especially corn and tomatoes.

Raccoons have become more difficult to dissuade from going after food in gardens than they used to be. Worse, some raccoons have learned that there is more food indoors and have learned to enter pet doors or open simple latches. Because they have become more habituated to human contact, they may become aggressive if accosted, rather than fleeing.

Your first defense is to remove temptations. Keep garbage cans tightly covered or put them in a tip-proof rack. Close off any openings that allow raccoons to take shelter in buildings, and do not leave pet food outdoors. If raccoons dig in your lawn, treat it with beneficial nematodes to reduce the number of lawn insects they can find to eat.

Gardening books list many different tactics for repelling raccoons from vegetable gardens, but these smart animals often learn to ignore our efforts. Ideas include leaving flashlights or radios on all night, putting a couple of shakes of ground red pepper on the silk of each ear of corn, and strategically placing dishpans containing ammonia-soaked rags. Motion-activated sprays of water may work, though local gardeners have reported that raccoons have ripped these apart.

Persistent raccoons may be stopped only by a fence. It is difficult to fence out raccoons, as they are very good climbers. Electrified wires provide the best barrier. If applied to an existing fence, use one strand 8 inches above ground and 8 inches out from the fence. Or create a low two-wire fence to protect your garden—one wire 6 inches high, a second one 12 inches high, on evenly spaced wooden posts. The charger need be on only dusk to dawn. (Don't let plants grow against the wires, or the fence won't work.)

Live trapping and release of raccoons elsewhere is no longer a legal option, as there is no longer any "area with fewer raccoons" in which to release them. While it is legal to trap a raccoon that has become a "nuisance animal," the only legal options for dealing with a trapped raccoon are to release it in the same place (well, you could take it out of your kitchen) or "humanely" killing it. Killing raccoons is not recommended, however, since in most areas the animals will be rapidly replaced by new ones. Exclusion, reducing attractants, and community education are your best bets in reducing the damage they can cause.

Rats

Long common and unwelcome where humans live, rats seem to be on the increase in our urban and suburban areas. Gardeners report damage to vegetables and fruits, and compost bins gnawed through to gain entry. Rats are particularly fond of avocados and citrus fruit. They will eat out the pulp of oranges or eat only the rind of lemons. They will also chew through twigs of citrus or ornamentals and carry them away for nest building.

High rat populations are generally a neighborhood problem. Attractants include open garbage bins, inadequately sealed buildings, pet food left outdoors, and spilled birdseed. Rats nest in dense underbrush, palm trees, and ivy that is over a foot thick on a wall. Ideally, education would lead to cleanup and seal-up activities, since these would be the most effective ways to reduce rat populations. Introduction of barn owl nests in a community can help, though probably not provide sufficient relief when populations are high and are sheltering indoors.

Two species of rats are common. Norway rats are ground dwellers. In gardens, they are most likely the species bothering a compost bin. They may enter redworm bins to eat the worms or go after meat scraps in any kind of compost setup. Roof rats, which are much better climbers, are the ones that eat fruit in trees. Either may eat vegetables or fallen fruit, though chances are greater that the ones eating vegetables are roof rats.

No material is known to repel rats, and no fencing method is recommended to exclude them from a garden area. A smooth metal band a foot wide on the trunk of a tree can prevent them from climbing it if there is no nearby fence or plant to climb and leap from.

When sanitation and exclusion fail, and populations of rats become large, trapping is usually the next step in providing relief. Trapping is far superior for the environment than poisoning the animals, since poisoned rats are often found and eaten by pets and wild animals, resulting in secondary poisonings. But rats are difficult to trap, since they are smart and suspicious of new objects in their territories. Large snap traps can work if used well. Please see other resources for details, but the bare minimum you need to know is that traps must be fastened down, or they will be dragged away, and they must be left unbaited at first until the rats are familiar with them. If pets are present, traps can be placed in boxes that pets can't enter.

Skunks

These native animals are minor pests in gardens. They are more likely to dig up a plant looking for insects in the soil, but they may eat berries or vegetable crops. I've included them mainly because they are another animal attracted by nesting sites under decks or porches, open garbage, pet food, and bird food. If you can reduce the availability of these amenities, you can reduce damage to gardens by skunks as well.

Tree Squirrels

Several species of tree squirrels live in our region. Some are native. One that is not native, the eastern fox squirrel, is the most damaging to California gardens. It can be identified by its brownish, red-orange fur. When these squirrels are numerous, gardeners may lose most or all of nuts, oranges, avocados, apples, apricots, and other crops. The squirrels may also browse on the ground, eating crops that include strawberries, tomatoes, and corn. They are most active in early morning and late afternoon.

Many people feed squirrels and provide them with nesting boxes. The animals are also attracted to bird feeders and are so agile that it is difficult to exclude them.

Protecting a tree is difficult, but covering it with bird net may work. Though the squirrels can easily chew through the plastic netting, they may become discouraged if they can find food more easily elsewhere. Chicken wire over soil can prevent squirrels from digging up just-planted seeds or bulbs, and chicken wire cages can keep them from harvesting strawberries or tomatoes. They don't like hot pepper, though protecting whole trees with this substance may prove a challenge. If a dog has free run, it may be able to keep squirrels out of a yard.

Eastern fox squirrels, which are considered pest animals, can be killed by any legal means. Kill trapping them is legal; poisoning them is not.

PLANT DISEASES

Most infectious plant diseases are caused by one of three kinds of organisms: fungi, bacteria, and viruses. Many of these organism will attack only certain species of plants or groups of related plants. For example, zucchini yellow mosaic virus will attack squashes and cucumbers, but no other crops, and celery late blight attacks only celery and, to a lesser extent, celeriac. Depending on the disease, it may be spread by one or more of the following agents: infected soil, seed, or plant debris, splashing water, wind, or insects. If a disease is insect borne, it spreads by an insect feeding first on an infected plant, then on healthy plants. Some diseases are spread on contact, so gardeners spread them by touching diseased plants with their hands or tools and then touching healthy plants.

Noninfectious diseases, or physiological problems, occur even though there is no pest organism present. They include, for example, conditions caused by not enough of particular nutrients or inadequate watering. They are treated by improving growing conditions. Sometimes certain varieties are better able to avoid particular noninfectious diseases than are other varieties. For example, some tomato varieties rarely develop catfacing, while others show this deformation often. See the tomato and summer squash entries in Chapter 11 for examples of noninfectious diseases. See also page 81 on nutrient deficiency symptoms.

Many infectious diseases have either no cure or no chemical treatment registered for home use, so prevention should be your main defense. First, try to get disease-free starts. To avoid diseases spread by infected seeds, seedlings, bulbs, or tubers, seek out ones that are certified to be disease-free. Especially avoid starting plants from potatoes, onions, garlic cloves, dry beans, or other starts that were sold in a grocery as food. Although they are wholesome to eat, these may spread diseases in your garden.

When you can find plant varieties that are genetically resistant to particular diseases common where you garden, it is always wise to choose them. Study descriptions on seed packets or in catalogs. Varieties described as *resistant* are usually able to avoid infection, although they may show symptoms if growing conditions are very poor. Varieties listed as disease *tolerant* are only somewhat resistant, perhaps showing signs of an infection but not succumbing to it.

Any variety will be better able to resist infectious disease if it has the best possible growing conditions. As with humans, a healthy plant can resist disease better than one suffering from deficiencies. For example, when the soil is too wet, so the plant roots lack air, plants are particularly susceptible to root disease. And plants grown too close together, so that the environment around them is humid, with poor air circulation, may become susceptible to foliage diseases.

Sometimes you will want to avoid conditions that are usually not harmful, because you know they can spread specific diseases. For example, celery leaves are not harmed by being wet, but they should be kept as dry as possible to discourage late blight. Or, though a much shorter rotation cycle is usually fine, you might wait three to four years before replanting onions in a soil infested with spores of downy mildew. And finally, while you would ordinarily compost crop plants at the end of the season, remove any diseased plants from your garden.

I have listed the diseases most likely to cause serious problems here. If you see that a plant is seriously damaged by a disease, pull it out and discard it, even if you can't identify the disease. Clean up all diseased plant debris and remove it from your garden. If a problem spreads to a large part of a crop or appears repeatedly, and it is not described here, try to get it identified so you can learn the best ways to avoid it in the future.

FUNGUS DISEASES

Fungi are typically made up of threads of tissue called mycelia that grow through the substance on which they are feeding. Then at some point they form fruiting bodies, relatively organized structures in which spores are formed. A familiar example is the mushroom, the fruiting body of a fungus that grows through soil or wood. While many fungi live on dead organic matter and are helpful in our gardens and compost piles, some attack living plants, the mycelia growing inside the plant cells and then producing spores on the plant surfaces. For example, powdery mildew spores cover plant leaves with white powdery spores. Some kinds of fungal spores live for many years in soil, awaiting a susceptible crop.

Celery Late Blight

If, in the cooler months, older leaves and stems of your maturing celery or celeriac develop yellow spots that turn brown, your plants have late blight. Tiny black dots will appear in the brown spots. Infected leaves eventually wither and the plants may die. While celery will often escape this disease, it is common enough that you should take precautions against it.

Celery late blight is also sometimes called septoria blight, after the fungus that causes it, *Septoria apiicola.* It is spread by infected seeds and by water splashed from infected plants or plant debris from these plants. It can live for up to eighteen months in plant debris, and for two years in infected seed.

If your celery or celeriac plants show symptoms of this disease, remove them immediately, together with any plant debris left on the ground. Don't grow either crop in that location for at least two years.

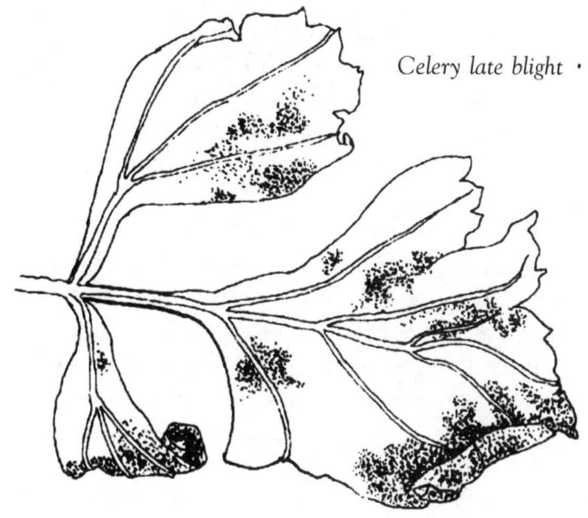

Celery late blight •

Late blight probably came into my garden via some infected nursery plants. For several years after that, I grew my own celery seedlings from seed I treated to make sure it was disease free. Here's how to treat seed: First tie the seed into a small, thin piece of cloth. Soak it in water at 118°F for 30 minutes. Use a meat thermometer to be sure the water temperature remains constant. Add more warm water if it starts to cool, but don't let it get over 120°F. Stir the water a little to keep the temperature even and to reach all the seeds. When 30 minutes is up, cool the seeds by dipping the cloth bag in cool water, then dry them.

Other means of prevention include using seed over two years old (sown more thickly, to compensate for the lower germination) and avoiding overhead watering. 'Emerson Pascal' celery is tolerant to the blight, but that doesn't mean it won't get some of the disease if it is present, and I prefer to eliminate late blight altogether rather than tolerate it.

Clubroot

Clubroot fungus infects cabbage family plants, causing them to turn yellow and often to become stunted. Plants wilt on warm days. When you pull the plants, you find that the roots are enlarged into club-shaped knots; they may be split open and decayed. Clubroot fungus lives in the soil, and while I have never seen it in San Francisco, it is common in soils from Salinas to Half Moon Bay. It is encouraged by warm moist weather.

If your area doesn't have clubroot, avoid bringing plants, soil, or manure from affected areas into your garden. Obtain seedlings from a reputable dealer or grow your own. Amend clay soil well to improve drainage. You can also reduce the chance of an outbreak by raising your soil's pH to 7.2

(see page 72), using ground limestone as well as hydrated lime, as limestone alone is not enough to prevent the disease. Pull all mustard family weeds from your garden, as they may harbor the disease, and plan as long a rotation as possible between cabbage family crops.

Once plants are infected, there is no cure for this disease. If you find infected plants, dig them up and remove them, getting as much of the root as you can. As the clubroot fungus is long-lived, in order to clear a soil of it you must use a crop rotation in which no cabbage family crops are grown for seven years. No variety is resistant to all races of this fungus. Check with local garden stores and Cooperative Extension offices to see if there are varieties that will resist the types of clubroot prevalent in your area.

Corn Smut

See the description on page 218.

Damping-off Disease

This scourge of seedlings causes them to fall over and wilt. The first point of damage is just at soil level. Some shriveling will be so complete that small, insubstantial seedlings such as lettuce and tomato can seem to simply disappear. Though it is a very serious problem, damping-off is generally preventable.

Damping-off is caused by various soil-inhabiting fungi. It is encouraged when seedlings are grown in too-moist soil, crowded too close together and grown at too high or too low a temperature. It also may be more likely to occur when the seeding mix contains ample fertilizer. As plants get larger, they become less susceptible, although mature plants can be damaged by damping-off also if growing conditions are extremely poor.

To avoid damping-off, start by using soil that is relatively free of infection. When starting seeds in containers, use a sterile seeding mix and sterile or well-cleaned containers (see instructions in Chapter 6). If you use a part of your garden as a seed bed, growing seedlings close together for later transplanting, rotate the area used for this purpose, to avoid a buildup of damping-off organisms.

A seeding mix for containers should be formulated so that it holds moisture without becoming soggy. In your garden, keep organic matter plentiful in seeding areas, especially if your soil has a high clay content. However, avoid adding fresh, uncomposted material to your soil just before you plant seeds. Don't plant seeds too close together, and if you are growing them indoors, move them to a well-aerated spot as soon as the seedlings break the soil surface.

I once overheard a gardener at a nursery, lamenting that all his seedlings had wilted and died. The clerk nodded sympathetically and handed him a bottle of fungicide with which to treat his potting mix. I too have lost seedlings to damping-off from time to time, but I can assure you, if you follow the preventive measures just outlined, you will see this disease so rarely that you will feel no need to resort to fungicides. (See also Root Rots in this section.)

Downy Mildew of Onions

All onion family crops, but especially onions and shallots, can get this fungal disease. The symptoms are sunken, water-soaked spots, either yellow or gray, on the leaves, followed by a coating of a dirty gray or violet-colored powder. This disease doesn't usually kill the plants, but leaf tips may die, and bulbs of badly infected plants are small and soft. The disease is favored by cool, wet nights and warm but overcast days. While downy mildew is not very common, it is common enough and serious enough that you need to watch out for it.

Prevent downy mildew by reducing excess moisture: amend heavy soil to improve drainage, don't overwater, and plant widely enough to allow the air to circulate among your plants. Once the disease appears, it will stay in the soil and in overwintering plants, and will break out again whenever conditions are right. You may escape chronic infection, seeing the disease only for one season, or it may appear several years in a row. If your plants do become infected, remove them, along with any plant debris. Don't grow any plants in the genus *Allium* in the affected spot for 3 to 4 years.

Fungal Leaf Spots

Plants infected with fungal leaf spots have discolored, round spots on their leaves. This is not a single disease, but several, each affecting one plant or several closely related ones. Strawberries get one kind of fungal leaf spot in our region. The disease doesn't damage the fruit directly, but it reduces plant vigor, and if spots form on the green caps over the berries, they may not ripen properly. Beets, chard, and spinach are affected by another disease, beet cercospora leaf spot. This leaf spot disease doesn't damage the roots, but it can reduce the size of beet roots by stunting the plants. (Despite the fact that spinach is susceptible, I have never seen the symptoms on my spinach.)

Spores of the organisms causing fungal leaf spot diseases live on plants and on infected plant debris

Wild Mammals and Disease

In addition to raiding our gardens and damaging homes, wild mammals also carry disease. A particular concern of gardeners is whether the contents of a raccoon latrine are entering garden soil. Raccoon latrines are communal, used by many animals. They can be in a garden or on a roof, from which rain can wash the mess into the garden. The latrines stink and often contain the eggs of raccoon roundworm. While this parasite doesn't seriously harm raccoons, it is more serious, even lethal, for rodents, birds, or humans who accidentally eat the eggs. If you have a raccoon latrine on your property, you may need drastic measures, such as an electric fence, to get the animals to abandon it.

Wild mammals carry other diseases humans or pets can catch. The best general advice is not to touch wild animals and not to handle dead ones or animal feces without gloves. Wash your hands after touching a dead animal or feces, even if you wore gloves. In addition, if you see raccoons that look ill or malnourished or are wandering in the daytime, contact the SPCA, since such an animal may have canine distemper.

and garden tools, but not in the soil. Beet leaf spot spores are also carried on seed. Spots usually appear first on lower leaves. If you notice spots just beginning to form, pick off the affected leaves. If many spots have already formed, pick off the leaves with the most spots and any dead leaves, and clean up any dead plant material from the soil's surface. A mulch on the soil forms a barrier that will prevent spores from splashing onto plants when it rains or when you are watering. In severe cases, remove the affected plants from the garden altogether and rotate the problem crop to a new site next season, using the affected site for susceptible crops only once every two or three years. In the case of beets, chard or spinach, do not save seed from affected plants. Sulfur is registered for use against some leaf spot diseases. Check the label.

Strawberries often show fungal leaf spot symptoms early in the season, especially if they are growing very rapidly (perhaps following over-fertilization with nitrogen). They also often outgrow the infection. You can reduce the likelihood of strawberries contracting leaf spot by planting them in well-amended soil and in unshaded locations, and by keeping the beds well weeded. Also, if your strawberries have become quite thickly massed, remove some plants until the remaining ones are no closer than 10 inches apart, or reset your plants, well spaced, into a new bed altogether. When you are shopping for strawberry plants, ask about resistant varieties suitable for your location.

Late Blight of Potato and Tomato

This is the same disease that caused the Irish potato famine in the 1840s. It is still active on potatoes and has also destroyed many tomato plants in our region.

The first sign that a plant has late blight is often a leaf or two with a brown area, or perhaps a brown area on a petiole—the stem of a leaf. Soon larger brown lesions appear on sections of the stems. On tomatoes, fruit develops greasy-looking brown shoulders; infected potato tubers have brown to purple surface patches with a dry, corky, reddish-brown rot underneath. Infected plants tend to rapidly turn brown and die. While what you see is mostly a dying plant, on very humid days, when the temperature hovers at around 70°F, you may see wispy, fuzzy white fungal growth on leaves, stems, or tomato fruits.

Tomato or potato late blight is caused by *Phytopthora infestans*, a fungus or a fungus-like organism, depending on who you ask. Plants become infected when spores are blown onto them by the wind or arrive in wind-driven rain. The fungus grows mostly inside the plants, only emerging at the surface in wispy threads to release more spores. Besides entering gardens with wind or water, it can also be brought by planting infected potato tubers or tomato plants.

The late blight presently in our gardens is a form that can survive only in a living plant. The spores (known as zoospores) live outside of a plant briefly as they float to another plant, but they can't survive in the soil. If a different "mating form" were to be present, the two would reproduce sexually, and the spores (oospores) they produced would be able to survive for several months in the soil. Fortunately, this is not the present case.

To reduce the spread of this terrible disease, use only certified disease-free potato starts. Grow your own tomato seedlings or buy them from a reputable source. There are now some resistant potato varieties (see page 251). One tomato variety for home gardeners, 'Legend', is resistant to some strains of late blight, but not at all to the strain of the disease present in my garden. In 2009, I conducted a trial of several varieties that gardeners have reported resist late blight (see page 275). I grew them in gardens in which tomatoes usually get late blight and compared them to a control variety I know gets the disease, just to be sure it was present. None of the varieties proved immune to the disease, though some did a better than average job of producing a good crop before dying. (More on this on page 279.)

Tomato late blight is more common where summers are often foggy. Hot inland area gardeners will have less of it. You can reduce the likelihood of infection by avoiding overhead watering and avoiding growing plants too closely together, to reduce surrounding humidity. Northwest gardeners grow tomatoes under clear plastic hoop houses to keep rain from falling on them.

You may be able to harvest healthy potatoes even if the disease shows up while they are forming. As potato plants grow, make sure no tubers are visible at the soil surface, covering them with soil if you see them. If your plants survive long enough that you are near harvest, even if they show blight symptoms, cut the plants off 1 inch below the soil level and take them out of the garden. Don't dig the tubers for another 10 to 14 days, so that spores on the surface will be mostly or all dead by the time you harvest. Dig when the soil is fairly dry, and cure the tubers as directed in the potato entry (page 251), but take them away from the garden to do it. Store them in a dry place. Check them occasionally for signs of the disease. If you find ones with small late blight lesions, eat those tubers first, after cutting the lesions out of them.

As long as there are only zoospores, you can break the annual cycle of late blight by removing all nightshade family crops and weeds from your garden from November to April. That includes ground cherry, tomatillo, eggplant, and weedy solanums. Pick up any fallen leaves or fruits under those plants and remove those as well. Harvest all the potatoes, and if any sprout in those months, dig the plants out. This will give the disease time to die out before you replant. If late blight appears, do not replant homegrown potato tubers.

Sprays for tomato or potato late blight need to be applied early and often if they are to succeed. Following the label, I once sprayed a fixed-copper fungicide every five days from when the plants first showed symptoms. It did not save them from late blight. Other sources suggest using copper from when the plants are 6 inches high, but I've since learned copper will eventually make the soil toxic. Serenade, a new fungicide based on the bacterium *Bacillis subtilis*, is registered for tomato late blight. The manufacturer suggests beginning early in the season and applying it at least every 7 days, or as often as every 4 days if conditions favor the blight and you know it is present nearby. In the unlikely eventuality that it should rain within 4 hours of spraying, spray again. You can spray Serenade up to the day of harvest.

The catch, of course, is that all this spraying takes time and energy. So while it is definitely worth a try, having a solidly resistant variety would be a superior solution.

Onion White Rot

See page 241 within the Onion, Bulb, entry.

Powdery Mildew

You have powdery mildew when leaves of your crops become covered with a light gray or white powdery substance. Several different fungi cause this symptom, each affecting one crop, or several—often related—ones. Squash, pumpkins, and sometimes cucumber get one kind. Peas and cole crops get another.

Powdery mildew diseases of fruit crops tend to infect growing tips of branches, destroying young leaves and damaging developing fruit. One disease infects apples and quince. Peach and plum can get either of two different powdery mildews, one of which also infects cherry. Strawberries and grapes each can become infected with still other powdery mildew fungi.

There is some cross-susceptibility with ornamentals. Pea powdery mildew *Erysiphe polygoni* infects sweet pea, lupine, and flowers ranging from California poppy to calendula. One of the two diseases of peach and plum is the same one that infects rose, and grape shares its powdery mildew with ivy. See references on pest control in Appendix VIII, Suggested Reading, for more information on the hosts of different powdery mildew diseases.

Check the listings for Squash, Summer, and Squash, Winter, in Chapter 11 for information about resistant species and varieties. You are likely to find resistant cucumbers, peas, and strawberries. American grapes resist grape powdery mildew, while American/European crosses vary in resistance.

To prevent powdery mildews, plant where your crops will get enough sunlight, water them adequately, and don't overfertilize them. Plant peas in the cooler times of year, when the fungus is less active.

Unlike most fungus diseases of plant leaves, powdery mildew can be disrupted early in its development by washing the plants. Wash fronts and backs of susceptible leaves with a gentle spray from a hose before the disease appears. This may not prevent it entirely, but will help reduce the infection.

Cucurbit crop plants will survive and bear longer if you remove the lower leaves as soon as the disease appears on them. These older leaves don't photosynthesize as actively as the upper, younger ones, and do so even less when covered with a disease, so the plant won't be much worse off without them. Be sure to carry such leaves out of the garden to avoid spreading the spores. And don't overdo this strategy. Be sure that at least half of the leaves remain on the plant. (Don't wait until more than half have signs of powdery mildew before you act!) If plants are hopelessly infected, remove them from your garden to reduce the spread of the disease. Keep grapes and fruit trees pruned to an open habit to discourage powdery mildew. Prune out affected twigs and leaves.

One local predator, the lesser ashy gray lady beetle, eats spores of powdery mildew on cucurbits. This tiny insect is rounded in shape, with mottled wing covers in shades of light gray and brown. Its larvae resemble those of the larger lady beetles, but are ash gray. Although it is pleasant to watch these beetles grazing on the mildew spores, they don't seem to contribute significantly to control, as they appear only when the leaves are covered with spores, and the plants succumb despite their help.

Some chemicals are protectant, preventing new infections from occurring. These include sulfur and the biological fungicide Serenade. Protectants are best applied on highly susceptible plants before symptoms appear or at the earliest symptoms.

Oil chemical sprays have the ability to eradicate existing infections, although it should be said that if the disease is extensive, control with any fungicide will be difficult. Use summer oils or a product containing a plant-based oil such as neem oil or jojoba oil. Gardeners have, in the past, made up sprays of baking soda (sodium bicarbonate), oil, and water. Because of the plant toxicity of sodium, a product based on potassium bicarbonate (such as Kaligreen) is better than the homemade mixture. Potassium carbonate is protectant, with some ability to eradicate the disease.

Some of these chemical treatments can cause damage to plants. Cucurbits, in particular, are often sensitive to sulfur. The best sulfur formulations to use, both to prevent plant toxicity and to prevent skin and eye irritation, are wettable sulfur with surfactants.

Heed label warnings about not spraying sulfur or oil when temperatures are high. Also, be aware that all plants are sensitive to oil and sulfur in combination, so never use these products closer together than two weeks. Some plants need even longer between times they are sprayed with these two substances. If you aren't sure whether a plant is sensitive to sulfur, or whether enough time has passed between using sulfur and oil, you can test spray a small area of the plant and wait 48 hours to see if it is damaged.

Root Rots

If plants are infected by a root rot, they wilt in the daytime, even though well watered, and are stunted. Leaves turn yellow and then die. The stem at the ground level and/or the root are dark brown and rotting. Root rots are caused by many different fungi, known collectively as water molds. Rhizoctonias are one common kind of root rot fungus. Many of these fungi are ones that also cause damping-off in seedlings.

Root rots can infect a wide variety of crops. The main way to avoid them is to make certain the soil isn't kept too wet. Be sure the soil drains well, and be careful not to water too often. If plants begin to yellow, remember that root rot could be the cause, and don't automatically water before checking whether the soil is wet enough already. Remove any infected plants from the garden when you pull them. Rather than try to cure these diseases with chemicals, it's better to prevent them next season with better growing conditions.

Vascular Wilts

Wilt diseases are infections of plants' water-conducting cells. When these cells are plugged by a fungal infection, the plant wilts and often dies. While a number of fungi cause wilt diseases of one crop or another, the ones you are most likely to see are verticillium and fusarium. Verticillium wilt is encouraged by cool summer weather, and once in the soil, it remains infectious for 20 years. There is no cure for this disease. The variety of fusarium that attacks tomatoes attacks only tomatoes. Another variety causes decline in asparagus. Tomato fusarium is more common inland because symptoms do not develop until temperatures are above 68°F and are worst at 80 to 90°F.

Verticillium infects not only tomato, but also apricot, avocado, blackberry, cabbage, eggplant, grape, horseradish, New Zealand spinach, olives, persimmon, pepper, potato, radish, raspberry, spinach, peach, plum, sunflower, and strawberry. It also affects a long list of ornamentals, including California poppy, chrysanthemum, dahlia, elm, foxglove, fuchsia, geranium, ice plant, lilac, marguerite, nandina, maple, privet, snapdragon, strawflower, and sweet pea. Even the common weeds dandelion and groundsel are susceptible.

Verticillium is a common reason for the decline of local tomato and strawberry plants. If a tomato is infected, the older leaves wilt, beginning at the edges. Leaves first develop a V-shaped yellow patch, which then turns brown. Often the leaves dry up completely. The plants remain stunted and do not grow even when well watered and fertilized. They may not bear fruit, or may bear small, malformed fruit with poor flavor. When you cut the main stem off near the ground, the water-conducting tissue in the center of the stem appears brownish, instead of pale green like the rest of the stem section.

If strawberries are infected by verticillium wilt, the outer leaves turn brown along the margins and veins, then die completely. The plants lie flat to the ground, forming few new leaves. There may be brown streaks on leaf stems or runners. The plants may recover to bear good fruit the next year, or they may not.

Cultural controls can be of some help in fighting verticillium wilt. Don't slack off watering toward the end of the season, as this increases stress, making susceptible crops even more susceptible. Giving tomatoes too much nitrogen fertilizer will also make them more susceptible to the disease. Rotate nightshade family crops together, since they are all susceptible. Solarization, if you have enough sunny weather to carry it out, can destroy verticillium in the soil. Choose resistant tomato and strawberry varieties. A "V" after a tomato variety name indicates it resists verticillium. And while conditions for development of verticillium and fusarium are different, a number of tomato varieties resist both diseases, and you may as well use these.

Among vegetables, some kinds are resistant to all kinds of verticillium. These include asparagus, bean, carrot, celery, corn, lettuce, onion, and pea. Of the flowers discussed in Chapters 13 and 14, the following are among those that are resistant: calendula, carnation, columbine, Johnny-jump-up, pansy, ranunculus, sweet alyssum, sweet William, and zinnia. Alternate susceptible crops with resistant ones in your rotation, even if the disease has not appeared.

BACTERIAL DISEASES

Bacteria are single-celled creatures that grow by dividing into more of the same kind of cells. As with fungi, many kinds of bacteria are helpful in soil and compost because they break down dead organic matter. In fact, relatively few bacteria attack living plants, and you will see far fewer bacterial diseases than ones caused by fungi. Also, while many kinds of bacteria produce spores, the ones that infect plants do not, so they are not able to live outside of their host plants as long as fungal diseases. A practical result is that crop rotations to avoid bacterial diseases rarely require more than a year or two.

Bacteria cause some kinds of superficial rots, as when cut Swiss chard stems decay. When the rot is superficial, I remove the affected part and try to keep the plants less moist. As for more serious bacterial diseases, the best prevention is to reduce moisture. Look to the soil, being sure it has good drainage. Keep plant leaves dry when possible and plant susceptible crops where air circulation is good. Also, don't use too much fast-releasing nitrogen fertilizer, as this can foster bacterial disease.

If you identify a bacterial disease in a crop, rotate planting so that the susceptible crop isn't replanted in the same place for the next couple of seasons. Look for resistant varieties or certified disease-free seed.

One common bacterial disease, fireblight, attacks many fruit crops in the rose family, especially apples, pears, and quince, causing limbs to die suddenly, as if by scorching. The main means of treating fireblight is by cutting out affected limbs well below the area of visible infection. Prevent outbreaks by planting resistant varieties.

Bacterial Soft Rot

Like damping-off, this disease is caused by several different organisms, in this case by several bacteria. It consists of a watery, mushy decay of the fleshy parts of plants, usually accompanied by a foul odor. This may destroy tubers, bulbs, or ripening fruit. Follow the preceding general instructions for reducing moisture, keep your crops well-harvested, and clean up plant debris and remove it from your garden to reduce the source of infection.

VIRUS DISEASES

When plants are infected with these diseases, their leaves often have discolored blotches. Plants are often stunted, with leaves that are puckered and misshapen, but no insect will be visible. Fruit may be blotchy or lumpy. Viruses are tiny living particles, not even complete cells. They can't usually live very long outside of a living creature, so they rarely survive in the soil. They are spread mainly by insects, by infected seed, and in some cases by contact with plants, tools, or gardener's hands with virus particles on them.

Since there are no biological or chemical cures for these diseases, control must focus on cultural methods. Some possibilities are choosing resistant varieties, buying certified seeds, bulbs, or rootstocks, growing extra crop plants (in case you lose some to a virus), removing infected plants, and planting when the infecting insects are least active.

Of course, it is also a good idea to control the specific insects that spread the viruses, but it is rarely possible to eliminate them completely. Aphids are the most common virus-spreading insects and also one of the most common of insect pests. Other common vectors of viral diseases are leafhoppers, whiteflies, and mealybugs.

Many viruses cause symptoms known as *mosaic*, a streaking or mottling of leaves with shades of green and/or yellow. Other viruses cause mainly stunting, sometimes along with curled leaves. Symptoms of different viruses may overlap, and plants may also be infected by more than one kind of virus.

Your most likely encounter with virus disease will be to notice that one plant of a particular crop is seriously malformed on them or that its leaves have very strange markings. And the most common control strategy you will use is to pull the infected plant. Often, that will be the end of that. However, several viruses are common enough to merit learning their specific symptoms and ways to prevent them from reducing your harvests.

Inland gardeners may have to contend with one virus that coastal gardeners usually do not. Curly top virus infects beets, beans, and tomatoes. It is spread by the beet leafhopper, an insect that does little damage other than spread the virus and is more common inland than near the coast.

Curly Dwarf Virus of Artichoke

See the description on page 178.

Tobacco Mosaic Virus

Tomatoes get several mosaic viruses, the most common being the tobacco mosaic virus. Most gardeners know not to let smokers handle their tomato plants, as they are likely to spread the disease from infected tobacco in cigarettes. But many gardeners are not familiar with the symptoms of the disease. Tobacco mosaic does not, as one might expect, cause tobacco-colored spots on the leaves. (These are more likely to be a less serious leaf speck or spot caused by a bacterium or a fungus.)

The symptoms of tobacco mosaic are subtle and varied. On young plants, or in cool weather, the leaves are likely to be malformed. They will be long and narrow, commonly called "shoestring," or may be more pointed than usual. On older plants, look for mottling of leaves. It will most commonly be a subtle pale and dark green mottle (looking at the leaf with the light behind it will help you to see this), but some strains of the virus produce a bright yellow mottle. Plants may wilt severely on a very sunny day following a foggy period. They may be stunted or have dying leaves or malformed and brown-spotted fruit.

Tobacco mosaic virus can infect soil briefly but probably doesn't linger until the next season. In fact, waiting as few as 20 days to replace an infected plant will greatly reduce the chance of reinfection. However, the disease is easily spread, not only by touching tomato plants after handling infected tobacco, but also by touching infected and then uninfected plants. When you remove an infected plant, it is safest to also remove any tomato plants that were adjacent to and touching it. Then wash your hands and any tools that touched the infected plant with a 3-percent solution of TSP (trisodium phosphate). Use the solution to wipe off door knobs, hose valves, and any other items you handled as well. Launder clothing that touched diseased plants.

Seek out resistant tomato varieties, identifiable by the initial "T" following their names. To be quite safe from reinfection by virus in the soil, wait a year before replanting a susceptible crop in the same location. Other tomato family crops can get tobacco mosaic virus as well, as can spinach, mustard, and tomato family weeds.

Zucchini Yellow Mosaic Virus

This viral disease has become common only in the past few years, and is wreaking havoc in local gardens. Spread by aphids, it affects zucchini and other summer squash, cucumbers, and pumpkins. The leaves develop yellow blotches and become stiff and brittle. Plants remain stunted, and the fruit becomes lumpy and misshapen.

It is best to halt the spread of this disease by removing infected plants from the garden. A good strategy is to plant a few extra seeds, to be sure you have enough plants left when the disease strikes. Also, if too much of your early planting is affected, remember you can replant cucumbers till late June and summer squash until mid-July. The aphids are less likely to spread the disease at these later planting times.

TEN

Growing Like Weeds

GARDENERS OFTEN ASK ABOUT an unknown green interloper, "Is that a plant or is it a weed?" Of course, we all know exactly what they mean; on the other hand, we also know that weeds are plants.

Before there were gardens, the Anglo-Saxons used the word *wèod* to refer to all small plants generally. As plants were invited into gardens they were withdrawn from the weed category, becoming instead such things as crops and flowers. Since then, the term *weed* has been reserved for any unmannerly wild plant that came into our gardens against our wishes.

Like gardeners of food crops and flowers everywhere, we must contend with many kinds of weeds: uninvited seedlings that blanket our seedbeds, wild vines that entangle our garden plants, and tough perennials that sprout each year from missed bits of root. We must control these weeds if we are to have productive and beautiful gardens. To save time and energy combating weeds, we need to understand the habits of these unwelcome plants.

JUST WHAT IS A WEED?

Some would have it that a weed is only a flower or vegetable growing in the wrong place, and this certainly can be the case. When you have carefully sown and tended nasturtiums, you call them flowers. With pleasure you watch them grow, enjoying their bright accents in your yard. You may even be charmed when nasturtiums reseed themselves, adding their cheeriness to other parts of your garden. However, when these fast-growing seedlings crowd out your delicate baby carrots, you are right to consider them weeds. Other domesticated plants that can make pests of themselves locally include Algerian ivy, calla lily, sweet alyssum, and our local onion lily (wild onion). Our most common wild blackberry was once a domesticated plant, but it succeeded so well in this region that it is now one of our most familiar and hard-to-control weeds.

Another definition of weed is a plant that grows mainly in places markedly disturbed by humans. Nature rarely clears and churns up the soil as much as we do when we are about to plant a garden. Plants have to be tough to survive such conditions, which occur naturally only after floods, landslides, and other natural disturbances.

Many of these denizens of disturbed places, such as dandelions, lambsquarters, pigweed, and dock, have followed humans over most of the earth. Carried unintentionally in grain, manure, animal fur, implements, and vehicles, their seeds have proved adaptable to a wide range of climates. Although plants native to California turn up as weeds in our gardens, they are rarely among the most difficult to control, maybe because they have not had centuries to adapt to our gardening practices.

The imported, worldwide weeds have adjusted in many ways to human efforts to control them. Some have evolved seeds that closely resemble those of commercial crops—understandable, since those were the seeds most likely to survive. One old-world weed common in California, yellow starthistle, makes two kinds of seeds, one smaller and darker than the other. The smaller seed is hard to separate from several kinds of commercial seeds, so the weed has been able to survive as a contaminant of crops. If you have ever tried to pull sowthistle, also called wild lettuce, from hard soil, you have encountered another adaptation. The stem will often break near the ground, then sprout again from buds near the soil surface.

THE PROS AND CONS OF WEEDS

There are many good reasons to control weeds. They can disrupt the design of ornamental plantings and make a vegetable garden look disorderly. They harbor pests, including diseases, that can spread to domesticated plants. Some weeds exude chemicals that slow the growth of plants around them, a process called *allelopathy*. They compete with intentionally planted vegetables and flowers for water, nutrients, and light—and if ignored for long, they will simply take over. Weeds can cover the ground in a solid mat that few vegetables or flowers can penetrate. Some weeds, such as fennel or blackberry, can eventually make your yard impossible to walk across, never mind using it for a garden.

On the other hand, there are reasons to tolerate weeds and even to encourage them. Some weeds are edible and make welcome additions to salads and omelets. As long as they haven't gone to seed, most weeds can be used to make compost, or they can be dug into the soil as green manure. Pulled before they go to seed, many weeds can be left on the soil surface to mulch it and to feed earthworms and other soil organisms. (Most annual weeds will not reroot if left on the soil surface in summer, but more care must be taken to avoid rerooting during the wetter winter months.) Certain weeds can even be tolerated for short periods as a living mulch. Many weeds also provide pollen for bees and serve as a refuge for certain helpful insects.

As Joseph Cocannouer explained in his classic *Weeds: Guardians of the Soil*, some deep-rooted weeds, which he referred to as deep divers, provide another crucial service—opening up the subsoil to water and to the roots of more delicate plants. Most of our garden crops have been bred for their tops and not their roots, and consequently they have relatively weak root systems that do not penetrate deep. Many weeds, because they have had to be tough to survive, have very strong, deep-reaching roots. These deep divers include lambsquarters, wild chicory, plantain, purslane, nightshade, sowthistle, and vetch.

You can use deep divers to improve your soil, growing them either before you plant your garden or while you are gardening. Of course, you mustn't let even these weeds take over. Lambsquarters and sowthistle are the easiest to control, because their flowers are mostly at the top and can easily be cut off as they form. Vetch is also a good choice, since it is rarely an aggressive spreader. Do not allow these weeds to grow close together, or their roots won't go as deep; one deep diver every few feet is plenty. When the weeds become large, cut them off at ground level, leaving their roots to decay in place. When added to the compost, the tops will enrich your garden with nutrients from deep in the subsoil.

Another reason to tolerate the occasional weed is that these intruders are interesting, adding a bit of serendipity to your garden. I had a friend who grew weeds in a window box in his San Francisco apartment, just watering and watching what came up. Learning to identify the plants that nature sends our way can be fun and educational, a little like bird watching. I let one plant of any unfamiliar weed grow in my garden until I am able to identify it. Until you learn to recognize the most noxious weeds, however, it is better to err on the side of control.

The Uses of Weeds

For Food: Chickweed, dandelion, dock, epazote, fennel, Himalaya blackberry, lambsquarters, miner's lettuce, mint, mustard, nasturtium, New Zealand spinach, onion lily, purslane, shepherds purse, sorrel, and wild radish.

For Ornament: Calla lily, Kenilworth ivy, nasturtium, and onion lily.

For Deep Diving: Lambsquarters, sowthistle, and vetch.

For Attracting Beneficial Insects: Fennel, mustard, wild radish, pigweed, and white sweet clover.

For Living Mulch: Chickweed and other annual weeds before they flower.

For Compost: Any weed that has not ripened seed and will not reroot.

DIFFERENT KINDS OF WEEDS

Like your garden crops, weeds have varying life spans. Some are annuals, completing their life cycle in less than a year. Others are biennials, starting from seed one spring, overwintering, blooming the following spring, and dying the second year. (In mild-winter regions such as ours, biennials may act like winter annuals, growing during the fall and going to seed in spring.) Still other weeds are perennials, living for three or more years.

Annual weeds sprout only from seed, dying at the end of one season. Biennials also sprout from seed, and they may die back in winter, then resprout from slightly thickened roots—although only once. Then they die, relying on seeds to carry on the generations. Perennial weeds sprout not only from seed, which most of them produce each year, but also from food storage structures—tubers, corms, bulbs, woody or starchy roots, or creeping stems—that stay alive in the soil from year to year. Because of these structures, perennials are much harder to eradicate than annuals or biennials.

In addition to the length of time that they live, weeds can be classified by the season of their most active growth. Some weeds grow the most in warm weather, sprouting as the soil warms and thriving on the water that you give your garden in summer. Common summer weeds include the annuals purslane, lambsquarters, mallow, and crabgrass, and the perennial bindweed. Other weeds are most active in winter, encouraged by our mild, rainy climate. They sprout as the winter rains begin and go to seed in March and April. Winter weeds include many grasses, chickweed, Cape oxalis, and our onion lily, or wild onion. Even if you don't plant a garden in winter, it is a good idea to keep winter weeds under control (see page 148).

HOW TO CONTROL WEEDS

The following tactics are based on the premise that we are smarter than weeds, and if they have gotten away from us it is only because we have not been paying enough attention to them. Of course, being smart, none of us want to spend all our weekends weeding. An hour spent reading about control strategies is likely to save many hours of actually pulling weeds.

Theoretically, if you killed every weed seedling that dared come up, soon you would have no weeds. However, weeds are not something you can ever completely eliminate. You will miss weeds here and there, and nature will bring new ones into your garden, so the struggle will always go on. Still, once you have eliminated the worst weeds, you will be able to stay in control with little day-to-day effort. (If you are facing a much-neglected yard, see page 148.)

Eradication Versus Limited Tolerance

Gardeners differ about the degree to which weeds should be controlled. One style of gardening insists that all weeds be cleared away. In a clean-culture garden, only the plants that the gardener has actually planted are allowed to survive. An opposing style, what I call selective weeding, involves a certain amount of laissez-faire. Selective weeders may let some weeds live at some times while controlling others. They may even encourage certain weeds, but with a clear understanding of when control is essential.

The clean-culture method is a good idea for a beginner because it is simple to learn. Clear the ground completely before you plant, and then remove anything else that comes up while your crops are growing. Period. Be thorough and stick with it. Selective weeding, on the other hand, requires knowing which weeds you have and how they are likely to interact with your crops. It also requires that you recognize flower and vegetable seedlings when they come up, whether you planted them or they seeded themselves. Perhaps the best approach is to practice clean culture when you are a beginner, then work toward a more selective approach as you learn more.

In my garden, I tolerate some purslane, chickweed, and onion lilies as food plants, and I sometimes let chickweed grow for a while as a living mulch (and salad green) in winter. Also, I am very tolerant of volunteer flowers and vegetables that sometimes come up without being planted. Johnny-jump-ups, forget-me-nots, and nasturtiums are among my flower volunteers, and potatoes, arugula, collards, mustard, parsley, salsify, and garland chrysanthemum are among my vegetable volunteers. Depending on where they appear and if I have room for volunteers, I may pull them, thin them, or transplant them to other spots in the garden. My goal is to encourage volunteer vegetables and flowers and useful weeds while reducing undesirable weeds. In time, a good gardener can change the makeup of the wild flora of a garden, so that much of what comes up is useful in one way or another.

Timing Is Crucial

Crops are most damaged by competition with weeds in their first six weeks after seeding. It is not enough just to clear the bed of weeds before you plant. In the first month or so after planting, you must think as much about keeping the seedbed weed-free as you do about watering and thinning the crop seedlings. And it is the weed seedlings that grow in the row, among the crop seedlings, that are most damaging—more so than the ones between the rows. Even clean-culture gardeners often weed too late to protect their crops during this critical period. The little weed seedlings look so innocent that no internal alarms go off to warn you of the serious competition for food and water that faces your desirable seedlings.

As crop plants get older and larger, they are less affected by weeds. Crops that grow tall quickly, such as corn, and crops that spread out fast to form a solid leaf canopy, such as bush beans, can hold their own against weeds sooner than crops that are shorter or have a less solid leaf canopy, such as radishes and onions.

SOME GENERAL CONTROL TACTICS

- **Mulching** Gardeners once hoed frequently between crops, not only to control weeds but also to maintain a dust mulch, which was believed to reduce surface evaporation. Hoeing was also supposed to open crusted soil so that water could penetrate more easily. However, it has been shown that dust is a poor mulch and doesn't prevent evaporation very well. Although hoeing will break up a crust, an organic mulch will accomplish the same purpose but with many additional benefits, including weed control, reduced evaporation, better water penetration, and improved soil structure and fertility. A thick organic mulch helps control weeds by reducing the germination of weed seeds beneath the mulch; also, any weeds rooted in the loose mulching material are easier to pull. However, mulching will not stop the sprouting of perennials weeds from their underground structures. Some perennials can even punch their way through a plastic sheet! (See page 147 for more about mulches.)
- **Shallow Cultivating** If you choose not to mulch, shallow cultivation is a good way to control weed seedlings. To keep from damaging the roots of your crop plants, cut no deeper than an inch. Choose a scuffle hoe, a short-handled cultivator, or any other tool with a blade that you hold parallel to the soil surface. This kind of tool will cut young weeds off just below the soil surface with minimal harm to the roots of crop plants.
- **Thick Planting** Another way to protect crop plants from weeds is to space them close enough together so that the leaves of adjoining plants touch at maturity. Fast-growing crops will shade out much weed growth.
- **Meeting Crop Needs** Growing your crops under the best possible conditions will give them an advantage when they compete with weeds. In general, provide loose and fertile soil, adequate water, and the proper amount of sunlight. Find out the special needs of each crop and try to meet them.

CONTROLLING ANNUAL (AND BIENNIAL) WEEDS

Seeds are an annual weed's only means of continuity. Combating the weed by eliminating its means of reproducing itself seems simple enough until you learn how many seeds an annual weed can produce in a season. Consider purslane, which doesn't appear to be much of a threat: it is squat, has small leaves, and is easy to uproot. But if you wait too long to pull it, purslane can drop fifty-two thousand seeds per plant! If you are wondering how so many seeds can germinate at once in a few square feet, they can't and they don't. What happens is worse.

The old adage "one year of seeds, seven years of weeds" is based on the fact that the seeds don't all germinate in the first year. The purslane that drops its thousands of little black seeds in your garden is ensuring that purslane seedlings will blanket your spring seedbeds for many years to come. Only 10 to 20 percent of the weed seeds will germinate each year. Assuming that 10 percent sprout yearly and that no new seeds are shed, 51 percent of the seeds will be left after seven years. At the rate of 20 percent each year, there will still be 21 percent left after seven years. In ten to twenty years, 1 percent of the original seeds will remain. So when you see your garden covered with annual weeds, understand that it is their seeding that you must prevent.

Many annual weeds bloom when they are quite young, and some have flowers so insignificant that you hardly realize that they are blooming until you look closely. Still others continue to ripen seeds after they have been pulled. These traits have developed or persisted because they allowed the weeds to survive eradication efforts. Here are some ways to control annual weeds before they take over your garden.

- **Hand Pulling** Start removing weed seedlings as soon as you can identify them. In small areas, if the soil is soft enough, you can use your hand to lift handfuls of soil with the seedlings, shake out the soil, and either place them back on the surface or remove them. Or use a weeding tool that cuts weed roots right under the surface (see Shallow Cultivating on page 144). If a weed seedling is located near to delicate crop seedlings, you can avoid harming the crop roots by cutting the weeds at soil level with scissors.

  Hand-pull larger weeds on days when the soil is moist and the weeds are easy to pull out. (Don't weed during soggy conditions, or you may damage your soil structure.) You may be able to pull more than one weed at once, but firmly rooted weeds often do not come out unless you pull them one by one. Reach down and grasp a weed near the base. If there are several branches at ground level, find them all and gather them into your hand before you pull. If you find that you are leaving the bottom of the plants in the ground, you are trying to pull too many at once or you are not reaching low enough. If a large weed is close to a crop plant, use one hand to hold the soil in place at the base of the weed as you pull, so that you won't pull up the crop plant too.

  As you gain experience gardening, you will learn the habits of various weeds and how to pull them, and you will be able to adjust your technique to different species. For example, you will need to hook a finger under crabgrass to pull out the base of the plant. Hand pulling will become easier as you continue to improve your soil. One day your soil will be so loose that you will pull out a really tough weed and realize that you did it with only a flick of your wrist!

- **Presprouting** Turning the soil even once before you plant will kill some weed seedlings. If your garden is heavily infested with weed seeds, however, a technique called presprouting will eliminate more weeds than just a single digging. This method works by tricking the weeds into using up their seeds faster. It takes some planning, but when you see the difference it can make for such hard-to-weed vegetables as carrots, you will agree that it is worthwhile.

  Begin by digging and amending your soil and raking it smooth. Water the soil and keep it moist, just as if you had sown crop seeds. In a week or two you will have a bed of little weed seedlings, mostly annuals. Kill the weeds by gently scraping the soil surface (it should be on the dry side) with a hoe or hand-weeding tool. Don't dig into the soil any more than necessary, because that will stimulate seeds that are deeper in the soil to sprout. If the plot is particularly weedy, water again, wait for more weeds to sprout, and destroy the seedlings before you plant. When you do plant, disturb the soil as little as possible to keep new weed seeds from sprouting.

  Weed presprouting must be done at a time of year when the weeds that you hope to control will germinate. Although some weeds will germinate almost anytime the soil is moist, others must wait for the soil to warm up in spring. I learned this the hard way presprouting weeds in an early carrot patch. The patch, which was perfectly clear in late March, was covered with tiny weed seedlings mixed with the young carrot plants by the middle of May. The late-starting weed seeds had escaped my hoe by remaining dormant. I presprouted in February and April the next time, and my June-planted carrot crop was practically weed-free. The earlier presprouting would have worked fine for a fast-growing crop, such as radishes, which would have been harvested before the weeds popped up in May.

  Even if presprouting doesn't work perfectly, it will reduce the number of weed seeds in your soil, hastening the day when a blanket of weed seedlings is a thing of the past. Presprouting also teaches you to recognize weed seedlings and helps you to distinguish them from crop seedlings. If you presprout weeds a couple of times a year, you will soon know most of the weeds that are likely to grow in your garden.

- **Postponing Delicate Crops** Even after presprouting, you may decide that an area is still too weedy for crops with delicate seedlings. If so, first plant a crop that quickly grows large, such as beans or potatoes. Keep the bed well weeded, and presprout again before you plant more delicate crops.

- **Planting in Rows** If there are still many weed seedlings coming up but you are impatient to start a delicate crop, plant the crop in rows. Rows are easier to weed than scatter-sown beds.

Deciding About Herbicides

Every gardener wishes for a magic way to make weeds vanish, and one result of this wishing is the development of herbicides. During the twentieth century, a number of synthetic chemicals were developed to kill unwanted plants. Some were even selective—killing, for example, only broad-leaved weeds in lawns, or only preventing seeds from germinating. They all sound good, but there are drawbacks.

Health hazards of synthetic herbicides give one pause. The EPA and the National Institutes for Health have reported cancer, reproductive effects, birth defects, as well as damage to nerves, kidneys, and liver for many of them. They may also harm other creatures and contaminate soil or groundwater. Because of these hazards, organic farmers and gardeners reject the use of any synthetic herbicides.

It is my opinion that herbicides should never be part of a regular garden maintenance program. I know weeding can be hard work. I hope you will learn from this chapter and from experience to weed smarter. But you won't escape weeding even if you use herbicides, so you may as well think of it as part of the game. Use preventative methods, compost weeds whenever you can, and keep the toxins out of your garden. However, I feel that I must address two concerns: (1) the development of less-toxic herbicides, and (2) whether there is ever a place for more toxic herbicides and, if so, which are least problematic.

Some new herbicides are based on materials from the EPA list of minimum-risk pesticides (for more on this, see Appendix IV). One of the earliest introductions was a soap-based spray. Soap is a mixture of potassium salts of fatty acids, some more toxic to plants than others. To make an herbicide, chemists selected for the plant-toxic ones.

There are also herbicides based on acetic acid (vinegar) or on clove oil that is acidified with acetic acid or citric acid. Studies show that the 5-percent acetic acid on your food shelf will kill many kinds of weeds, and that you may get better results with the 8- to 20-percent concentrations in some commercial herbicides.

These minimal toxicity pesticides are not selective, meaning they will harm or kill any plant they strike, so they are useless where weeds are intermingled with crop plants. They are also contact herbicides, not translocated through plants to roots, so perennial weeds like bindweed or oxalis may survive. Even if these weeds can be killed with repeated applications, the process may be more trouble than digging or pulling them.

Herbicides are most useful in two situations. The first is when a weed is growing in a crack in pavement or rocks and cannot be pulled. A less-toxic herbicide may do the trick—or even boiling water, if the weed isn't far from your kitchen.

The other situation is when you are trying to reclaim land from woody weeds such as Himalaya blackberry or Algerian ivy prior to planting a garden. Hand removal requires the two-step cut-and-dig method. That is, you have to cut top growth and then dig up the roots, or roots will regrow. Wildland weeders report that they feel the best use of time and resources in such a case is to cut as much of the woody weeds as possible, then paint the stumps with an herbicide to finish the job. They paint the stumps, rather than spray, to avoid breathing herbicide droplets and to limit the amount of herbicide used (thus greatly reducing soil or water contamination). For this purpose they typically use an herbicide containing glyphosate. Much controversy surrounds glyphosate, a product of Monsanto Corporation, which also bioengineers crop plants to withstand the chemical. I am not recommending its use but do want readers to know that it is used by wildland weeders in preference to other synthetic herbicides. Note that glyphosate is not registered for use in a food garden. (See page 394 for more on glyphosate.)

- **Avoiding New Infestations** Be aware of the possible sources of new weed seeds that may enter your garden. Think twice when your neighbor offers a pile of weeds for your compost. Unless you make a hot compost, you may end up with your neighbor's weed species as well as the ones you already have. Notice whether the weeds in nearby vacant lots form wind-borne seeds; if so, cut them down before the seeds form and blow into your garden. Keep new weed seeds out of your garden while working to eliminate the weed seeds already there, and over time you will have to contend with fewer and fewer annual weeds.

CONTROLLING PERENNIAL WEEDS

Although perennial weeds are sometimes big seed producers, they have an additional—and formidable—survival strategy of asexual reproduction from bulbs, corms, tubers, underground stems, or fibrous or thickened roots. When a perennial weed sprouts from one of these underground storage structures, it has more energy to draw on than if it were sprouting from a small seed. When you pull a dandelion and don't get the whole root, in a couple of weeks the part left in the ground can generate a plant that would have taken months to grow to that size from seed. Some perennial weeds almost never grow from seed, whereas others use both means of reproduction. If dock grows in your garden, you will soon learn to tell the difference between a robust sprout growing from a thickened root and the smaller, more delicate dock seedling.

The following techniques will help you prevent perennial weeds from gaining a roothold in your garden.

- **Digging Out** Although pulling and hoeing will remove perennial weed seedlings as easily as they do annual weed seedlings, these techniques are rarely sufficient to control more mature perennial weeds. You must also dig and remove the underground structure that allows the weed to spring back each season. Remember, some perennials will resprout from *every fragment* of runner or root that you leave behind, while others regrow from tiny bulbs or tubers. Yes, this digging can be hard work if the weeds have had several years to get a roothold. However, once you remove these structures, it is relatively easy to keep perennial weeds from ever becoming so well established again. After initial control efforts, keep pressure on perennial weeds by continuing to dig them whenever you see them and never letting them go to seed.

  Although you can dig out perennial weeds anytime in their life cycle, a particularly effective time is after they have just bloomed but before seed heads form. At that point, they are storing the least amount of energy underground. Another good time to dig them out is when they are just beginning to come up for the season, since you can use the technique of presprouting to find missed bits of root. Dig first, removing as many root pieces as you can, then water and wait for new sprouts to mark the location of the roots that you missed. Dig a second time to remove the sprouting fragments.

- **Cutting the Tops** When noxious perennial weeds are mixed with your crops, you won't be able to get into the soil to remove the roots, bulbs, or other underground structures. But at least you can keep the weeds from storing more food underground by cutting or pulling off their shoots. For instance, I try to pluck bindweed shoots before they are a couple of inches tall. You can do a more thorough job of removing the weeds during a break in crops.

- **Mulching to Smother** If your initial control efforts seem futile or if the area needing control is large, a smothering mulch may do the trick. To be effective against perennial weeds, a mulch must block light from reaching the soil and it must be difficult for weeds to penetrate. Ideally, the mulch will allow water to pass through and will decay slowly into the soil to improve it. Finally, the mulch should be relatively attractive.

  Black plastic will block light and stop most weeds, but it doesn't let water penetrate, will not decay into the soil, and is unsightly. Both newspaper and corrugated cardboard from boxes meet the criterion of effectiveness against weeds, and they will allow water through and decay into the soil. (For more information about newspaper as a gardening material, see page 93.) Commercially available weed mats can also be used, although they are more expensive and do not decay into the soil. On perennial weeds that are not very large, a layer of straw or wood chips at least 6 inches thick may be enough.

  Before spreading the mulch, clear an area as well as you can and water the soil thoroughly. If you are mulching with newspaper, spread it least six sheets thick. Double or triple the layer if you are dealing with very pushy weeds, such as fennel or blackberry. If you are using cardboard, spread a layer three sheets thick. Overlap the pieces of any smothering mulch material generously, so that weeds cannot grow between sections of the material.

Underground structures, such as this bindweed runner, allow perennial weeds to resprout.

Weight black plastic, commercial weed mat, newspaper, or cardboard here and there with soil as you go. Cover any of these materials with 2 to 4 inches of an organic mulch, such as straw or wood chips, to improve the appearance.

Keep the mulched area moderately moist, unless you are using black plastic. You can dig in an organic mulch anytime from several months to a year after the normal sprouting time of the perennial weeds that you are fighting. (Remove any black plastic and any large pieces of newspaper or cardboard that have not decayed.) Straw, wood chips, newspaper, and cardboard are low in nitrogen, so if you dig these in you will have to add nitrogen before planting.

- **Avoiding New Infestations** Just like annual weeds, perennial weeds can come into your garden as hitchhikers. A plant from a friend's yard or a nursery can be a Trojan horse, bearing Cape oxalis bulbs or nutsedge tubers hidden in the soil. If you accept plants that you suspect are contaminated by perennial weeds, be on guard. Remove any visible weeds and weed storage structures from the soil around your new plants, then watch for new sprouts. As a precaution, you may want to keep the plants in containers for a few months until you are sure that the soil around the roots is free of perennial weeds. Remember that the weed that doesn't get into your garden in the first place is one you won't have to control, and one you get out before it can multiply is one you won't spend years trying to get rid of.

HOW TO CONTROL (AND USE) WINTER WEEDS

Our mild, rainy winters give local gardeners a special concern: winter weeds. As the hills turn green, so do our gardens. From our windows the green looks pretty, and the chilly, wet weather makes it easy to ignore the fact that those plants are weeds. Although the weeds offer the soil some protection against the pelting winter rains, they will lead to big trouble if they are ignored for too long.

As the days grow shorter and colder, winter weeds will outgrow most fall-planted garden crops. Soon they will be shading them and usurping scarce nutrients. By March or April, weed seeds will begin to ripen. If you wait for fine spring weather to begin weeding, you will be pulling large, tough weeds from drying soil. They will require more care and effort in composting because of the seeds and the woody stems. You will probably prefer to throw the weeds, along with the nutrients they have removed from your soil, into the trash.

Winter weeding is the undoing of many clean-culture gardeners, who tend to keep summer gardens immaculate but fall down on the job in winter. It is important to continue weeding the year around. Even if you are a selective weeder, do not, under any circumstances, let winter weeds grow past January or February, when they begin to go to seed.

Although keeping winter weeds under control is crucial, there are also several ways to make use of the weeds. Sometimes I allow them to grow as a living mulch for a few weeks (I've let chickweed grow among cabbages, yanking it out in handfuls when it got too tall), but I do not tolerate aggressive perennials or let weeds overgrow my winter crops. Since garlic, onions, and winter legumes cannot endure competition from weeds, I always keep those beds weed-free. I often leave pulled chickweed and similar weeds on the soil surface as a mulch not only in summer but also in winter, even though the risk of rerooting is greater during the rainy season. Grasses are particularly likely to reroot and should be placed roots up after they are pulled.

Rerooting is less likely if you turn the weeds into the soil as a green manure. This should be done when they are still small enough to decompose easily and on a day when the soil is not too soggy from rain. If I have many weeds that may reroot or have grown a little too large for green manure, I use them to make a sheet compost (see page 92) to be dug under later in spring.

I find edible weeds more welcome in winter than summer. In summer, purslane comes up just as my cactus pads are ready and when there are large harvests of zucchini, cucumbers, and green beans. In winter, I take great delight in tossing together salads of domesticated lettuce with plenty of miner's lettuce, chickweed, and onion lily (wild onion) leaves, topped with onion lily flowers, borage, and Johnny-jump-ups. Steamed dock leaves are a great treat when the last of the brussels sprouts are gone and the early spring greens are only just beginning to break through the earth.

HOW TO RECLAIM NEGLECTED LAND

After a garden is abandoned, the first weeds that appear are mostly annuals. In a few years, the harder-to-control perennials take over. We have all seen

Soil Solarization—If You Have Enough Sunshine . . .

A relatively new technique to control most weeds and some soil pests, soil solarization involves covering the soil with clear plastic sheeting for six to eight weeks. If the days are warm enough, the soil near the surface will get hot enough to kill weed seeds, fungus spores, and other pests. Unfortunately, coastal gardens may never get warm spells that last long enough for this technique to be effective. Several consecutive warm spells may be enough to produce results in the sunnier parts of the region.

Soil solarization works work best in an area at least 6 by 9 feet. Clear the soil, then smooth it so that the plastic covering will be in contact with as much soil as possible. Water the soil thoroughly and cover it with one or two layers of sturdy clear plastic (recent studies showed that two layers are more effective than one). If you must piece together the plastic, use transparent tape, duct tape, or a heatproof and waterproof glue. Tuck the edges of the plastic into the soil—and hope for a lot of sunshine!

abandoned lots in our neighborhoods. In winter, they are a riotous green, blanketed with grasses, Cape oxalis, and other winter weeds. In summer, only large, deep-rooted perennials, such as arching blackberries and towering fennel, remain green; the smaller plants turn brown, just as the small plants on the coastal hills do.

You can't expect to prepare an untamed, overgrown yard for planting in a day. You may not even be able to walk across it. Although I hope you won't have to face a badly neglected yard, especially if it is to be your first garden, the truth is that you may have to tackle one someday.

The following is a plan that, begun in fall or winter, will allow you to plant by early to midsummer. Begun in summer, it will allow you to plant by late winter or early spring. Be sure to put as much as you can into your initial attack. Enlist volunteer or paid help if there is too much work, since success or failure in the initial stages may mean the difference between an actual garden and a perpetual "someday" garden.

1. **Cut** Start by cutting and removing all the plants you don't want, including woody plants. Use hand pruners, loppers, or even a machete (if you are skillful with one) to cut the aboveground parts of blackberry brambles, fennel stalks, grasses, and other unwanted plants. Alternatively, consider using goats or sheep to do your initial clearing. Check Internet listings for companies that rent these four-legged weeders. (They eat most plants, so if there are any desirable plants, you'll need to fence them off temporarily.)

2. **Dig Out** Set about chopping and digging out what is left. Don't try to dig out weed roots when the soil is dry. Water the soil thoroughly several days in advance, so that it will be moist but not soggy when you are ready to dig. A mattock or grub hoe is a good tool for cutting up and removing the base of tough weeds, such as fennel or wild pampas grass. (You can rent these heavy-duty tools inexpensively from a tool rental company.) A garden fork is a good tool for finding and removing trailing roots. If you have perennial weeds that spread by root fragments, don't be tempted to use a rotary tiller. Rototilling will make the situation worse by chopping the roots into fragments from which new plants can sprout.

3. **Discard** Although it is possible to compost some of the debris, it will contain many seeds and storage structures from which new weeds can grow. You would have to sort carefully and put any dubious material in a hot compost pile. Since you are probably impatient to finish clearing the yard, I suggest that you just put all the debris—the brambles, brush, grasses, rootstocks, runners, bulbs, corms, and tubers—into the trash or, if you have them, municipal compost containers, and save your own composting for later.

4. **Presprout** Although the cleared area looks bare, there will be many seeds and roots lurking in the soil. Let them start to grow, keeping the soil moist during the dry season to encourage their growth. Turn the soil when the weeds are a few inches high but before they have a chance to go to seed. Turn the seedlings under, and dig out any weeds that are sprouting from roots or other underground structures. Put these sprouting perennial weeds in the trash or municipal compost container.

5. **Presprout Again** Wait for more weeds to grow, watering if necessary to encourage growth. When the weeds are a few inches high, kill the seedlings by lightly scraping the soil surface with a hoe. Keep presprouting, hoeing, and digging every few weeks for the next four to six months.

6. **Plant** Dig in organic amendments, add fertilizer, and plant. Having come this far, you may want to grow a cover crop, or a green manure (see page 76) or make a sheet compost (see page 92) before you plant.

7. **Keep Watch** Although this program will clear your garden well enough for you to start planting crops, you must be vigilant for the next couple of years. Watch especially for winter-sprouting perennials in fall and summer-sprouting perennials in late spring and early summer. A "rotation" of bindweed in summer and Cape oxalis in winter is a common one in neglected local gardens. Plan on continuing to dig out some underground structures for several years.

If you find yourself losing the battle against perennial weeds in your garden, because either the area is so large or you can't seem to dig out enough of the storage structures, consider using a smothering mulch on the cleared ground (see page 147). Gardeners in sunny, hot parts of the region can try soil solarization (see the previous page). Woody weeds regrowing from stumps can be difficult to remove. If you didn't hire help, but find you can't dig them, you might want to hire someone just to dig these out. Wildland weeders sometimes also use an herbicide, painted on the stumps, at this stage (see page 146).

You are undoubtedly thinking, "Six months to a year is a long time to wait before I can garden. Can't I get something growing sooner?" For the understandably impatient would-be gardener, here are two good options. One is to garden temporarily in containers. A relatively inexpensive method is to plant in plastic garbage bags filled with compost or a mixture of compost and a purchased soil mix. Unattractive at first, the bags will gain considerably in charm when they are bursting with healthy crops. When your garden is ready, just dig the planting medium into your soil.

Here is another good way to have your garden and prepare it too: Leave small openings, no more than a foot in diameter, in the smothering mulch and set individual plants in them. In these openings amend the soil, making one more effort to remove perennial underground storage structures as you mix in the amendment. Plant and water thoroughly. When the seedlings are well established, lay on more mulch until it almost touches the stems. Large individual plants, such as tomatoes, cabbage, and broccoli, and hills of squash, corn, and pole beans are good choices for this treatment. You run a risk that perennial weeds will burst though the openings, but it's a controllable risk.

WEEDS YOU'RE LIKELY TO SEE

The chart on the following pages lists the weeds that I have encountered frequently in my San Francisco garden or have heard are a problem in other gardens in this region. I have grouped annual and biennial weeds and listed perennial weeds separately. The chart falls within more detailed descriptions of weeds that are the most troublesome, the most useful, or just plain interesting. (Seed sources for some of the edible weeds or their edible relatives are listed in code at the end of the descriptions. For an explanation of the codes, see Appendix IV.) The illustrations scattered throughout will help you to identify certain weeds, and the chart will allow you to make educated guesses about others. For more illustrations of the listed weeds, do an Internet search for the scientific name of the weed, as a phrase, and you will find many photos to help you figure out which you have.

If you need help identifying a weed, first show it to neighbors who garden, since they probably know the most common weeds in your neighborhood. If they can't help, refer to a good weed identification book (see Appendix VIII, Suggested Reading), check out weed-related websites (see Appendix VII, Resources for Gardeners), or consult an expert. People who know local weeds include nursery employees, Cooperative Extension agents, instructors of horticulture classes, and staff members of various gardening organizations. If no one recognizes the weed, take it to an herbarium, where experts can identify it by comparing it with pressed specimens. (See Appendix VII for a listing of herbaria.) You are much more likely to get a positive identification if your specimen has flowers on it; seedpods are helpful, but not crucial.

Compendium of Weeds

ANNUAL WEEDS

California Burclover

Medicago polymorpha (*Medicago hispida*)
Legume Family ❖ *Fabaceae* (*Leguminosae*)

Despite its common name, this weed is one of the ones that came from Europe, probably during the Spanish Mission Period. It has been used as pasture, as hay, and as a green manure crop. As a legume, it does have the ability to put nitrogen into soil, but it seeds itself too aggressively to tolerate in your garden.

This is a rangy plant, low to the ground, with clover leaves—little trefoils—and small yellow pea-type flowers in groups of three to eight. It is best to pull it before it can mature seeds, but if you do find seedpods, take a close look at them. They are miniature bean pods, typical of a legume, but rolled up in spirals with curved burrs along the outer edges for catching onto animals' hair. This hitchhiking ensures seed distribution. And, as you pull the plants, look for the little nitrogen-fixing nodules on the roots.

Chickweed

Stellaria media
Carnation Family ❖ *Caryophyllaceae*

Sprouting mainly in the fall and greening up winter gardens, chickweed seems to grow everywhere. It is a weak-stemmed, sprawling plant, with small bright green leaves and ¼-inch white flowers (*Stellaria* refers to the star shape of the blooms). Chickweed grows so fast that it often shades winter vegetable seedlings, but it is the most bothersome when it becomes entangled in perennial herbs and flowers. Growing through other small plants, it can be difficult to extricate and pull out. I have let chick weed grow as a living mulch under larger crops, such as broccoli, pulling handfuls of it now and then and leaving them on the soil.

Chickweed

Chickweed is edible and, in fact, was sold in the markets of Old England as a potherb. It has a fresh, mild flavor. Try flowering stem tips in salads, either with lettuce or as the main green. Chickweed can also be steamed or cooked in just the water that clings to it when you wash it; season it with butter and a squeeze of lemon juice.

Cotula (or Australian Brassbuttons)

Cotula australis
Sunflower Family ❖ *Asteraceae* (*Compositae*)

Domesticated relatives of this aggressive little spreader are used as ground covers. Left alone, the weed will cover your garden with a low dense feathery mat. Before it blooms, cotula looks very much like swine cress (see page 162) and thus its seedlings, like those of swine cress, are occasionally mistaken for carrot. However, you can distinguish cotula from swine cress by its flowers. Cotula has small flat greenish-yellow flowerheads borne on wiry leafless stems, rather like those of English chamomile.

Crabgrass (or Hairy Crabgrass)

Digitaria sanguinalis
Grass Family ❖ *Poaceae* (*Graminae*)

Hairy crabgrass germinates as the soil warms in spring. Its leaves are a light gray-green. On crabgrass seedlings, the leaves are almost as broad as long. Left to grow, crabgrass produces rosettes of grassy leaves, then flower stalks that reach out sideways. Wiry flower stems, arranged like fingers on an outstretched hand, branch out from the tips of the stalks. *Digitaria* refers to the digits of these imaginary hands.

If your soil is well amended, you can just scrape crabgrass seedlings off with a weeding tool. Once they have sent down their larger roots, they are hard to pull, even in loose soil. The trick is to hook a finger under each plant to make sure that you pull all of it out.

Young crabgrass plant

Some Weeds You May See

PERENNIAL WEEDS

Common Name (Latin Name)	Family	Source	Reproduction	Comments	Use
*Bermuda grass (*Cynodon dactylon*)	Poaceae	Old World	Seed, rhizomes, stolons	Very invasive	Lawn grass
*Bindweed, wild morning glory (*Convolvulus arvensis*)	Convolvulaceae	Europe	Taproot, rhizomes	Grows from root fragments	—
Birdseye speedwell (*Veronica persica*)	Scrophulariaceae	Europe, Asia	Runners, seeds	—	—
*‡Blackberry, Himalaya (*Rubus discolor*)	Rosaceae	Europe	Runners, seed	Very invasive	Edible berry
Calla lily (*Zantedeschia aethiopica*)	Araceae	South Africa	Rhizomes	Spreads slowly	Cut flower
Chicory (*Chicorium intybus*)	Asteraceae	Europe	Seed	—	Coffee substitute (roots)
Cineraria (*Pericallis* × *hybridus*)	Asteraceae	Europe	Seed	Purple daisy	Ornamental
Coast dandelion (*Hypochoeris radicata*)	Compositae	Old World	Seed, taproot	—	—
*Dandelion (*Taraxacum officinale*)	Asteraceae	Europe	Seed, taproot	Root breaks when pulled	Edible
*Dock (*Rumex crispus*, *R. obtusifolius*)	Polygonaceae	Europe, Asia	Rootstocks, seed	Grows from root fragments	Edible
Ehrharta grass (*Ehrharta erecta*)	Poaceae	South Africa	Seed, rooted stem joints	Invasive	—
*‡Fennel (*Foeniculum vulgare*)	Apiaceae	Mediterranean	Seed	Large plants	Culinary herb
‡German ivy (*Delairea odorata*)	Compositae	South Africa	Seed, runners	Climber	Houseplant
*Grasses, perennial (various species)	Poaceae	Various	Seed, rhizomes, stolons	—	—
Horsetail (*Equisetum hyemale*, *E. arvense*)	Equisetaceae	Native	Rhizomes	Probably poisonous	Ornamental
‡Ivy, Algerian (*Hedera canariensis*)	Araliaceae	Canary Islands	Runners, seed	Invasive	Ornamental
*‡Ivy, English (*Hedera helix*)	Araliaceae	Europe, East Asia, North Africa	Runners	Invasive	Ornamental
Judean pellitory (*Parietaria judaica*)	Urticaceae	Europe	Seed	Leaves sticky	—
Jupiter's beard, red valerian (*Centranthus ruber*)	Valerianaceae	Europe, Mediterranean	Seed	—	Cut flower, Ornamental
Kenilworth ivy (*Cymbalaria muralis*)	Scrophulariaceae	Europe	Seed, runners	Small, nice in cracks	Ornamental

** means it is a particularly troublesome weed (common in gardens and hard to control)*
‡ means it is problematic as a wildland weed

Some Weeds You May See

Common Name (Latin Name)	Family	Source	Reproduction	Comments	Use
Mints (*Mentha* spp.)	Lamiaceae	Various	Runners	Invasive	Edible, tea
*Nutsedge (*Cyperus esculentus*)	Cyperaceae	Old World	Tubers, seed	Tough to pull	—
*Onion lily, wild onion (*Allium triquetrum*)	Amaryllidaceae	Mediterranean	Bulbs, seed	Invasive	Edible, cut flower
*‡Oxalis, cape, Bermuda buttercup, (*Oxalis pes-caprae*)	Oxalidaceae	South Africa	Bulbs	Invasive	Edible (small amounts)
*Oxalis, creeping (*Oxalis corniculata*)	Oxalidaceae	Europe	Runners, Seed	Invasive	Edible (small amounts)
‡Pampas grass (*Cortaderia jubata*, *C. selloana*)	Poaceae	South America	Seed	*C. jubata* is the worse spreader	Cut flower
Plaintain, broadleaved (*Plantago major*)	Plantaginaceae	Europe	Seed	—	Edible
Plantain, narrowleaved (*Plantago lanceolata*)	Plantaginaceae	Europe	Seed	—	Edible
*Quackgrass (*Agropyron repens*)	Poaceae	Eurasia	Rootstocks, seed	—	—
‡Scotch broom (*Cytisus scoparius*)	Fabaceae	Europe	Seed	Invasive	Cut flower
Sorrel, sheep sorrel (*Rumex acetosella*)	Polygonaceae	Europe, Asia	Rootstocks	Acid soil	Edible (small amounts)

ANNUAL AND BIENNIAL WEEDS

Common Name (Latin Name)	Family	Source	Reproduction	Comments	Use
Annual bluegrass (*Poa annua*)	Poaceae	Europe	Seed	Dormant in summer	Lawn filler
Bull thistle (*Cirsium vulgare*)	Asteraceae	Europe, Asia	Seed	Sharp thorns Biennial	Ornamental seed heads
California burclover (*Medicago hispida*)	Fabaceae	Europe	Seed	Clinging seeds	Soil improver
*Chickweed (*Stellaria media*)	Caryophyllaceae	Europe	Seed	Heavy seeder	Edible
*Cotula (*Cotula australis*)	Asteraceae	Australia	Seed	—	—
*Crabgrass, hairy (*Digitaria sanguinalis*)	Poaceae	Europe	Seed	Heavy seeder, summer weed	—
Cranesbill (*Geranium* spp., esp. *G. Rotundifolium*)	Geraniaceae	Europe	Seed	—	—
Cudweed, pussy-toes (*Gnaphalium luteo-album*)	Asteraceae	Old World	Seed	—	Dry flower
Epazote (*Chenopodium ambrosioides*)	Chenopodiaceae	Tropical America	Seed	—	Culinary herb

Some Weeds You May See

ANNUAL AND BIENNIAL WEEDS (continued)

Common Name (Latin Name)	Family	Source	Reproduction	Comments	Use
Fumitory, white ramping (*Fumaria capreolata*)	Fumariaceae	Europe	Seed	Climbs in low plants	—
*Groundsel, common (*Senecio Vulgaris*)	Asteraceae	Europe	Seed	Heavy seeder	—
Hedge mustard (*Sisymbrium officinale*)	Brassicaceae	Europe	Seed	—	Edible
Herb Robert (*Gerianium robertianum*)	Geraniaceae	Europe	Seed	Pink flowers, strong odor	Pressed flower/ leaf art
Horseweed (*Conyza canadensis*)	Asteraceae	United States	Seed	—	—
Ivyleaf morning glory (*Ipomoea hederacea*)	Convolvulaceae	Tropical America	Seed	Climber	Ornamental
Lady's thumb (*Polygonum persicaria*)	Polygonaceae	Europe	Seed	Matlike	—
Lambsquarters, nettleleaf goosefoot (*Chenopodium murale*)	Chenopodiaceae	Europe	Seed	Leaf backs green-mealy	Edible, deep-rooted
Lambsquarters, white goosefoot (*Chenopodium album*)	Chenopodiaceae	Europe	Seed	Leaf backs white-mealy	Edible, deep-rooted
*Mallow, cheeseweed (*Malva* spp., esp. *M. parviflora* and *M. minicaensis*)	Malvaceae	Europe	Seed	Heavy seeder	Edible
Milk thistle (*Silybum marianum*)	Asteraceae	Europe	Seed	Biennial	Edible
Miner's lettuce (*Montia perfoliata*)	Portulacaceae	California	Seed	—	Edible
Mustard, wild (*Brassica* spp., esp. *B. juncea*, *B. kaber*, *B. nigra*, *B. rapa*)	Brassicaceae	Europe, Asia	Seed	—	Edible
Nasturtium (*Tropaeolum majus T. minus*)	Tropaeolaceae	South America	Seed	Some climb	Edible leaf and flower, cut flower
Nettle, small (*Urtica urens*)	Urticaceae	Europe	Seed	Stinging hairs	Edible if cooked
New Zealand spinach (*Tetragonia tetragonioides*)	Aizoaceae	New Zealand	Seed	Matlike	Edible
Nightshade, black (*Solanum nodiflorum*, *S. furcatum*)	Solanaceae	Europe, South America	Seed	Poisonous	—
*Pellitory (*Parietaria hespera hespera*)	Urticaceae	California	Seed	Leaves a little sticky	—

** means it is a particularly troublesome weed (common in gardens and hard to control)*
‡ means it is problematic as a wildland weed

Some Weeds You May See

Common Name (Latin Name)	Family	Source	Reproduction	Comments	Use
*Petty spurge (*Euphorbia peplus*)	Euphorbiaceae	Europe	Seed	—	—
Pineappleweed (*Matricaria matricarioides*)	Asteraceae	Probably California	Seed	—	—
‡Poison hemlock (*Conium maculata*)	Apiaceae	Europe	Seed	Poisonous biennial	—
Popweed, hairy bittercress (*Cardamine hirsuta*)	Brassicatceae	Europe, Asia	Seed	Seeds jump from pods	Edible
Prickly oxtongue (*Picris echioides*)	Asteraceae	Europe	Seed	—	—
Prostrate knotweed (*Polygonum aviculare*)	Polygonaceae	United States, Europe, Asia	Seed	Matlike	—
*Prostrate spotted spurge (*Euphorbia maculata*)	Euphorbiaceae	Eastern United States	Seed	Matlike	—
*Purslane (*Portulaca oleracea*)	Portulacaceae	Europe	Seed	Heavy seeder	Edible
Rough pigweed (*Amaranthus retroflexus*)	Amaranthaceae	Tropical America	Seed	—	Edible
Scarlet pimpernel (*Anagallis arvensis*)	Primulaceae	Europe	Seed	Poisonous	—
Shepherds purse (*Capsella bursa-pastoris*)	Brassicaceae	Europe	Seed	—	Edible
*Sowthistle, wild lettuce (*Sonchus oleraceus*)	Asteraceae	Europe	Seed	—	Edible if young, deep-rooted
*Spiny sowthistle (*Sonchus asper*)	Asteraceae	Europe	Seed	—	Deep-rooted
Storksbill (*Erodium* spp., esp. *E.botrys*, *E. cicutarium*, *E. moschatum*)	Geraniaceae	Europe	Seed	—	—
*Swine cress (*Coronopus didymus*)	Brassicaceae	South America	Seed	Heavy seeder	—
Vetch, common (*Vicia sativa*)	Fabaceae	Europe	Seed	—	Deep-rooted, improves soil
Wall bedstraw (*Gallium parisiense* and probably *G. aparine*)	Rubiaceae	Europe	Seed	—	—
Wild radish (*Raphanus sativus*)	Brassicaceae	Europe	Seed	—	Young seed pods edible
Yellow foxtail (*Setaria glauca*)	Poaceae	Europe	Seed	—	—
‡Yellow star thistle (*Centaurea solstitalis*)	Asteraceae	Europe	Seed	Sharp spines under flowers	Poisonous to horses

Groundsel, Common (or Senecio)

Senecio vulgaris
Sunflower Family ❖ *Asteraceae* (*Compositae*)

Here is a little weed with no redeeming value. It isn't pretty or edible. Also, it uses a great deal of nitrogen, competing strongly with crops. Furthermore, the weed blooms when it is quite young, and its flowers continue to ripen seeds even after the plant has been pulled. If it lacks enough nutrients, light, or water, it just produces a smaller plant, which can bloom at only a couple of inches high, though it can grow to about 15 inches high when conditions are good.

Common groundsel is an upright plant, with larger leaves at the base and gradually smaller leaves up the stem. Narrow with toothed edges, groundsel leaves resemble small, narrow chrysanthemum leaves. The flowerheads, about ⅜ inch across, consist of many tiny yellow flowers. The seeds are carried on white fluff that floats over a wide area to ensure a larger and thicker stand of seedlings in the following year.

Hoe or pull groundsel seedlings when they are still small. If a plant has flowers, remove it from the garden.

Judean Pellitory

Parietaria judaica
Nettle Family ❖ *Urticaceae*

This old-world weed and the similar native *P. hespera hespera* are widespread in our region. *P. judaica* and other native European pellitories are common in Mediterranean Europe, where they grow, as they do here, very successfully in the cracks between sidewalks and buildings or between the rocks in retaining walls. The small, thin leaves are covered with short hairs that cause them to adhere slightly to clothing. The tiny flowers are borne along the stems at the leaf joints. Both stems and flowers are often pinkish.

Judean Pellitory

Pellitory isn't a major pest, but it can be hard to eliminate, especially when it grows wedged between bricks, concrete, wood, or other elements of garden construction. In such cases, it is difficult to pry out the whole plant.

Lambsquarters (or White Goosefoot or Fat Hen)

Chenopodium album

Lambsquarters (or Nettleleaf Goosefoot)

C. murale
Goosefoot Family ❖ *Chenopodiaceae*

Several members of the genus *Chenopodium* are known as lambsquarters. They are upright plants with one main stem that can grow several feet high. Their leaves are roughly triangular with wavy or toothed edges, and their flowers are almost unnoticeable, resembling a cluster of tiny unopened buds.

Two species are particularly common in local gardens. *C. album* has a white mealy substance on the undersides of the leaves. The mealy coating is also on the upper surfaces of the leaves near the top of the plant, giving the growing tip a pleasant dusty white appearance. *C. murale* has a dull green mealy substance on the backs of the leaves, and a red tinge on the leaves, stems, and flower buds.

Neither of these weeds is very difficult to manage. If you let seed mature, seedlings will follow, so it's best to pull them young. Young plants are good for green manure or compost, and mature plants are among those that serve well as deep-diving weeds. They are also edible, and reasonably palatable. Both are among the plants that were widely eaten in Europe before the introduction of spinach from Persia in the 1500s. Try very young plants in salad or steamed, perhaps mixed with other greens.

Worldwide, a number of other *Chenopodium* species are eaten. Good King Henry, *Chenopodium bonicus-henricus*, is a European species still grown for its tender shoots, leaves, and flowerheads. Magentaspreen is a plant of possibly Asian origin that is usually classified as *C. giganteum*. It has a bright magenta meal on its young leaves at the top of the plant. (Children call it lipstick plant and enjoy applying the magenta powder to lips and eyelids.) The magenta leaves and young, growing stem tips are striking in salad, and their leaves make a good steamed vegetable. Left to themselves, the plants grow to over 6 feet high and will reseed, but if you pull most before seeds drop, you can have just a few volunteers each year to transplant and use.

From the U.S. Southwest into South America, other species have been used for greens or grain. One, known as Huazontle by the Aztecs, is classified as *C. berlandieri*. The variety usually sold has red leaves when it matures. Its leaves are used like spinach, the flowerheads are stir-fried before the flowers open, and the mature seeds are also eaten. It is one of the weeds gathered in Mexico and often served as mixed greens, with wild amaranth and perhaps other wild greens, as *quelites*. *Chenopodium quinoa* is the species grown in the Andes to produce grain. For more on quinoa, see page 254.

A near relative of *Chenopodium* is orach (*Atriplex hortensis*). Orach was known as a vegetable by the Greeks and Romans. The most commonly grown variety in today's gardens is known as purple or red orach. The smallish leaves, which are a dusky magenta purple, are a nice addition to salad.

Mallow seedling

A possible downside to growing wild or domestic *Chenopodiums* in your garden is that they can attract pests of beets and chard, such as beet leafhopper and beet leafminer. However, the leafhopper is rare in cool microclimate gardens, and though I have big problems with the leafminer, I have not noticed it damaging my magentaspreen.

Sources

C. *album* or C. *murale* seed: BG, JG, JLH, RH
C. *berlandieri* seed: ABL, JLH, RH, SOC
C. *bonus-henricus* seed: BG, RH
C. *giganticum* (magentaspreen) seed: BG, JLH, JSS, NGN, SOC
Red orach seed: BCS, BG, JG, JLH, NGN, PGS, RH, SESE, SOC, TERR

Mallow (or Cheeseweed)

Malva (various species)
Mallow Family ❖ *Malvaceae*

If your seedbed is covered with seedlings that have pairs of little heart-shaped leaves, don't ignore them—you have a mallow problem in the making. This is a plant to eliminate early on, because it can grow large and become extremely difficult to pull. At 3 to 4 feet high, a well-rooted mallow can take the strength of two people to wrestle it out. A specimen 6 to 8 feet high means hard work with a mattock—I know from experience. So whenever I see the mallow seedlings with their pretty, dark green, elongated hearts, I become quite heartless and start cultivating.

The mature leaves of a mallow are dark green and more or less round, with radiating veins and a toothed edge. They may have shallow lobes. The flowers, most often pinkish lavender, are borne where a leafstalk joins a main stem. The blooms are followed by intriguing seedpods that look like little cheese wheels—hence the name cheeseweed. The seeds are the wedge-shaped sections of the wheels.

Mallow seed head

The weedy mallows are edible plants (very high in vitamin A), although their flavor is not particularly interesting. The leaves can be used as a potherb and the immature seedpods are fun to nibble.

Closely related but less weedy mallows are among our favorite garden flowers: flowering mallows, lavateras, hibiscus, and hollyhock.

Milk Thistle

Silybum marianum
Sunflower Family ❖ *Asteraceae* (*Compositae*)

Milk thistle is a common sight along our roadways, and you may very well see its rosettes of basal leaves getting a start in your garden. The weed is easy to identify, as the leaves have spiny edges and very noticeable white markings. A biennial weed, milk thistle usually does not bloom or mature its seeds until the second year, so you will probably have time to get it out.

I have seen this plant grown for its ornamental leaves in Bay Area gardens. In North Africa, the young leaves, stems, roots, and bases of the flowerheads are boiled and eaten—after removing any spines. (The flowerhead bases are said to resemble artichoke.) The dried flowerheads, with their large, recurved spines, also make spectacular additions to dried flower bouquets. Despite these possible uses, I'm more comfortable pulling this plant when it is young, before it gets really prickly and the wind blows its seeds around.

Miner's Lettuce

Montia perfoliata (*Claytonia parviflora*)
Purslane Family ❖ *Portulacaceae*

A California native, miner's lettuce is an attractive and unusual plant, clear green and up to a foot tall when it is growing in reasonably fertile soil with enough water. It is smaller and reddish when it is dry or in too much sun. The youngest leaves are strap-like, the slightly older leaves are broadly triangular, and the mature leaves are nearly round with the flower stems growing unexpectedly right up through their centers. The small flowers are white or pinkish, and the tiny seeds shiny black.

Miner's lettuce

Unless miner's lettuce is crowding your crop seedlings or mature plants, save some plants to harvest. One of the most succulent of greens, rather like a mild spinach, it is delicious in a green salad lightly dressed with a vinaigrette.

Miner's lettuce may properly be called a wilding instead of a weed. In fact, perhaps it ought not to be called a weed at all. Although it may come up wild in your garden, it can be rather difficult to get started there intentionally. You will see it in spring, growing wild on the north side of hills or among grasses in light shade.

Start harvesting the triangular immature miner's lettuce leaves when they are over an inch across and continue harvesting the mature leaves until the flowers begin to form seeds. Don't take more than half of the leaves of any plant at once. The best way to harvest is to pick off just the leaf tops, so that you don't have to remove the leaf stems later in the kitchen.

When the seeds are ripening, around April, you can pull some plants and lay them on newspaper in a dry place. The seeds will fall out and can be collected to plant the following October. When you are harvesting, avoid leaves with leafminer damage. Not the hungry 49er gold miner for whom these plants were named, this is an insect that mines into leaves, creating a pale blotch. The proportion of damaged leaves is usually small.

Sources

Miner's lettuce seed: ABL, BG, CG, GS, IST, JSS, NGN, PGS, RCS, TERR

Mustard (or Wild Mustard, Field Mustard, or California Rape)

Brassica (various species)
Mustard Family ❖ *Brassicaceae* (*Crucifae*)

Wild mustard is a general term for a number of similar plants in the genus *Brassica* that appear wild in gardens and fields. Many are escapees from gardens or wild relatives of the mustards that we grow on purpose. The flowers are like those of domesticated mustard: yellow, four petaled, and with four long and two short pollen-bearing stamens. The plants typically bear large leaves at the base and smaller ones higher on the flowering stems. Long narrow pods, each containing two rows of small round seeds, form along the stems behind the flowers. Mustards are most often winter annuals, blooming in early spring.

If you grow domesticated mustard, you will soon learn to recognize the reseeded or wild plants. I usually leave the wild seedlings alone, as long as they are not too close to my garden plants, then pull them to eat when they are a few inches high. The leaves of most mustards are mild and tender when young, tougher and more bitter when older.

Wild mustard may attract aphids, loopers, and other pests of domesticated members of the mustard family. However, their shallow-necked flowers may also attract predators of these and other pests. In general, tolerate wild mustards in small numbers, examining them to see if they are attracting many pests.

Nettle (or Small Nettle)

Urtica urens
Nettle Family ❖ *Urticaceae*

Small nettle is a dark green, erect plant up to 2 feet high. The leaves, arranged alternately on the stems, are oblong, toothed, and pointed at the tips. Very small green flowers form in little bunches where the leafstalks join the stems.

Small nettle makes a very good addition to a compost pile, and the young plant can also be cooked and eaten as a nutritious vegetable. However, from the time that small nettle is a couple of inches high, it is covered with hairs that are hollow and filled with an irritating chemical. If you brush against these stinging hairs, your skin will itch and burn for at least a few minutes.

Nettle (*half-size*)

Wear gloves when harvesting small nettle. You can usually avoid a sting if you reach in and grasp the plant at the very bottom, almost below the soil line. Cooking the stems and leaves destroys any trace of the irritant.

Nightshade

Solanum (various species)
Nightshade Family ❖ *Solanaceae*

Any rangy, upright weed with small round black berries is likely to be in the nightshade family, which also includes tomatoes, potatoes, peppers, and eggplants. The leaves of nightshade weeds generally are triangular with wavy edges, and they are sometimes lobed. The flowers, plain white or tinted with purple, look like tomato flowers but are usually smaller. The berries, quite soft when ripe, contain several seeds. The plants may reach 3 feet high and wide, or they may mature at a much smaller size if they are growing in the shade or in competition with other plants.

Several closely related solanums are considered part of the black nightshade group. These plants look so much alike that even botanists and farmers have trouble telling them apart. *S. nodiflorum*, known as American black nightshade or deadly nightshade, is common throughout California, especially along the coast. I have seen the similar *S. furcatum*, known as South American black nightshade, in San Francisco. There may be other species growing near you.

There is disagreement about which black nightshades are poisonous, how deadly they are, and which parts of the plants contain the poison. Black nightshades generally are known to contain nicotine and other poisonous alkaloids, traits they share with domesticated members of the nightshade family. Leaves of our local *S. nodiflorum* have been suspected of poisoning livestock. Potatoes are in the genus *Solanum*, and tomatoes, once classified in another genus, are now also considered to be another *Solanum*. Potato tubers and tomato fruits are safe and healthful foods, but not the other parts of these plants.

As far as local wild nightshades are concerned, the research is not complete, but we should assume that all parts of the plants are poisonous until proved otherwise.

Despite the fact that wild nightshades contain various amounts of toxic alkaloids, particular species have entered local diets here and there around the world, and seeds for some of these are sometimes found in seed catalogs. Two species with edible fruit are the most commonly available. *Solanum melanocerasum*, which is commonly grown in the tropics of West Africa, has ½-inch shiny black berries and is sold as "garden huckleberry." *Solanum burbankii*, a plant developed by Santa Rosa plant breeder Luther Burbank, has ¼-inch deep blue fruits with a white bloom. Burbank sold his creation, which he claimed was a cross between the garden huckleberry and *Solanum villosum*, as "sunberry." Burbank sold the rights to the plant to another plant dealer, who changed its name to "wonderberry," a name Burbank thought far too grand. I have not grown either of these, but those who have report that the garden huckleberry and sun- or wonderberry are not very interesting raw, but tasty cooked with sugar and perhaps some lemon juice.

Because of the confusion about identification of similar black-fruited solanums, it is unwise to eat the fruit of wild ones. Even if you ate fruit or leaves of a wild one in a different part of the world, the ones you see here are likely to be different species. Therefore the wisest choice is to eat only ones sold as food plants and eat only the parts suggested by the seller. The fruits of edible species may even contain toxins until they are fully ripe.

Another genus of wild plants in the same plant family that is beginning to be explored by North American gardeners is *Jaltomata*. Mexico and south into the Andes are home to many species, some of which have edible fruit—again, perhaps not so good unless cooked with plenty of sugar. The seeds are sold with warnings not to eat the fruit until it is completely ripe and not to eat any other parts of the plants.

Meanwhile, back to the weeds; a good reason to get rid of wild nightshades is that they act as alternate hosts for spider mites and for many diseases that attack their domesticated relatives. It is advisable to rotate domesticated members of the family and to remove any doubtful or useless family members. For a discussion of the nightshade family and its edible members, see page 249.

Sources

Garden huckleberry seed: BCS, JG
Wonderberry seed: JLH, SESE
Jaltomata species: BCS

Pigweed (or Rough Pigweed, Green Amaranth, or Wild Beet)

Amaranthus retroflexus
Pigweed Family ❖ *Amaranthaceae*

If you have ever seen domestic amaranth growing, you will recognize this common weed. Its leaves and bushy flower spikes look much the same. The leaves, arranged alternately along the stems, are oblong to roughly triangular and somewhat hairy. Although the flower spikes at the tops of the stems are clearly visible, the individual flowers are so insignificant that you have to look closely to see whether the plant is blooming or has already gone to seed. Domesticated amaranths often have red leaves or red flowers, or both. However, pigweed is completely green, its flower spikes a paler green than the leaves. The only touch of red appears at the top of the taproot, which is pink or reddish.

Pigweed is an upright plant that usually grows several feet high, with flower spikes up to 2 inches long. It has deep roots and can be used as a deep diver, loosening the soil for plants with shorter roots. Unless you are planning to use pigweed this way, it is best to pull it young because the deep roots will put up a fight later. When young, it is a good weed to dig under as green manure or add to your compost pile. Tender young plants may be eaten as a potherb. (In fact, you can buy pigweed in some produce stores and farmers markets.)

You may come across other wild amaranths, either upright types or prostrate ones that trail along the ground. These can be used and controlled in much the same way as pigweed. (See page 174 for information about domesticated amaranth.)

Poison Hemlock

Conium maculatum
Carrot Family ❖ *Apiaceae* (*Umbelliferae*)

Although I had long known that *immaculate* means clean, I didn't realize that it literally means spotless—that is, lacking spots—and that the opposite, *maculate*, means spotted. That I discovered one day upon learning that poison hemlock's species name refers to the small purplish splotches on its stems. Semantics aside, this common weed of wild places and some local gardens is a very poisonous plant that is related to and resembles many of our domesticated vegetables and herbs.

The leaves of poison hemlock are finely divided like those of carrot or fennel, but have broader surfaces than either of those leaves. The purple blotches aren't present on stems of younger plants, but you will see them as the plant gets older. The plant does have a pungent, unpleasant odor from an early age. A biennial weed, poison hemlock grows through a winter to bloom in spring. A blooming plant can reach 10 feet high, but will probably be shorter. Like other members of the carrot family, it has small flowers in flat heads called *umbels*. In this it resembles fennel, but you won't confuse the two plants because fennel has yellow flowers and those of poison hemlock are white. Bottom line: if you aren't sure about any plant, especially if you know it could be mistaken for a poisonous one, don't eat it unless someone can positively identify it for you.

Incidentally, you may have thought that the hemlock with which Socrates ended his life was the tree, but it was this very weed. Its poison, an alkaloid called *coniine*, is contained in all parts of the plant. You needn't be afraid to pull or compost this plant—just don't eat it!

Purslane

Portulaca oleracea
Purslane Family ❖ *Portulacaceae*

Both the stems and the ¾-inch, oval, dull dark green leaves of purslane are thickened, even fleshy. They may have a red tinge, particularly if the plant is growing in bright sun or dry soil. Bright yellow flowers, just over ¼-inch across, bloom along the stems, opening only in sunlight. A prodigious seeder, purslane forms small shiny black seeds in capsules that split open at maturity. Some say that purslane will also spread by rerooting from any pulled plants left on the ground, but I have never noticed that.

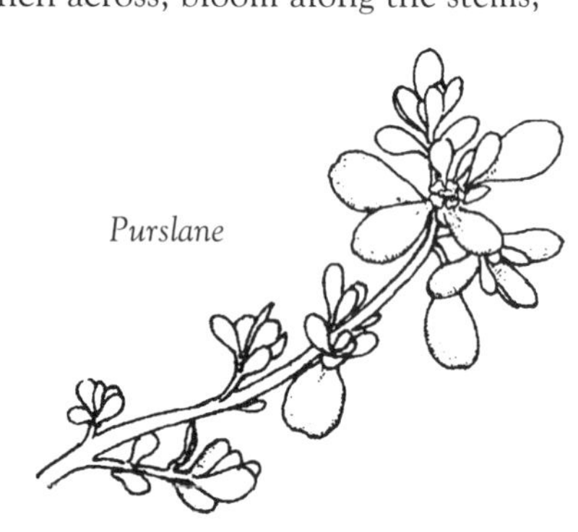
Purslane

Purslane seedlings usually begin to appear in May—a sure sign that the soil has warmed. They grow very fast in their first few weeks, so you must keep them from competing with your spring seedlings. Each plant forms a low mat a foot or more across. Only the central stems have roots, not the side branches. (If you have spent time in a climate with hotter summers, you may know *P. grandiflora*, a related ornamental flower known as *portulaca* or *moss-rose*. Forming a similar mat but with narrower leaves and large vivid red, orange, pink, or yellow flowers, it succeeds in warmer parts of our region.)

Purslane is a weed that elicits varying reactions. Some gardeners would be happy if it disappeared from the face of the earth, and others enjoy it as a staple vegetable. At San Francisco farmers markets you will find bunches of purslane sold as *verdolaga*, its name in Mexico. Purslane is eaten wild or cultivated in many countries of Europe and the Middle East as well as in India, Pakistan, China, and the Philippines. In Europe it is cultivated under various names including *portulaca* (Italy), *pourpier* (France), and *postelein* (Holland). In the United States, most gardeners don't even know that it is edible. In some areas it is called *pusley*—a name guaranteed to spoil anyone's appetite.

If managed properly, purslane can serve as a "free" summer green without intruding on your intentionally planted crops. Try adding the stems and leaves of some pulled seedlings to a green salad. Or let a few purslane plants that aren't too near your crops grow a bit longer, and harvest them when they are about 6 inches across but before they have bloomed. Eat the stems and leaves raw or cooked. Purslane is high in vitamin C and contains a moderate amount of oxalic acid, similar to that of domestic spinach. It has a pleasantly fresh, slightly tart taste.

Although you may be harvesting purslane to eat, you will still want to keep it from seeding itself widely in your garden. Even if it becomes a favorite green, pull it early or your garden will be blanketed with purslane next year.

Domesticated varieties of purslane are larger and more tender, but they probably spread just as freely as wild purslane. You may want to keep intentionally planted purslane in a separate planting box if you don't already have it as a weed in your garden. Purslane prefers sandy soil and needs only light fertilizing, although moist soil and partial shade will improve its size and tenderness. Grow successive plantings from May through August, harvesting young plants whole.

Sources

Purslane seed: ABL, BCS, BG, CG, JG, JLH, JSS, NGN, RH, SESE, SOC, TERR, WCS

Radish (see Wild Radish)

Scarlet Pimpernel (or Poorman's Weatherglass)

Anagallis arvensis
Primrose Family ❖ *Primulaceae*

This pretty little weed can be left alone if it is growing away from crop seedlings. A low plant spreading from a central stem, scarlet pimpernel has small leaves and tiny five-petaled flowers. The blooms are most commonly salmon, but they may be white or, in the case of one variety (*A. arvensis* var. *coerulea*), blue. A particularly common weed along the coast, where it blooms all year, scarlet pimpernel is poisonous.

Poorman's weatherglass refers to the weed's role as a weather indicator, since the flowers are reputed to close at the approach of bad weather. That's not much help in our region, since the plant doesn't distinguish between fog and storm clouds.

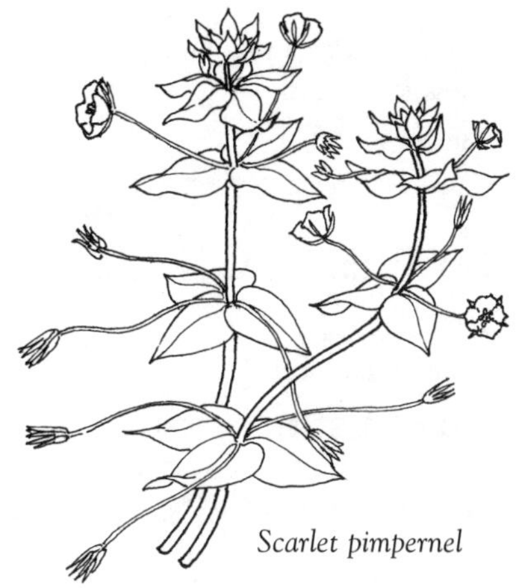
Scarlet pimpernel

Yes, this is the plant for which the novel *The Scarlet Pimpernel* was named. In this turn-of-the-century fiction by a Hungarian countess, Scarlet Pimpernel was the code name for a Royalist hero who rescued nobles during the French Revolution.

Shepherds Purse

Capsella bursa-pastoris
Mustard Family ❖ *Brassicaceae* (*Crucifae*)

Shepherds purse is a winter annual, sprouting mainly in the fall. The plant first forms a small rosette of coarsely toothed dark green leaves, which lies very flat to the ground. Then it forms a flowering stem, rarely over a foot high, with very small mustard-type white flowers. As new flowers open at the top of the stem, spent flowers form tiny heart-shaped pods below them. You will soon learn to recognize shepherds purse by these distinctive heart-shaped "little purses."

A few plants are not much bother, although you wouldn't want to let them reseed until they formed a thick mat in your garden. If shepherds purse appears, dig it in as green manure or eat the whole plant before it forms seeds. The leaves have a mild, pleasant flavor and can be used in salads, omelets, curries, and casseroles. Late one November long ago, it was among the wild plants that, together with leftover Thanksgiving turkey, saw me through a very lean week in fine style. I had only recently begun a garden and little was available to eat from it. However, I found shepherds purse, chickweed, and onion lilies to combine with the few domesticated greens and herbs from my garden. Our meals included turkey and weed salad, turkey and weeds a la king, turkey and weed soup. . . .

Apparently others agree that shepherds purse tastes good, since the seeds can be purchased. I have never tried to grow it intentionally, but I think that you could do so without worrying that it would take over. Still, as a precaution, harvest the plants before they go to seed.

Sources

Shepherds-purse seeds: RH

Sowthistle, Common (or Wild Lettuce)

Sonchus oleraceus

Sowthistle, Prickly

S. asper

Sunflower Family ❖ *Asteraceae* (*Compositae*)

These are summer annuals that normally come up in late spring. Upright plants, they can grow 5 feet high, although mine rarely reach as much as 2 feet before I pull them. The leaves are several inches long, with toothed and lobed edges. The leaves of *S. asper* are dark green and quite prickly, whereas those of *S. oleraceus* are blue-green and much smoother. Both plants form deep taproots that are hard to pull out. Although these weeds are called thistles and one is rather prickly, their prickles aren't as tough or dangerous as those of true thistles. Sowthistles have a milky sap, visible when you break a stem or leaf. The flowerheads are similar to those of dandelions, but smaller and a paler yellow. Fluffy seeds carried by the wind spread the plants all over your garden.

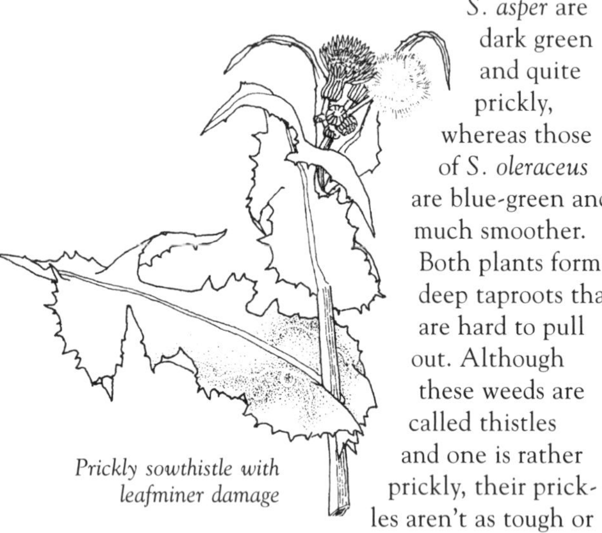

Prickly sowthistle with leafminer damage

I have often been surprised by sowthistles growing up through my maturing crop plants. When I try to pull the plants, they frequently break off at the ground—a handy survival mechanism, since they can quickly regrow new side shoots to replace the missing central stem.

Hoe or pull sowthistle seedlings. The plants are edible, OK in salad when small, tougher when mature. Dig out larger plants if possible; if this would damage crops, just keep the top broken off so that the plants can't go to seed. Although their roots will provide the benefits of any deep-diving weed, sowthistles are large plants and should not be allowed to crowd your crop plants. They can spread leafminers to other sunflower family plants.

Swine Cress

Coronopus didymus

Mustard Family ❖ *Brassicaceae* (*Crucifae*)

This low-growing, nondescript weed is common to both gardens and sidewalk cracks The flowers, which form at the tips of the stems, are tiny and without petals. The flat, rounded, light green seedpods are also tiny, and they spiral up the stem very much like those of sweet alyssum.

I once saw the vegetable bed of a beginning gardener whose carrot seedlings had been completely shaded and crowded out by swine cress. She had assumed that the plants were carrots but began to wonder when they didn't act like carrots as they matured. It is certainly possible to confuse the two at first, as they have similar finely divided leaves. However, carrots soon grow upright, each tall stem holding aloft a feathery plume, whereas swine cress stems branch and remain close to the ground. (See illustration on page 205.)

Vetch (or Common Vetch)

Vicia sativa

Legume Family ❖ *Fabiaceae* (*Leguminosae*)

Common vetch is a low, open, spreading plant with small, bright magenta pea-type flowers. The leaves have a twining tendril at the end of the leaf stem and two rows of small leaflets arranged along the sides. The seeds are borne in small pods resembling those of peas.

I usually notice only a couple of these plants a year and leave them to mature out of respect for the nitrogen-fixing capacity of their roots. In fact, some farmers and gardeners sow common vetch as a cover crop. It makes an excellent addition to your compost pile, contributing nitrogen and other minerals. Don't assume vetch is edible, however; despite its resemblance to pea, it contains toxic substances.

If broad bean weevils have infested your fava or scarlet runner bean plants, eliminate weedy vetch, as it is an alternate host for this pest. You can see the little notches it eats in the edges of the vetch leaves. (See page 185.)

Wild Radish

Raphanus sativus

Mustard Family ❖ *Brassicaceae* (*Crucifae*)

I have never seen wild radish become a serious problem in areas that are actively gardened, but it does

Black Bean Tostadas

This is one of the first recipes I learned to make after moving to California many years ago. To simplify last-minute preparation, you can cook the beans way ahead of time and reheat them before serving. Serves 3 or 4.

1 cup dried black beans
4 cups water
3 to 4 cups torn lettuce, spinach, and/or edible weed greens (such as chickweed, young purslane, miner's lettuce, shepherds purse, or lambsquarters)
Edible flowers, such as nasturtiums or pansies (optional)
4 tablespoons virgin olive oil
2 tablespoons red wine vinegar
¼ pound Monterey Jack or cheddar cheese
1 cup plain yogurt (nonfat is OK)
One 4-ounce can chopped black olives
1 medium to large avocado
Green taco sauce
Oil or nonstick spray for frying tortillas
6 to 8 corn tortillas

Pick over and rinse the black beans. Soak them in water overnight, then put them in a saucepan with the water and bring to a boil over medium-high heat. Reduce heat and simmer for 2 hours, or until they are tender.

About 30 minutes before you plan to serve the tostadas, make a tossed green salad. Wash the greens. Pat the leaves dry and tear them into pieces no bigger than 3 inches across. For color, you can add edible flowers, if desired. Add the olive oil and toss to coat the salad. Sprinkle the salad with the vinegar and toss again. Refrigerate.

Grate the cheese coarsely and put it into a small bowl. Put the yogurt into a second bowl and stir it briskly with a spoon for about 30 seconds. Put the olives in another small bowl. Peel the avocado and slice it into strips; place in a fourth bowl. Reheat the beans, if necessary. Before you start frying the tortillas, put all four bowls of food on the table along with the salad, the warm beans, green taco sauce, and any necessary utensils. (Tortillas cool quickly and are best eaten immediately.)

Add 2 tablespoons of oil to a medium skillet and heat it until a sprinkle of water dropped into the pan jumps and sizzles. Add a tortilla and cook 1 to 2 minutes on each side. The tortilla should be crisp, but not brown. Transfer it to a plate. As soon as the first tortilla is cooked, someone can begin to build a tostada on it. Here is a suggested order of ingredients, although some diners will have their own preferences or even want to leave some out:

- 4 to 6 tablespoons black beans (use a slotted spoon to remove beans from liquid)
- 2 tablespoons yogurt
- ½ cup salad
- 2 to 3 tablespoons grated cheese
- 1 tablespoon chopped black olives
- 2 to 3 strips avocado

grow wild in abandoned lots and may sometimes appear in your garden. A winter annual, it sprouts during the rainy season and soon reaches 2 to 4 feet high. Blooming in spring and into summer, its typical mustard-family flowers, about ¾ inch across, are white, pink, or lavender. The pointed green seedpods, which form along the sides of the flower stems, taste just like radishes. When they are still young and tender, pick them for a tasty nibble or add them to spring salads. Flowers and very young plants are also edible. No one grows wild radish as a crop, but rat tail or podding radish, a domesticated relative, is raised for its large edible pods (see page 255).

PERENNIAL WEEDS

Bermuda Grass

Cynodon dactylon
Grass Family ❖ *Poaceae* (*Graminae*)

When you realize how Bermuda grass reproduces, you will understand why it is so invasive. It spreads through the soil not only by underground stems, called rhizomes, but also by aboveground stems, called runners. Both types of stems may extend several feet from the parent plant, where the main roots are. Roots can form anywhere along these stems. And worse news—any broken pieces of stem can root to form new plants.

The stems are wiry, flat, and smooth. The leaves, 1 to 4 inches long, are rough on the upper surface and smooth underneath. There is a conspicuous ring of white hairs at the base of each leaf blade. Upright stems, 4 to 18 inches high, bear four to seven narrow flowering stems arranged like fingers. The flowering stems resemble those of crabgrass (see page 151) but are smaller.

This hard-to-control weed is a lawn grass that often escapes to overrun other garden areas. Except for tolerating drought and salinity, Bermuda grass is not well suited to lawns in our area. It does poorly in our cool weather and prefers sun to shade or fog. It also tends to turn brown in winter, unlike several other lawn grasses including bluegrass, ryegrass, and bent grass. However, it is very persistent as a weed.

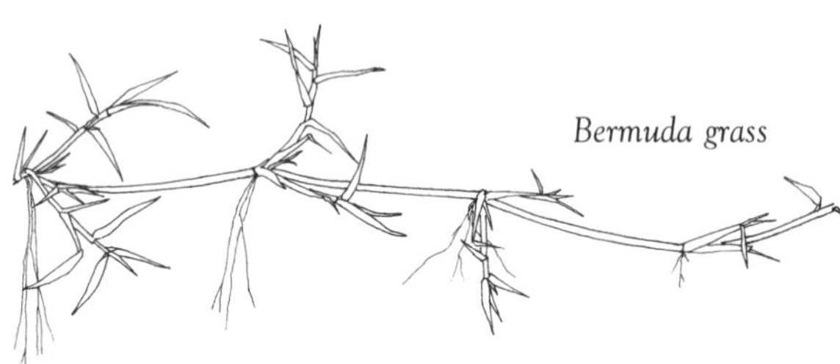
Bermuda grass

Mount an effort to eliminate Bermuda grass from your garden in fall or spring. Fork out all the stems, and take care to sift through carefully for any stem particles left in the soil. Water the soil and remove any new growth before you plant your crops. A smothering mulch is also an effective tool in destroying this weed.

Bindweed (or Wild Morning Glory)

Convolvulus arvensis
Morning Glory Family ❖ *Convolvulaceae*

Bindweed can be recognized by its arrow-shaped leaves, ½ to 1½ inches long, arranged alternately on stems that twine around any available support. All too often a new gardener is charmed by the pretty morning glory flowers, white on the inside and pink on the backs of the petals. Unfortunately, by the time you see bindweed blooming, it has already established a vigorous and persistent root system ready to send up shoots all over your garden. If you ignore it for even a month, you are likely to face a veritable sea of bindweed.

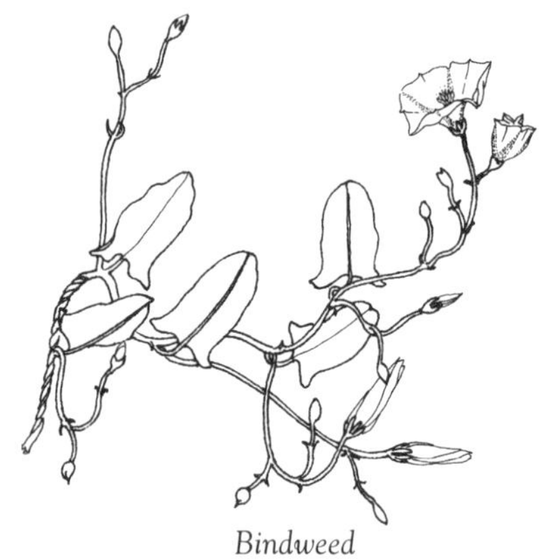
Bindweed

This is obviously a weed to which you should give no quarter. If it begins to invade your garden in the middle of a growing season, pull shoots whenever you see them. If you can get them before they are 2 inches high, the plant will be unable to enlarge its root system. When there is a break in crops, dig out as many bindweed roots as you can. Search for roots that look like dirty beige string. Some grow vertically, whereas others grow horizontally 6 inches or more beneath the soil surface. If you just pull up individual shoots with some vertical roots attached, the horizontal roots will soon send up new growth.

In a small area you can combat a heavy bindweed infestation with a thick newspaper mulch. Two years of summer fallow with once-weekly turning of the soil will also kill the weed.

If you enjoy bindweed's flower, you may like to know that bindweed is in the same genus as three very pretty, well-behaved domesticated plants. *C. cneorum*, bush morning glory, is a small perennial with silvery leaves and white or pink blooms. *Convolvulus sabatius* (*C. mauritanicus*), ground morning glory, another small perennial, has soft blue flowers. *C. tricolor*, dwarf morning glory, is a 1-foot-high annual with striking flowers that are rose-pink or bright blue with a yellow center surrounded by a white band. The first two are widely available as nursery plants and the third as seeds.

The domesticated morning glory vines are members of the same family, but in the genus *Ipomoea*. *I. hederacea*, the blue-flowered ivyleaf morning glory, is included in the weed chart (see pages 152–55), because it often escapes to spread over large expanses of ground and fencing.

Blackberry Brambles

Rubus (various species)
Rose Family ❖ *Rosaceae*

The blackberry bramble in a neglected yard or vacant lot in our area is overwhelmingly likely to be *R. discolor*, Himalaya blackberry, a formerly domesticated plant of European origin that escaped from cultivation and is very common in the coastal areas of Northern California. Although you could encounter other kinds of escaped blackberries, few have taken to our local habitat with the vigor of *R. discolor*. *R. vitifolius*, the native California blackberry, is also found in the central coastal area. You are more apt to see it in less developed areas, such as native woods, coastal scrub, or open oak woodlands. *R. laciniatus*, the common blackberry sold in nurseries, may be a weed if it has been neglected and left to grow on its own.

Here's how to tell which blackberry is growing in your yard. If the flowers and fruit are borne sparsely in small clusters, usually along single stems, and the thorns are slender, the plant is California blackberry or another native blackberry species. If the flowers and fruit are borne in heavy bunches at the ends of the stems and the thorns are stout, the plant is an escaped domesticated type. In the case of *R. laciniatus*, the backs of the leaves are greenish. Also, the leaflets (five to fifteen to a leaf) are deeply cut, forming lobes. Himalaya blackberry leaves, which consist of three to five leaflets, have a whitish underside. A hand lens will reveal that this whiteness is due to a covering of short dense hairs.

Blackberries spread easily. They are carried to new sites by birds, which pass the seeds through their digestive tracts. Once a plant is established, it starts new plants quickly along underground rhizomes and from the tips of long (up to 20 feet) arching stems. Himalaya blackberry is particularly vigorous. Within a few years, its brambles can cover a neglected yard so thickly that the yard becomes impassable.

Himalaya blackberry will not politely share garden space, so you must remove it completely from any area that you intend to cultivate. Pull seedlings when they are quite small, before they have a chance to develop a root system that can survive after the top is pulled. Cut back mature plants and grub out the roots. If your neighbors have blackberries that threaten to spread into your garden, several times every summer you will have to cut stems and dig out runners as they reach over, through, and under the fence and into your yard.

When cutting Himalaya blackberry, wear gloves to avoid the sharp, recurved thorns. Don't try to compost the plants. Even if they don't resprout, they will leave thorns in your compost. Remove all parts of the plant from your yard. I cut the canes into short pieces and put them in my "green bin," the contents of which, in San Francisco, will go to a very hot municipal composting system. For more on clearing gardens overrun by aggressive woody weeds such as Himalaya blackberry, see How to Reclaim Neglected Land on page 148.

Dandelion

Taraxacum officinale
Sunflower Family ❖ *Asteraceae* (*Compositae*)

Although this widespread weed is more common in the eastern United States, where it spreads freely in lawns, it is also often seen here. The plant has a low rosette of smooth, irregularly toothed, bright green leaves. Each flower stem, which is hollow and produces a milky sap when cut, bears one bright yellow head. Winged seeds form a fluffy sphere atop the stem, before the wind disperses them.

If dandelions happen to be new to you, you may at first confuse them with some other local weeds. The biennial prickly oxtongue (*Picris echioides*) has similar flowers, although they are borne several to a stem, and its leaves are dark green, coarse, hairy, and dotted with raised glands. Another similar plant is the perennial coast dandelion (*Hypochoeris radicata*), which has hairy leaves and several flowers to a stalk.

Dandelions do not serve a vegetable garden well, and they are difficult to eradicate. They use much nitrogen and iron, robbing your crops of these nutrients. They also exude ethylene gas, which hampers the growth of nearby plants. Worse yet, they make many seeds and resprout from a broken taproot. When you try to pull a dandelion, its long thin taproot breaks partway down. Buds form on those broken roots, and soon the plant is growing merrily as if nothing had interrupted it. Control dandelions in your vegetable garden by digging

Dandelion

Taming Himalaya Blackberry

Instead of removing all the wild Himalaya blackberry from your yard, you may have considered keeping some of it as a crop. The plant bears tasty fruit that ripens over a long season. Although it has been grown commercially to some extent, it is not very popular with growers, because it is a particularly thorny type. Also, aggressive pruning is required to keep the plants accessible for picking. You will probably be better off removing Himalaya blackberry and planting a domesticated variety, which will be much easier to control and may even offer the luxury of being thornless (see page 344). However, here are some tips for those brave souls who wish to tame the wild Himalaya blackberry.

At a minimum, you will need to make paths into the patch every few feet so that you can get to all the plants to pick fruit. Get rid of any that become rooted in the paths, and keep the others pruned so that they won't fill in the paths. Several times a year, cut aggressive root runners, prune back arching canes, and pull out seedlings.

Blackberries are a cane plant, meaning that they consist of many long stems that rise from the ground and arch up, then fall over. They branch very little. A blackberry patch is maintained by pruning out all the canes that fruited this year, since they won't fruit again, and preserving some of the new canes, which will fruit next year. Himalaya blackberry differs from the other domesticated blackberry plants in that some of the canes may become perennial, living more than two seasons, but it is still best to prune out any canes that have fruited and allow vigorous, new shoots to grow. In fact, Himalaya blackberry produces so many canes each year that it is more likely to form an impenetrable thicket than suffer for lack of its older canes.

Himalaya blackberry is considered a trailing blackberry. This type is commonly trained by growing the fruiting canes along one or two wires stretched between posts 2½ to 3 feet high. Because Himalaya blackberry is a heavy plant, it should be supported on 12-gauge wire, a heavier wire than is used ordinarily. Train the fruiting canes on the wire, but let the summer's new canes trail along the ground. When the new canes reach 8 to 10 feet long, cut off their ends. At the end of the season, cut all the fruiting canes to the ground. Save the four to seven strongest new canes and train them on the wire.

Himalaya blackberry begins to ripen in early July, and the best wild stands continue to ripen until the middle of August. In well-watered gardens, they will ripen a month or so longer and bear larger fruit. The berries are sour until they are quite ripe, when they suddenly become mellow and sweet. For pie, cobbler, jam, or any recipe to which you will be adding sugar, pick all the fruit that is black or almost completely black. For eating fresh, you want only the quite ripe fruit that is still shiny. Overripe fruit becomes dull.

them out, being careful to remove the entire taproot. Add the roots to your compost pile only if you are making a very hot compost. Otherwise, remove them from your garden.

Dandelions have a useful side. When I was a child, our midwestern lawn doubled as a dandelion farm. We ate dandelion buds and tender young greens every spring, and Dad made dandelion wine from the blossoms. At Thanksgiving and Christmas, he poured us all a sample of the wine—a sweet and often bubbly reminder of the sunnier times of year. In late winter or early spring, try young dandelion leaves steamed and flavored with butter or vinegar. Older leaves are likely to be too bitter, although you may enjoy the zest from just a few mature dandelion leaves in salads or mixed cooked greens.

To serve only the buds or make wine, you need more plants than most local yards contain. We plucked the flower buds from deep in the center of the plants or from stems that had grown no more than an inch or so, steamed them, and served them with butter. The milky sap stained our fingers in payment for this delicacy, but we always thought it a small price to pay. For wine, Dad had to pick at least a couple of quarts of blossoms.

There are domesticated dandelion varieties, bigger and somewhat milder versions of the wild kind. Much more commonly sold are chicory varieties known as "Italian dandelion" (see page 222). These have leaves that look and taste similar to those of dandelion.

Sources

Dandelion seeds: BG, CG, GS, IST, JG, JSS, NGN, RH, SI

Dock (or Curly Dock)
Rumex crispus

Dock (or Broad-Leaved Dock)
R. obtusifolius
Knotweed Family ❖ *Polygonaceae*

Several species of *Rumex* are commonly called *dock*. The two listed here are common in our area. They resemble domesticated sorrel, although their upright leaves, arising directly from the ground, are darker green than those of sorrel. Dock leaves also appear to be more leathery, and they are straplike rather than arrow shaped. Their tall spikes of tiny pinkish flowers are very similar to those of sorrel.

Dock grows through the winter months, blooming and setting seeds in summer. It spreads by both seed and root and is one of those persistent plants that regrows vigorously from even small bits of missed root. You will soon recognize the difference between a dock plant growing from seed and a root sprout. A seedling begins with small rounded seed leaves, flat to the ground, whereas a root sprout springs up with large, upright, elongated leaves. The first kind can be dealt with simply by pulling the plant and leaving it on the ground. To control root sprouts, you must dig out the whole root carefully and remove it from your garden.

Dock makes a good cooked green vegetable. When steamed, its leathery-looking leaves become surprisingly tender. Some people like to flavor the leaves with butter, others with vinegar. Eat them in moderation (once a week should not be a problem), because they contain oxalic acid. If you are going to leave a plant for greens, be sure to relegate it to an out-of-the-way area of your garden, and cut the flower stalks in summer to prevent seeding.

Ehrharta Grass (or Panic Veldtgrass)
Ehrharta erecta
Grass Family ❖ *Poaceae* (*Graminae*)

A South African native grass, *Ehrharta erecta* is well adapted to our Mediterranean climate. In the past 10 years, it has suddenly entered urban California areas and began to spread. You will recognize it by its long, slender, branches that spread horizontally or climb into other plants and have very narrow seed heads with tiny oval seeds. It seeds all year, and it also reproduces when its branches lie on the ground and root. It is easier to stop it from spreading than to get rid of it once it has shed seeds all over an area, but repeated pulling while it is young will eventually get ahead of it. When it is growing through other plants, start by grasping one branch and follow it to the ground, then use a spiraling motion to gather up the bases of all the plant's other branches before you pull.

False Garlic (or Slender False Garlic)
Nothoscordum gracile (*N. inodorum*)
Lily Family ❖ *Liliaceae*

Here is a weed with potential to be worse than Cape oxalis or bindweed. It can easily slip under the radar, since it is kind of attractive, like a white *Brodiaea*, with its bunches of little flowers facing mostly upward on bare, rounded stems. The leaves are straplike, floppy, a slightly grayed green, and up to a foot long. It does not have a garlic or onion odor.

Once established in a garden, this plant will take years of hard work to get rid of. The bulb of mature plants can be deeper than the average shovel can reach, and each plant forms many rice-like bulblets around the central bulb. When you dig out the bulb, loosely attached bulblets readily fall off into the soil. Young bulblets are white, but mature ones are brown—that is, soil color. The ones you miss will all grow into new plants, starting out as tiny green threads. In addition, this plant grows readily from seed.

The best advice is that if you think you have one of these plants, you should excavate carefully, dig it out, and discard it with the soil around its bulb. (I rarely choose to discard any precious soil, but this weed warrants it.) To dig tiny plants growing from bulblets, dig down and be sure you remove each bulblet. If you see a slender false garlic blooming before you have time to dig it out, break off and discard the flowers before they can form seed.

Fennel (or Wild Anise)
Foeniculum vulgare
Carrot Family ❖ *Apiaceae* (*Umbelliferae*)

This is the tall feathery-leaved plant with flat heads of yellow flowers you will see in many a vacant lot in our region. Locals know it as anise, but it is really a wild variety of fennel (for more on domestic fennel, see pages 223 and 300). Wild fennel is an acceptable substitute for domesticated fennel for some uses, and its flowers attract beneficial insects, but it can become problematic in a garden. It will seed itself profusely, and if left from year to year, will make huge clumps that require serious cutting and digging to remove. Even domestic fennel can become a pest if it reseeds. So take care about letting any fennel mature seed, or live from year to year, in your garden. Pull out unwanted seedlings young, before they develop deep taproots. Consider collecting leaves, seeds, or the latest fennel rage in culinary circles, fennel pollen, from plants in untended places.

Grasses, Perennial

Grass Family ❖ *Poaceae* (*Graminae*)

Besides Bermuda grass (see page 164), ehrharta grass (see page 167), and quackgrass (see page 172), many other perennial grasses can become established in local gardens. Some spread by rhizomes or rootstocks, others have only a mass of fibrous roots, but they all reroot easily. If a grassy weed has only thin, fibrous roots, you can probably kill the roots by shaking off the soil, then putting the plant upside down for a while, or by putting them deep in a compost pile or under sheet compost (see page 92). However, if a grass has any kind of horizontal runner or rhizome, you should be very careful about composting it, putting it into only a very hot pile.

Be sure to pull grassy weeds before they can go to seed in the spring. If you look closely at newly formed flowering stems, you will be able to see the dangling stamens of the flowers, which lack petals. It is hard to tell when grass seeds are mature, but you know it will be at least a couple of weeks after the plants bloom.

Horsetail (or Scouring Rush)

Equisetum hyemale and *E. arvense*
Horsetail Family ❖ *Equisetaceae*

These are ancient plant species that bear no flowers and reproduce by spores instead of seeds. They have hollow, jointed stems with slender vertical grooves. *E. hyemale* has many unbranched green stems, up to 4 feet high. The small black-and-tan fringed bands at each stem joint are primitive leaves. Spores are produced in the conelike structures, called *strobili*, at the tops of the stems.

E. arvense has two kinds of stems. Short, brown, unbranched fertile stems come up in early spring, make spores, and then die. Green branched stems follow and grow all summer. These are 1 to 3 feet high, with airy whorls of narrow, jointed side branches extending from each joint of the main stem.

In the wild, horsetail thrives along stream banks or wherever moisture is seeping. It prefers sandy soil. Although horsetail is very pretty as a wild plant and is sometimes used in ornamental gardens near pools, it is very invasive, spreading by deep perennial rootstalks. Be careful where you allow it to grow, because it is very hard to get rid of. Control horsetail by digging out all the roots and improving the drainage. Also, improve the fertility of your soil to help your crops compete successfully with horsetail.

Native Americans used horsetail to polish arrowheads, and the name *scouring rush* probably comes from the fact that these plants were used by early European settlers to scour cooking utensils. They are abrasive because of a high silicon content. *E. arvense* (and probably all horsetails) is poisonous to livestock and likely to people as well.

Ivy, Algerian

Hedera canriensis

Ivy, English

H. helix
Ginseng Family ❖ *Araliaceae*

Algerian ivy is the large-leaved, dark green ivy used frequently in public and home landscaping. English ivy has smaller leaves and is used in outdoor landscaping and as a houseplant. Both types of ivy spread by rooting along their creeping stems, and both can become pests, although Algerian ivy is probably the more common pest. If your garden is overrun with ivy, you will have to eradicate it before you can grow much else. If your neighbors grow ivy, you will have to fight it when it grows over, under, and through your fence. The stems will reach out over the soil and then root at every joint. The roots will anchor themselves to the fence, contributing to its decay if it is made of wood. If all that weren't enough, ivy patches are notorious as hiding places for snails and rats. And if ivy matures and forms berries, these will be digested by birds and carried into wildlands. Escaped ivy is destructive of native plants in wildland habitats.

To keep an intentional planting in bounds, you will have to prune the edges several times a year and cut it back to prevent it from maturing and fruiting. To eradicate ivy, pull out all the aboveground stems and dig out all the roots. Remove all the plant parts from your garden, as they are likely to sprout and grow if left on the ground or composted. It is safer to use less invasive vines and ground covers in gardens; however, if you plant either kind of ivy, confine it to an area that it cannot easily escape or contain it in planters.

Nutsedge (or Yellow Nutgrass or Chufa)

Cyperus esculentus
Sedge Family ❖ *Cyperaceae*

Nutsedge is another interesting, pretty weed that is hard to eliminate once it gets established. It has bright green grassy leaves—as broad as crabgrass leaves, but much stiffer. Its flower stalks remind me of papyrus: At the top of each stalk is an umbrella rib arrangement of small leaves and stems bearing brownish flowers. In fact, papyrus (*C. papyrus*), a member of the same genus, has escaped to the wild in some moist areas of our region from Marin County southward.

Nutsedge seedling

Although nutsedge doesn't spread as fast as some other weeds, it grows into a large plant that is hard to pull. I have never been able to hand-pull this weed once it matured. Instead, I have had to hack it out laboriously, even in fairly loose soil. Often my labor was for naught, because I missed some of the small tubers, which proceeded to grow into new plants. Also, if it forms seeds, it will resow itself prodigiously. Your best bet is to learn to recognize this plant when it is small and pull it early.

Decaying nutsedge leaves have been shown to inhibit the production of corn and soybeans. Therefore, it would seem best not to use nutsedge as a green manure or mulch, although putting a little of it in a compost pile should be safe. However, even one tiny tuber will sprout a new plant, so discard all the roots.

Nutsedge does have edible tubers. The wild variety has tiny ones, but gardeners sometimes grow a variety bred for its large tubers, *C. e.* var. *sativus*, known as *earth almond* or *chufa*. It rarely flowers, and it produces many tubers, up to ¾ inch in diameter, crowded on short underground stems. The tubers have a pleasant almond flavor and their texture is reminiscent of partially dried coconut. They can be eaten raw or roasted, or they can be ground into flour. I remember munching them in an aunt's Indiana garden.

Nutsedge seed head

You can order chufa seed (tubers) from Glendale Enterprises, Inc., 297 Railroad Ave., Rt. 3, DeFuniak Springs, FL, 32433, (850)859-2141, www.chufa.com. They sell them as food for wild turkeys, but also for human consumption. Although this crop could conceivably become a nuisance, the tubers are large enough that they could probably be removed easily. My one effort to grow it failed. That is, the plants grew, but I found no tubers, and the plant that I left to overwinter died out by spring. My guess is the chufa would do better in the warmer areas of our region than in a foggy San Francisco garden.

Onion Lily (or Wild Onion)

Allium triquetrum
Lily Family ❖ *Amaryllidaceae*

Onion lily sprouts in September from rounded bulbs less than an inch in diameter. The leaves are flat and reminiscent of leek leaves, although not as large, and with a strong ridge, or keel, on their undersides. In late winter the flower stems appear, each bearing several nodding, bell-shaped white flowers. Each petal is marked with a pale green stripe. The flower stems, a foot or more tall, are triangular in cross section. When bruised, the entire plant smells strongly of onion. Each flower forms several black seeds in a roundish pod. The plant dies back in April or May, disappearing without an aboveground trace until next fall.

This wild onion of our urban backyards is not native to our part of the world, but is a Mediterranean plant that has escaped to the wild in California. Although pretty enough to grace an ornamental flower bed, and edible, it bears controlling because it can seriously hinder a winter or spring garden.

To rid an area of onion lily you will need to dig up all plants and bulbs, as well as make sure that seeds don't fall. The best time to pull plants is in late fall or winter, when they are growing vigorously and the stems are sturdy. At this time you are likely to get the whole plant, and it may not have formed the dormant bulb offsets that will remain in the soil to reinfest the area the following year.

All parts of onion lily are edible, and once you get the plant under control, you may like to leave a patch behind for continuous harvesting. However, I advise preserving onion lily only in small numbers and in out-of-the-way corners, since left on its own it can blanket a garden. If you maintain a bed for eating, you will want to control seeding by picking off the blooms as soon as they fade, before they fall over and shed their seeds.

Lately I have been experimenting with using my onion lilies. I harvested the leaves for salads and cooking throughout winter. The plants grow well even in deep winter shade, where scallions will not grow. In March, I pulled clumps of sprouting seedlings to use in salads. They made a wonderfully tasty and attractive addition, although I have decided not to let the plants seed anymore, since it is too easy to miss seedlings and end up with more plants than intended. In May, when the plants were just dying back, I harvested the bulbs, using some right away and saving the rest. They can be used in cooking much as you would use pearl onions. I served them in beef bourguignon, skinning them first by dropping them in boiling water for a few seconds and then popping their skins off. I also used onion lilies as houseplants. In the summer, I planted some of my saved bulbs in 6-inch-deep clay pots. They grew outdoors through the winter. In February, when they were about to bloom, I carried them indoors, where they made a graceful display, blooming prettily for several weeks.

Onion lily (wild onion)

Oxalis (or Creeping Oxalis)

Oxalis corniculata
Oxalis Family ❖ *Oxalidaceae*

O. *corniculata*, known as creeping oxalis, is a European native that has established itself throughout the United States. I called it sour clover when I was a child, and while at play I used to nibble its leaves.

The leaves are rather like those of clover, with three heart-shaped leaflets, although the small, five-petaled yellow flowers could not be mistaken for clover blossoms. Some plants have purple leaves.

Even though it appears delicate and not much in the way, creeping oxalis can make quite a pest of itself, especially if allowed to get a start among perennial herbs. This aggressive spreader can trail, rooting at every leaf attachment point, and climb, draping itself over low plants. It spoils the look of the plants, but more than that, it harms the plants by cutting off their sunlight. Removing the weed is unexpectedly difficult, because it is hard to trace the slender stems back to their origins through the supporting plant.

Creeping oxalis is a very successful seeder. Its seeds pop out of little rocket-shaped pods when they are ripe, scattering all around the parent plant. I try to pull creeping oxalis while it is young, before it can show its skill at spreading and eluding the weeder's hand. I do not return pulled plants to the garden as mulch unless they are not yet blooming, and then only if the weather is dry enough so that the weeds will shrivel and die instead of rerooting.

Oxalis, Cape (or Bermuda Buttercup)

Oxalis pes-caprae (O. *cernua*)
Oxalis Family ❖ *Oxalidaceae*

Cape oxalis is usually a taller plant than creeping oxalis. Introduced from South Africa as an ornamental, it escaped from gardens and spread so successfully that its showy yellow blooms are a common sight in late winter. It sprouts in September and dies back in May, although a few plants may hang on into summer in well-watered soil. An area infested with Cape oxalis can be used for a summer garden but is usable in winter and spring only if weeded frequently.

Like creeping oxalis, Cape oxalis leaves look like those of clover, though neither is related to clover, nor do oxalis plants add nitrogen to soil. The plants are variable in height, lying flat in full sun or where mowed, up to nearly a foot when reaching through other plants for sunlight. The leaves grow from a common base, which is at ground level on low plants, but several inches above the ground on taller ones—the leaf stems radiating like umbrella ribs. Leaves often bear a few reddish dots.

Cape oxalis grows from teardrop-shaped brown bulbs. These may be quite tiny or nearly an inch long. Early in the season, there is a thickened, fleshy, underground structure above the bulb. Later in the season, new bulblets, nearly white at first, form along this structure, and it shrivels to a thread. When the plants become dormant, the mother bulb and all the small ones remain to grow the following season. Bulbs can be quite deep in the soil, and there are often so many that digging for them or sifting soil is arduous. There is no evidence that the flowers ripen viable seeds in California.

Still, gardeners do get Cape oxalis under control without resorting to chemicals through a combination of digging out bulbs and pulling plants. It will probably take several years.

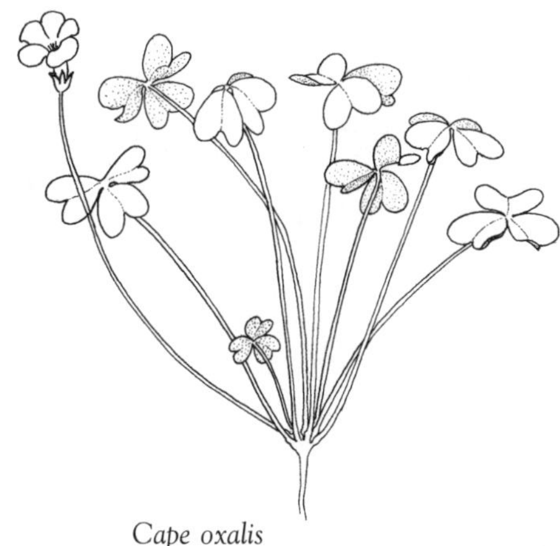

Cape oxalis

Whenever possible, dig Cape oxalis plants out in fall or early winter, before they have a chance to make more bulblets. Dig deep enough to get the mother bulb if at all possible. Digging later is also good, but the later you wait the greater chance that bulblets will detach as you dig and will be mature enough to grow.

If the plant is growing near desirable plants, digging it will damage their roots. In this case, pulling the tops off early in its season and repeating if they return will at least weaken the oxalis and reduce bulblet formation. If you must pull instead of digging, be sure to grasp the stem below the point of attachment of the leaves. If this point is low to the ground, try to dig at least an inch or two to be sure to get the place where new leaves can form.

Don't use oxalis in compost if there is any chance there are bulbs on it, as the likelihood of their surviving is great. If you don't have this pest, be vigilant, ready to destroy any that appear in your garden. Also, beware of accepting plants from gardeners who do, since tiny Cape oxalis bulbs may well be hidden in the soil around their roots.

A less bothersome relative is redwood sorrel (*O. oregana*), a native of California and the Pacific Northwest. The leaves look like those of Cape oxalis, but the flowers are pink or white instead. It is less invasive, sometimes spreading in shade but generally stopping when it reaches a sunny area.

Any oxalis can be nibbled in the garden or used as flavorings for salads and sauces. English cooks in the Middle Ages made a fish sauce from leaves of a native oxalis. However, none should be eaten in large quantities, since the oxalic acid content is rather high. The acid interferes with the ability of our bodies to absorb essential minerals.

Many other, less invasive oxalis species are grown ornamentally, and some are treasured as miniature rock garden plants. Oca (*O. tuberosa*), a Peruvian species that forms an edible starchy tuber, is occasionally grown locally for food or as a curiosity. (See page 237 for more on oca.)

Plantain, Broadleaf (or Common Plantain)

Plantago major

Plantain, Narrow-Leaved (or Buckhorn Plantain)

P. lanceolata

Plantain Family ❖ *Plantaginaceae*

Both of these plants have rosettes of leaves with prominent parallel veins. As the common names indicate, one has broader leaves than the other. The leaves of broadleaf plantain lie flat on the ground, with a spread of 4 to 12 inches. Narrow-leaved plantain leaves are more upright, growing 3 to 12 inches high. Both plants have tiny flowers borne on the sides of leafless unbranched stalks. Narrow-leaved plantain flowerheads, about an inch long, appear at the top of the stems, whereas those of broadleaf plantain cover several inches of stem.

Both plantains spread by seed and by new shoots growing from the roots. They don't spread as aggressively from their roots as many other perennial weeds, but their numerous tough fibrous roots can make them very hard to pull. Hook your fingers under the plants to make sure that you get the whole plant and not just the leaves. Otherwise, the base will be able to grow new leaves. Control light infestations by hand pulling. To fight heavy infestations, turn the soil and dig out each plant completely.

Tender young plantain leaves can be eaten raw in salads, and slightly older ones are tasty when cooked. Don't bother harvesting the mature leaves, as they are bitter and tough.

Italians eat the young leaves of yet another plantain, *Plantago coronopus*, which they call *erba stella*. It's also known as minutina and staghorn plantain. This last name is also a common name used for narrow-leaved plantain. But *erba stella* leaves have "prongs" along their edges, making them more "staglike" to my eyes and more decorative in a salad. I have seen it growing wild above Ocean Beach, so, like the other two European plantagos listed here, it could become weedy. Also like them, it is less tender and more bitter when mature.

Sources

Erba stella seed: GS, IST, JSS, NGN, SI

Quackgrass (or Witchgrass)

Agropyron repens
Grass Family ❖ *Poaceae* (*Graminae*)

This perennial grass has some of the toughest roots I have ever seen. The plant itself is often small, short, seemingly insignificant, but growing underground are yards of horizontal, pale-yellowish, wirey rootstocks with sharply pointed tips. At each joint is a brown sheath, a ring of short roots, and the potential to grow a new above-ground plant. The rootstocks are so tough that they can grow right through a potato! And if you break up the rootstocks when you are digging, every fragment can grow.

Quackgrass thrives in cool, moist conditions, and is spreading in the coastal parts of California. Its seed can enter a garden as a contaminant in hay or straw.

Combat early infestations by removing as much as you can by hand, digging to get out all of the rootstocks. Their very toughness betrays them when you pry them up and tug on them, as they are more likely to come out whole than to break, if your soil is reasonably loose. Smothering mulch made with cardboard doesn't stop quackgrass, but the rootstocks tend to grow near the surface in such a mulch, rendering it much easier to pull.

A quackgrass seed head looks like a narrow head of wheat. Even seed that is immature can ripen and grow after it falls, so try to remove this weed even before it can form its flowering stems.

Sorrel (or Sheep Sorrel)

Rumex acetosella
Knotweed Family ❖ *Polygonaceae*

Sheep sorrel is a tiny wild relative of the domesticated French and garden sorrels (see page 259). Its leaves also resemble arrowheads, although it is a low-growing plant with a rosette of leaves only a few inches across. Sheep sorrel can be a serious invader, but in my garden it is only an occasional visitor in late winter and early spring.

If you see more than a few specimens of this plant in your garden, check your soil pH, since it is an indicator of acidity. To control sheep sorrel, dig it out and be sure to remove all the roots. Sheep sorrel has the same tart taste as its domesticated relatives, so I gladly add bits of it to my winter salads. Like any plant that contains a significant amount of the sour-tasting oxalic acid, sheep sorrel should be eaten only in small quantities, but a few of these small leaves in a salad now and then should not be a problem.

ELEVEN

Vegetables from A to Z

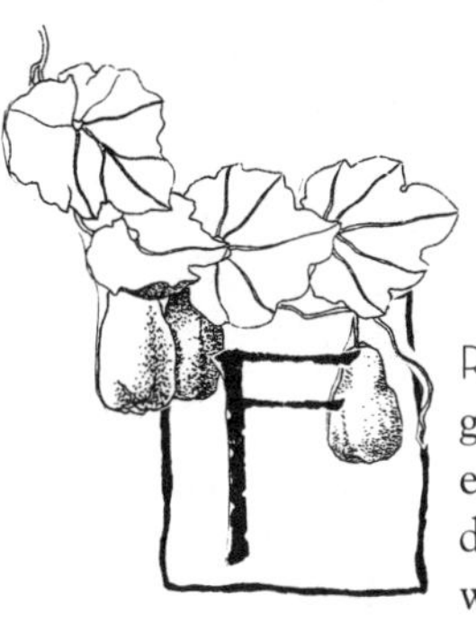

FROM THE TIME I BEGAN TO garden in San Francisco, I deliberately set about growing as many different vegetables as possible to see what would succeed here. I wanted to know how well a crop would thrive in summer fog, how much cold and wet it would tolerate in winter, the best times to plant it, and how to get a longer harvest. I've planted the common and the uncommon, from tomatoes to Bolivian sunroot, in search of crops that perform well and are worthwhile growing. I've tried many different varieties and growing techniques to coax more out of reluctant crops. I've talked with people who garden in a number of microclimates, and I've collected reports of successes and failures.

I discovered that we can grow a wide variety of vegetables and that warm pockets make it possible to grow an even wider assortment than I would have expected in some neighborhoods. I also found that certain crops are not likely to give satisfactory results in the foggier areas. I'm not saying that those crops are impossible to grow here, only that success may be the exception rather than the rule, a triumph to celebrate and not a harvest to depend upon.

For instance, a resident of the outer Richmond district of San Francisco, just a few blocks from the ocean, told me that her husband once harvested a watermelon from their garden. "Really?" I inquired. "How did it taste?" She replied, "I don't know. He shellacked it and we had it around the house for years." My own melon triumph was the harvest of a single cantaloupe from my San Francisco Mission district garden. My noble melon attained a diameter of just over three inches, but it was passably sweet.

The yard-long bean, also known as the asparagus bean, is a prime example of a crop that has trouble even getting to first base in cool summer parts of our region. There, the plant grows to about a foot high, then declines and dies. From a plant that short, you can bet you won't get yard-long bean pods!

Farther inland, gardeners can add summer crops, such as eggplants and melons, which require more heat, although the cool ocean breeze blows inland even where less fog reaches, slowing summer crops by lowering and delaying maximum summer temperatures. Conversely, inland gardeners will find that cool-season crops, like peas and spinach, must be grown before or after summer's intense heat.

But even if you live where summers are at their coolest and foggiest, and you can't grow summer crops you'd love to grow, you can still raise a great many crops. In fact, discovering what you can grow is half the fun of gardening. I encourage you to be adventurous!

THE VEGETABLES

The listing for each crop includes the following information in the same order. If any element is missing, it is because there is nothing relevant to say—for example, when a crop has no significant pest problems or there is only one variety on the market.

- **A brief introduction**, including information on how the crop copes with the microclimates of our region.
- **Growing Instructions** Here you will find details on how to start the crop, whether to plant directly in the garden or sow seeds indoors, when to plant, and so on. If the crop's watering

need is not mentioned, assume that it is average for vegetables—about an inch a week in summer. If there is no mention of sunlight, assume that the crop needs a minimum of four hours if it is leafy and six to eight hours if it bears fruit. "Any good garden soil" or "average garden soil" means soil to which organic matter and fertilizer have been added.

- **The Harvest** This section includes tips on when and how to pick a crop, as well as how to cure, store, and prepare the harvested crop.
- **Varieties** Here are the varieties that I, or other local gardeners, have found to be especially well adapted to our climate, superior in production, particularly flavorful, or just plain interesting to grow. (In some cases, closely related species are cited as well.) Certain crops, such as lettuce and cabbage, are so well adapted to our climate that most types will succeed. For such crops, choose heat-tolerant varieties to grow in summer, cold-tolerant ones to grow in winter. For crops that require heat, such as tomatoes and corn, the variety listing consists of those that mature early and are tolerant of cool weather. A factor other than climate will sometimes limit your choice. Disease resistance may be the key consideration if a crop is susceptible to powdery mildew or verticillium wilt—two common diseases in our area. The number of vegetable varieties available to gardeners is too great to be described fully and is always changing, so many good choices are left for you to discover on your own.
- **Pests** The insects, diseases, and other pests that most commonly damage the crop are cited here. Many of these problems are described in greater length, and control measures given for them, in Chapter 9.
- **Sources** At the end of each entry, you will find a source list for the crop or for some of its varieties. If it is carried by only a few sources, you will find codes for them. For example, you will find that one of the sources of Bolivian sunroot (yacon) is NGN, which stands for Nichols Garden Nursery. You will find a list of seed and plant sources with their codes in Appendix VII, Resources for Gardeners. If a crop or variety is so common that you are likely to find it in nine out of ten seed racks, general seed catalogs, or local nurseries, I simply say that it is widely available. (Although the listings were accurate when they were compiled, seed companies often change their offerings. Refer to the most current catalogs for up-to-date information.)

SO MANY CHOICES, SO LITTLE TIME AND SPACE

There are so many crops to grow, even in the foggiest areas, that a gardener must be selective. As you read this chapter or browse through a seed catalog, you may be tempted to try everything the first year. But think carefully before ordering. There is no sense in growing more plants than you have the time to tend or harvest. Also consider the amount of space you have. Plants are not polite to each other, and fast growers are not shy about shading out slow growers. I am still learning this lesson. Not too long ago I planted several kohlrabi seedlings between my summer squash hills and potato patch—a space that looked big enough but obviously wasn't. I was a little chagrined to see the squash and potatoes meet and intermingle over the tops of the kohlrabi.

Compendium of Vegetables

Amaranth

Various species of *Amaranthus*
Pigweed Family ❖ *Amaranthaceae*

Several species of amaranth are grown in various parts of the world for their tender leafy greens and nutritious seeds. Despite efforts by the Rodale Institute, of *Organic Gardening* magazine fame, they have not become a popular American crop. However, gardeners may still be interested in them for their nutritional qualities and because they are easy to grow, given a reasonably warm summer location. The leaves provide vitamins A and C, phosphorus, iron, copper, magnesium, and manganese. The seeds have a high protein content, and the balance of amino acids in the protein complements that of other grains. Some amaranths are highly ornamental, since red or variegated leaves and red flowers are common among the species.

People in many areas of the world use amaranth leaves as greens. The Asian native, *A. tricolor* (also known as *A. gangeticus*) is called tampala in India, hin choy in China. In the Caribbean, *A. dubius* is the favored leafy green used in a popular stew known as callaloo. In Greece, leaves of *A. viridis* are gathered wild and served cooked with sprinklings of olive oil and lemon juice. Africans use many species of amaranth as leafy greens, and the plants have probably hybridized so much there that some species are no longer separate.

In the American Southwest, Central America, and South America, where historic use of amaranth seed as a grain goes back thousands of years, it is still grown for both seed and leaves. The American species *A. caudatus*, *A. cruentus*, and *A. hypochondriacus* have been introduced to Africa and Asia, where they are all used as greens and sometimes as grains. Grain of *A. hypochondriacus* is used in Himalayan cultures.

The main hindrance to amaranth becoming a common crop for American gardeners is that it is unfamiliar. The greens are mild-flavored, rather like spinach, and become tender with little cooking. Grain varieties are heavy producers, easy to thresh, and can be used as a cooked cereal, added to baked goods, or popped like popcorn.

Some amaranths, such as the also edible *A. retroflexus* (red-root pigweed), are weedy, but the ones grown for food aren't likely to become serious weeds if their seed falls in the garden.

Growing Instructions Sow seed to produce grain, or your first successional planting of amaranth for leafy harvests, at the beginning of May, or even a few weeks earlier if the weather is warm. Grow the plants in full sun and in soil that has had fertilizer and organic matter added. Don't overdo nitrogen fertilizer if you plan to allow the plants to produce grain. Water as you would for any rapidly growing vegetable crop. Underwatering will result in flowering at a young age, which will cut short leafy green production or, if you are growing the plant for grain, reduce the grain harvest.

Plants can be sown thickly, then transplanted to the desired spacing, or sown as they will stand. If you plan to pull entire young plants for greens, you can plant them about 3 inches apart. If you plan to cut several times and let the plants regrow, plant them about 9 inches apart. To let the plants mature and bear seed, plant them about a foot apart.

The Harvest Pull entire plants for greens when they have about 10 leaves. (If you harvest this way, plant more every couple of weeks for a continuous harvest.) Or, harvest by cutting back to no fewer than 2 leaves (4 to 6 inches from the ground) when plants are about a month old, then cut again every 2 or 3 weeks for a month or two. Very young leaves are sometimes used raw, in salads, while more mature leaves are better cooked.

Or, instead of harvesting leaves, you can let the plants mature, flower, and set seed. To harvest seeds, wait until just before the mature heads are dry and brittle. Ideally, you'd harvest them after the first frost, but in practice, in this area you need to do so before rains begin. Cut them, tie paper or cloth bags over the heads, and hang them upside down in a shady place to finish drying. Each plant may require more than one cutting as seed heads mature. When the seed heads are dry, remove the seeds. Try shaking or beating the stems so that the seeds fall into the bag, or rub the seed heads between your hands (gloves recommended). Sieve out the chaff with a small mesh screen. Spread the seeds on trays and dry well in a warm place before you store them in a closed container, or the seeds may mold. Plants are expected to produce on the order of a pound of grain per square yard, or about ½ cup (¼ pound) per plant.

Amaranth grain can be used whole as a cooked cereal or added to other cooked cereals. They can also be sprouted or milled to a flour that can be mixed with 3 or 4 parts wheat flour in baked goods. Amaranth flour used alone can be cooked into chapatis, a fried flatbread (see recipe on page 211).

Varieties and Related Species Here is a quick rundown of the species of amaranth most used for food. You may find them labeled correctly in a seed catalog, or you may have to deduce the species from the description. (Classification is somewhat confused, and seeds may be mislabeled.) I have included the common names, including ones used when a species is also grown as an ornamental. Height is of the plant in flower, and it may vary among cultivars and with growing conditions. Light-colored seeds tend to have a more pleasing texture when cooked, but dark-seeded ones are still sometimes offered as grain plants.

A. blitum (*A. lividus*; purple amaranth; to about 3 ft. tall): Grown as a leafy green in the Mediterranean since ancient times, this species is still grown in vegetable gardens of Southeastern Europe, India, and Africa, and gathered wild in many places. It is called vleeta in modern Greece, norpa in India.

A. caudatus (grain amaranth, Inca wheat, African spinach, love-lies-bleeding, tassel flower; 3 to 5 ft. tall): This native of Andean countries has been used there for grain for at least 2,000 years. While primarily a grain crop, its young leaves are also sometimes eaten. Its flower tassels, often drooping or hanging, may be red or green.

A. cruentus (red amaranth, blood amaranth, prince's feather; to 6 ft. or taller): Grown for grain as much as 6,000 years ago in its native Central America, it is still eaten there, often popped and mixed with honey or molasses to form a confection. It is also grown as a grain in India and Nepal, and as a green throughout South Asia, Africa, and the Caribbean. Its seeds are most often pale brown, but may be dark, almost black.

A. *dubius* (spleen amaranth; to 5 ft. tall): Originating in Mexico, Northern South America, and the Caribbean, this species is used as a leaf crop. It is featured in callaloo, a gumbolike stew that is central to Caribbean culture and cuisine. A choice cultivar is 'Claroen'.

A. *hypochondriacus* (prince's feather; to 6 ft. tall): From Mexico or the Southwest, this species, which may be a relatively recent hybrid between A. *cruentus* and A. *powellii* (a weedy species), is now widely grown in Central and South America and in Asia, mainly as a grain, but also for leaves. Its crimson flowers are held in erect spikes.

A. *tricolor* (sometimes called A. *gangeticus*; tampala, hin choy; to 4 ft. tall): A native of Southeast Asia, this species is grown widely there and in other parts of Asia as a leafy crop. Of the species listed here, it probably needs the most heat to thrive. The kinds in cultivation often have variegated leaves. One variety, 'Joseph's Coat', has leaves streaked in red, green, and yellow. It is grown as an ornamental, and the young leaves are used in salads.

One kind of A. *tricolor* is often sold as "elephant's head amaranth." It has thick, ungainly, upright heads of red flowers in which some see an elephant's head and more or less upright trunk. In the United States, it is mainly grown as an odd ornamental, but South Asians eat the leaves when the plant is young.

A. *viridis* (slender or green amaranth; to 3 ft. tall): A green-leaf amaranth, possibly originating in Asia, and used mainly as a leaf crop. It's a weed that is often wild-gathered, including in Greece, where it is commonly cooked, sprinkled with olive oil and lemon juice, and served with fried fish.

(For more on amaranth relatives to grow for leafy greens, see Lambsquarters, page 156. For a grain crop similar to amaranth, see Quinoa, in this chapter.)

Pests Slugs and snails may damage amaranth, but mine hasn't been bothered by other pests.

Sources

Amaranth seed:

For a leaf crop: BCS, BG, BI, EE, GS, JG, JLH, JSS, KIT, NGN, NSS, PGS, RCS, RH, TERR, WCS

For a grain crop: BCS, BG, JLH, NSS, PGS, RH, SOC

Artichoke

Cynara scolymus

Sunflower Family ❖ *Asteraceae (Compositae)*

The Romans probably discovered artichokes growing wild in North Africa. These wild plants had small, tough thistles, but the Romans ate the leaf midribs, as they did those of cardoons. Introduced to rich soil and ample water, the plants responded with larger, more tender flower buds. By selecting the best plants, gardeners developed our modern vegetable.

Growing artichokes is a challenge to those who live in places where snowy winters alternate with hot summers. In such places, they require the kind of fuss and worry the Bay Area's coastal gardeners save for tomatoes. However, in the Bay Area, the closer artichokes grow to the coast, the better they like the climate. The mild winters provide just enough chill to stimulate bud formation, but rarely enough cold to cause damage, and the cool springs and summers produce large, tender buds. The suitability of this delicious crop for local gardens is attested to by the commercial artichoke fields lining the coast south of San Francisco and in Monterey County.

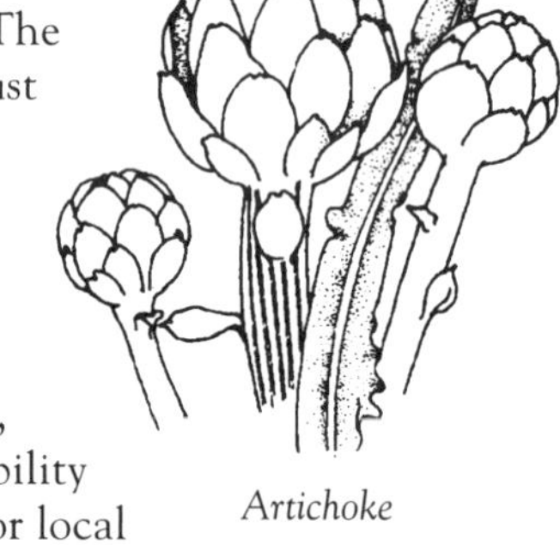

Artichoke

The artichoke is a perennial plant averaging 3 to 4 feet high, but sometimes growing to 6 feet. It is 3 to 4 feet wide. The vegetable we eat consists of bracts surrounding many immature flower buds and the tender stem base where those buds are forming. The flowerheads form on tall stems, usually three to a stem but sometimes as many as ten. Plant at least two plants per person in your household.

A new development in artichoke growing is the use of varieties that are grown from seed planted fresh each year, treating the plants as if they were annuals. These are useful in places with less than ideal artichoke climates, but they have advantages for our region as well.

Growing Instructions Ideally, a site for artichoke would get at least 6 hours of sun—that is, unshaded light—including some unshaded light in winter. When an artichoke is to be grown as a perennial, you need to make sure that perennial weeds, such as Bermuda grass or oxalis, are under control where you plant it, since these will be difficult to get rid of when something is growing in the bed from year to year. Add plenty of compost or other humus-producing organic matter and a slow-release fertilizer. Space plants 3 to 4 feet apart.

Until recently, artichokes were most commonly started from rootstocks that were grown from divided plants. These are still available, bare-root or planted in pots. The ideal time to plant either is in late summer to fall, with winter next best, though you can plant potted artichoke starts whenever they are available.

Artichokes can also be grown from seed, which will produce seedlings ready to plant out in 8 to 12 weeks. Plant a few more seeds than you think you need, since seeds of all varieties have a relatively low germination rate (70 percent) and then, of the seedlings that do come up, maybe 20 percent will be rather small or albino (chlorophyll-lacking) plants, which should be discarded. Among the healthy seedlings you have allowed to continue to grow, there will be some variation in eventual production. Josh Kirschenbaum, product development director at Territorial Seed Company, says that he thinks the ones with smoother, less serrated or lobed leaves will be more productive than the ones with serrated or lobed leaf edges. If you have too many seedlings, favor the ones with less serrated leaves. (You can also plant them all and then, at the end of the first year's harvest, remove any that didn't produce well, testing for yourself whether there is any connection between leaf shape and productivity.)

Because the traditional varieties, such as 'Green Globe' and the various purple-choked ones, require up to 500 hours of winter chill (under 50°F) before they can start to flower, their seeds are best started in late summer or early fall to ensure they will get their chill early enough for a spring harvest. If they are planted out in spring, expect a first crop in late fall. The newer 'Imperial Star', one of the varieties farmers now treat as an annual plant, requires only 200 to 250 hours of winter chill, so it can be sown indoors in November or December, planted out in February or March, and produce a late spring into summer crop. Just be sure there are likely to be 10 to 12 days of temperatures under 50°F when you plant out 'Imperial Star' seedlings. You can also sow 'Imperial Star' seed earlier, if you choose, which will allow it to begin to bear a couple of months earlier.

When artichokes are actively growing they appreciate a monthly booster of high-nitrogen liquid fertilizer. They also need consistent watering while they are growing, including during dry spells in fall or spring.

A modern artichoke growing in poor soil with inadequate water will not revert to the original Mediterranean weed, but the plant will be stunted and will not produce well. On Alcatraz Island, artichokes survived forty years of abandonment between the closing of the federal penitentiary in 1963 and the beginning of garden restoration in 2003. Such plants can be coaxed back with proper care, and if you like the buds they produce, they can be used as rootstocks to start new plants.

Artichoke plants are not harmed badly by temperatures a few degrees below freezing, but if there are buds on the plants, even light frost will cause cosmetic damage. Frostbitten buds are scaly, which is unsightly, but the damage doesn't affect eating quality. Below 25°F the buds may blacken and become inedible, though the plants can survive to at least this temperature. Where ground may freeze, gardeners cut the plants to 8 to 10 inches and mulch over them with straw or leaves, but in our milder winters, with wet ground and rainy days, mulch over any perennial is likely to increase the chance of decay.

Commercial growers control harvest times by cutting all the stems and leaves of perennial plants to just below ground level, letting the plants rest. In the Monterey area, about 75 percent of the acreage is cut back in May. These fields are kept on the dry side for several weeks, and then watering is resumed. The plants rebound to make a September to May crop. Fifteen to 20 percent of the acreage is cut back in August or September, which results in a summer harvest. A few fields are not cut back at all, which gives a longer harvest but allows pest buildup.

About 25 percent of the artichokes grown in the Monterey region and all of those grown in Southern California are now grown as annuals from low-chill varieties. They produce midsummer to fall and are then dug under. Because they aren't left in the ground from year to year, the plants are smaller, so they can be planted a bit closer together than perennial plants. The process also interrupts the life cycle of pests more completely than can be done with perennial plants.

If you allow a plant to remain in the ground from year to year, it grows many new whorls of leaves from the enlarging rootstock. It isn't necessary to divide a plant each year—do it when the clump becomes overgrown. Divide and replant rootstocks at the beginning of the rainy season, so that the plants can reestablish themselves during cool, humid days.

The Harvest The buds are ready to harvest just as the tips of the lower bracts begin to lift away from the bud. Each stalk will make one bud at the top. When that has been cut, the buds lower on the stem will enlarge, although they usually don't get as big as the top one.

Sometimes gardeners harvest some of their artichoke buds when they are less mature, when they haven't reached their full size and their bracts are still tightly closed, to use them as tender baby artichokes.

As soon as you cut the last bud from a particular stalk, cut the stalk off just below ground level with strong pruning loppers held at an angle. (Don't twist or pull it out, because you risk pulling out a new shoot that will increase your plant's size.)

When a bud opens, revealing its purple blossoms, it will inhibit the rest of the plant from making more buds. If you want to see the showy flowers, leave one plant unharvested or let some of the side buds bloom at the end of the season.

Varieties and Related Species Most artichoke rootstocks and potted nursery plants available are 'Green Globe', and you can get seed of 'Green Globe' as well as improved strains of it that may bear more heavily than the original strain. You may also find seed of 'Violetto', a variety that require a similar amount of chill. Though handsome in the garden, its buds turn green when cooked.

Among low-chill varieties, you are most likely to find seed of 'Imperial Star'. It is particularly useful in places less well adapted to artichoke growing. If winter is too cold or too mild to provide enough chill for 'Green Globe', seedlings of low-chill varieties can be kept where they will experience 60 to 70°F in the daytime and 50 to 60°F at night, then planted out when frost danger is past but when they will still get 10 to 12 days below 50°F.

If you live where other artichokes are also adapted, you may still choose a low-chill variety just to get a faster crop, and you may choose to let it become a perennial.

Pests Commercial growers often have severe problems with the artichoke plume moth. Growing artichokes as annuals is one of their best tactics for avoiding damage. Turning the crop into the ground each fall prevents the pest from overwintering. You may not ever see the dark trails the larvae of this moth eat into the buds, but if you do, add growing artichokes as annuals to your list of ways to fight this pest. (For more on artichoke plume moths, see page 114.)

You are more likely to see aphids. Two kinds often feed on artichoke buds, attracting ants that feed on the honeydew they produce. Bean aphids are dark green to black, and oleaster-thistle aphids are pale yellow to green. A minor infestation does little damage, but a heavy outbreak may result in smaller, tougher buds. Aphids are difficult to wash out when they get under the bud scales. (For more on aphids, see page 113.) Another reason to control aphids is that they can spread diseases, such as curly dwarf virus (see below).

In spring, you may see the white foam that covers pale green spittlebug larvae on the leaves and under the bud scales. These sucking insects are rarely present in large enough numbers to cause much damage, but you may want to hose them off with a strong spray of water every few days.

Slugs and snails occasionally do some damage, although they rarely make the buds inedible. Earwigs sometimes make a nuisance of themselves by living under the scales and emerging in the kitchen or, worse, getting cooked in the choke. If they invade your crop, shake the chokes firmly before you bring them into the house, then submerge them in water for a few minutes before you cook them.

Curly dwarf virus is a disease spread from infected plants to healthy ones by aphids and leafhoppers. When your plants are infected, you will gradually realize that they have become stunted and misshapen. Try to prevent the virus by pulling any milk thistle (*Silybum marianum*) growing nearby (see page 157) and by controlling aphids and leafhoppers. Since there is no cure, pull any infected plants and start again with fresh seeds or with roots from a source guaranteed to be free of the virus.

Sources

Green Globe artichoke seed: Widely available

Artichoke seed (purple varieties): BCS, BI, CG, GS, IST, NGN, PGS, SI, TERR, WCS

Imperial Star artichoke seed: ABL, BCS, BUR, CG, JSS, NGN, PGS, SESE, SOC, TERR, WCS

Artichoke plants: RH

Arugula (or Rocket or Roquette)

Eruca vesicaria subsp. *sativa*

Mustard Family ❖ *Brassicaceae* (*Cruciferae*)

In my experience, people are rarely indifferent about arugula—they either love it or hate it. It has a strong and complex flavor, often described as sharp or nutty. Some people use the term "arugula eater" as shorthand for "food snob," but the irony, for the gardener, is that arugula is a fast, easy crop. It's almost a weed, a plant that still grows wild in

Mediterranean Europe. It can be a minor or a major note in salads. It's often included in a spicy mesclun mix (see page 236), which you can add to lettuce in just the right amount so it won't overpower the salad. When it is cooked, arugula has a milder flavor. You can steam it lightly and put it on a pizza; use it as one of several mixed greens to steam and serve Greek style, with a sprinkling of olive oil and lemon juice; or sauté it with onion and garlic, add a bit of feta or goat cheese thinned with milk to create a creamy consistency, and serve it with pasta. The flowers, which are cream-and-maroon or, less commonly, pale yellow, share the arugula flavor, and are pretty on a salad or a soup.

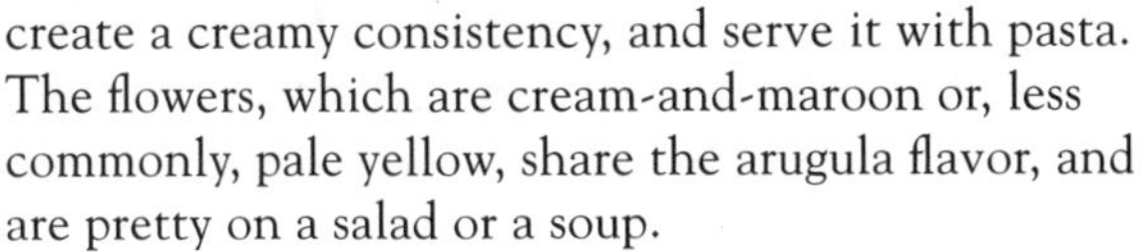

Growing Instructions Try planting this very hardy mustard-family green in early fall, again in February, and once more in spring. Scatter-sow the seeds, covering them ¼ to ½ inch deep. Thin the plants until they stand 4 to 6 inches apart, and use the thinnings in salads.

The Harvest You can harvest whole small plants or individual leaves. You may find the leaves too strong-flavored when they are older, or you may still enjoy them either raw or cooked. In any case, let some of your crop flower so you can use the blossoms. Let some seed pods mature, too. Then you can either cut the plants and harvest the seed for replanting, or let some seed fall and surprise you when arugula seedlings appear.

Varieties and Related Species Until recently, only one variety was available, but now there are several open-pollinated selections. Some promise more heat tolerance or less bitterness. One, 'Surrey', is said to bolt (bloom) late, so you have longer to harvest the leaves. (I tested a noncommercial, experimental strain that was said to be slow to bolt, and found only a small difference. When a regular strain was bolting, the experimental strain had about 20 percent fewer bolting plants.) There is considerable variation in leaf shape, with an occasional plant having strap-shaped, unlobed leaves. One variety, 'Astro', has been selected for these.

A different species, *Diplotaxis tenuifolia*, is sold as "wild arugula," "rustic arugula," or "sylvetta." It's a perennial, the advantage of which is that you will nearly always have a bit of it to harvest, but it generally has smaller leaves, so you may not have much at a time. Also, it seems to bloom most of the year, making long, wiry stems topped with bright yellow flowers. I cut most of these stems off before they elongate, because they take energy from the leaves, and also because the plant will reseed a bit more than I would like. Several strains of wild arugula are now sold, including "olive-leaved," a type with unlobed, strap-shaped leaves.

Pests My arugula has had only one pest problem: flea beetle damage in warmer months. The damaged leaves are edible, though not so attractive. (See Flea Beetles on page 118.)

Sources

Arugula seed: Widely available

Wild arugula seed: ABL, BCS, BI, CG, GS, IST, JSS, NGN, PGS, RH, SI, SOC, SSE, TERR, T&M, WCS

Olive-leaved wild arugula seed: GS, IST, JSS, SI

Asparagus

Asparagus officinalis

Lily Family ❖ *Liliaceae*

A native of marshy areas of Europe and Asia, asparagus thrives in cool, humid summers and so is well adapted here. Our winters are just cold enough to provide the necessary yearly dormant period.

Every spring, asparagus sends up thick shoots from perennial roots. You can harvest these shoots for a certain number of weeks, depending on the age of the plant. Then you must stop cutting and let the last shoots grow into 3- to 5-foot-high feathery shrubs. The mature plants are attractive enough to grace the back of a flower border or to add to bouquets. After all, they are related to the lacy ornamental asparagus fern.

This is not a crop for the gardener in a hurry, because it requires careful soil preparation and takes several years to reach full harvest. In a few years, however, asparagus can be one of your most carefree and rewarding crops.

Growing Instructions Because asparagus is a perennial that produces harvests for fifteen or more years in the same site, it needs a well-prepared permanent home away from areas that you dig up each season. The soil should be very rich and well amended. It is best not to plant an asparagus bed until you have gardened in a new site for at least a year. This gives you time to get persistent perennial weeds under control and to let organic matter mellow in the soil.

How many asparagus plants will you need? You can always grow a few plants for fun, but each plant makes only a couple of stalks at a time, so it takes from five to twenty plants to supply one person with meal-sized portions all season long. Each plant requires a minimum area of 1½ by 1½ feet, so five plants need an area 7½ by 1½ feet, or 11¼ square feet. Twenty plants, an asparagus lover's dream, need an area 3 by 15 feet, or 45 square feet.

Asparagus is usually grown from crowns, or dormant rootstocks. One-year-old crowns are cheaper and transplant better than older crowns. Seeds are even cheaper, but they take more skill and effort. Research has shown that both seeds and crowns mature to allow a full harvest in the third spring after planting. And, though some newer varieties are advertised as being ready the second spring, caution is advised—previous research showed that harvesting plants before the third spring weakened the plants and could keep them from reaching full production.

In early spring presprout the seeds (see page 49), then sow them in a seedbed to which you added plenty of organic matter. Thin to 3 inches apart when the plants are still quite small. Tend the bed carefully to prevent weeds from taking over these slow-starting, wispy seedlings. You can start the seeds indoors, but you will need a setup that will accommodate the plants for two or three months. Transplant the seedlings to an interim bed in the garden until fall.

In fall, in an area that has already been amended and is free of perennial weeds, begin preparation for a permanent asparagus bed by digging in several more inches of organic matter. Transplant seedlings right away. Plant crowns anytime from January through March, being sure to put them in the ground the same day that you obtain them.

To plant either seedlings or crowns, prepare planting trenches as follows. On a day when the soil is dry enough to dig, make a trench 10 to 16 inches deep and 12 inches wide. Put 2 to 8 inches (2 inches if the trench is 10 inches deep and 8 inches if it is 16 inches deep) of compost or well-rotted manure in the bottom, mounding it slightly every 18 inches where the plants will be set. You may also want to work in another organic fertilizer, such as hoof and horn meal, or a slow-release synthetic fertilizer. Then place a 1- to 2-inch layer of soil in the trench. After you have done this, the trench should still be 6 inches deep at the top of the mounds. Set the seedlings or crowns in the trench, spreading the roots over the mounds. Fill in the trench so that the soil is level and the tops of the crowns are covered with 1 to 2 inches of soil. If you are using seedlings, pull 1 to 2 inches of soil around the base of each plant. The trench should still be about 4 inches

Asparagus unfolding

deep. Fill it gradually as the plants grow taller, so that the soil is level by winter of the following year.

If your soil is heavy clay, you must modify this system to reduce the danger of decay. Dig the initial trench only 6 to 12 inches deep, then follow the rest of the preceding directions. When you are finished, the asparagus plants will be planted in level soil rather than in a 4-inch trench. As the plants grow, mound soil around the stems, adding 2 inches by the next fall and 2 inches more by the next summer.

Keep the soil moist and free of weeds all year. When your plants are well up, you may want to apply a mulch. In early spring, before the plants begin to produce, apply a high-nitrogen fertilizer. If the plants appear healthy except that the ferns yellow or die back before fall, it is probably a sign that they need more fertilizer. When the plants die back for the winter, cut them at ground level and compost or discard them. It is always better to wait until the tops are dead before you cut them, but you can do it a bit earlier if they are an eyesore.

The Harvest Beginning the third spring after planting (whether you started from seed or crowns), you can harvest early spring shoots when they are 6 to 10 inches high. To avoid injuring the roots, just snap off the shoots right above the soil level. The first harvest should last no more than two or three weeks, since most of the plant's energy should go into forming fleshy storage roots. It is these roots that allow the plant to send up succulent shoots after each winter's dormancy.

You can harvest shoots for six to eight weeks in the fourth year, and every spring thereafter you should get about two months of delicious asparagus spears. Never harvest after the largest spears become thinner than a pencil or you will harm next year's yield. If you pick any of the ferny stems for bouquets in summer, do it sparingly; they are supplying the roots with energy.

Varieties The old varieties 'Mary Washington' and 'Martha Washington' are rust-resistant and widely adapted, with large spears. 'UC Davis 157' was developed especially for mild-winter regions such as ours. It is tolerant of fusarium, and plants are about 75 percent male, a good thing, since female plants put energy into berries at the expense of more shoots. The 'Jersey' series is also mostly male, and various strains resist or tolerate fusarium and rust. Some European types are bred to be blanched (made white) by covering them with a thick mulch in spring, but they can be allowed to develop green as well. They should do all right near the coast. Purple-speared types would probably do better inland.

Pests Given adequate care, your asparagus bed will probably reward you with years of pest-free harvests, but some pests are possible. Examine young shoots for slug or cutworm damage, rust spots, and common asparagus beetle eggs (laid in rows). Check ferns once or twice a week for aphids, rust, or beetles, since they will reduce the next spring's crop.

Rust appears as elongated spots containing reddish masses of fungal spores. Try to avoid it by using resistant varieties, planting where air circulation is good, and watering only at ground level. Cut diseased shoots or ferns and remove them from the garden.

Tiny, light-green asparagus aphids can be detected by beating a fern over a white surface, to see if they fall out. Serious infestations give plants a blue-green cast and cause bushy "witches' brooms," but it is best to wash them off or apply soap spray before the plant is that damaged.

As a preventative, keep all shoots, even small ones, picked until the harvest is over. This may starve the aphids as they hatch. If you find aphids, remove badly infested ferns and spray remaining ferns with soap or oil.

Small gray larvae and ¼-inch adults of asparagus beetles feed on shoots and ferns. The adult may be metallic blue-black with yellow markings or, less commonly, reddish with twelve black spots. Handpick the insects or (if you have them) pen chickens with your asparagus. Lady beetles and a tiny wasp are asparagus beetle predators. Clean up weeds before spring to reduce overwintering of beetles. Dust the plant with bone meal or rock phosphate to discourage the beetles, or use soap/pyrethrin spray.

If you have found rust spots, aphids, or beetles, remove the ferns from the garden in fall and do not compost them.

Sources

Asparagus seed:
- UC 157: WCS
- Jersey series: JSS, TERR, WSC
- Washington series: BCS, BUR, GS, PGS, VBS
- Purple varieties: GS, TERR
- White varieties: BCS, IST, JG, SI, TERR

Asparagus crowns:
- UC 157: SOC
- Jersey series: BUR, CG, JSS, NGN, PGS, SOC

Asparagus Pea (or Winged Pea)

Lotus tetragonolobus (*Tetragonolobus purpureus*)
Pea Family ❖ *Fabiaceae* (*Leguminosae*)

Here's a good example of a crop trading on the name *asparagus* without the qualifications. The pods are edible when they are under 1 inch long, but they don't have the promised succulence of asparagus. Still, it's a charming plant that always attracts attention in my garden. A Mediterranean-region native, asparagus pea makes a circular mat of gray-green clover-like leaves. The winsome pea-type flowers are two-tone red and deeper red. It tolerates cool weather and, as a legume, would make a useful cover crop.

Growing Instructions I first planted seeds in June; planting as early as March should be fine. Direct-sow the seeds ½ inch deep and about 4 inches apart. This plant is very vigorous and will require little pampering, although it benefits from good garden soil and consistent watering.

The Harvest Pick the pods when they are about an inch long, since they become stringy when they are larger. They will bear for up to 10 weeks in cool weather. Steam them or sauté them in butter or olive oil.

Asparagus pea

Pests I left my June-sown plants in the ground over the winter. They suffered from a powdery mildew during the winter but recovered in spring. I don't know if the disease would strike often, but apparently the plant can fight it off in the warmer months.

Sources

Asparagus pea seeds: BCS, EE, KIT, PGS, SSE, T&M

Bean, Asparagus (or Yard-Long Bean)

Vigna unguiculata subsp. *sesquipedalis*
Pea Family ❖ *Fabiaceae* (*Leguminosae*)

This is the yard-long bean used in Chinese cuisine. A close relative of the black-eyed pea grown in the South, it requires warm temperatures to produce well. It has produced crops in Palo Alto, but even in sunnier parts of San Francisco, my plants grew barely a foot high and didn't even bloom. When asparagus bean does grow well, it needs a tall support.

Bean, Dry (including Kidney, Pinto, and Black Beans)

Phaseolus vulgaris
Pea Family ❖ *Fabiaceae* (*Leguminosae*)

Within the same bean species that is grown for snap beans (see page 188) are a number of cultivars that are grown mainly to be ripened into dry or soup beans. While any snap bean variety would eventually form dry beans, these varieties are particularly tasty, productive, or both, and often have particularly attractive markings on the mature seeds. If your location has cool, foggy summers, you will be most likely to succeed with earlier—that is, faster-maturing—dry bean varieties. Cool weather slows their growth, and they need to be harvested before damp, cold fall days encourage decay. Inland, you will have more choices of variety. (See also Beans, Shell, on page 188.)

Growing Instructions Choose a site that gets sun in early fall, and plant as early in the season as your site and the weather allow. In all other respects, grow dry beans as you would snap beans.

The Harvest Harvest the pods as soon as they are crisply dry—this will not be until at least six weeks after the pods begin to form. It is important not to leave drying pods on the vine too long. Cold, wet weather can rot the beans through the pods even if the pods are dry. If they are still moist when such weather arrives, pod decay is even more likely. You may want to harvest not-quite-dry pods to save them. Even if they aren't quite mature, the beans will still be fine for eating after you dry them, although they might not be mature enough to grow if you planted them. If the pods are damp when you pick them, or if you aren't sure the beans are fully ripe, shell the beans right away. Throw away any flat, withered beans or ones that have brown spots or other signs of decay. If you plan to store the beans before cooking them, spread them in a warm, dry place for a week or two to be sure they are well dried. Then store them in a cool, dry location.

You usually have to grow a lot of plants to collect a good supply of dried beans. Scarlet runner beans (page 186) are the only type I've found to be remarkable for the amount of dry beans produced in a small space. However, you may have other reasons for growing dry beans. They are fun to grow: it always seems a miracle to put bean seeds in the ground at the beginning of the season and then discover more of the same handsome seeds inside the pods at the end of the season. Even shelling the beans is a satisfying activity. Perhaps you remember a certain kind of dry bean fondly from another time, place, or way of life. Even if your microclimate isn't favorable and the harvest is small, you may enjoy growing that type of bean just for the pleasure of holding a few of the newly harvested seeds in your hand again.

Varieties and Related Species If you live in a cool-summer microclimate, start with dry bean varieties that require 85 or fewer days from seed to harvest. You may or may not actually be harvesting in that number of days, since cold summers may slow growth. Following are several early varieties, though you will find others:

- 'Indian Woman Bean', yellow beans, smaller than some, but productive, 60 to 75 days.
- 'Yin Yang', a black and white bean that looks to some like the yin and yang symbol. Seems to be synonymous with 'Calypso' and 'Orca'; as few as 75 days.
- 'Jacob's Cattle', a red-and-white-spotted bean with a whole string of alternate names, including 'Trout', 'Dalmatian', 'Coach Dog', and 'Anasazi'; 85 days. Similar beans, with slightly different coloration, are 'Jacob's Cattle Gold' (80 days) and 'Jacob's Cattle Gasless' (70 to 75 days and 50 percent less gas, they say).
- Several red beans (not kidney beans, which tend to be later, but smaller red beans) such as 'Red Ryder' (80 to 85 days) and 'Red Mexican' (85 days).
- Black beans vary a bit, but 'Black Turtle' is rated at 85 days.
- 'Soldier' beans have maroon markings in which some see a human figure; 85 days and good for cool climates.

Dry bean varieties rated at 100 days or more will require inland heat to mature. This is also true of some dry beans of other species, such as mung (*Vigna radiata*), aduki (*Vigna angularis*), black-eyed pea (*Vigna unguiculata*), and tepary bean (*Phaseolus actuifolius*).

See also Shell Bean on page 188, where you will find beans that can be used at more than one stage.

Pests See Snap Bean.

Legume Family

Beans and peas, which belong to the legume family, Leguminosae or Fabaceae, share many traits. They bear similar flowers, pods, and seeds, and they have similar habits of growth. Both crops have short bush varieties that grow only 1 or 2 feet high and pole varieties that reach 5 to 10 feet high and require a strong support. Both beans and peas get help from special nitrogen-fixing bacteria that live in nodules on their roots, so they don't have a high need for nitrogen fertilizer. In fact, while they need a good supply of phosphorous and potassium, it's best not to give legume crops much nitrogen fertilizer, because it will inhibit the action of the nitrogen-fixing bacteria. I seldom fertilize beans or peas, instead planting them the season after a crop that was fertilized. If they are your first crop in a particular soil or if you are planting when the soil is colder than the seedlings like, fertilize lightly with nitrogen when you sow the seeds. It is possible to purchase innoculant, to make sure the correct nitrogen-fixing bacteria are present, though if legume crops or weedy legumes have been growing in your garden, the bacteria are probably already there.

Legumes will grow in any soil, but they perform best in well-drained, organic soil with a pH of 6.5. Water adequately or the plants will become stunted and vulnerable to pest attack. Diseases can spread among wet plants, so avoid getting water on the leaves. At the end of the season, if your plants were healthy, either compost them or cut the tops and leave the nitrogen-rich roots to decay in the soil.

Peas and beans can be harvested at three stages. When pods are young, before seeds have formed, we harvest snow peas and "green beans." When the seeds have formed, but are still tender enough to be punctured by a fingernail, we harvest green peas and shell beans. When the seeds are hard and dry, and the pods dry and crisp, we harvest soup peas and beans.

Beans at the shell stage are a treat not often found in grocery stores. You can eat fava, lima, scarlet runner, and snap beans at this stage. Some types of snap beans, such as horticultural beans and French flageolet beans, are particularly good at the shell stage, but any snap bean will make a reasonably good shell bean. If you miss any bean pods that you intended to pick young, just shell the beans and cook them with the young pods.

To prolong the harvest of all but dry beans or dry peas, pick all the pods before they mature. If any pods form dry seeds, the plant will slow down or even stop production of new pods. Check the bottom of the plant, where the first pods form, to be sure that you didn't miss any. If you planted a bean variety that is used for both snap and dry beans, you'll get the biggest harvest if you pick all the young pods that form early in the season, then stop picking and let the rest mature as dry beans.

Beans and peas have fragile vines. To avoid cutting production short, hold the vine with one hand and pick pods with the other hand. Of the two crops, beans produce bigger harvests, although peas can be grown over a longer period. You can grow peas almost all year where summers are coolest. We usually think of beans as a crop that grows best only in warm summers, but scarlet runner beans will produce well in foggy gardens, and fava beans will make a crop in winter.

Once bean and pea seedlings survive snail attacks, they don't have many problems in our area. They may be bothered by aphids, mites, and whiteflies, but plants grown under good conditions can usually withstand the assault. A virus may infect an occasional bean or pea plant, but it doesn't usually wipe out a crop. Powdery mildew on pea is the only disease that may cause a serious loss of plants locally.

Sources

Dry bean seed:
Indian Woman: SOC
Yin Yang: SSE, TERR, T&M
Jacob's Cattle: BCS, PGS, SESE, SOC, VBS
Jacob's Cattle Gold: SSE
Jacob's Cattle Gasless: ABL, SSE
Red Mexican: SOC, VBS
Red Ryder: VBS
Black Turtle: VBS, WCS
Soldier: BCS, VBS

Bean, Fava (or Broad Bean or Horse Bean)

Vicia faba
Pea Family ❖ *Fabiaceae* (*Leguminosae*)

The only bean known to early Europeans, the fava bean has been discovered among Iron Age relics in Britain and on the Continent. When you read that the Roman army carried beans in its food supply, favas are what the soldiers were eating.

The fava bean is still widely grown in the milder regions of Europe and in the Middle East. It is seldom grown in most areas of the United States, because the summers are too hot and the winters are too cold. But favas are perfect for our region, growing extremely well from fall to late spring and other times of the year in cool summer microclimates.

Favas are most often eaten as shell beans, either when the seeds are still small and tender or when they are larger but not yet dry. Favas can also be harvested after they are dry and boiled in soups, or used to make a spread or dip similar to hummus, or used salted and roasted. They are the large brown roasted beans in some kinds of Japanese party mixes.

Some people have a genetic metabolic disturbance that causes anemia when they eat fava beans or even inhale fava bean pollen. The problem, called favism, is most common among those whose parents are from the Mediterranean area (particularly near Sardinia) and Asia (particularly Taiwan). Symptoms are more common among men than women, and among adults than children. Some Americans of African descent also have the genetic defect, but they rarely show symptoms of the disorder.

The anemia results from destruction of older red blood cells, but not younger ones. Because younger blood cells are unaffected, it is usual for a person to recover fully once exposure to the beans is stopped.

Many people eat fava beans, including those in parts of the world where the problem is more common. There are seasonal outbreaks of favism in those places, and most victims recover. I have encountered a couple of local people who have had alarming, if not life-threatening reactions to fava beans. The prudent path is to ask questions of your family; then, if no evidence of a problem emerges, eat a small amount of the beans at first, followed by a few days' break to be sure you feel OK.

You are most likely to find seeds in a local nursery if there is an Italian-American population in the area, although the nursery will probably stock a single unnamed variety. For more choices, try seed catalogs.

Growing Instructions Plant the seeds 2 inches deep and 3 to 4 inches apart in blocks or in rows separated by 18 inches. Make sure that you will be able to reach the center of a block to pick the beans. The best planting times generally in the region are February and March for a late spring harvest and September through November for a winter harvest, although year-round planting is possible in the foggier areas. If you plan to use an inoculant, purchase one specifically for fava beans.

What to Do with Fava Beans

To eat fresh favas as shell beans, you will need to push each one out of its tough skin. First remove the beans from the pods, then drop them in boiling water for 30 to 60 seconds. Drain the beans and pour cold water over them. Carefully open each bean and slide out the tender, bright green center. Now you are ready to use them in one of a number of ways. You can just eat them as is. They make a nice snack, appetizer course, or salad ingredient. Or they can be sautéed lightly with olive oil with some finely chopped garlic, and maybe some chopped tarragon. They can also be added to any dish that includes sautéed or stir-fried vegetables, right at the end of the cooking, or to a pasta primavera recipe as one of the vegetables, or to a couscous dish.

Fresh, green, skinned favas can also be mashed or put into a blender with seasonings and then spread on toasted bread or used as a dip for crisp vegetables. Try adding a little garlic, thyme (or dill), a bit of olive oil and lemon juice, salt, and pepper. If you like, you can put some Parmesan cheese in the spread.

If your favas mature into dry beans, you can use them to make a hummus-like dip or spread called ful mudammes that is eaten in Egypt and other parts of the Middle East. It is traditionally served with fried eggs and pita bread for breakfast but can be used in any way you would use hummus. Soak a cup of dry favas in water for 24 hours, then boil them for an hour or two, until they are very soft. In a small skillet, using nonstick spray, sauté ½ cup chopped onion until soft. Add 3 cloves garlic, minced, and a large tomato, chopped. Sauté for about 2 more minutes. Add the drained cooked favas and simmer for 10 minutes. Season with ½ teaspoon each of chili powder, curry powder, and ground cumin; a dash each of cinnamon and ground cloves; ¼ teaspoon salt; and 1½ tablespoons lemon juice. Blend in a food processor until smooth. Stir in 1 tablespoon olive oil. Adjust seasoning if desired.

The plants are handsome—the smooth leaves are gray-green and the edible flowers a dramatic black and white. They grow actively through the winter, reaching 2 to 4 feet high. They don't need much attention, but give them some support to keep them from blowing over in stormy weather. Form a grid by placing sturdy 4-foot-high stakes every 2 to 3 feet around and inside the planting, then connect the stakes at 1 and 3 feet above the ground with garden twine or strips of rags.

The Harvest While the developing beans are still small and tender, pick some to shell. If beans are very young, you can eat them whole, but as they get larger, you need to pop them out of their skins (see the What to Do with Fava Beans sidebar on the opposite page).You can also pick very young pods before the seeds form and eat them like snap beans. I thought that was a great idea, since the thick pods look very succulent, but I didn't find them very tasty. The foliage is a mild-flavored green that can be used in curries and other dishes in place of spinach. You can harvest leafy tops from young plants without harming later production. Older leaves are tougher.

Even if you don't find fava beans to your taste, there is still a good use for the plants. They make an excellent green manure. Sow the seeds in fall or late winter, then dig the plants under when they are 8 to 10 inches high, so they will decay in time for your spring planting. As an alternative, compost the mature plants after you harvest the beans, although they will not return as much nitrogen as the young plants. Cut the plants to the ground, leaving the roots in the soil to rot, and chop the tops for your compost pile.

Fava bean flowers, leaves, and pod

Varieties All varieties do well here. If the variety was developed to withstand warm days, plant it anytime from late winter to midsummer. There used to be only two types of favas—windsors, a short-podded bean with four or so large seeds, and longpods, which contain around eight smaller seeds. Now there are many hybrids, which fall into neither category. Although small-seeded varieties are said to be better tasting, I have not found any great difference among varieties—but I have never been a fan of fava beans.

Pests The only pest that I've seen on fava beans is the bean aphid, sometimes called the black fly, which attacks the tender growing tips of plants. Some gardeners wait until a good crop of pods has set and then remove the tops of infested plants, blooms and all, where the aphids congregate. This trick not only reduces the insect population and its favored habitat but also allows the plant to put its entire energy into ripening the beans that it has already set.

Sources

Fava bean seed: Widely available

Bean, Lima

Phaseolus lunatus

Pea Family ❖ *Fabiaceae* (*Leguminosae*)

Lima beans, the large flat beans in succotash, are very sensitive to cool weather. I had always been told that San Francisco's climate wasn't warm enough for them, but I tried some in my garden in a sunny part of San Francisco anyway. I planted pole and bush lima seeds on the same day in late May that I sowed pole and bush romano beans.

Pods first appeared on the bush limas in early August, when the bush romanos were already halfway through production. The pole limas grew so intertwined with the pole romanos that I couldn't tell the plants apart at first. Finally, toward the end of August, when the pole romanos had been bearing for several weeks, I noticed the distinctive ridged edges of the first lima pods. By the middle of September, I began to see the shadows of small beans in the pods of both bush and pole limas. In the middle of October, I harvested the bush limas as shell beans. I got a grand total of ⅓ cup of shelled beans per plant. The pole limas reached the same stage by the last week of October and made about the same amount of beans per plant.

My conclusion is that, although the climate is not ideal, limas will ripen to the shell bean stage in the warmer parts of the city—good news for fans of this delicious bean. It would take several more weeks for the seeds to ripen to dry beans, and I'm not sure they would make it before the rainy season. I recently learned that shell limas grew in the Santa Clara Master Gardeners' demonstration garden, where the harvest began in July.

Growing Instructions In early May sow seeds in place 2 to 3 inches apart and 1 inch deep. Limas transplant so poorly that seedlings started indoors rarely catch up to plants sown in place. Otherwise, grow limas as you would snap beans.

Sources
Lima bean seed: Widely available

Bean, Romano

Phaseolus vulgaris
Pea Family ❖ *Fabiaceae* (*Leguminosae*)

Instead of having pods that are round in cross section, Romanos have broad, flat pods. These wonderful varieties, which in seed catalogs may be mixed into the snap bean listings, are well worth seeking out. They are delicious and also have a distinctive texture, less crunchy than other bean pods, more buttery. Take care not to overcook them or they will become too soft.

While Romanos are not common in stores, and are usually pricey when available, they are just as easy to grow as any other bean.

There are both bush and pole Romano varieties, with green, yellow, and even purple pods. One of the most common green bush Romanos, which I have often grown, is 'Roma II', but there are several others. 'Romano Gold' and 'Supernano Marconi' are yellow bush types. 'Purpiat' bears purple pods. Among pole Romanos, 'Helda' is a popular green variety, but any you find is worth a try. You will find several pale yellow-podded pole types as well, including 'Gold Marie' and 'Marvel of Venice'.

Sources
Romano bean seed:
Green-podded bush varieties: Widely available
Yellow-podded bush varieties: GS, TERR, VBS
Purple-podded bush varieties: BUR, SOC, TERR
Green-podded pole varieties: ABL, BG, BUR, JSS, NGN, SOC, TERR, VBS, WCS
Yellow-podded pole varieties: GS, IST, JSS, PGS, SI, SOC, WCS
Purple-podded pole varieties: BUR

Bean, Scarlet Runner

Phaseolus coccineus (*P. multiflorus*)
Pea Family ❖ *Fabiaceae* (*Leguminosae*)

This perennial plant owes its tolerance of cool summers to its origin in the highlands of Central America. It gives gardeners in foggy locations a good chance for success with a warm-season bean. And what a fine bean it is! The handsome seeds, usually mottled pink and black, grow into large vines that quickly blanket a fence or arbor. A profusion of flowers, red on most varieties, make the plants handsome enough to use as ornamentals. The flowers often attract hummingbirds, although the birds aren't required for pollination. The large pods are tender and tasty when they are picked young. When the pods are left on the vine, the seeds ripen into large, well-flavored shell or dry beans.

Scarlet runner bean

Growing Instructions Most runner beans are climbers that grow to 8 feet or more. Give them a 6- to 8-foot-high trellis or pole tepee. Since bean vines twine, vertical supports are more important than horizontal ones. Plant seeds 1 to 2 inches deep and 3 to 4 inches apart along a trellis and thin the plants to 6 inches apart. Or plant five or six seeds around each pole in the tepee and thin to the three strongest vines.

These beans can take slightly cooler soil than ordinary snap beans. Although they will succeed from a May planting, they can be sown in April or even earlier if the spring is unusually warm. The plants begin to bear in late June or early July and may continue to make new pods as late as the middle of October. Keep the plants well watered, since production drops if they get too dry.

You can often overwinter scarlet runner beans. Leave the plants intact in fall after you have harvested the beans. The tops may die back completely, or some vines may remain alive. When it is clear which parts are dead, remove them. Any vines that are still alive will leaf out in spring and begin to bear pods a few weeks before runner beans that are planted that same spring. The plants that survive become larger each year.

I add a couple of new seeds each spring where last year's roots don't sprout, to ensure a continuous supply of beans. I have also successfully moved plants by digging the dormant roots in winter. (Some sources claim that the tuberous roots are edible, and others maintain that they are poisonous. The father of a friend sampled some from his garden and became very ill, so I suggest that you assume they are poisonous.)

The Harvest Pick runner bean pods to use as snap beans before any seeds have formed and when the pods are ½- to ⅝-inch wide. Once the seeds begin to fill out, the pods become tough and unpalatable. If a pod escapes notice, you can harvest the seeds to cook as shell beans. As an alternative, wait until the pods are crisply dry on the vine and save the seeds to

Trellises

You can save space and grow the more productive pole bean and pea varieties, or have more success with cucumbers, by constructing a trellis. Remember that beans climb by twining, peas and cucumbers climb with tendrils. This means that beans use only the vertical supports, while peas and cucumbers use both vertical and horizontal ones. Supplying both verticals and horizontals makes your trellis more versatile. Two good materials for this purpose are nylon trellis mesh (available at most nurseries) and hog wire fencing (available at most hardware stores). Hog wire is sturdy galvanized metal fencing with 2- by 4-inch openings. Nylon trellis or hog wire fencing can be mounted on a board fence, a few inches out. Or you can hang nylon trellis or hog wire on freestanding wooden stakes or more sturdy posts. These can be driven into the ground or mounted on the side of a wooden raised bed.

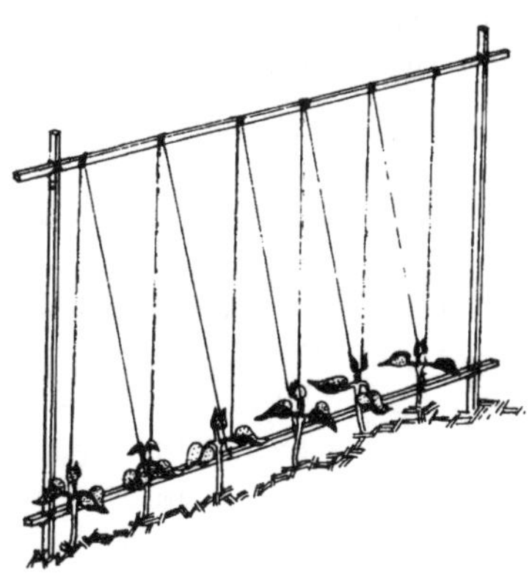

Beans can also climb simple vertical strings, tied to nails on a fence every few inches or from a narrow board mounted between two upright poles. If you have enough space, you can use 3 to 8 bamboo or redwood poles to make a bean tepee. Lash 8- to 12-foot-long poles together near the top with nylon cord, then push them into the ground in a circle 1½ to 3 feet in diameter. A larger tepee—one with a diameter of 4 feet or more—can also serve as a playhouse. Just leave an opening through which the children can crawl inside.

If you hang nylon trellis or strings on a fence, you will need to anchor them at the base. You can use metal "earth staples" designed for irrigation systems or attach a board or pole to the bottoms.

Always have supports in place before plants are tall enough to need them, and watch for wayward plants that need help finding the supports. You can weave these through, ever so gently, or attach them to a support with string or a twist-tie until they find their way.

cook as dry beans or to plant the next year. Be careful not to overplant runner beans. The crop of both green pods and dry beans can be huge. From five plants I harvested enough pods for two people to eat and share with friends for almost three months, then picked enough dry beans to fill several quart jars.

Remember also, that if you leave pods on the plant long enough for them to form beans, green pod production will slow or stop. So it's best to eat green pods, even picking them smaller than ½-inch across and eating them as "baby beans," early in the season, then stopping your harvest to let the later pods mature for storage beans. Adding some compost in late summer may stimulate the plants to make a bigger late harvest.

Some people find runner bean pods "too different" due to their slightly rough surface when raw and their slightly different texture, but many love them for their excellent, sweet, beany flavor. (Several recipes in this book feature runner bean pods.)

Varieties Scarlet runner bean seeds sold as an ornamental may not be a variety bred for flavor or production. One year I grew some seeds from a mail-order vegetable seed catalog and some from the flower section of a local seed rack. The seeds sold as a vegetable produced pods for a full month and a half longer than the ones sold as a flower. In seed catalogs, look for a separate listing for runner beans in the vegetable section or check the broader category of pole beans.

In your search for varieties that offer good flavor and production, you don't have to give up beauty. My productive vines had flowers just as colorful as those on the ornamental vines, and a lot more of them. Several varieties have white flowers (and white seeds). 'Painted Lady' has two-tone red and white flowers.

Pests Be on guard against earwigs, slugs, and snails when the plants are small, since these pests can do major damage at this stage. Pick the plants over for snails as you harvest the pods, since small snails sometimes congregate on the plants in late summer, and the leaves they eat won't be able to send nutrients to the storage roots for winter.

Sources

Scarlet runner bean seed:
Red-flowered varieties: Widely available
White-flowered varieties: NSS, T&M, WCS
Red-and-white-flowered varieties: BCS, RG, SSE, TERR, T&M, VBS
Pink-flowered varieties: CG, SSE, TERR, T&M, VBS

Bean, Shell

Phaseolus vulgaris
Pea Family ❖ *Fabiaceae* (*Leguminoasae*)

Although any common garden bean variety can be eaten at the shell bean stage, when the seeds have fully formed but have not yet hardened, some varieties are sold specifically for harvest at this stage. They include French and Italian types like flageolet, cannellini, and the colorful group known as "horticultural beans." While these types can be eaten as green snap beans (pods) or dry (soup) beans, the shell stage is their best use. Fresh shell beans appear at farmers markets briefly in late summer. Other than that, they are a treat mostly experienced by gardeners. They can be used any way you would use dry beans—soup, succotash, baked beans, and so on—but cook faster and have a pleasant texture.

You will have to search in catalogs to find these varieties. They are often there, but they may or may not be listed separately from other *Phaseolus vulgaris* kinds of beans. One group has red-striped pods and red-flecked seeds. Look for them as "horticultural beans" or "cranberry beans" (and see more on varieties in this section).

Growing Instructions See Beans, Snap. Most shell bean varieties are bush beans, but you will find an occasional pole variety.

The Harvest Beans are ready to harvest as shell or "shellie" beans when the pods are like flexible leather and you can easily shell out the fully formed beans. You should be able to split the pod at a "seam" and open it up lengthwise. If you have to pry out each bean, the pod isn't mature enough yet. If the pod has become hard and brittle, you waited too long. The beans should be full sized, but you should be able to easily puncture one with a thumbnail.

Most kinds of shell beans are used fresh out of the pods, but one, the flageolet, is often used "green dried." To achieve this, pull flageolet plants when most of the pods are at the shell stage and hang them in a warm, dry location. (This allows them to be stored, but if you grow only a few, you may as well eat them fresh unless you have a fond memory of green dried flageolets that you want to reproduce.) Flageolet beans are often not stringless at the snap bean stage, so are best not grown for that purpose.

Varieties and Related Species Horticultural beans are sold under a variety of names. You may find them sold as 'Tongue of Fire' (in Italian, that's 'Lingua de Fuoco'), 'Dragon's Tongue', 'Cranberry', 'Wren's Egg', or 'Borlotto'. Look for the red-streaked pods and beans with red or maroon flecks. They are often described as "triple use" beans since they can be used as snap or dry beans as well. Most, but not all, are bush beans.

Cannellini beans are a variety of white-seeded bean. While they can also be used as dry beans, in Italian cuisine they are often used fresh, at the shell stage.

The most common flageolet variety has white seeds, but there are varieties, known as chevriers, that are pale green at the shell stage, so they dry to a pale green. In France, freshly picked or dried flageolets are considered to be the perfect accompaniment to a leg of lamb.

Garbanzo and soy beans may require too much time to form dry beans, but can be harvested earlier, at the shell stage. Garbanzos (*Cicer arietinum*) can be planted in early spring. The lacy plants produce pods with only two beans each. Soy beans (*Glycine max*) are cooked in the pod at the shell stage to produce the Japanese snack edamame. They should be sown in late spring when soil has warmed. In both cases, early varieties will give you the best chance of good results in cooler microclimates.

Sources

Shell bean seed:
Cranberry: PGS, SI, SSE, TERR, VBS
French Horticultural: NGN, VBS
Bush Dragon Tongue: ABL, BCS, BG, BUR, CG, PGS, SSE, TERR, VBS, WCS
Bush Tongue of Fire: GS, IST, JSS, SI, VBS
Pole Tongue of Fire: GS, IST, SI, TERR, T&M
Cannellini: CG, GS, IST, SI, SOC, T&M, VBS
Flageolet: JG, NGN, JSS, VBS
Garbanzo: BCS, BG, GS, IST, JLH, NSS, PGS, SI, SOC, VBS
Soy bean (edamame): Widely available

Bean, Snap (Bush and Pole)

Phaseolus vulgaris
Pea Family ❖ *Fabiaceae* (*Leguminosae*)

Snap beans are the common green beans, such as 'Kentucky Wonder' and 'Blue Lake', which are eaten when the pods are young and before the beans form. They used to be called string beans, because of the

Minestrone

This is a wonderful, full-meal soup in the Italian tradition. Make a double batch and freeze half for later. Just be sure to remove the portion you intend to freeze before you add the pasta, as pasta doesn't freeze well.

Stock

- 1½ pounds fresh (uncured) pork or beef hocks
- 1½ pounds pork or beef soup bones
- 2 tablespoons vinegar
- 4 quarts water
- ½ cup coarsely chopped celery leaves
- 1 carrot, coarsely chopped
- 1 onion, quartered

Soup

- ¾ cup dry garbanzo beans
- 1 medium carrot, thinly sliced
- 1 small onion, chopped
- 1½ cups potato cut into large dice
- 1 cup green beans (you can use scarlet runner beans), cut in 1-inch pieces
- 2½ cups tomato sauce, canned or homemade (see page 365)
- 1 teaspoon chopped fresh thyme leaves
- 1 tablespoon chopped fresh basil
- 1 tablespoon chopped fresh parsley
- 2 small summer squash, chopped
- ¼ cup small pasta (such as small shells, alphabet macaroni, or spaghetti broken into short pieces)
- 1 cup grated Parmesan cheese

To make the stock, the day before, put the meat, vinegar, water, celery leaves, carrot, and onion into a large pot and bring to a boil. Lower heat, cover, and let simmer for 2 to 3 hours, until the meat is very tender. Cool. Refrigerate overnight.

The next day, use a slotted spoon to skim off the hardened fat. Remove and discard the vegetables. Remove the meat and bones. Reserve all of the lean meat, discarding the bones, fat, and gristle. Cut or tear any large pieces of meat into bite-sized chunks and place in a medium bowl. Strain the remaining broth through a sieve or colander into a large container. Scrub the pot well and return the strained broth and lean meat to the pot.

To make the soup, rinse and pick over the garbanzo beans and add them to the broth. Bring it to a boil, lower heat, cover, and simmer for 1 hour, or until the beans are nearly tender.

Add the carrot and onion and simmer for 5 minutes. Add the potatoes, green beans, and tomato sauce. Simmer for 20 minutes more. Add the thyme, basil, parsley, squash, and pasta and cook 10 to 15 minutes longer. Serve with Parmesan cheese to sprinkle on top.

fibrous string that ran the length of each pod and had to be removed before the beans were cooked. Now that plant breeders have all but eliminated the string, the produce industry has popularized the name "snap bean."

Snap beans and all other bean crops in the species *Phaseolus vulgaris* have similar growing requirements. They mostly succeed, both inland and near the coast, but microclimates in either part of the region can challenge them. What they like is humidity (not a problem near the coast), 70 to 80°F daytime temperatures, and no temperatures below 50°F. Below 50°F (which can happen on near-coastal nights) or above 90°F with dry air (as often occurs inland), pod set may be reduced.

Growing Instructions Plant your first successive crop of bush snap beans after the soil has warmed, usually on May 1 but earlier during a particularly warm spring. Plant the seeds 1 to 2 inches deep and 2 inches apart in a small block or in rows spaced 12 to 18 inches apart. Bush beans mature quickly, in just a couple of months, and produce for a few weeks. You can plant additional successive crops until the middle of July.

Pole beans can be planted any time from May 1 to early June. Sow the seeds 1 inch deep and 2 to 3 inches apart on one or both sides of a trellis, or plant three or four seeds around a pole. Leave 1 foot or more between poles. Pole beans begin bearing a couple of weeks later than bush beans, but they produce longer.

For best germination, plant bean seeds with the flatter narrow edge down. Plant after your garden soil is above 60°F at 2 inches deep, which is usually the case by May. Planted when soil is too cold, especially in clay soil, bean seeds will take a long time to germinate and may rot first. Presprouting or soaking the seeds will only encourage decay. However, you can get a head start in the spring by sowing the seeds indoors 3 to 4 weeks before the soil is warm enough for planting outdoors. If you do this, plant a single seed in each container (do not pot them up) and get them into the garden as soon as they have two or three true leaves.

If bean seeds manage to germinate in soil that is too cold, the seedlings will have yellow leaves because they can't get enough nutrients, and they will grow very slowly. As the soil warms, the leaves will become greener, but because the plants are growing so slowly, they may succumb to pest damage they would have otherwise outgrown.

The Harvest Pick snap beans while the pods are still smooth, with no swellings visible where seeds are forming. When they are more mature, the pods are likely to be tough and stringy. How large they can get and still remain tender depends on the variety.

Although you can pick any snap bean very young, you may get a more flavorful baby pod from French filet varieties, which were developed especially for picking at this stage. If you are growing these French delicacies, pick them when they are less than ¼ inch (some say less than ⅛ inch) in diameter, steam them briefly, and serve them whole. They require daily harvesting to keep them from growing past their prime, and when they get past the baby bean stage, they may not be as tasty or tender as regular snap bean pods.

Varieties Bush and pole snap beans come in three colors of pods: green, yellow, and purple. Yellow-podded snap beans are also called wax beans. They have a firmer texture when cooked than other varieties. If you can grow any standard pole or bush bean, you can probably grow them all. 'Blue Lake' and 'Kentucky Wonder' and their various strains are good bets here. And 'Kentucky Blue' is said to combine the best of both. Try others as well and compare your results.

The purple-podded varieties are tasty and are said to tolerate cooler weather and soil than most green or yellow beans. They can be planted a couple of weeks earlier or grown in a cooler microclimate. Their flowers are a lovely violet, and their deep purple pods turn an unexpected bright green when cooked. Common purple-podded bush varieties are 'Royalty' and 'Royal Burgundy,' and there are several pole varieties, including some that are called violet- or even blue-podded beans.

There are many French filet varieties, most of them introduced to American gardeners in the past few years. You may find them listed as baby beans or *haricot vert*, which is French for green bean.

If you find that all the varieties you try struggle in your cool summer microclimate, you may want to grow scarlet runner beans instead.

(See also Beans, Romano, on page 186.)

Pests Slugs and snails inflict great damage on snap bean seedlings, and earwigs do occasional damage. There are several strategies for protecting seedlings: Plant twice as many seeds as you need and either thin the extras or transplant them to fill gaps when the pests strike, plant the seeds under a floating row cover, or start the seeds indoors and move them into the garden when they have several leaves and are better able to survive the pest damage. Late in the season the summer's baby snails may turn your bean leaves to lace, although they won't seriously reduce the nearly completed harvest. Still, crush as many small snails as you can and continue to control snails through winter and spring so that there won't be as many to breed and produce small snails to plague next summer's beans.

Other pests that I've seen on snap beans include aphids, spider mites, and whiteflies. All are more likely if the plants are grown under poor conditions, especially if they are underwatered. Beans also get aphid-transmitted virus diseases. Remove infected plants from your garden to keep such diseases from spreading.

In parts of the country that get summer rain, beans are susceptible to a number of bacterial and fungal diseases, so gardeners there are cautioned not to water with overhead sprinklers and not to work among wet plants. In dry-summer areas like ours, these diseases are rare, but it is still wise to water at

Cheesy Italian Sausage Stew

This dish is almost a full meal, needing only a green salad and maybe fruit for dessert to round it out. Serves three or four.

6 Italian sausages, hot or mild (or turkey Italian sausages)
3 cups green beans, cut on the diagonal into 1½-inch pieces (scarlet runner or Romano-type beans are especially good)
2 cups boiling potatoes, unpeeled, cut into 1-inch chunks
4 tablespoons butter or margarine (or use half olive oil)
4 tablespoons unbleached flour
2 cups milk (lowfat or nonfat are fine)
¼ cup grated Parmesan cheese
Salt and pepper, if desired

Put the sausages in a saucepan of boiling water and simmer them for 10 minutes. Cut the cooked sausages into ¼-inch slices and set aside. Steam the green beans and potatoes 10 to 15 minutes, until tender but firm, and set aside.

Melt the butter in a skillet over low heat and stir in the flour. Turn the heat up slightly and cook the mixture for about 2 minutes, until it is bubbly. Turn off heat. Stir milk in very gradually, working rapidly with a fork to break up lumps and keep the flour dispersed. When all of the milk has been mixed in, bring the mixture to a simmer and cook till it thickens, stirring continuously and scraping the sides and bottom often to keep the sauce from burning.

Add the cheese to the thickened sauce and stir to mix it in well. Add salt and freshly ground black pepper to taste. Stir in the sausages and vegetables and serve hot.

ground level. It is also important to obtain disease-free seeds. Commercial bean seeds are the safest, and locally homegrown seeds are probably safe—but avoid using seeds saved from bean plants grown in wet-summer areas.

Sources

Snap bean seed: All types are widely available.

Beet

Beta vulgaris
Crassa Group
Goosefoot Family ❖ *Chenopodiaceae*

At their best when daytime temperatures are 55 to 75°F, beets thrive in all parts of our region. Like other root crops, beets make the best-shaped roots in either sandy soil or soil well amended with organic matter. They are almost always direct-seeded, but I have discovered that they can be transplanted successfully when very young. Being able to transplant allows you to have beet seedlings growing while another crop is finishing production. You can start the seeds indoors, or outdoors in a corner of your garden.

Growing Instructions Plant in rows or scatter-sow in small blocks. Plant seeds ½ inch deep and 1 or 2 inches apart. Since each beet seed really consists of several seeds, the seedlings must be thinned. If you sow the seeds in place, wait until the seedlings have two true leaves, then thin to 3 inches apart and to one plant per cluster. Use scissors to snip off the excess plants. If you grow seedlings to transplant, separate them carefully and plant them in the garden 3 inches apart. You must water regularly to produce sweet, tender beets with good color.

Begin sowing seeds outdoors as early as February, whenever the soil isn't too wet for planting. In areas closest to the coast, you can continue to plant until around the end of July. The July-planted beets will be able to mature in the warmth of late summer, and they can be left in the ground to be dug up in fall and winter. In protected sites or farther from the coast, you may be able to plant a month or two later. If you plant too late, however, the beets won't have time to form big roots before they are stopped by cold weather. In spring you may be tempted to leave small beets in the ground

Marinated Beets

Make a couple of cups of these vermilion pickles and keep them at the ready in your refrigerator. They make a tangy, colorful addition to salads.

- 2 cups beets, cut into ⅛-inch strips, as described
- ½ cup cider vinegar
- ½ cup water
- 2 tablespoons sugar (optional)

Scrub the beets. They don't have to be peeled, but trim away any brown corky matter or hard-to-clean bunches of rootlets. Cut the beets into vertical slices ⅛-inch thick and then into strips ⅛-inch wide. Cut any extra long strips in half.

Steam the beets until tender, 20 minutes or longer. Put them in a jar or plastic refrigerator container with a lid and set them aside.

In a saucepan, heat the vinegar, water, and sugar to just below a simmer. Pour the hot mixture over the beets. If the beets are not covered, add a little more unheated vinegar and water till they are completely submerged. Chill overnight before using. They will keep for at least a couple of weeks in the refrigerator.

hoping that they will get bigger, but they will go to seed instead and then die.

The Harvest You can harvest beets for tender greens before the roots have even formed. The next harvest can be for baby beets, when the roots are only an inch or so in diameter. For regular use let them reach at least 2 inches in diameter, but check the seed packet to find out the optimum size for the variety you are growing. Some beet varieties remain tender when they get bigger, but most toughen up. Almost all beet varieties reach the size listed on the seed packet in about two months.

Varieties When choosing a beet variety, don't limit yourself to early varieties, since beets aren't hampered by cool summers. Standard round red beets, such as 'Early Wonder', 'Detroit Dark Red', and 'Ruby Queen', do just fine here. 'Winterkeeper' (also called 'Lutz'), although not very shapely, is a good red variety for late summer into fall cropping, since it stays tender for a long time. 'Bull's Blood' is popular for the deep red of its leaves, which can be used in salads when still small. When its red roots are sliced, they show lighter red rings. 'Chiogga' shows alternating white and red rings. While this "zoning" is normal for these two varieties, when other varieties show this trait, it is because the days were too warm when the roots were maturing. There are also yellow- and white-rooted beets. Both are reputed to germinate poorly, which I was quite relieved to hear after my first effort to grow 'Burpee's Golden' produced a very thin stand.

Pests Spinach leafminers are my worst beet pests. The larvae tunnel inside the leaves, making unappetizing blotches. They don't harm the roots directly, but extensive leaf damage will stunt the roots. To my great delight, leafminers didn't damage the leaves of 'Bull's Blood' beets. (For more on leafminers, see page 118.)

Overwintering beets often get either cercospora leaf spot (see page 134) or beet rust. The same prevention methods help you avoid both.

Sources

Beet seed:
Red varieties: Widely available
Chiogga: Widely available
Bull's Blood: Widely available
Yellow varieties: Widely Available
White varieties: BCS, BG, JG, JLH, JSS, NGN, PGS, SSE, TERR, T&M, VBS

Bitter Melon (or Balsam Pear or Foo Gwa)

Momordica charantia
Gourd Family ❖ *Cucurbitaceae*

A standard vegetable in Chinese cuisine, bitter melon is a vine that can be trained to climb a trellis in the same way that cucumbers are. The distinctive bitter flavor of this crop is due to quinine. Startling at first, the flavor appeals to many people once they get used to it. If bitter melon is new to you, buy it at a grocery store and make sure that you like the taste before you grow it.

Bitter melon is a borderline crop even in the warmer parts of our region. It may produce fruit in a sunny microclimate or a minigreenhouse (see page 33). Still, the plant is pretty, and even if fruit doesn't form you can use the young leaves and stem tips as a potherb.

Growing Instructions Start seeds indoors in a bottomless milk carton, in the same way that you would start any other fast-growing plant with delicate roots (see page 51). Start the seeds during the third week of March to plant out in early May. (The seeds will take two weeks to germinate, and the plants should grow indoors for three to four more weeks.) Fertilize your garden soil well and set plants 6 to 8 inches apart near a trellis. Keep the soil well watered and apply a booster of manure or compost tea (see page 81) or fish emulsion every two weeks.

The Harvest Since bitter melon becomes too bitter to eat when it is ripe, it is only eaten green. Try the immature fruit while it is under 6 inches long. Sample larger fruit until it becomes too bitter for your taste. (The ripe fruit is interesting to look at, turning yellow and then orange and finally splitting open to show its red seeds.)

To prepare a bitter melon fruit, cut it in half lengthwise. Scoop out and discard the seeds, which are poisonous at any stage, and cut the melon into ¼-inch slices. Drop the melon slices into boiling water and boil them for three minutes to reduce the bitterness. Bitter melon is often stir-fried and served with fermented black bean sauce.

Sources

Bitter melon seed: BCS, BI, EE, JSS, NGN

Bok Choy (or Pac Choy)

Brassica rapa (*B. chinensis*)
Chinensis Group
Mustard Family ❖ *Brassicaceae* (*Cruciferae*)

This crop is the handsome white- or pale green-stemmed, nonheading Chinese green. It is a near relative of turnip, tender-green mustard, and heading Chinese cabbage. Grown similarly to Chinese cabbage (see page 202), bok choy is somewhat easier. Since both crops attract slugs and snails in hordes, they should be attempted only if the pests are under control, or grown under a row cover frame (see pages 48–50).

Growing Instructions Bok choy needs organic, fertile soil. Sow the seeds in place ¼ to ½ inch deep. When the plants are about 4 inches high, thin them to 6 to 8 inches apart. Water bok choy regularly, so that it will grow fast and stay tender. It should be possible to grow bok choy from February through April and again from late summer into fall. You may be able to grow it all summer if your site is cool enough. Warm days will cause the crop to go to seed prematurely, or bolt, before it gets very big. It may also bolt during the longest days of the year, but it is less likely to do so than Chinese cabbage.

The Harvest Start by eating the small plants that you pull to thin the crop. Then harvest outer leaves of growing plants, or pull whole plants at any stage before the flower stalk has grown taller than the leaves. Eat leaves and stems in salads, in soups, or stir-fried with sliced mushrooms in oyster sauce.

Bok choy

Varieties Tall, white-stemmed types used to be the main ones available, but now we can also grow the delicious short, or "baby" bok choys, including pale-green-stemmed types such as 'Mei Quing' or 'Ching-Chiang'. A similar Chinese green of the same species, 'Tah Tsai', has flat rosettes of shiny, dark green leaves with bok choy-like white stems. It is good in salads or stir-fried.

Pests Bok choy has the same pests, including clubroot, as other members of the mustard family (see page 198).

Sources

Bok choy seed:
Tall varieties: Widely available
Short-stemmed varieties: BCS, BUR, EE, GS, JSS, KIT, NGN, PGS, RG, TERR, WCS
Purple varieties: CG, JSS, KIT, TERR, T&M
Tah Tsai/Tatsoi: ABL, BCS, BG, BI, EE, JG, JSS, KIT, NGN, PGS, SESE, TERR, VBS, WCS

Bolivian Sunroot (or Yacon or Strawberry Jicama)

Polymnia edulis (*Polymnia sonchifolia*)
Sunflower Family ❖ *Asteraceae* (*Compositae*)

It took me nearly three years to find a start of this plant, but the wait was worthwhile. Nearly pest-free, Bolivian sunroot produces a generous supply of large, sweet, juicy tuberous roots. A native of South America, it is grown for food in several Andean countries.

Bolivian sunroot leaps skyward to a bushy 8 feet or higher. Its huge triangular gray-green leaves are covered with soft hairs. Weighing up to a couple of pounds apiece, the edible roots are between jicama and watermelon in texture, and between jicama and sunchoke in flavor.

In fact, the plant is related to sunchoke (see page 266). You can see the family resemblance in the daisies, which on Bolivian sunroot are orange and a little over an inch across. Less impressive than those of sunchoke, the flowers are barely noticeable blooming atop the tall plants in fall.

Growing Instructions Bolivian sunroot is grown from rhizomes, which can be easily divided and transplanted during the winter when the plant is dormant. When you buy a crown, what you are getting is a rhizome division, usually one with several buds. Plant it in late winter, before the shoots start to grow, with the highest buds just at soil level. Leave 2 or 3 feet between crowns.

Bolivian sunroot needs good garden soil and deep watering while it is actively growing. Be especially careful not to let it dry out in late summer or early fall. (When the plant is thirsty, its leaves droop dramatically.)

The Harvest In mid- to late fall, the top of the plant dies back. Lop off the stems a foot or so above the ground, so that the stumps will clearly mark the site of your underground treasure. When the weather has cooled, dig around looking for the tuberous roots. The edible structure is not the rhizome that you see at the soil surface, but rather the large storage roots that have formed beneath them, each connected to the rhizome by a thin attachment root. You will find them by carefully digging in from one side of the plant. When you locate one, remove the soil around it until you can lift it out and detach it.

What you will have in your hands is a large, homely brown object, either elongated and pointed at the ends or almost spherical. Wash it, cut off a portion, peel off the thin brown skin, and enjoy.

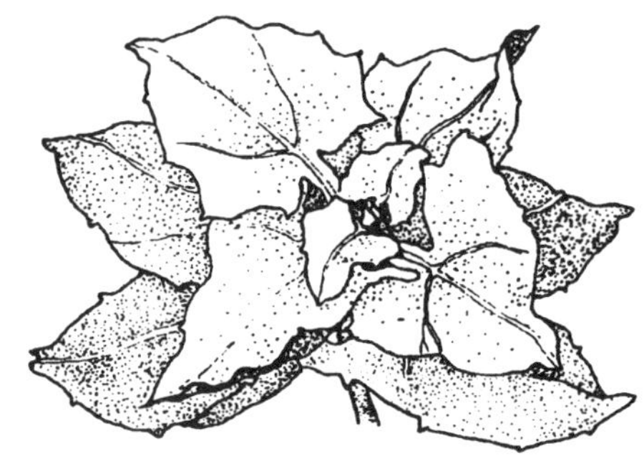
Bolivian sunroot leaves

You can harvest roots gradually or all at once. It is best, though, to renew the plant each spring, or it will develop a mass of rhizomes but few new storage roots. By March, when the plantings begin to grow again, you should have harvested all the roots made that year. Before you reset the plant, dig in some organic matter and fertilizer. Divide the rhizomes and replant a small start of them. You will have quite a few extra rhizomes, which you can either use to grow more plants yourself or share with gardening friends.

So far I have only enjoyed Bolivian sunroot raw. The crisp roots enliven a bag lunch or make a good vegetable relish for dipping. The textures and flavors of Bolivian sunroot, romaine lettuce, and a jar of artichoke hearts with the marinade all blend delectably in a salad.

Varieties Although there is probably more than one variety of this crop in its native South America, the local sources do not give any variety names.

Sources
Bolivian sunroot (Yacon) crowns: NGN, SOC

Broccoli

Brassica oleracea
Italica Group
Mustard Family ❖ *Brassicaceae* (*Cruciferae*)

The Bay Area climate is ideal for growing broccoli—and, in fact, Italian market gardeners who grew the crop in San Francisco and on the peninsula introduced it to the American market. If you time your plantings well, plant both short- and long-season varieties, and grow types that resprout when you cut them, you can harvest broccoli most of the year.

Growing Instructions See Mustard Family (page 198) for general growing requirements for cole crops. Unlike cabbage, young broccoli plants may stunt if the temperature approaches freezing, so I never set them out until the middle of February. There is also some risk of stunting when plants are set out too late in the fall. Where summers are cool, August is the safest last planting time for fall

Bolivian Sunroot and Blood Orange Salad

This is an arranged salad on a lettuce-leaf bed. Similar salads are made with jicama, but the tender, crisp Bolivian sunroot is exquisite in this dish. Serves four.

¼ cup orange juice (use prepared juice or buy an extra orange)
¼ cup olive oil
1½ tablespoons red wine vinegar
⅛ teaspoon garlic powder
Salt and freshly ground pepper
1 medium red onion
4 large or 8 small lettuce leaves
1 or 2 blood oranges (or 2 navel oranges)
Bolivian sunroot (enough to make about 1½ cups of slices)
1 large or 2 small avocados

To make the dressing, combine the orange juice, olive oil, vinegar, garlic powder, and salt and pepper to taste in a small jar with a lid.

To make the salad, slice the red onion thinly and put it in a small bowl. Put the lid on the dressing jar, shake vigorously, then pour the dressing over the onion. Let it marinate in the dressing for 1 hour.

Divide the lettuce leaves among four salad plates. Peel and thinly slice the blood oranges (or regular oranges). Divide the orange slices among the four salads.

To prepare the sunroot, wash it, peel it with a potato peeler or small knife, then cut out any dirty cracks or other blemishes. Rinse it again, then cut the roots into ¼-inch-thick slices. Out of each slice, cut triangles about 1½ inches on a side. Arrange 6 to 8 of these triangles on top of the orange slices.

Cut the avocado into thin slices and arrange on top of the sunroot.

To serve the salads, put ¼ of the onion on each salad, then pour ¼ of the remaining dressing over each salad.

broccoli, though where late summer is warmer, September or later may work. Nurseries sometimes don't stock fresh broccoli seedlings until September, so if you want them for a midsummer planting you may have to start them yourself. Start seeds indoors beginning in the middle of December and continue to grow more seedlings as you need them until the end of July. You can also start seeds outdoors in a seedbed between March and July. Transplant small varieties of broccoli to stand 8 to 12 inches apart and larger ones 18 to 24 inches apart.

Short-season varieties take 50 to 85 days from transplanting; long-season ones 85 to 220 days. When long-season broccoli is overwintering, it may take a month or two longer than listed. I usually set out short-season plants in the middle of February or March for a late spring harvest. Then I usually seed both short- and long-season varieties indoors in early to late June and set them out in mid-July to mid-August. The short-season plants will mature in late summer or fall, the long-season ones sometime between December and March. Either may mature earlier or later depending on the weather and the variety.

Stunted broccolis will have central heads smaller than those described in catalog entries. The diameter of the central head is determined by the diameter of the main stem when the head starts to form. Broccoli plants vary in normal height, from as short as 1½ feet to over 3 feet high.

The Harvest Cut broccoli when the central head stops enlarging and its flower buds are still tightly closed. If the variety is a sprouter (as most are), you can cut the stem several inches below the head and smaller heads will form from the base of the remaining leaves. You can keep cutting these side heads, which become smaller and smaller, for months. I once cut a sprouter for a year and a half, just to see how long I could do it. Most of that time it yielded a large handful of very small sprouts twice a week, enough to add to a casserole or to stir-fry. It made more during cool spells and less when the weather turned warm. Remember not to let the yellow flowers open on a plant kept for side sprouts, since they will reduce side-shoot production. It's easy to overlook flower stems when you are harvesting side sprouts, so make a point of searching for them and snapping them off.

Varieties There are numerous broccoli varieties, both open-pollinated and hybrid, to explore. I will mention some of them but also offer some criteria for you to consider. Breeders who are catering to farmers seek to create plants that mature all at the same time and have ever larger central heads, with less emphasis on the side shoots. This allows farmers to harvest in one go-through and get impressively large heads to market. As a home gardener, you'd probably rather not harvest all on the same day (unless you are planning to freeze your broccoli). Staggered maturity helps you have a steady supply for a longer time. Another trait that helps you get this is a long period of side shoot production. Large heads are exciting, but most of us cut them up before we serve them, so smaller ones will suffice.

Most of the cultivars you will find today are rather fast-growing ones that do not need to be exposed to cold before they form the flower buds that we eat. Some are said to be particularly able to withstand heat or cold, so they are good for planting inland where summers are warmer and winters chillier. Among short-season open-pollinated varieties that also offer staggered maturity and plenty of side heads are the old varieties 'De Cicco' (48 days from plant-out, 3- to 6-inch central head), 'Calabrise' (58 to 90 days), and 'Green Goliath' (55 days, "large" central head). Two newer nonhybrid cultivars are 'Umpqua' (60 days, generous side shoot production) and 'Nutribud' (58 to 65 days, 4- to 6-inch central head, moderate side shoot production), which was bred to be high in glutamine, an important amino acid. Popular hybrid cultivars with larger central heads and plenty of side shoots include 'Premium Crop F_1' (58 days) and 'Packman F_1' (55 days, best planted summer or fall).

Varieties that grow best in late summer and early fall include the old open-pollinated 'Watham 29' (85 days, 4- to 8-inch central heads, "some side shoots") and Romanesco broccoli. Romanesco is a visual treat, with its chartreuse heads made up of pointed spears. It has a mild flavor and a different, pleasing texture. Some call it a cauliflower, since it doesn't make any side shoots. But unlike cauliflower, spears can be cut from the outer edge of the head, and the inner ones will continue to mature, extending the harvest. (Still, some seed sources list it as a cauliflower.)

Romanesco-type broccoli is represented in current catalogs only by hybrids such as 'Veronica F_1' (85 days, 7-inch head). In its heirloom, nonhybrid form it made heads up to a foot across that made for an extended harvest. For my money, these were preferable. I am hoping someone will go to Northern Italy, its origin, and bring back seed for the original Romanesco.

Finally, there are heirloom long-season sprouting broccolis that require longer exposure to winter cold and don't form a large central head. Their small central head is followed by numerous side sprouts that are almost as large. They require 120 to 220 days from plant out, for harvest in December through March. Plant them at the same time as you plant other late-summer broccolis and get a winter harvest without having to plant in the winter. These are more popular in English than U.S. gardens, but you can locate seed for some of them. 'Rudolph' is listed at 150 days, 'Purple Sprouting' at 120 to 220 days; 'White Star' takes about 6 months. So that you can sample them, Territorial Seed Company offers a mix of several kinds. These are big, productive plants, perfect for large families or for school gardens, where there are many children each of whom wants to snap off a broccoli shoot or two.

Pests Broccoli is subject to the usual mustard-family pests (see page 198). Aphids can be particularly troublesome if they get into the developing heads.

Sources

Broccoli seed:

Short season varieties:
- De Cicco: Widely available
- Calabrise: Widely available
- Nutribud: ABL, NGN, PGS, SESE, SOC, WCS
- Premium Crop: NGN, PGS, SESE, TT

Summer- and fall-planted varieties:
- Packman F_1: JSS, NGN, PGS, PS, TERR, T&M, VBS
- Waltham 29: BCS, GS, PGS, SESE, SOC
- Rudolph: TERR
- Purple-sprouting: BCS, BG, GS, NGN, PGS, TERR, T&M, WCS
- White Star: WCS
- Romanesco: BCS, BG, GS, IST, JG, JSS, PGS, SI, SSE, TERR, T&M, WCS

Broccoli, Chinese (or Gai Lan, Kailaan, Chinese Kale)

Brassica oleracea alboglabra
Mustard Family ❖ *Brassicaceae* (*Cruciferae*)

Although one of my main goals in writing this book has been to develop a cuisine based on what we can grow in local gardens and to try new foods with the intent of matching what I eat to what I can grow, it is a testament to how entrenched food habits can be that it took me until a few years ago to understand that this plant tastes good and is easy to grow. Asian-American students often bring gai lan with oyster sauce to my vegetable gardening class potlucks. I finally bought some and tried the recipe, and it quickly became a favorite in our meals.

Gai lan is, like hon tsai tai or broccoli raab, primarily a stem crop, harvested just as the flower buds form. It's a white-flowered variety of *Brassica oleracea*, the species that includes Western broccoli, cabbage, and so on. This means it is as easy to grow as those plants—that is, easier than bok choy or heading Chinese cabbages. Though its place of origin isn't certain, gai lan may have evolved in the Mediterranean region.

Growing Instructions Start seeds indoors in January or February, or in midsummer, and plant the seedlings out six weeks later. Or sow seeds in place in February or March and again in late summer. Plants should stand 4 to 6 inches apart. In areas with the coolest summers, try later spring plantings as well. Grow in full sun, in fertile, well-drained soil.

The Harvest You can use whole plants when the first stem has flower buds about to open, or you can cut the center stem to a lower leaf and let secondary stems develop for a second or third cutting. To make gai lan with oyster sauce, blanch whole stems with leaves and flower buds for one minute in boiling water, then toss them into a skillet in which you have cooked a bit of minced garlic in oil for about a minute. Stir-fry until mostly tender, then add some bottled oyster sauce, maybe a bit of rice wine. Stir and cook a bit longer. Gai lan can also be used in stir-fries that include meat or tofu, or steamed like broccoli. It tastes similar to broccoli but is more flavorful, and it is not bitter.

Varieties and Related Species There are several hybrid varieties, including 'Green Lance' and 'Ryokuho', which offer better heat resistance than open-pollinated ones. This means that one of our random spring or summer hot spells is less likely to make the plants flower before they are big enough to support good-sized edible stems.

The Italian vegetable *spigariello liscia* also has white flowers, so it is probably closely related to gai lan. It is grown for its tender leaves and its small broccoli-like heads.

Note that neither of these plants are broccolini, which is a patented hybrid between Western broccoli and gai lan and looks like miniature gai lohn (Chinese kale). While broccolini is good, you won't find seed for it, since only one agribusiness owns the rights to grow it. (But gai lan is just as good, in my opinion.)

Pests Gai lan is subject to the same pests as other cole crops. It has not had any significant problems in my garden.

Sources
Chinese broccoli seed: BCS, BG, BI, NGN, PGS, RH
Hybrid varieties: EE, JSS, KIT
Green Lance variety: JSS, KIT
Ryokuho variety: KIT
Spigariello liscia seed: GS, IST, JSS, NGN, SI

Broccoli Raab

Brassica rapa
Mustard Family ❖ *Brassicaceae* (*Cruciferae*)

Here's another crop with "broccoli" in its name, but it is really a kind of turnip, grown for its leaves and for the young flower stems, cut just before the buds open. The somewhat strong flavor is tamed, deliciously, in Italian cuisine, by serving the vegetable cooked.

Broccoli raab can be planted in late winter through late summer, but it will produce longer if it's maturing in a season that provides cool weather. Give it rich, organic soil and plenty of water.

Start the harvest when the plants are 10 to 15 inches tall and with still unopened flower buds, cutting near the ground level or at the lowest point that the stem is still tender. If weather is cool, you may be able to cut once or even twice more. Leaves, stems, and buds of broccoli raab are often boiled briefly and then sautéed with garlic, similar to the Chinese way of cooking gai lan, except the oil is olive oil, and instead of oyster sauce, what is added at the end is salt, pepper, and a bit of lemon juice.

The names raab and rapini are often used interchangeably, though some would say that rapini is a variety that must be planted in late summer or early fall to form its flower stems after winter cold.

The Asian vegetable choy sum or flowering pak choy is closely related to raab and rapini and is also

Mustard Family

Many of our most common vegetables are members of the mustard or cabbage family, *Brassicaceae*. Although the family members differ somewhat in leaf shape and general form, you can see that they are related if you study their flowers, which are cruciform, or shaped like a cross, with six stamens: four long and two short.

The mustard family includes the cole crops—broccoli, Chinese broccoli, brussels sprouts, cabbage, cauliflower, collards, kale, kohlrabi, and flowering kale—all of which belong to the same species. The family also includes arugula, cress, horseradish, mustard, radish, and turnip. All mustard-family plants thrive in cool weather. Although they tolerate slightly alkaline soil, they grow best when the soil pH is 6 to 6.8. They need ample water and plenty of nitrogen, calcium, and potassium.

Mustard-family crops are the ones most likely to be attacked by pests, in local gardens, but there are effective controls for most of the pests and the harvest is well worth the effort. Common pests of mustard-family plants include aphids, cabbage loopers, cabbage root maggots, cutworms, earwigs, imported cabbageworms, slugs, snails, and powdery mildew. In some areas clubroot, a fungus disease, poses a problem. While you certainly won't have all of these pests, read the entries on cabbage root maggots and imported cabbage worms in Chapter 9 before you plant your cole crop seedlings.

The big four cole crops—broccoli, brussels sprouts, cabbage, and cauliflower—grow well throughout our region and during most of the year. In fact, one or more of these crops can be harvested every month of the year. Their smooth, water-repellent leaves help them resist decay in our cool, damp weather. They are large plants, requiring 1 to 4 square feet per plant, depending on the variety.

Since cole crops often perform badly in hot weather, breeders have created small, early-season varieties. In hot-summer areas they are often planted so that they will mature before the summer heat hits. We can also benefit from these quick varieties, planting them in spring, early fall, or—in microclimates with the greatest ocean influence—right through the summer. The larger, late-season varieties don't succeed in much of the United States, but they are ideal for late-summer plantings to grow into our mild winters. They are the preferred varieties in England and Mediterranean Europe, which have a climate similar to ours.

The big four cole crops are usually grown from transplants about six weeks old. When seed packets or catalogs give the "days to harvest" for these crops, note that the figures do not include the approximately six weeks to grow the transplants. When you plant cole crop seedlings, set them a bit deeper than they were growing in the pot. Removing seed leaves or a lower leaf is OK.

It is important to avoid stunting cole crops. A stunted plant produces an undersized crop—a wee central head of broccoli or a few tiny brussels sprouts. Stunting follows a period of stopped growth due to cold, heat, lack of water, low soil fertility, or delayed transplanting. Cabbage is the least sensitive to these stresses and broccoli a little more so. Brussels sprouts and the prima donna cauliflower are probably best left until you have succeeded with one of the easier cole crops, although you can't rule out beginner's luck.

Crucifer flowers

grown for its succulent flower stems. Look for both green and purple-stemmed varieties. (The purple-stemmed ones may also be called hon tsai tai.) Sow seed in midsummer to early fall and harvest stems when the yellow flowers at the tops have just begun to open.

Sources

Broccoli raab seed: Widely available
Asian choy sum seed: EE, GS,IST, JG, JSS, KIT, NGN, WCS

Brussels Sprouts

Brassica oleracea
Gemmifera Group
Mustard Family ❖ *Brassicaceae* (*Cruciferae*)

These miniature cabbages grow up the stem of the plant, giving the impression of a plant creature from Mars. This crop thrives everywhere in our region. If you grew up eating (and hating) brussels sprouts that were picked too mature or boiled too long, give them another chance. Steam fresh sprouts until they are just fork-tender, then serve them with butter or a small dollop of a dipping sauce made from mayonnaise and soy sauce. Or, even better, slice them lengthwise, with just a bit of the base on each slice to hold it together, and then steam until just tender. Now you can use them in a stir-fry or cool them, then serve them in a green salad that is dressed with balsamic vinaigrette (3 parts extra virgin olive oil, 1 part balsamic vinegar, salt, pepper, garlic powder).

In addition to being a welcome winter crop, this big four cole crop is fun to harvest. The sprouts make a satisfying snap when you dislodge them from the sturdy stem with your thumb. It takes willpower not to harvest them all at once.

Growing Instructions See the opposite page for general growing requirements for mustard-family crops. Brussels sprouts are among the crops that do best when planted to mature into fall and winter. Use the formula in the Counting Backward for Brussels Sprouts sidebar below to choose the sowing and transplanting dates for the variety you choose to grow. Even if you see brussels sprout seedlings in a nursery in early to mid-spring, resist buying them. Seedlings set out in March or April tend to produce small, strong-flavored sprouts that burst open quickly, and the plants often suffer aphid infestations.

Counting Backward for Brussels Sprouts

Plant brussels sprouts so that the crop begins to produce around the first expected frost. In San Francisco, that's December 1. By then, the combination of cold weather and short days effectively slows growth, even if there is no frost. To calculate a transplanting date for a long-season variety that takes 150 days to mature, count back 150 days, or five months, from the first frost date. Five months before December 1 is July 1. Count back another six weeks—to May 15—for the last date to start seeds. Similar calculations for a short-season variety that takes 90 days to mature result in a last transplanting date of September 1 and a last seeding date of July 15.

Short-season varieties, ones requiring 100 days or fewer to maturity (from transplant date), are sometimes called dwarf varieties, since they don't grow as high as long-season varieties. Where winters are very cold, short-season types are the only ones possible, but throughout our region we can also grow long-season types, ones that require 100 to as many as 220 days from plant-out to first harvest. They grow through the rainy season with little attention and then reward us with their tasty buds in late winter. The plants are not damaged by light frosts. In fact, I have read that frost is necessary for flavorful brussels sprouts, but I can attest that this is not true.

You can start seeds either in containers indoors or in a seeding bed in the garden. Transplant short-season varieties to stand 12 to 15 inches apart and long-season ones 15 to 24 inches apart. If your location is windy or the plants begin to grow sideways, drive a 4-foot bamboo or redwood stake into the ground near each plant and tie the plant to it.

The Harvest Brussels sprouts can be harvested for two to four months, because they mature a few at a time from the bottom of the stem up. To get enough sprouts for a meal, pick a few from several plants. As each sprout matures, the leaf beneath it turns yellow and eventually drops. When you pick the sprouts, pull off that leaf and any other yellowing leaves.

Sometimes it is hard to tell when sprouts are ready for picking. They should be like mature tiny cabbages—firm and even a bit shiny on top. The first ones to mature are usually smaller than the sprouts that will develop higher on the stem. A common error is to wait for the lowest sprouts to get bigger. You will know you waited too long if they begin to open. Discard any that open and pick the sprouts on the next three inches of stem. They will be ready to eat.

You may find that none of the sprouts get very big if the plant has stunted. Once you realize that this has happened, don't wait too long to harvest the small tasty sprouts. Keep checking their growth and pick any sprouts that haven't enlarged for a week or two. Try a different strategy when you grow brussels sprouts next year—perhaps choosing another variety, changing the planting date, adding more organic matter to the soil, or fertilizing or watering more often in late summer.

Varieties Most varieties should do well throughout the region. I have grown several short-season varieties with good success, as well as several long-season ones. I have grown only one red-sprouted cultivar, 'Rubine', which in my garden produced small sprouts set far apart. There are several red-sprouted types now, all worth trying, as they are certainly spectacular in the garden and at the table.

Pests A hazard of leaving sprouts on the stem too long is that aphids may get into them. The longer you allow the aphids to build up on the plant, the harder they are to eliminate. The best course of action is to spray them off with a strong jet of water and to harvest in a timely manner. The problem should lessen as cool fall days kill many of the aphids. The crop is also susceptible to all of the common mustard-family pests (see page 198).

Sources

Brussels sprouts seed:
Short-season varieties: Widely available
Long-season varieties: BG, GS, JSS, TERR, T&M, WCS
Red varieties: BG, NGN, PGS, TERR, T&M, WCS

Cabbage

Brassica oleracea
Capitata Group
Mustard Family ❖ *Brassicaceae* (*Cruciferae*)

Cabbage heads are not much to look at in the produce market, but a maturing cabbage nested in a wide ring of unfurling leaves is one of the prettiest sights in a vegetable garden. If plain flat-leaved green cabbage is pretty, a plant with purple or savoyed (crinkled) leaves is spectacular. Sure you can buy cabbage cheap, but you don't have the pleasure of watching it grow! And freshly harvested cabbage is so sweet and crisp that I often cut a wedge and eat it right there in the garden. Fortunately, cabbage is in its element in cool, foggy weather and can be grown nearly the year around in much of the region.

Cabbage

Growing Instructions Cabbage is the easiest of the big four cole crops. (See Mustard Family on page 198 for general growing requirements.) Still, although you can set out cabbage transplants during most months, doing so from November through January is risky. The plants won't be killed by frost, but they will grow very slowly during frigid weather and may become permanently stunted. They may also suffer snail and slug damage if they grow too slowly to replace damaged leaves.

Some cabbage varieties make a quick crop, whereas others mature more slowly. Short-season varieties are rated at 50 to 75 days from transplant size, midseason varieties at 75 to 90 days, and long-season varieties at 90 to 150 days or more. The long-season types are worthwhile planting out in late summer for harvests from December through March.

I often start short-season or midseason cabbage seeds in the middle of November and set out a few of the plants in January. If the weather is mild and sunny, these plants will produce my first spring cabbage crop. I reserve some seedlings to plant in February or March, just in case the first ones don't make it. (I make sure the reserve seedlings are in 4-inch pots and that they get enough fertilizer and water so they won't stunt.) Although you can seed cabbage most of the year, you probably won't need enough to warrant starting plants every month. In addition to the November sowing, I often start cabbage in April or May for transplanting in June or July, and more in July for transplanting in August or September. If you garden where summers are hot, see Appendix III, Inland Planting Calendars.

A cabbage plant produces a wide ring of open leaves before it forms a head. It ranges from two to four times the diameter of the mature head. Cabbage is usually planted far enough apart that the leaf tips of mature plants will touch, 12 to 30 inches apart, depending on the variety. However, a recent trend is to plant some early varieties as close as 8 inches apart, so that they will produce "mini-heads." Each head is smaller, more convenient for a small family. (I once grew a 15-pound head of a late cabbage variety—and believe me, that's a lot of cabbage!)

The head will split open if it grows too fast or the watering is uneven. Although splitting doesn't affect the flavor, it ruins the leaves for recipes like stuffed cabbage. As the spring days warm, keep the soil moist but don't overwater. If a head is mature and you aren't ready to harvest it, grasp the plant and give it a one-quarter turn. This will break some roots and slow the growth of the plant, making a split in the head less likely.

The Harvest When a cabbage head feels firm, it is ready to harvest, even if it hasn't reached the advertised size. It will usually hold unharvested for a while, up to several weeks for later varieties. If the top of the head looks tight and shiny, however, don't wait much longer. To harvest, you can pull the plant and cut the head off with a knife, or cut the head without pulling the plant. Plants left in the ground after harvest may grow a second crop of tender leaves. In spring, you may even get several

Stuffed Cabbage Leaves

Variations of this dish are made throughout Eastern Europe. Serves four.

1 large head cabbage
1 pound ground beef, lamb, or turkey
1 small onion, chopped
1 egg
1 cup cooked rice
½ teaspoon paprika
2 tablespoons chopped parsley
Two 14.5-ounce cans tomato sauce (or 2 to 3 cups Quick Homemade Tomato Sauce, see page 365)
¼ cup water
1 or 2 lemons, very thinly sliced (optional)

Carefully remove the leaves from the head of cabbage, trying to keep them intact. Start by cutting across the base of the outermost leaf, then gently pry it off, lifting the bottom first, then working the top loose. Repeat until you have 12 unbroken leaves. (Use the remaining cabbage and any badly torn leaves for another dish.) Cut a shallow V at the base of the good leaves, removing the thick stem end. Steam or parboil the leaves briefly, until flexible, but not fork tender.

Preheat the oven to 350°F.

In a medium bowl, thoroughly mix the ground meat, onion, egg, rice, paprika, and parsley. Divide the meat mixture into 12 equal portions. To make the rolls, place a portion of the meat in the middle of a cabbage leaf. Fold the ends of the leaf over the stuffing, then fold in the sides, overlapping in the center. Fasten the roll with a wooden toothpick, or just place each roll with the folded edges down. Repeat to make 12 stuffed leaves.

Place the rolls in a casserole, forming a single layer, and pour one can of tomato sauce and the water over them. Arrange a lemon slice on each roll. Bake for 40 minutes or until the cabbage is fork tender. Heat the remaining tomato sauce and offer it for pouring over the served rolls.

small, loose heads. Or snap off all but one of the new buds and see if the remaining bud will form a larger head.

Varieties I suspect that any cabbage will thrive in our region, but I will give you a few starting suggestions. Some of the early varieties suggested for producing "mini-heads" are 'Gonzales F_1' (55 to 66 days, a spicy sweet flavor), 'Super Red 80 F_1' (73 days, red cabbage), and 'Parel F_1' (50 days, holds for 3 weeks). 'Early Jersey Wakefield' is a very old variety that produces pointed 2- to 4-pound heads, 60 to 75 days from plant-out.

For midseason cabbage, consider heirloom 'Winningstadt' with its pointed heads to 9 inches high or a red variety such as 'Red Drumhead' (75 to 90 days) or 'Ruby Perfection F_1' (75 to 85 days). I have often grown the midseason 'Savoy King F_1' (70 to 125 days) into the fall and enjoyed its "savoyed," crinkly leaves and large (to 5 pounds), sweet heads. (It is also reputed to handle summer heat well.)

The king of winter cabbages is 'January King', an old northern European variety with ruffled, lavender-tinged outer leaves. It is pure art in the garden, and a tender, mild cabbage. From fall planting, it will head up in 3 to 5 months, or even longer, and will reward you with late winter beauty and 3- to 5-pound heads. Late cabbage varieties also include 'Danish Ballhead' (120 to 125 days, 5- to 6-pound heads) and 'Tundra F_1' (180 to 220 days), a savoyed selection.

A nice opportunity for those who want to explore cabbage varieties—and have a staggered harvest—are packets that offer several kinds mixed together.

Pests See the Mustard Family sidebar on page 198 before you plant cabbage. A cabbage plant should be examined regularly for pests. It is especially important to do this when the plant is young and also just as the head is beginning to form. The leaves and developing head may be attacked by aphids, cabbage loopers, cutworms, earwigs, imported cabbageworms, slugs, and snails. Generally, these pests do less damage as a cabbage head gets larger and firmer, although cutworms can burrow a short distance into a mature head. Damage by aphids, cabbage loopers, cutworms, and imported cabbageworms decreases in fall and may stop between October and March. Savoy and red cabbage varieties are more resistant to imported cabbageworms and cabbage loopers than are plain green cabbage varieties. Although you should keep leaf-chewing pests to a minimum, be aware that damage can look worse than it really is. A plant may look horribly chewed even though the head is still almost entirely intact. Cabbage is also susceptible to cabbage root maggots and to the fungus disease clubroot.

Sources

Cabbage seed:
Early varieties:
- Gonzales F_1: JSS, TERR, PGS
- Super Red 80 F_1: JSS, WCS
- Parel F_1: TERR

Midseason varieties:
- Winningstadt: BG, SSE
- Red Drumhead: BG
- Ruby Perfection F_1: JSS, NGN, PGS, TT, VBS
- Savoy King F_1: PGS, T&M

Late season varieties:
- January King: BG, TERR, WCS
- Danish Ballhead: PGS, TERR, WCS
- Tundra F_1: T&M, TERR

Mixed Cabbage Varieties: BG, NGN, PGS, PS, T&M

Cabbage, Chinese (or Napa Cabbage)

Brassica rapa
Pekinensis Group
Mustard Family ❖ *Brassicaceae* (*Cruciferae*)

The upright heads of Chinese or Napa cabbage are mild, sweet, and never tough—they're delicious in salads, soups, and stir-fries. This vegetable is a little harder to grow than its close relative bok choy, since it is more likely to go to seed prematurely, or bolt, during warm or long days. Like bok choy, it is very susceptible to attack by snails and slugs. And, because it stands a bit longer than bok choy and has more crevices in which pests can hide, there is more opportunity for damage. If you've never tried to grow Chinese cabbage, you may want to try bok choy first.

Growing Instructions Most Chinese cabbage varieties do best when they are planted after the longest day of the year, June 21, and allowed to mature as the days shorten. A long warm spell in late summer may cost you a crop, but planting too late may result in cold-stunted plants. July or August is usually a good time to plant, but experiment to find just the right planting time for late summer and early fall harvests. You can also try early spring plantings if you choose varieties selected for their ability to do well early in the season.

Chinese cabbage is usually seeded in place, since it transplants badly. Sow seeds ½ inch deep and 2 to 3 inches apart in very fertile, well-amended soil. Thin the smaller seedlings until you have a plant every foot or so. Water well to fuel rapid growth. Quick varieties mature in 45 days, late ones in as long as 90 days. Some late varieties may overwinter.

The Harvest It is best to wait and harvest whole plants after the head has filled out, though you can eat thinnings. The mature heads are solid, but not as firm as a European cabbage.

Varieties Most of the available varieties are hybrids, since hybrid vigor helps this crop grow quickly. Some varieties have been bred to withstand spring planting without bolting, and some of these can be planted in mid- to late summer as well.

Pests Snails and slugs love Chinese cabbage, so growing this vegetable will be difficult unless the pests are under control. The crop may fall prey to other mustard-family pests (see page 183), especially cabbage root maggots, which cause the plant to collapse from the center and wilt.

Sources

Chinese cabbage seed:
Summer to fall sown varieties: Widely available
Spring to summer sown varieties: EE, JSS, KIT
Spring or fall sown varieties: EE, KIT

Cabbage, Flowering (see Kale)

Cactus, Prickly Pear (or Indian Fig)

Opuntia ficus-indica or *Nopalea cochenillifera*
Cactus Family ❖ *Cactaceae*

Here is a crop that thrives in poor soil with little water. Great, you are probably thinking, but how can anybody eat it with all those prickles? I admit to an occasional ouch, but this low-maintenance crop is worth it. A common vegetable in Mexican cuisine, young prickly pear pads are cooked and used hot in egg, cheese, and vegetable dishes. The cooked pads are also served cold in salads. The canned nopalitos sold in the Mexican food section of the grocery store pale next to fresh ones

Nopalitos in Tomato Sauce

Nopalitos are strips of nopales, the prickly pear cactus pads. The fresh cactus has a slightly gelatinous quality. I don't mind it at all, and it is largely masked by the tomato sauce in the recipe, but if you find this unpleasant, boil the cactus strips for 10 to 15 minutes, and rinse them several times in fresh water before adding them to the onion in the skillet. Serve this dish with Black Bean Tostadas (page 163). Serves three or four as a vegetable side.

1 or 2 pads young prickly pear cactus
2 tablespoons oil (olive oil is good)
1 small onion, chopped
One 8-ounce can tomato sauce (or 1 cup Quick Homemade Tomato Sauce, page 365)
½ or more pickled or fresh jalapeño pepper, finely chopped

Cut the spines from the cactus pads, using a sharp knife, or, if you are good at such things, you can probably pinch out the spine-bearing bumps faster with your fingernails. Wash the pads. Cut them into ½- by 2-inch strips. Parboil them if desired.

Heat the oil in a skillet and sauté the onion until tender but not browned. Add the nopalitos and cook over medium heat, stirring occasionally, until they turn from bright to dull green. It will take about 5 minutes. Turn heat to low. Add the tomato sauce and jalapeño and cook a few more minutes, until the cactus is tender.

picked from your own plant. In addition to the pads, prickly pear fruit (tunas) are eaten raw or cooked.

Although edible cactus is not a crop to interplant with standard vegetables, it may be just the thing for a corner of your garden. This large, striking perennial makes a lot of food for little work. It grows well throughout the region, isn't fussy about soil as long as the drainage is reasonably good, requires very little water, and is almost pest-free.

Growing Instructions Although prickly pear can be grown from seed, starting it from a pad is much faster. However, locating either seeds or pads may be difficult. Prickly pear cactus is rarely sold with other cacti, since it is not a popular ornamental. And it isn't grown often enough as a vegetable to be marketed by nurseries with the other vegetables. Still, persistence should pay off. If a local nursery doesn't stock rooted pads, ask if it can order them. If not, try to find a gardener who will give you pads, or ask a farmer who brings fresh nopalitos to a farmers market. Friends in Southern California or the Central Valley may have or know of a plant from which you can get a start. The California Rare Fruit Growers (see Appendix VII) may also have pads. If you get unrooted pads, start with two or three, since pads sometimes decay before they root.

Pads sold for eating are usually too young to plant and are apt to wilt and die instead of growing. You stand a good chance of success with mature pads, no matter when you get them. Pads cut in summer will probably root before winter, and pads cut in winter (a good time to prune and shape prickly pear cactus) should root in spring.

To root a pad, some gardeners advocate burying two-thirds of the pad in soil, either in a temporary bed in the garden or in a pot. Others advise just laying the pad on the soil surface, making sure the whole surface is in contact with soil. Both methods work. Even though well-amended soil isn't necessary later, adding organic matter to the temporary bed will help the developing roots grow better. Keep the soil moist, but don't overwater. Roots should form in a couple of months, but it won't hurt to allow extra time if the unrooted pad still looks healthy.

When a pad is well rooted, plant it in its permanent site. Since the cactus will eventually reach 6 to 8 feet high, choose the north side of an area suitable for growing sun-loving vegetables and flowers. Give it a minimum of 5 by 5 feet—the smallest you

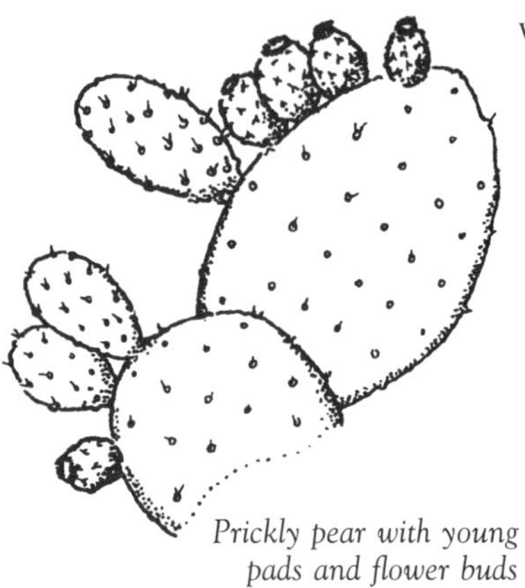
Prickly pear with young pads and flower buds

will be able to keep the plant, even with careful pruning. Locate it where you will have maximum access for harvesting and pruning.

Once the plant is established, it will need very little moisture. I never water the soil under my prickly pear, since I am already watering nearby soil. In a very dry site, you can give it a couple of waterings in summer, but don't overdo it or the plant may rot.

Prickly pear plants enlarge slowly for the first few years. Every year one to several pads will grow from each of last year's pads until finally you have a sizeable plant. From then on, you must control the plant or it could develop into a huge, impenetrable thicket up to 18 feet high. Although that may be acceptable in a large garden, it isn't usually welcome in a small urban yard—and besides, you want to keep the plant short enough to harvest without a ladder.

Control the growth of prickly pear by pruning. You can eat your prunings if you cut the pads when they are at the right stage. Be selective when you harvest: remove wayward growth, crowded pads, or pads growing into the center of the plant. Eventually you may find that harvesting won't get rid of all the excess growth, and you will have to do additional pruning. When this happens, just lop off the unwanted pads at any time before they begin to bud again in spring, but be careful to leave "mother pads" low on the plant so that they will make new pads and fruit where you can reach them.

The Harvest The year's first young pads may be ready to harvest as early as April, when they are at least 6 inches long. Some people won't eat them if they are more than 8 inches long, but I have found them tasty and tender as long as they are still a brighter green than the mature pads. The peak of the harvest is usually May and June, although a few new pads may develop later in summer. Use leather gloves or wrap a rag around the pad, then either snap the pad off at the base or cut it with a sharp knife.

You will notice that some buds stay small and cylindrical instead of flattening out. These flower buds open in summer, revealing cheery yellow flowers. The base enlarges and in late summer and fall forms fruit, which usually ripens to a bright red but may be paler. The interior is juicy and has many seeds. The surface is usually studded with tiny prickles, so beware when picking or eating.

I suspect that sweet fruit is a result of climate and genetics. I got my starter pads from an abandoned plant growing in San Francisco, and my plant has always made rather bland fruit. Try to get your starter pads from a plant that you know has sweet fruit, then cross your fingers and hope that the fruit will be equally sweet where you live. Wear leather gloves to pick ripe fruit. Roll it on firm, dry ground to remove the prickles. Wash it, cut it in half, and spoon out the pulp. In Mexico the fruit is eaten raw, cooked in desserts and preserves, and used to make a fermented drink.

Varieties and Related Species Edible plants of two different genera, *Nopalea* and *Opuntia*, are known as prickly pear. They aren't easy to tell apart, the main difference between them being that *Nopalea* has showier flowers. The most commonly grown species is *N. cochenillifera*, which in its native habitat attracts the cochineal insect. This is a kind of mealy bug that produces a red dye used in cosmetics.

The most commonly grown *Opuntia* is *O. ficus-indica*, which has sprawling as well as upright varieties. 'Burbank's Spineless Cactus,' a variety developed by Luther Burbank, sounds like a good choice but hasn't proven consistently spineless.

Pests I am not aware of any serious local pests of prickly pear cactus. The older pads, which lose most of their spines, provide a smooth, flat surface on which snails like to rest in the daytime. Although they may scrape at the pads, they don't do much damage. The main problem is that they attack nearby plants. To keep your cactus from becoming a snail haven, prune the center so that you can reach in to handpick snails.

Sources

Prickly pear cactus starts: See Growing Instructions.

Cardoon (or Cardoni)

Cynara cardunculus

Sunflower Family ❖ *Asteraceae* (*Compositae*)

Cardoon resembles its close relative, the artichoke. However, the part of cardoon that is eaten is the tender leaf midrib rather than the flower bud. Cardoon has been a favorite vegetable in the Mediterranean region at least as long as the artichoke and maybe longer. It is a favorite among Italians, who call it cardoni.

Growing Instructions Cardoon has requirements very similar to those of artichoke. Regular watering produces tender, mild-flavored leafstalks. Cardoon does well in foggy weather, although it doesn't need cool days to produce a crop.

Although cardoon is a perennial, gardeners usually grow it as an annual to avoid having to provide space for the mature plant, which can reach 6 to 8 feet high and wide. Plants grown as perennials need the same careful site selection and preparation as artichoke, whereas those removed after one season can be mixed with other crops. As an annual, cardoon will grow in any organic, moderately fertile garden soil.

You can grow cardoon from a rootstock if you can find someone with a mature clump. The best time to divide the clump is early spring. Just dig it up and cut sections with roots and young shoots on them.

Cardoon can also be grown from seed. The plants should be up in February if you sow seeds in late fall. You can also sow seeds from the middle of February to April for a summer harvest, or in early July for a fall and winter harvest. Plant the seeds ½ to 1 inch deep and 2 inches apart in groups of five or six. Space the groups 2 to 3 feet apart if the plants are to be grown as annuals, or 5 to 6 feet apart if they are to be grown as perennials. When the seedlings are 2 to 3 inches high, thin to the best one in each group. Be wary of overplanting, since each plant will make a large harvest.

The Harvest A plant should bear in four months or sooner. You can begin to harvest the outer leaves when they are 1 to 2 feet long. For a larger proportion of tender stalks, blanch the plant when it reaches 3 feet high. To blanch cardoon, secure the leaves with string and fasten heavy brown paper or burlap around the plant. Pile soil around the base of the plant, then uncover it in about a month and cut the entire blanched plant at the base.

If you have space to allow the plant to mature, harvest only the young outer leaves and stop cutting when the plant gets over 3 feet high. You will get a tower of striking gray-green leaves, topped in summer or fall by flowering stalks bearing small artichokelike flowers. Cardoon will die back in late fall, then sprout again in early spring. (Clean up the dead leaves and cut out dead stalks during the winter.)

Since the leaves are bitter, remove all traces of leaf from the stalks. Cardoon is always cooked. The stalks may take from twenty to fifty minutes to become tender, depending on their size and whether the plant was blanched. After the stalks have been steamed or boiled, cut sections can be served hot in a butter sauce, breaded and deep fried, or marinated in an Italian dressing and served cold in antipasto or salads. If you have never tasted cardoon, buy some from a produce store before you decide to grow it.

Varieties Although several cardoon varieties are available in Europe, the cardoon sold in seed catalogs in this country doesn't have a variety name.

Pests If you have trouble with the artichoke plume moth, that is a good reason not to let a cardoon plant mature near your artichoke planting. The plume moth caterpillar enjoys cardoon plants just as much as it does artichokes.

Earlier this century cardoon itself became a pest in an area at the edge of the region covered by this book. It had escaped to cover thousands of acres near Benicia on the Carquinez Strait. Although it has been controlled to some extent, there are still some infested areas. It looks so remarkably like artichoke that one local gardener collected the seeds, planted them, and grew the crop for a year before realizing his error.

Sources

Cardoon seed: Widely available

Carrot

Daucus carota

Carrot Family ❖ *Apiaceae (Umbelliferae)*

Carrots are a productive crop throughout the region. By sowing seeds from February through July (or even later in protected areas), you should be able to have carrots to pull almost every day of the year. Carrots grow best in sandy or fine loamy soil, often forming forked or otherwise misshapen roots in rocky or clay soil. If you don't have the best soil for carrots, here are a couple of strategies to try. Grow short carrot

Carrot seedling (2× life size)

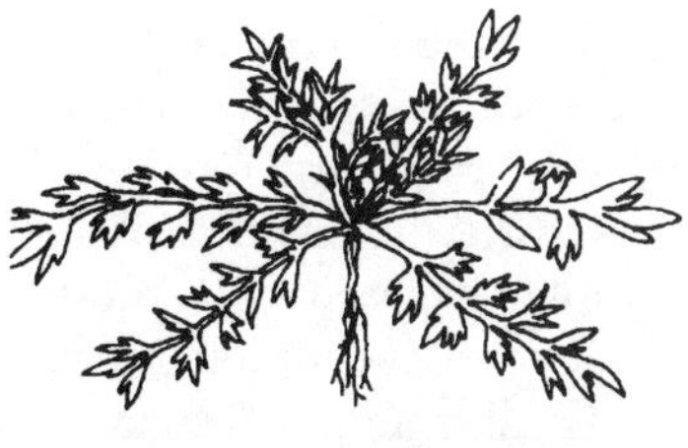

Swine cress seedling (2× life size)

varieties, which need to push away only a little soil. Or improve your soil in just a small area and grow carrots there. Sieve out all rocks more than ¼ inch in diameter to a depth of 6 inches. Then spread a 6-inch layer of fine-textured compost or other organic amendment (but not fresh manure) and dig it in, mixing it with the sieved soil. You should be able to grow medium-sized carrots nicely in this bed.

Growing Instructions Carrots have traditionally been grown from seeds sown in place. Although the plants may survive ordinary transplanting methods, the roots will not develop properly afterward. Some gardeners take this as a challenge, creating transplanting trays with sliding, removable bottoms or other ingenious methods to avoid disturbing the roots, but sowing in place is definitely the path of least resistance.

Sow carrot seeds from February through June for spring and summer harvests, and, depending on your microclimate, in July or as late as October for fall and winter harvests. Near the coast, a crop sown later than August is a gamble. Planted too late, carrots don't get very big and will just go to seed in spring.

Carrot seeds can be sown in single-file rows, wide rows, or small blocks. The sowing depth—from ¼ to ¾ inch—depends on your soil type and the weather. For example, plant the seeds closer to the surface in clay soil during cold weather and deeper in sandy soil during warm weather. Carrots are usually sown thicker than needed and then thinned. Beginning gardeners are usually surprised to find out that carrots are tricky to get started. A tongue-in-cheek maxim is that if you sow carrots thickly they will all come up, but if you sow them thinly you'll be lucky to get any at all.

Carrot seeds take 10 to 17 days to germinate, which can seem like a very long time. You can hurry germination a bit by soaking the seeds in water several hours or overnight before you plant them. Presprouting the seeds (see page 49) may improve your chances of success.

Another useful technique is to cover the carrot seedbed with something that will hold moisture and prevent the soil from crusting. You may want to cover the seeds with sieved compost instead of soil, especially during warm weather. (Don't use bone-dry compost, which will be hard to moisten when you sprinkle the seedbed.) Another option is to lay a floating row cover or toilet paper on top of the soil or the sieved compost. You can water right through either material. Remove the covering once the seedlings are up.

It's easy to forget to keep the carrot bed watered after all your other plants have long since come up. To help you remember where your carrot bed is while you wait for something to appear, sow a few radish seeds mixed with the carrot seeds. The radishes will come up quickly, marking the place to water the carrots. The radish seedlings will also loosen the soil surface for the more delicate carrot plants. And, conveniently, when the fast-growing radishes are ready to harvest, the carrots will be ready for thinning.

The carrot seedlings are so tiny that they are easy to miss in the first few weeks, especially if they become covered by quick-growing weed seedlings. Try the weed presprouting technique described on page 145 to avoid this problem. A few weed seedlings, notably swine cress (see page 162) and cotula (see page 151), look very much like carrot seedlings. I once saw a garden in which a mat of swine cress completely covered what was to have been the carrot patch. But they are possible to tell apart: Carrot leaves always stand upright, whereas cotula and swine cress leaves lie flatter to the ground.

Once the carrot plants are about 2 inches high, they usually need to be thinned. You can wait until there are fingerlings and eat the largest ones as you thin, or you can ruthlessly pull the smallest plants so that the remaining ones stand 1½ to 2 inches apart. With the first method you probably get more carrots to eat, but with the second you get bigger carrots faster.

All this worrying over getting carrots up and thinned will cease as soon as you have a little experience. Once you get the knack, carrot are an immensely satisfying crop, maturing quickly into plump, delicious roots that can be washed off and munched on the spot.

The Harvest Carrots are mature two to three months after the seeds are sown. They can be eaten young as baby carrots, but they usually get sweeter as they get larger, attaining maximum sweetness when they are close to their full size. To check for maturity, brush aside the soil around the stem and see how wide the shoulders are. Pull up one of the larger roots and taste it. Seed catalogs and seed packets will show you the mature shape of the variety you are growing, but in most varieties, the bottom end of a mature carrot should be filled out rather than narrowly tapered.

Carrots that have overwintered should be pulled by February, because they will soon put all of their energy into producing tough seed stalks. On second thought, let one or two go to seed. The flowers attract helpful hover flies, and everyone seems to enjoy the rare sight of carrot flowers. They look very much like the flowers of wild carrot, or Queen-Anne's-lace, which are sometimes added to florist bouquets.

Varieties Most carrot varieties will do well here, but your soil may limit your choices. If your soil is rocky or a very heavy clay, start with an almost round variety, such as 'Thumbelina' or 'Oxheart' or any other very short type. If you have reasonably loose soil, try 'Nantes' or 'Chantenay' (or related varieties), all of which make good medium-sized roots. Very long carrots, such as the commercial 'Imperator', need deep, loose, well-amended soil and are not for a garden with poor soil or one in which you have just begun to improve the soil.

Cultivated carrots used to be white, pale yellow, purple, red, and even black, but ever since Dutch breeders created some orange ones in the 1500s, orange has been the standard. In recent years, carrots of colors other than orange have become more and more commonly offered. My bouts with rust flies have limited my exploration of these rainbow roots, but they are worth a try if you have a reasonably loose soil. (Most of them are relatively long varieties.) Some are F_1 hybrids, others are open-pollinated heirlooms. Some that seem most interesting are 'Cosmic Purple', a 7-inch root that is purple on the surface, orange inside, yellow-cored, and holds its color when cooked better than most; 'Solar Yellow', 7 inches, pale yellow clear through; 'Yellowstone', 9 to 10 inches, good sweet flavor; and 'White Satin F_1', 8 inches, all white. In general, the paler the color, the milder the flavor. You can also find packages of mixed colored roots, including one, 'Rainbow F_1', which produces white, yellow, and orange roots in one variety (7 to 8 inches).

Two varieties, 'Flyaway F_1' and 'Resistafly F_1' were bred to resist carrot rust fly. Of the two, I have gotten better protection from the 'Resistafly'. My February-planted carrots were completely pest-free when I harvested them in a timely manner, though if I left them in the ground until August, the fly did damage them.

Pests The parsleyworm—the larva of the black swallowtail butterfly—will occasionally munch on a carrot plant, but rarely in large enough numbers to cause significant damage. I see one or two of these smooth-skinned, bright green, black, and yellow caterpillars a year. I move them over to a wild fennel plant, which they also enjoy.

The most serious local pest of carrots is the carrot rust fly. This spoiler lays eggs that hatch into maggots, which eat their way into the carrots. The only way to exclude the flies is to cover the plants with a floating row cover or a cage made of window screening. The flies are less active during cool weather. So carrots left in during summer are particularly at risk. If they get chewed, I just cut away the damaged parts and use the rest, but it is best not to leave infested carrots in the ground because the pupae will fall out and lie in wait for next year's carrots. Predatory nematodes, released after soil warms in spring, will help control carrot rust fly.

Sources

Carrot seed:

Medium and long varieties: Widely available

Round and short varieties: BI, BUR, BCS. GS, JSS, NGN, SI, SOC, SSE, TERR

Other colored varieties:

- White Satin F_1: CG, JSS, PS, TERR, WCS
- Rainbow F_1: BUR, JSS, NGN, PGS, T&M, TT
- Cosmic Purple: BCS, GS, JSS, KIT, PGS
- Yellowstone: ABL, CG, JSS, NGN, SOC, T&M, VBS
- Solar Yellow: GS, KIT
- Flyaway F_1: T&M
- Resistafly F_1: NGN, T&M

Cauliflower

Brassica oleracea
Botrytis Group
Mustard Family ❖ *Brassicaceae (Cruciferae)*

When you first glimpse a pristine white head of cauliflower forming deep in the wide nest of leaves, you will know that this crop is worth the wait. Although cauliflower requires attention to timing and growing conditions, it is a reliable crop once you catch on to its needs.

Growing Instructions Cauliflower needs growing conditions similar to those of other big four cole crops (see Mustard Family on page 198) but is a little more sensitive to imperfect care. It is likely to form a stunted plant, with a small head, if it is held in a pot too long before it is transplanted, or is lacking in nutrients or water as it grows. In fact, cauliflower is so

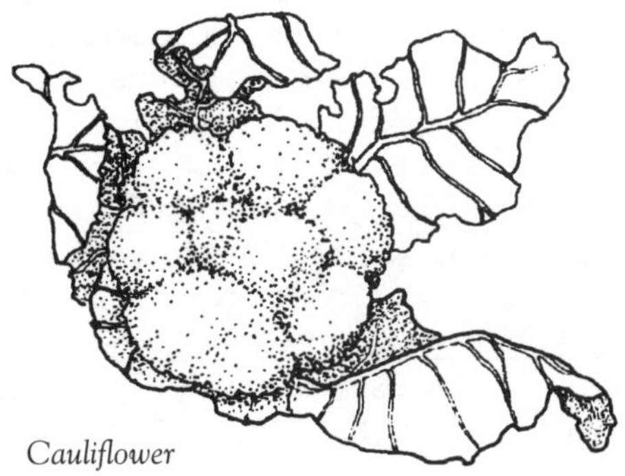

Cauliflower

prone to stunting, that there is a special name for it—buttoning. A prime reason for this tendency to button is that the root system of cauliflower is shallow and not so vigorous. Because of this, the plant also doesn't do well in clay soil that has not been adequately amended with organic matter.

The short-season types of cauliflower, which are rated at 45 to 70 days from transplanting, can be seeded between January and April for harvest between April and July or in July and August for September and October harvest. If you live in a hot-summer microclimate, avoid having cauliflower heading up in your garden in the summer months. Try seeding the long-season types (90 to 200 days or more) anytime from June through August for harvest between fall and late winter. Allow 18 to 24 inches between plants. If you are growing a long-season variety, add a high-nitrogen fertilizer near plants as growth picks up in late winter, and be sure to keep soil moist if late rains fail.

Some cauliflower varieties need to be blanched or the sun will discolor the head, usually turning it pinkish. To blanch cauliflower, pull the leaves over the nearly formed head and tie them together. Break the leaves if necessary. Some types are self blanching—that is, their leaves curl over naturally and shade the developing head. If you forget to blanch a variety that needs it, don't worry; a discolored head usually tastes just as good, although it may be received better at the table if it is blended in a cream soup or a soufflé.

The Harvest A long-season variety can take six months to form a head, and it may take another month or two when it is overwintering. That can seem like a long time. I once watched a neighboring community gardener disgustedly pull her huge, seemingly unproductive summer-planted cauliflower plants in January. I interceded as diplomatically as I could, and we were both happy to see the one remaining plant form a fine large head in late March.

The other harvesting error I've noticed is leaving cauliflower heads on too long. As they do with brussels sprouts, gardeners hope that cauliflower heads will reach the size of the largest ones in the grocery stores. You may get heads that big, but smaller ones are more likely. Harvest a head whenever it stops enlarging. Otherwise, it will begin to open up, and the white florets will send up ungainly flower stalks. Although edible, the stalks are tougher and less flavorful than the head. Don't make a large planting of cauliflowers that will mature at the same time unless you plan to freeze cauliflower, as they don't hold very long in the garden.

Varieties 'Snow Crown' is an excellent and easy early cauliflower cultivar, ready in 50 to 60 days from transplanting, and holding in the garden for 10 days at maturity. I've harvested it in June from a March sowing, in July from an April sowing, and in September from a July sowing. Overwintering cauliflowers are also available, allowing harvests from December and as late as the following May, depending on the variety you choose.

There are also cauliflower varieties, both old and new, in colors other than white. 'Purple Cape' (200 days), 'Rosalind' (60 to 75 days), and 'Graffiti F_1' (80 to 90 days) are all purple. 'Purple Cape' and 'Rosalind' turn green when cooked, but 'Graffiti F_1' stays bright purple. Several F_1 hybrids are yellow-green, and they vary from the early 'Green Harmony F_1' (55 days and heat tolerant) to the late 'Emeraude F_1' (125 days, best planted for maturing in fall). 'Cheddar F_1' (90 days) is orange. It has produced very nicely in my garden from an August plant-out.

Some would classify Romanesco-type broccolis and 'Rosalind' purple broccoli as cauliflowers. They seem more broccoli-like to me, especially Romanescos, since you can harvest outer spears while the center ones continue to mature, but look for them in both places in seed catalogs. I have put 'Rosalind' here and Romanesco types among the broccolis.

Pests Cauliflower has the same pests as other members of the mustard family (see page 198). Snails and slugs can make a cauliflower head less appetizing by munching away the surface.

Sources

Cauliflower seed:

Snow Crown F_1: CG, JSS, NGN, PGS, T&M, TERR, TT, VBS, WCS

Overwintering varieties: T&M, TERR, WCS

Other colored varieties:

- Purple Cape: BG, SSE, TERR, WCS
- Graffiti F_1: GS, JSS, NGN, PGS, T&M, TERR, TT, WCS
- Green Harmony: PGS
- Emeraude F_1: T&M
- Cheddar F_1: GS, JSS, NGN, PGS, PS, T&M, TERR, TT, WCS
- Rosalind: WCS

Celeriac (or Celery Root or Turnip-Rooted Celery)

Apium graveolens var. *rapaceum*
Carrot Family ❖ *Apiaceae* (*Umbelliferae*)

This variety of celery is grown for its globe-shaped taproot instead of its stalks. The root is sweet, has a mild celery flavor, and makes an intriguing salad. It is not grown much in the United States, although it is a popular vegetable in Eastern Europe. Well suited to our entire region, it has similar needs to celery but isn't as fussy.

Growing Instructions Plant seeds from April through June to mature into fall. You can also try planting as early as February and as late as August, since celeriac is fairly adaptable. Seed in place or transplant with care to avoid damaging the root.

Plant the seeds ⅛ inch deep. Final spacing between the plants should be 8 to 12 inches. Read on for other requirements. Although celeriac is less particular than celery about soil fertility, it will probably grow larger roots in rich soil.

The Harvest Encourage bigger roots by pulling soil from the tops of the roots several times as they are enlarging and removing yellowed lower leaves. You can begin to dig up roots when they are about 2 inches in diameter, but it is more common to harvest them when they are 4 or 5 inches across. Celeriac has entered our cuisine mainly from Northern Europe. Common uses there are shredded raw in a salad called a rémoulade, cooked and served with a sauce, or mashed with potatoes. However, this delicious root vegetable began its journey to our table at the eastern end of the Mediterranean, and a search will reveal it in recipes from that region, such as spiced lamb (or vegetarian) stew over couscous. Celeriac leaves are strong flavored and the stems tend to be pithy, but they will flavor a soup stock nicely.

If the plants are left in the garden until spring, they will bloom. They become ungainly, growing 4 to 5 feet high, and their roots are too tough to eat, though the flowers attract beneficial insects. If a plant forms seed, it will probably reseed itself, adding to the serendipity of next year's harvest.

Varieties 'Alabaster' and 'Prague' are two old, popular open-pollinated varieties, but there are many others, including some new European hybrids.

Pests I've found celeriac to be nearly pest-free. Although celery late blight doesn't affect celeriac as much as celery, it shouldn't be tolerated, since it can live on celeriac waiting for the next celery crop to appear. Pull any plants showing evidence of a virus.

Sources

Celeriac seed: Widely available

Celery

Apium graveolens var. *dulce*

Carrot Family ❖ *Apiaceae* (*Umbelliferae*)

I've had many successes with celery, but I've also had failures. During some winters homegrown celery stalks with peanut butter were a lunch staple. During other years I had to pull most of my crop in midsummer because it was going to seed prematurely or the stalks were bitter and tough. Although celery is a very demanding vegetable, it can produce a crop anywhere in the region.

Wild ancestors of celery were first cultivated in the Middle East, where they were found growing wild in the marshy lowlands. Modern celery is a much larger, milder, and more succulent version of those plants, but it has retained the need for constantly moist, very rich soil.

Celery likes cool, but not cold, weather. Chilly night temperatures in spring and fall may cause young plants to go to seed before they make full-sized stalks. The safest period to plant out celery seedlings in areas nearest the coast is April through August, when normal night temperatures are at least 49°F. You may have to wait until May in inland locations, where the nights are slightly colder. Other planting times may work, but you will run a greater risk of the crop going to seed early because of exposure to cold.

Growing Instructions Celery can be seeded directly, but it is most often grown from transplanted seedlings. Start seeds indoors in January through March for transplanting into the garden in March through June. Sow the seeds ⅛ inch deep. Move the seedlings to larger containers when they are about four weeks old, then grow them for four to eight more weeks before setting them out. Be sure to give the seedlings ample water and fertilizer when you repot them. (See chart on page 52.)

As an alternative, you can sow seeds in a seedbed in the garden in spring, then transplant the seedlings to a permanent location when they are 2 to 3 inches high. Celery seeds will germinate in as little as a week at 60° to 70°F, but they can take up to three weeks in cooler weather. You may want to use the same techniques that are suggested for germinating carrot seeds (see page 206).

Set transplants 8 to 12 inches apart in organic, fertile soil (celery would like pure compost if it could get it). Celery may be the crop on which you use the most fertilizer. Fertilize at transplanting time, and give a booster of liquid fertilizer every two to three weeks during active growth. You will improve your chances for a large crop of crisp celery by keeping the soil constantly moist. Add a thick mulch to conserve moisture, especially if your soil is sandy. The stalks become pithy when the plants dry out.

The Harvest You can begin to pick the outer stalks of a young plant when it is 6 to 8 inches

Year-Round Vegetable Curry

Whatever the season, there are likely to be vegetables you can use to make this curry. Substitute whatever is available, making sure there are different colors among the ingredients. Rather than a prepared curry powder, this recipe contains a curry blend. Serves four as a side.

4 cups vegetables, cut in ½-inch to 1-inch pieces (dice them if necessary)
2 teaspoons ground cumin seed
2 teaspoons black mustard seed
2 teaspoons turmeric
1 teaspoon ground coriander seed
1 teaspoon cayenne pepper (optional)
2 tablespoons butter or cooking oil
1 cup plain yogurt (nonfat is OK)
1 tablespoon unbleached wheat flour or chick-pea flour

Steam the vegetables until they are just tender. If their cooking times are very different, you can steam the vegetables separately. Combine the five spices in a small bowl. Heat the butter in a skillet, and add the spices all at once. Stir well for a minute or so, being careful not to burn them. Add the vegetables to the skillet and stir, heating them through. Add the yogurt and mix it in. Stir in the flour. Bring to a simmer and cook until the sauce has thickened.

Note: Just use what is available in your garden or try one of the following combinations:

- 1 cup each carrots, potatoes, broccoli, and peas (shelled, or cut-up snap pea pods)
- 1 cup potatoes, 1 cup carrots, and 2 cups green beans
- 1 cup carrots, 1 cup leeks, 1 cup Jerusalem artichokes, and 1 cup (or more, because they cook down) turnip greens
- 1 cup each broccoli, cabbage side shoots, green beans, and zucchini

high. Continue to harvest outer stalks until the plant begins to go to seed. Or you can harvest the whole plant at any time. Celery leaves contain more vitamins than the stalks. Use them, either fresh or as dried flakes, to flavor soups or to add in small amounts to salads.

Traditionally, celery was blanched to produce pale, tender stems, but this is rarely done today because modern cooks know that blanching drains vitamins. However, you may want to try blanching to rescue a crop that has become tough and strong flavored. To blanch celery, tie heavy brown paper around the plant, leaving a few inches of leaf at the top. Blanching takes about two weeks.

Varieties The most commonly grown varieties today were developed to stay tender and mild without blanching. These include 'Golden Self-Blanching' as well as the 'Utah' types and their derivatives. (For celery varieties developed to be used as seasoning, see Chinese Celery on page 296.)

Pests Pick over celery for slugs and snails, which will eat holes in the stalks. Celery is susceptible to a number of other pests, including aphids, cabbage loopers, cutworms, leafhoppers, leafminers, parsleyworms, and spider mites. Luckily, I haven't had any serious problems with any of them.

Several diseases are also possible, although I have seen only one—celery late blight. A fungus disease occurring in fall and winter, it begins as spots on the leaves but can lead to the death of plants. (See also page 133.) Pink rot is another fungus disease affecting celery. It begins with a soft, watery rot low on the outer stems, then moves up. A white to pinkish cottony mold with small black dots develops next, turning the affected parts of the plant a light pink. The disease is more common when the plants are overwatered, which can easily happen in poorly amended clay soil. Prevent pink rot by working in plenty of organic matter and watering carefully. Remove infected plants as soon as you see symptoms of pink rot.

Celery is also susceptible to several viruses spread by aphids. Since there is no cure, remove diseased plants and control aphids in the future.

Sources
Celery seed: Widely available

Celtuce (or Stem Lettuce)

Lactuca sativa var. *angustata*
Sunflower Family ❖ *Asteraceae* (*Compositae*)

This variety of lettuce produces leaves for salads when it is young and a tender stem when it is mature. After the stem has been peeled to remove the bitter outer layer, it becomes a mild crisp vegetable that can be eaten raw or stir fried.

Growing Instructions Celtuce is an easy, fast-growing crop. Sow celtuce seeds as you would lettuce seeds (see page 230). Planted at the same time as lettuce, it will bear usable leaves faster. Try sowing it in February or March and again in late summer. If you are going to let the plants mature, thin to 8 inches apart.

The Harvest Eat the leaves when the plant is young, since they toughen later. Plants grown for stems will be ready to harvest in about three months.

Pests Celtuce seedlings may be nibbled by any of the pests that attack lettuce seedlings: birds, cutworms, earwigs, slugs, or snails. However, celtuce plants seem less susceptible to attack than lettuce.

Sources
Celtuce seed: EE, KIT, NGN

Chayote Squash (or Vegetable Pear)

Sechium edule
Gourd Family ❖ *Cucurbitaceae*

Most types of squash are warm-season crops, producing fruit in summer, but there is one cool-season squash—chayote (pronounced shy-OH-tay), which bears fruit in November and December. It is firmer and sweeter than zucchini but may be used similarly. The young leaves and stems as well as the tuberous roots are also edible.

Chayote is a native of tropical America; its name derives from the Aztec word *chayotli*. The plant is now grown in most of the tropical and subtropical world, and it has picked up new names along the way. It is part of the cuisine of old New Orleans, where it is called mirliton. In Australia it is called choko, in Southeast Asia choco, and in India chow-chow. In the Philippines the name is pronounced sigh-OH-tay.

Once you learn to recognize chayote, you will notice its attractive 5-inch-wide squash-type leaves peeking over many backyard fences throughout the region, even in quite foggy microclimates. Since

Chapatis

Serve this simple fried Indian bread with Year-Round Vegetable Curry (page 210).

½ cup whole wheat flour
½ cup unbleached white flour
1 tablespoon butter, melted
About 6 tablespoons warm water

Measure the flours into a medium bowl. Mix in the butter, using your fingers. When it is well blended, add water, a little at a time, mixing it in with your other hand. When you can form a ball of dough that cleans the bowl of flour, stop adding water. Knead the dough for a couple of minutes. If it is sticky, add a bit more flour.

Divide the dough into four balls. Put a bit of flour on a large cutting board and roll each ball of dough out into a thin even round, about 6 inches in diameter.

Heat just a little butter in a skillet. Fry the chapati about 30 seconds on each side, then repeat the procedure so you cook it twice on each side. If necessary, add a little more butter as you cook the chapati. The chapati may puff up as it cooks. If so, press it down with a spatula to flatten out the bulges and keep it in contact with the skillet.

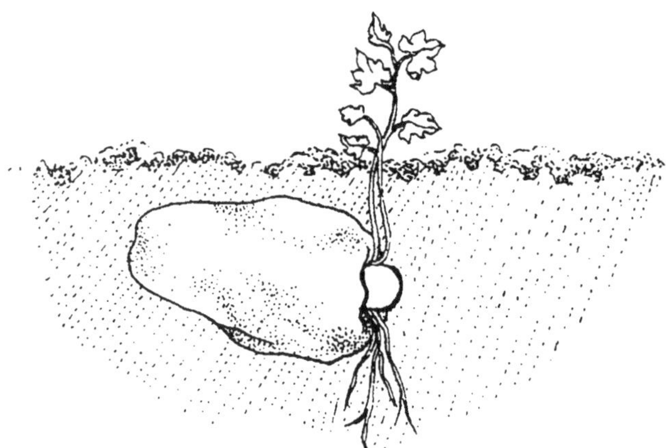

Plant a whole chayote squash to grow a new plant.

chayote is a plant of the tropical highlands, it can grow where the nights are cool—and, in fact, cool nights help production. Chayote is able to live from year to year wherever the soil remains unfrozen all winter.

Although the plant can become huge, it can work in a small garden because it is attractive and a climber. Chayote can climb straight up a stairway, blanket a fence or garage roof, or cover a trellis to conceal a compost bin. It may be the only crop that succeeds in some shady pockets because it grows up to the light.

Growing Instructions This tropical plant grows from seeds that never become dormant, but just grow out of the mature fruit a few months after it falls to the ground. To start plants, get two or three chayote fruits from another gardener in December or January or buy some at a produce market. You are most likely to find them at a store that carries Central American or Filipino specialties. Choose fruit that is fairly large and free of blemishes. Keep the fruit in a warm room for a few weeks and watch for a seedling to emerge from the large end. The seedling sort of backs out of the squash, with the roots leading the way. The ends of the seed leaves remain inside, and the shoots grow sideways between the leaves and the fruit. As this occurs, the chayote shrivels up a bit. (If the seedling doesn't emerge by the end of March, the fruit is not viable.)

Sprouting chayotes can be planted in a pot or outdoors in the ground in March. I first learned to plant the fruit tipped, so that the emerging roots were beneath the soil surface and the shoot and most of the fruit were above the ground. However, Filipino gardeners bury the whole squash just below the soil surface. In a comparison planting, the Filipino way worked better. When you are growing seedlings in a pot indoors, don't let the plants become spindly. If a shoot grows more than a foot long before you can move the plant into your garden, cut it back to 6 inches or to three or four leaves.

In choosing a site, give some thought to how you will control the size of the plant and reach the fruit to harvest it. Given 30 feet to climb, the vine will make a run for it. Planted too near a tree, it will grow into the branches. It will grow horizontally if there is no way to grow upward, so it can be trained on a fence or a wide trellis, but if you let it cover a fence, it may bear a good part of its crop on the other side. Think about a defensible space. You want to be able to prevent the plant from climbing where you don't want it by judicious pruning, and you want it to bear fruit you can reach.

Prepare your planting site well, adding plenty of organic matter and slow-release fertilizer, since chayote is a perennial. Although there are male and female flowers on the same plant, production improves when there are two plants for cross-pollination. If no one near you is growing chayote, set out two plants. One San Franciscan of Central American origin refers to a neighbor's plant as his chayote's *novia*, or bride. Space your chayote plants at least 3 feet apart.

Water during the summer months and into fall. Typically, the plant grows rapidly, 10 to 15 feet the first season, but with few stems and quite possibly without any fruit. In subsequent years the plant grows larger, produces more stems, and bears increasingly larger crops that eventually total as many as 350 fruits per plant! Each winter the plant dies back. You will need to remove dead stems at least every couple of years to avoid a messy buildup. Robust growth begins again by about March.

You can help chayote climb open areas by hanging a nylon trellis (such as those sold for trellising

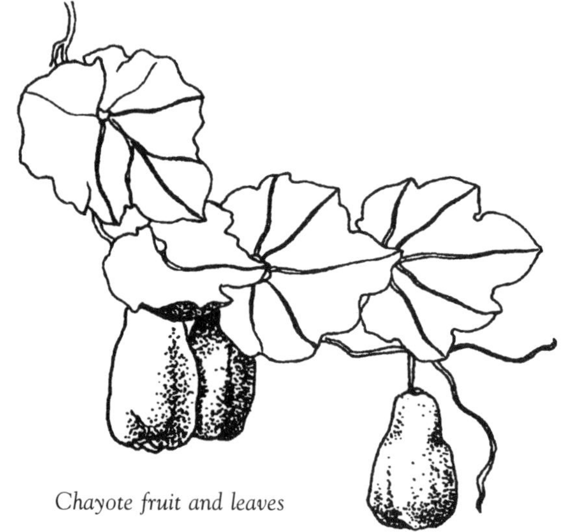

Chayote fruit and leaves

Chanclette

This Guatemalan dessert is made with chayote squash. My friend Maria-Marta Herrara taught me how to make it. She says it is not considered an elegant dish—that is, you wouldn't go buy chayote for it. You'd make it when your vine was so loaded that the chayotes were "falling on your head." The word chanclette translates to "old shoe." Serves four.

- 2 medium chayotes (best if they are not too mature)
- 4 egg yolks
- 2 tablespoons brown sugar
- ½ teaspoon cinnamon
- 2 to 4 tablespoons almonds, slivered or coarsely chopped in a blender
- About 20 raisins
- 2 Mexican sugar cookies, crumbled (or ½ cup bread crumbs sprinkled with ½ teaspoon vanilla)

Cut the chayotes in half lengthwise, cutting in the direction of the crease in the large end. Steam them until they are barely tender. Remove from heat and cool a bit. Using a teaspoon, scoop out the centers, leaving a shell about ⅜ to ½ inch thick.

Preheat the oven to 350°F.

Place the removed pulp and seed in a medium bowl and mash them with a fork or cut into small bits with a knife. Beat the egg yolks and add them to the mashed chayote along with the brown sugar, cinnamon, almonds, and raisins. Stir to combine. Add the cookie crumbs and mix well. Spoon the filling into the squash shells, mounding it to get it all in. Bake on a baking sheet until set, about 30 minutes.

beans) and pushing the branches through weekly to manage stragglers. Redirect or cut off branches that are trying to grow where you don't want them. Pruning done after spring and early summer will harm production, although you may choose to do it anyway to remove wayward stems and to curb runaway growth.

The Harvest In Central America chayote is so plentiful that the spring harvest consists only of tendrils! Entire stem tips of about 1 foot, including tendrils and young leaves, are tender and tasty added to soups, sautéed lightly in butter and garlic, or stir fried. Stop harvesting tendrils, stems, and leaves by the end of May.

Small yellow-green flowers appear as early as July or as late as October. Look closely to see the male flowers, several to a stalk, and the female flowers borne singly where the leafstalk joins the stem. The first fruit may form as late as December. One of the pleasures of having your own chayote vine is being able to pick young fruit, which has a better texture and flavor than the more mature fruit usually sold in produce stores.

Another edible part of this versatile plant is the large tuberous root. Of course, you sacrifice the plant when you eat the root, and I have not done so. After cooking one, my parents concluded that it was passable but not distinguished. "It was just another starchy vegetable," they reported.

Always eat the whole chayote fruit, including the seed. The single large seed develops a nutty flavor as the squash matures. If the chayote is so mature that the skin has toughened, simply peel it. Young fruit may be eaten raw, sliced and served with a dip, or cut up in a salad. Mature fruit is best cooked.

In Mexico and Central America, the squash is served many ways. It is added to vegetable soups or cooked in a tomato sauce with onions and jalapeños. Cooked chayote is chilled and added to salads. In addition, the squash is sometimes treated as a fruit, as in Guatemalan chanclette—a sweet baked stuffed chayote (see page 213). Other cultures that have adopted chayote treat it as they would similar vegetables in their cuisine. For example, cooks from New Orleans stuff it with sausage and shrimp, Australians braise it in a pot roast, and Filipinos stir-fry it with brine shrimp.

Chayote is comparable to scallop squash in nutritional content—not as vitamin-rich as many other vegetables but a solid source of minerals and fiber. The stems and leaves provide vitamins A and C.

Chayote squash will keep for a few weeks in the refrigerator, but a mature plant produces so much fruit that you will probably have to share the bounty just to get rid of it. Or follow the example of one gardener I know in San Francisco's Mission district and sell the fruit to a grocery.

Varieties The fruit can be pale or dark green, round or pear shaped, thorny or spineless. The one sold most often in grocery stores is light green, pear shaped, and spineless. I have heard that the spiny ones taste better. If you see them in a market or are offered starts of them, compare them to the spineless ones first to see if you like them, since their spines will make them harder to prepare for dinner. (In one local community garden, spiny chayotes were a favorite not for their flavor, but because they were less likely than smooth ones to be used as baseballs by the local youths!)

Pests The plants I have grown had no pests except snails. Use a floating row cover to protect young plants. Snails don't significantly damage a mature chayote plant, but they can be a bother when they use the vine as a staging area for forays to other crops—a good reason to grow only as much chayote plant as you can reach. However, if you leave fruit on the vine too long or allow fallen fruit to lie on the ground, the seeds will begin to germinate. Snails will find them and eat the tender seed leaves, making the fruit useless for starting new plants.

Sources

Chayote starts: Local produce market or another gardener

Chicory (see Endive)

Collards (or Collard Greens)

Brassica oleracea
Acephala Group
Mustard Family ❖ *Brassicaceae* (*Cruciferae*)

Collards produce a lot of food for the space they occupy. The plants are easy to grow and produce nutritious greens most of the year, although I've found them to be more tender and sweeter in winter and spring than in summer and early fall. I have only recently come to relish the hearty flavor of this vegetable.

Growing Instructions Collards require the same growing conditions as other cole crops (see Mustard Family on page 198). The crop is usually seeded in place, although it can be transplanted if that's more convenient. You can seed collards in the garden from January until late summer. In summer sow by July if your microclimate is very near the coast; try as late as September in a more protected site. Plant seeds ½ inch deep. If the plants are to overwinter, space them 2 to 3 feet apart. For summer harvests space them a foot apart.

The Harvest You can begin to pick outer leaves when the plants have 10 or more leaves. In a few weeks the plants will be strong enough to withstand heavy picking, up to one-half to two-thirds of the leaves at a time. Let them grow back for a week or so before you pick again. As a plant gets larger, begin to pick the medium-sized leaves near the center, leaving the outer leaves to feed the plant and the inner ones to grow a bit longer.

Collards are known mainly in America as part of Southern cooking. In that cuisine, they are most commonly boiled for a long time with a ham hock. However, should you prefer to forgo the ham or the long cooking, there are many other ways to prepare them. When you start looking, you find recipes from all around the world.

Collards

I find collards to be very good when they are simply cut up and steamed until tender, which takes 10 to 15 minutes, depending on how tender they are. I also add collards to mixed greens, which I chop small, steam lightly, and serve with a light drizzle of olive oil and a few drops of lemon juice. This Greek-style dish can include several domestic or wild greens. Use a mixture of mild and stronger greens, to your taste, such as collards, magentaspreen, spinach, Swiss chard, kale, chickweed, shepherds purse, young mustard or wild dandelion leaves, escarole, or chicory.

Plants started in late summer usually flower by February or March. Spring planted ones often flower in summer. For some, the appearance of small side shoots that will bear flowers marks the time to pull the plants out. But I have learned that the young shoots are a delicious vegetable. I keep them picked before the flower buds open and either steam them as I would the leaves or use them in ways that one uses broccoli raab or gai lan, or in stir-fries, curries, or omelets. The plants may look awful, but they keep bearing these tender shoots for months.

If you let seedpods form, shoot production will slow, but if seed forms, it is easy to save.

You may need to put a mesh bag over the stems to keep birds from eating the seeds.

Varieties Almost any collard variety will do well here. Seeds given to me by another gardener, surprised me with an occasional purple-tinged plant. Most varieties grow 2 to 3 feet high, with seed stalks reaching about 5 feet high. A tall perennial type, commonly called tree collards, may grow to 10 feet or more. Usually grown from cuttings, tree collards can be planted in February and picked whenever it isn't going to seed. Prune the stems in late summer. Many enjoy tree collards, but I found the leaves unpleasantly tough.

Pests Collards share all of the mustard-family pests (see page 198).

Sources

Collard seeds: Widely available

Tree collard plants: Common Ground in Palo Alto (see Appendix VII, Resources for Gardeners)

Corn, Sweet

Zea mays

Grass Family ❖ *Poaceae* (*Graminae*)

Corn is a warm-season crop that produces consistently in all but the foggiest parts of the region. You can grow early varieties even in sunnier San Francisco neighborhoods. However, if the summer is too cool and foggy, corn may respond by forming tassels and silks at different times. The tassels contain the male flowers and the silks are the female flowers. If they aren't ready at the same time, there is no fertilization and no corn. Once fertilization takes place, cool days don't seem to affect the sweetness of the kernels.

Growing Instructions Corn expects the red-carpet treatment—sunshine, good rich soil, and ample water. Dig in plenty of compost or well-rotted manure at planting time and some high-nitrogen fertilizer. Give corn a booster of nitrogen while it is growing, especially if there is any sign of yellowing in the lower leaves. If you let corn dry to a point where the leaves are dull and curled, it will be stunted.

Direct-seed corn anytime from April 15 to the middle of July. A foot between plants is the usual recommended distance. If corn varieties with standard-sized plants are spaced closer than 8 to 10 inches apart, they will bear fewer and poorly filled out ears. Ample spacing is especially important when fog limits the amount of light. Plant the seeds 1½ to 2 inches deep. I usually plant two kernels in each spot, spacing them 1 or 2 inches apart. When the plants are 3 or 4 inches high, I pull the extras or transplant them to fill gaps left by poor germination or pest damage.

Corn female flower

Always plant corn in a block at least 4 by 4 feet. This is important because corn depends on wind for pollination. Grains of pollen from the stamens, which dangle from the tassels, must blow onto the ends of each individual silk. Every pollen cell then grows an extension that goes all the way through a silk until it reaches the ear, fertilizing one kernel. In a smaller or linear planting, much of the pollen is apt to blow uselessly over other crops. A 4- by 4-foot block will produce twenty to forty ears of wonderfully sweet corn.

Corn seeds are most often sown in place. However, germination in cold soil (less than 60°F) may slow future growth. So if you intend to plant before the middle of May, when the soil is still cold, presprout the seeds (see page 49) or grow them in containers indoors for three to four weeks. You may also decide to start corn indoors to give it a jump on pests.

You've probably heard of the Native American "three sisters" plantings, ones that combined corn, beans, and squash. In near-coastal gardens, be cautious of beans climbing corn, since the corn will need all the sunlight it can get between foggy days. Even inland, pole beans can overwhelm corn unless the seed are put in after the corn plants are at least 12 inches high. If squash or cucumbers are grown under corn, they will be the ones shaded, which will slow their growth where fog is common.

Gardeners used to remove the suckers—the nonproductive little side shoots—from corn, in the

Couve Mineira (Sautéed Collard Greens)

The following recipe, taught to me by Erica Junghans, is served on Fridays in restaurants in the Brazilian state of Minas Gerais. It's a side dish served with fejoada *(a black bean and pork stew), rice, and roasted cassava or corn flour to sprinkle on the food. When the collards are left crunchy, they are almost a new vegetable.*

1 bunch collard greens (8 or so leaves)
Vegetable oil for sautéing the garlic
2 cloves of garlic (or to taste), minced
Salt and freshly ground pepper to taste

Rinse and dry the collards; cut off the stems. Stack the leaves, then roll them up into a very tight roll. Slice it as thinly as you can with a large, very sharp knife. Undo and reroll the bunch as needed, as that makes it easier to slice thinly. The result will be very voluminous, so make sure you have a large enough container to put it all in before you cook it.

In a large skillet, on medium low, heat the oil. Add the garlic and sauté it for a few seconds. Add the sliced collards. You can dump them in all at once and toss them carefully until they reduce in volume, or add in two parts, making sure there is enough garlic to mingle with the second batch. Sprinkle with salt and pepper and serve as soon as you can. (Be careful not to add too much salt, as collards have a naturally salty taste.)

Note: Some cooks fully cook the collards, while others "just let the greens touch the bottom of the skillet" and become well-coated with garlic, oil, salt, and pepper—less than a minute— and take them off the heat so the collards are still crunchy when served. Other variations are the addition of broken-up fried bacon or a drizzle of lime juice at the end of the cooking.

belief that doing so increased yield. Recent studies have shown that these suckers either don't affect yield or may even increase it, so save yourself work by leaving them on the plants.

If you are trying to grow corn in the foggier parts of the area, you can try to protect it in a mini-greenhouse (see page 33). Using a short-stalked or dwarf variety, enclose a block of corn in a structure 5 or 6 feet high. When you see the pollen being released, shake the plants lightly to be absolutely sure that it falls on the silks.

On more than one occasion I have found my corn in a horizontal position after a storm in late spring or early fall. You can usually save the plants by propping them upright, since most of the roots are still in the ground. However, it is much easier to put in supports before the damage happens. If your garden tends to be windy, build a corn corral. Drive in 5-foot stakes at the corners of the block and every 2 feet across the north and south ends, since the wind here comes primarily from the west. Then tie rope or strips of cloth about 4 feet high around the perimeter and between the plants, connecting each pair of north and south stakes.

The Harvest Fertilized corn silks shrivel as the ear swells. When the visible part of the silks is dry and brown, the corn is ripe—or soon will be. To check for ripeness, make a small vertical slit in the husk near the top of an ear. Keep the slit small, since it provides an entry for insect pests. See if the kernels have filled out. If they are still tiny, look a little lower down, because kernels at the very top sometimes never fill out. Puncture a kernel with your thumbnail. If the liquid inside is watery, the corn isn't ready yet. If it is thoroughly opaque, you waited too long. Sweet corn is just right when the liquid is milky but still translucent. After a season or two you will be able to gauge ripeness by the appearance of the kernels without a thumbnail test. While you are harvesting, try chewing on a fresh green cornstalk—

Corn That's Sweeter Than Ever

There has been much excitement over two new kinds of sweet corn that produce ears that are sweeter and stay sweeter longer on the plant and in the refrigerator. With this type of corn, there is no need for the proverbial dash from the garden to the pot of boiling water. Much of the corn sold in markets is now one of these new hybrids.

I once harvested some ears of Kandy Korn, an Everlasting Heritage (EH) hybrid, stored them overnight in the refrigerator, traveled to San Diego with the ears in the bottom compartment of a Greyhound bus, refrigerated them overnight again, and served them to my parents for dinner the next day. The corn was still much sweeter than regular corn sold in grocery stores. These hybrids, which are also called Sugar Enhanced (SE), carry a gene that makes them sweeter, more tender, and able to hold their sweetness longer. They do not need to be isolated to prevent cross-pollination.

The other new varieties, known as Super Sweets or Xtra Sweets, carry the gene Shrunken 2, or sh2 for short, which makes them even sweeter and able to hold their sweetness a week or more. Some gardeners even complain that they find these varieties too sweet! 'How Sweet It Is', a white-kerneled Super Sweet, did fine in my garden and wasn't too sweet for me. Super Sweet seeds are sensitive to decay in cold soil, so if your seed isn't fungicide-treated, delay planting till mid-May or start seed indoors. 'Northern Xtra Sweet' is said to have good germination in cold soil. Plant Super Sweets at least 25 feet from other varieties to avoid cross-pollination, as this will reduce the sweetness of your Super Sweet corn.

Note: These are not bioengineered varieties.

it's as sweet as sugarcane. (You might also like to dry some cornstalks for fall decorations.)

Varieties Seed companies rate corn varieties at 50 to 92 days, but don't be surprised if the crop takes half again as long to mature in our cool summers. Concentrate on the earlier, short-season varieties, especially if your microclimate is borderline.

The first corn I grew in San Francisco is still a good choice. 'Early Sunglow F_1' is listed at 62 days but takes 90 days here; it is said to be vigorous in cold weather. It makes two or more 7-inch-long ears on 4- to 4½-foot-high plants. I found that in my garden in a sunnier San Francisco neighborhood, I could sow it twice: once in early May, for a late July harvest, and again in mid July, for an October harvest.

If you can grow 'Early Sunglow F_1', try others that are said to tolerate relatively cool conditions—I've given sources for a few. 'Peaches and Cream SU' is a 70-day bicolor. 'Northern Xtra Sweet F_1' (Sh2) is a white corn.

In addition to sweet corn, which is eaten immature, there are varieties that are harvested mature. Some of these are used for making cornmeal or cracked corn, others are used for popcorn, and still others are grown mainly to produce ornamental ears. These varieties take longer than sweet corn, since the seeds must be dry before the ears are picked. You run the risk of decay if the ears are still ripening on the stalks into the rainy season. If you want to try these types of corn, choose a relatively early variety and plant it in early May.

If you can grow sweet corn, you can probably also grow popcorn, and it is such fun to grow that you should try. Dry popcorn until three test kernels pop well, then store in a closed jar. There are a number of interesting varieties. In a garden in a sunnier part of San Francisco, I grew 'Early Pink' (85 days, 5- to 6-inch ears), and, emboldened by that success, planted 'Calico' (90 to 100 days, average two 6-inch ears per plant). Planted in early May, it ripened in mid-October, just before the first rains, on stalks 6 or 7 feet high, some with purple leaves. The mixed-color ears were fun to pop and made nice gifts. The dry husks made great cornhusk dolls. I think my next ones will be 'Wisconsin Black' (80 days, black to maroon-black kernels) and 'Cherokee Long Ear Small' (100 days, mixed colors, 5- to 7-inch ears).

If you enjoy the miniature ears used in Chinese cooking, you may like to grow some. They are just tiny, unpollinated ears—corn flowers, if you will—picked when the silks first emerge. This crop has potential for moderately foggy areas, since no pollination is required. You can harvest any regular corn when it is tiny, before the kernels form, or you can buy a baby corn variety that produces several ears per stalk. I tried a baby corn variety thinking that it would take up garden space for a much shorter time than regular corn, but it took about as long. By the time the silks form, corn plants are pretty close to the end of their life cycle. After I stripped off the husks and silks and made my first little pile of tiny ears, I couldn't help thinking that it wasn't much food for all the time and effort. One rare variety, 'Chires Baby', produces up to twenty miniature ears per plant. Worth consideration, but still mostly a novelty in a small garden.

Pests Various chewing pests eat corn seedlings: birds, cutworms, earwigs, slugs, and snails. If they pose a problem, either start the corn under a floating row cover or sow the seeds indoors and move the seedlings to the garden when they are three to four weeks old and have a better chance of surviving pests. If birds are a problem, discourage them by propping a piece of bird netting over short sticks placed around the perimeter of the seedbed.

Maturing plants may become infested by aphids, which can get into the ears but usually get only as far as the tips by the time you harvest. They wash off easily.

Corn earworms may enter the ends of the ears and chew the kernels, although this has happened to me only twice in fifteen years of growing corn. If these small striped caterpillars catch you by surprise, just cut off the ends of the affected ears before you cook them.

Raccoons are notoriously fond of corn. There are plenty of raccoons in our area, even in the urban neighborhoods, but they aren't necessarily a problem. I know they live around my community garden, because they once killed our ducks, but they have never damaged a corn crop there.

Common corn smut is a fungus disease that produces gray galls on the ears, stalks, and leaves. Although it is more common in hotter regions, it sometimes appears in the warmer parts of our area. While they are immature, the galls are edible and considered a delicacy.

Sources

Sweet corn seed:
- Kandy Korn F_1 (SE): BUR, CG, TERR, VBS
- How Sweet It Is F_1 (Sh2): TERR
- Peaches and Cream SU: BUR, VBS, WCS
- Early Sunglow F_1: BUR, NGN, PS, VBS
- Northern Xtra Sweet F_1 (Sh2): BUR, VBS

Popcorn seed:
- Calico: TERR, WCS
- Cherokee Long Ear Small: SESE
- Early Pink: TERR, WCS (Pink Popcorn, 85 days: http://tinyurl.com/cdbgff)
- Wisconsin Black: SESE

Baby corn seed:
- Chires: BCS, JLH, SESE, SOC

Corn Salad (or Lamb's Lettuce or Mache)

Valerianella locusta
Valerian Family ❖ *Valerianaceae*

An annual valued in colder climates as a winter salad green, corn salad is a rather small plant with spoon-shaped leaves that have a buttery texture and subtle flavor. If you want to give it a try, you may find that you enjoy this European favorite.

Growing Instructions Sow seeds in August or September for harvests throughout winter into spring, or sow in February for early spring salads. Plant the seeds in place, and thin the plants to stand 3 to 4 inches apart.

The Harvest Pick leaves individually from the low rosettes or pull whole plants. Plants will go to seed in a few months and may seed themselves in your garden.

Varieties Several European varieties are available, and they should thrive here. Look for large-leaved varieties—a desirable feature in a plant so small.

Sources

Corn salad seed: Widely available

Cucumber

Cucumis sativus
Gourd Family ❖ *Cucurbitaceae*

This warm-season crop is more sensitive to cold than summer squash, a close relative. It does well in the sunnier parts of the region, including sunnier San Francisco locations, but not in the foggiest locations.

Cucumbers need organic, nitrogen-rich, well-drained soil that is kept constantly moist but not soggy. Grown in excessively wet soil, cucumber plants may die from root diseases. They grow best when kept out of strong breezes, which are all too common in coastal gardens. In a very windy site, plant cucumbers where taller plants will protect them without shading them too much, or provide some other windbreak.

Cucumber flowers

Cucumbers and the Birds and the Bees

Most cucumber varieties are dependent on bees for pollination. Some varieties have male and female flowers on the same plant, whereas others bear female and male flowers on separate plants. When you buy a variety that has separate male and female plants, the seed packet will usually contain mainly female plants with just enough male plants to provide pollen. Even without these pollinator plants, you would probably still get some fruit, since bees bring pollen from plants up to a mile away.

'Sweet Success' is a variety with only female flowers on all plants, and these flowers don't need to be fertilized to develop fruit. Thus the fruit is mostly seedless, although you may find an occasional seed due to chance pollination.

Growing Instructions Plant cucumber seeds outdoors from early May to the middle of June. A May-planted crop will start to bear in July and continue until the fall rains kill the vines. For a jump on the season, you can use three- to four-week-old transplants started indoors as early as March (see chart on pages 52–53). Indoor seeding may also allow you to avoid heavy snail damage.

I can't speak too strongly in favor of trellising cucumber plants. Trellised plants produce more and straighter cucumbers. The cucumbers are also more likely to escape snails and slugs, which can scar the surface of the fruit so badly that it is stunted. You can make a trellis from a length of 4- to 6-foot-high hog wire fencing or similar fencing with at least 2-inch openings. Mount the fencing on stakes that are either fastened to a raised bed or driven into the ground.

Plant a row of cucumber seeds 2 inches from each side of the trellis. Sow the seeds in pairs, leaving 4 inches between pairs, and thin to the stronger of each pair when the plants are 4 to 6 inches high. Alternatively, you can grow cucumbers indoors for 3 to 4 weeks and then plant them out, taking care not to disturb the roots.

Although cucumber vines have tendrils, often they aren't very functional. Every few days as the vines grow, I gently guide the growing tips through higher openings in the wire.

If you don't trellis, at least use a straw mulch under the vines to keep the fruit off the ground. When the cucumber vines are young, guide them in the direction in which you want them to grow.

The Harvest It is important to keep cucumbers picked, since even a single overmature cucumber on a plant will slow down or stop production. That means harvesting as often as every two days at the height of the season. Overmature cucumbers turn yellow and become tough. Also watch out for partially fertilized fruit. You may see only the skinny, pale green undeveloped part near the stem and overlook the fat, yellow overmature tip.

Cucumbers are usually ready for harvest when they are 1 to 1½ inches in diameter. Cut open a seeded variety and taste it. The seeds should be visible in the cross section, and they should be just as tender as the rest of the cucumber. Peel homegrown cucumbers only if the skin is tough.

Varieties There are three kinds of elongated green cucumbers: slicers (the supermarket standards), picklers (harvested small for making into pickles), and long green ones, which include traditional Asian and Middle Eastern ones, greenhouse varieties, and hybrids that are called "burpless." The so-called "English" cucumbers in grocery stores are of this type, and probably greenhouse-grown.

In my search for delicious cucumbers, I tried the traditional 'Japanese Long' and Middle Eastern 'Amira', but they did not thrive. Then I discovered the hybrid "burpless" types, and have grown them exclusively ever since. They are long and mild-flavored, have thin skins that usually need no peeling, and are able to produce abundantly in warmer parts of San Francisco. Try 'Sweet Success' or 'Burpless Tasty Green'. (One year I planted a generic "burpless" variety from seed purchased in a local store, and the fruit quality did not approach that of the named varieties.)

Bush cucumbers promise a crop in less space, but I have found that they are less productive per plant than vining types, and also less productive per garden area if the vining types are trellised.

Grow lemon cucumbers the same way you do other cucumbers. At first the small round fruit is pale yellow. Harvested at this stage, it is very mild and tender. When the fruit turns bright yellow it is tougher and has a stronger flavor. An advantage of growing your own lemon cucumbers is being able to harvest them at their prime.

Southeast Asian Cucumber Salad

A wonderful mix of flavors sets off the refreshing taste of cucumbers. I grind the peanuts in a mortar and pestle. Whatever you do, don't grind them to a powder. Just break them into several pieces each. Serves two to four.

1 medium cucumber, peeled (if necessary*) and sliced thinly
2 tablespoons onion, cut into thin slivers
¼ teaspoon crushed red chile pepper
2 tablespoons rice vinegar
1 tablespoon water
1 teaspoon sugar
¼ teaspoon salt
¼ cup coarsely chopped coriander or mint leaves
¼ cup unsalted dry roasted peanuts, crushed

Put the cucumber slices in a medium bowl. Sprinkle the slivers of onion and the red chile pepper over them. In a small bowl, mix the vinegar, water, sugar, and salt. Stir until the sugar and salt are dissolved. Pour the dressing over the cucumber and onions. Toss. Sprinkle with the coriander leaves and the peanuts.

Cucumber Raita

You can serve this Indian dish as a salad or as an accompaniment to curries. Serves six.

2 cups grated cucumber (peeled, if necessary*)
1½ cups plain yogurt
1½ teaspoon ground cumin
½ teaspoon salt

Press the grated cucumber lightly and pour off the excess moisture, but don't try to squeeze all the moisture out. Add the yogurt, cumin, and salt and mix well. Serve immediately or chill first.

*One of the joys of homegrown cucumbers is that they are not waxed and needn't be peeled as long as the skin is not tough or bitter.

Pests In addition to getting root rot when they are overwatered, cucumbers sometimes suffer from leaf diseases, such as powdery mildew. Although the crop thrives in our coastal high humidity, the damp air encourages many diseases. 'Burpless Tasty Green' and 'Sweet Success' are among the cucumber varieties that resist powdery mildew.

Cucumbers are susceptible to several virus diseases, including beet curly top virus, cucumber mosaic virus, and zucchini yellow mosaic virus. There is no cure for these diseases, so look for resistant varieties and remove infected plants as soon as you notice them.

Sources

Cucumber seed:
Slicing varieties: Widely available
Pickling varieties: Widely available
Lemon cucumber: Widely available
Sweet Success F_1: BUR, NGN, PGS, PS, T&M, TT, VBS
Burpless Tasty Green F_1: BUR, EE, KIT, T&M, TT, VBS, WCS

Eggplant

Solanum melongena
Nightshade Family ❖ *Solanaceae*

Eggplants were domesticated from wild plants growing in India and Southeast Asia, small plants with prickles and bitter fruits. We now see a tempting range of cultivated eggplants, developed in both Europe and Asia, in many colors and shapes, but alas, all eggplants need more warmth than either tomatoes or peppers, members of the same family. Cold nights will slow the plants' growth, and when the plants finally bloom, temperatures under 60°F will keep fruit from setting. In moderately foggy microclimates, you may get a few fruits, especially when a particular summer has a spate of warm weather. In warm summer parts of our region, a respectable harvest is possible, though the plants still resent the cool nights.

In a sunny San Francisco garden, I once planted six eggplants and harvested a total of two small fruits. In a more favorable growing area, I could have picked as many as four dozen fruits from the same number of plants. In my garden, flowers dropped unfertilized all summer long, and the plants didn't set any fruit until nearly the end of September.

Growing Instructions In the middle of May, set eggplant seedlings in a sunny, protected spot out of the path of strong winds. The crop grows best in organic, fertile soil. To warm the soil, you might like to try a black plastic mulch. Cut holes for the plants 18 inches apart. A floating row cover or minigreenhouse (see page 33) will help warm the air around the plants. Add a booster of compost or manure tea (see page 81) or liquid seaweed a month after transplanting. Reduce watering after fruit sets.

The Harvest For the best flavor, pick the fruit small, when it is one-third to two-thirds full size. No matter what size the fruit is, pick it if it stops enlarging. You will know you waited too long if the seeds are brown when you cut open the fruit. Don't pull up the plants until the weather turns chilly, since fruit may still ripen during a warm fall.

Varieties Local gardeners have long been searching for the magic eggplant variety that will bear well in cool summers. Choosing an early, vigorous cultivar is of some help, but it is cool temperatures, day and night, that are the main problem. Look for varieties that promise ability to set fruit in cool temperatures. No guarantees, but worth trying in borderline microclimates, are ones that have succeeded in Pacific Northwest gardens, such as 'Millionaire F_1' (54 days, 8-inch slender, deep purple Japanese-type fruits). Another with promise is 'Fairy Tale F_1' (63 days, lavender with white stripes, Japanese-type, best eaten at about 4 inches long). Where summers are a bit warmer, start with 'Dusky F_1' (80 days, rounded, deep purple, Italian-type fruits, 8 to 9 inches long). Among unusual colors, the best bet for cooler areas may be 'Applegreen' (62 to 70 days, rounded, 5-inch, pale green fruits), said to "do well even in cool weather," though of course it depends on what they mean by "cool." (Note that, as with tomatoes, the days to harvest for eggplant are counted from the time of transplanting seedlings into the garden.)

Pests In the warmest parts of our region, flea beetles may chew tiny holes in the leaves. Spider mites may be a problem in any garden, especially if plants are underwatered. Eggplant occasionally develops verticillium wilt, and it is also susceptible to tomato or potato late blight, so rotate eggplant along with other tomato family members to reduce the chance of spreading these diseases. Watch for the serious malformations caused by viruses, and remove infected plants from the garden if you see them.

Sources
Eggplant seed:
Millionaire F_1: BUR, EE, KIT, T&M, TERR
Fairy Tale F_1: BUR, JSS, NGN, PS, TERR, TGS, VBS, WCS
Dusky F_1: NGN, PGS, TERR, WCS
Applegreen: BCS, SESE, SSE, TGS

Endive (includes Escarole, Frisée)

Chicorium endiva

Chicory (includes Radicchio, Witloof Chicory)

Chicorium intybus
Sunflower Family ❖ *Asteraceae (Compositae)*

Endive and chicory are two different species, often confused. They are even often sold as lettuce, but while they are in the same (daisy) family, they are really not lettuce. (This becomes apparent if the plants bloom. Lettuce has small yellow flowerheads; chicory and endive blossoms are light blue.) Both chicory and endive have a mildly to strongly bitter flavor, which some like as the main green in a salad, while others prefer it as a minor note or prefer these greens slightly cooked, which reduces their bitterness.

There are two main types of endive (*Chicorium endiva*). One, escarole, has broad leaves with wavy edges. The plants look like heads of loose-leaf lettuce. The other, frisée, has narrow, spiky, curled leaves. You will often find young frisée leaves in supermarket salad mixes.

Vegetable chicories (*Chicorium intybus*) are more likely than endives to form heads, which may be shaped like head lettuce or romaine. Radicchio forms a small, spherical head of red leaves with white veins. When you grow it, you can see that each head is surrounded by a ring of red-tinged green leaves that provide photosynthesis for the plant, but are usually discarded at harvest. Several other kinds of heading chicories, not as commonly grown, have more of a romaine lettuce form. One is the source of the nearly white buds of shell-like leaves sold as witloof chicory. To get these pale buds—which are also sometimes called chicons or, confusingly, Belgian endive—you must cut the plants to the ground and let them resprout in complete darkness.

Catalogna chicory is nonheading, with narrow, dandelion-like leaves that are eaten when young, especially in winter. It is sometimes sold as "Italian dandelion." One variety, 'Catalogna Puntarelle', has thick stems that are sautéed in olive oil in Italian cuisine; these are often compared to asparagus. The roots of other nonheading varieties are dried, ground, roasted, and used as a coffee substitute.

If an endive or chicory variety forms a head, like that of radicchio, this blanches the interior leaves, making them milder-flavored. Such varieties are called "self-blanching." Open forms, such as the endives, are sometimes so packed with leaves that the inner leaves remain pale, and therefore milder. Others may need to be tied up to block light from the inner leaves before harvest.

Growing Instructions Both *Chicorium* species appreciate an organic, fertile soil. Sow seeds in place or start them indoors four to five weeks before transplanting. Space the seedlings 6 to 18 inches apart, depending on the variety. Keeping the soil constantly moist will produce plants with a mild flavor and also discourage the plants from going to seed prematurely, or bolting.

Endive and chicory are more tolerant of cold than lettuce, and it is satisfying to watch them grow heartily in our usual winter temperatures. Be wary of overplanting—a little endive or chicory in a salad goes a long way. Most varieties are planted in July or August to mature in the cool days of fall and winter. You can also try a quick crop from seeds started in January or February, but plants of most varieties will bolt if they are planted much later. Some newer varieties have been developed especially for planting in early spring, and some of these can also be planted into summer. As a component of mesclun (see page 236), chicory or endive may be planted most of the year and cut while it is still young and mild flavored.

The Harvest Although endive is a biennial and chicory a perennial, both are grown as annuals, meaning we harvest the whole plants before they flower. Looseleaf endive as well as red- and green-leaved chicory varieties can be harvested unblanched by the leaf or by the plant. Heading varieties like radicchio are harvested whole.

To blanch escarole or frisée on a dry day in fall or winter, gather the leaves of mature plants and tie them together. Then cover the plants with overturned flowerpots and plug the bottom holes to exclude sunlight and rain. Check the plants occasionally: they should be blanched in two to three weeks. Whether blanched or not, endive heads placed in plastic bags will keep for months in the refrigerator if they are dry when you bag them. For both endive and chicory, storage reduces bitterness even more.

Witloof chicory is produced by a process known as forcing. This means that the top of the plant is cut off and the base allowed to resprout in darkness. Commercially, the roots may be dug and grown in boxes of moist sand or in hydroponic systems. If you are adventurous and want to try to grow these, don't overfertilize with nitrogen, since it is good root growth you want, not excess leaves. In our mild climate, it is possible to force the plants where they are growing. To try this, in November or December cut mature chicory plants 2 inches above the ground and pile 6 to 8 inches of soil on them. Keep the soil just moist, but don't overwater. (If rains are heavy, cover the area with a tarp.) In late December, dig cautiously and look for the pale shoots. Harvest them when they are 3 to 4 inches long. Cover the cut stumps with soil to let new shoots form. Use stakes to mark your place in the underground harvest as you move down a row or across a bed.

Varieties Choose an endive variety based on whether you prefer the broad-leaved escarole (also sometimes called Batavian endive) or the narrower, curled leaves of frisée.

There is more to think about in choosing a variety of chicory. If you are planning to force the plants, in order to form witloof chicory, choose a variety intended for this purpose. Among non-forcing types, you have a choice of green-leaved or red-leaved varieties. Be sure to check whether you are buying seed meant to be fall-planted (which in foggier areas really means July or August), or one that can also be planted in early spring.

Radicchio—those pricey little heads of mildly bitter red leaves—are not the easiest of crops to grow, as even the best varieties can be a little erratic in behavior. A certain proportion of the plants tend to bloom before they form good heads. Plant breeders are trying to make the crop more predictable, so new varieties appear fairly often. Check variety descriptions for bolt resistance and reliability, as well as whether they can be planted in late winter and spring or can only be planted in summer for a fall crop.

I haven't tried the Catalogna-type chicory, but I did once try to prepare chicory root coffee and found it a lot of work for the amount of beverage, although the flavor was interesting. If you are curious, try some chicory coffee from an herb store to see whether you like it before you grow your own.

Pests Endive and chicory are often described as pest-free, and in fact I have had little trouble with pests. Snails and slugs may attack young plants, but they pretty much ignore older plants, since they prefer so many other kinds of greens. Be prepared to control aphids if they appear.

Sources

Endive seed:
- Broad-leaved: ABL, BCS, BI, EE, GSI, IST, JG, JSS, NGN, SESE, SI, WCS
- Frisée varieties: Widely available

Chicory seed:
- Red-leaved heading (radicchio): Widely available
- Green-leaved heading: BCS, GS, IST, NGN, SI, WCS
- Catalogna chicory: BCS, BG, GS, IST, JLH, JSS, NGN, PGS, SESE, SI, TERR, WCS
- Witloof chicory: BCS, BG, GSI, IST, JG, JSS, SI

Fennel, Florence (or Finocchio)

Foeniculum vugare var. *azoricum*
Parsley Family ❖ *Umbeliferae*

The large white bulb of Florence fennel is thickened leaf bases that form just at ground level. Like other fennels, it is often mistakenly called "anise," and is even sold as such. The bulbs are crunchy and do have a strong anise or licorice flavor when raw. Cooked, they become a mild, sweet vegetable with a unique, non-anise flavor. This Mediterranean crop is well adapted to our region, growing well in cooler seasons and microclimates. Ordinary wild or domestic sweet fennel won't necessarily form a bulb, so be sure you start with seed for Florence fennel.

Growing Instructions Florence fennel will do best in a rich, moist, well-drained soil. Gardeners usually sow seed in place, but it can be sown inside and transplanted while still small. It has a tap root, so transplant it before that root gets malformed by the container. Seeds germinate in 6 to 17 days. For large bulbs, thin to or plant out at least 6 inches apart, up to 8 or 10, since plants too close together will start bolting to flower without having formed a bulb. It is also important to keep the soil moist, since dry soil will also stimulate bolting. Some varieties are best planted in late summer or early fall, but a few are bolt-resistant enough for late winter or early spring planting as well. If a flower stem begins to emerge, cut it off early to try to get the plant to make a bulb instead.

The Harvest Harvest Florence fennel bulbs when they are at least 3 and up to 5 inches across, by pulling the plant and cutting the root off. You can use the leaves from these plants in any way you would use those of sweet fennel (see page 301). The raw bulb is used in salads. It may also be sautéed, roasted, braised, or boiled.

Varieties While some sell a "dual use" fennel, for leaves and bulb, I'd trust more a variety sold for good bulb production. If you want to plant in spring, read descriptions to find ones recommended for spring as well as fall planting, such as 'Finale', 'Perfection', 'Zefa Fino', and 'Selma Fino'. (For fennel grown mainly for leaves or seeds, see page 300.)

Sources

Florence fennel seed: Widely available
Varieties for spring sowing: ABL, CG, GS, IST, JSS, NGN, PS, SI, SOC, TERR, WCS

Flowering Kale (see Kale)

Garden Cress (or Peppergrass or Upland Cress)

Lepidium sativum
Mustard Family ❖ *Brassicaceae* (*Cruciferae*)

Garden cress is a mustard family crop, similar in flavor and appearance to watercress. Since it doesn't require the moisture that watercress does, it can be grown in an ordinary garden bed. A fast-growing annual, garden cress makes a rosette of tasty leaves, then quickly goes to seed. It is best to make small plantings every few weeks.

Growing Instructions Garden cress is more likely to produce a good crop of leaves in cool weather. Scatter-sow the seeds in place in rich soil from February to April or from July to September. Provide part shade for the July to September crops, perhaps by planting the garden cress behind taller plants.

The Harvest Pick the outer leaves or pull entire plants.

Varieties and Related Species There are broad-leaved and curly-leaved varieties. Garden cress is sometimes called upland cress, which can lead to some confusion, since there is another plant, *Barbarea verna*, called upland or winter cress. It is a biennial that overwinters, then goes to seed in spring. One variety has pale yellow-variegated leaves that add pizzazz to a salad. The two species are grown the same way and their flavors are similar, so there isn't much practical difference.

Sources

Garden cress seed:

Barbarea verna seed: BG, JLH, JSS, KIT, NGN, PGS, SESE, T&M, TERR

Lepidium sativum seed: BCS, BI, GS, IST, JG, JSS, KIT, NGN, SESE, SI, SOC, TERR, WCS

Variegated cress: JLH, T&M

Garland Chrysanthemum (or Shungiku or Sukiyaki Greens)

Glebionis coronaria (*Chrysanthemum coronarium*)
Sunflower Family ❖ *Asteraceae* (*Compositae*)

Although the scientific name of this plant has changed—part of botanists' reclassification of the genus *Chrysanthemum*—the English common name will probably remain garland chrysanthemum. It's an annual plant that grows to 4 feet high and then bears bright or pale yellow daisies. It should be eaten long before it matures, however. The young leaves are commonly used in Asia in sukiyaki, soups, and stir-fries.

Garland chrysanthemum

Growing Instructions Garland chrysanthemum prefers cool weather and can be grown most of the year throughout this region. It grows readily from seeds sown from February to September and is ready to harvest about a month and a half later.

The Harvest Begin to pull whole plants when they are about 5 inches high, or harvest by cutting the leaves. If you cut plants to an inch or so from the ground, the stubs will resprout for another harvest. The leaves have a distinctive, pungent flavor. Mild at first, the flavor becomes stronger as the plant matures, until it is too strong for many palates.

Let some plants bloom. In addition to attracting syrphid flies and other beneficial insects, the flowers can be cut for bouquets. The petals can also be eaten in soups and other dishes. Garland chrysanthemum will seed itself, rewarding the gardener who spots it amid the weeds with early spring greens. However, try to keep seed out of wild areas and vacant lots.

Varieties You can buy this chrysanthemum species as an ornamental, but any variety sold as a vegetable is probably more succulent. When you are looking in a seed catalog, try the Asian greens section.

Sources

Garland chrysanthemum seed: EE, JSS, KIT, NGN, RH, WCS

Garlic

Allium sativum
Amaryllis Family ❖ *Amaryllidaceae*

You can use a tiny corner of your garden in winter to produce an entire year's supply of garlic. One year I grew 6 pounds of this useful seasoning in a plot measuring only 3 by 3 feet.

Growing Instructions Start with purchased garlic bulbs, preferably from a nursery rather than a grocery store. Ask if they are certified disease-free; the nursery person should be able to find out. Plant the garlic in a bed that gets as much sun as possible in winter. Dig in a few inches of aged manure or compost and some fertilizer that provides more phosphorous and potassium than nitrogen.

To plant, gently separate the cloves and gather up all but the smallest center ones. Do not peel them. Set the larger cloves in moist soil, blunt (root) end down and pointy end up, with the top about 1 inch below the surface. Space the cloves about 4 inches apart. Don't water on the same day that you plant—in fact, wait until shoots emerge before watering for the first time.

You can plant anytime between October 15 and February 15, although fall-planted garlic will be the largest, since it has the most time to mature. The bulbs are ready to be harvested in late June or July.

When the plants begin to grow rapidly in late winter and early spring, add a fertilizer that provides more nitrogen than phosphorus or potassium. Watch out for dry spells, especially in spring, and water when necessary but don't keep the bed soggy. Between May and late June, the tips of garlic leaves will turn yellow even with adequate watering. This means that the bulbs are nearly mature and should be watered less frequently. If you have a drip system, pull back the drip lines or turn off the valve watering your garlic. In softneck varieties, the stem near the ground will begin to flatten and the mature plant will fall over. Hardneck types produce a flower stem, which is stiff, so it doesn't fall over.

The Harvest When garlic is ready to dig, the leaves should be at least 60 percent brown. If you want to check maturity, dig a bulb. A mature bulb has well-developed cloves throughout and four to six dry leaves wrapped around the entire bulb.

Dig up mature plants carefully and brush off as much dirt as you can. Cure the whole plant in a warm, dry place out of direct sunlight for two to three weeks. Then clean the cured bulbs. Using the ball of your thumb, brush off dirt and the outer one or two layers of loose and broken skin. With scissors cut the roots to 1 inch. Braid the stems or cut them 2 inches from the bulb. Store garlic out of the sun in a cool, dry, airy place.

You can use fresh garlic leaves during the winter and spring. They are milder than the bulbs and higher in vitamins A and C. A good use for the smallest cloves in the bulb: plant them close together and use their leaves.

Varieties Softneck garlic is best adapted to our mild winters. It tends to have a spicier flavor than hardneck and stores for up to a year. The tops are good for braiding. Examples are: 'California Early', 'California Late', and 'Silverskin'. You can experiment with hardneck types such as 'Spanish Roja' and 'German Red', but they may perform badly or have less flavor and quality in this climate.

Hardneck garlic is sometimes called "rocambole," or that name may be reserved for hardneck varieties with flower stems that make a double twist before they bloom. Bulblets may form in the flowerheads of hardnecks, and these may be eaten or planted, though it is probably wiser to cut off the young flowering stem to direct more energy to the underground bulbs.

Note that garlic for planting is usually available only in the fall until October. By November you may have to wait until next year. Local nurseries usually sell a variety or two, but for more choices, try mail order sources.

Pests The only insect pest that has attacked my garlic is a black aphid. Examine the plant bases and leaf undersides regularly for this pest. If you see it, begin twice weekly spraying with insecticidal soap (see page 100) until it is under control. Examine nearby bunching onions, garlic chives, nasturtium, and artichoke for black aphids and control them on these plants as well.

If your garlic rots before it matures, the cause could be overwatering. If there are white fungal mats on the bulbs, suspect onion white rot or lettuce drop. Dig out the affected bulbs and seek positive identification of the disease. White rot affects other onion family crops (see page 241); lettuce drop affects lettuce and many other vegetables and flowers (see page 234).

Sources

Garlic sets (bulbs): BCS, BUR, CG, JSS, NGN, PGS, RPF, SESE, SI, SOC, SSE, T&M, TERR, VBS, WCS

Garlic, Elephant

Allium ampeloprasum
Ampeloprasum Group
Amaryllis Family ❖ *Amaryllidaceae*

This is the garlic that makes huge mild cloves. The whole bulb is about the same size as an ordinary garlic bulb, but it consists of only three to seven cloves.

Growing Instructions Plant individual cloves in October or November and grow them in the same way that you would ordinary garlic. Although an elephant garlic plant looks like a robust version of an ordinary garlic plant, it has slightly different habits. In spring it is very likely to form a flower stalk, which should be cut before it blooms so that more energy is funneled into forming bulbs. Elephant garlic also forms small bulblets at the base of a bulb, and these will make mature bulbs in two or three years.

The Harvest Collect the mature bulbs as you would ordinary garlic, but check for small bulblets. Separate them from the bulbs as you harvest. Refrigerate the bulblets for at least a month, then plant them in fall. They won't all come up (20 percent is considered good), but after one year those that do grow will make small bulbs resembling boiling onions. Leave them in the ground and during the third summer you will get the familiar bulbs with their several giant cloves.

Elephant garlic has a nice mild flavor that makes it very useful in cooking, but don't plant more than you can eat in a couple of months since it doesn't keep well.

Pests Elephant garlic is subject to aphid attack, just as ordinary garlic is. It is also susceptible to white rot—a good reason to start with certified disease-free cloves.

Sources

Elephant garlic sets (bulbs): BCS, BUR, JSS, NGN, SESE, SSE, TERR, VBS

Gourd

Cucurbita species
Gourd Family ❖ *Cucurbitaceae*

Gourds, which are members of several cucurbit species, are used more for decoration than food. They require a long, warm summer to ripen fruit until it forms the rock-hard shell that is so attractive and useful. Don't let visions of large decoratively carved containers entice you beyond the very limited possibilities of this crop in near-coastal microclimates. The coastal central California region is not gourd country. However, you may want to try a packet of the smallest gourd varieties, which are strains of C. *pepo*. With a little luck, these may mature even in foggy areas.

Growing Instructions Grow a gourd just as you would winter squash (see page 263). It forms a long vine that trails along the ground, but you can save space by trellising the plant. Check every few days and help weave the vines through the trellis if necessary.

Sources

Small gourd seed:
Goblin Eggs (small egg-shaped): BI, JSS, NGN, PGS, TERR, WCS
Small mixed gourds: BCS, BUR, CG, GS, JSS, NGN, SESE, TERR, VBS

Ground-Cherry (or Cape Gooseberry or Husk Tomato)

Physalis peruviana (*P. edulis*) and *P. pruinosa*
Nightshade Family ❖ *Solanaceae*

When you pop a ground-cherry into your mouth for the first time, your eyes will probably open wide with surprise. This relative of the tomato can be used as a dessert fruit, although it may take a little getting used to. About the size of a cherry tomato, the yellow-orange fruit is very sweet but also tart and tangy. It is borne in little papery "lanterns" similar to those of the tomatillo (see page 270). The plants are rangy, with grayish green, softly fuzzy leaves and small pale yellow flowers. As with other nightshade family crops, parts of this plant contain toxins. Don't eat leaves or unripe fruit. Ground-cherry is worth trying even very near the coast, since it will mature in a cooler climate than tomato will. It grows well in poor sandy soil.

Growing Instructions Ground-cherry is easy to start from seed. It can be started indoors, but you may as well sow it directly in the garden. Thin or transplant the seedlings to stand 2 to 3 feet apart. Ground-cherry needs about three months to begin ripening fruit, then goes on producing for several months. Planted in spring, it bears into fall. My plants have seeded themselves to sprout in midsummer and bear fruit in spring, so midsummer sowing is a second option. An unusually cold winter may kill ground-cherry.

Some varieties sprawl on the ground; others grow up to 4 feet high. Taller ones should be staked or corraled. To corral a plant, surround it with several stakes, then tie twine or cloth strips around the stakes to keep the plant within bounds.

The Harvest When ground-cherry ripens, its papery husk turns from green to brown, and the fruit inside takes on a rich golden color. Ripe fruit often falls to the ground. To harvest, start by picking up fallen fruit and peeking inside the husks to be sure that it is still good, then pick over the plant, checking others for full ripeness. I eat many of my ground-cherries right in the garden as a snack, but they can also be used in fruit salads, pies, and jams. If you are saving the fruit until you have enough for a recipe, you can store it in its husk for several weeks. Collect it when it is ripe, then spread it in a single layer in a cool, dry place. Once the husks are removed, the fruit will not keep unless it is frozen. Fruit that has been frozen and thawed tastes best cooked.

Ground-cherry

Varieties and Related Species At least two separate species are called ground-cherry. You may also find either listed as husk tomato, yellow husk tomato, husk cherry, or even strawberry tomato. *P. peruviana*, a perennial that grows 3 to 4 feet high, is sometimes sold as cape gooseberry or 'Golden Berry'. This plant is the source of poha jam, which tourists often buy in Hawaii. *P. pruinosa*, an annual that grows to about 1½ feet high, is sometimes called dwarf cape gooseberry. Unfortunately, not all seed catalogs are clear about which species they are offering.

Pests This crop seems to be completely pest-free, although it is a potential host for tomato russet mites and nightshade-family diseases. If your tomatoes have russet mites, don't let ground-cherries overwinter, since they will allow the pest to survive. Also rotate ground-cherry along with other members of the nightshade family to keep diseases from building up in the soil.

Sources
Ground cherry seed:
P. pruinosa: JSS, NGN, SSE, T&M, WCS
P. peruviana: BCS, JLH, KIT, TT

Horseradish

Armoracia rusticana
Mustard Family ❖ *Brassicaceae* (*Cruciferae*)

If you enjoy the sharp taste of horseradish, you may like to grow it yourself and make fresh sauce. However, it is usually at its best only after several weeks of frosty weather—an unlikely occurrence in this region. Also, the roots are thinner and not the best flavored here. Still, I know of several local gardeners who have grown horseradish and were satisfied with their harvests.

Growing Instructions Horseradish will grow in any well-amended, fertile soil. Add plenty of organic matter to sandy soil, since horseradish plants need constant moisture for the best growth. Don't use fresh manure because it will cause forked roots. Also be sparing with nitrogen, since too much will encourage leafy growth at the expense of roots. Horseradish needs a large amount of potassium. Although this nutrient is usually sufficient here, you may want to add some kelp meal or greensand if your soil is very sandy.

Horseradish plants are grown from root cuttings. The custom is to sell roots with the top cut flat across and the bottom cut at a slant so you can tell which end is up when planting. In February plant the roots right side up and at a 45-degree angle. The top of the roots should be 3 inches below the soil surface. You may also find potted horseradish plants at a nursery. Plant them 12 inches apart.

The Harvest Dig up the roots in November, after cold weather has had a chance to add some bite. If the flavor is still too mild, try again in a month or so. Either dig up roots as you need them or refrigerate harvested but unprocessed roots in moist sand in a plastic bag. Prepare the roots by cleaning them, peeling them, and grating them finely. Mix any unused grated root with vinegar and refrigerate it in a closed jar. As an alternative, peel the roots and run them through a blender with a little white vinegar.

Horseradish is a sturdy perennial that will grow from any root fragments left in the soil. If you harvest the whole crop and plan to grow something else in that spot, try to get every root fragment. In spring check again for missed pieces of root. You can start a new planting with freshly dug roots or roots that you stored in the refrigerator. (Be sure to cut the ends of stored roots in the customary way so that you won't accidentally plant them upside down.) If you are leaving plants in the ground from year to year, don't maintain any particular plant more than two or three years, because the root will become too tough to eat.

Pests Horseradish may attract some mustard-family pests, such as cabbage loopers and imported cabbageworms. Although horseradish sometimes gets a leaf spot disease, the roots are rarely affected.

Sources
Horseradish roots: BUR, CG, JSS, NGN, RH, TERR, VBS

Jerusalem Artichoke (see Sunchoke)

Jicama

Pachyrhizus erosus
Pea Family ❖ *Leguminosae*

These big, crisp, sweet roots (pronounced HEE-ka-ma) require a long warm summer. I once started some jicama seeds in my garden in the Mission district of San Francisco and in my nearby apartment. The plants in the garden grew less than a foot high and died before the summer was over. The one that grew in a pot in my living room made several twining stems, each bearing typical pea-family leaves with three leaflets each. I put up string for the stems to twine on and directed them around my living room window. They framed it nicely, each stem growing about 10 feet long. The plant was so dramatic that it got a lot of comments, but when it died down in fall and I dug up the root, I found that it was woody and only about 2 inches across. So jicama is not for the coast, but is worth a try in areas with the hottest summers.

Kale (or Borecole) and Flowering Kale (or Flowering Cabbage)

Brassica oleracea
Acephala Group

Siberian Kale (or Russian Kale or Hungry Gap)

B. napus var. *pabularia*
Pabularia Group
Mustard Family ❖ *Brassicaceae* (*Cruciferae*)

The plant most commonly called kale is *B. oleracea*, the same species as collards. It even looks like handsomely curled collard greens. *B. napus*, a related plant known as Siberian kale, is similar but stays mild and tender enough to be eaten raw for a longer period.

In the East, varieties of kale are often grown ornamentally, as "flowering kale." They aren't really used for their flowers, but are bred to form low rosettes of leaves, often with inner leaves of pink or white contrasting with the green outer ones. Varieties with less curly leaves are known as "flowering cabbage," though all of them are really kale. The pretty leaves are useful as garnish, but we don't grow them as often here, in part because we have so many other ornamentals that bloom in the fall, and perhaps because our milder climate allows imported cabbageworms to continue to attack cole crops into the fall. We may be willing to keep a close eye on our vegetables, but would rather grow a pest-free ornamental, given the choice. In any case, many kale varieties grown for food are also ornamental. Their frilly, crinkled, sometimes pink or pink-veined leaves are pretty enough to grow among the flowers.

If you live in a cool-summer microclimate, you can harvest kale most of the year. As with many of the cole crop vegetables (see page 198), kale will bolt, meaning it will form flower stems and then seedpods instead of tender leaves, after it has gone through sufficient chill. (I have not found these to be as tasty as those of collard plants.) Therefore you don't want to set plants out too late in fall, or they will stay small and then bolt, not giving you much to eat.

Growing Instructions Grow kale from transplants or seeds sown in place. Start seeds in midsummer for fall and winter harvests or as early as January for a spring crop. The final spacing depends on the cultivar and whether you want to harvest whole young plants or leaves from mature plants. Leave only a few inches for whole young plants, and 10 to 24 inches for mature plants. Grow Siberian kale the same way, but sow it in place, since it doesn't transplant well. The final spacing for mature plants should be 18 inches.

The Harvest Pull whole young plants or pick leaves from plants as they grow. Try kale leaves from young plants raw. Later, when the leaves have become sturdy and flavorful, cook them. If the leaf stems are tough, cut or strip them out of the leaves.

Varieties All varieties of kale grow well here. As with collards, most of the available *B. oleracea* kale varieties are the shorter ones, which grow to 18 inches high at most. Tall varieties reach 3 or 4 feet. The name of the variety often suggests the height—such as 'Dwarf Scotch' or 'Tall Curled'. Some, such as 'Redbor', have magenta-purple leaves.

Look also for the Italian variety popularly known as dino kale for the prehistoric impression it gives. Its leaves are long and narrow, heavily savoyed (blistered), and a dark blue-green. It goes by a host of other names, here and in Italy, including 'Black Palm', 'Lacinato', 'Braschetti', 'Cavolo Nero' (which means "black cabbage"), and 'Nero di Toscana' (meaning "Tuscan black"). This kale figures in classic Tuscan recipes such as *ribollita*, a vegetable and cannellini bean soup usually served over toasted bread.

Russian or Siberian kale differs from true kale in having less ruffled leaves, and many think it's more tender than other kales. While it's sometimes sold as *B. oleracea* var. *fimbriata*, most sources agree that somewhere in its history lies parentage from *B. napa*, which is the species of rutabaga (see page 256). Leaves of 'Dwarf Siberian' and 'White Russian' are green. Those of 'Red Russian' or 'Ragged Jack', a variety reputedly brought into Canada by Russian traders, have purple veins and stems.

Pests All types of kale are subject to mustard-family pests (see page 198).

Sources

Kale seed:

B. oleracea kale seed: Widely available

Redbor kale seed: CG, JSS, NGN, PGS, PS, TERR, VBS, WCS

Tuscan black kale seed: Widely available

Russian kale seed (including Red Russian kale seed): BCS, BG, BI, BUR, GS, JLH, JSS, NGN, PGS, RH, SESE, SOC, SSE, TERR, WCS

Flowering kale seed: GS, IST, JSS, PGS, TERR, VBS, WCS

Kohlrabi

Brassica oleracea
Gongylodes Group
Mustard Family ❖ *Brassicaceae* (*Cruciferae*)

Kohlrabi is yet another member of the versatile species that includes cabbage, cauliflower, collards, and kale. In this case the part eaten is the stem, which enlarges to form a mild, sweet, crisp globe commonly called a bulb. Although you can cook kohlrabi bulbs, they are at their

Kohlrabi

best peeled and eaten raw as a snack or relish. (See Mustard Family on page 198.)

Growing Instructions You can sow kohlrabi seeds in place or grow transplants. I have had the best results from a sowing in June or July, but plantings a month or so later or in early spring are also worth trying. (Bulbs that mature in very warm weather are likely to become tough and peppery.) The seedlings must be transplanted or thinned to stand 8 to 12 inches apart. Plants that are too close together simply refuse to make big round bulbs.

The Harvest Begin to harvest when the bulb is the size of a golf ball. This will take at least two months. You can let some bulbs get larger, up to about 4 inches across. Don't go for record-breaking bulbs, however, because they will be tough and tasteless. Peel bulbs before eating them.

Varieties Both green and purple varieties are available. Although the purple ones are pretty in the garden, all kohlrabi bulbs are white inside when peeled.

Pests Kohlrabi is subject to the usual mustard-family pests (see page 198).

Sources
Kohlrabi seed:
Green or white varieties: Widely available
Purple varieties: Widely available

Leek

Allium ampeloprasum
Porrum Group
Amaryllis Family ❖ *Amaryllidaceae*

Leeks deserve wider planting in local gardens. They are easy to grow (largely because they are resistant to many of the pests and diseases affecting onions), and they produce a very welcome fall and winter crop. Their flavor is sweet—much milder than that of onions. Although they can be used young as tender baby leeks in summer, they are in their glory full grown and standing firm through the cold and rain, ready to be harvested for a soup or an elegant quiche.

Potato Leek Soup

Have you ever pulled a leek while holding an umbrella? Hint: It is easier if someone else is holding the umbrella. Be sure to put some leeks in your garden so you can enjoy this simple, hearty soup on a cold, rainy winter day. To make it, you will need one huge leek or two large ones. Serves two to three.

- 2½ cups diced unpeeled potato
- 2 cups water
- 2 cups leeks, cut in ¼-inch slices (at least ⅔ should be the white part)
- 2 cups milk
- Sprinkling of freshly ground black pepper
- ½ teaspoon salt (optional)
- 1 tablespoon butter or margarine
- 1 tablespoon chopped fresh parsley
- ½ cup coarsely grated Monterey Jack or cheddar cheese
- ¼ cup chopped chives (or green onion tops or onion lily tops)

Boil the potatoes in the water until tender, about 15 minutes. Do not drain them. Mash them well in the cooking water, using a potato masher or the bottom of a clean glass. Add the leeks to the potato mixture. If there isn't enough water to cover the leeks, add a bit more, but the mixture should remain quite thick at this stage. Simmer, covered, until the leeks are tender, 10 to 15 minutes.

Add the milk. Heat through, stirring occasionally, but don't boil. Stir in pepper and salt. Melt the butter on the surface of the soup and sprinkle the parsley over all. Put the grated cheese and chives in separate bowls and pass them, so diners can sprinkle them on the soup as they desire.

Growing Instructions Give leeks organic, fertile soil and keep them well watered during the dry season. For the biggest leeks, plant seeds indoors from December through January or outdoors from January through March. Seeds planted later won't produce very large leeks before cold weather slows their growth. Although you can plant outdoors in fall, it is a gamble. The plants will probably go to seed in late winter or early spring of the next year, or if they are very small in winter they may continue growing into large leeks in spring and summer. Of course, if you plan to harvest them young, you can plant them almost anytime.

Leek flower buds emerging from bract

Sow the seeds ½ inch deep and ¼ to ½ inch apart in a seedbed for later transplanting. Otherwise, direct-seed them slightly farther apart and thin the seedlings to 3 to 6 inches apart. Another good option is to plant purchased seedlings. Nursery packs of leeks are usually a good buy, since they contain many seedlings for a low price, and leek seedlings are easy to separate and transplant.

I either sow seeds close together in a seedbed or start them indoors and transplant them to stand an inch or two apart in the seedbed when they have three or four leaves. They stay in the seedbed until they are approximately the diameter of a pencil. Whenever a large enough area of my spring or summer garden is bare, I transplant the leeks to stand 4 to 6 inches apart. Although some sources recommend clipping the leaf tops when you transplant, I never do. Since the leeks will be there all fall and often into winter, I don't interplant them with summer crops but instead give them their own out-of-the-way site.

The most tender part of the leek is the white portion of the shaft. Leeks are bred to make long shafts, which are tender and white only if they are blanched by being underground. Traditionally, gardeners achieved this by planting seedlings in a trench and gradually filling it in or by mounding soil around the growing plants. Since I don't have the extra soil to do either in my small raised-bed garden, I prefer a newer method of blanching that works just as well—burying the leek to the base of the first leaf joint when I transplant.

The Harvest Pull up baby leeks whenever you like. For mature leeks, dig the plants when they are more than 1 inch in diameter, usually not until September. Harvest as needed during the winter, but finish picking before the middle of March or the plants will go to seed. Some use only the white part in cooking, but I find that adding some of the light green lower leaves too works fine. Use the rest of the green part to flavor soup stock (see page 372).

Varieties Some varieties are listed as winter leeks, others as summer leeks. Winter leeks can overwinter in climates that are colder than ours and would kill a summer leek. In my experience, all leeks overwinter very well in our mild climate. If you are growing the crop specifically for baby leeks, you may as well grow a summer leek, since this type is often more tender. For fall and winter harvests, choose a winter leek. I have no particular variety to recommend, since I have had great success with every variety I've tried.

Sources

Leek seeds: Widely available

Lettuce

Lactuca sativa

Sunflower Family ❖ *Asteraceae* (*Compositae*)

Lettuce grows best and is most delectable when the days are cool. In ocean-moderated Bay Area microclimates, gardeners can harvest lettuce virtually all year. Lettuce doesn't stay at its prime as long in the heat of an inland summer, though providing some shade can help. It is also important to choose the best variety for the microclimate and the season. Whether you are growing looseleaf, butterhead, romaine, or crisphead, you will find some varieties are better adapted to heat or to cold than others.

Growing Instructions Lettuce needs soil that is fertile, loose, and well drained. It will grow very poorly in unamended clay soil. Give it plenty of water from the time it first sprouts until it is harvested. Chronically underwatered plants will be stunted, tough, and vulnerable to pests. Overwatering is also hazardous. Constantly wet soil encourages root rot.

Direct-seed lettuce ¼ inch deep from February to early July for crispheads such as 'Iceberg', and from February to August for the others. Outdoor sowings from September to January are chancy—success depends on the variety, your microclimate, and the weather during that particular year. I sow lettuce indoors at this time, getting it off to a good start before putting it out to brave the elements. When you are sowing lettuce in containers, barely

Leek Quiche

Quiches are pricey by the slice when bought at a deli. They are really not hard to make and are great at a brunch or as a light supper dish, so why not make it yourself? Use the classic pie crust recipe here, or any unsweetened crust recipe that you prefer. For fewer calories, steam the leeks. Serves six to eight.

Pie Crust

½ cup butter or margarine (1 stick)
1¼ cups unbleached flour
½ teaspoon salt (optional)
2 to 3 tablespoons ice water

Filling

1½ to 2 cups sliced leeks (at least ⅔ should be the white part)
3 tablespoons butter or margarine
3 eggs
1½ cups milk (can be low or nonfat)
6 ounces Swiss cheese, grated (Gruyère is nice, or try Jarlsberg)

Preheat oven to 325°F and prepare the pie crust. Have ready a 9-inch pie pan, rolling pin and a clean rolling surface. (If your kitchen doesn't have a good rolling surface, use a sheet of brown paper cut from a large grocery bag.)

Put the butter in a medium bowl and cut it up with a knife until no piece is over ½ inch in diameter. Add the flour and salt. Working quickly, rub the butter into the flour with your fingertips until the mixture looks like coarse meal. Try to keep the mixture loose; don't encourage the particles to stick to each other.

Put 3 tablespoons of water in a cup with an ice cube. Sprinkle half of the ice water over the flour mixture and immediately begin to try to form a ball of dough. Handle as little as possible. If some of the flour mixture is still not adhering to the ball, add just a bit more water until it does. (You may not need to add all of the water.) When the dough is ready, it should clean the bowl of the flour/butter mixture and it should not be sticky.

Sprinkle a little flour on your rolling surface. Center the dough and flatten the top slightly with your hand. Sprinkle the dough with a little flour. Roll the dough out into a round slightly larger than the pie pan, adding just a bit more flour if needed to prevent sticking. Put the crust in the pie pan, cut any excess dough away with a knife, and use your fingers to mold a thickened wavy edge. Set the pie crust aside.

Sauté the leeks in the butter until tender but not browned. Spread them in the bottom of the raw crust.

In a medium bowl, gently beat together the eggs and milk, then stir in the grated cheese. Pour the cheese mixture over the leeks.

Bake until a knife inserted in the center comes out clean, about 30 minutes.

Variations:

- Blend 1½ cups New Zealand or regular spinach with the milk and eggs in a blender. Stir in the cheese and pour the mixture over the leeks in the crust. Bake as directed.
- Spread ¼ pound small cooked shrimp over the leeks before you add the milk, egg, and cheese mixture.

cover the seeds with fine potting soil. The ideal temperature for lettuce germination is 60° to 75°F.

Although all lettuce varieties transplant easily, seedlings of looseleaf and some butterhead varieties are remarkably tolerant of being held in containers. They recover so well from being crowded and root bound that you can transplant seedlings as you need them and hold the rest in containers for several more weeks. Just add some weak fertilizer solution periodically and provide adequate light and water. Otherwise, the seedlings will become fragile and hard to transplant.

When you are direct-seeding lettuce, you can sow the seeds in single-file rows, wide rows, or small blocks. Try to sow thinly, or actually set each seed 1 to 2 inches from the next one. Cover the seeds with ¼ inch of soil. When the plants are 2 to 3 inches high, thin crisphead varieties to 12 inches apart and other types to 6 inches apart. If you like, remove the extra plants with a small trowel and plant them elsewhere. The transplanted seedlings will grow a bit slower, giving you a slightly staggered crop.

Our warmest and coldest days are difficult for lettuce. Look for varieties that cope best with the weather at the time of year you intend to plant. Even when summer is relatively cool, even a brief hot spell may cause lettuce to become bitter, go to seed prematurely, or both. If you live in a sunny part of the region or are planting lettuce to mature in September or October, plant it where it will be shaded by another crop for part of the day. Don't expect it to remain at its prime for very long.

Local truck farmers grow baby lettuce the year around, starting it every two weeks in a greenhouse, planting it in raised beds kept free of snails and slugs, and harvesting it in four to five weeks. When I asked one farmer how his lettuce grows in winter, he replied dryly, "Very slowly." During our dark, cool months, lettuce may grow so slowly that it can't keep ahead of pest damage. In warmer weather the stressed lettuce would just lose a leaf or two, but in winter it may actually diminish in size. If you can't eliminate snails and slugs, combat them by growing the lettuce under a floating row cover or in a pestproof cold frame (see pages 50 and 58).

The Harvest You can begin to harvest lettuce by adding thinned seedlings to salads. When looseleaf, butterhead, or romaine have developed a number of leaves, you can take one or two of the larger leaves per plant. As these plants grow you can continue to pick them by the leaf, always leaving enough so that the plant can keep growing. You can also harvest by cutting or pulling the entire plant at any time. Harvesting by the leaf has the virtue of prolonging the harvest, but if you overplanted, you may prefer to take whole plants to reduce the total crop. Romaine lettuce is most often harvested as either whole baby lettuce or whole mature plants. Crisphead varieties are usually harvested at maturity, when the head is large and firm.

Cutting lettuces are varieties, usually looseleaf, that resprout vigorously from a cut stem. Just use a knife or scissors to cut the plant near the ground. These varieties are good additions to mesclun (see page 236) and are best cut and recut while they are fairly small.

Estimate how much lettuce you will use before you plant. Small successive plantings are usually better than a single large planting. When gardeners ask me what to do with lettuce besides making salads, I take it as a sure sign that they overplanted. Having said that, I offer two uncommon recipes from my father's childhood on a farm in Indiana. They won't take up much of your surplus (your nongardening friends are probably your best bet for that), but they do offer variety. The first is Bibb or Buttercrunch lettuce with honey. This simple treat is nothing more than a bowl of very fresh young butterhead leaves drizzled with a little honey. The other is wilted lettuce (see opposite page). If you're looking for alternatives to these European ways of using lettuce, Asian cuisines include it too. Lettuce is used to make informal wraps for morsels in Vietnamese cuisine. Chinese cooks may use it to wrap meat fillings, or they may stir-fry it or use it in soup.

Varieties Looseleaf varieties are ones that form no heads. They include green-leaved 'Black Seeded Simpson', 'Salad Bowl', and 'Oakleaf', and red-leaved 'Red Sails' and 'Red Oakleaf'. Looseleaf varieties mature in only 45 to 60 days, though you will probably be picking outer leaves before then.

Butterhead varieties have a tender, buttery texture. They may not form much of a head, or may have a loose head and a blanched center. They

Left to right: Bibb, romaine, crisphead, butterhead, looseleaf

Wilted Lettuce

Wilted lettuce reflects the German contribution to the Midwest melting pot, and it's a dish I remember from my childhood there. The heated sweet and sour dressing wilts the lettuce, resulting in more of a vegetable dish than a salad. These days, I make it only when I've purchased some nitrite-free bacon at a natural foods store. Serves four.

- 2 medium heads looseleaf or butterhead lettuce, torn into pieces (about 8 cups)
- 3 tablespoons cider vinegar
- 2 tablespoons water
- 1 tablespoon white or brown sugar
- 4 slices nitrite-free bacon
- ½ medium onion, cut into small pieces

Put the lettuce pieces in a large bowl and set it aside. In a small bowl, combine the vinegar, water, and sugar, stirring until the sugar dissolves. Set aside.

Fry the bacon in a skillet until it is crisp, then set it on a paper towel to drain and cool. Measure out and reserve ¼ cup of bacon drippings; discard the rest. Crumble the bacon and set it aside.

Return the ¼ cup of drippings to the skillet and fry the onion over medium heat until soft but not browned. Stir in the vinegar mixture. Add the crumbled bacon. Heat this dressing to the boiling point, stirring all the while. Immediately pour the hot dressing over the lettuce, and toss it to mix.

Variation: To make this even more of a vegetable dish, let the lettuce cook briefly in the dressing. Leftovers of either version are delicious.

include the old green variety 'Bibb', the newer 'Buttercrunch'—which is larger and more heat tolerant—and many other varieties. Red-tinged 'Continuity' and 'Four Seasons' (or 'Merveille des Quatre Saisons') are probably the same variety. Butterhead varieties mature in 60 to 75 days, but as with looseleaf you can pick whole plants or leaves much earlier.

Romaine, or cos, lettuce is upright and columnar in habit, has a crisp texture, and is considered the slowest to bolt. Some references advise gardeners to plant it only in spring, but seed companies offer winter varieties, and local market gardeners are able to grow some kinds through our winters. A good summer romaine is 'Little Gem', a green-leaved type that grows only 6 inches high. For all seasons try 'Rouge d'Hiver', a red-leaved type. Most romaine varieties take more than 75 days to mature, although dwarf ones may mature more quickly. 'Little Gem', for instance, is listed at 65 days.

'Iceberg', commonly sold in supermarkets, is a kind of crisphead best suited to the Imperial Valley, where it is grown commercially. Try instead varieties bred for home gardeners. Two good varieties are 'Diamond Head' and 'Summertime'. Crispheads take about three months to mature. If you like the firm, crisp, thick leaves of iceberg, but would like to reap nutritional benefits from a more open head that lets the leaves stay greener, try Batavian or summer crisp varieties. Some, such as 'Nevada', are green-leaved; 'Sierra' and 'Magenta' (an improved 'Sierra') are bronzy.

A number of varieties of all lettuce types have green leaves speckled with dark red. They include the butterhead 'Speckles' and the romaine 'Flashy Trout's Back' (known in Europe as 'Forellenschluss'). I am particularly fond of 'Flashy Butter Oak', a looseleaf with broad oak-type leaves nicely splashed with bright maroon. It has proven particularly slow to bolt and tolerant of cold as well.

There are a legion of lettuce varieties, and most will do well here, so try several a year. Try heirloom and new ones, redleaf and green. You will notice that the main types have strains with similar names or descriptions. For example, there is a 'Simpson Elite'—an improved 'Black Seeded Simpson'. And a number of varieties are really red oak leaf types, though they are called 'Purple Oak Leaf', 'Brunia', or 'Mascara'.

Pests Lettuce seedlings are often the most tender morsels in a garden, so they understandably fall prey to birds, cutworms, earwigs, slugs, and snails. As lettuce plants mature they remain attractive to snails and slugs, and they may also attract aphids and spider mites. To the dismay of unsuspecting gardeners, slugs often live deep in the plants at the bases of leaves. Occasional night slug-picking forays, flashlight in hand, will reduce damage considerably. Earwigs often feed on lettuce, especially in the spring. Set out earwig traps among your lettuce plants and see what you catch (see page 117). If leaves are nibbled from the edges all around, suspect bird damage, and try covering the planting with bird netting. Cabbage loopers are potential pests, though they have not been so in my garden.

Overwatered lettuce can succumb to bacterial or fungal root rots and die suddenly. If this happens, it is best to water less and rotate to something else next season. But check under your wilted lettuce plants for a white fungal mat studded with pea-sized black resting bodies. This would indicate you have lettuce drop, caused by the fungus *Sclerotinia sclerotia* or another member of this fungal genus. If you see the white fungal mat, remove affected plants, fallen debris, and a handful of infected soil, since this disease can infect many other kinds of vegetables—corn being one of the only ones immune to it. Soil solarization (see page 149) will control this disease.

Angular brown spots caused by downy mildew sometimes appear on lettuce leaves. Remove damaged plants, rotate with another crop, and seek downy mildew–resistant lettuce varieties.

Sources

Looseleaf lettuce seed: Widely available
 Flashy Butter Oak: NGN, TERR
Butterhead lettuce seed: Widely available
 Speckles butterhead: RH, SESE, TERR, WCS
Romaine lettuce seed: Widely available
 Flashy Trout's Back: JSS, TERR
Crisphead lettuce seed:
 Summertime: BUR, CG, NGN, PGS, TERR, VBS, WCS
Summer crisp lettuce seed:
 Nevada: ABL, JSS,SOC, TERR, VBS
 Sierra or Magenta: JSS

Melon (includes Cantaloupe and Honeydew)

Cucumis melo

Watermelon

Citrullus lanatus
Gourd Family ❖ *Cucurbitaceae*

Every few years I come across a listing for a "very early" cantaloupe that is supposed to bear fruit even in cool weather. So far, my success has been limited to the 2½-inch cantaloupe reported earlier in this chapter. And cantaloupe is probably the melon most likely to succeed here! Watermelon is even more heat-loving, although I have heard reports of small watermelons ripening in various San Francisco gardens. I expect I will be tempted again by another early melon variety.

Over the years, the Master Gardeners of Santa Clara County have experimented with melons in Cupertino and San Jose test sites, and their results in some of the warmest parts of the Bay region serve as a bookend to my failures in the area with the coolest summers. Using soil warming methods and early varieties, they had pretty good success.

Growing Instructions If you garden in a protected, relatively sunny site and are tempted by melons, be sure to give your plants an early start indoors. In late March or early April, start melon seeds in 4-inch, bottomless containers, such as cut-off milk containers, from which you can transplant them without disturbing the roots (see page 51). Plant the seedlings out in late April or early May, when they have two or three true leaves. Do not be tempted to start much earlier and grow large transplants indoors, as these will not transplant well and are likely to be stunted.

Be sure the soil in which you plant the melons is well amended (to be able to grow in pure compost would delight these demanding plants) and well fertilized. Set the plants 3 to 5 feet apart (check recommendations on the seed packet). Water regularly, but don't let the soil stay soggy or the flavor of the fruit may be ruined.

When Cooperative Extension researchers conducted melon variety trials in San Jose in 1987 and 2000, they went to great lengths to provide good growing conditions. Several weeks before the planting date, they buried a drip irrigation line under the bed (you could use a soaker hose instead). In 1987, they laid black plastic over the soil to warm it. In 2000, they tried a special infrared transmitting plastic film. They planted the seedlings in slits cut in the plastic, then placed a floating row cover over the whole bed to warm the air above the soil. (If you do this, remember to tuck the edges of the plastic into the soil to keep snails from hiding under it, and then, when you add the row cover, tuck its edges into the soil outside the edges of black plastic.) They removed the row cover when the plants began to bloom, to allow pollination, and stopped irrigation as soon as they picked the first ripe fruit. Although these Herculean efforts don't guarantee a good crop in cooler parts of the region, they will improve your chances.

Some of the conclusions the Cooperative Extension researchers drew were the following: The soil warming performed by the black plastic or IRT plastic (up to 5 degrees) was important in allowing the melons to perform better. You have to be on the ball to remove the row cover during the periodic heat waves we get in the Bay Area, or the plants will die from overheating. Also, the plastic keeps the soil under it so wet that overwatering is a hazard.

The Harvest Cantaloupes and other netted skin types "slip" or pull off easily when ripe. Smooth-skinned types, like honeydews, change from hairy to smooth and slippery, and then, finally, to waxy when the fruit is ripe.

Varieties Look for varieties rated as early or able to grow in cool, northern, or mountain climates. The top variety for both flavor and production in the Santa Clara 2000 trials was 'Earliqueen F_1'. You are now more likely to find 'Halona F_1', an improved 'Earliqueen' with more resistance to powdery mildew. 'Halona' is rated at 73 days to harvest, a day earlier than 'Earliqueen'. The Master Gardeners didn't report whether 'Earliqueen' really was that early in their location, but reported it produced about five 3- to 4-pound melons per plant. 'Burpee's Hybrid' rated second for taste, but wasn't quite as productive. Others that rated well for taste and production were 'Galia', 'Galia Passport', and 'Haogen'. Not in the trials, but worth trying, is 'Diplomat', a new Galia-type melon with added powdery mildew resistance.

Pests Melons often fall prey to powdery mildew, so resistance to this disease is a plus. (See page 136 for information on combating powdery mildew.)

Sources

Melon seeds:
Halona F_1 seed: JSS
Burpee's Hybrid F_1 seed: BUR, TT
Galia F_1 seed: T&M
Galia Passport F_1 seed: JSS, PGS, TERR
Haogen seed: BG, BI, SSE, T&M
Diploma F_1 seed: JSS, WCS

Mustard Greens (or Southern Mustard)

Brassica juncea

Tendergreen (or Mustard Spinach) and Mizuna

B. rapa
Perviridis Group
Mustard Family ❖ *Brassicaceae* (*Cruciferae*)

All kinds of mustard greens do very well throughout our region. Some are *B. juncea* and others are *B. rapa*, the species that includes Chinese cabbage and turnip. Although all culinary mustards are probably Asian in origin, some have become staples in American cooking, especially in the South, and some varieties are being added to trendy salad mixes. Mustards vary considerably in flavor, tenderness, and susceptibility to snails and slugs, but most make quick, short-standing crops of greens. Experiment to see which ones you like and which do well for you.

Growing Instructions Mustards often go to seed prematurely, or bolt, during long days and thus are best sown in late winter, early spring, or mid- to late summer. Since they vary in resistance to cold, some can be planted later than others in fall. Although they will succeed in any good garden soil, they grow faster in soils that warm quickly. (If your soil is clay, be sure to amend the area where you are growing spring mustards.)

All mustards are seeded in place, about ½ inch deep, and thinned as they mature. They are very quick crops listed at 20 to 45 days. If you plan to eat them young, sow a few more every couple of weeks. Most kinds go to seed soon after reaching maturity, so you must use them quickly. However, some will hold in the winter months from a fall planting, not bolting until spring. As with all quick-growing crops, be sure to keep mustards well watered.

The Harvest Harvest whole plants or outer leaves at any stage, or cut young plants near the base and let them regrow. Use mild-flavored mustard in salads (young mustards are part of many mescluns) or stir-fries. Stronger-flavored leaves are generally cooked—boiled or used in stir-fries or soups. The key to preparing strong-flavored mustards is to use sturdy seasonings able to stand up to their strong flavor. In Southern cooking, the seasonings of choice are often onion, a little smoked bacon or ham, and a dash of bottled hot sauce. In a typical dish, the pork is sautéed with the onions, the mustard and some water are added, and the hot sauce is tossed in at

Mesclun

Our practice of sowing only one kind of seed at a time has not always been the case in agriculture. Often different kinds of grain or vegetable seeds have been sown together. Mesclun is a mix of greens, sown together and harvested young, as practiced traditionally in Italy and Mediterranean France.

Mesclun is not a particular combination of greens. It might consist of only several kinds of lettuce, or a mix of lettuces and other greens, or it may not include lettuce at all. Any fast-growing green is fair game, including arugula, chervil, chicory, corn salad, cress, endive, fennel, kale, and mustard. The idea is to select species and varieties that grow at about the same rate. When the plants are several inches tall, they are cut near the ground, leaving the growing point so they can sprout again for another cutting.

Many seed companies sell mesclun mixes, with varieties selected for matched growth rates and a pleasing combination of flavor, form, and color. You can choose ones that range from spicy to mild, and you can also grow different mixes separately and then blend spicy and mild greens to your taste in the kitchen. Mesclun is traditionally for salad, but you will also find mixes intended for stir-fries.

Begin to sow seeds for mesclun in February. Unlike other crops, which need plenty of room to mature, plants grown in mesclun are crowded together, because they will be cut while still young. Sow seeds about a half inch apart, either in blocks a couple of feet square or in bands 6 to 12 inches wide. Cover the seed with about ¼ inch of fine soil.

Make a small planting, then sow another area when the first mesclun is nearly tall enough for the first cutting. Practice until you get the supply right; that is, coordinated with your salad needs. Plant more mesclun as long as the weather isn't too hot or cold for salad crops. When plants are 4 to 6 inches tall, use scissors to cut a section of plants ½ inch to 1 inch from the ground. You will get two or three cuttings per section. While the cut-and-come-again method is traditional, some prefer to harvest by hand picking the largest leaves of their mesclun.

Of course, instead of growing mesclun, you can also combine young leafy greens that you have grown separately to create a mixed salad. In the grocery, you find mixed greens sold as "spring mix." Are they mesclun? Possibly, or they may be grown separately and mixed for the market. (One thing for sure is that any torn-up radicchio leaves were added later, since this plant makes those glorious white-veined red leaves only in the mature head. Its young leaves are green.)

The Achilles heel of mesclun is weed seedlings. If you plant it in a plot that will sprout many weeds, you will have some of them in the mix when you cut it. That is inconvenient, and if you can't tell the weeds from the edibles, you could accidentally eat something you shouldn't. So plant where weeds are few, or consider using a wide but shallow planter box containing potting mix. Six inches should be deep enough.

For more on choosing and blending salad ingredients, see page 379. Mesclun seed mixes are widely available.

the end. Although this dish is usually cooked much longer, it is fully cooked and more nutritious boiled about 20 minutes. In Asian cooking, the seasoning for strong-flavored mustard is likely to be sesame oil and soy sauce. (See the recipe for Mustard Greens, Noodles, and Tofu Sauté on page 239.)

Varieties and Related Species The hot, spicy mustard varieties are *B. juncea*. Their broad leaves, which are sometimes ruffled or lobed, may be green, red, or almost purple. Newly available *B. juncea* varieties 'Golden Streaks' and 'Ruby Streaks' are small plants with narrow, lacy leaves. In my variety trials, I learned that the chartreuse-leaved 'Golden Streaks' is hot and spicy even when quite young, but the red-leaved 'Ruby Streaks' is milder at first. 'Ruby Streaks' also grew faster in cold late winter weather than 'Golden Streaks', and both outgrew mizuna varieties. Use both young in salads in just a few weeks, steam or stir-fry older leaves. Both would attract comments in an ornamental planting as well.

The most common *B. rapa* mustard is tendergreen, or mustard spinach. It is so mild that some find it bland. 'Tyfon Holland Greens' are a mild-flavored cross between genetic turnip and Chinese Cabbage.

Young 'Mizuna' leaves are often sold as part of "spring salad" mixes. They are narrow and spiky with a mild flavor. These *B. rapa* variety *japonica* greens are now also available in a purple-tinged variety called 'Purple Mizuna', which in trials grew larger than the green-leaved variety and was equally mild in flavor. Mizuna is an easy and excellent crop for local gardens that can be used young in salad or cooked when older.

To grow mustard seed as a spice, see page 307.

Pests Mustard greens are susceptible to slug and snail damage and can be infested by cabbage aphids. However, they often escape damage by cabbage moths that harm other crops, though attacks are possible, especially in warmer weather. Watch for viruses, which stunt and curl mustard leaves. Remove infected plants.

Sources

Mustard greens seed:
Large-leaf red or purple *B. juncea* seed: Widely available
Lacy-leaved salad *B. juncea* seed: BI, EE, JSS, KIT, NGN, TERR
Mizuna *B. rapa* (green leaf) seed: Widely available
Mizuna *B. rapa* (red leaf) seed: GS, JSS, KIT
Tendergreen seed: BCS, BUR, EE, JSS, KIT, NGN, RH, VBS, WCS
Tyfon Holland Greens seed: NGN, PGS, TERR

Oca

Oxalis tuberosa
Oxalis Family ❖ *Oxalidaceae*

The Andean mountain region of South America is the native land of not only our familiar potatoes, but also other edible tubers, roots, and rhizomes that are less known outside of that region. Oca has remained mainly a crop of Peruvians and Bolivians, who use it in soups and stews. I have kept it going in my garden for years, though I admit that I eat it only occasionally.

The part eaten is an underground structure usually described as a tuber but more correctly called a rhizome, since it grows horizontally in the ground. The rhizome may be yellow or pink and more or less starchy. Its flavor is on the tart side because of a moderate oxalic acid content. Mine are pink and grow to about 3 inches long and an inch wide. A plant will produce a pound or two of these, in various sizes.

Oca plant and edible rhizome

The leaves are cloverlike, but if you garden in the Bay Area, you will clearly see that this is not clover but a relative of the weedy South African *Oxalis pes-caprae* that blankets winter gardens wherever it can get away with it. In fact, though it

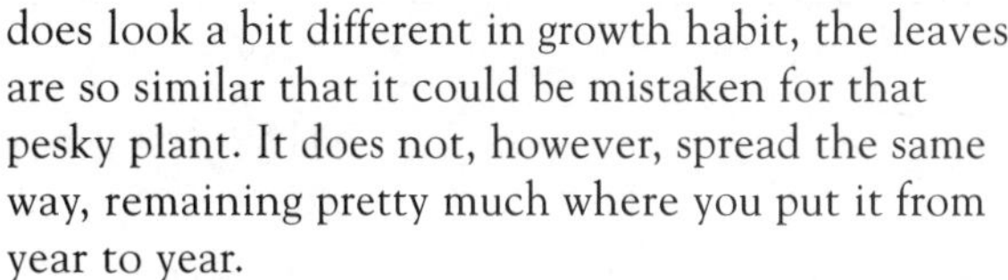

does look a bit different in growth habit, the leaves are so similar that it could be mistaken for that pesky plant. It does not, however, spread the same way, remaining pretty much where you put it from year to year.

Plant rhizomes in spring and let them grow into autumn. The rhizomes continue to develop until the tops die back, or at least decline, in winter. The rhizomes will be fine in the ground unless the temperatures drop below the low twenties. Dig as needed. My oca has never been bothered by any pests.

Sources

Oca rhizomes: NGN, SOC

Okra

Abelmoschus esculentus
Mallow Family ❖ *Malvaceae*

Okra is grown for its immature pods, used in soups or alone, boiled or fried. It is probably out of reach for Bay Area gardeners in cool summer parts of our region because it wants soil over 70°F and daytime temperatures over 85°F, and it does best when nights are warm. In San Francisco, where soil temperature reaches the low sixties in May and summer highs are around 70°F, my results were less than stellar. Although I used an early variety, the plants were small, and they caught a rust disease from nearby mallow (*Malva* sp.) weeds before pods formed (not that pods would necessarily have formed).

To try okra, plant in May or June. You can try germinating seed indoors 4 or 5 weeks before plant-out, keeping the seeding mix at 80° to 90°F until the seedlings emerge. Plant out 1 to 1½ feet apart, taking care not to disturb the roots.

If your okra starts setting pods, pick them while they are 2 to 3 inches long, and never let any mature on the plant. Pick often, every day or two, to keep the plant producing well.

To increase your chance of success in a marginal location, grow an early variety, such as 'Cajun Delight', which is rated at 50 days from seeding. However, be aware that cold nights and cool days may not just slow growth but also prevent pod formation. In warmer microclimates, try standard varieties such as 'Clemson Spineless' or the red-podded 'Red Burgundy'.

Control the related mallow weeds to avoid rust infections (see page 157) Okra can also be damaged by aphids, mites, or corn earworms.

Microgreens and Sprouts

Mesclun greens are traditionally cut while still young; microgreens carry this one step further. They are harvested when the plants have only their seed leaves, or their seed leaves plus two or three true leaves. Microgreens are typically grown in shallow planting trays. Trays sold for this purpose allow 1 to 1½ inches of planting medium and have a clear plastic cover that holds in humidity. Microgreens can be grown in soil but are also often grown in seeding mix or even pure vermiculite. You can cover the seeds with a moist paper towel instead of soil or mix.

You can sow a flat with the same kind of seed, or mix them as for mesclun. Some microgreen mixes are available, formulated to ensure that the plantlets will develop at more or less the same rate. In addition to individual or mixed salad greens, microgreen growers may grow such surprising selections as popcorn, basil, celery, or sunflower. Harvest is in 2 to 3 weeks. The little plants are cut at soil level to remove the roots, washed, spun-dried in a lettuce whirler, and ready for use. They can be stored in the refrigerator for later use.

The simplest use for microgreens is as salad or salad ingredients. They are also used, with great finesse, to add interest and flavor to high cuisine, and here they would be highlighted, used sparingly so the diner can focus on their individual forms and flavors.

Microgreens require close attention to timing, more so than most crops, and so need high motivation from the gardener. They could certainly serve the purpose of allowing a cook with little or no garden space to grow fresh greens, needing only a reasonably warm and sunny spot that could be on a balcony or even indoors.

Microgreens are just a bit more mature than sprouts, another option for the landless gardener. Sprouts typically have only pale, tiny seed leaves when they are eaten. The simplest method of sprouting seeds is to put them in a quart jar with an old style two-part metal Mason canning lid. Instead of the metal cover, however, you cut a circle of metal screen to fit, so that the ring part of the lid holds it in place. Add 2 tablespoons of seeds, soak in water overnight, and drain. Then rinse and drain the seeds twice a day until they reach the size you want. You can also buy jars with screen lids, or newer seed sprouting containers that allow for larger amounts or keep sprouts upright and untangled.

Be sure that seeds you use for microgreens or sprouts are ones sold for that purpose, and be sure to keep your equipment clean to avoid bacterial contamination.

Sources

Seed for microgreens: BE, BUR, CG, JSS, T&M, TERR

Seed for sprouting: BI, BUR, CG, GS, IST, JSS, PGS, PS, T&M, TERR, TT, VBS, WCS

Seed sprouting equipment: BUR, CG, GS, IST, JSS, PS, T&M, TERR, TT, VBS, WCS

Sources

Okra seed:

Clemson Spineless: BCS, BG, BI, BUR, GS, JLH, NGN, PGS, SESE, SSE, TT

Red Burgundy: BCS, BG, GS, JLH, PGS, PS, RCS, RH, SESE, SSE, T&M, TERR, TT

Cajun Delight F_1: JSS, KIT, NGN, PGS, PS, TERR, VBS

Onion, Bulb

Allium cepa
Cepa Group
Amaryllis Family ❖ *Amaryllidaceae*

Bulb onions are a cool-season crop that can be grown successfully in all parts of our region. They are satisfying to dig and use fresh when their flavor is at its peak, and some varieties keep well for later use. Yet gardeners often find that their plants go to seed before the bulbs form or that the bulbs never get very big. Onions are a bit ornery, and some of your plants may misbehave no matter what you do. Still, you can increase your success rate dramatically if you learn what this crop needs: well-prepared soil, ample moisture, minimum weed competition, the right variety, and proper timing.

Growing Instructions Amend your soil well for onions. This is especially important if the soil is very sandy or clayey. Without organic matter, you will find it too difficult to keep sandy soil moist enough, and in heavy clay soil onions often form small bulbs. Heavy clay also has a tendency to become waterlogged—a condition that encourages soilborne onion disease. Be sure to fertilize when you plant.

Give onions plenty of water during their first few weeks of growth, since the surface roots that form during that time are essential to the future vigor of the plants. Keep weeds under control,

Mustard Greens, Noodles, and Tofu Sauté

Here is a delicious dish that uses mustard greens or the small Asian-type turnips along with their greens. For a spicier dish, use sesame oil with chile oil. Serves two generously.

6 cups of water

6 to 8 ounces chuka soba or other Asian-style wheat noodle

3 to 4 tablespoons vegetable oil

4 cups coarsely chopped mustard greens (or small Japanese-type turnips, thinly sliced, with their greens, wild mustard, young radish greens, or any combination of these)

1 pound firm tofu, cut into bite-sized pieces

1 teaspoon toasted sesame oil

2 tablespoons Japanese soy sauce, or more to taste

Bring the water to a boil in a saucepan. Add noodles and boil for 3 minutes (following directions on the package). Drain in a colander.

Spray a large skillet with nonstick spray (it will help prevent the noodles from sticking later). Add 1 tablespoon or so of oil. If you are using turnips, put them in first and sauté them over medium heat until half-tender, but not browned. Add the greens and sauté them until limp. Add the drained noodles and fry them, turning with a spatula. Add more oil if the noodles stick.

Add the tofu and mix into the noodles and greens. Season with the sesame oil and Japanese soy sauce. Serve hot with additional soy sauce.

Note: Chuka soba is a fat-free wheat flour noodle, usually sold in 6-ounce packages. If you can't find it, you can use any Asian type of wheat flour noodle intended to be boiled and then fried—read the label. (Ramen noodles work but are high in fat.)

because they will compete for water and shade out young onion plants.

Make sure that the variety you are growing will form bulbs in our region. Most onions are sensitive to day length—that is, they begin to form bulbs when spring days reach a certain length. If the variety you planted needs longer days than we get at our latitude, it will never form bulbs. Even when a day-length-sensitive variety is adapted to our day length, it still won't do well unless it is planted at the right time. If it is planted too late, it will not be mature enough when day length stimulates the bulb to form and, as a result, will produce small bulbs. If it is planted too early, winter cold will cause all or some of the plants to bloom and go to seed instead of making bulbs. (See Onions and Environmental Factors on page 244.) New day-length-neutral varieties take some of the calculation out of growing bulb onions. They will form bulbs wherever they are grown, as long as they are growing by reasonably early in spring. Some of them can also be started in fall, if you can time them so they are still small when cold weather hits, to avoid "bloomers."

The most common way of starting bulb onions is from small purchased bulbs called sets. As an alternative, you can start your own seedlings, or you can buy seedlings or bunches of bare-root plants from a nursery. (Don't plant sprouted grocery store onions, because they will go to seed right away and never form good bulbs. Also, they may be diseased.)

Onion sets are a popular way to grow onions, since they are easier to handle than seeds or small plants. It's true that you are likely to get a few "bloomers" from a planting of sets, but the proportion is small enough that most gardeners don't mind the risk.

If you are planting onion sets to produce bulb onions rather than green onions, choose sets that are less than ¾ inch in diameter, because these are less likely to bloom. Plant them, pointy end up, just below the soil surface, and leave 3 to 4 inches between sets. (Save the larger sets and plant them to grow green onions—see page 243.) Plant onion sets in January or February to give them the entire spring to make big plants before the bulbs begin to form. March is risky, and sets planted in April or May definitely won't have enough time to make big bulbs. (Gardeners who plant late often leave the small bulbs in the ground hoping that they will mature into big bulbs next year, but that is unlikely to happen. The onions are more apt to bloom and go to seed the following spring.)

Starting onions from seed gives you the widest choice of varieties. If you are starting seeds before October 1 or after January 1, you can seed directly in the garden. From October through December start the seeds indoors, allowing eight to ten weeks from the seeding date to the correct transplant time for the variety you are growing. If seedlings are getting their start outdoors in fall, allow an extra month or so, since they will grow more slowly as the days get shorter and colder. Your goal is to get as early a start as possible but avoid having plants with a stem diameter bigger than a pencil in the ground during the coldest months.

Sow onion seeds ¼ to ½ inch deep. You can plant them 2 inches apart and thin the seedlings to 3 to 4 inches apart. As an alternative, sow more thickly in a small area and transplant the seedlings to stand 3 to 4 inches apart when they have at least three leaves.

Some mail-order seed companies offer bare-root onion seedlings. Make sure that the variety is well suited to our latitude and that the company will ship it at the right time—January or February. Bare-root plants are sold in bunches of 50 to 225 (depending on the source), so you want to share your order with other gardeners. Seedlings in containers sold at local nurseries are also a good option, as long as you choose a suitable variety and plant at the proper time. Be sure to separate the plants and plant them 3 to 4 inches apart.

Bulb onions

Keep the plants well watered through the spring, until the necks (the stems right above the bulbs) begin to be less firm. When this happens, stop watering. When the necks are quite flat, the bulbs are fully formed. At this point, most of the leaves are dead and the plants often fall over.

If at any time while your bulb onions are growing you see a flower stem beginning to emerge—a tall central stem topped by a pointy, pale green flower bud cover—you may as well dig the plant and eat whatever you can right away. You could try, instead, cutting out the flower stem, but once an onion starts to grow this stem, it rarely forms a good bulb, and is very unlikely to form a bulb that can be stored. You might like to let one or two onions flower, just to see how they look and because they are prime attractants for beneficial insects.

The Harvest You can eat onion bulbs fresh, digging them up when they are mature or nearly so. Or you can store them for up to several months—but if you plan to store them, don't dig them up too soon. Commercial onion growers keep the plants in the ground until they are completely dry, then leave them there for five to ten more days. Don't plan to put a summer crop, such as beans or tomatoes, in that spot next or you will be tempted to dig the onions too soon. Instead, plan to follow onions with a mid- to late-summer planting of a fall crop, such as carrots or a cole crop.

If you intend to braid the tops, do it immediately after digging up the bulbs. To cure onions, spread them in a single layer or hang them by their braids in a warm, dry place out of direct sunlight for a week or two. Check them every couple of days to be sure that they are drying well. When they are cured, gently brush off dirt and loose scales. If you didn't braid the stems, cut them 2 inches from the bulbs at this time.

Once onions have been cured, they keep best in a cool, dry place, ideally between 32° and 40°F. A refrigerator won't do, since the high humidity encourages sprouting and decay, and most local basements and garages are too warm. Hang the onions in the coolest, driest part of your home. If they are braided, hang the braids. If they are loose, hang them in mesh bags or in bags fashioned from panty hose. Store onions away from apples or bananas, since these fruits exude ethylene gas, which make onions sprout. Check stored onions often for sprouting, rooting, or decay—and eat undamaged parts of any affected onions immediately. Among onions of the same variety, use the biggest onions first. Also, use any onions that are more elongated than others of the same variety. Yellow onions are usually the best keepers, red intermediate, and white the worst. Other rules of thumb are that hotter varieties of onion keep better than milder ones, and long-day types keep better than short-day ones.

Varieties Read catalog descriptions carefully to assure the varieties you choose will succeed in our region. (See Onions and Environmental Factors on page 244 for details.) The following varieties are some that we can grow. The list includes a number of intermediate and long-day onions, as well as the new day-neutral ones. It is by no means intended as a list of all varieties that may succeed. If you have questions about any specific variety you find as seeds, sets, or bare-root seedlings, contact the seed company involved and ask for more information.

Mid-Keeper White and Yellow Types

- 'White Sweet Spanish' and 'Yellow Sweet Spanish' are designations that seem to cover a wide range of strains, many of which will thrive at this latitude. I have grown a 'Yellow Sweet Spanish' strain in San Francisco with great success. Read carefully—and if there is any doubt about whether the one you find will grow here, ask the supplier.
- 'Utah' strains of 'White Sweet Spanish' or 'Yellow Sweet Spanish' should be fine here. You may find named substrains, such as 'Valencia', which is listed as a "Utah strain of Yellow Sweet Spanish."
- 'Walla Walla Sweet' is a large, sweet variety much grown, as its name suggests, in the Northwest, but Bountiful Gardens sells a strain they say is good from 35° to 55° latitude. It can be fall planted if your timing is right, to produce larger bulbs.

Short-Keeper Reds

- 'Red Torpedo' is an intermediate type with an elongated red or purplish-red bulb. It is sweet and mild. 'Italian Blood Red Bottle' and 'Rossa Lunga de Firenze' are very similar or the same variety.
- 'Stockton Early Red' (also known as 'Fresno Red' or 'Early Red') is an intermediate-day onion that can tolerate high temperatures. It is globe-shaped, mild-flavored, and white-fleshed with light red ringing.

White and Yellow Storage Types

- We are probably at the southern end of the range of 'Southport White Globe', but it is worth a try.
- 'Giant Zittau' forms a 4- to 5-inch golden-brown bulb that keeps very well. It has good flavor and a wide range of day-length adaptability.
- 'Ailsa Craig' is another variety considered suitable for intermediate day length, due to its wide adaptability. It is straw yellow, with bulbs that weigh up to two pounds each.

Red Storage Types

- 'Rosso di Milano' is a medium-sized, mildly hot onion with a flat top and a rounded base. It is rated as "long to intermediate day" and said to be "tolerant of cool climates."
- 'Tropeana Tonda', described as top shaped, is similar in form to the preceding onion, but is said to be "short to intermediate day." It is large and violet red, with an excellent flavor.
- 'Rosso di Toscano' is a "somewhat flattened" onion from a different region of Italy and is a long- to intermediate-day onion.

Day-Neutral Varieties

These day-neutral varieties are all available as seeds, and bunches of bare-root plants are often available as well. All are best used fresh; that is, don't depend on them for long storage.

- 'Superstar F_1': A large, mild white onion.
- 'Candy F_1': A flattened, yellow-skinned, 3 to 4-inch onion.
- 'Red Candy Apple F_1': Deep red, flattened globe-shaped bulbs to 4 inches across. Very sweet flavor.

Pests If an onion plant dies suddenly, it very likely has succumbed to onion root maggots. (See page 95.) Fortunately, snails and slugs show little interest in onions, but black aphids can be a problem. Downy mildew is a fungus disease favored by cool weather, especially when there is rain or heavy dew. The first symptom is yellow areas on the leaves. During very moist weather, the spores emerge and cover the leaves with a dirty gray or violet powder (see page 134).

Like garlic, onions are susceptible to white rot. The disease can be carried on sets or transplants, but not in seeds. Once white rot is in your soil, it stays a long time, so it is very important to use only certified disease-free sets and plants.

If you don't allow onion bulbs to dry thoroughly before you harvest them or if you don't cure them

Storing Onion Sets

Storage temperature affects whether onion sets will form good bulbs or immediately flower. They should be stored at 32° to 35°F or above 65°F. If you buy sets at a good nursery, they will have been stored correctly before you buy them. If you buy some but don't plan to plant them right away—and you may not, since they may be available a couple of months before you are ready—keep the sets in your warm house, since your freezer is too cold and your refrigerator's temperature will prime them to bloom.

well, they can develop neck rot in storage. This decay works its way down from the still-moist stems. Poorly cured onions may also be damaged by black mold, which makes black spore masses between the layers of scales. Be sure the storage area is cool and dry, and check the bulbs often for signs of decay. Remove affected onions, which can still be eaten after you trim off damaged parts. Aphids may attack onions in storage. Keep aphids under control while you are growing onions, and check for the insects when you inspect stored bulbs.

Sources

Onion seed (day-length-sensitive varieties):
Sweet Spanish types: GS, PGS, SESE, SOC, VBS, WCS
- Utah Strains of Sweet Spanish: GS, SOC
- Walla Walla Sweet (intermediate day strain): BG, NGN, PGS, PS, RH, T&M, VBS, WCS
- Red Torpedo strains: BCS, BG, BUR, CG, GS, JG, JLH, JSS, NGN, PGS, RPF, SI, SSE, TERR
- Stockton Early Red: SOC
- Southport White Globe: BG, SOC
- Giant Zittau: BG
- Ailsa Craig: BG, JSS, PGS, SSE
- Rosso di Milano: CG, SOC
- Tropeana Tonda: GS, IST, SI
- Rosso de Toscano: GS

Onion seed (day-neutral):
- Superstar F_1: NGN, PGS, PS, RPF, WCS
- Candy F_1: JSS, NGN, PS, TT, VBS

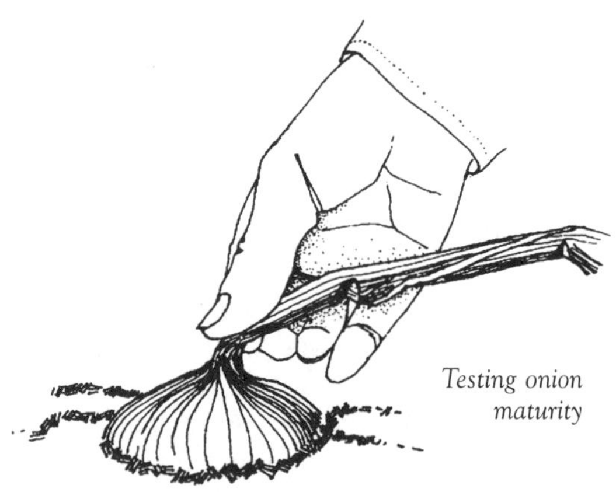
Testing onion maturity

Onion sets: BUR, PS, T&M, VBS
Onion plants, bare-root:
- Day-length sensitive: BUR, CG, JSS, NGN, PGS, PS, RH, TERR, VBS
- Day-neutral: CG, JSS, PGS, PS, TERR, VBS

Onion, Bunching (or Welsh Onion)

Allium fistulosum
Amaryllis Family ❖ *Amaryllidaceae*

Bunching onions are large sturdy plants that have been the main garden onion of China and Japan since ancient times. Although they are also known as Welsh onions, they have never been commonly grown in Wales. The plants look much like those of bulb onions, except that the leaves are round in cross section rather than indented on one side. Each plant of a perennial bunching onion will form many green onions from a single base. The advantage of growing this type of onion is that you can harvest during most of the year. To get more green onions the following year, all you have to do is separate the remaining clump and replant the onions.

Growing Instructions Bunching onions are most often grown from seed. Plant them in spring to early fall for green onions in summer, fall, and spring. In winter the plant is so small and scraggly that you would want to harvest it only in a pinch. Mature clumps should stand 6 to 8 inches apart, but you can start seeds much closer together and either transplant seedlings or pull them to eat young. Cut flower stalks in summer before they have a chance to bloom. This will encourage the plants to put their energy into multiplying instead.

The Harvest Eat some plants when they are the size of small green onions and let others mature into clumps of larger onions. It would seem that you could pull bunching onions one at a time from the edge of the clump, but in practice this is sometimes difficult. You may have to use a trowel to dig away a little soil next to a clump to remove plants without breaking them. You can maintain a planting for

Growing Green Onions

You can get green onions, or scallions, by planting bulb onion sets and digging the plants when they are about six weeks old. For a continuous supply, plant sets every few weeks all year long, except possibly in December. For green onions, plant the sets 3 inches below the soil surface, spacing them 1 to 2 inches apart. As an alternative, plant onion seeds close together and harvest when the stems are the diameter of green onions that you buy at the grocery store. (For other ways to grow green onions, see Bunching Onion on page 242 and Top Onion on page 245.)

many years. Divide large clumps every two or three years in fall.

Varieties All varieties should do well here.

Pests Beware of the same pests and diseases to which bulb onion plants fall prey.

Sources
Bunching onion seeds: Widely available

Onion, Pearl, Boiling, and Cipollini

Allium cepa
Cepa Group
Amaryllis Family ❖ *Amaryllidaceae*

Pearl, boiling, and cipollini onions are all onions intentionally grown to produce small bulbs. While this could be done with any bulb onion variety, particular varieties are generally chosen for this purpose.

Pearl onions are ¾ to 1¼ inches in diameter, and boiling onions are up to 2 inches across. Cipollini are harvested at 1 to 2 inches across and are particular varieties that form flattened bulbs. There are red, yellow, and white varieties of all three kinds. Some kinds can be dried and stored, others should be eaten fresh. All are meant to be used whole, in soups, stews, or casseroles or in kabobs, and pearl onions are sometime pickled.

It is common to use short-day varieties of onion to produce pearl onions, various day-length types to grow boilers. Cipollini types also vary in day-length classification.

Growing Instructions Grow varieties of bulb onions that are intended to make these small onions as you would bulb onions, but carefully follow the package directions for distance apart and depth to plant seeds. You may be planting seeds as closely as ¼ to ½ inch apart to produce pearl onions, and 2 inches apart to grow cipollinis. Close spacing keeps the bulbs small. Don't sow seed deeper than suggested, or the bulbs may elongate, ruining their round or flattened profile. Plant seed in January through April, and thin only if you have sown seed more thickly than was suggested.

The Harvest You can begin to harvest pearl onions for fresh use as soon as they reach the desired size. Continue to harvest until they are ready for storage. Pearl onion tops are so small and weigh so little that they may not fall over as the leaves of larger onions do, so you will have to watch the plants more closely to determine when the bulbs are the maximum size. When the leaves die back, you can be sure that they are ready. If you have grown a variety that will store well, dig them up, cure, and store them as you would bulb onions.

To remove the skins of pearl onions, drop the onions in enough boiling water to cover them. Drain them immediately, dip them in cold water, and slip the skins off.

Varieties and Similar Species A classic, short-day-length, white pickling variety is 'Barletta White'. 'Purplette', a day-neutral variety, is bright purple when raw, a pastel pink when cooked or pickled.

To grow boiling onions, try planting bulb onion varieties that are suited to the day length of our latitude at the appropriate time, but closer together.

'Pompei', a white cipollini onion, is a short-day variety. Another white one, 'Bianco de Maggio', is short- to intermediate-day. Yellow-skinned 'Borretanno' is intermediate to long-day. 'Gold Coin' and 'Red Marble' are rated as long-day onions. South of 38° latitude, the necks of long day varieties may be thick, reducing storage life. (San Francisco is at 37°, 8" north. For more on day length and onions, see page 244.)

Some varieties of onions sold to grow pearl onions are really bunching onions (*Allium fistulosum*) that happen to form small round bulbs instead of only narrow scallions (for example, 'Pacific Pearl'). This variety is also fairly day-neutral, so it can be planted later in the season and still make bulbs. They are not suited for dry storage.

Onions and Environmental Factors

Bulb onions are biennial plants, meaning that they grow most or all of a year, overwinter, bloom in the spring, drop their seed, and then die. In their first year, they form a bulb to store up food. In the second spring, they use that food to regrow and bloom. As a garden crop, we manipulate and then interrupt their life cycle. We time the planting to produce the largest possible bulb, and then we eat it.

Most varieties of bulb onion form bulbs as the days lengthen. Different varieties start to form their bulbs at different day lengths, so we need to be sure the ones we choose will form bulbs where we garden.

On the earth, at the equator, days and nights are equal all year—12 hours each. As you move north or south, winter days are shorter than the nights, and summer days are longer. At the latitude of San Francisco, the longest summer day is 14 hours and 47 minutes.

Day-length sensitive onions can be divided into roughly three groups. Short-day varieties require 12- to 14-hour days before bulbs begin to form. Intermediate-day varieties need 14-hour days, and long-day varieties need 14 to 16 hours. As you can see, a long-day onion is a risk in our area unless we know it is at the low end of that 14- to 16-hour requirement. These days, seed sources often inform us whether an onion variety is suitable at our latitude—information that is far more useful than the "days to harvest."

You will find some long-day varieties listed as best north of 38°, others best north of 36°. These differences show the variation within the long-day category. With the equator at 0° and the poles at 90°, San Francisco is located at North 37°8" (Mendocino is at 39°30"; Monterey at 36°60").

In addition to choosing an onion variety that will form bulbs in our location, we also want to plant our day-length-sensitive onions early enough that they have time to form big plants before the length of the day stimulates bulb formation. Seeds or bare-root plants that start growing in late winter will make bigger bulbs than ones that start out in late spring.

Then we begin to think about starting even earlier, before the coldest months of December and January, in hopes of having even bigger plants ready to bulb up at their day length of choice. This idea, however, runs into the second climatic factor that affects bulb onions: vernalization. This term means that exposure to sufficient hours of chill stimulates the plant to flower, whether or not a bulb has formed. An onion plant can flower if the stem near the ground is bigger than a pencil before the cold of winter begins. When an onion flowers, it becomes all flower stalk—all woody, unpalatable stem, with no succulent bulb underground.

Early plantings require a bit of dancing about to avoid vernalization. Planting can be timed so that the seedlings are still smaller than a pencil on December 1, or they can be kept in a greenhouse and allowed to grow bigger, then planted out after winter cold has passed. What can be done varies a bit depending on your particular microclimate. At the coast, fall growth may be slower, due to foggy, windy days, allowing a fall planting to work, when the same timing would let the plants get too big in a warmer inland autumn. Experimentation is called for.

If you are using onion sets, never plant them before most of the winter's coldest weather has passed, because the plants that grow from them are often already bigger than a pencil in diameter when they start to grow. Even cold weather in February and March may produce a certain number of "bloomers." Another way to reduce the number of "bloomers" when you are using sets is to choose the smaller sets for bulb production and save the larger ones for growing scallions.

Short-day onion varieties include some of the milder, sweeter ones like 'Bermuda'. It would seem, at first glance, that we could grow these north of their best-adapted latitude simply by planting them earlier. Then, when they start to bulb up in March or April, the plants would be big enough to make sizeable bulbs. Alas, if we plant them in fall or early winter, we run up against vernalization. In addition, these more southern varieties tend to be more frost sensitive, so to succeed, you'd pretty much have to grow them in a greenhouse until February.

One use we can make of short-day varieties is to grow pearl or boiling onions, the small ones that are used in soups and stews. (See Pearl, Boiling, and Cipollini Onion on page 243.)

When old-time farmers said of someone that they "know their onions," it was meant as a high compliment. The new day-length neutral bulb onion varieties simplify the situation quite a bit, but there is still plenty for the adventurous gardener to learn.

Pests Pearl onions are susceptible to the same pests as bulb onions.

Sources

Pearl, boiling, and cipollini onion seed:
Barletta White: GS, JG, PGS, SI
Purplette: JSS, RPF, SOC, TERR, WCS
Pompei cipollini: GS
Bianco de Maggio cipollini: BCS, GS, JSS, PGS, RPF, TERR
Borretanno cipollini: CG, GS, IST, SI, TERR
Red Marble cipollini: CG, JSS, PGS, RPF, TERR
Pacific Pearl (*A. fistulosum*): TERR

Onion, Top (or Tree, Walking, or Egyptian Onion)

Allium cepa
Proliferum Group
Amaryllis Family ❖ *Amaryllidaceae*

Top onions are perennial green onions that multiply like bunching onions, forming new plants at the base. But they also make clusters of bulblets at the top of what would otherwise be flower stems. These bulblets, which are fully formed by about the middle of July, often begin to sprout into small plants while they are still attached to the stems. These little plants sometimes even make their own sets of tiny bulblets. The heads of sprouting bulblets are often quite picturesque, with their tiers of bulblets and curving stems and leaves. The weight of the bulblets eventually pulls the stem over and the sprouting bulblets grow where they land—"walking" the onions to a new location. Like bunching onions, they offer the advantage of providing green onions for harvest much of the year with little effort.

Growing Instructions Either buy sets or plant harvested bulblets. Rather than letting the bulblets plant themselves, it is better to pick them as soon as they are fully formed, separate them, and plant them where you want them, either immediately or within a couple of weeks. Set them about 3 inches apart, or as close as 1 inch if you plan to harvest them as green onions. If you set bulblets at the bottom of a 4- to 8-inch-deep trench and fill it in as they grow, you will have green onions with very long white shafts for winter and spring harvests. The plants are undemanding, growing well in good garden soil with average water.

Top onion bulblets

The Harvest Bulblets planted in July make tender green onions in fall. The same plants that you harvested in fall are tender and very mild when they start to grow again in late winter and early spring. Clumps of plants live for many years, eventually becoming crowded and unsightly. You need to find a balance among harvesting plants to eat, leaving some plants to produce summer bulblets for the next season's green onions, and removing the oldest, least productive clumps.

Pests Top onions are susceptible to the same pests as bulb onions. Onion root maggots have never infested my top onions, but black aphids have often attacked them in winter.

Sources

Top onion sets: BUR, NGN, PGS, PS, RH, RPF, SESE, TERR, VBS

Oyster Plant (see Salsify)

Parsley, Root (or Turnip-Rooted Parsley or Hamburg Parsley)

Petroselinum crispum var. *tuberosum* (*P. hortense* var. *radicosum*)
Carrot Family ❖ *Apiaceae* (*Umbelliferae*)

Root parsley has a parsnip-shaped root that tastes very much like celeriac, and the leaves are an acceptable substitute for parsley. Since the crop tolerates part shade and thrives in cool weather, it is a good choice for our region.

Growing Instructions Start root parsley from seed, either indoors in November or December or outdoors in February or March. Try a July sowing for harvests into fall and winter, especially in very cool areas near the coast. Plant the seeds ¼ inch deep, and transplant or thin plants to stand 6 to 9 inches apart. Root parsley seeds takes several weeks to sprout. (You can use the same techniques recommended for starting carrot seeds; see page 206.) The crop grows best in loose, moisture-holding, fertile soil. Like other root crops, root parsley may make deformed roots in soil containing fresh manure or too much nitrogen fertilizer.

The Harvest Harvest a leaf or two as the plant grows, leaving most of the foliage to help the plants form large roots. The roots take about three months to mature and are most tender when they are less than 7 inches long. They can be left in the ground to be dug up during the winter. Cold weather is said to improve the flavor of root parsley, but be sure to harvest before the plants go to seed in spring.

Scrub the root well before you cook it. You may want to peel it, although it will discolor if you peel it raw. Drop it into boiling water for about five minutes, then peel it. Use root parsley in soups, stews, and salads and as a boiled vegetable.

Pests I don't know of any pests or diseases that attack root parsley in our region.

Sources
Root parsley seed: Widely available

Parsnip

Pastinaca sativa
Carrot Family ❖ *Apiaceae* (*Umbelliferae*)

Although these long white roots are not among the most commonly eaten vegetables, you may find that you're partial to them. They are tough when raw, but tender when baked or cooked in soups or stews. If you have never tried parsnip, prepare some store-bought ones first. Scrub the roots and halve them lengthwise. Add a little butter, some brown sugar, and a tablespoon of water, then cover and bake at 350°F for about 30 minutes.

Growing Instructions A member of the carrot family, parsnip has many of the same needs as carrot (see page 205). Like carrot, it thrives in all parts of our region. I have planted parsnips in February, later in spring, and again as late as August, all with good results. The crop holds well in the ground in winter. In fact, parsnip not only is frost hardy but actually gets sweeter after a frost.

Like carrot, parsnip needs a deep, fine-textured soil, and it makes inferior roots in rocky soil or poorly amended clay. Sow seeds thickly, ½ inch deep, and later thin the seedlings to 4 to 6 inches apart. Parsnip is even slower to germinate than carrot, taking 15 to 25 days. All the tricks that work to get carrot seedlings past their slow start (see page 206) will also help with parsnip. Unlike carrot, however, parsnip will endure a careful transplanting while it is still very small.

The Harvest Parsnip roots mature in three to four months, but a crop started in summer can be left to pull as needed through the winter. Pull the roots before spring growth begins, or they will become woody and the plants will go to seed.

Pests Although parsnip plants are susceptible to bean aphids and to the carrot rust fly, mine have never been attacked by either. I have had some damage from a leafminer—presumably the parsnip leafminer—but since the damage is minor, and one doesn't eat parsnip leaves, picking damaged leaves should be a sufficient control.

Sources
Parsnip seeds: Widely available

Pea

Pisum sativum
Pea Family ❖ *Fabiaceae* (*Leguminosae*)

Shelling peas grow well in our cooler months, but they aren't the best crop for a small garden because by the time you shell them out and discard the tough pods the weight of peas isn't much for the amount of space the plants take up. You may enjoy growing a few just for the pleasure of shelling the peas, but think in terms of a few to add to a risotto or curry rather than large individual servings of peas.

On the other hand, snow peas and snap peas are among the best crops for small-space gardens. Both are high-value crops, meaning you save money by growing them. And in the case of snap peas, you get more weight of harvest per plant, since you eat the thick, sweet, crunchy pods along with the peas themselves. Snap peas are one of the garden's finest treats for eating fresh off the vine. If you get them to the kitchen, use the whole pods in a fresh vegetable tray, or cut the pods up, peas and all, to use in salads or other dishes.

Like beans, peas need well-drained soil high in organic matter. Although they have the nitrogen-fixing root bacteria typical of legumes, peas will grow better if they get a little nitrogen fertilizer at planting time. (For more on the legume family, see page 183.) Also like beans, peas are available in bush and pole varieties.

Growing Instructions Peas are a cool-season legume, typically planted in November and February in near-coastal gardens. Peas planted in November will bear their delicate blossoms after the worst winter storms have passed. A February-planted crop will bloom and fruit while spring is still cool. Inland, where heavy fronts are expected, it is safer to plant peas in February or March and again in August or September. Peas planted in late spring or in summer may succeed in foggier microclimates or during cool years, but they

Peas

may stop production and die during a hot spell. Also, powdery mildew (see page 136) is more likely to strike in summer and early fall.

Peas are generally seeded in place, although they are occasionally sown indoors three to four weeks before being planted out. You may want to start them indoors to circumvent very wet weather or to escape the predation of snails. Plant all peas 1 to 2 inches deep. Sow peas two inches apart, in double rows 6 to 8 inches apart, and put supports between them. Separate double rows by a foot or so.

Put your supports in when you plant or at least by the time the peas are 3 inches tall. If you wait too long, the plants will twine on themselves and you will damage them when you try to separate them and train them to climb something else. The supports should be 3 to 4 feet high for bush peas and 6 to 8 feet high for pole peas. Since peas use tendrils to climb, they use both vertical and horizontal elements of a trellis. Well-supported hog wire or chicken wire fencing, or nylon mesh with no more than 6-inch openings, work well. (When you are constructing a frame for peas, don't be tempted, as I was one year, to construct a flimsy one of wood scraps, or the spring winds will keep you laboring at repairs.) (More on trellises on page 187.)

For bush peas, the British insert "pea sticks"—brushy prunings from trees or hedges—along the rows. It's a charming idea, but unless you have good, sturdy, very branch like trimmings that are still 3 to 4 feet long after you have inserted them a foot into the soil, you probably should construct a frame for a trellis. It is very difficult to harvest peas from plants that have fallen over and intertwined due to lack of adequate support. You will break the plants trying to do it—and still miss many of the peas.

Pea seedlings may need some help finding the mesh at first. Gently guide them, perhaps tying wayward seedlings in place.

The Harvest Peas will begin to bear in 8 to 10 weeks, or up to four months if they are growing during the winter. Their first pods will form at the bottom of the plant. Pick these as soon as they are ready, even if there are only a few. This will encourage the plant to grow and make more pods. Although bush peas are touted for small gardens, if you are looking for a good-sized crop, remember that pole pea plants will bear up to five times as much.

Harvest old-fashioned garden peas when the peas are large but not quite fully developed. You will soon learn to recognize pods whose peas are plump but not so mature that they are tough and starchy. Snow peas are at their peak of flavor, and therefore ready to be picked, when the pods are still quite flat, with only a hint of peas visible. You can harvest snap pea pods at any stage you like, but the pods are at their sweetest when the peas are fairly large.

Pea plants are easily bent or broken, so use care as you harvest the pods. Either use a pair of hand pruners or flower shears, or use both hands to pick. In the two-hand method, you steady the stem with one hand while you pluck the pod with the other.

Snow peas, garden peas, and snap peas

Young pea leaves and tendrils are edible and taste the same as the peas, so be sure to try the seedlings you thin out of the planting. Or you may like to try pea varieties sold specifically for this purpose.

Varieties Home gardeners grow three main types of peas: old-fashioned garden peas, snow peas (sugar peas), and snap peas. Garden peas must be shelled, since the inner lining of the pods is too tough to eat. (Some people peel the lining before they munch the pods, but that's an arduous task.) Most varieties of garden peas should succeed here. 'Maestro' and 'Oregon Trail' are resistant to powdery mildew. Some garden pea varieties, known as petit pois or "tiny peas," are intended to be harvested when the peas are still quite small. These are valued for French cuisine, but because they are so tiny, you will need a relatively large planting to get enough to go very far.

Snow, or sugar, peas are grown for their edible pods. 'Oregon Sugar Pod II' and 'Oregon Giant' promise powdery mildew resistance. The peas grown for edible stem tips, with their leaves and tendrils, are snow pea varieties. In Japan, pea stem tips, with leaves and tendrils, are known as *tobyo*. A Chinese name for them is *dau miao*. In both cuisines, they are served steamed or stir-fried, alone or with meat or other vegetables. They are also a delightful addition to a salad.

Snap peas revolutionized pea growing, when a breeder discovered in his 1979 trial planting a plant bearing thick, crisp, edible pods like those of a snap bean. The pods remained tender and sweet even as the peas filled out. The first variety on the market was the pole pea 'Sugar Snap', which unfortunately lacks resistance to powdery mildew. However, many of the new varieties, including the pole 'Super Sugar Snap' and most of the bush varieties, including 'Sugar Bon', Cascadia', and 'Sugar Sprint', are resistant.

A footnote to the discovery and development of snap peas is that after the snap pea became popular, researchers discovered descriptions of just such peas in gardening books from at least a century earlier. Since then, an Amish heirloom pea has been discovered with the same traits. Apparently this is an example of an heirloom variety nearly lost but rediscovered by chance during a breeding program.

Pests Slugs, snails, and other pests of seedlings love young pea plants. They are especially tempted by them in winter, when peas are among the most tender plants in the garden. Protect peas by starting them indoors, or grow them outdoors under a floating row cover until they are at least 3 to 4 inches high.

As weather turns warm, peas become susceptible to powdery mildew, which coats the leaves in a white dust. (Don't confuse it with the lacy, whitish natural markings that appear on most pea leaves.) Fight the disease by planting resistant varieties or planting nonresistant ones only during the coldest time of year. If plants do get powdery mildew, let them bear until the disease becomes debilitating, then remove the plants from the garden. Preventative sprays can slow the disease, though these may not be worth the trouble for a few plants. (See page 136.)

Control aphids that appear on pea plants; they sometimes spread viruses. Of the many possible pea viruses, one, pea enation, is common in the Northwest, and while I haven't seen it here, it is always wise to remove any plants that seem to be disfigured by a virus (more on viruses on page 139).

Sources

Pea seed: Widely available

Shelling pea seed:

Maestro: ABL, BUR, PS, TERR

Oregon Trail: NGN, SOC, WCS

Snow pea seed:

Oregon Sugar Pod II: ABL, BCS, BUR, EE, KIT, NGN, PGS, T&M, TERR, VBS

Oregon Giant: CG, EE, JSS, KIT, NGN, RG, SESE, SOC, TERR, WCS

Snow peas for edible leaves seed: EE, KIT

Snap pea seed:

Super Sugar Snap: BUR, JSS, PGS, PS, RG, TERR, VBS, WCS

Sugar Bon: BUR

Cascadia: BG, BI, CG, NGN, PGS, SESE, SOC, T&M, TERR, WCS

Sugar Sprint: CG, JSS, NGN, PS, TERR, VBS

Pepper, Sweet and Hot

Capsicum annuum var. *annuum*
Nightshade Family ❖ *Solanaceae*

These sweet or fiery delights are perennials in their native tropical America. Beyond the tropics they are grown as annuals, planted to mature in the warmest months. Occasionally they survive a very mild winter to bear during a second summer. One plant I grew even came back a third year, but by then it had become woody and set only one or two small peppers.

In cool, foggy summers, pepper plants rarely reach full size or maximum production. Pepper plants very near the coast are unlikely to set fruit at all, their blossoms falling unfertilized. In my foggy San Francisco yard, an unprotected 'Ace' pepper plant grew as large as the ones in my sunnier community garden, but not a single blossom set fruit. Night temperatures under 60°F inhibit fruit set. Harvests will be larger in gardens with warmer summer temperatures, day and night. However, days over 90°F will also reduce fruit set. You can improve your chances in cooler microclimates by choosing varieties carefully and using aids to warm the soil and the plants.

Growing Instructions Because this region's climate is marginal for peppers, we need to pay special attention to the needs of this crop. They require a moderately fertile soil, so use a complete fertilizer at planting time. Supplement with a high-nitrogen fertilizer when the blossoms open. Water pepper plants adequately, because water stress will cause blossoms and developing fruit to drop. Since pepper roots extend 4 feet or more into the soil, water deeply. Don't keep the soil soggy, however, as this will also reduce fruit set and may encourage root rot. Maintaining the right moisture level will be easier if the soil contains plenty of organic matter.

Since peppers are susceptible to cold, they are usually seeded indoors to give them an earlier start. Many local gardeners grow their own seedlings, since nurseries may not carry the varieties best suited to this climate.

The ideal temperature range for pepper seed germination is 70° to 85°F. The plants grow best when daytime temperatures are in the low eighties and night temperatures are above 55°F. Try to give peppers the warmth they need while they are indoors, since they will have to contend with less favorable conditions soon enough. The minimum time required to grow pepper seedlings indoors is six to eight weeks. ("Days to harvest" for peppers does not include the time it takes to grow seedlings.) Some gardeners keep them indoors longer to get a bigger head start. You can start seeds as early as January, but you must be sure to give the plants enough light and fertilizer and move them to larger pots before their roots become crowded. If you can't meet these needs, you are better off with younger but healthier seedlings.

Wait until the weather is quite warm before you move transplants into the garden, since pepper plants may become stunted by cold. Temperatures hovering around 45°F, common on April nights in much of this region, can cause temporary shock. The nights are usually warmer by May. Still, the plants won't reach full size in most areas, since temperatures under 55°F (possible any night of the summer) will slow their growth.

Set the plants 12 to 15 inches apart. A protective covering will help peppers brave the hostile elements. In early spring try setting plants in a Wall O' Water, or use a floating row cover to hold in heat and cut down on wind. Black plastic mulch will help warm the soil. If you combine black plastic with a floating row cover, be sure to extend the row cover beyond the edges of the plastic sheeting, so that both can be tucked into the soil to keep pests out. Later, try a clear plastic minigreenhouse (see page 33) to protect the maturing plants from wind and cold.

The Harvest The first peppers may be big enough to pick sometime in July or August, but they may not even set until the warmer weather of late

The Nightshade Family

The nightshade family, the *Solanaceae*, includes four well-known crops—tomatoes, potatoes, peppers, and eggplants—as well as a few lesser-known ones, like tomatillo and ground tomato. All of the ones listed in this book are tropical perennials, all except eggplant native to tropical Central and South America. Species and varieties of species that are more cool-tolerant are probably related to ancestors that grew at higher altitudes, where the climate is cooler.

Potatoes are the most cool-tolerant of the group, growing best at 59° to 63°F. They can be planted from February through late summer in all of our region. Tomatoes, peppers and eggplants need progressively more heat. The most cool-tolerant varieties of tomatoes can succeed in much of the region, including protected areas near the coast. Even cool-tolerant varieties of pepper, however, need greater warmth than near-coastal gardens can generally offer for best production, and eggplants may be a disappointment except in the warmest microclimates and the warmest summers.

If night temperatures are too cool, nightshade crops will drop blossoms unfertilized. This is not a problem with potatoes, since we are after the tubers instead of the fruit, but it does limit our ability to grow tomatoes, peppers, and eggplants.

Tomatoes, peppers, and eggplants are grown from transplants to give them an early start in a protected environment. As with cabbage family crops, the "days to maturity" rating on seed packets doesn't count the approximately six weeks to transplant size. Seedlings mustn't be set out too early, either, since cool weather will stunt them. Still, many gardeners do set tomatoes out early in hopes of getting early growth. If the spring is unusually warm, or if you use protective coverings to raise the temperature around the plants, you may get a jump on the season. But if it's too cool, your early plantings may end up no bigger—or even smaller—than later planted ones. Peppers are more likely to stunt in cool weather, and eggplants even more so.

We may chuckle to remember that many people once believed that the tomato was poisonous, but do keep in mind that, except for the parts generally eaten, the rest of potato, tomato, eggplant, and pepper plants do contain toxins. Never eat any part of a plant from this family but the one you *know* is edible.

Solanaceous crops share the same pests, although the bugs that will eat these crops don't seem to be serious pests, at least in the cooler parts of the region. One disease, tobacco mosaic virus, can be spread by cigarette smokers if they do not wash their hands after smoking and before working in the garden. Another, tomato or potato late blight, has become a serious pest, spreading to all the nightshade family crops through airborne spores (see page 135).

summer in foggier locations. Plants may continue to bear through November if there are no heavy rains.

Pick sweet peppers as soon as they stop enlarging, which may happen before they reach the size promised in the seed catalog. You may have as few as three or four peppers per plant, although up to fifteen peppers are possible in favorable conditions. Cut the peppers with scissors or hand pruners to avoid damaging the plant.

All peppers start out green. Left alone, they mature into red or yellow peppers. (Some turn purple before they turn red.) Although red and yellow peppers are very pretty and have more vitamins than green peppers, the ripening process keeps the plant from setting new fruit—and peppers ripen very slowly in our cool climate. If peppers are marginal in your microclimate, it is wiser to aim for a good-sized crop of green peppers instead of trying to grow types that, given enough time, may ripen to exotic colors.

Hot peppers are picked green or red, depending on the variety. Green hot peppers are used fresh. Hot peppers picked red can be used fresh, or they can be dried and kept for later use.

Varieties and Related Species The colorful photos in seed catalogs make you want to grow every pepper variety they sell, but if you are in a cooler microclimate, careful selection will be necessary for success. Look for early varieties (60 to 70 days from transplanting) and high productivity.

Among full-sized bells, 'California Wonder' is early (65 days) and reasonably adapted to cool growing conditions. You can expect 4 to 5 fruits per plant if it is able to set fruit. 'Ace F_1' or 'New Ace F_1' (50 to 60 days to green fruit) is reputed to resist blossom drop in adverse (cool) weather.

In both sunny and foggy San Francisco gardens, I have found that 'Gypsy F_1' (60 to 70 days) will produce at least some fruits. They are yellow-green and smaller than standard bells, but still good eating. Another that is at least as likely to bear—and, if it does, may have more fruits—is 'Sweet Banana' (about 70 days), an elongated yellow Hungarian-type pepper. Both ripen to red.

Another idea, akin to the "cherry tomato strategy" is to grow pepper varieties that produce many small fruits. This gives the plant more chances to have flowers ready for pollen on rare nights that are warm enough to allow pollination. There are a number of early (55 to 65 days) "minibell" offerings you might try, including some that ripen to mixed colors. They would be ideal for stuffing as hors d'oeuvres (see page 271).

Many hot peppers require long, warm seasons to bear well, but a few are early. I've grown jalapeños successfully in a sunny neighborhood in San Francisco. Try 'Early Jalapeño' (60 to 70 days) if you like really hot ones, or one of the milder hybrids, such as 'Señorita F_1' (60 days) or 'Dulce F_1' (65 days). Two jalapeño-type peppers are quite tame: 'False Alarm F_1' (62 days) has little heat, and 'Fooled You F_1' (62 days) has none at all. For small, round, hot peppers that ripen to red, consider 'Cherry Bomb F_1' (65 days) or 'Big Bomb F_1' (62 to 67 days). A traditional variety, 'Hungarian Hot Wax' (58 to 70 days) produces mildly hot, long yellow peppers up to 6 inches long. I have also succeeded with tiny Thai peppers in a sunny San Francisco garden, maybe due to the cherry tomato strategy. (Note that all days to harvest are for peppers at full size but still green, or yellow. Peppers take about 20 days longer to ripen, probably more where temperatures are low.)

You might also like to try the perennial Rocato pepper (*Capsicum pubescens*). Its origin in the mountains of Bolivia and Peru prepared it to thrive in cooler microclimates. It becomes a 4-foot-high shrub with small purple blossoms, then apple-shaped fruits (1¾ by 1¼ inches) that start green and ripen to red or yellow. A distinguishing feature is its black seeds, unlike those of *Capsicum annuum*, which are white. Rocato fruits are very hot when ripe, slightly less so when green. Plants are damaged at 30°F. In spring, remove damaged branches and cut plants back by one third.

Pests Peppers don't suffer much from diseases or other pests. About 70 percent of the varieties on the market are resistant to the most common pepper diseases. However, they can get and spread tomato late blight. (See page 135.) If any of your plants seem discolored or misshapen from disease, remove them from the garden. Smokers should wash their hands well before handling pepper plants, since peppers can fall prey to tobacco mosaic virus.

Pepper plants are susceptible to attack by aphids and several caterpillars, including cabbage loopers and corn earworms. However, pepper is rarely the first crop these insects will attack.

Sources

Sweet pepper seed:

California Wonder: Widely available

Ace F_1 or New Ace F_1: JSS, PGS, TT, VBS

Gypsy F_1: BUR, NGN, T&M, TERR, TGS, TT, WCS

Sweet Banana: BUR, NGN, PS, SESE, TGS, TT

Minibell (single or mixed): Widely available

Hot pepper seed:

Early Jalapeño: Widely available

Senorita Jalapeño F_1: NGN, TERR, TGS

Dulce Jalapeño F_1: JSS
Senorita Jalapeño F_1: NGN, TERR, TGS
False Alarm F_1 Jalapeño: BUR
Fooled You F_1 Jalapeño: NGN, PGS, TGS, TT
Cherry Bomb F_1: JSS, TGS, TT
Big Bomb F_1: TERR, TGS, TT
Hungarian Hot Wax: Widely available
Rocato pepper seed: RCS, SSE, TGS, TT
Rocato pepper plants: AA

Potato

Solanum tuberosum
Nightshade Family ❖ *Solanaceae*

You may have read that potatoes aren't a good choice for a small garden because they take up a lot of space, and anyhow they don't cost much to buy. But I think they are a splendid choice: I enjoy growing unusual varieties, I like eating them fresh from the garden, and digging potatoes is one of the highlights of vegetable gardening. Moreover, fresh high-quality potatoes, especially unusual types, are no longer cheap items.

Native to the Andean highlands and the cool Chilean coast, potatoes do well throughout this region. They thrive in the humid air and produce tubers best in cool weather—59° to 63°F is ideal. They prefer sandy soil, but they will grow in clay soil and actually help loosen it.

Growing Instructions Potatoes are traditionally grown from pieces of tuber that have at least one bud, or eye. You can buy these pieces, known as sets, precut, or you can purchase whole seed potatoes and prepare the sets yourself. Leave one to three eyes on each piece. Let the sets cure in a warm, humid place for a couple of days, so that their cut sides will harden a bit before you plant them.

You can also grow potatoes from small whole tubers, 2 to 3 inches in diameter. This is a common practice in England, and it often produces a greater yield than cut sets do. Most of the "seed potatoes" on the market are now these small whole tubers. You can buy them or set them aside from your harvest. (But if you save your own, don't save the very smallest ones; egg-sized tubers will make a better crop.) Buy certified disease-free potatoes at local nurseries or through mail-order catalogs. If you plant potatoes from the store, you take the risk that they may be diseased and that the disease might spread through your soil.

Potato plants are capable of blooming and setting true seed in little round (poisonous) fruits. It is much easier to grow them from whole tubers or pieces, but potato breeders saw reasons to develop a variety that made enough seed to sell, and you can now buy these and try your hand at them. If you buy true seed, it will come with instructions. In general, it must be started indoors, timing is important, and the seedlings are slow and delicate. Mine did grow up and produce potatoes, but for most home gardeners, I think they are more novelty than practical choice. In the international seed market, they are more practical than tubers, because they are far less expensive than tubers to ship and are definitely disease-free. In addition, while the tubers will remain viable for only a year, seeds can be stored longer.

Potatoes will grow the year around in our region, producing a crop in a little over three months, so several plantings are possible. Many gardeners plant spring potatoes on March 17, an easy date to remember given the historical link between the Irish and the potato, but the soil is often dry enough to plant a month earlier. If you plant in February, May, and August you will have three harvests a year. (Of course, plantings are also possible anytime between February and August.) Potatoes planted after September 1 will still be growing in December and January, when frost is possible. Ever since I lost a winter crop to a light December frost I have not made large plantings later than August, but it is fun to try to sneak a few potatoes past the winter. You can always cover them if frost threatens. (Seed potatoes aren't available for sale all year round, but you can save and plant your own.)

Gardeners often wonder about the wisdom of planting sprouting potatoes. If the sprouting potato is one you bought for food, the answer is not to plant it, because it is not certified disease-free for planting. However, some gardeners purposely let short sprouts

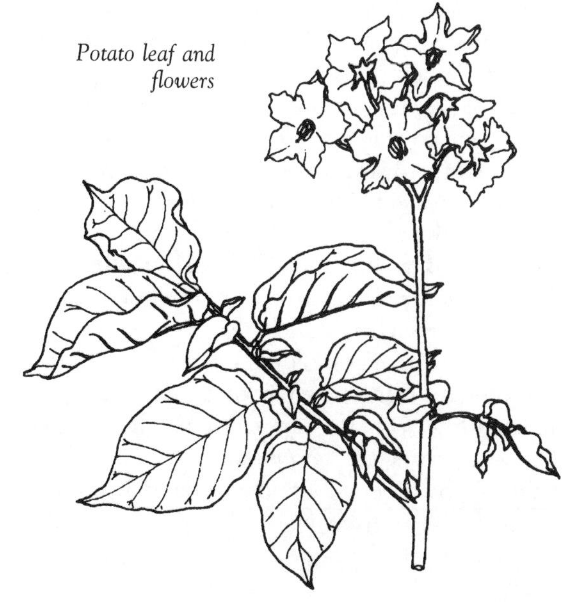

Potato leaf and flowers

Potato Towers

You can grow more potatoes in a small space by planting them vertically in a tower of wire mesh. The potatoes will form in the tower, and you can harvest them simply by removing the tower.

To build a wire-mesh tower, construct a ring of fencing that is 3 to 4 feet high and 1½ to 2 feet in diameter. It should have openings at least 1 by 1 inch. Lay four or five potato sets on the soil surface 4 inches from the mesh frame. Add 10 to 12 inches of compost or compost-rich soil, then four to five more sets. Repeat until you get to the top of the mesh. The top layer of potatoes should be at least 4 inches below the top surface of the compost. The plants will grow out the sides of the mesh. This tower works best in late spring and early summer, when the sun is high in the sky and the north side of the tower gets some sun.

form on their sets before planting them. This is OK, though mine always sprout fine without this extra help. If the sprouts get long and spindly, they will tend to break off during planting. Also, because the plant needs energy to make the maximum number of buds for new tubers in the first few weeks after sprouting, you really want it in the ground, with access to water and nutrients during this period.

Potatoes will make the best growth in highly organic, moderately fertile soil. Dig in a few inches of aged manure or compost and some fertilizer that provides more phosphorous and potassium than nitrogen. (For more on fertilizing, see page 81.) Plant sets cut side down and 10 to 12 inches apart. You can bury sets or whole small tubers 4 inches under the level surface of the soil. However, there is much to be said for the practice of hilling potatoes—burying them deeper as they grow. Since tubers form only between the original set and the soil surface, hilling encourages more to form. A standard method is to dig a trench 8 inches deep and plant the potatoes at the bottom. Then fill in 4 inches of soil or compost. When the potato shoots have been up for a week or so, fill more soil or compost around them. It's all right to bury a few leaves, since the plants will just keep on growing, but leave a little of the greenery above the soil. After about three weeks, pull soil up around the plants or add compost, burying part of the stem and making a mound. You can also cover the mounded surface with a thick layer of straw or other loose mulch.

However you grow potatoes, be sure to watch for exposed tubers and cover them with soil or mulch. Otherwise, the exposed skin will turn green. The green parts of potato plants, including any green on the tubers, contain a moderately poisonous substance called solanine.

The Harvest Potatoes are ready to harvest beginning two weeks after the plant blooms, typically about three months after planting. But often potato plants don't bloom. If you don't see the white or purple flowers or at least the small branched flower stalks at the tops of the plants, the next hint that harvest time is near is yellowing of the leaves despite regular watering. As soon as the plant blooms or begins to turn yellow, cut back on watering. You can dig potatoes from the time about 20 percent of the plant is yellow to the time it has completely died down. Don't leave plants unharvested long after that, since the tubers may decay.

Dig your potatoes on a day when the soil is relatively dry, so it won't stick to the potatoes. Use a digging fork if you have one. Insert your fork or shovel well back from the plant stem and dig straight down so that you won't cut across the tubers. You will find large and small tubers, which you can sort later to use for different purposes. If you plan to eat the tubers within a few days, just wash them well and store them in the produce section of your refrigerator. If you want to store them longer, leave the unwashed tubers outdoors for a while if it's warm. Otherwise, put them in a warm, dry room for a few hours. Then brush off most of the dirt and store the tubers in a dark, dry, cool (about 60°F) place for two weeks. After this curing period, move them to a dark, humid, cooler (40°F) spot with good air circulation. Most of us don't have an ideal potato storage location. Our basements are usually warmer, and refrigerators lack circulation. Still, potatoes will keep pretty well for at least a few weeks in either of these places.

Be very careful not to leave harvested potatoes in the light for more than a day, or the skins will begin to turn green. If this happens, peel away the green part. The rest of the potato is safe to eat.

Tibetan Hot Potato Curry

Potatoes, tomatoes, and bell peppers from the Americas were carried across Europe and Asia, into the mountainous lands of Tibet. One result is this delicious curried potato dish, which I've adapted from the book Food in Tibetan Life, *by Rinjing Dorje. Serves four.*

- 4 medium potatoes (boiling varieties are best)
- ½ cup chopped tomatoes (or Quick Homemade Tomato Sauce, page 365)
- 1 or 2 cloves garlic, minced
- 1 teaspoon freshly grated ginger
- ¼ teaspoon turmeric
- Salt to taste
- 1 medium shallot, chopped (or 2 tablespoons minced onion)
- 2 tablespoons olive or vegetable oil
- ½ teaspoon fenugreek seeds
- ½ cup thinly sliced bell pepper

Steam the potatoes for 15 minutes, then dice them into bite-sized pieces. Put the tomatoes, garlic, ginger, turmeric, salt, and shallot in a blender and purée to create a sauce. Heat the oil in a skillet and brown the fenugreek seeds, being careful not to burn them. Add the mixture from the blender, stir well, and cook over high heat for 1 minute. Pour the mixture over the potatoes and mix gently until well blended. Garnish with the slices of bell pepper.

If you plan to save your own seed potatoes for cutting into sets or planting whole, dig up the tubers when the plants are only partly yellowed or have just died down. Tubers left in the ground long after the plant has died won't be as vigorous. Choose tubers that weren't injured in digging—either large tubers for cutting into sets or 2- to 3-inch tubers for planting whole. Do not save any that show signs of disease or were harvested from plants that had a disease. Don't save the smallest tubers either. You may as well eat them, since they won't make a very big crop if you plant them.

Don't replant homegrown sets right away; they usually need a couple of months of rest before they will sprout. Store them in a plastic bag in the refrigerator. Insert a note with them and in your calendar to remind yourself when they were harvested and when to plant them.

Potato plants will also grow from tubers you missed while harvesting. These will sprout in spring and summer, having rested underground. When you see a potato growing, you have the choice of discarding it, letting it grow, or moving it to a different location. If you move it, dig carefully with a trowel to get the tuber as well as the shoot and root. Although these volunteers often grow from very small tubers and may not produce prolifically, I have enjoyed many meals from such plants growing in out-of-the-way corners of my garden.

Varieties Potatoes are such fun to grow that I encourage you to try different varieties. The sets at your local nursery will probably be cheaper than those ordered by mail. Most nurseries carry old standard varieties, which may be sold by name or by color. 'Irish Cobbler' or 'White Cobbler', introduced to this country in the 1870s, is an early maturing, brown-skinned potato that is delicious baked or boiled. 'Kennebec' yields brown-skinned potatoes a little later, which are good for all uses. The oval, red-skinned 'Red Pontiac' is easy, early, and very flavorful. 'Bison' is a round, red treasure that is early and delicious.

Potato varieties with less familiar shapes and colors are becoming increasingly available. 'All Blue'—blue outside and inside—is great baked or boiled. 'Yukon Gold' and 'Yellow Finn' are yellow inside and out. 'Yukon Gold' is early, and great for french fries. 'Yellow Finn', which matures a bit later, makes wonderful mashed potatoes. Fingerling potatoes, such as 'Russian Banana', are long and skinny. You can steam them and serve them whole, or cut them into round chunks for potato salad or soup. There are many others for you to try. Some are more productive than others or better for certain uses than others. Read the descriptions and try out a few. Of the sources listed, all carry at least one brown, yellow, red, blue, and a fingerling.

Late blight of tomato and potato can dash your potato-growing plans, so read up on it (see page 135) and use preventive techniques. There are no fully late blight–resistant potato varieties currently available for home gardeners, but 'Kennebec' and 'Russian Banana' are said to show some resistance.

Pests Scab is a fungus disease that causes rough scabs on the surface of the tubers. Although unsightly, they are just surface blemishes that can be peeled off. Commercial growers keep the soil pH between 4.8 and 5.4 to prevent this disease, but lowering the pH for just one crop is awkward in a small garden. Besides, potatoes grow best in pH 6 to 6.5—so if you haven't encountered scab or have only an occasional spot of it, no heroic acidifying effort is necessary. Reduce the chance of scab by starting with certified disease-free seed potatoes, planting in fertile soil, and watering well until the plants bloom.

Early and late blight are two fungus diseases that can cause plants to collapse before they mature and can make the tubers inedible. They are spread through diseased tubers, so the first defense is to buy certified disease-free tubers. Another precaution against both diseases is to avoid overhead watering. Late blight, described on page 135, has been very prevalent in regional gardens in recent years.

We are fortunate to live in an area unaffected by the Colorado potato beetle, a common pest in most of the country. Slugs and snails—and sometimes earwigs—nibble on potato leaves, but they rarely destroy an entire planting. Wireworms may damage tubers.

Sources

Potato sets:
- 1–5 varieties: CG, WCS
- 6–10 varieties: ABL, BUR, JSS, SESE, TERR
- 11–20 varieties: PGS, SOC, SSE, VBS
- 50+ varieties: RPF
- Kennebec potato sets: BUR, JSS, PGS, RPF, VBS
- Russian Banana potato sets: ABL, JSS, PGS, RPF, SOC, TERR

True potato seed (Catalina variety): NGN, TERR

Pumpkin (see Squash, Winter and Pumpkin)

Quinoa

Chenopodium quinoa
Goosefoot Family ❖ *Chenopodiaceae*

This South American traditional staple grain resembles amaranth but is in a different plant family, which it shares with spinach and beets. Its Andean mountain origin gives it the ability to thrive where nights are cool; in fact, the best seed set is where nights are below 60°F and days below 90°F. The small seeds are high in protein with a good amino acid balance and have a low glycemic index, making quinoa ideal for diabetics or those at risk for diabetes.

Growing Instructions Quinoa will be taller and more productive in well-fertilized soil. Sow the seeds in April or May, when the soil has warmed. Make a finely prepared seedbed, since the seeds are very small, and plant no deeper than ¼ inch. Thin, eventually to 6 to 18 inches. Keep weeds under good control. Plants grow slowly at first, then, after they are a foot high, they grow faster. Water regularly, but a bit less than other crops once the plant's growing well, as they are somewhat drought tolerant. Late in the season, if frost is expected, let the soil dry. Mature plants are 2 to 6 feet tall depending on variety and conditions.

The Harvest Leaves of young plants pulled to thin quinoa can be used in salad. Older leaves can be eaten cooked. You can expect to harvest 1 to 6 ounces of grain per plant. When the grain is ready to harvest, the leaves will have fallen from the plant. Use a gloved hand to strip the seed heads from the stalks. (Rain can cause mature seeds to germinate in the heads. They are likely to be harvested before autumn rains begin, but if rain threatens, you can still harvest the seeds if they are firm enough that your thumbnail will barely indent but not easily puncture them.)

Clean seeds as you would amaranth, by forcing them through screens or by winnowing out the chaff with a fan. Spread the seed in trays and dry it well in a warm place before you store it in a closed container, or it may mold.

Quinoa seeds are covered with a bitter material called saponin. It has been rinsed off of the quinoa sold in stores, and it is best if you rinse it off before you eat the grain you grow. This can be done in a blender on the lowest speed, changing water about five times, or until it is no longer soapy or frothy. Another method is to put some grain in a loosely woven muslin bag or a pillowcase and run it through the cold water cycle of a washing machine. You may be able to get away without following this step if you are mixing only small amounts of quinoa grains into other grains or beans. (See Amaranth for a similar grain crop you may want to grow.)

Varieties and Related Species Part of the pleasure of growing quinoa is the brilliant colors of its flowerheads, which may be yellow, orange, purple, or red. Try different varieties and compare flavor of the seeds. The Seeds of Change catalog reports that the lighter the quinoa seed, the less bitter the saponin coating. 'Temuco' is "a particularly white and delicious" variety, but darker seed can also taste good if it has been rinsed well.

For other Chenopodium species used in cooking, see pages 156 and 300.

Sources

Quinoa seed: ABL, BG, JLH, SOC

Radish

Raphanus sativus

Mustard Family ❖ *Brassicaceae (Cruciferae)*

Wild ancestors of the radish abounded from Europe through Asia, and domesticated versions were developed on both continents. Most American gardeners grow the small-rooted types, but in Europe and Asia the large-rooted varieties are also popular. All offer a crisp, peppery treat, and as a gardener you can explore the many colors and shapes available.

Growing Instructions Radish seeds can be planted almost anytime, except during very wet periods or prolonged hot periods. Radishes appreciate organic soil, but they will make poor roots if the soil is too rich in nitrogen. They can take some shade in the sunniest sites. In foggier sites or during dimmer times of year, plant radishes in full sun.

Radishes are always direct-seeded in the garden. Sow the seeds thinly and ½ inch deep. To ensure room for the rapidly developing roots, thin the seedlings early to 1 inch apart for small radishes or to the diameter of a mature root for large-rooted varieties. (The thinnings are tasty in a salad or omelet.) Provide plenty of water for mild, juicy roots. During periods of high temperatures, radish plants form flower stems. If this happens, pull and compost the plants, since their roots will no longer be succulent.

Small-rooted radishes are ready a month or less from the day of seeding. The larger radishes need 40 to 70 days to mature. Many of the larger types are best planted in mid- to late summer to mature into fall and winter—in fact, they are commonly called winter radishes. A few of the large-rooted varieties are also suited to spring planting.

Radishes become tough and woody if they are allowed to stand too long. For a steady supply of the quick-growing, small-rooted types, make successive plantings every two weeks. Larger radishes can be harvested for a longer time from a single sowing, since they keep better in the soil. Still, be careful not to overplant, since a single large-rooted radish can equal or exceed the size of three grocery-store bunches of the little ones.

Varieties Almost any radish variety will succeed in our climate, though some are more vigorous or more interesting to grow. Read the catalog descriptions if you are looking for one that is particularly mild or peppery. Besides the familiar small, round red types, you will find the French breakfast types, which are slightly elongated and two-tone—red at the top, white at the bottom. You will also find small white radishes, including round ones and the 5-inch-long 'Icicle'. Newly available are small, round varieties of a delicate pale yellow. For a novelty, you can grow 'Easter Egg', a mixture of small round roots in red, white, lavender, and purple.

Large-rooted types for summer planting vary from 2-foot-long slender roots to short round ones up to 7 inches in diameter. Most large radish varieties are best planted in late summer to mature into fall, but some can be spring sown as well. Check descriptions.

In the grocery stores you may see the long white radishes that the Japanese call daikon. Shredded raw daikon is a traditional accompaniment to sashimi, and the root is pickled whole to make pungent yellow takuan, which is used as a condiment for rice. In addition to daikon and other large all-white varieties are radishes of other colors. 'Round Black' and 'Black Spanish Long' have white flesh with matte black skin. 'Misato Rose', which is also known as 'Red Meat' or 'Watermelon', is white or pale green with bright pink flesh. The skin color is deep enough to give the cut root the appearance of a watermelon with pale "rind."

Asian cuisine includes radish leaves, and you will find varieties especially for this purpose.

Podding radish (*R. sativum* 'Caudatus'), sometimes called rat tail radish, doesn't produce thickened roots. Instead, it is grown for its young seed pods, which reach 9 inches long and can be eaten raw or used in a stir-fry. They taste much like a radish root, wonderfully sharp and crisp. All radishes, including wild radish (see page 162), produce edible pods, but no others approach the dimensions of the podding radish.

Pests Radishes often get cabbage maggots, which burrow into the roots, making them unappetizing. Radishes growing in fall and before the end of March are likely to escape damage, as the adult fly is inactive in this period. (For more on this pest, see page 115.) One note here: I tried a floating row cover frame over radishes to try to avoid this pest, but in spring and summer, when the pest is active, it made the air too warm around the radishes, so they didn't form good roots.

Sources

Radish seed (small roots):
French Breakfast seed: Widely available
Round yellow variety seed: ABL, BCS, PGS, SI, SSE, T&M, TERR
Easter Egg II seed: BUR, JSS, NGN, PGS, RG, TERR, TT, VBS, WCS
White Icicle seed: Widely available
Radish seed (large roots):
Black Spanish Long seed: BCS, GS, NGN, WCS
Round Black seed: Widely available
Daikon (long white) seed: Widely available
Red Meat seed: Widely available
Rat Tail (for pods) seed: BCS, BG, JLH, NGN, SSE, T&M
Radish for leaves: EE, JSS, KIT

Rhubarb

Rheum rhabarbarum
Knotweed Family ❖ *Polygonaceae*

This perennial vegetable is a large plant with a small but enthusiastic following. Its long red stems are very tart, but they are used as a fruit, cooked with sugar, often in a pie. I don't grow it myself, because it bothers me to have to pour so much sugar into anything. If rhubarb pie is one of your favorites, however, you will be glad to know that we can grow rhubarb here.

A native of Siberia, rhubarb needs colder winters than ours to make the thickest stems. But narrow stems are still tasty, and it is such a big plant that even a few narrow stems constitute a sizeable harvest. You may also find that stems are paler here, since winter chill is needed for good red color.

Rhubarb

Growing Instructions Rhubarb can be grown from seed, but if you want only a plant or two, it is wiser to plant dormant roots or plant divisions known as "crowns," either of which are available in local nurseries in fall or spring. Pick a cold, unprotected planting site. Rhubarb won't mind cold or shade in winter or cool days in summer. One plant is probably enough, and it will take up 3 or 4 square feet. As with other perennials, prepare the site well, mixing plenty of compost or aged manure deep into the soil. Plant so that the top of the dormant root lies 1 to 2 inches below the surface, or set a container plant at the same level it was growing in the container. It may go dormant in periods when days are above 90°F but will probably grow back again when weather is favorable. Water less if the plant is dormant.

Each fall fertilize with manure. This will allow the plant to grow in the same spot without being divided for 5 to 10 years. If it becomes too big to survive on the available nutrients in the site, rhubarb will produce big stalks of white flowers. Remove these as soon as they form and plan to fertilize well or divide the plant in the fall. To divide rhubarb, you can dig the whole plant, separate it into two or more pieces, and replant the pieces—but you will have to wait two or three years for each to return to full production. To avoid the wait, use a shovel to detach and remove one or more rosettes of leaves with roots attached. This lets the parent plant continue producing while you wait for the new plants to get started.

The Harvest Like asparagus, rhubarb is harvested only in spring, when it begins to grow again after winter dieback. (In our mild climate rhubarb plants don't die back completely, and the first flush of spring growth suitable for harvest is likely to occur in late winter.) Then it is allowed to replenish its energy during the rest of the year. Harvest not at all the first year and for only two weeks the second year. After that you may take stems for two months every spring. Gently pull or twist the largest stems. Never yank so hard that you injure the crown, and never cut rhubarb, because the stub may rot. Harvest when the stems are at their prime—just after the leaves open up and before they are completely flat. Remember that rhubarb leaves and roots contain poisonous amounts of oxalic acid. Eat only the leaf stems, making sure that no trace of green leaf blade remains.

Varieties Local nurseries carry varieties suited to our region. 'Red Cherry' and 'Giant Cherry' have a low-chill requirement, important in our mild region. Or try 'Strawberry', another variety that has done well here.

Sources

Rhubarb roots or plants: NGN

Rutabaga

Brassica napus
Napobrassica Group
Mustard Family ❖ *Cruciferae*

Rutabaga is a starchy root, a winter vegetable of the sort that you butter and mash. It is much like turnip in flavor and texture, but sweeter. The plants produce a lot of calories for the amount of garden space they use. My father never forgot a field of rutabagas he grew with his Uncle Ervin and shared with the extended family during the Great Depression of the 1930s. Although rutabaga can be grown here, it is one of those crops that would be improved by a little colder weather in late fall.

Growing Instructions Give rutabagas soil that is organic, holds moisture well, and is not too high in nitrogen. Sow the seeds ¼ to ½ inch deep, and thin the seedlings to stand 6 to 8 inches apart. Sow in early spring, or wait until mid- to late summer so that the roots will mature in cool fall weather. If rutabaga is planted too late in summer, the roots won't attain full size before winter cold slows their growth.

The Harvest Rutabagas are ready to dig about three months after you plant the seeds, when the roots are 3 to 5 inches in diameter. They hold in the soil over the winter, but they will go to seed in late winter or early spring.

Pests Although rutabaga can succumb to the same pests as other mustard-family plants, it is not affected as often.

Sources
Rutabaga seeds: Widely available

Salsify, Common (or Oyster Plant)
Tragopogon porrifolius

Salsify, Black
Scorzonera hispanica

Salsify, Spanish Oyster Plant
Scolymus hispanicus
Sunflower Family ❖ *Asteraceae* (*Compositae*)

These three plant species, all known as salsify or oyster plant, belong to the sunflower family. They are grown for long, mild-flavored roots that can be harvested into winter. The name oyster plant derives from the flavor of the steamed or sautéed roots, which many people find reminiscent of oysters.

Growing Instructions Since salsify does best when the temperature is between 55° and 75°F during most of its growing period, it is a good crop for the cool-summer parts of the region, where it can be planted with assurance from February through July. In hot-summer climates, plant it in early spring and late summer. An August planting may also succeed.

Although it differs botanically from carrot and parsnip, salsify is just as slow to get started and has similar cultural needs. It needs the same loose, deep, rich soil; rocks and fresh manure will cause it to fork. Sow the seeds 1 inch deep and 2 inches apart. Thin to 4 inches apart, or 3 inches if the soil is very loose and rich. Salsify seeds may germinate in as few as seven days, or they may take as long as twenty. The seedlings grow slowly at first and have linear leaves that can be mistaken for young grass. Like carrot, salsify makes poor roots if it is transplanted. Black salsify and Spanish oyster plant have growing needs much like those of salsify.

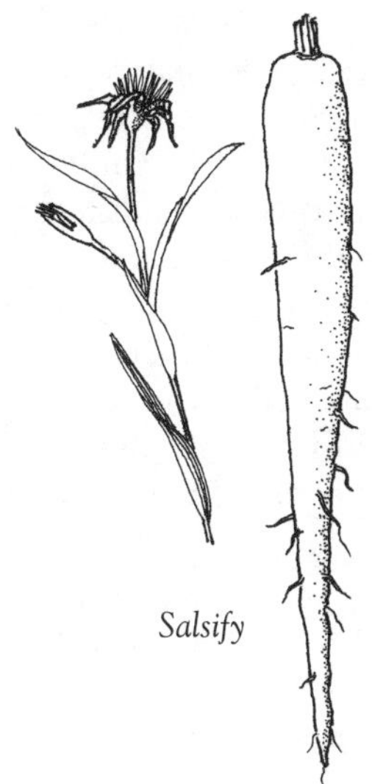
Salsify

The Harvest Salsify, black salsify, and Spanish oyster plant roots mature in four to five months. In cold-winter areas they are harvested after a few light fall frosts. In this region you can pull salsify whenever it is 1½ inches in diameter at the shoulder. If your roots aren't that large in four or five months, you may have planted too late in the year, or perhaps you didn't supply enough nutrients or water. The root of salsify is brown; black salsify is dark brown; and Spanish oyster plant has white roots.

Dig the roots of these crops the day you plan to prepare them, using a digging fork to avoid damage. It used to be thought you should boil them 7 to 15 minutes and then rub off the skin, but you can also peel them raw and drop the pieces into acidulated water (water to which you have added a little lemon juice) to keep them from discoloring. The roots can be served steamed, sautéed, or in soup or casseroles, avoiding recipes with strong flavors that will overwhelm the delicate flavor of the roots.

Salsify blooms if the roots aren't dug up by March or April. I often leave one or two plants intact so I can enjoy the flowers and seed heads. The pretty lavender flowers of common salsify are the domesticated version of the wildflower goatsbeard. They are followed by 4-inch dandelionlike heads of pale brown winged seeds. You can collect the seeds to grow the following year or let them fall to the ground. Some of the fallen seeds will germinate in spring, producing a free crop for gardeners who welcome such bits of serendipity.

Varieties and Related Species Of the three crops, salsify is most commonly grown and its seed the most commonly available. If you like salsify, you will probably like black salsify—which is often sold as scorzonera—even better, as it has more flavor. It's a perennial, so it will live for several years, but in practice it is best to eat the root during the first year, when it is most tender. Flowers of scorzonera are yellow. Spanish oyster plant, by all accounts, is the least desirable of the three, having prickly leaves and a mild, or some say insipid, flavor. It's a biennial with yellow flowers. I have not been able to find a source of seeds for Spanish oyster plant. But with so many imports appearing in seed catalogs, it may turn up one day soon.

Sources
Salsify seed: BCS, GS, IST, JG, JSS, NGN, SESE, SI, T&M
Black Salsify seed: BCS, BG, GS, IST, JSS, NGN, SI, T&M

Sea Kale

Crambe maritima
Mustard Family ❖ *Brassicaceae* (*Cruciferae*)

A native of the sea cliffs and beaches on the English, Irish, and European coasts, sea kale is a large perennial plant with bluish green leaves and small white flowers. Before the plant was domesticated, people ate the wild spring shoots. In the eighteenth century they began to grow it in gardens, blanching the shoots to make them milder and more tender. Once a popular crop, it is now rarely grown.

Growing Instructions Sea kale is well suited to ocean-influenced microclimates, although it appreciates a sunny site. Sow seeds 1 inch deep in early spring in a temporary bed of good garden soil. When the seedlings are well up, thin them to 6 inches apart. The following spring move the plants to a permanent bed, spacing them 2 to 3 feet apart.

The Harvest Begin to harvest sea kale the third spring after you planted seeds. When the shoots begin to poke through the soil, blanch them by placing large clay pots upside down over the plants. Plug the bottom holes. Pale shoots, with tiny leaf blades at the top, will continue to grow under the pots. Harvest outer shoots when they are 6 to 9 inches long. When leafier growth begins to appear, uncover the plants and stop harvesting.

Let the plants mature—the flowers make an airy addition to bouquets and will attract bees. However, you will probably want to cut the flower stalks back before seeds form, since you want the plant to direct its energy into forming storage roots for the next year's crop. A plant should bear for up to ten years.

The flavor of sea kale is nutty and slightly bitter. Shoots can be eaten raw with cheese or in salads. They can also be steamed and served with butter. You can substitute sea kale in any recipes calling for cardoon.

Sources
Sea kale seeds: BG, RCS

Shallot

Allium cepa
Aggregatum Group
Amaryllis Family ❖ *Amaryllidaceae*

A shallot plant looks like a smaller version of bunching onions, except it makes small, usually elongated storage bulbs with a distinctive, mild flavor. The plants can be used fresh, leaves and all, like green onions, or you can dry the bulbs and store them for later use. Either way, shallots add a wonderfully delicate onion flavor to sauces and salad dressings. They are especially common in French and Southeast Asian cooking.

Growing Instructions According to a folk saying, you should plant shallot sets on the shortest day of the year, December 21st, and harvest them on the longest, June 21st. This is about right, but you should probably plant in November, before the weather turns chilly. Plant shallot sets about 6 inches apart and no deeper than an inch.

The newly available shallot seeds should be sown outside in February, or inside 10 to 12 weeks earlier. Plant them ½ inch deep and 1 to 2 inches apart for single bulbs, wider apart to get clusters. Shallots are sensitive to overwatering, so they are probably a poor choice for unamended clay soil. Keep shallots moist during dry spells, but leave them dryer in June, as the bulbs mature.

The Harvest You can cut shallot leaves to use like chives, dig up the entire plant to use like green onions, or wait until the tops fall over and the leaves begin to die back, then harvest the bulbs for storage. Overusing the greens will reduce the size of the bulbs. Cure and store the shallot bulbs like onions (see page 238), being careful to check frequently for decay. Shallots do not keep as well as onions, so use them up by winter, or replant them to make next year's crop.

Varieties and Related Crops I've had the best crop so far with French shallots, but there are many kinds to try, as both sets and seeds.

Old-fashioned potato onions are the same species and variety as shallots, but they have a more oniony flavor. To grow them, plant a mixture of large (to 2 inch) and small sets; the small ones enlarge, while the larger ones multiply, so you have a harvest each year of green onion and bulb onions. Plant sets in fall or midwinter and dig in early summer. The bulbs keep well.

Pests Shallots are susceptible to the usual pests affecting onion and its relatives. They are especially vulnerable to downy mildew and onion root maggots. If your garden is infested with onion root maggots, you may be able to grow shallots only for greens in winter, taking them out before the maggots become active in late March. Try to reduce the chance of disease by purchasing your shallot sets from a nursery rather than a food market.

Sources

Shallot sets: BUR, CG, JSS, NGN, RPF, SESE, T&M, TERR, TT, VBS
Shallot seeds: JSS, NGN, PGS, T&M, TERR, VBS, WCS
Potato onion sets: BCS, RPF, SESE

Siberian Kale (see Kale)

Sorrel, Garden

Rumex acetosa

Sorrel, French

R. scutatus
Knotweed Family ❖ *Polygonaceae*

Cool weather and fog are no hindrance to garden sorrel or French sorrel, perennial plants that bear tart, tender leaves the year around. As well as adding a kick to mixed green salads, sorrel is the key ingredient of some Old World soups and is an interesting addition to omelets and stuffing.

Growing Instructions Buy a small sorrel plant, which you will probably find among the herbs at your local nursery. Since you will probably only need one plant, it is easier to buy it than to grow from seed. Prepare a planting site as you would for other perennials, controlling weeds and mixing in plenty of organic matter. Allow 1 to 1½ feet between sorrel and neighboring plants. A fall or spring planting is best, but you can plant sorrel whenever you buy it. Keep the soil moist all year.

The Harvest Until the plant has two or three dozen leaves, harvest lightly. Once the plant is mature, it can handle frequent harvests throughout the year, although leaf production will slow in summer when the plant blooms. Pull out flower stalks to increase leaf production. The long stems of tiny pinkish flowers make an attractive if unconventional cut flower. Divide the sorrel clump in spring or fall if it gets too large.

Varieties and Related Species French sorrel grows 1 to 2 feet high, whereas garden sorrel reaches 2 to 3 feet high and has larger leaves. Which sorrel you have won't be evident when you purchase it, since the height refers to the flowering stems not yet formed. However, the plants are so similar that the question is of minor practical importance. When your plant does bloom in summer, pull out the flowering stems as soon as you notice them to direct more energy to leaf formation.

A third species grown in gardens, *Rumex sanguineus*, red-veined (or blood-veined) dock (or sorrel), has red or maroon veins. It has been touted as a salad green, when very young, but in my experience it grew extremely slowly and had a bitter taste. I wouldn't put it in my salad, but it's an interesting ornamental.

All three plants are related to weedy docks (see page 167), which are edible and not as sour as sorrel.

Pests Although snails hide in my sorrel plant, they do only minor damage. I go to the trouble of removing them because they use the sorrel as a home base from which to attack nearby plants.

Sources

French sorrel seed: BG, GS, JLH, NGN, TERR
French sorrel plants: JG, RH
Blood-veined dock seed: JLH, JSS, NGN, RH, T&M

Spinach

Spinacia oleracea
Goosefoot Family ❖ *Chenopodiaceae*

Spinach is an annual plant, unlike its close relatives beet and Swiss chard, which are biennial. A fast-growing crop, spinach makes a low rosette of large, tender leaves in a little over a month. When the crop is grown in unsuitable conditions, it responds by making only a few small leaves and then rushing to form a tall seed stalk. Even spinach grown under good conditions is short-lived. Although it may keep producing leaves for several weeks in fall, it will often go to seed soon after reaching maturity.

Growing Instructions To grow spinach successfully, choose the best variety for the season in which you are growing it and apply ample organic amendment, fertilizer, and water. Spinach has very high nitrogen needs. One gardener even reported success from seeds spilled in fresh horse manure. If you are working fertilizer into your soil before planting spinach, add it to the top few inches only, since spinach has shallow roots. Spinach is usually seeded in place. Sow ½ inch deep and 2 inches apart in blocks or in wide rows separated by 8 to 12 inches. Thin the seedlings to stand 4 to 6 inches apart, and use the thinnings in salads.

Sow seeds from February onward, and experiment to see how long you can plant in your particular microclimate before spring warmth and lengthening days cause spinach to bolt to seed early. Start seeding again in mid-July and see how late into fall you can plant before cold weather slows growth too much. As fall progresses, it becomes too cold for spinach to grow large. It may overwinter and grow again in late winter, then flower when spring weather warms. A cold frame will allow you to extend fall planting.

Sow successive plantings of spinach every three weeks to a month for a more or less steady supply. Small plantings, just a dozen or two plants tucked in a corner, are best until you get a feel for the needs and rhythm of this crop.

The Harvest You can harvest spinach as baby leaves, by the leaf, or as whole plants. You can also pull and eat larger plants, or you can pick just outer leaves, allowing for a longer harvest period. While you are perfecting your spinach growing technique; plants may be smaller than you expect. Just be sure to pull and eat the plants if they begin to elongate and show signs of forming a seed stalk, and keep trying to improve conditions so plants will grow large next time.

Varieties Because I am interested in high production in a small space, I prefer large-leaved varieties. For spring or late summer/fall seeding try 'Monstreaux de Viroflay' (45 to 50 days, leaves to 10 inches long), 'Oriental Giant' (35 days, 14 to baby leaf size), and 'Giant Nobel' (plants to 25 inches across). 'Giant Winter' is semi-savoyed and very cold and hardy for late summer or fall seeding. 'Tyee F_1' has leaves to 10 inches and is worth trying in warm as well as cool weather. Two varieties offer particular heat tolerance for those whose summers are warm: 'Okame F_1' (53 days) and 'Spaulding F_1' (45 days).

A new option is spinach with red stems and leaf veins, which is especially nice as a baby salad green. There are several red-stemmed cultivars, including 'Bordeaux F_1' (21 days to baby leaves).

Pests Spinach shares leafminer problems with beets and chard (see page 118).

Sources

Spinach seed: Widely available
Monstreaux de Viroflay seed: BCs, BG, GS, JG, SOC
Oriental Giant seed: NGN, RG, VBS
Giant Nobel seed: BCS, JLH, PGS,
Giant Winter seed: ABL, BCS, BG, GS, IST, SI, SOC
Tyee F_1 seed: JSS, PGS, TERR, VBS, WCS
Okame F_1: KIT
Spaulding F_1 seed: TERR
Bordeaux F_1 seed: JSS, T&M, TERR, WCS

Spinach, Malabar

Basella alba
Basella Family ❖ *Basellaceae*

Malabar spinach is a crop with thick, succulent, mild-flavored leaves that serve as a spinachlike crop in weather that is too warm for regular spinach. Alas, ocean-influenced microclimates are barely warm enough for it to survive, let alone thrive. In my sunny San Francisco garden it grew only 6 inches high, whereas in a warm Southern California garden or even in the Napa Valley it can sprawl or climb several feet. If you live where summers are warm enough, you can try the green-leaved variety or the red-leaved one, which is *B. alba* 'Rubra'. Both have mild, succulent leaves.

Sources

Malabar spinach seed:
Red-leaved variety: BCS, EE, JLH, JSS, KIT, NGN, PS, SSE, T&M
Green-leaved variety: BG, EE, JSS, KIT, PGS, TERR

Spinach, New Zealand

Tetragonia tetragonioides (*Tetragonia expansa*)
Carpetweed Family ❖ *Aizoaceae*

New Zealand spinach is not a true spinach but a similar-tasting green that does well everywhere in the region right up to the beach. It can be found growing wild at the beach end of Golden Gate Park and even on the ocean side of the Great Highway in San Francisco. Although New Zealand spinach is one of the plants that saved Captain Cook and his crew from scurvy during their voyages of discovery from 1771 to 1775, no one seems to know whether the people native to New Zealand ever considered it edible.

New Zealand spinach is often advertised as a hot-weather spinach. Although it grows well in hot temperatures, it also thrives in our foggy summers and often grows actively enough for harvests in winter. I have had tender young leaves from midwinter plantings very near the coast. It also seems to be entirely pest-free.

Like regular spinach, it tastes a bit sharp and contains some oxalic acid. Rapidly growing young stem tips are the mildest. Enjoy New Zealand spinach in salads, as a steamed vegetable, or in a mixed dish such as quiche or spanakopita.

Growing Instructions Here is one crop that isn't choosy about soil, fertility, or watering regularity. Although it appreciates rich soil and grows faster when well watered, it matures in most soils and tolerates some drought. It seems to grow bigger, milder leaves when it is growing through other plants, in part shade.

In early spring plant the seeds after soaking them overnight for quicker germination. Use mail-order seeds, or collect seeds from wild plants or a friend's garden. Sow them ½ inch deep, either in flats or directly in the garden. Thin or transplant to 2 feet apart. Plants grow very slowly for the first couple of months, but once established they sprawl over several square feet. You may decide to keep just one or two plants, but it is a good idea to start extra plants to allow for accidents during the maturing process.

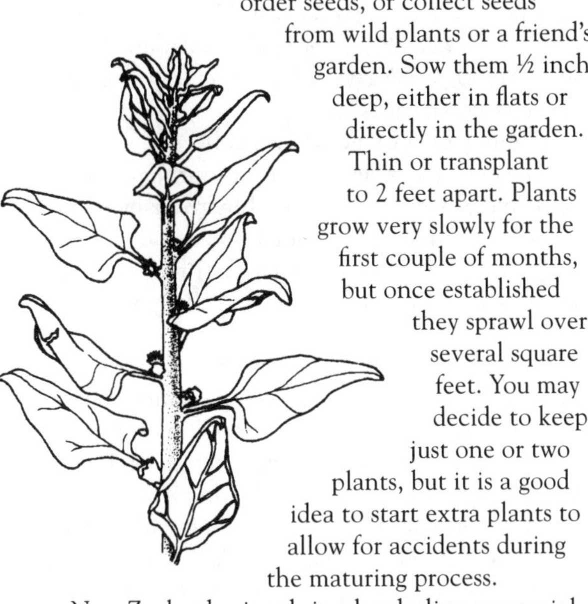

New Zealand spinach is a borderline perennial here. It will live through the winter in relatively frost-free areas, but it can be damaged by even a mild frost. If the seeds fall to the ground, some will probably come up next spring. Sometimes I just pull the old plant and let a couple of the seedlings have the spot. If volunteer seedlings pop up where I intended to grow something else, I dig them up and transplant them where I want them.

The Harvest Starting in early summer you can harvest small whole plants from spring-planted seeds. Or you can wait until the plants are larger and pick 3- to 4-inch stem tips, then pick some more when the plant has regrown. Once the plants have bloomed and the small knobby seedpods form, the stems are likely to be too tough and the leaves too strong for your taste. In late summer try cutting the plants back to 1 foot across to stimulate fresh growth.

Varieties Only one variety is available, and it seems to be the same one that grows wild locally. You will often find it listed in seed catalogs under the heading "Spinach."

Sources

New Zealand spinach seed: Widely available

Squash, Summer (including Zucchini, Crookneck, and Scallop)

Cucurbita pepo

Gourd Family ❖ *Cucurbitaceae*

Like other members of the cucurbit family, summer squash is a warm-season crop that should be planted after the soil has heated up in spring. Both summer and winter squash are good bets for the entire region, requiring less heat than other family members, which include cucumber, gourd, and melon. Summer squash requires a rich soil and ample water to produce good harvests. It makes large plants, each requiring 3 square feet or more. Although the plants will be smaller in cooler parts of the region, their fabled productivity makes them worthwhile even there. If you live in a foggy location or if you haven't improved your soil sufficiently, try zucchini first, since it tends to be more vigorous than other types of summer squash.

Growing Instructions A summer squash planted in May will begin to bear fruit in July. It will continue to bear until it succumbs to the chill and damp in October or November—unless it falls victim to powdery mildew earlier. Planted as late as the middle of July, it will still be productive for a month or longer.

You can try starting summer squash outdoors as early as February. Many plants started before the soil and air are warm enough don't make it, but those that do survive produce early crops. To increase your chance of success with extra early plantings, try covering your seedlings with a floating row cover. Like the other cucurbits, summer squash can be started indoors if you are careful to plant them in the garden before they outgrow their containers. Cucurbit seedlings that have become root bound or that have become mature enough to bloom in their containers are unlikely to ever grow very big. Sow the seeds in a bottomless container so that you can transplant the seedlings without disturbing the roots (see page 51). Move the plants into the garden after about four weeks, when they have two true leaves. If you purchase squash seedlings, buy only very young ones with few leaves and only a few roots showing.

Summer squash is usually planted in hills (a grouping of several seeds or plants) rather than rows. Although hills do not have to be actual mounds, they are commonly mounded for squash. Mounding creates a warm, well-drained environment for the seeds. That allows the seeds to germinate faster and makes them less vulnerable to decay.

I plant summer squash seeds (as well as winter squash and pumpkin seeds) in a special mound I have designed to make the soil warmer, more aerated, and easier to water. Here's how to construct the mound. After preparing the seedbed, form a circular trench 3 to 4 inches deep and wide. Use the soil removed from the trench to make a 1-foot-diameter, flat-topped mound in the middle. Form a lip at the edge, press the lip to firm it, then plant five or six seeds in a ring around the level top of the mound. Water the top of the mound and the surrounding trench until the plants have a couple of true leaves. Thin all but the largest two plants, and from then on water only the trench. If you are using transplants, just make the circular trench and not the special mound. Plant two seedlings about 6 inches apart in the area circled by the trench.

At the same time you plant squash seeds, consider planting a quick crop between the hills to mature before the squash grows over the area. Try radish seeds, lettuce seedlings, or onion sets for green onions.

Summer squash is a good candidate for the sunken-can technique of watering (see page 62). Periodically add a nutrient boost, such as manure or compost tea or fish emulsion, when you water.

The Harvest One benefit of growing your own summer squash is that you can harvest the flowers, which are delicious in soups or fried. Squash plants have both male and female blossoms, which can be distinguished by the tiny squash fruit behind the female flower. A plant usually makes several male flowers first. You may as well eat them, since there is nothing for them to fertilize. Then it makes both male and female flowers at the same time. There are usually more male ones than necessary for pollination, so a judicious harvest won't slow production. Harvested female flowers have the added bonus of a baby squash. Of course, eating female flowers will limit overall production, but that may be just what you want to do.

We've all heard jokes about gardeners with too many zucchini and stories about fruit the size of baseball bats. It is best never to let the fruit get too big, not only because it is tough and bitter but also because production of tender new fruit slows and eventually stops.

The smaller the squash when you pick it, the better it will taste—and, almost as important, the smaller the total production of the plants. After years of dissatisfaction with too many big summer squash, I have finally learned to pick all the fruit while it is small. I pick it as baby squash with blossoms, or I wait until it is 4 inches or slightly longer, but never more than 10 inches. This means picking it as often as every two or three days. If an occasional zucchini grows to 12 to 15 inches long, it can still be used for stuffed squash (see page 364). You may as well discard any zucchini fruit longer than that.

Varieties If you are growing in the most fog-challenged parts of our region, you will want to start with a vigorous summer squash variety, perhaps one that resists powdery mildew. In a trial, I found 'Burpee Hybrid F_1' zucchini to be moderately resistant. Newly available 'Anton PM F_1' and 'Romulus PM F_1' are powdery mildew resistant. Another, 'Seneca F_1', is more cool-tolerant than most, and so, at 42 days, a bit earlier. All of these bear dark green squashes.

A group of cultivars known collectively as "Romanesco" types generally bear fruit that starts out larger than some, so the just-pollinated babies you pick will be 6 to 8 inches long instead of the usual 4 or 5 inches. They are ridged and striped. Look for names such as 'Costata Romanesco', 'Largo', and 'Striata d'Italia'.

In warmer microclimates, where cucumber beetles and squash bugs can attack summer squash, varieties that don't need bees for pollination will allow you to plant under a row cover "hoop house." Two such varieties are 'Sultan F_1' and 'Partenon F_1'.

In my Mission District San Francisco garden, I've also had good luck with 'Black Beauty', various yellow crook- and straight necks, 'Peter Pan' green scallop, 'Sunburst' yellow scallop, and 'Kuta', one of the pale green types favored in the Middle East. My experience has been that the yellow squashes are more susceptible to powdery mildew, so I welcome the development of 'Sunray PM F_1', a yellow straightneck with powdery mildew resistance.

I have also grown tromboncino squash, which bears long, curved, pale green fruits with bulbous tips. Its texture is firmer than other summer squash, and its flavor slightly different. Because it is the species *Cucurbita moschata*, it has some resistance to powdery mildew, but it will not bear well in the foggiest gardens. (It is sold under several names, including zucchini rampicanta.) Another *C. moschata* squash eaten at the summer squash stage is 'Early Bulam F_1', a Japanese specialty with oval, 4- by 6-inch fruits.

Some gourds are eaten young, like summer squash. You may see snake gourds, *Trichosanthes anguina*, which are the cucuzzi of Southern Italy, or laginaria (such as *Laginaria siceraria*). Luffa squash, *Luffa cylindrica*, is eaten when young, used as bath sponges when mature. All of these will be at their best only in warmer microclimates.

Pests Some of the most common problems of squash are actually caused not by pests but by physiological factors—from inconsistent watering to lack of pollination. Gardeners sometimes have many squash blossoms but little fruit, or they have fruit that begins to form but never matures. If the female blossoms drop off without setting fruit or if the small fruit shrivels and turns yellow from the tip, your problem is probably lack of pollination. This can happen anytime, but it is more likely to occur very early or very late in the season or during prolonged foggy periods, when bees are less active. For pollination insurance, you can hand-pollinate, using a cotton swab or even your finger to gather pollen from the center of male flowers and dab it on the yellow structures in the center of female flowers (identifiable by the tiny squash behind the flowers). You can also find varieties, such as 'Sultan' and 'Partenon' that set fruit without being fertilized.

Squash may also remain unfertilized as a kind of natural birth control, setting fruit in several waves during the season with brief rests between. Also, if you've left large fruit on the plant too long, new fruit won't set. Sometimes the stem end of the fruit is pollinated and swells, but the blossom end stays narrow. You must pick any half-formed fruit, because seeds can mature in the large end, signaling the plant to stop making new fruit.

If the fruit begins to mature but the tip decays, you may have a condition similar to blossom-end rot in tomato. The cause is probably calcium deficiency caused by uneven watering. Root damage, heavy soil, or a nutrient imbalance could also be at fault. In a humid, foggy microclimate the problem may simply be a rot spread by blossoms that stay moist and stick to the fruit rather than drying up and falling off. Remove the blossoms as soon as the fruit begins to swell, carefully scraping away any decay on the end of the fruit. Do this soon enough and the fruit will dry, heal, and continue to develop normally.

Check summer squash blossoms and growing tips occasionally for aphids. Those found on squash are usually pale green. Zucchini yellow mosaic virus, a disease spread by aphids, sometimes strikes summer squash. See page 139 for more information on this disease. Some varieties, including 'Sungreen' and 'Plato', offer resistance.

Most summer squash varieties are susceptible to powdery mildew, a fungus disease that covers the leaves with a white dust. Unless a variety is resistant, this disease is almost inevitable late in the season. The small circular clusters of spores appear first on the undersides of lower leaves, so you should examine your plants for them as summer progresses. (Don't confuse the normal white or silvery markings on the upper surface of the leaves of some zucchini varieties for powdery mildew. See page 136 for more on powdery mildew and resistant varieties.)

Inland gardeners may find their young squash plants being eaten by green-and-black cucumber beetles or brown, shield-shaped squash bugs. (There is more on cucumber beetles on page 116.) Check for rows of squash bugs' bronzy eggs and small white to grayish nymphs on leaf undersides. Removal of the egg masses and removal of squash plants at season's end is very helpful. You can protect from either pest by starting your squash plants under a row cover. Remove it when the plants start to flower, unless they are a variety that doesn't need bees for pollination (see varieties in the preceding discussion).

Sources

Summer squash seed:
- Anton PM F_1: JSS
- Romulus PM: TERR
- Seneca F_1: NGN
- Romanesco type: ABL, BUR, CG, GS, IST, JG, JSS, NGN, PS, RCS, RG, SESE, SI, TERR, WCS
- Sunray PM F_1: BUR, JSS
- Sultan F_1: JSS
- Partenon F_1: GS, TERR
- Tromboncino squash: BCS, CG, GS, IST, NGN, PGS, RG, TERR, WCS
- Early Bulam F_1: KIT
- Edible gourd: BCS, EE, GS, JG, IS, JLH, JSS, NGN, RH

Squash, Winter and Pumpkin

Cucurbita species
Gourd Family ❖ *Cucurbitaceae*

Winter squash includes acorn, butternut, hubbard, and spaghetti squash. They are called winter squash because, although grown in the summer, they can be stored unrefrigerated to be eaten in winter. Pumpkin is grown in the same way as winter squash. Winter squash and pumpkin have needs similar to those of summer squash. They differ mainly in usually taking up more space and in needing a longer period of growth before harvest.

All prefer warm, sunny summers, but they are worth a try in foggier areas. Pumpkin generally does well in

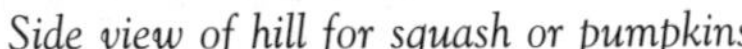

Side view of hill for squash or pumpkins

the fog, and winter squash varieties vary in their ability to produce in foggy climates.

Growing Instructions Plant winter squash and pumpkin anytime from the middle of April to the middle of June. Gardeners in the foggiest areas must get seeds in by May 15, so the fruit has time to ripen on the vine before the weather turns cold.

Like summer squash, winter squash and pumpkin are usually planted in hills. The warm, well-drained environment of a raised hill (see page 261) is even more important to get these seeds off to a good start, since they need every available day in which to mature. You may want to sow them indoors to get the earliest start. Do it just as you would summer squash, planting them in bottomless containers to avoid disturbing the roots when you transplant. Move the seedlings into the garden in about a month. A few varieties form zucchini-like bushes, but most form long vines that can eat up a lot of garden space. Use the seed packet as a guide for the distance between hills. It will range from 3 feet apart for bush types to 10 feet for the largest vines.

You can guide winter squash and pumpkin vines as they grow to keep them from invading other plantings or direct them into a corn patch that has been given a head start. You can also train them up vertical frames. This may sound strange since the fruit is so big, but you can support it in cloth slings. Like cucumber, winter squash and pumpkin will need hand weaving every few days to help it climb. Make sure the frame is strong and has wide openings. If you're growing the vines on the ground, prop the developing fruit on a dry board or flat stone to keep the bottom from coming into contact with damp soil or decaying vegetation.

At Green Gulch Farm, which is quite near the west coast of Marin County, gardeners stop watering winter squash in the middle of August to hasten ripening and to keep the water content of the fruit down. Experiment with this, but be aware that the soil at Green Gulch is quite clayey. If your soil is sandy, you may find a total water cutoff too extreme.

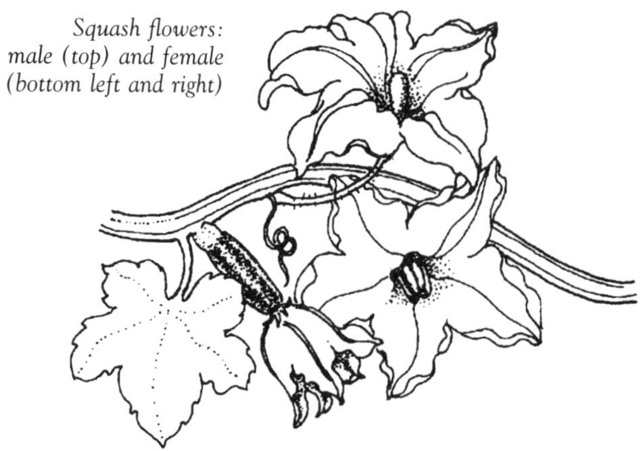

Squash flowers: male (top) and female (bottom left and right)

The Harvest Harvest male blossoms from winter squash or pumpkin plants only when no female blossoms are present, as each plant makes only a few female blossoms, and if they don't get pollinated, you will have no fruit production. In fact, pumpkins and winter squash typically set so few fruits per plant that you may want to try hand-pollinating the female flowers. Typically, a large-fruited pumpkin or winter squash vines ripens 1 or 2 fruits; a medium-sized vine 3 or 4 fruits; and a vine with small fruits, like 'Baby Bear' or 'Jack-Be-Little' pumpkins, 8 to 12 fruits.

Do not harvest pumpkins and winter squash until they have formed a hard shell. It's better to leave them too long than not long enough, since they will sweeten only on the vine. To be sure the fruit is ripe, leave it unpicked for a few weeks after it has reached maximum size and has stopped changing color. Also, wait for the stem to turn brown. There is no point in leaving fruit on after the vines have died, and it should definitely be removed by the time the winter rains begin, since rain will foster decay.

When cutting a winter squash or pumpkin from the vine, leave a 2-inch stem and keep the fruit in a warm, dry place for a week or two. Then store the fruit, making sure that one doesn't touch another, in a dry, dark place as close to 50° to 60°F as you can find. If the shell is not damaged, pumpkin and winter squash will last at least two months and often much longer (although the sugar content will suffer by spring). If you are storing both pumpkins and winter squash, use the pumpkins first since they do not keep as well. Pumpkins and winter squash can be used interchangeably in many recipes.

Varieties and Species The commonly grown pumpkin is *Cucurbita pepo*, like summer squash. If you plan to carve a big jack-o'-lantern, you will want a variety that makes 15- to 20-pound, relatively smooth fruits, such as 'Howden' or 'Connecticut Field Pumpkin'. 'Spirit' is a space-saving short-vined variety that makes large fruit. If powdery mildew on cucurbits has been an issue in your garden, consider 'Charisma', which is resistant to the disease. While these are all adequate for use in cooking, the classic pie pumpkin is 'Small Sugar', weighing in at 5 to 8 pounds. 'Baby Bear' has a classic pumpkin shape, but weighs only 1½ to 2 pounds. It is good for pie, and has semi-hull-less seeds for easy roasting. Even tinier, 'Jack-Be-Little' is flattened and cute, useful for decorations or stuffing.

The Winter Squash Family Tree

Both pumpkin and summer squash belong to the species *Cucurbita pepo*, and they can cross-pollinate. That explains why the seeds that you save from a pumpkin or zucchini or the seeds that sprout from a mature zucchini tossed into the compost pile may make plants with zucchini-shaped pumpkin fruit or pumpkin-shaped zucchini fruit. Acorn, delicata, and spaghetti squash are members of the same species.

Another species, *C. maxima*, includes many types of winter squash, such as banana, buttercup, hubbard, and turban. It also includes several varieties of squash that are more commonly called pumpkins, such as 'Atlantic Giant' and 'Big Max'.

C. mixta (*C. argyrosperma*) is represented mainly by cushaw, a type of squash native to the southern United States and Mexico. Cushaw is an elongated, curved-necked squash, often with a striped skin.

A fourth species is *C. moschata*, which includes tromboncini, butternut, golden cushaw winter squash, and winter crookneck. It differs from the other species in having softer fuzz on its leaves. Moschata is the species I've found to be the most resistant to powdery mildew, although breeding is creating particular resistant varieties of other species.

Pumpkins of different colors add interest. 'Lumina' has pure white skin and weighs 10 to 12 pounds. 'Baby Boo' is white and tiny, like 'Jack-Be-Little'. Other varieties offer speckled, netted, or blistered surfaces.

'Rouge Vif d'Etampes' makes big, decorative, "Cinderella-type" pumpkins, while 'Dill's Atlantic Giant' and 'Big Max' are among those grown for competition-size fruits. All three are really *Cucurbita maxima* and not the best for eating, nor is their thick flesh ideal for carving.

Among winter squash varieties, choose ones with long vines and large fruit for your main crop. That way, if cool weather limits the crop, you will at least have *something* to harvest. I have found production from bush types, including acorn squash, to be disappointing.

Our best bets are hubbards and any variety in the species *Cucurbita moschata*. Both types have thick orange flesh with excellent flavor and texture. Among hubbards, some, such as 'Sweet Meat' and 'Sugar Hubbard', have been passed down in the Northwest as heirlooms, but other hubbard types should thrive as well.

C. moschata winter squashes generally resist or tolerate powdery mildew better than other winter squash species, but the butternut varieties 'JWS 6823' and 'Metro' are particularly resistant. Butternut squashes are buff-colored, elongated, medium-sized squashes with the seeds in a slightly bulbous end. Other moschata squashes form round fruits with ridges that make them look like wheels of cheese. Examples are 'Long Island Cheese' and 'Musquee de Provence'. For the adventuresome, Native Seeds/SEARCH offers ten Native American and Mexican traditional varieties of *C. moschata*.

Finally, I should mention two *C. pepo* squashes. 'Cornell's Bush Delicata', a 1½- to 2-pound squash, white with green stripes, is resistant to powdery mildew. The other is spaghetti squash, filled with pasta-like threads that are used as a spaghetti substitute. I mention it because it is popular, though it has no powdery mildew resistance. Expect 4 or 5 fruits per plant if it is growing well, which it may not do in the foggiest microclimates.

Pests Powdery mildew seems to be the primary local pest of pumpkins and winter squash, although cucumber beetles (see page 116) or squash bugs (page 263) could appear in warmer inland microclimates. Pumpkin vines may succumb to powdery mildew before the fruit is even ripe—and once the vine is dead, the fruit stops maturing. For more on powdery mildew, see page 136. Other hazards are pill bugs and sow bugs, which will nibble fruit that has been in contact with soil and has begun to decay.

Sources

Pumpkin seed:

Howden: ABL, BCS, BG, BI, JSS, PGS, SOC, TERR, VBS, WCS
Connecticut Field: BCS, BUR, PGS, SESE
Spirit F_1: NGN, PGS
Charisma PMR F_1: JSS
Small Sugar: Widely available
Baby Bear: BUR, JSS, NGN, PGS
White pumpkin: BCS, BI, BUR, GS, JSS, PGS, TERR, WCS
Jack-Be-Little: BCS, BI, BUR, JG, JSS, NGN, PGS, PS, TERR, WCS
Rouge Vif d'Etampes: Widely available

Winter squash seed:
Hubbard squash: Widely available
Sweet Meat hubbard: BCS, NGN, PGS, SESE, TERR, WCS
Sugar Hubbard: TERR
C. *moschata* seed:
JWS 6823 PMR F_1 butternut: JSS
Metro PMR F_1 butternut: JSS
Long Island Cheese: BCS, BUR, CG, GS, JSS, PGS, SSE, TERR
Musquee de Provence: BCS, CG, GS, IST, JSS, PGS, SI, SSE
Delicata squash seed: Widely available
Cornell's Bush Delicata: BUR, CG, JSS, NGN, TERR

Sunchoke (or Jerusalem Artichoke)

Helianthus tuberosus
Sunflower Family ❖ *Asteraceae* (*Compositae*)

This perennial native North American relative of the sunflower produces edible tubers. European settlers, who were introduced to the sunchoke by native Americans, carried some of the tubers back to Europe. They were grown there and renamed in several European languages. Eventually the tubers were reintroduced to the United States, where they became known as Jerusalem artichoke. Why Jerusalem? The most cogent theory I've heard is that it is a distortion of the Italian name for the plant, *girasole*, which means turning to the sun. Sunchoke is a newer name, meant to be more descriptive and less confusing.

The crisp, low-calorie tubers are very easy to grow in all parts of our region. They appreciate a sunny location, but because they grow 10 to 12 feet high, they will reach for the sun. If you plant them in a shady spot, such as next to a fence, their tops will soon be in sunlight, although they may lean out on the way up, reaching for just a bit more light. Sunchoke will produce a crop in relatively infertile soil. However, the crop is likely to be smaller and the tubers misshapen if they are grown in very heavy, poorly amended clay soil. The plants grow all summer, the tops dying back around October. The tubers can be dug from October to the following March.

Growing Instructions You can plant a sunchoke you bought at the grocery store as long as the buds haven't been cut off. You can also buy tubers from mail-order seed companies.

The best time to plant sunchoke tubers is March or April. If you can't get them in the mail at the right time for our climate, just plant when you can. Planted in fall, the tubers should stay dormant until spring. Those planted in spring will get a late start this year but will sprout earlier next year. If the soil is too wet when your tubers arrive, refrigerate them in a plastic bag until the soil is the right moisture for planting.

Choose firm, unblemished tubers and plant them 2 inches deep and 1 foot apart. Sunchokes are very productive, so two or three tubers per person are plenty to plant, unless you know you will use them as staples. Put them where they won't shade shorter plants, then stand back and watch them shoot upward. Water well all summer.

The Harvest In late summer you may see groups of 2- or 3-inch sunny yellow daisies atop the plants. The flowers may not form if the summer is very foggy, but they are a bonus anyhow, since the plants don't need to bloom to be productive. When the leaves begin to turn brown in October, dig up the first crisp, mild tubers. What you don't need will keep best in the ground. You can break off the stalks, leaving just a little to mark the place, then harvest throughout the winter. If you need to store harvested tubers for a few days, put them in a plastic bag in the refrigerator. To prepare the tubers for eating, scrub them well. There is no need to peel them, even if they are green. (Green parts on a sunchoke tuber are harmless, unlike those on a potato.)

In March, you will notice that the buds on your earth-stored tubers are beginning to swell. The tubers are still edible, but it is time to renew your sunchoke bed for the next year. Dig up the remaining tubers, add organic matter to the soil if you wish, then replant a few large tubers. When the new shoots appear, dig out any extra plants so that you have just the number you want to grow. A sunchoke bed tended this way once a year will not get overcrowded or spread out as the years go by.

What you must avoid doing is getting sunchoke tubers spread around your garden. Remember where they are and don't move the soil around, and do not try to compost extra tubers. Kept in one place, they should cause no problem, but spread around, they could make a pest of themselves.

Varieties Sunchoke flowers reportedly don't make viable seed, so the plants must be grown from tubers. 'Stampede' is a knobby type of tuber that is said to be extra early. Others are smoother and elongated. 'Fuseau' has tubers nearly 4 inches long and one inch in diameter and 'Golden Nugget' has small elongated tubers with a nutty flavor.

Pests Sunchoke is practically pest-free. Although something chews a leaf of my plants now and then, it doesn't affect the productivity of the crop.

Sources
Sunchoke tubers: JSS, NGN, RPF, VBS
Stampede tubers: JSS & RPF
Fuseau tubers: RPF
Red Fuseau tubers: RPF

Sunflower

Helianthus annuus
Sunflower Family ❖ *Asteraceae* (*Compositae*)

Sunflower is a warm-season crop that tolerates some fog. Given organic, fertile soil and plenty of water, it will reward you with 6- to 10-foot-high plants that are topped with huge yellow flowers eventually studded with deliciously munchable seeds.

Although sunflower isn't a very demanding crop, overconfidence can result in disappointment. If you are counting on the plant's tremendous vigor to help it survive wretched soil or severe under-watering, don't be surprised if you get pint-sized flowers on 3- to 4-foot-high stalks and only a few well-filled-out seeds. Sunflower may also respond to extremely foggy periods or to a too-late planting by producing hollow seeds.

Growing Instructions Although unshelled raw sunflower seeds from a food store may grow, you will be more certain of good results if you buy seeds selected and packaged for gardeners. In early May sow the seeds directly in your garden in a place where the plants won't shade other sun-loving crops. Plant the seeds 1 inch deep, sowing groups of three seeds 1 foot apart. Thin to the best seedling in each group. Sunflower may succeed if it is planted as late as the beginning of July to mature in late summer.

A single sunflower is really many flowers. Each flat head is covered with hundreds of small fertile flowers, with a narrow fringe of infertile flowers forming the yellow "petals" around the edge. The seeds, which form under the fertile flowers, have creamy white hulls at first. Later, dark stripes become visible. When the flowers fall from the seeds at the brush of a hand, test a couple of seeds for ripeness. If the meat is well formed in them, cut the seed head.

Keep cut seed heads in a warm, dry place for a few days, then brush the seeds out of the heads. The fleshy heads have a tendency to decay in a damp climate, so don't leave the seeds in them too long. You can crack the seeds and eat them immediately. As an alternative, spread them to dry for a couple of weeks, then store them in closed containers. Eat shelled seeds raw, or salt and roast them in the shell.

Pests Don't leave a mature seed head uncut for too long, since birds may peck out the seeds and ants may crawl into the seed heads. Although ants don't do any damage, they make it unpleasant to dry a head indoors.

Varieties Ever-increasing numbers of ornamental sunflower varieties vie for your attention. Most of these make small seeds—suitable for bird feed, perhaps—but to grow large sunflower seeds to roast and eat, you need an agricultural variety. Large-seeded sunflowers are more likely to be mixed in with the ornamental ones than listed among vegetables, so you have to read carefully. The most common edible-seeded one is a large-headed one called 'Mammoth', 'Giant Russian', 'Mammoth Grey Stripe', or some other combination of these words. There are a few others, like 'Sunzilla' and 'Miriam'. Native Seeds/SEARCH offers several that are grown by Native Americans of the Southwest.

Sources
Large-seeded sunflower seed: ABL, BCS, BG, BUR, CG, NSS, PGS, RG, SSE, SOC

Sweet Potato

Ipomoea batatas
Morning Glory Family ❖ *Convolvulaceae*

Sweet potatoes are not related to Irish potatoes or yams. It has become customary to sell some sweet potatoes as yams, but the yam is a tropical root in the genus *Dioscorea* and is rarely seen in our grocery stores.

Also tropical in origin, sweet potatoes require a long, hot summer—a reason they are a popular crop in the South. I tried planting sweet potatoes one year to see how close I could come to success. Even on the sunny side of San Francisco, the plants produced about a pound of roots each. Gardeners report 1 to 6 pounds of usable roots per plant, so my results were definitely on the low end. Given good soil and adequate water, you are likely to harvest more sweet potatoes in warmer microclimates. Still, it is a very pretty plant and the leaves are used in Filipino cuisine, so you may like to give it a try in cooler microclimates.

Growing Instructions Planting the roots directly can spread disease, so it is best to purchase certified disease-free starts or start your own slips from store-bought roots. Buy some medium-sized, unblemished roots in early November. Store them at room temperature in a light-filled room, but out of direct sunlight, until early February. Then, in a container of sand or potting soil, bury most of the root at a 45-degree angle, leaving the thicker, sprouting end exposed. Alternatively, lay them on their sides, about halfway buried. Each root will make up to a dozen sprouts, known as slips. Keep the sand or potting mix damp and the container in a warm place in bright light until the slips are 6 to 12 inches high. Sprouts will grow best if the sand or mix is 80°F, so a heating mat will help.

Cutting the slips an inch from the root ensures that you won't transfer any diseases from the parent root to the soil, but it means the new slips will have no roots. Now you need to transplant them into clean potting mix and grow them indoors for six more weeks. Cover the slips with a plastic bag and keep them out of bright light for a few days after transplanting them. (For more on root cuttings, see page 59.)

In May, plant rooted slips in rich, organic garden soil. Plant them 4 inches deep and 1 foot apart. For more warmth, try planting in raised beds or on mounds. Use black or clear plastic mulch to help heat up the soil. Plastic will also discourage vines from rooting at several places, which would reduce yield. If the plants do try to root at the joints, lift them to discourage this.

The Harvest Dig sweet potato roots in fall. Give them as long as you can, but dig while the weather is still warm. You can eat them right away, but they get sweeter after curing, because some of the starch turns to sugar. To store sweet potatoes, cure them in a warm, humid place (about 80°F) for two weeks. Then wrap each root in newspaper and store at 55° to 60°F. Take care not to injure the roots, since this will encourage decay.

Pests Sweet potatoes are quarantined in California, so you can't order roots for planting from sources outside the state. The cause of the quarantine is the sweet potato weevil, which thus far has been kept away from California sweet potato crops. Other pests of commercial sweet potatoes crops include two diseases—black rot and scurf. My plants didn't have any pests, although something might have found them had I grown them for several consecutive seasons. I gather, from reports I have read, that if gophers, voles, field mice, rats, rabbits, or deer find your sweet potatoes, they are sure to judge them as delectable as you would have.

Sources

You can obtain clean, rooted, organically certified slips sent to California from Sand Hill Preservation Center, 1878 230th Street, Calumus, Iowa, (563) 246-2299, www.sandhillpreservation.com. Order early to be sure to get some, though they don't start shipping until near the end of May. Another source will ship small quantities of plantable roots within California: Jim Alvernaz, P.O. Box 255, Livingston, CA 95334. Order in March or April.

Swiss Chard

Beta vulgaris
Cicla Group
Goosefoot Family ❖ *Chenopodiaceae*

Swiss chard, the ancestor of beets and a leafy green with no storage root, is one of the stalwarts of local gardens. It grows easily from seed and provides ample greens for months. It is so at home here that it grows wild in some of the marshlands near San Francisco Bay.

Growing Instructions Swiss chard will grow all year. You can sow seeds indoors in December or January, and inside or in the garden mid-February through mid-August. Swiss chard appreciates organic matter and fertilizer. Although Swiss chard can be transplanted, it is so easily started in place that direct seeding is common. Sow the seeds ½ inch deep and 2 inches apart. Let the plants crowd each other a bit before thinning them to 10 to 12 inches apart. Eat the thinnings.

The Harvest Cut whole young plants, or leave them to mature and harvest one or two outer leaves at a time. If you are harvesting during rainy months, remove the whole leafstalk by pulling sideways. Don't leave a stub or it may rot and damage the rest of the plant.

Like beets, Swiss chard is a biennial—meaning that it will overwinter and go to seed the following spring. I have been told that you can force the plant to make more leaves by cutting back the flower stalk, but I have never found this to work well. Instead, I just pull out the blooming plants.

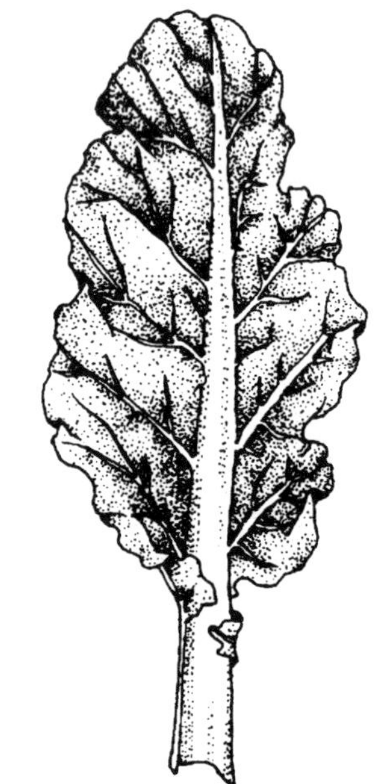

Chard was one of the first crops I grew in San Francisco. I didn't have many ideas for using it beyond cutting it up and steaming it. I got bored and stopped growing it. But I have since learned many more ways to use it. See recipes for Mexican Vegetables and Italian Sautéed Swiss Chard. I also chop the brightly colored stems very small and sprinkle them on a salad as "vegetable confetti."

Italian Sautéed Swiss Chard

This is easy enough for everyday meals and elegant enough to serve as a vegetable dish for a Thanksgiving dinner. Nuts and greens are a delicious combination. Here the crunchiness of the nuts masks any residual crunch left in the chard stems. Makes four small servings.

2 tablespoons pine nuts or sliced almonds, toasted
2 tablespoons olive oil
8 to 10 leaves of chard
½ medium onion, cut into ¾-inch pieces
1 clove garlic, minced
Salt
Pinch of red pepper flakes (if desired)
½ teaspoon freshly squeezed lemon juice

If you are starting with raw pine nuts or sliced almonds, turn the heat to medium under a dry 10- or 12-inch skillet. Add the pine nuts or raw sliced almonds and toss them constantly by shaking the skillet or with a spatula. When they just start to brown, turn off the heat. Immediately place the toasted nuts in a small bowl and set it aside.

Cut the stems from the chard leaves, folding the leaf sides together and cutting the stem out of their bases in a deep V. Chop the stems in half-inch slices and chop the leaves coarsely, keeping stems and leave separate.

Heat the olive oil in the same skillet. Add the onion and sauté over medium to high heat, turning often with a spatula, for three minutes, until it is about halfway to tender. Add the chard stems and sauté again, until they are partway tender. Add the leaves and continue to sauté and turn until the leaves are cooked.

Clear a small area of the skillet and add the garlic. Sauté for about 30 seconds, until you can smell it, then mix it into the greens. Cook gently another minute or two, then add salt, pepper flakes, and lemon juice. Mix well. Taste and add more seasonings if you like. Stir in the toasted nuts.

Variation: You can put the chopped chard stems in a microwave on "cook" setting for 2 minutes, covered with a paper towel, then add them to the skillet when you add the leaves.

Varieties All varieties of Swiss chard will thrive in this region. (In fact, Swiss chard brought by Italian farmers has escaped along the west side of the Bay, and you may still find wild plants there.) Swiss chard varieties differ mainly in the color of the leaf stems, which can be white, cream, yellow, pink, orange, or red. When the leaf stem is red, the leaf can be green or red. The most famous old varieties include 'Lucillus', with light green leaves and cream leaf stems, and 'Rhubarb', which has red-stemmed green leaves. There are a couple dozen others with names that describe stem color: 'Golden', 'Pink Lipstick', 'Ruby Red', and so on. All of these will be easy to find. There are also mixes, with different colored stems in the same package, such as the recently developed 'Bright Lights', which has five stem colors and some plants with red leaves. Many consider the thick stems to be a savory part of the vegetable, but if you prefer thinner stems, grow 'Perpetual Spinach', which is also sometimes sold as 'Spinach Beet'.

Pests Swiss chard is susceptible to the same leaf-blemishing pests (leafminers, cercospora leaf spot, and beet rust) as beet. (See the chapter entitled "Managing Bugs & Blights" for more information about these pests.)

Sources

Swiss chard seed:
White stems and single colors: Widely available
Bright Lights chard: BI, BUR, CG, JSS. NGN, PGS, RG, T&M, TERR, TT, VBS, WCS
Perpetual spinach: BG, CG, GS, IS, KIT, T&M, TERR

Tomatillo

Physalis philadelphica (P. ixocarpa)
Nightshade Family ❖ *Solanaceae*

Raw or cooked tomatillo is the main ingredient in Mexican green sauces. You'll find it in taco sauce, enchiladas, and many other dishes. Although a component of piquant dishes, tomatillo itself isn't fiery—in fact, it tastes very much like green tomatoes.

The tomatillo is a relative of the tomato and has similar needs. However, if tomatoes are difficult in your cool microclimate, you may still find tomatillos worth a try since they are usually harvested green. The 1- to 2-inch fruit forms in husks like that of another relative, the ground-cherry. The tomatillo plant is loose and sprawling like ground-cherry, but the leaves are smooth instead of furry. Also, tomatillo fruit bulges out of the husks instead of being neatly contained like ground-cherry fruit.

Growing Instructions In May, direct-seed tomatillo in a well-prepared garden bed. As an alternative, start the seeds indoors by the middle of March, then transplant the seedlings into the garden, spacing them 1½ to 2 feet apart. Stake the plants if you want to economize on space. Keep the soil moist through the summer.

The Harvest Tomatillos are often picked for salsa while still unripe, when the husk has just turned light brown. They can also be used when they are riper, when they may fall from the plant. When riper they develop some sweetness, but they are not sweet like a tomato. They can be stored at room temperature in their husks for at least a couple of weeks. Keep them in a cool, dry area and spread them in a single layer. You might want to do this if you are accumulating enough that are ready to use from a small planting.

To make a batch of salsa, start with two cups of tomatillos—a couple dozen medium-sized ones. Husk them and rinse them with warm water to remove the sticky coating. You can puree them as is or, if you like, roast or boil them first. (Roast on a broiler rack for a few minutes, turning them a couple of times, or boil for 5 to 10 minutes.) To make a salsa, blend with a medium onion, a clove or two of garlic, up to ½ cup cilantro, and salt and fresh chilies to taste. Another idea is to add some tomatillos to guacamole instead of tomatoes.

Varieties Many sources carry 'Toma' or 'Tomate Verde', a golf ball-sized green tomatillo, and 'Purple', which is smaller with purple fruit. You will find others with larger green fruit, and 'De Milpa' or 'Purple de Milpa', which is blushed purple and smaller, with perhaps a sharper flavor. Seeds/SEARCH sells a couple of small-fruited varieties grown by Native Southwest Americans or in Mexico. You will find that tomatillo often has a bit of an identity crisis in seed catalogs, sometimes listed among the tomatoes, sometimes mixed up with various ground-cherries (see page 226), which are different species and more useful for jam than for salsa.

Sources

Tomatillo seed:

Toma or Tomate verde: BCS, BI, BUR, CG, JSS, PGS, RG, SESE, SOC, TGS, WCS

Purple tomatillo: ABL. BCS, JG, JSS, PGS, RG, SSE, TERR, TGS

Purple De Milpa: BG, JSS, SESE, SOC, SSE

Tomato

Solanum lycopersicum
Nightshade Family ❖ *Solanaceae*

Tomato is America's favorite home garden crop, so it's no surprise that it is the first crop that many beginning gardeners try to grow. It is also not surprising that gardeners—novices and old hands—in cool summer parts of our region are frustrated by the typical performance of tomatoes in their gardens. At best, tomato plants bear later and bear lighter crops than they do in warmer microclimates.

At worst, they may produce no ripe fruit at all. The plants may not set fruit, set it too late to ripen, or succumb to disease before most of the green fruit can ripen. I used to think that you could predict success with tomatoes simply by knowing how far you live from the ocean. But I've seen plants two blocks from the ocean outdo ones several miles inland. That tells me that a well-prepared, wind-protected, unshaded spot with no tomato diseases in the soil can be more important than a neighborhood that gets very little fog.

Cherry tomatoes

Broiled Tomatoes with Herbs and Cheese

This works well with tomatoes about 1½ to 2 inches in diameter, such as are often produced by 'Early Girl', 'Stupice', or the paste tomato varieties. Serves three or four as an appetizer or a side dish.

- 4 tablespoons grated Parmesan cheese
- 4 tablespoons chopped scallion, onion lily (wild onion) tops, or garlic chives
- 2 tablespoons minced Italian parsley
- 4 tablespoons mayonnaise
- 6 small ripe tomatoes

Preheat the broiler. In a small bowl, combine the cheese, scallion, parsley, and mayonnaise. Cut the tomatoes in half. Cut a shallow depression in each half, removing some of the core. Cover each tomato half with a dollop of the topping, mounding it slightly and being sure it extends to the edges. Broil the tomatoes for 2 to 3 minutes, until the tops are golden brown.

Variation: You can also use the topping on chunks of bell pepper or as a filling for mushroom caps. Broil them as you would the tomatoes.

A perennial tropical plant, tomato needs a long, warm season to ripen fruit. The "days to harvest" ratings for tomatoes are from the time of transplanting six-week-old seedlings to the first ripe fruit. In my garden tomato seeds sometimes germinate from last year's fallen fruit, giving me a demonstration of what would happen if I were to seed them in place when the soil is warm enough. The seeds begin to grow in the middle of May, when I am often transplanting the last of the tomato plants from my windowsill. These volunteers never bear ripe fruit by the time the transplants do. Unless the fall rains are late, the fruit that does set on the volunteers may not ripen in time.

Cool days and nights will slow the growth of tomato plants, and fruit will not set if the nights are below 55°F. Tomato flowers are mostly self-pollinating, with pollen falling from the male part (stamens) onto the female part (pistil) in the same flower. When the temperature is too low, the cells fail to unite and the unfertilized flower usually falls off. Unfortunately, in the most ocean-influenced microclimates, night temperatures can dip below 55°F during any month of the year. If you observe closely, you may notice fruit set increasing and decreasing as cool and warm spells pass. Shaking the blossoms will get the pollen onto the pistil, but it won't get the germ cells together. Fruit-setting hormones, such as 4-CPA, sometimes allow fruit to develop without fertilization, but are not always effective. Your two best strategies for aiding fruit set are doing what you can to increase night temperatures around your plants and choosing varieties that cope best with cool weather.

Growing Instructions Purchase tomato seedlings or grow them yourself. Among the easiest seeds to start indoors, they are ready to transplant into your garden in five to seven weeks. If you grow them indoors longer, be sure to move them into larger pots so that their roots aren't crowded. Put them next to a very sunny window and provide adequate fertilizer and water.

It is generally warm enough to transplant tomatoes into the garden in late April or early May. For the best results, get them into the ground no later than the end of May. They can succeed when they are planted as early as February if the weather is particularly warm that year, the site is well protected, or you are using a special protective structure, but it is also quite possible that early plantings will have no advantage over later ones, and they may be more disease-prone.

Choose the warmest, sunniest spot in your garden for your tomatoes—preferably one with a southern exposure. You may also want to try special techniques to generate more heat and light. Some of the best ideas include planting in front of a white wall, using mirrors or foil-covered boards to catch more light, mulching with black or clear plastic, using a floating row cover or Wall O' Water to protect a young plant, or making a minigreenhouse to hold the heat around a larger plant. If you are going to cage tomatoes for support (see page 272), try wrapping black plastic

Staking, Caging, and Pruning Tomatoes

When you are growing tall (indeterminate) tomato varieties, you must support them. Staked or caged plants take up less space, and the fruit is more protected from pests and decay. Support is optional for determinate varieties, but it has the same advantages.

Gardeners often stake tomatoes, tying the plants as they grow to one or two tall stakes that have been driven into the ground. Staked tomatoes usually get pruned so they won't be so heavy that they pull the stakes over. The plants so staked and pruned will bear fewer fruits per plant, but can be planted as close as a foot apart, so should produce more fruits in the same garden space than unpruned plants. However, pruned plants will have fewer total flowers, so fewer chances to set fruit. In microclimates with cool summer nights, it is probably wisest to cage your plants and leave them unpruned to increase the chances of having flowers ready for pollination on the occasional mild summer night.

To stake your plants, at planting time drive one or two 6- to 8-foot-long redwood or bamboo stakes a foot into the ground about 4 inches from each plant. Starting when plants are small, use plastic plant tape or soft cloth strips to tie the plants to the stakes, making a figure eight with the plant in one loop and the stake in the other.

Prune staked tomato plants by pinching off the suckers—the leafy shoots that grow where the leafstalks grew from the stems. Let a sucker develop a couple of leaves, then pinch out the end of the shoot. If you do this from the time the plant is small, you can limit growth to one or a few main stems—three is typical. To keep a plant so drastically pruned, you must remove suckers every week or two.

Staking and pruning removes much of the foliage, exposing the soil surface and making it more difficult to keep the plants well watered. Inconsistent watering may lead to blossom-end rot. Lessen the problem by mulching under staked plants. Heavy pruning may also result in sunscald in the warmest microclimates. Prune less drastically, or erect a shade structure to protect the fruit if your summers are hot.

Caging is less work than staking, and it causes fewer problems with water balance. Although caging has the disadvantage of requiring a higher cash outlay, the cages will last several years. The best cages for indeterminate tomatoes are made from 5- to 6-foot high galvanized fencing with openings large enough to reach through and pick fruit. To make a cage about 18 inches in diameter, you will need about 5 feet of fencing. For a cage about 24 inches in diameter, you will need about 6.5 feet of fencing. (Nurseries sell prefabricated wire tomato cages, but most of them are too small for indeterminate varieties.)

Tomatoes growing in cages need virtually no pruning, but you can pinch occasional suckers to let in light and air. Tuck the branches into the cage as the plant grows, lopping off the occasional wayward one. The wider plant base of a caged plant shades the soil, so a mulch is less important.

Gardeners often prune the tips of their staked or caged plants late in the season when no more fruit is likely to set. The theory is that the plant will then ripen the fruit that it has instead of continuing to grow taller. Try this in the middle of September and see how it works for you.

If you are growing short (determinate) tomato varieties, formal staking or caging is less important. If your site is windy, however, support may be necessary to keep the plants from blowing over or breaking. Some gardeners provide support in order to space plants closer together or to keep fruit off the ground. Here is a use for those 3- to 4-foot-high prefabricated wire cages sold at nurseries. As an alternative, insert two 4-foot-long bamboo stakes into the soil, and wrap the plants and stakes with soft ties at several levels as the plants grow.

around the bottom foot of the cage to absorb and reradiate heat back to the plants.

Before planting, work in plenty of organic matter. Dig planting holes 12 to 15 inches deep, and put a big shovelful of compost at the bottom of each hole. Tomatoes need soil that is fertile, but not too high in nitrogen, since too much will inhibit fruiting. If you are using a synthetic fertilizer, use one that has more phosphorus and potassium than nitrogen. Also avoid adding too much nitrogen-rich organic fertilizer, such as blood meal or cottonseed meal. Since tomato plants have an especially high need for phosphorus and calcium, you may want to add a handful of bonemeal if you haven't already used a fertilizer that provides these nutrients. Stir the bonemeal into the bottom of the planting holes, cover the amendments and fertilizers with an inch or more of soil, and set the plants into the ground.

Space tomato plants 1 to 4 feet apart, depending on the variety and whether they will be staked or caged. Unlike most transplants, tomatoes should be planted deeper than they were growing in the container. Pinch off the bottom leaf, or several leaves if the plant is large, and bury about half the stem. This allows roots to form where the leaves were attached and makes for a stronger root system. If you are going to stake your tomatoes, drive the stakes on the day you plant to avoid disturbing the growing roots. If you are going to cage them, it is best to set the cage the same day as well.

Tomato roots reach as deep as 4 to 5 feet into the soil, so they need deep watering. Diseases will get a foothold if you keep the soil soggy—but, on the other hand, don't let the soil dry out more than 3 inches deep. Underwatering is a cause of blossom drop, undersized fruit, and various fruit defects (described earlier).

Although tomato plants will produce a crop without extra fertilizer during the growing season, they are heavy feeders and will probably make more fruit if they get a couple of booster applications as they grow. Apply either an organic fertilizer or a synthetic one with a moderate amount of nitrogen (such as 5-10-10 or 5-10-4) when the first tomatoes have just formed and again about a month after that. If the stems 6 inches from the ends of major branches are thicker than ½ inch in diameter, the plant probably has too much nitrogen; if the stems are smaller, the plant is lacking in nitrogen.

The Harvest Tomatoes ripen at least a month and a half after they set. A fast-growing tomato variety may produce its first ripe fruit in July, but don't be surprised if it takes until September in an unfavorable microclimate or during a particularly foggy summer. Some tomato varieties continue to grow taller and set more fruit until they are felled by winter rains and cold; these are called indeterminate varieties. Others, called determinate varieties, are short and bushy they ripen fruit over a shorter period. Look on plant labels and in seed catalogs for the designations *I* or *Ind* and *D* or *Det*. Occasionally a variety is called semideterminate, indicating that it falls between the two major types.

Leave the fruit on the plant to ripen as long as you can, although you may have to pick some before it is totally ripe if you are having trouble with pests. Keep in mind that most tomatoes in the grocery stores are picked green and ripened with ethylene gas. The ones you pick after they color up, although not absolutely ripe, should turn out better than any gas-ripened fruit.

When you pick tomatoes, try to break the stem at the natural separation point about ½ inch above the fruit, leaving the short stem and little green cap attached. This will keep you from tearing the fruit as you pick and allowing decay to enter. If you harvest more tomatoes than you can eat the same day, store them out of direct sunlight at room temperature. Refrigeration ruins their flavor.

Even the healthiest indeterminate tomato plant will usually die in October, or later if the fall has been dry. There will usually be quite a few green tomatoes left on the plant. They can be ripened indoors by a process called force ripening. One method is to pull the whole plant, hang it upside down, and pick fruit as it ripens. Another method is to pick all the fruit that has reached full size, with stems attached, and wrap each separately in newspaper. In either case, ripen the fruit in a dry place away from direct sunlight at a temperature of 60° to 70°F, and check it often. (Tomatoes gives off ethylene gas, which is needed for ripening, and the paper holds it near the fruit.) Don't give up on green tomatoes on a live plant—fruit has been known to ripen on plants in the garden as late as February, especially when rain is scarce. However, don't leave tomatoes in the garden into winter if late blight has appeared in your garden (see page 135).

Tomato truss with "stubs" where cold nights caused blossom drop

I often pick green tomatoes to eat fried during the summer and at the end of the season. When the plant is in decline in fall, I harvest all the green tomatoes that are too small to force-ripen and chop them up for chutney or relish.

Varieties If you are like most gardeners, by the end of summer you have forgotten which varieties of tomatoes you grew. By the time you are eating ripe tomatoes, the little tags that came with the tomato seedlings have long since disappeared. I encourage you to keep track of the tomatoes that you try, since the variety can make such a difference. Write their names in your calendar or datebook, with a little

A Tour of Tomato Types

Small-Fruited Tomatoes

Fruit is under 2 inches in diameter, often under 1 inch. Plants are usually indeterminate; fruit form in trusses of up to 20 and are intensely flavored. Round types are called cherry tomatoes; oval ones, grape tomatoes; and there are also pear-shaped varieties. Often planted in cool summer areas in hopes some of the many flowers will set fruit—the "cherry tomato strategy."

Salad or Saladette Tomatoes

These hover in size between small and standard fruits, in the 2- to 4-ounce range. Barely big enough to slice, they are often cut into chunks for salad and are very useful to halve and make into hors d'oeuvres (see recipe on page 271). Includes early varieties such as 'Early Girl F_1' and 'Stupice'.

Standard-Sized Tomatoes

At least some of the fruit on these plants are over 2 inches in diameter, and often larger. Usually round, but may also be flattened, oblong, or irregularly lobed. They're big enough to slice, vary in color, flavor, texture, and earliness. Includes determinate and indeterminate varieties.

Beefsteak Tomatoes

These are large, juicy tomatoes, usually wider than tall, with more "meat" than seed cavities. Some fruits may reach a pound or even two pounds in good growing conditions. These are typically rather long-season varieties, 80 or more days from transplant. In cool areas, look for the earliest varieties. Gardeners in reasonably warm microclimates report some success with 'Brandywine' strains, which are rated at 80 to 85 days from transplant size.

Paste Tomatoes

More pulp than juice means these tomatoes produce more tomato sauce or sun-dried tomatoes from the same volume of fruit. They make firm chunks in salads. Most paste varieties are determinate, but there are exceptions. The typical paste tomato is oblong, taller than wide, typically 2 to 3 inches long, but some are round, and some are long and narrow, like a banana pepper. The old standby is 'Roma', but it isn't necessarily the best performer.

Heirloom Tomatoes

In markets, the tomatoes labeled "heirloom" are typically large and often purple, yellow, or green, rather than red. But heirlooms can be any color or size. Traits they often share are thin skin and rather soft fruit, since the idea of developing thick-skinned, hard tomatoes for commercial shipment postdates the time these fruits were developed. Among familiar heirlooms are 'Brandywine', 'Black Krim', 'Green Zebra', and 'Yellow Pear'. Recently we've seen heirloom introduced directly from Russia, Eastern European countries, and other far reaches of the earth. 'Stupice' is an open-pollinated selection from the former Czechoslovakia.

Currant Tomatoes

A different species of tomato, *Solanum pimpinellifolium*, is sold as currant tomato. The indeterminate plants bear clusters of fruit the size of the smallest cherry tomatoes. The intensely flavored fruits may be red, yellow, or creamy white.

map of your tomato planting so you will remember even when the tag is gone, or use a hole punch on the tag and attach it to the plant or to the plant stake. Also notice what your neighbors are growing. (When you see one of their plants doing really well, you'll wish they had saved their tag.)

Here are some hints to guide you as you compare catalog descriptions of tomato varieties. If your garden is in a particularly foggy or windy location, choose only the earliest varieties. Early tomato varieties are those listed at less than 70 days from transplanting. Also watch for descriptions such as "bears well under adverse conditions" or "sets well in cool weather." Tomatoes said to be "good for short northern summers" may produce here, but remember that northern summers, though short, have longer days than ours and are warmer than our coolest microclimates. In moderately warm locations in this region, you can try midseason varieties, which are listed at 70 to 80 days from transplanting. Unless you live well inland, where summers are hot, be wary of long-season varieties, which are listed at more than 80 days.

Although you will want to know whether a tomato is a hybrid or not, this is not a deciding factor in whether it will produce well in your region.

Fried Green Tomatoes

1 to 2 medium-size green tomatoes per person
About 1½ tablespoons olive oil per tomato
A small bowl of water
About ½ cup whole wheat flour
Salt and freshly ground pepper

Select firm, completely green tomatoes. Slice them ¼-inch thick. Add enough olive oil to cover the bottom of a large skillet and heat the oil over medium heat. Dip each tomato slice in water and then in whole wheat flour. Fry, turning once, until the slices are browned and offer no resistance to a fork. Add more oil if necessary. Drain the tomatoes on paper towels and serve immediately, with salt and pepper to taste.

If you want to save seeds, get an open-pollinated variety. Otherwise, feel free to choose varieties based on other characteristics.

You may notice that some varieties are parthenocarpic. This means that the fruit is able to develop even though the nights are so cold that flowers cannot be fertilized. This means the fruit will be seedless or nearly so. (Fruit texture may not be as good as that of seeded varieties, and when you grow it from seed, you may find that you have to sow more thickly, since some seeds will not be fertile.)

Indeterminate varieties have the potential to make larger crops than determinate ones, because they grow taller and produce flowers over a longer period. They are more likely to have flowers ready for pollination during our sporadic warm spells in summer, and they are able to take advantage of warm weather in early fall to ripen the last fruit set. However, if a determinate variety is particularly good at setting fruit in cool weather, it is worth a try.

To compare varieties for resistance to diseases and other pests, look for the letters V, F, N, T, A, and St, which stand for resistance to verticillium wilt, fusarium wilt, nematodes, tobacco mosaic virus, alternaria, and gray leaf spot (caused by species of the fungus *Stemphyllium*). For example, a tomato with the letters VFF after its name is resistant to verticillium wilt and two races of fusarium wilt. You may never see these diseases, but if you have identified them in your garden, you will want to grow resistant plants.

Of the resistances or tolerances available, verticillium and alternaria are most important in near-coastal regions, since they develop in cool weather. Fusarium is more common in warmer microclimates, and the others could be present in either. The one resistance we wish we had is to tomato late blight. While late blight varieties have been developed for commercial growers of hard, shippable, processing tomatoes, there is no perfect choice for home gardeners. Only one variety, 'Legend', has been bred and formally tested for tomato late blight resistance, and it is not resistant to all of the races of the disease present in our gardens. (See the Physiological Problems of Tomatoes sidebar on page 276, as well as disease listings in Chapter 9.)

As for flavor, you probably can't learn much by reading the catalogs or seed packets. They will either tell you that the fruit is delicious, or they will decline to mention the matter. This points up an important truth: you can't really find out all you need to know by reading catalogs. That goes for productivity as well—rarely will the descriptions allow you to predict accurately how much fruit you will get in this region. Even earliness, although more reliably calibrated than flavor or productivity, is not entirely reliable, since different varieties may be affected to different degrees by unfavorable conditions.

It was because of just such questions that I undertook—with the help of the San Francisco League of Urban Gardeners (SLUG) and many volunteers—tomato variety trials in San Francisco. In 1987 I tested ten tomato varieties. All of them were red-fruited, with either saladette or full-sized fruit. In 1988 I tested an additional four. In 1989 I put five paste tomatoes to the test. In these variety trials, volunteer gardeners grew, counted, measured, weighed and ate tomatoes in three locations: one in the Mission, one in Visitacion Valley, and another in the Outer Richmond. I reported the results in this book's earlier editions.

Although even three years of formal tests revealed only a limited amount of information, we did get some answers. The trials bore out my prediction that indeterminates—that is, tall plants—would be the biggest producers. Although not every indeterminate variety produced well, none of the determinate, or short, plants, were among the top producers. A determinate type might be rated as very early by the seed company that sold it, and might be said to bear well in cool weather, or even to set fruit without pollination ('Oregon Spring') but none of them bore as much fruit as the best of the indeterminates.

We were also able to see that some varieties did produce earlier crops than others, though none produced ripe fruit as quickly as their catalog descriptions promised. From our early May plant-outs, the first fruits ripened near the end of July—80 to 90 days later. The two earliest varieties—the ones that started to ripen at the end of July—were 'Oregon Spring' (variously rated at 60 to 80 days) and 'Stupice' (rated at 52 days). Plants rated with the same days to harvest might vary somewhat in actual days to harvest in San Francisco's conditions. For example 'Marmande', which is rated at about 70 days, produced relatively early, while 'Celebrity', also rated at 70, was one of the latest to ripen.

I also learned that 'San Francisco Fog', which many gardeners believe to be the very best for coastal gardens because of its name, is not among the earliest or most productive—and its flavor was rated as only "fair." Flavor proved tricky to study. We did find some tomatoes in our trials with a flavor that appealed to the majority of tasters, but there was a wide variation, with some liking them all, some panning them all, some preferring a sweet fruit, and others wanting a tart one.

We didn't try as many paste tomatoes, and we tested them only for one year, so they resulted in fewer conclusions that remain useful. Only one of

Physiological Problems of Tomatoes

All crops have some problems that are not caused by insects, diseases, or other pests, but tomatoes seem to have more than their share. When a physiological problem is caused by something you can change, such as watering or soil fertility, you may be able to reduce or eliminate the problem. You can do only so much, however, when the cause of a problem is unfavorable climatic conditions, such as cold nights.

Sometimes the blossom end of the fruit (the end away from the stem) turns brown and begins to decay. This can happen even before the fruit is ripe. Blossom-end rot is caused by a shortage of calcium in the plant, seemingly hastened by uneven watering. To prevent the problem, work in plenty of organic matter and add bonemeal at planting time, don't let tomato plants dry out, and mulch plants that are staked and pruned. Some varieties are more susceptible than others, although you probably won't learn this from catalog descriptions. Just be aware that if the variety you grew this year was affected, a different variety next year may be fine.

Catfacing is another problem that appears most often on the blossom end of fruit. It shows up as rough, dry brown blotches or lines often accompanied by deformations, such as deep folds in the fruit surface. The brown lines often have little cross bars reminiscent of a zipper. Catfacing, which happens when the flower is first becoming a fruit, is believed to be caused by cool weather. There is little you can do to prevent catfacing. Many varieties will escape this blemish, although once again the problem is rarely mentioned in catalog descriptions.

Tomato fruit may crack, usually at the stem end. Cracking is most common when the plant has been very dry and is suddenly well watered. Cracked fruit does not keep well, since decay organisms can get in through the cracks. The best way to prevent cracked fruit is to water consistently.

You may notice that the leaves of your tomato plants have rolled up. If the leaves are not an unusual color, curling is not a serious problem. The disorder is more common on heavily pruned plants, and some varieties are more likely to develop it than others, although it is so slight a problem that no one seems to pay much attention it.

Tomato fruit may also occasionally develop sunscald. Although it is not as likely to occur in foggier areas, it is possible, especially when plants are heavily pruned or losing leaves to russet mites or a disease. Sunscalded fruit develops a whitish patch on the side facing the brightest sun, usually the southwest. As the fruit ripens, the scalded spot often decays.

Although all these problems are a nuisance, affected fruit can still be eaten. Just cut away any unsightly parts and the rest of the fruit will be just as tasty and wholesome as an unblemished tomato.

our two best varieties, 'Ropreco', seems to still be on the market. Our best kind, 'Sprinter' (not to be confused with 'Crimson Sprinter'), seems to have disappeared. The most useful tip I can derive from our paste tomato trial is that the old favorite 'Roma' isn't necessarily the best.

In this edition, I have moved information on the methods and results of the original trials to Appendix V. I also reported sources for as many of my original trial varieties as possible, even the losers, in case someone wants to repeat any of the trials or compare those varieties to other ones.

Since then, many new tomato varieties have been found or developed. I have grown some of them, and nearby Master Gardeners have used some of them in trials. In the chart Some Tomato Varieties Worth Trying, I have listed ones that did well in either my trials or later Master Gardener trials (see codes), plus others that I have grown with success, or that were recommended to me by seed suppliers as having promise for our region. The descriptive details in this chart are from seed catalogs or from other published descriptions.

In the chart, I have also included a few varieties that gardeners have reported show some resistance to tomato late blight. I tried these varieties in the summer of 2009 and didn't find any to resist the disease completely, though some produced respectable crops before succumbing in a garden with heavy exposure to late blight spores. (For more on tomato late blight, see page 135.)

Inland gardeners will detect a coastal microclimate bias in this chart. As with other warm-season crops, your choices will be wider, and other sources will help you further as you explore more varieties.

I encourage you to try new tomato varieties often, since there are hundreds of varieties and new varieties are constantly being developed, so maybe the next one you try will be the tomato of your dreams.

Pests Tomato plants often exhibit alarming symptoms: leaves that are spotted, curling, or dying, or fruit that is blotched or misshapen. Some symptoms are caused by poor growing conditions (see the Physiological Problems of Tomatoes sidebar on the opposite page). Others are evidence of virus, bacterial, or fungus diseases, most of which are incurable. Tolerate minor spots and blemishes of unknown origin on tomato leaves while you learn what may be causing them. However, if it is clear that a plant is in very serious trouble and you can't find out why, it is best to remove it from your garden to avoid spreading the problem.

Verticillium wilt, one of the most common tomato diseases locally, is spread by infected soil and encouraged by cool temperatures. The first symptom is the wilting of older leaves, followed by yellow, then brown V-shaped patterns on the edges of some leaves. (See Vascular Wilts, page 137.)

Tomato late blight, another common tomato disease, causes dark brown stem areas, with green stem above and below, and brown, wilting leaves. Infected fruit has greasy, brown shoulders. (See Late Blight of Potato and Tomato on page 135.)

Since tomatoes and potatoes are in the same family and share many of the same diseases, planting infected potatoes can spread diseases that will attack your tomato plants. That is why it is important to get certified disease-free potato starts. Once the diseases are introduced, they can be spread in soil or by wind and water. I first saw tomatoes with late blight in San Francisco in 1990, but now it is quite common.

Tobacco mosaic virus can be spread by smokers, since it is usually present in cigarettes. The disease can also enter your garden on nursery transplants. Some diseases are spread by insects. Spotted wilt, a virus diseases spread by onion and flower thrips, turned up on a tomato plant in one of my experiments. The most obvious symptom is concentric rings of yellow, green, and red on the fruit. Several diseases are spread by splashing water, so avoid spraying the leaves of tomato plants when you water (see page 139).

Tomato diseases that live in the soil from year to year can end your efforts to grow tomatoes in your garden. If your plants succumb, try to identify the problem using books or enlisting the help of an expert. The next season, plant tomatoes in a different location, try varieties with as broad resistance as you can find, add plenty of organic matter, and take care not to overwater. If the problem persists, you may want to try soil solarization (see page 149) if you are in a warm microclimate. Soil diseases eventually die out, but the wait can be long. For example, verticillium can live in the soil for twenty years or more, and it is carried by many other crops and ornamentals when tomatoes aren't being grown. When all else fails, get some big containers, fill them with sterile potting mix, avoid contact between the potting mix and your infected soil and between the containers, and get on with your tomato growing.

Before you assume that your tomatoes have a disease, consider whether they may have tomato russet mites. The microscopic russet mites swarm over a plant, sucking sap and soon turning the stems and leaves a greasy dirty yellow or bronze. The fruit

Some Tomato Varieties Worth Trying

Variety[1]	DTH[2]	Det/Ind?	Resistance[3]	Comments
SMALL-FRUITED VARIETIES				
Chocolate Cherry	70	Ind	—	Red-brown, 1" fruits with excellent flavor in trusses of 8, ripens well off plant, crack-resistant.
Currant, Red	65–75	Ind	—	Tiny fruits, under ½" with strong, sweet flavor. A different species: *S. pimpinellifolium.*
Currant, White	70–75	Ind	*++	Same species as red currant. Tiny creamy-white fruits with unique, sweet flavor.
Gardener's Delight	65–72	Ind	—	Red fruits ¾" in diameter, 6 to 12 fruit trusses. Sweet flavor and crack-resistant. MMG
Juliet F_1	60	Ind	*++	Oval, red, grape-shaped fruits, to 1½", less likely to fall from plant than other small-fruited tomatoes. MMG
Koralik	61	Det	*+	Red, 1" fruits ripen at the same time on 6 to 8 fruit trusses, heavy crop for plant size.
Matt's Wild Cherry	70–80	Ind	*+	Seed from wild plant in Mexico, fruit tart early in season, sweeter later, marble-sized.
Sungold F_1	57	Ind	—	Deep orange when fully ripe, very sweet, unique flavor, long trusses. Bred in Japan. SMCMG, MMG
Sun Sugar F_1	62	Ind	—	Golden yellow fruit with sweet-tangy flavor, crack-resistant. MMG
Sweet 100 F_1 (Supersweet 100 F_1)	65	Ind	—	Known for super-long trusses of fruit—up to 100 fruits that are 1", red, sweet. SMCMG
Tommy Toe	70	Ind	*+	Ozark Mountain heirloom with red ½ to 1" fruits, round to oval, mild flavor.
Yellow Pear	78	Ind	—	Old-time favorite, yellow pear-shaped fruit 1 to 2", mild flavor, can grow very tall.
PASTE VARIETIES				
Black Plum	75–80	Ind	—	Vines are short indeterminate, fruit is red-brown, green and purple inside, good fresh, dried, or in sauces.
Principe Borghese	75–80	Det	—	Italian variety grown mainly for drying, but good for uncooked or cooked sauces.
Ropreco	70–75	Det	—	Red, angular, pear-shaped fruits. One of the earliest paste varieties; did well in my tomato trials. SFTT
San Marzano	75–85	Ind	—	Classic Italian variety with heavy production and good flavor. Some strains are open-pollinated, others are F_1 hybrids.
Viva Italia F_1	80–85	Det	VFFNASt	Not so early, but it bears well and has good-flavored fruit.
RED SALADETTE AND STANDARD-SIZED TOMATOES				
Brandywine	72	Ind	—	Many strains of this large-fruited heirloom exist. The best have good flavor and texture, few defects. Brandywine OTV considered very good.
Bush Champion F_1	70	Det	VFFASt	Large fruit, excellent flavor, good for containers. MMG

Variety[1]	DTH[2]	Det/Ind?	Resistance[3]	Comments
Early Girl F_1	52–60	Ind	VFF	Perennial favorite in our region. Early, bears well, smallish fruit that is sweet-tangy. SSTT
Jetsetter F_1	64	Ind	VFFNASt	Good production of 2½" fruits with rich, well-balanced flavor. SMERMG
Legend	68	Det	*	Bred to be late blight tolerant, but it died completely in my trials. Parthenocarpic. MMG
Matina	58	Ind	—	Smallish fruit that rivals flavor of beefsteaks. Fruit in clusters. German heirloom. MMG
Oregon Spring	58	Det	V	One of the earliest in my tomato trials, large flavorful fruit, light crop. Parthenocarpic. SFTT
Sophie's Choice	55	Det	—	Large, tasty fruit, orange w/red interior. Best quality in cool climate. Canada heirloom. MMG
Stupice	52	Ind	—	Top-rated in my trials for earliness, production, and flavor. Smallish fruit. Czech heirloom. SFTT
OTHER COLORS—SALADETTE AND STANDARD-SIZED FRUIT				
Black Krim	69	Ind	—	Brown-red fruits, very thin-skinned, nice flavor and texture. Good production in SMERMG trials.
Cherokee Purple	80	Ind	—	Heavy crop of mild-flavored, red-purple fruit. In SMERMG trials, some had to be ripened indoors.
Green Zebra	75	Ind/Det	—	Green on green stripes when ripe, with maybe some yellow. Seem to be det. and ind. strains. Fruit is 1½ to 2" in diameter.
Jaune Flammée	70–80	Ind	—	Tall, thin vines with good production of orange fruits with reddish interior the size of a small apricot. Sweet flavor. SMERMG
Lemon Boy F_1	72	Ind	VFNASt	Lemon yellow when ripe. Has large, mild fruit and good production in warmer parts of SF.
Old German	75	Ind	—	Earliest of the red-yellow bicolors. Large fruit, juicy, meaty, and tasty. Virginia Mennonite heirloom.
Taxi	65–70	Det	—	Yellow fruits to 1½" with mild flavor, meaty texture. Heavy production for size of plant. SMERMG

Tomato Trial Codes: SFTT=my San Francisco trials in 1987–89, MMG=Marin Master Gardeners 2007 trials, SMERMG=San Mateo Elkus Ranch Master Gardeners 2007 trials, SMCMG=San Mateo (Coastal Location) Master Gardeners 2007 trials

[1]The symbol F_1 indicates a variety is a hybrid.

[2]DTH=Days to Harvest (estimated days from planting out of the seedlings to the first ripe fruit, as suggested by commercial sources of the variety).

[3]Codes are for disease resistance (see page 275 for discussion).

In 2009 I performed a trial of 'Legend', which was bred for late blight tolerance as well as several varieties that a person on the Internet claimed resisted tomato late blight. Plants in these trials are indicated by *. None of these plants proved resistant, but some showed enough tolerance to produce good crops. If the plants showed enough tolerance to produce some fruit, I've added a +, if they were among the more productive of the tested varieties, I have added ++.

is usually not attacked, but it may sunburn when the leaves die.

Damage to tomatoes from chewing pests is less common here than in many other parts of the country, although earwigs may do major damage to young tomato plants. In warmer microclimates, large green tomato or tobacco hornworms may feed on your plants (see page 120). Slugs may eat holes in your tomatoes, especially if the fruit is in contact with the ground.

Sources

Tomato seed (small-fruited varieties):
- Chocolate Cherry: BG, PS, TERR, TT
- Currant, Red: ABL, GS, NGN, PGS, PS, RH, SESE, TERR, TGS, TT
- Currant, White: ABL, BCS, TERR
- Gardener's Delight: BG, BI, BUR, CG, PGS, T&M, TGS, TT, WCS
- Juliet F_1: BUR, JSS, PS, T&M, TGS, TT, VBS, WCS
- Koralik: ABL, BCS, TERR
- Matt's Wild Cherry: JSS, SESE, SOC
- Sungold F_1: BI, BUR, CG, EE, JSS, KIT, NGN, PGS, RG, T&M, TERR, TGS, TT, WCS
- Sun Sugar F_1: NGN, PGS, TGS, TT, VBS
- Supersweet 100: BUR, CG, KIT, PS, TGS, TT, VBS
- Tommy Toe: SSE, T&M, TGS, TT
- Yellow Pear: ABL, BCS, BG, BI, BUR, CG, GS, JSS, NGN, PGS, RG, SESE, SOC, SSE, TERR, TGS, TT, WCS

Tomato seed (paste varieties):
- Black Plum: SESE, SOC, SSE, TERR, TGS, TT
- Principe Borghese: BCS, BG, GS, IST, SESE, T&M, TERR, TGS, TT, WCS
- Ropreco: SOC
- San Marzano: CG. GS, JSS, PGS, SI, TERR. TGS, TT, VBS
- Viva Italia F_1: BUR, NGN, PS, TERR, TGS, TT, VBS

Tomato seed (saladette and standard-sized varieties):
- Brandywine (OTV Strain): SESE, TGS
- Bush Champion F_1: TGS, TT
- Early Girl F_1: BUR, GS, NGN, PGS, TERR, TGS, TT, VBS, WCS
- Jetsetter F_1: NGN, TGS, TT
- Legend: ABL, NGN, SOC, T&M, TERR, TGS, TT, VBS
- Matina: CG, GS, SOC, T&M, TERR, TGS
- Oregon Spring: ABL, JSS, NGN, PGS, SOC, TERR, TGS, TT, WCS
- Sophie's Choice: SESE
- Stupice: ABL, BG, CG, NGN, PGS, SESE, SOC, SSE, T&M, TERR, TGS, TT, WCS

Tomato seed (other-colored varieties):
- Black Krim: BCS, BG, BI, BUR, CG, GS, JLH, NGN, PGS, SOC, SSE, TGS, TT, WCS
- Cherokee Purple: ABL, BCS, BG, BI, BUR, GS, JG, JLH, JSS, NGN, PS, SESE, SOC, SSE, TERR, TGS, TT
- Green Zebra: BCS, BI, CG, GS, JSS, NGN, SESE, SOC, SSE, TERR, TGS, TT, WCS
- Jaune Flammée: JLH, SSE, TGS, TT
- Lemon Boy F_1: BUR, NGN, TGS, TT
- Old German: GS, SESE, TERR, TGS, TT, VBS
- Taxi: JSS, PGS, TERR, TT, WCS

Turnip

Brassica rapa
Rapifera Group
Mustard Family ❖ *Brassicaceae* (*Cruciferae*)

When someone mentions turnips, do you think of big starchy boiled root—sand are you overcome by boredom? If so, I encourage you to try an Asian variety like 'Tokyo Cross Hybrid' or 'Tokyo Market', or one of the other varieties meant to be eaten when the roots are small. They make crisp, mild-flavored white roots as quickly as radishes. They can be added to salads or used in a stir-fry (see page 239). Or try heirloom golden or red varieties.

Growing Instructions The crispest and most tender turnips are produced in rich soil with plenty of water. Plant turnips every few weeks for successive crops from February to August. Direct-seed ½ inch deep and 1 to 2 inches apart. Don't let weeds compete with the rapidly growing seedlings. Thin the seedlings as soon as they begin to crowd each other, and eat the thinnings as greens.

Varieties The heirloom 'Purple Top White Globe' forms the iconic turnip—a white globe, up to 5 inches across, with bright purple shoulders. Some strains are mild enough to eat raw when they are 2 to 3 inches across, but they are traditionally eaten cooked. 'Golden Ball' offers a sweet, mellow, golden yellow flesh that is attractive cooked and mashed.

Red is an unexpected turnip color offered by several varieties: 'Sweet Scarlet Ball' is white skinned, red within. 'Scarlet Queen' has red skin and white splashed with red inside.

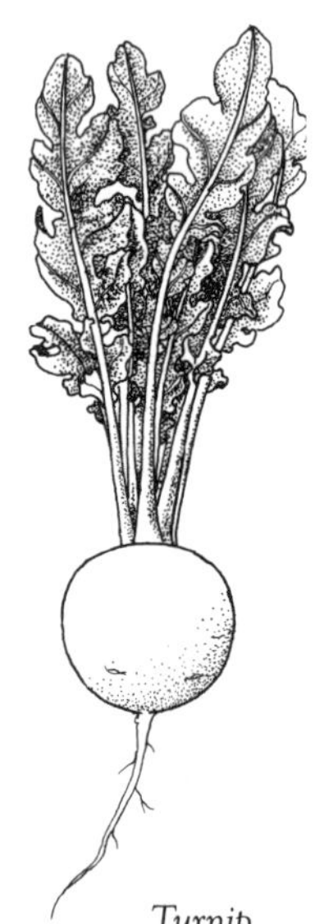
Turnip

'Tokyo Cross F_1' and 'Tokyo Market' can be harvested in around a month at 2 inches or later at twice that size. 'Shogoin' is often grown for its large leaves, which are ready in 30 days. After 60 days, it has 4-inch roots.

Pests Turnips get cabbage maggots as often as radishes do, so they need protection when they are grown during the warmer months of the year. Try beneficial nematodes applied in mid- to late March, or plant under a row cover frame. Turnips may also attract cabbage aphids.

Sources
Turnip seed:
Purple Top White Globe: Widely available
Golden Ball: BCS, GS, JLH, PGS, SESE, TERR
Tokyo Cross F_1: BUR, EE, KIT, PGS, VBS, WCS
Tokyo Market: EE, GS, KIT, NGN

Watercress

Nasturtium officinale
Mustard Family ❖ *Brassicaceae* (*Cruciferae*)

Watercress grows wild in running streams, but you can grow it in your garden if you keep the soil very moist. It is a good choice for a site where water seeps or near a hose attachment where you rinse vegetables. Since it does best in light shade, it is also a candidate for a shady corner. As a potted plant, it is suitable for growing in a bright north-facing window or an apartment light well. Watercress is happiest in the cool seasons and the coolest microclimates.

Growing Instructions Plant watercress in soil containing lots of organic matter. Sow the seeds directly, scattering them thinly and barely covering them with soil or sand. Thin the seedlings to 2 to 3 inches apart. When they are 6 inches tall, pinch the tips to encourage branching.

You can also start watercress from a purchased bunch. Cut off any injured or decayed stem bottoms. Cut the healthy stems in half and stand all the pieces in a small jar, with the bottom ends down. Add water to cover the stems halfway. Change the water daily until roots appear. The stem cuttings may also root well if you insert them in garden soil, burying them about halfway and keeping the soil very moist. Plant the cuttings, rooted or not, about 3 inches apart. Once the cuttings are well rooted and begin to grow, pinch the tips to encourage branching.

Watercress can also be grown in a pot of soil standing in a container of water. Be sure to put gravel in the bottom of the pot to keep the soil from leaking through, and change the water in the outer container daily to keep it fresh. Apply a liquid fertilizer once a week.

The Harvest When the plants have made substantial growth, harvest several inches of stem tips. Watercress seeds are rated at 50 days, but you will probably be picking sooner. If you use cuttings, you may be harvesting in just two weeks. Pinch back any stems that are forming flower buds. Although the plant is a perennial and lives on after flowering, the flowering and seeding stems are too bitter to enjoy. Plants that form seeds may reseed themselves in moist soil. If the plants are becoming ungainly, just take fresh cuttings and reroot them to start again.

Pests Watercress sometimes gets aphids. Take them as a sign that something is wrong: overcrowding, inadequate fertility, not enough water, or too little light (possible in deep shade or indoors). If the infestation is severe, pull up the plants and try to improve conditions for the next planting.

Sources
Watercress seed: BI, CG, EE, JG, JLH, JSS, KIT, NGN, PGS, RG, RH, SESE, T&M, TERR, WCS

Winter Melon (or Wax Gourd or Doan Gwa)

Benincasa hispida
Gourd Family ❖ *Cucurbitaceae*

An ingredient in Chinese cuisine, winter melon will mature in the warmer gardens of this region. The plant is large and productive in warmer parts of San Francisco. It is a vine that can be trained on a fence or trellis, although you will need to support the fruit. Each pumpkin-shaped melon can weigh as much as 25 pounds.

Winter melon is not a sweet fruit; it is used as a vegetable in stir-fries and soups. It is the basis for a classic Chinese dish in which the intricately carved melon shell serves as the soup tureen. In addition to using the mature fruit, you can also eat the immature fruit, young leaves, and flower buds.

Growing Instructions Give winter melon an early start, although it will not help to plant it out before the soil warms up, usually in early May. To gain four or five weeks, start the seeds indoors in a bottomless container to avoid disturbing the roots when you transplant (see page 51). Before you move the seedlings into the garden, add plenty of compost and fertilizer to your planting bed. Space the plants 8 to 10 inches apart and keep them well watered.

The Harvest When winter melons are ripe, they are covered with a white waxy substance. Cut the fruit, leaving a couple of inches of the stems. Stored in a cool spot (but not under 50°F), the fruit will keep for six months to a year—hence the name winter melon.

Sources
Winter melon seed: BCS, EE, KIT

Zucchini (see Squash, Summer)

TWELVE

Herbs for All Seasons

OU CAN GROW MOST OF THE commonly used culinary herbs in even the foggiest microclimates and harvest most of them throughout the year. You will find herbs easy to grow, delightful to have in the kitchen, and thought-provoking as well—taking you through history, around the world, and into many of the world's cuisines.

EASY AND REWARDING TO GROW

Even if you have only a tiny plot to devote to food gardening, herbs are among the most satisfying plants you can grow, because many common herbs are among the easiest of crops—and an herb garden can be one you use every day. Think how many meals contain a bit of oregano, a little chopped parsley, a pinch of thyme. And it takes so little of an herb to transform a dish. One oregano plant is usually sufficient for a household. A few basil plants will keep you amply supplied with pesto sauce through the summer. And a half dozen potted herbs on a sunny porch can brighten your menu all year.

You'll be glad to know that some herbs will tolerate less than ideal garden conditions. Some don't mind deep shade, so they can be grown in sites as shady as an apartment light well. Others will survive the extreme winds and sun of an exposed roof site, and some tolerate fairly poor, dry soil. Herbs can even be grown indoors with some success, although they are not at their best there.

You can easily integrate both annual and biennial herbs into your vegetable garden. A few parsley plants, some basil, a patch of cilantro make good neighbors to your other crops. (In a rotation, consider these fast-growing, succulent herbs to be heavy feeders.) Perennial herbs, on the other hand, are most commonly separated from the vegetables—at the corners of beds or grouped together in a separate area where they needn't be disturbed every time you replant annual crops. Many perennial herbs are light feeders, needing only reasonably fertile soil.

Annual or perennial herbs can also be used in ornamental plantings. Use annual herbs to fill in small spaces among more permanent plants in an ornamental border, replacing the herbs when they decline or when you have pulled them to eat. Perennial herbs, on the other hand, can provide the framework of an ornamental planting. They tend to stay green or gray-green all year. Many bloom for several weeks, and though the flowers are usually small, they are an attractive background for your showier blossoms and an attractant for beneficial insects.

The most formal ornamental use of perennial herbs is to create intricate and carefully manicured patterns of low herbs called knot gardens. While these are lovely, they do take time to maintain. Also, you will often find the species used are herbs grown mainly for scent, rather than for cooking. This is probably because harvesting fresh leaves for cooking tends to disturb the uniformity of the pattern, whereas you can collect clippings for dried sachets whenever you need to prune for aesthetic reasons. And consider that any ornamental pattern with many plants of the same culinary herb will probably produce far more of it than you can eat.

WHAT'S INCLUDED?

The chart on pages 286–287 shows the herbs covered in this chapter. In deciding whether to include an herb, I considered first whether it would grow in all or at least most of the region. Many familiar herbs, such as sage, oregano, and rosemary, are right at home in our climate. Native to the European countries bordering the Mediterranean, they are accustomed to similar day lengths, winter temperatures, and patterns of rainfall. Summers in the Mediterranean Basin tend to be warmer than summers in the foggiest California microclimates, but even in foggy gardens, these herbs develop plenty of flavor. Other familiar herbs, like parsley, coriander, and garlic (see Chapter 11) originated in the Middle East. While that region has hot summers, winters are mild. This means that their winter herbs do well in our winters also, and they sometimes grow through cool summer days as well.

Most of the herbs listed in this chapter will thrive in the entire Bay Area. (If I don't mention that an herb can grow only in one area, you can assume it will grow everywhere here.) But a few will have to struggle in foggier, colder gardens. Basil, in particular, may survive, but won't grow much, if summer temperatures are too low.

Among the many herbs that will grow here, I have included mainly the ones local gardeners grow most often and find most useful. But popularity wasn't my only criterion. Few have grown our native mint, yerba buena, a tasty and historically interesting plant. The hops vine is attractive and fun to grow and could tempt you to try home brewing. Winter tarragon is a little-known but delicious herb, waiting to be more widely discovered. And in at least one case, that of comfrey, I have explained why I no longer eat or even grow a once-popular herb.

Most of the herbs I've included are used in cooking, although I've described such uses as tea or sachets when they are common. And my cat insisted that I include catnip and similar feline favorites. I have not attempted to cover medicinal uses. I have also largely ignored the many claims that herbs can protect other crops from attacks by pests. Other books have covered the subject thoroughly, and the verdict is currently out on many of these claims. (See Herbs and Pests on page 288.)

In cooking, herbs are generally the plants used as flavorings, while vegetables are the foods that might be flavored by them; but in truth there is no clear line separating herbs and vegetables. Onions and garlic, for example, are often used as seasonings, but can also be vegetables. Cutting celery, which belongs to the same species as regular celery, is used as an herb. One person may like strongly flavored salads in which arugula or basil are a major green; another may see arugula or basil only as herbs to be chopped small and added sparingly. And sometimes what is an herb in one part of the world is a flower or even a weed in another. For all of these reasons, any listing of herbs is bound to be a bit arbitrary. If you don't find a plant listed in this chapter, check the index—it might be among the vegetables, flowers, or weeds.

GROWING HERBS

Nursery herbs in their identical 2-inch pots tend to give the impression that all herbs should be treated in the same way. Sometimes herb garden plans or photographs also give that impression when they show herb plants all the same size, growing in tidy clumps. But to successfully grow herbs, you need to learn the differences blurred by those matching pots and neat arrangements. Some herbs never grow more than a few inches tall, others are trees. Some stay politely in one spot, while others spread rampantly by underground runners. Some are annuals, some biennials, some perennials. Some need sun, others suffer unless they are shaded. Some need rich, well-watered soil, and others actually taste better when grown in poor, sandy, dry soil.

Still, those nursery herbs in 2-inch pots are the best way to get many kinds of herbs started in your garden. They are almost as economical as starting plants from seed, since you usually want only one or a few plants of each herb. They are considerably more convenient, since many kinds of herbs grow very slowly from seed, while you can be harvesting from a nursery plant in only a few weeks. And when you buy herb plants you can decide if you like their scents before you buy them. (Just gently rub a leaf and sample the aroma.) This is important when you are buying an unfamiliar herb, and also because the scent is likely to vary among cultivars of the same herb or even among plants with the very same name.

Some herbs are so easy to grow from pieces of the mature plant that they are rarely grown from seed. For example, mint is usually started by planting a piece of stem, which then grows roots. And a few kinds of herbs cannot be grown from seed at all. You will never find French tarragon seed, because this tarragon cultivar never blooms. All French tarragon is started by cuttings from existing plants. (If you do buy tarragon seed, it will grow into the much less tasty Russian tarragon.)

At the other extreme, cilantro, chervil, summer savory, and dill are much more likely to succeed if they are started from seed, because they transplant badly. If you buy nursery seedlings of these herbs, not only will you be spending a lot for plants you could easily grow from seed, but you will also give them a poor start by subjecting them to transplanting.

In the listings you will find advice on whether to grow an herb from seed or purchased plants, assuming that you are not planning to make a major project of herb propagation. The chart on pages 286–287 lists whether an herb is best grown from seeds, plants, or, if, given ample attention and time to grow, both are equally good. If you want to try more kinds of herbs from seed, either for the challenge or to have more plants, refer to the chart for general seeding requirements. For more information, see the books in Appendix VIII, Suggested Reading.

Keep perennial herbs tidy by pruning them back each year, as recommended under individual instructions. Many low-growing perennial herbs thrive for several years, then decline. Some grow in clumps that can be dug up, then cut apart and divided; others need to be renewed by layering, or by root or stem cuttings, as described in Chapter 6. Replace any herbs that do not thrive or that have declined seriously.

Remember that each type of herb is a new plant to learn to grow and use. If you've never used fresh herbs in cooking at all, start with only a few that you already purchase and use as dried herbs. Introduce only one or two new herbs each season so you will learn to grow and cook with them, not forgetting them as you use instead, out of habit, the ones you already know. As you look through cookbooks for recipes using vegetables you grow, remember to look for uses for herbs as well (see page 371).

Some herbs you grow may never find a place in your kitchen. Many a gardener has brought home a wonderfully aromatic and mysterious treasure, only to find no way to use the mature plant that has now sprawled over a large part of the herb garden. Unless you are enjoying such plants as ornamentals, find the courage to toss them into the compost heap and give something else a try instead.

Herbs in Containers

Herbs grow well in containers, so you can grow a few even if you have only a stair landing or porch. Choose tough, drought-tolerant ones for windy spots, shade-tolerant ones for shaded spots. Use a good potting mix, high in organic or other materials that hold moisture well, and plan to add some fertilizer regularly while the plants are actively growing. Choose 8- or 10-inch pots for most individual herbs, or larger boxes for several plants at once. Almost all herbs will be smaller when grown in pots, and perennials will be shorter-lived, but you will still be amply rewarded for your efforts.

Potting is one way to keep large herbs in bounds. Bay trees, for example, can be container-grown, keeping them well pruned so that they don't outgrow the pot too fast, and transplanting them to larger pots as they grow. Pots are also a good option for rampant spreaders, like mint, although you must remember that mint needs ample water. Use a very moisture-retentive soil mix and as large a container as you can arrange, water often, and don't try to grow potted mint on a windy roof.

If you want to try growing herbs inside, start by getting them out of their 2-inch nursery pots and into something more comfortable. Herbs do stay smaller when grown inside, but give them at least a 4-inch or 6-inch pot. Try them in your sunniest window—one that gets five or more hours of sunlight a day. If they still seem spindly, you may need to supplement with fluorescent lights. Just as for seedlings, the lights must be hung a few inches from the tops of the plants (see page 54). Also, wash your herbs in plain water once a week to avoid pests, which thrive indoors because there aren't enough natural predators there. Be sure to inspect and wash the backs of the leaves, too. If aphids, whiteflies, mealy bugs, or mites do appear, use a soap or oil spray to combat them. Check the source list in Appendix VII also, for sources of the tiny predator insects or mites that are suitable for indoor release.

Gardeners who have any outdoor space at all can have the best of both worlds by alternating environments. Grow the herbs you use the most in two separate sets of pots. Bring one set inside for a few days of harvesting, then put it back outdoors and bring in the second set for harvests instead. (For more on growing plants in containers, see pages 36–38.)

Herb Chart

HERB	TYPE	STARTED BY	FERTILITY	WATER	SUN	HEIGHT	VEG REPRO
Anise hyssop	Perennial	Plant/seed	Rich	Moderate	S	1–3'	Division, cuttings
Basil	Annual	Plant/seed	Rich	Moist	S	8"–2'+	—
Basil, African blue	Perennial	Plant	Moderate	Moist	S	2–6'	Cuttings
Bay laurel	Tree	Plant	Moderate	Dry	S/PS	40'	Cuttings
Bay, California	Tree	Plant	Moderate	Moderate	S/SH	60'	Cuttings
Borage	Annual	Seed	Most	Moderate	S/PS	3'	—
Catnip	Perennial	Plant/seed	Mod/rich	Dry/mod	S	2–3'	Division
Chamomile, English	Perennial	Plant	Moderate	Moderate	S/PS	1'	Division
Chamomile, German	Annual	Seed	Moderate	Moderate	S	1–2½'	—
Chervil	Annual	Seed	Mod/rich	Moist	PS/SH	2'	—
Chinese celery	Biennial	Seed	Rich	Moist	S/PS	2'	—
Chives	Perennial	Plant/seed	Rich	Moist	S/PS	1–1½'	Division
Comfrey	Perennial	Root	Moderate	Moist/ mod	S/PS	3'	Root cuttings, division
Coriander	Annual	Seed	Moderate	Moist	S	2–3'	—
Dill	Annual	Seed	Rich	Moist	S	3'	—
Epazote	Perennial	Plant/seed	Moderate	Moderate	S	2–4'	Stem cuttings
Fennel	Biennial	Seed	Moderate	Moist/mod	S	5'+	—
Garlic chives	Perennial	Plant/seed	Rich	Moist	S/PS	1–2½'	Division
Ginger	Perennial	Root	Rich	Moist	PS	3–4'	Root cuttings
Hops	Perennial	Root	Rich	Moist	S	10–30'	Division
Lavender	Perennial	Plant	Low	Moderate	S	18"–4'	Division, stem cuttings
Lemon balm	Perennial	Plant/seed	Rich	Moist	S/PS	2–3'	Division

Started By—Best way to get started. When either plant or seed can be used, they are both given, in order of preference; for example, "plant/seed" means it's best to start with a plant, although it isn't too hard from seed.

Fertility—Will thrive with low fertility, moderate fertility is fine, rich fertility required, or most levels are fine.

Water—Water requirements (dry, moderate, moist).

Sun—Sun requirements (S-sun, PS-part shade, SH-shade).

Height—Usual height (sometimes it varies by cultivar).

Veg Repro—Means of vegetative reproduction, when applicable.

Herb Chart

HERB	TYPE	STARTED BY	FERTILITY	WATER	SUN	HEIGHT	VEG REPRO
Lemon verbena	Shrub	Plant	Moderate	Moist	S	3–10'	Stem cuttings
Lemongrass	Perennial	Plant	Moderate	Moderate	S	1–2'	Division
Marjoram	Perennial	Plant/seed	Moderate	Moderate	S	1–1½'	Cuttings
Mint	Perennial	Plant	Rich	Moist	S/PS	1–1½'	Rooted runners
Mustard	Annual	Seed	Rich	Moist	S	2–3'	—
Oregano, Greek	Perennial	Plant	Mod/low	Rather dry	S	1–1½'	Cuttings, layering, division
Parsley	Biennial	Seed/plant	Rich	Moist	PS/S	6–12"	—
Parsley, Japanese	Perennial	Seed	Rich	Moist	SH/PS	1–3'	Division
Perilla	Annual	Seed	Moderate	Moist	S/PS	1–3'	—
Rosemary	Perennial	Plant	Low/mod	Rather dry	S	6" to 4'	Cuttings
Sage, garden	Perennial	Plant/seed	Moderate	Dry/moist	S	2'	Cuttings, layering
Sage, clary	Biennial	Seed	Moderate	Dry	S	3'+	—
Sage, pineapple	Perennial	plant/seed	Moderate	Moderate	S	3'+	—
Stevia	Perennial	Seed/plant	Moderate	Moderate	S/PS	1–2'+	Seed/cuttings
Summer savory	Annual	Seed	Rich	Moderate	S	18"	—
Winter savory	Perennial	Plant	Low/mod	Dry/mod	S	6–12"	Division, layering
Sweet woodruff	Perennial	Plant	Rich	Moist	PS/SH	6–10"	Rooted pieces, root cuttings
Tarragon, French	Perennial	Plant	Moderate	Moderate	S/PS	1–2'	Division, root cuttings
Tarragon, winter	Perennial	Plant/seed	Moderate	Moderate	S	1'+	Division
Thyme	Perennial	Plant/seed	Moderate	Dry/mod	S	6–12"	Cuttings, division, layering
Yerba buena	Perennial	Plant	Rich	Moist	S/PS	Creeping	Cuttings, layering

HERBS AND PESTS

Herbs grown out-of-doors tend to have few pest problems. Their aromatic oils often make them unattractive to insects. So unless an insect pest or a disease is mentioned for an herb, you can assume it is not likely to be affected by them here.

In fact, herbs are often mentioned as "companion plants" that can save nearby plants from insects, disease, or general malaise. Scientific testing of these theories has shown mixed results. A few relationships seem to work, although most concern insects that are not common here. And when an herb does repel an insect, to do so it often must be growing so thickly that the protected crop is stunted by the competition. A more promising research direction has been using extracts of repellant herbs to spray on crops. (For more on companion planting research, see Appendix VIII, Suggested Reading.)

A new and useful interpretation of companion planting is growing flowers to attract beneficial insects. Parsley and mint family flowers provide nectar and pollen for bees and other pollinators (see also page 106).

HARVESTING HERBS

We imagine that we will be able to pick the herbs we grow whenever we need them for a particular purpose. While this is true for many herbs—among them oregano, thyme, and chives—others are harvested according to other schedules. French tarragon can be harvested only in warmer months, as it is dormant in winter. Dill and most basils are annuals that grow in the warm season. They die each winter and must be replanted every spring. Parsley is a biennial. It goes to seed in the spring (and sometimes at other times). While parsley can be harvested much of the year, you need staggered plantings to be sure of having it all year. A few herbs, like cilantro or chervil, must be replanted every few weeks to provide a steady supply of young plants.

Herbs that have groups of single leaves growing from a central point, like parsley, are harvested by cutting off entire individual leaves with their stems. Chives, which have grasslike leaves, can be harvested by clipping the tops of leaves, like mowing. Herbs with leaves borne on the sides of stems, such as basil or oregano, are harvested by pinching back the stem tips. (By pinching off ungainly shoots, you can also shape plants as you harvest.)

Because herbs are generally used in such small quantities, you are more likely to be underpicking than overpicking them, but there are limits to how much you may safely harvest. You can begin to pick when the plant is quite small, but even if you are picking only a little bit at a time, if the plant is getting smaller, you are picking too much. You may harvest larger plants quite heavily several times a season. A good rule of thumb is never to harvest more than 50 percent of the plant at one time, and if you do harvest that much, let it grow back before you harvest again. A few herbs, among them mint and chives, can withstand even heavier harvesting. Both will spring back even if they are leveled, as long as it is during a season when they are actively growing. However, you will probably not want to chop them quite so severely very often, as it will interrupt your harvest.

Left to right: Thyme, basil, sage, oregano

PRESERVING HERBS

No matter how small your herb garden, you will occasionally grow more of something than you can use fresh. If you have time, dry some of your harvest, or freeze it. Most herbs dry very well at room temperature, in a few days to two weeks. Hang small bunches upside down in a well-ventilated room, or spread the herbs on a screen. Don't put them in direct sun or in a damp place. If you are drying seeds, like those of coriander or fennel, on their stalks, hang them with their tops in a paper bag. The bag will catch any seeds that fall from the stalks as they dry.

Oven drying is faster, from three to six hours. The oven temperature should be no higher than 150°F. Exceptions are basil and chervil, which should be dried at about 90°F. Dry herbs until they are crisp. If they brown, you have used too high a temperature. After you dry herb plants, you often need to separate the part you want from the part you don't want. For example, you need to strip leaves from oregano or thyme stems and sift any bits of plant out of coriander or fennel seeds. If they are dry but you aren't quite ready to prepare them, store the dried herbs in a closed plastic bag, to keep the flavor in. Then, after you've cleaned them, store in a tightly closed bottle.

You can also freeze herbs. Either freeze whole herb leaves, in plastic bags from which you have forced most of the air, or put herbs in the blender with just a bit of water and freeze the resulting paste in ice cube trays. When your herb ice has frozen, store the cubes in closed and labeled plastic bags until you are ready to use them in soups or sauces. You can blend and freeze a favorite combination of herbs together. And pesto base, frozen in the summer basil season, can extend that season to most of the year (see recipe on page 291).

We use herbs in such small quantities that you will often have a plant that is producing more than you can use. Extra home-grown herbs, fresh, dried, or frozen, make excellent gifts for nongardeners. Other ideas for easy herbal gifts include herbal vinegars, sauces, and mixes of dried herbs and flowers for use in fragrant potpourris or sachets.

Cooking with Fresh Herbs

Having a source of fresh herbs expands your options in the kitchen. For example, dried or fresh herbs can be used to season a salad dressing, but fresh herbs can also be chopped and added directly to the salad. Basil leaves in a tossed salad, cilantro in a salsa, mint in tabouli, or anise hyssop leaves and flowers in a fruit salad are delicious examples. Here is another advantage of growing herbs: their flowers are pretty and scented as pleasantly as the leaves. See Chapter 13 for more on edible flowers.

When making a stock or broth for soup, use fresh herbs in a bouquet garni—a small bundle of herbs tied together with a string. They are left in until the stock is cooked or may be taken out earlier if they have imparted as much flavor as you desire. Dried herbs can also be used to make a bouquet garni, though they must be contained in a small cloth sack, since they are not in large, easily removed pieces. Basic herbs for this purpose are parsley, bay leaf, and thyme, but you can vary the components as you desire. See the recipe for Homemade Chicken Stock on page 373.

In sautéed dishes, fresh herbs may be added to the oil, to flavor it, then removed. The fresh herb is better able to release its aroma for this style of cooking than are dried ones. Chopped fresh herbs can also be added at the end of the cooking, especially ones that do not keep their flavor well when cooked, such as chervil or marjoram.

The possibilities go on: fresh herbs in scrambled eggs, omelets, or frittatas, in sauces, casseroles, or breads. And, if you wish, try brewing tea with freshly picked herbs. Just put sprigs in a teapot or a cup and pour boiling water over them. However you use the fresh herbs from your garden, you will enjoy the convenience and zest they bring to your kitchen.

Compendium of Herbs

Anise Hyssop (or Licorice Mint)

Agastache foeniculum
Mint Family ❖ *Lamiaceae* (*Labiatae*)

Grow this herb for the delicious, sweet tea that can be made from its fresh or dried leaves, and for its edible flowers. Although small, each blossom contains a burst of flavor. Use them in green or fruit salads or to ornament a dessert. Flowering stems are also handsome in bouquets. Anise hyssop is a native of the north central United States, where the Plains Indians discovered how good it tastes.

Anise hyssop plants are a bushy 2 to 3 feet high. They resemble the related mints in having opposite pairs of leaves on square stems. However, they differ in their licorice flavor, and they clump rather than spread aggressively by runners like mint. In addition to the common purple-flower, dark green-leaved variety, you will find 'Snow Spike' with white flowers and 'Golden Jubilee' with yellow-green leaves.

Growing Instructions Start anise hyssop from a nursery plant, or, if that proves hard to find, you can also grow it easily from seed. Start seed inside in the spring. The plants will grow in any soil with good drainage and will grow lushly in rich garden soil. They more or less die back to the ground in winter and usually regrow in spring, though they sometimes winterkill. If plants live from year to year and enlarge, they will become big enough to divide, or sometimes seedlings come up in spring where last summer's seeds fell, so you can get more plants simply by transplanting them.

Sources

Anise hyssop seed: JLH, JSS, NGN, PGS, RH, SESE, SS, TERR, T&M
Anise hyssop plants: RH, TERR
Snow Spike anise hyssop seed: RH
Golden Jubilee anise hyssop seed: JLH, TERR, T&M
Golden Jubilee anise hyssop plants: AA

Basil (or Sweet Basil)

Ocimum basilicum

Holy Basil (or Tulsi)

Ocimum sanctum

Mint Family ❖ *Lamiaceae* (*Labiatae*)

I never saw much reason to grow basil until I tasted fresh garden pesto, a wonderful basil-based sauce for pasta. Then I became a basil evangelist. More basil, yes! Bigger basil leaves! Basil earlier and longer! And, while basil pesto is delicious, there is more; this is a wonderfully aromatic herb that can have many other uses in your cooking.

Basil does well in the sunnier parts of the region, but may not succeed in foggier gardens. If you are trying out basil in a very foggy area, include a dwarf variety like O. *basilicum* 'Minimum', which may do better than the larger-leaved varieties. One fog zone gardener starts many large-leaved basil seedlings each spring, growing some in a small greenhouse and trying others in the garden. He reports that some years the plants outside fail, other years they thrive.

The big news is that a new variety, African blue Basil, grows into a shrub in warm summer gardens and can grow well enough to be worth trying even in foggy locations. Where winters are frost-free, it is a perennial plant.

Growing Instructions *Ocimum basilicum* is an annual plant that grows in the warm months. May is always warm enough to plant basil; earlier times may work out fine, but are chancy. Give the plants a protected spot that will be sunny on clear days.

To grow annual basil for occasional use as seasoning, start with just one or two plants. But to have enough for pesto, buy one or two six-packs of seedlings of a large-leaved variety. Basil is also relatively easy to start from seed. For an early start, seed your basil indoors. Sow March through May, maybe even as early as February if you have a good place to grow it till the weather warms, or if you are planting it out early into a very protected spot. The seedlings will be ready to transplant in three to four weeks, either into the garden or into a larger pot. I usually pot mine up and grow them to 5 or 6 inches tall before I set them out, to give them the best chance against slugs, snails, and earwigs.

Basil does best in well-fertilized soil that has good drainage. Plant full-sized basil 8 inches apart, dwarf varieties 4 inches apart. When basil has three to four sets of true leaves, pinch out the tip of the plant. This will make side branches grow, creating a bushy plant. Keep basil evenly watered; it is not one of the herbs that thrives in dry soil.

The Harvest To get the most production from your plants, don't harvest whole plants. Pick by pinching back the leafy stem tips, always being sure to leave at least half of the plant intact. Take 1 to 4 inches from each tip, pinching back to where there are small leaves sprouting at the base of a pair of large leaves. Keep harvesting tender tips all season.

Soon spikes of flower buds will begin to form at the stem tips. You can use these, or even opening flowers, just as you would leaves. However, if a plant blooms very much, and the flowers begin to form seeds, it will begin to lose its lower leaves and will not make many new leaves. Therefore try to keep flower buds picked before they open. After you have completed a day's harvest of leafy tips, check the plants over again for any opening flowers you have missed, and pick them off.

When weather turns wet and cold, Mediterranean basil leaves fall off and the plants eventually die. This commonly happens in October or November, but the exact time varies with the weather patterns of a given year. Watch your plants for a decline and try to pull them while the leaves are still usable. Strip the plants and either freeze or dry the leaves. Dry basil at no more than 90°F, just until crisp, or freeze fresh leaves in freezer bags, or use in a pesto base (see the opposite page).

African blue basil will become a 5- to 6-foot-tall, woody shrub if you let it. The leaves have purple-speckled undersides or may be purple-tinged on top as well, and the flowers are purple, making it pretty enough for an ornamental garden. I have grown it into a shrub, letting it bloom all over, and have found it is a tremendous attractant of beneficial insects, from bees to lady beetles to butterflies. I have harvested stem tips along with their flowers most of the year, frequently trimming off long, spent flower stems to keep the plant looking tidier. My plant, in a San Francisco Mission District garden, has survived three winters so far, with some dieback that I prune out in spring.

A second plant has been in for one summer, and I have been harvesting by pinching every

California Pesto and Pasta

I call my version of this classic sauce "California" Pesto because of the two changes I've made in the traditional recipe. First, I replace some of the olive oil with water. This reduces the fat content and lowers the calorie count, but still leaves plenty of flavor. Second, I substitute almonds for the traditional but more expensive pine nuts. (Sometimes I use pecans, which are also very good.) Try it and I'm sure you'll find that this pesto is as delicious as a traditional pesto. In this recipe, the pesto is served with spaghetti, but you can use it with any other pasta. Serves two to four.

Spaghetti (¾- to 1-inch diameter bunch per serving)
⅓ cup cold water
¼ cup virgin olive oil
2 cups packed fresh basil leaves (no tough stems), coarsely chopped
3 cloves garlic
¼ cup almonds (or pecans)
¾ cup grated Parmesan cheese
¼ cup or more hot spaghetti water, as needed

Let the spaghetti cook while you make the pesto. Bring a large pot of water to a boil and add the spaghetti. Bring the water back to a boil, turn to low, cover, and set the timer for 7 to 12 minutes, depending on the thickness of the spaghetti and how well cooked you like it.

To make the pesto sauce, pour the cold water and olive oil into a blender. Gradually add the basil and blend until smooth. Add the garlic and almonds and blend again. Pour the pesto into a medium bowl and stir in the Parmesan cheese.

When the spaghetti is cooked, spoon boiling water from the pot into the pesto and mix. Add enough water to make a thick sauce. You want it not too solid or too runny. Drain the spaghetti and serve it with pesto to spoon on top, or toss with the spaghetti before serving.

Variation: Pesto is most commonly used as a pasta sauce, but it has many other uses. For instance, you can stir it into soups, add a little to salad dressings, or use it as a pizza topping. You can even use it as a seasoning for baked fish: spread a ¼-inch-thick layer of undiluted pesto in the cavity of a trout, wrap the fish in aluminum foil, and bake at 350°F for about 20 minutes.

Note: Pesto sauce freezes well, but it will taste better if you do not add the cheese until after it is thawed. You can blend just the basil, cold water, olive oil, garlic, and almonds to freeze as a pesto base. When you need a pesto sauce, thaw the base, add the cheese, and spoon in enough boiling water to thin the sauce to the desired consistency.

stem before flowers can open. This lets it put more energy into forming larger leaves and lets you avoid the chore of deadheading. It's a bushy 18-inch-tall clump, although, of course, without flowers it hasn't served the beneficial insects.

Some people, on crushing an African blue basil leaf, are put off by the scent, but I've used the leaves to season salads or to make pesto for many people, and all have given it rave reviews. I have also found that the leaves make a nice dried herb.

Besides being used in pesto, basil is commonly used in dishes with raw or cooked tomatoes, in soups, in meat and fish dishes, and in salads and salad dressings. Try a few basil leaves finely chopped in a green salad. Or make a salad of just tomatoes, avocado or cucumber, some chopped fresh basil, and a sprinkling of pine nuts. Add basil to omelets or use it to season vegetables. A good combination is basil—either chopped fresh or crumbled dry—sprinkled on chunks of steamed winter squash.

Varieties and Related Species There are several dozen varieties of *Ocimum basilicum*, grouped mainly by whether they have large leaves, small leaves, purple leaves, or variations on the basic basil scent such as hints of lemon or cinnamon. To get plenty of large leaves for pesto, grow sweet basil or its strains such as 'Genovese'. Even larger-leaved cultivars, such as 'Mammoth', are sometimes used as "wrappers" for other foods. Small-leaved types, usually classified as *O. b. minimum*, include 'Green Globe' and 'Bush Basil'. These are fine for those who want just a pinch of the herb now and then or want to use a stem to flavor vinegar.

Purple-leaved basils are available with leaves from big wrapper size, like 'Red Lettuce Leaf', down to tiny, such as those of 'Dark Opal'. Scented varieties bear leaves that remind the taste buds of lemon, cinnamon, or anise.

Lemon basil (*O.b. citriodorum*) has medium-sized green leaves with a lemony touch. Cinnamon and anise basil both have rosy pink flower stalks. An anise-scented basil known as Thai basil was introduced to the U.S. by Southeast Asian immigrants.

Another favorite of that part of the world is the clove-scented perennial *O. sanctum*. Considered holy by Hindus in India, this plant is grown near temples and dwellings and is valued in Asian cuisine. *O. sanctum* may be sold as Holy basil or as Tulsi.

The presumed parents of African blue basil are *Ocimum kilimandscharicum*, from East Africa, and *Ocimum basilicum* 'Dark Opal'. The African parent is a tropical shrub used to make a salve because of its camphory scent. Because the two plants are different species, it is not surprising to know that the flowers make no seeds; it has to be propagated from cuttings. Look for plants in the spring in local nurseries or order from a mail order source. To propagate the plant, you need to make a stem cutting in June or July and then make sure it survives winter well, perhaps inside or in a greenhouse, so it gets a good start in spring.

Pests Basil grown indoors is likely to be attacked by aphids or whiteflies. For information on both, see Chapter 9, Managing Bugs and Blights. Outdoors, protect basil seedlings from snails, slugs, and earwigs by growing them under row cover until they are 6 to 8 inches tall. A serious new threat is a soil disease, fusarium wilt. While I have not seen it yet, you should obtain seed that has been tested to be sure it isn't infected (called FT0 seed). This information should be provided by websites or catalogs. If your basil plants suddenly wilt, remove and do not compost them. Two basil varieties, 'Nufar' and 'Aroma 2', are resistant to the disease.

Sources

Many varieties of basil seed are widely available.
Nufar basil seed: BUR, JSS, NGN, PS, RH, WCS
Aroma 2 basil seed: JSS
African blue basil plants: RH, TERR

Bay Laurel (or Sweet Bay, or True Laurel)

Laurus nobilis

California Bay (or California Laurel)

Umbellularia californica

Laurel Family ❖ *Lauraceae*

The bay laurel (*Laurus nobilis*) is the tree that bears the classic culinary bay leaf. It is also the tree from which laurel wreaths were made, in ancient Greece, to celebrate winners in the Pythian games, and in which Roman generals wrapped announcements of victories before sending them to the Senate. And a striking tree it is, its branches covered thickly with lustrous, deep green leaves. Its small yellow flowers are sometimes followed by attractive (but inedible) berries. Although it naturally grows up to 40 feet tall, it can be kept much smaller by constant pruning and snipping. Gardeners without room for a large tree can keep a bay pruned as a shrub or grow it in a container. It can also be trimmed into fanciful shapes, a pruning style called topiary.

The California bay (*Umbellularia californica*) is a native plant from the same family. Its leaves are similar to those of the bay laurel, but a bit narrower. Californians often use them like bay laurel, although *Laurus nobilis* is the preferred culinary herb because the flavor of California bay is decidedly harsher. In the wild, California bay can grow to 60 feet, often with several trunks. It thrives among the redwoods, its silhouette lovely in a soft fog. Under redwoods it grows tall and narrow, reaching toward sunlight, often leaning so far that it falls over. In an open area it grows straighter and fuller.

Growing Instructions Buy a bay tree as a small potted plant. They are often sold in 1-gallon pots, and occasionally as even smaller plants.

Both of these trees will do well in partial shade. The California bay will even grow in deep shade. (Beware of planting either one where it can grow up and cast its shadow on your garden, as both create quite deep shade themselves.)

Soil for these trees needn't be rich, but both require good drainage. Mature bay laurels need little water. The California bay does well with moderate watering, though it will tolerate drought. However, if you grow either of the bays in containers, you will have to pay closer attention to watering it than you would if it were in the open ground, since neither should ever go bone dry. Use a good potting mix and mulch with well-rotted manure. You may want to fertilize once in a while, but don't do so often or use too much fertilizer at a time, as you don't want to encourage rapid growth.

Either is guaranteed to outgrow its pot eventually, it roots reaching out the bottom. Before it gets pot bound, repot it in a slightly larger container, adding fresh potting mix and trimming the roots back. (See page 341 for more on root pruning containerized trees.) You may be able to keep it in larger and larger containers for ten years or more, putting it in a half wine barrel when nothing smaller will hold it.

The Harvest Prune culinary bay frequently to keep it small, and don't remove lower limbs, so you will be able to pick the leaves. Harvest leaves when you are pruning, or break off a leaf or two as needed. Leaves can be used fresh or dried. Some cooks prefer to use the leaves dry, since the flavor is mellower. To dry the leaves, make single layers between sheets of newspaper or brown bag paper and press the layers under heavy books for two to three weeks. Store the dried leaves in closed jars to preserve their flavor. In cooking, bay is used in soups, stews, tomato sauces, and marinades, and as a pickling spice. Bay leaves are a standard ingredient in the French bouquet garni. Since the California bay is stronger flavored, use only one California bay leaf in place of two or three bay laurel leaves.

Varieties One variety of the true bay laurel is worth seeking out. *L. nobilis* 'Saratoga' was developed at the Saratoga Horticultural Foundation. It resists scale and another pest, the psyllid, and is a vigorous plant. It is worth a try as a container plant, although it has a slightly more open habit, so won't make quite the dense bush of leaves that the common bay laurel will.

Sources

Bay laurel plants: Widely available

California bay plants: Often available in local nurseries or at plant sales or through the California Native Plant Society (see Appendix VI, Seed and Starter Plant Sources).

Borage

Borago officinalis

Borage Family ❖ *Boraginaceae*

This is a big, exuberant plant with rough-hairy, grey-green leaves and striking blue flowers about ¾ of an inch across. Borage grows wild in southern Europe and on the chalk downs of southern England. It also grows wild in my garden, reseeding itself in both the spring and the fall. I weed out, and sometimes eat excess seedlings, but let it mature here and there. I really don't use much of the mature plant, but I like the fact that it encourages bees to visit my garden. I have sometimes planted it in fall by a fruit tree to attract bees to the area in time to pollinate the tree's flowers.

Borage

Though it is not in the cucumber family, the whole borage plant has a definite, and very refreshing, cucumber flavor.

Growing Instructions Borage is an annual that grows 2 to 3 feet high. It is best seeded in place, since it does not transplant well. It isn't fussy about soil, just growing a bit less high if the soil is poorer. Sow in the late spring to early fall, in full or nearly full sun. Thin so that mature plants stand a foot or two apart. Keep plants evenly moist.

The Harvest The first time you see borage seedlings, you are likely to think they are squash seedlings, as they have similar big flat seed leaves. The true leaves of borage, however, are simple ovals, not lobed like a squash leaf. If you planted the seed thickly, do harvest the extra seedlings as you pull them. In subsequent years, the borage will self-sow, giving you plenty of extra seedlings to add that mysterious hint of cucumber to your salads. Use them when they have only seed leaves or at most one or two small true leaves. After that, the raw true leaves become a bit too prickly for most people's taste.

I am learning that borage has been traditionally used as a vegetable in its native Spain and is so used in other parts of Europe as well, despite the rather rough hairs that cover the plant. The young stems are peeled, revealing a crisp, slightly mucilaginous, light green core, and the leaves lose their prickliness when cooked. For use as a vegetable, the plant parts are harvested while young and tender, generally before the plant has bloomed. In the Netherlands, plants are sold as a vegetable when they are only 4 to 6 inches tall. However, it must be said that leaves of borage contain traces of the liver toxins found in the related comfrey, so I suppose one wouldn't want to subsist on them.

You can eat borage flowers with or without their soft-furry sepals. (To remove the sepals, pull on the stamens.) Use the flowers in salad, or float them in iced tea or punch. Victorians candied them. For tea, harvest the blooming tops with their leaves and steep them in boiling water.

Sources
Borage seed: Widely available

Catnip
Nepeta cataria
Catmint
Nepeta mussinii
Cat Thyme
Teucrium marum
Mint Family ❖ *Lamiaceae* (*Labiatae*)

These are herbs to grow primarily for your cat, although catnip also makes a passable, but not psychotropic, tea for people. Many cats enjoy these herbs, both fresh from the garden and dried. In fact, some cats enjoy these herbs so much that they will nibble them or roll in them until they kill the plants. (On the other hand, some cats are bored by all three herbs, and recent research has shown that response or lack of it are genetic traits among cats!)

All three herbs are perennials. Catnip grows 2 or 3 feet high, blooming in summer. Its small flowers are white with red or lavender dots. Catmint and cat thyme are prettier plants, worthy of a border or rock garden if neighborhood cat attention isn't too intense. Both are low growing, under 1 foot high and sprawling. Catmint has blue flowers and cat thyme flowers are rosy pink to purple.

Growing Instructions Of the three plants, cat thyme is best grown from a transplant, while catnip and catmint can be grown from either transplant or seed, though for one plant, you would do best to use transplants. When you set transplants in the soil, you will bruise the leaves, releasing the odors. To keep cats from nibbling or crushing young plants to death, you may need to cover them with something firm, like a wire cage, while they establish themselves. In an extreme situation, you might need to resort to moving them to safety in a hanging pot. Sometimes plants grown from seed are more likely to escape cat notice, because if you don't touch the seedlings, and your cat doesn't walk through them, they won't give off much cat-attracting odor at first.

Plant any of these species in a sunny place. They all thrive in sandy soil, but will do well in any soil but heavy, unamended clay. Sun and good drainage will increase the strength of their scent.

The Harvest Cut leafy stems as desired. Cut the flowering stems before the seed sets to prevent plants from self sowing and becoming a weed, or at least cut plants back once a year to improve their appearance.

You may decide to just let your cat enjoy these herbs fresh, or you can dry them. For drying, harvest the flowering stems. These dry easily if hung or spread in a dark, well-ventilated place. Give your cat a teaspoon or so of the dried herb, or brush the dried leaves and flowers from the stems and sew or tie them into a piece of cloth, perhaps with a bell added for merriment.

Sources
Catnip seed: Widely available
Catnip plants: JG, RH, TERR
Catmint seed: JSS, NGN, RG, RH, T&M, WCS
Catmint plants: BUR, PGS, PS, RH
Cat thyme plants: RH

Chamomile, English (or Roman Chamomile)
Chamaemelum nobile (Anthemis nobilis)
Chamomile, German (or Hungarian Chamomile, or Sweet False Chamomile)
Matricaria recutita (*Matricaria chamomilla*)
Sunflower Family ❖ *Asteraceae* (*Compositae*)

Two plants are championed as the true chamomile. The English and the Germans have each historically preferred the flavor of one over the other, and you will still find opposing claims in modern books and seed catalogs! The flowerheads of both are used to make a soothing tea with a strong apple-like scent.

English chamomile is a creeping perennial ground cover, under one foot tall. It makes a thick, low mat of feathery leaves and, from the second year after seeding, small flowerheads on wiry stems. These may have white petals around the edge, like little daisies, or may be just yellow buttons. English chamomile can be grown between stepping stones or even, with occasional mowing to remove its flowers, as a lawn.

German chamomile, an annual, is a taller, much looser plant than English chamomile. It makes no mat of leaves near the ground. In my garden it reaches only about 1½ feet, but it is said to grow as high as 2½ feet. Its flowerheads are quite similar to the white-petalled form of English chamomile.

Growing Instructions Start English chamomile from purchased plants, from either the herb or the ground cover section of your nursery. However, if

English chamomile plants are being sold as a ground cover, be sure the variety you buy is one that blooms, as it is the flowers that you will be harvesting. Grow German chamomile from seed. It can be started indoors, and transplanted until it is 2 inches high, but it is easier to sow it in place.

Both chamomiles grow well in full sun. English chamomile will tolerate some shade and prefers days that aren't too hot. Grow both in good garden soil, and keep them well watered.

The Harvest Because the tea is made only from the flowerheads, you will need a number of plants. Plant a few square feet of either of the chamomiles to get enough for a steady supply of tea. Harvest the flowerheads when the yellow centers are taller than they are wide, but don't wait too long or they will be less flavorful. If you harvest more than you can use at one time, dry them at room temperature.

You can propagate English chamomile by division, digging 1- to 2-inch-diameter sections of the plant and transplanting them. Once you've let German chamomile go to seed in your garden, it will probably continue to reseed itself. These volunteers can be a free source of tea, but they can get in the way of your other plants, so don't let very many plants drop their seed.

Varieties and Related Species If you are buying English chamomile plants, beware of nonblooming cultivars. At least one, 'Treanague', has been bred bloomless for use in lawns.

Two other locally common plants are also sometimes called chamomile, but their flavor is clearly inferior to both English and German chamomile. One is pineapple weed (*Matricaria matricarioides*), a low-growing plant with yellowish-green flowerheads, often found growing wild in the cracks of the pavement. The second is feverfew (*Chrysanthemum parthenium*) (see also page 328), a small-flowered perennial chrysanthemum that grows about 2 feet high. It is used in landscaping, but often comes up wild in gardens. The flowerheads of feverfew are white, usually double, with yellow centers. The leaves look like miniature chrysanthemum leaves. I tolerate volunteer plants of feverfew because they make nice cut flowers, but for tea, I choose one of the true chamomiles.

Sources

English chamomile plants: Local nurseries
German chamomile seed: Widely available

Chervil

Anthriscus cerefolium
Parsley Family ❖ *Apiaceae* (*Umbelliferae*)

Given a window box in Paris big enough to grow only one herb, many French people would certainly choose *cerfeuil*, or chervil. Chervil is as common in French cooking as it is rare in American. It thrives in cool, shady places, so it grows very well in our region.

Chervil is an annual plant that, like coriander, makes a low leafy rosette, then a tall seed stalk. Like coriander, the parts eaten are the young leaves. Cool days, fog, and shade stimulate leafy growth, while heat and sun stimulate seeding. I haven't grown it long enough to be sure of all the planting times that will succeed, but clearly it can be grown more of the year in foggier areas than elsewhere. I grew it in early spring in my foggy San Francisco garden, and it reseeded itself in midsummer to make a plentiful harvest again in September. Try plantings in late winter through midsummer, and again in the early fall. Sow once a month for a continuous supply of leaves.

Growing Instructions Sow chervil seed in the place where you want it to grow. Choose a location that is partially shaded, especially in early summer. Chervil will grow well in any good garden soil, but if you have heavy clay, plant chervil only after you have amended your soil for a couple of years. Mulch can help keep the soil cool in warm periods. Stimulate leaf production by cutting the plants back to near the ground when they are 3 inches tall.

The Harvest Thin small plants to 6 inches apart, making use of your thinnings in cooking. Then, as plants get larger, begin to harvest older leaves or whole plants before they form flower stems.

Chervil has a lovely taste, like a mild anise or tarragon, with a hint of parsley. It is used particularly in omelets, but also with meat, fish, oysters, in sauces, in sorrel or spinach soup, and in salads. Add it at the end of cooking, or even after food leaves the stove, to preserve its delicate flavor. It is almost always used, fresh since its flavor does not survive drying well, but you can try drying it at 90°F.

Varieties Two varieties of chervil, plain and curled, are commonly available. If the variety is not identified in a description, it is probably the plain-leaved. Both are used as seasoning, with the curled variety also favored for visual effect in a salad, or for use as a garnish instead of parsley.

Pests and Diseases Chervil may be nibbled by the various chewing pests, especially in the fall, when small hungry snails and summer's larger sow bug population are looking for something tender to eat. See Chapter 9 for controls for these pests.

Sources
Plain chervil seed: Widely available
Curly chervil seed: BUR, CG, JG, NGN, RH, T&M

Chinese Celery (or Kintsai, Heung Kun, Seri-na Cutting Leaf Celery, or Celery Dinant)

Apium graveolens var. *dulce*
Carrot Family ❖ *Apiaceae* (*Umbelliferae*)

Ordinary celery is often used as a flavoring. Pieces of stalk and leaves are boiled and then discarded in the preparation of many soup stocks, and we also value celery for the zest it can add to a variety of salads. In China, and also in Europe, smaller and particularly strong-flavored types of celery are used exclusively as a flavoring ingredient, much as we would use chopped parsley. These plants are left standing in the garden, and their stalks, or sometimes only their leaves, are harvested as needed, to use fresh or in soups.

Cutting celeries, both Asian and European, are strains of the same species and variety as regular celery, and they are grown in the same way. (See page 209.) While they are probably just as sensitive to cold as regular celery, and need just as much water and fertilizer to thrive, they don't have to be grown quite as perfectly, since the leaves will be usable even if the stalks are not very tender. Scan seed catalog herb listings under its various names, or look for it under celery. While cutting celery could be grown from purchased transplants, I have never seen them for sale.

Sources
Chinese celery seed: CG, EE, KIT, PGS, PS
European cutting celery seed: Widely available

Chives

Allium schoenoprasum
Amaryllis Family ❖ *Amaryllidaceae*

Chives are smaller cousins of bunching onions. One of the most popular herbs, chives are easy for a beginner and quite useful in the kitchen. The tubular leaves of these perennial plants can be harvested with a pair of scissors, cutting back the tops and letting more grow from the base.

Growing Instructions Chives can be grown fairly easily from seed but are very slow to mature, usually growing to cutting size only in the second year. Because of this, gardeners usually save at least a few months by purchasing a clump or two of plants from a nursery. Chives will grow in most garden soils, doing best in a well-amended one that drains well and at the same time holds moisture well. Since they are perennial, you should choose a spot for them that is as free as possible from weeds. Grassy weeds are especially difficult to remove from an established chive clump. Chives also do very well in an 8- or 10-inch pot. They can live permanently in a pot near your back door, or they can be transplanted when you have prepared a garden spot for them.

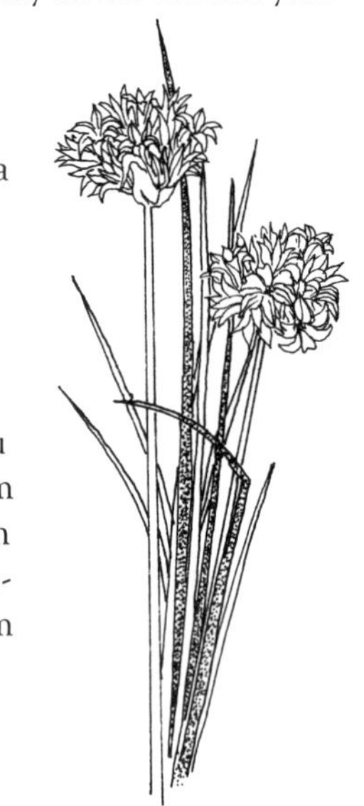

Fertilize chives growing in the garden a couple of times a year to help them withstand heavy cutting. Fertilize potted chives every two weeks, while they are actively growing, with a liquid fertilizer at half the recommended strength. Divide your chive clumps every two to four years, replanting in groups of six to ten bulbs per clump, and leaving 8 inches between clumps. You can do this any time of year, but the spring or the fall is best. If you haven't developed a need for more chives by the time you thin your clumps, pot some up for budding gardener friends.

The Harvest Harvest chive plants by clipping their leaves with scissors. Cut leaves nearly to the ground, rather than just halfway down. This stimulates the plant to make more new growth, preventing flowering. If you would rather harvest smaller amounts more frequently, try cutting just a few plants in the clump each time, but cutting them low. Use your chives fresh, or freeze them, chopped small, to use in winter, when growth will slow.

Chive blooms are attractive lavender pompoms. They can be used in salad or to make an herbal vinegar (see French Tarragon Harvest, page 315), but unless you have a use for them, it is better to pick them off before the buds open. This lets the plants put more energy into growing leaves.

Chives are appealing snipped small into cottage cheese or sour cream; try them also in omelets, scrambled eggs, creamed vegetable soups, and salads. Try sprinkling whole chives or at least half-length ones over a salad. While finely chopped chives will often migrate to the bottom of the bowl during tossing, these longer ones won't, and they add an intriguing visual touch to your salad.

You may prefer a longer, thicker chive leaf. Cultivars such as 'Staro' and 'Grande' are somewhat larger than usual, and a variety known as *Allium schoenprasum sibericum* is sometimes sold as "giant chives." While the species has leaves about 1⁄16 of an inch in diameter, those of giant chive are up to 3⁄16 of an inch and the plants are up to two feet high.

Pests Chives are susceptible to a black aphid. Check low in the plants for aphids, especially in winter. See page 113 for more on aphids.

Sources
Chive seed and plants: Widely available
Grande chive seeds: RH
Staro chive seeds: JSS, SOC, T&M

Chives, Garlic (see Garlic Chives)

Comfrey (or Russian Comfrey)

Symphytum × uplandicum (*S. peregrinum*)
Borage Family ❖ *Boraginaceae*

I have decided to stop growing comfrey, although it hasn't yet stopped growing in my garden. Once established, this perennial keeps coming back from missed bits of root. When I first planted it, I used the leaves or roots for tea, and found the very young leaves mildly pleasant to munch in early spring. Then recently, scientists discovered dangerous amounts of a substance that is a liver toxin and possible cause of cancer, pyrrolizidine, in comfrey leaves, so I stopped eating it. Comfrey is still an excellent ingredient for the compost, but I strongly recommend that you do not eat any part of it, make tea from it, or feed it to animals.

Comfrey has quite a reputation as a healing herb. It was used in the Middle Ages of Europe both as a tea and as a poultice for wounds. Comfrey has also been used as food for chickens and other livestock. Modern study of the plant revealed a substance that does indeed aid healing. This has been named allantoin, and it is now extracted from comfrey roots, as well as made artificially, for use in medicines.

Growing Instructions Should you wish to grow comfrey, it is best to start it from a small plant or from a 1- to 3-inch piece of root. Lay the root in the ground horizontally, 3 to 6 inches deep, 3 feet from any other plants. It will form a rosette of large, hairy leaves and, in the late spring and summer, tall stalks of small, bell-like flowers. The flowers are most likely to be purple, although white, rose, or yellow flowers are also possible. If you have a variety that forms viable seeds, remove flower stems to avoid seed formation.

The Harvest Chop leaves for use in compost. Do not compost any bit of root, as it will grow into a new plant.

Varieties Most of the available comfrey plants are not common comfrey (*Symphytum officinale*) but *Symphytum × uplandicum*, which is a cross between common comfrey and *S. aspersum*. It generally doesn't form viable seeds, which will help prevent its spread. 'Bocking 14' is said to have the highest allantoin content.

Sources
Comfrey roots or plants: NGN, RH

Coriander (or Cilantro or Chinese Parsley)

Coriandrum sativum
Carrot Family ❖ *Apiaceae* (*Umbelliferae*)

Few people are neutral about the flavor of cilantro—the name by which most of us know the leaves of the coriander plant. Some find the flavor delectable, others, awful. I can testify that this can be an acquired taste. The flavor used to remind me of soap, but now I enjoy it and use cilantro in many delicious recipes. I also cook with coriander seeds, which have a different flavor from the leaves.

Gardeners' most common problem with coriander is that they expect it to stand all year like parsley, and they are surprised when it flowers after only a few weeks of harvest. Coriander is an annual plant, maturing seed in three to four months. For a

Coriander stem with seeds (left) and flowers (right)

Thai Fish Soup

I used to order a soup much like this at a Thai restaurant in the San Francisco Mission District. Sharply tart and wonderfully savory, it was just right on a cold winter evening before a bike ride home from work. I learned to make it by asking what was in it and experimenting on my own. That restaurant is gone, but now I can make the soup myself. Fish sauce is a very common ingredient in Thai and Vietnamese cooking. It is made from an extract of salted fish. You can buy it at Asian grocery stores. Serves four.

1½ pounds red snapper or similar white fish

2½ quarts water

3 or 4 fresh leaves lemongrass, cut in 1- to 2-inch lengths (or 1 bulbous leaf base, chopped)

⅓ cup lime juice

⅓ cup fish sauce

⅛ teaspoon crushed red chile pepper

One 14-ounce can coconut milk

⅓ cup fresh coriander leaves, chopped

¼ cup green onion tops, onion lily leaves, or garlic chives, cut into 2-inch pieces

Cut the fish into ¾-by-1½-inch pieces, removing any bits of bone you find. Bring the water to a boil in a large pot. Add the lemongrass and simmer for 10 minutes. Stir in the lime juice, fish sauce, red pepper, and coconut milk and simmer the soup for a few more minutes. Add the fish, lower the heat, and simmer 5 to 10 more minutes. Just before serving, add the coriander leaves and onion greens. Taste and adjust seasonings, adding more lime juice, fish sauce, or crushed red pepper if needed.

continuous supply of leaves from young plants, you must resow every few weeks. If you eat only a little of it, try sowing a dozen or two seeds at a time, as larger plantings may only go to seed before you can eat them.

Growing Instructions Coriander grows well in cool temperatures, even in the winter months. Its maturation is slowed down when the weather is cool or the garden site shady—which means a longer production of leafy greens before the inevitable bolt. In fact, plants that mature in a very warm period may send up flower stems after producing only a few usable basal leaves.

Coriander will thrive in any moderately rich, well-draining garden soil. It needs even moisture to make lush growth. Since it is set back a bit by transplanting, it's best to sow your seeds in place. Plant them ¼ to ½ inch deep, then thin plants to 4 to 8 inches apart. Each "seed" is really two seeds, so expect to thin out one each of a lot of plant pairs. You might want to use scissors to clip plants out, avoiding tearing the roots of the twins. Or, if you have good, loose soil, you might be able to separate and transplant pairs. To try this, work when the plants have only one or two true leaves.

Warning: Cilantro is often sold in 2-inch pots, but if the pot contains a tight clump of many seedlings, they should be separated. This will damage some seedlings beyond saving.

The Harvest Begin your harvest by using your thinnings. Continue to pick leaves, always leaving some to grow. You can also pick and use the young flower stalks while they are in bud; picking the stalk will delay flowering a bit.

After the flowers open, you can still cut the flower stems and use the small side leaves in cooking, but eventually the leaves will turn yellow and die; by the time seeds ripen, the plant will be dead. Reseed as soon as you begin to harvest leaves from a young planting, so you will have plants to replace them before they decline.

Coriander flowers are pale lavender and are borne on 2- to 4-foot stalks, in the flat umbels typical of the carrot family. They make a pretty addition to a salad or to a delicate bouquet. I usually don't let the seeds form, because they are inexpensive to buy and I generally want the garden space for something else. However, seeds will ripen here easily. Harvest them when about two-thirds of them have turned from green to brownish. Cut the stalks and put their tops into a large paper bag. Tie it around them and hang them upside down to dry. If you harvest seeds on a damp day or in the early morning, the seeds will be less likely to fall before you can get the stalks into a bag. To harvest mature seeds for planting, let most of them reach the dry, brown stage before you cut the stalks, then cut carefully to avoid seed fall, and dry them as for culinary use. Or you can let a few plants drop seed in your garden and seed themselves.

Both the leaves and seeds are used in cuisines around the world. Although many Americans know coriander leaves only as the cilantro in Mexican salsa, they are also used in South America, the Middle East, through India, and into China, Southeast Asia, and Japan. Middle Easterners use them in their vegetarian patties called falafel, and in the hot sauce traditionally served with it. In India, the leaves are an ingredient in many curries. In China, they are traditionally added to a stir-fry near the end of cooking. Southeast Asians enjoy them in soups and salads.

Coriander seed, which is used in the United States mainly as a pickling spice, is used more widely in all cuisines of Arab and Arab-influenced countries in the Near and Middle East, North Africa, Spain and various New World cultures influenced by Spain. There, it is often used as a seasoning for fresh or cured meat. In India, coriander seed is a prime ingredient of curry.

Varieties and Similar Species Until recently there was only one variety of coriander. Now there is a new one said to be slow to bolt. If you plan to grow coriander for its leaves, look for this one. It doesn't seem to have an official name, but it is described in seed catalogs with terms like "slow-bolt" and "grow for leaves."

At least two other species have a flavor similar to that of coriander and are used as substitutes. Both have the advantage of a longer harvest period from the same plants, but their leaves are harder, less delicate in texture. *Polygonum odoratum*, sold as Vietnamese coriander, rau ram, or hot mint, is perennial. It may overwinter, though it does decline in the colder months. Look for it in local farmers markets. It will often root in potting mix from purchased stems. The biennial *Eryngium foetidum* is sold as culantro, Mexican coriander, ngo gai, or, confusingly, Vietnamese coriander. It grows best in moist, rather shady locations. Culantro holds its flavor well when dried and when cooked.

Sources

Coriander (cilantro) seed: Widely available
Rau ram plants: RH
Culantro seed: BCS, EE. JSS, KIT, NGN, PS, RH

Dill

Anethum graveolens
Parsley Family ❖ *Apiaceae* (*Umbelliferae*)

Dill resembles its cousin fennel in appearance, but it is smaller. While fennel towers to a bushy 6 feet or more, dill is a thinner plant reaching only 2 to 4 feet. In fact, dill seems to be less than what most local gardeners expect. I think this is due to an incorrect assumption that it should grow as tall as the more robust wild fennel, in combination with the fact that dill may not reach its full size in this region's less than ideal conditions. Dill is a summer annual that requires full sun, moderate warmth, and some protection from strong winds. It will not grow well in a too foggy or too windy garden.

Growing Instructions Soil for dill should be loose and rich. Because dill transplants badly, sow your seeds in place, covering them only lightly. Sow the first planting in April, then, for a steady supply of dill leaves, sow more seed every few weeks through mid-July. Keep the soil evenly moist as the dill grows. Thin plants to stand 6 to 12 inches apart, depending on whether you plan to harvest plants small for leaves or let them grow to form seed stalks.

The Harvest Dill leaves are best when harvested before the plant comes into bloom. The plants produce few new leaves once flowering begins. Sometimes cutting out the growing tip will delay flowering, but if the weather turns hot, flower stalks will form quickly anyway. To dry a leaf crop, cut plants when they are at least two months old, but before they bloom, and spread leaves to dry in a warm, shady place. The dried leaves are often called dill weed.

Seeds ripen when the plant is four or more months old. To save dill seed for cooking, cut the heads before the last flower falls, and dry them well in a warm room, or in a paper bag, as for coriander.

Then knock the seeds from the stems. If you want to save seed for growing more dill, leave it on the plant longer, until it is brown. For pickling purposes, cut whole plants when the seeds are only half ripe, and bend these green plants to fit pickling jars. Plant dill for pickling in early May, for the best chance of making your dill harvest coincide with your cucumber harvest.

Dill is a popular flavoring in northern, central, and eastern European cooking, as well as in Russia and Turkey. It grows wild in Southern Europe, but it is not much eaten there except in Greece. In the cuisines in which they are a popular ingredient, dill leaves are used to flavor many vegetables, especially potatoes and cabbage family vegetables. They are also added to meats, fish, eggs, salads, breads, and soups. Dill seed is used in cabbage and potato dishes, in fish dishes, and in breads.

Varieties If you are growing dill for leaves, choose 'Dukat' or 'Fernleaf', varieties that are promised to be especially leafy. Fernleaf is a short plant, suitable for container growing.

Sources
Dill seed: Widely available

Epazote (or Jerusalem Oak Pazote, or Mexican Tea)

Chenopodium ambrosioides
Goosefoot Family ❖ *Chenopodiaceae*

Epazote, an herb native to Mexico, is commonly used in Mexican cuisine as a seasoning for beans, hence it is known as the bean herb.

It's a perennial plant, closely related to the weed lambsquarters. The plant in my garden is quite vigorous, growing to 3 feet tall and almost as wide. The leaves are a rich green, to about 4 inches long. The green flowers that form late in the summer are so tiny that you won't notice them unless you look closely. The plant has a strongly pungent aroma.

My experience growing epazote began one day in early summer, when a Mexican-American family stopped during a stroll to ask me about my community garden. I invited them in and gave them some purslane and mint. When I told them I was trying to find some epazote, they offered to show me some that was growing in a nearby vacant lot. It was a small, struggling plant that I would have overlooked myself. I took several cuttings, and, though I'm not sure early summer is the best time to take cuttings, one of them did grow.

At the time, I didn't know where to buy epazote, but now you will find plants and seeds both locally and from mail-order sources.

Growing Instructions One plant is enough for many a pot of beans, but if you want to grow more, it grows easily from seed. Grow from plants you purchase in spring or early summer, or sow seed in the spring. Epazote survives in the lean, summer-dry soil of local vacant lots, but it will grow much larger in more fertile and well-watered garden soil. I would expect it to suffer in poorly drained, soggy soil. It grows well in full sun but will also tolerate shade.

The Harvest Cut leaves as needed and use them fresh or dried. The leaves dry well if spread in a dark, airy place. Look for epazote in Mexican recipes as an ingredient in dishes that contain tortillas and/or beans.

This herb can be so vigorous, and reseed itself so profusely, that you will want to spend some energy keeping it in bounds. It may grow so fast that you will want to prune it a couple of times during the summer to keep it from overgrowing other plants. My plant reseeded thickly, and it took considerable weeding to get rid of the extra plants. To prevent this, time one of your prunings to remove flowering stems before seeds can form. Cut the plant back one last time in the fall, to make way for fresh spring growth.

Sources
Epazote seed: Widely available

Fennel (or Sweet Fennel)

Foeniculum vulgare var. *dulce*

Fennel, Bronze (or Red Fennel)

Foeniculum vulgare var. *rubrum*
Parsley Family ❖ *Apiaceae* (*Umbelliferae*)

Wild sweet fennel is one of our most common and visible weeds. It grows in tall, dense thickets in many vacant lots or neglected backyards. The plants reach over 6 feet high, with feathery leaves, and are topped in the summer with loose, flat heads of small, yellow flowers. You have probably heard it called "wild anise." Fennel does have a taste similar to that of anise, but the plant that produces commercial anise seed is another species (*Pimpinella anisum*).

Fennel originated in the Mediterranean region. Sweet fennel is a common weed there too and is also widely cultivated as an herb. Some say that the flavor of wild sweet fennel is inferior to that of the domestic varieties, that it is bitter and hasn't much anise taste. Still, local cooks do use it, and the particular wild sweet fennel near my garden tastes strongly of anise to me. If you do like the flavor of wild fennel leaves or seeds, harvest them from vacant lots, but don't let it set seed in your garden, as it is a nasty weed. (See page 167 for more on fennel as a weed.) If you want the sweet, white fennel bulb, you need to grow Florence fennel, a variety bred to produce it (see page 223).

Growing Instructions If you decide to grow sweet fennel, sow seed in place in February or March, or in midsummer. Sweet fennel will succeed in most soils, but will do best in one that is light and well drained but kept moist.

Thin plants of varieties grown for leaves to 6 to 12 inches apart.

The Harvest Collect sweet fennel leaves from the time of thinning on. Fennel leaves are well known as a seasoning for fish; they are also good with pork and veal and in soups, salads, and salad dressings.

The plants are biennials or short-lived perennials that bloom in the second season or after exposure to cold weather. Seeds are used in sausages, breads, and cookies. In India, they are nibbled after a meal. If you want seed, cut off the seed heads when the seeds begin to turn brown and dry them in a paper bag as you would coriander seed.

Varieties In addition to ordinary green sweet fennel, a variety with bronze or dark red leaves is pretty enough to use in an ornamental border.

Pests and Diseases Other than an occasional parsleyworm (see page 310), which does little damage, fennel seems pest-free.

Fennel has a reputation for inhibiting the growth of other plants; however, I have not tested this theory and have seen no hard proof.

Sources

Sweet fennel seed: Widely available
Bronze fennel seed: Widely available

Garlic

See the Compendium of Vegetables in Chapter 11.

Garlic Chives (or Chinese Leeks, Gow Choy, or Nira)

Allium tuberosum
Amaryllis Family ❖ *Amaryllidaceae*

The first time I grew this herb, in a foggy garden on the coast side of the San Mateo County hills, was from a packet labeled "Chinese Leeks." I grew a whole row of them and let them stay for most of a year, hoping they would eventually get bigger. I thought they were awfully small leeks. Now I appreciate garlic chives for what they are: broad-leaved chives with a mild garlic flavor and flowers pretty enough for an ornamental garden. The leaves of mature garlic chives are 12 to 15 inches high and about ¼ inch wide, with graceful curves at the tips. Attractive white flowers bloom in late summer, on stems as much as twice as high as the leaves.

Growing Instructions Nurseries sell small clumps of these perennial plants as potted herbs, and you can also easily grow them from seed. The best time to sow seed, either indoors or directly in the garden, is between January and April. The seedlings look like onion seedlings, little green threads, but they soon become sturdy and easy to transplant.

Garlic chives will grow best in fertile, well-prepared garden soil. They are most productive if kept evenly moist. Grow a clump of them or plant them in a wide row.

The Harvest You can harvest whole plants, then replant for the next year, or pick individual leaves as you need them, leaving the plants to grow. If you do let the plants grow year round, harvest fewer leaves in late summer, while the plants are blooming.

Divide perennial clumps every few years. Just dig the whole clump and cut it into two or more parts with a shovel. Discard any plants badly damaged by the shovel, then replant the clumps at least 18 inches apart.

In China, garlic chives are known as gow choy, and in Japan, nira. In both cuisines they are often used like scallions, the whole plant chopped in stir-fries. They are also an ingredient in Southeast Asian cuisines. I use whole plants or just the cut leaves. I toss whole leaves, or pieces no shorter than 4 inches, in a salad, or add 2-inch lengths of leaf to soup just before serving, or chop the leaves finely in an omelet. I use the white flowers, too, in salad, to float in soup, or to add to a bouquet.

Pests and Diseases Check low in the plants for incipient black aphid infestations, especially in the winter. Cut or pull out any dead flower stalks that remain in the fall, to let the center of a clump get more light and air and, incidentally, to make it easier to see any aphids. (See page 114 for aphid control tips.)

Varieties and Related Species You will find a similar, but lavender-flowered plant sold as "Mauve Garlic Chives." It has flattened leaves and a similar onion-garlic flavor, but with lavender flowers. I suspect it is a different species.

Sources
Garlic chive seed: Widely available
Garlic chive plants: RH, TERR
Mauve garlic chive seed: RH

Ginger

Zingiber officinale
Ginger Family ❖ *Zingiberaceae*

Ginger prefers warmer weather than this region provides. Yet although it is borderline if planted in the open ground, it grows well in a container. That way you can grow it in a bright room or move it outside to a protected spot whenever days are warm. You can grow a significant amount of ginger in containers. In fact, ginger is so productive that if ignored for too long it will break the pot by simple root pressure!

Growing Instructions In the spring or early summer, purchase ginger rhizomes from a grocery store. Look for plump, fresh-looking rhizomes, preferably with active buds. The buds begin as cream-colored bumps, then grow to minaret-shaped protrusions. Either stage is fine for planting.

If you can't find rhizomes with active buds, buy the healthiest ones you can find and plant them anyway. Dig them up and check them in two weeks to see if buds are beginning to form. If not, just wash the rhizomes, dry them, and set them aside to eat—some ginger rhizomes just won't grow—and try rhizomes from another source.

If you find rhizomes with good buds, or if your buried rhizomes do begin to sprout, break off 3- to 4-inch pieces of rhizome with one or more good buds and plant them. A 10-inch terra-cotta bulb pot should be big enough for three of these pieces. (Bulb pots are shallower than the standard kind.) Plant rhizomes horizontally, about 2 inches under the surface, in good potting mix, with some compost or well-rotted manure mixed in. Keep the container indoors in a warm place, as the rhizomes will rot if the soil isn't warm. However, keep the container out of direct sun, or where it will get only a little sun, until the shoots are well up. Even then, ginger prefers a warm, bright place to hot sun. It would actually not be bothered by foggy days, if only they were warmer and less windy!

If the rhizomes sprout successfully, they will grow several stems up to 3 or 4 feet high, each bearing two rows of fragrant narrow leaves. The plants may bloom on short stems near the ground, but this is not common. The closest mine has come so far was to form buds that then shriveled and fell off.

Keep the soil moist at all times, but not soggy, and never let the pot stand in water. Add liquid fertilizer, such as manure tea, fish emulsion, or 10-10-10, every couple of weeks. However if you plan to grow your ginger over the winter, cut back on fertilizer then to let it rest, fertilizing again when the plant begins more active growth.

The Harvest You can dig ginger in four or five months and eat the young rhizomes, or let them grow eight or nine months to maturity. You can even wait a full year if you like. Whenever you harvest, be sure to save some of the rhizome to replant. If you are keeping a plant for a long time, harvest younger parts of the rhizomes to eat, as the older ones will become less flavorful.

Ginger rhizomes will keep for a week or two at room temperature or for several weeks in the refrigerator in a closed plastic bag or jar. They can also be frozen, in which case the best way to use them is to grate what you need while they are still frozen, then return the rest to the freezer.

Varieties Ginger has several varieties, but generally only one will appear in U.S. groceries. Ginger plants sold as ornamentals are not necessarily edible.

Sources
Ginger rhizomes: Buy in local produce markets

Hops

Humulus lupulus
Hemp Family ❖ *Cannabaceae*

Hop vines can grow over 30 feet in a single summer if the summer is long and warm enough. The coolest summers may not allow for maximum growth, but the truth is that a full-sized plant would be too big for many of our urban gardens anyway. Although references agree that hops need full sun, I know of two hops plants growing successfully in a shady backyard (in the northeastern corner of San Francisco). These plants grow over 10 feet each summer and produce plenty of hops, the fruits used in making beer.

Hop vines, with their attractive grape-like leaves, fit nicely into an ornamental garden. They are perennial plants, twining up their supports all summer, dormant in the winter, then sending up new shoots in February or March. If your garden gets enough sun to need summer shade, a hop vine will provide it very prettily. It will also create welcome privacy for summer entertaining.

Growing Instructions Plant roots in the spring, 18 inches apart. Be sure the soil is rich and deeply dug. Keep moist and once growth becomes rapid, give ample water. Plants will need support a couple of months after first shoots appear; they will climb vertical supports more readily than horizontal ones. You will need a sturdy fence, a trellis, or several poles 10 to 12 feet tall. When plants die down in winter, you should remove dead vines. Omit the winter mulch suggested for cold-winter areas, as it will only encourage decay in our mild, wet winters. The clump of vines from a single hop root becomes more extensive each season. To keep a plant in bounds, dig straight down all around it in a circle one foot away from the stem. This cuts running roots. Dig out any roots outside of this circle.

Hops bear male and female flowers on separate plants. Only the female flowers produce the resins used in beer making. Because the flowers produce the resins whether or not they are pollinated, you don't need to grow any male plants. Female blossoms are borne under green, papery bracts that make the flower bunches look like little cones.

Hops

The Harvest Cones that are ready to harvest no longer feel damp to the touch, but instead feel papery and light. After touching them, your hand will pick up their odor and feel slightly sticky from the powdery yellow resin called lupulin. (Wear long sleeves and gloves to handle the plant as you harvest; its hooked hairs may slightly irritate your skin.) Spread the cones of female flowers to dry in a sunny room or in an oven. If you use an oven, keep the temperature below 150°F and leave the door ajar. These dried fruits, called hops, are used to flavor beer. If you do make beer, be sure to return the spent hops to the compost pile.

In most places where hops are grown as a crop for beer production, people also eat the young shoots as a vegetable. They may not be vigorous enough the first year, but after that hop plants sprout so vigorously from the root in spring that you may have to thin out some of the later shoots to keep the plant under control. You can eat these extra shoots, or, if your plant is well established, you can blanch the first shoots to eat, let a few mature, and still eat some of the late ones. To blanch, pile earth over the roots in late winter and dig out the tender stems when the tips emerge through the mound. Sources say to eat these as an asparagus substitute; a San Franciscan friend who tried them said they were OK, but not especially good.

Sources
Hops root cuttings: NGN, PGS

Lavender
English Lavender
Lavandula angustifolia (*L. officinalis*)
French Lavender
Lavandula dentata
Spanish Lavender
Lavandula stoechas
Mint Family ❖ *Lamiaceae* (*Labiatae*)

Lavenders are plants of the Mediterranean, native to the eastern Pyrenees, throughout Spain and into Portugal. Only occasionally used as culinary herbs, they are grown in local gardens primarily as ornamentals, thriving in gardens that require little water. Lavender is a popular scent for soaps and a common ingredient in sachets and potpourris. The handsome plants have narrow, gray-green leaves and small lavender to purple flowers borne at the top of slender stalks. Lavenders prefer full sun, so should be grown in an unshaded spot, but they will grow and bloom in foggy areas too.

Growing Instructions Lavender is best grown from purchased plants, since plants grown from seed will take a couple of years to reach full height. Herb nurseries sell several varieties of lavender in small containers, and you will also often see larger, one-gallon cans of lavender in nurseries. Space the plants from 8 inches to 4 feet apart, depending on the mature size of the variety you are growing. Lavender will grow best in light soil, with good drainage, and does not require much fertilizer.

The Harvest For dried lavender to use in sachets or potpourris, cut the stems just as color shows on the flowers, hang them in a dark, airy place, and then strip the dried flowers from the stems. You can also use fresh flowers in bouquets, eat them in salads, or use them to make lavender vinegar or lavender-flavored sugar. To make the latter, add them to sugar and store the mixture in a closed jar for a couple of weeks. You can use the flowers or leaves in cooking, such as stews and sauces, or in baked goods, as you would rosemary. Be careful to use only a little lavender in a dish, or your food will taste bitter and perfumy. (See Chapter 13 for more on edible herb flowers, and page 315 for an herb vinegar recipe.)

If you did not cut the flower stems to use in some way, you should cut them all back when they finish blooming, or the plant will start to look untidy. Cut to the top of the leafy part, and don't leave ugly little stubs sticking up from the leaves. To shape or limit the size of plants somewhat, you can cut into the leafy part, but too heavy pruning of the leaves will weaken the plants.

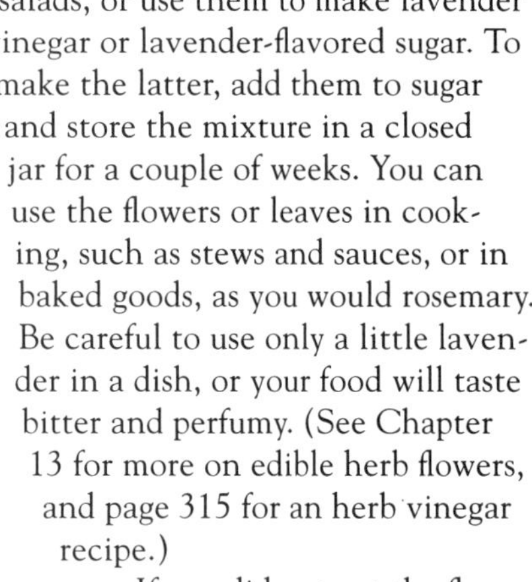
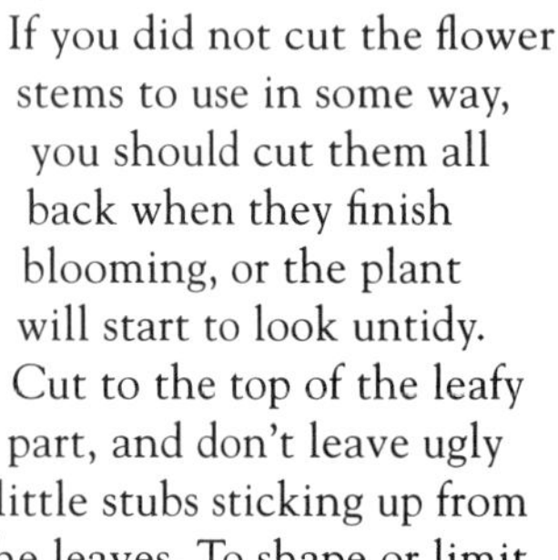
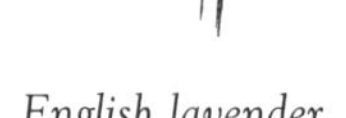

English lavender

Varieties and Lavender Species English lavender, the most widely planted species, is also the tallest—to 4 feet high. Its leaves are up to 2 inches long, with smooth edges. It blooms in the summer, with flowerheads an inch or two long. Several dwarfed cultivars are popular for small spaces and for edgings. 'Munstead' is only 18 inches high with deep lavender flowers. 'Lady', a compact 8- to 10-inch-high plant, is the first type to bloom consistently from seed in the first year.

French lavender—as its scientific name, *L. dentata*, suggests—has toothed leaves. You can recognize it by the distinctively square-angled teeth on the edges of the 1½-inch-long leaves. Its flowerheads are topped by a prominent ring of bright purple, petal-like bracts. These plants reach 3 feet high, and in areas with mild winters they bloom almost all year.

Spanish lavender has tiny leaves, only ½ inch long, with smooth edges. It is 1½ to 3 feet high. Its flowerheads are topped with a tuft of large purple, petal-like bracts. Flowers form only in the summer.

Sources

Lavender plants: BUR, JG, NGN, PS, RH, TERR, CG, SOC, SS
Lady Lavender seed: BUR, NGN, JSS, RH, TERR, VBS, WCS

Lemon Balm

Melissa officinalis
Mint Family ❖ *Lamiaceae* (*Labiatae*)

Lemon balm is a perennial with a fine lemon scent. It grows and is used similarly to mint. The leaves are oval, an inch or two long, with toothed edges. Its small white or pale blue flowers bloom in the summer. Lemon balm is well adapted to cooler microclimates, preferring cool days and not minding a bit of shade or some fog. One plant is usually enough for a garden, since the plants are up to 2 feet high and rather bushy.

Growing Instructions While lemon balm isn't hard to grow from seed, you will probably not want to bother for only one plant. Better to buy it already started. It's an easy herb to grow, although it requires a certain amount of attention to grow well. It needs a site with soil that is rich and kept moist. If it is grown too dry, its leaves will be pale and not as succulent.

The Harvest Clip leafy stems as you need them, or shear the tops several times a summer, which will also prevent seed production. Lemon balm may seed itself and become a bit of a nuisance if the seeds fall. Cut back any tall, ratty-looking stems in fall. Harvest much less in fall and early winter, since the plant will grow little then, but new stems will grow by late winter. After several years, the clump will become too thick and will benefit by being dug, in winter, and divided into 6-inch sections.

Lemon balm can be used as if it were just another kind of mint, good for a refreshing tea and in fruit salads, tabouli, and mint sauce. It can be dried, but its lemon scent is much more potent when it's fresh.

Sources

Lemon balm seed: Widely available
Lemon balm plants: JG, RH

Lemon Verbena

Aloysia triphylla (*Lippia citriodora*)
Verbena Family ❖ *Verbenaceae*

This is one of the best of the lemon-scented herbs because it holds its scent when dried and also after cooking. Lemon verbena is a shrub native to mild-winter parts of Chile, Argentina, and Peru. It can grow to 10 feet high and may approach that height in Bay Area gardens with the mildest winters. Its

3- to 4-inch leaves grow from its stems in whorls of three, and it may bear small white to lavender flowers in midsummer.

Growing Instructions Start your lemon verbena by purchasing a rooted plant, rather than starting from seed. Plant it in full sun, in soil that is well drained but fertile, and keep it moist. Avoid a windy site if you can, or stake the plant if wind makes it begin to lean. While this area's winter temperatures are not cold enough to kill this perennial, don't be surprised if it drops leaves or looks generally unkempt in winter: remember, it is a tropical plant. When it begins to leaf out again in spring, you can prune out any branches that winter has killed. You may also want to remove some branches that have grown out far enough to crowd other plants, or thin out some branches to let light into the plant, and/or remove water sprouts (vertical branches that form on other branches and shoot up through the center of the plant).

The Harvest Pinch tips to use leaves as you need them during the summer growing season. The plant tends to be ungainly, and you can improve its shape by your choice of places to pinch it when harvesting. For drying, harvest in August and dry at room temperature. In addition to using it for tea, try lemon verbena in poultry or fish dishes. It also makes an aromatic addition to potpourri.

Sources
Lemon verbena plants: JG, NGN, RH, TERR

Lemongrass, West Indian

Cymbopogon citratus
Grass Family ❖ *Graminae*

Lemongrass plays a central role in providing Southeast Asian dishes with their unique lemony taste. The grass is a native of Southern India and Ceylon and is frequently found growing in gardens throughout Southeast Asian countries. In the tropics this plant can grow to 6 feet high, but in our area it grows to only a foot or two. Individual leaf blades are about ⅝ inch wide and feel rough and dry. Groups of leaves grow from somewhat bulbous bases, each mature clump divided into many of these bases with their leaves. This plant will grow throughout the region; however, it will grow faster and larger in warmer, sunnier microclimates.

Growing Instructions Lemongrass rarely flowers, having been propagated by plant divisions for so many centuries. Get it started in your garden by buying a plant or two from the nursery. Or you might be able to root lemongrass stalks you buy at a grocery store. In the spring, look for stalks that are not too dried out and have some roots still attached. Put two or three of these in containers of seeding mix and keep them moist until they start to grow new leaves, then plant them in the garden.

Plant lemongrass in full sun. It is not fussy about soil, but since it is a perennial, it should be in a site that has been cleared of perennial weeds. Water evenly and moderately. Growth will slow in the winter and the plant may take on a reddish cast and look weatherbeaten. It will be damaged or killed by prolonged frosts. Trim out dead or unattractive leaves in the spring.

The Harvest Usually the bulbous base of a section of leaves is cut up and added to a soup or other dish. Part of this is tender and can be eaten, and any part that is too tough is removed by diners as they eat. Use lemongrass to season soup, fish, or curries. (See Thai Fish Soup on page 298.)

To harvest the bulbous leaf bases, reach close to the ground and separate out a section of leaves joining one base. Use a knife to cut it near the ground. Cut off the leaf tops and peel off the outer, tough leaves.

Pests Lemongrass rust affects only lemongrass. It causes small linear lesions on the leaves. On leaf undersides, you may see the rust-colored spores bulging from the lesions. Carefully examine purchased plants or stalks you plan to root for signs of this disease. Remove any plants with rust from your garden and clean up all plant debris. Next season, plant lemongrass only in another part of the garden. To help prevent this disease, avoid overhead watering.

Sources
Lemongrass plants: JSS, NGN, PS, RH
Root from grocery store stems.

Marjoram (or Sweet Marjoram, Knotted Marjoram, or Annual Marjoram)

Origanum majorana (*O. hortensis*, *Majorana hortensis*)
Mint Family ❖ *Lamiaceae* (*Labiatae*)

Marjoram is one of the easiest herbs to grow in our region. With very little care, it grows into a rangy, 2-foot-high perennial plant. Its leaves are ¼ to 1 inch long, oval, and gray-green. Its flowers are very small, usually white, although they may be pink. Marjoram is sometimes called knotted marjoram, because of the characteristic rounded "knots" formed by the green bracts of the flowerheads.

Many gardeners grow marjoram but call it oregano, and this is not the only confusion surrounding this plant. First, you will sometimes find it sold under its obsolete names, *Origanum hortensis* or *Majorana hortensis*. Also, you may find it listed in gardening books as an annual, because winters only a little colder than this area's will kill it. In fact, where winters are really cold, gardeners often substitute *Origanum onites*, a plant commonly, and confusingly, known as pot marjoram—and sometimes sold as oregano (see oregano listing, this chapter). In this region, however, marjoram lives through the winters very well.

Growing Instructions To grow just a plant or two, purchased marjoram plants are certainly the easiest way to go, although marjoram is not hard to grow from seed. If you do use seed, sow it indoors in early spring. Plant seedlings or purchased plants in a sunny spot, in fertile garden soil, and keep plants moderately moist. (This is not one of the herbs, like sage and oregano, that tastes better when it is grown hungry and dry.) Marjoram plants begin to look straggly after a few years and should be replaced or restarted by layering (see page 59).

The Harvest For fresh use, harvest marjoram leaves any time. Just cut some stems and strip the leaves from the somewhat woody stems. In this part of the world, marjoram grows most of the year and tends to outproduce our kitchen needs. To keep it from taking up too much space, and to reduce its woody growth, cut the plants to several inches above the ground when you first see forming flower buds. Then cut a second time when more flowerheads are forming. Hang these bunches of stems to dry in a dark place with good ventilation.

The flavor of marjoram is strong and sweet and holds up well after drying. Cooking, however, may damage it, so it is often added near the end or used in dishes that are not cooked long. Try in omelets or to season meats, or use it fresh in salads, salad dressings, or herbal vinegar.

Sources

Sweet marjoram seed: Widely available
Sweet marjoram plants: RH, TERR

Peppermint

Mentha × piperita (a cross between M. *aquatica* and M. *spicata*)

Spearmint (or Mint)

Mentha spicata

Apple Mint

Mentha suaveolens

Pineapple Mint

Mentha suaveolens 'Variegata'

Bergamot Mint (or Orange Mint)

Mentha × piperita var. *citrata*

Corsican Mint

Mentha requienii

Mint Family ❖ *Lamiaceae* (*Labiatae*)

Yes, there really are a peppermint plant and a spearmint plant, though not a doublemint plant. The mints are easy to grow; in fact, some gardeners consider them too easy, since these perennials spread aggressively via horizontal underground stems. Though they can be a nuisance to keep in bounds, they offer plenty of interesting flavors for teas and for seasoning foods.

Oil of peppermint is used to flavor gum, candy, and ice cream. While you probably won't go to the trouble of extracting oil from your plants, you can use fresh peppermint to flavor jellies or a sauce for meats, or make peppermint tea from fresh or dried leaves. Peppermint is the kind of mint tea that is most soothing to an upset stomach.

Spearmint can also be used for sauces and teas, and it is the mint most commonly used fresh in the recipes of several cuisines. It is in the Middle Eastern tabbouleh, Indian chutneys, and Southeast Asian cooking.

Besides these well-known mints, there are a host of other mints with good but less familiar flavors. Some of these are apple mint, pineapple mint, and bergamot mint. Gardeners often buy them but can't always think of ways to use them. Still, any of these might become personal favorites for any of the various mint uses. All mints make good tea, and a small amount of any mint is good in fruit or lettuce salads, especially if the salads have flowers in them or a dressing containing a bit of honey.

Corsican mint (*Mentha requienii*) differs from the others in that it is more often used as an ornamental ground cover than for culinary uses. It's under an inch tall, with tiny leaves—almost mosslike. It's especially nice between stepping stones, because if it is bruised by a passing foot it releases a very heady mint scent. It is probably not planted more widely because

The Mint Family

Mint family plants (oregano, sage, savory, and catnip, to name just a few) all share certain traits, and mint itself is a clear example. The stems are usually squarish in cross section, the leaves are arranged in opposite pairs, and the flowers appear in whorls at the tops of stems. The flowers are small, and most often lavender, but sometimes white, pink, blue, or even yellow. They are two-lipped, the lower lip providing a convenient platform for pollinating insects. When you know these traits, you will discover many a wild or domestic mint relative on your own, although not all mint family plants have pleasant scents or can be used in cooking.

it is a delicate plant, hard to maintain at its peak all year. It may die back in the winter or during a warm spell. Corsican mint usually prefers 50-percent shade, but you can try it in full sun in foggy areas. Though its main culinary use has been to flavor liqueurs, it can be used as other mints. Try it as a tea, in combination with lemon balm.

Growing Instructions Mints are best grown outside of your main garden area, since they will spread aggressively. At a minimum, keep mint out of the way of perennial crops like asparagus and away from perennial herbs like oregano. You won't want to disturb the roots of those plants, but you may have to, to remove the competing mint plants.

You should be able to keep a mint under reasonable control by pulling out its runners as you work the nearby soil each season, but you will probably find mint coming up in unexpected places now and then. You might try sinking a section of terra-cotta pipe, or a wood or metal barrier, at least 18 inches deep around a mint bed to slow its spread, but even this may not totally contain it. The only sure way to confine a mint is to grow it in a container. If you do this, give your mint a pot 10 or more inches in diameter and be sure to keep the soil constantly moist.

Mint is most often started from a rooted stem or runner. Plants started this way will grow to productive size much more quickly than plants started from seeds. Also, if you buy a plant grown from a cutting or runner, the scent you smell will be the one you get, whereas mint plants you start from seeds may be highly variable in scent. Buy your small mint plants in a nursery or get stems or runners with some roots on them from another gardener. You may want to set the pot in a saucer to help keep the potting mix constantly moist.

Soil for the mints should be rich and moisture-retaining, but with good drainage. Grown without enough water or in poor soil, the mints will be sorry-looking and slow-growing plants. Mints thrive in full sun in foggy areas, as long as they get enough water. They prefer partial shade in warmer areas. If they are not in containers, plant mints 2 feet from each other or from other plants.

The Harvest Harvest mint stem tips or whole branches as needed. Mint grows more rapidly in the summer, allowing more frequent harvests. Cut off any flowers, to encourage leafy growth. Some mints, like spearmint, grow well enough in the winter to allow moderate harvests all year; others, like peppermint, will decline drastically in winter and put out a flush of growth in the spring.

Pests and Diseases Peppermint is subject to a rust, which does not change the flavor and rarely kills the plant, but disfigures the leaves with rust-colored spots. Since mine got the rust, I just harvest leafy stem tips early in the season, before they are infected. Later, when rust spots appear on the upper leaves, I stop harvesting. Despite this, I am still able to fill my large tin with dried leaves each year from only one or two plants.

Sources

Various mint plants: AA, JG, NGN, RH

Mustard Seed, Black

Brassica nigra

Mustard Seed, Brown

Brassica juncea

Mustard Seed, White

Brassica hirta

Mustard Family ❖ *Brassicaceae (Cruciferae)*

Mustard seed is used as a seasoning in both Indian and Western cuisines. The seed used in Indian cooking is likely to be black mustard seed. In a jar of American mustard, the seeds used are usually somewhat less spicy brown or white types or mixtures of the two. The main ingredients of commercial mustard are crushed mustard seed and vinegar, although they may also contain honey or other ingredients. In any case, the seed is easy to produce. Grow the mustards as you would mustards for greens, in rich, well-watered soil. Thin them to stand 8 to 12 inches apart. (See page 235 for more on growing mustards.)

Harvest the seed stalks when the pods are brown and some are just beginning to split open. You may have to cover the ripening seed stalks with mesh bags or other porous material to avoid sharing your crop with birds. After cutting the stalks, dry the seed pods for several days in a dark, warm place, then break them open and winnow out the seeds.

Use black mustard seed in curries and in Indian cooking in general, as well as in such European-style soups as split pea. In Indian cooking it is usually used whole, just toasted slightly in oil before the other ingredients are added. In European cooking, mustard seed is usually crushed before it is used. Florida broadleaf mustard seed is sometimes mixed with black mustard seed to impart a slightly different flavor to mustard condiments.

Sources
Black mustard seed: PGS, JLH
Brown mustard seed: PGS, RH
White mustard seed: PGS, RH

Oregano

Oregano (Greek Oregano, Sicilian Oregano, Winter Sweet Marjoram)
Origanum heracleoticum (*Origanum vulgare hirtum*)

(Oregano, Sicilian Oregano)
Origanum × *majorana*

Pot Marjoram
Origanum onites
Mint Family ❖ *Lamiaceae* (*Labiatae*)

Plants of several separate species in the genus *Origanum* are called oregano. Complicating the picture, commercial oregano often contains several herbs, blended for flavor. It may contain more than one *Origanum* species and may also contain leaves of sage and thyme, a Mexican herb called *Lippia graveolens*, or several other plants.

I can't tell exactly what is in your store-bought "oregano," but I can tell you that you will get good oregano flavor from plants of *Origanum heracleoticum*, sometimes called O. *vulgare hirtum*. As an alternative, try a new hybrid between oregano and sweet marjoram, which is in the same genus. It is sold as *Origanum* × *majorana*, or Sicilian oregano.

O. *heracleoticum* is a low plant, whose flower stems may grow to a foot or so. The leaves are oval to longish oval, less than an inch long, and a muted green. Flowers are small and white, in loose whorls at the ends of the stem. The leaves are somewhat hairy. O. × *majorana* also has white flowers and does not set seed.

Origanum onites is sometimes listed as oregano, sometimes as pot marjoram. It may be grown in cold-winter areas as a substitute for sweet marjoram, or it may be offered as oregano. In either case, its flavor will probably be less sweet than marjoram and less pungent than oregano.

Other oregano species and cultivars promise strong flavor, so you may want to try them, but be aware that some kinds are mainly ornamental. You will sometimes find the species *Origanum vulgare* or cultivars of it other than *hirtum*. The species itself may be sold as Italian oregano, wild marjoram, or, confusing the matter further, even Greek oregano. It is similar in appearance to O. *heracleoticum* when it is small, but it grows taller, to 2½ feet. Its lavender blooms are borne atop the stems in bunches that are loose and flat across the top. This plant has a weak scent and flavor. It is better for cut flowers or dried and used in a wreath. Another mainly ornamental plant is golden oregano, O. *vulgare* 'Aureum'. And Dittany of Crete, *Origanum dictamnus*, is grown mainly ornamentally for its pretty pink conelike blooms.

Greek oregano

Growing Instructions All the oreganos can be grown fairly easily from seed sown indoors in the spring, but as the flavor of the seedlings tends to vary significantly, even within a species, this is not the recommended procedure. The most certain way to get the scent and therefore the flavor you want is to buy a plant you have been able to smell first. As you will not need more than one or two plants, this will not be expensive to do.

Plant your oregano in a sunny spot, in light, well-drained, not overly rich soil. Keep it moist at first, but don't overwater it as the season progresses. Too rich or too wet a soil will lessen the flavor of this native of the dry Mediterranean hillsides.

In fact, cool, damp air probably reduces the flavor of oregano, but if you start with a good, strongly scented O. *heracleoticum*, you will still have an herb worthy of great pizza and lasagne.

The Harvest Harvest fresh leaves as needed and cut stems for drying as the plants come into bloom. Hang stems to dry in a dark, well-ventilated place. Besides in Italian dishes featuring tomatoes, use oregano in beef, lamb, fish, cheese, or bean dishes, and in soups and salads.

Shape oregano plants as you harvest, by cutting back long, rangy stems. This will also encourage the plant to send up new shoots from the ground. Never cut off more than 50 percent of the leaves at one time, though, so it will have enough energy left to regrow quickly. Despite your pruning and shaping, oregano plants tend to become unattractive in a few years. If you layer a few stems, they will root and provide new plants to replace the aging one (see page 59).

Sources

O. *heracleoticum* seed: ABL, BG, GS, JG, JLH, JSS, NGN, PGS, PS, RH, SSE, TERR

O. *heracleoticum* plants: JG, RH, TERR

O. × *majorana* plants: NGN, TERR

O. *onites* seed: BUR

Parsley

Petroselinum crispum var. *crispum* or *P. crispum* var. *neapolitanum*

Parsley Family ❖ *Apiaceae* (*Umbelliferae*)

Even if you ignore the parsley sprig at the edge of the restaurant plate, there is still plenty of reason to grow parsley. Chopped fresh parsley is a great addition to many dishes and is a major ingredient in the Middle Eastern cracked wheat salad, tabbouleh. You can grow enough parsley to replace dried parsley flakes with the fresh herb in your recipes throughout the year, in all parts of the region.

Growing Instructions Most nurseries carry small parsley plants, and these are the easiest way to get parsley started. Two to six plants are usually plenty. Parsley also grows easily from seed, but you must have patience during its long germination period. Folklore has it that parsley seed goes to the devil and back nine times before it sprouts. Actually, that seems an ambitious journey to complete in three to six weeks, but six weeks can seem like an eternity to water a flat in which no seedlings have appeared. It is probably safest to start parsley indoors, even when outside temperatures are warm, since it is easier to keep track of it in a container in the house than in a patch of the garden.

Sow parsley seed indoors in December through February for an early crop, as late as May if you forget to do it earlier. Seed you sow in late summer or early fall will grow fine too, but the life of the plants will be shorter, as they will probably go to seed in the spring, along with plants you started earlier in the year. You can get the seed to germinate a few days faster by soaking it overnight in warm water. After it has been soaked, pat the seed dry with paper towels, so it is easier to handle when you sow it.

Plant parsley in rich soil that you can easily keep moist. While parsley thrives in full sun, it tolerates part shade and, in fact, is able to grow well even in open shade. Set your plants 6 to 12 inches apart. Keep them free from weeds.

Parsley flowering stem

The Harvest If your purchased or homegrown plants are ready to go in the ground in February, you can begin to harvest them beginning in March or April, as soon as they have ten or twelve leaves. Cut leaves at the soil level, even if you don't choose to use the stems. Biennials like parsley will usually produce leaves all year long, then bloom and go to seed the following spring. Though some references say that overwintered plants become tough and bitter, our cool, moist springs seem to bring out the best in even last year's parsley.

When a plant first begins to form flower stalks, they are still tender and you can cut them to eat. By cutting them, you stimulate the plant to make more leaves and flower stalks. Eventually the seeding process takes over. The stalks become too tough to eat, and the plant stops making new leaves. Even then, however, you can use parsley stalks to flavor soup stocks, discarding them before you use the broth (see recipe on page 373). Occasionally plants will go to seed in the first summer, particularly where nights are cool. When you see this beginning to happen, just purchase a few nursery plants to replace them.

If you let a parsley plant go to seed in your garden, it will often reseed itself, the new plants coming up the following winter or spring. You can move these volunteer plants to a different location, if you do so while they are very young. After the plants grow much over 4 inches tall, they will be set back seriously by a move. This is because parsley depends mainly on a tap root—one long, central root, like a carrot's but skinnier, which is easily damaged in a transplanting. (If you really want to move a larger parsley plant, do it like this: Holding a shovel at a slight angle, push it into the roots several times, cutting the tap root eight or nine inches below the surface. Water the plant, and leave it alone for 10 to 14 days to let its side roots grow. At the end of this time, water it again. The next day, lift the plant and transplant it.)

Parsley may be added at the beginning of cooking, as when it is cooked to flavor broth. It can also be chopped and sprinkled over food when it is fully cooked, just before it is served. Use it in salads, salad dressings, sauces, soups, casseroles, and stuffings for poultry. It is also a major ingredient in some recipes, such as parsley pesto and the bulgur wheat salad called tabbouleh.

Varieties and Related Species The parsley most often used for a garnish is curled leaf parsley, *P. crispum* var. *crispum*. Several cultivars of curled leaf parsley are available, some more curled than others. While some people eat their parsley garnishes and others ignore them, few realize that the traditional purpose of a parsley garnish was to sweeten one's breath after a meal. Certainly try eating it if you want to be rid of garlic or other strong odors. Curled leaf parsley is also decorative when cut coarsely and sprinkled over salads or cooked vegetables.

Flat leaf or Italian parsley (*P. crispum* var. *neapolitanum*) is more productive, and some cooks think it's better flavored. Its flat leaves are easier to chop than curled ones. Flat leaf parsley is also the better choice for drying, as it holds its flavor better when dry. To dry it, discard the thick stems and dry the thin stems and leaves only. Dry them at 200°F to keep their green color.

A third variety of parsley is grown mainly for its thickened root, although its leaves are also acceptable as a parsley substitute. This is *P. crispum* var. *tuberosum*, known as Hamburg or parsnip-rooted parsley. (For information on how to grow this vegetable, see page 245.)

Another plant very similar to parsley is Japanese parsley (or mitsuba). This Asian herb is really in another plant genus: *Cryptotaenia*. Directions for growing it follow.

Pests Parsley is generally pest free. Spittlebugs can cause minor damage in the spring (see page 119). Parsley may also attract an occasional parsleyworm. This handsome green, yellow, and, black caterpillar is the larva of the very pretty western swallowtail butterfly. If it were common enough to destroy our garden parsley and fennel, we'd probably try to kill it anyway. However, since you will rarely see many, I suggest capturing any you see and placing them on a wild fennel plant in a vacant lot, or you might even leave one on garden plants so you can watch it grow.

Sources

Flat and curled leaf parsley seed: Widely available

Parsley, Japanese (or Mitsuba)

Cryptotaenia japonica

Carrot Family ❖ *Apiaceae* (*Umbelliferae*)

Japanese parsley looks like a cross between celery and parsley and tastes much like Italian parsley. This perennial plant grows to 3 feet high. Here is a denizen of moist, shady places that actually suffers if it is exposed to too much sun. It should be grown in at least partial shade to prevent it from becoming pale and mottled, or in full shade if your garden gets a lot of sun.

Sow seed for Japanese parsley in rich soil in early spring, and keep the soil moist during the entire time it is growing. It is usually grown as an annual, sown as a succession crop, and harvested whole while young and tender. However, you can harvest by the leaf from older plants. Leave a plant or two to produce seed for replanting. Chinese and Japanese cooks use the leaves and stems to add their distinctive flavor to stir-fries. They can be used whenever you would use parsley or cutting celery. Try them with fish or shrimp, in an omelet, as a seasoning for vegetables, or in cucumber salad.

Sources

Japanese parsley seed: EG, JG, KIT, NGN, RH

Perilla (Beefsteak Plant), Shiso (Japanese), Ji Soo (Chinese)

Perilla frutescens

Mint Family ❖ *Lamiaceae* (*Labiatae*)

Here's an herb quite unfamiliar to Western palates, but common in Korean, Japanese, and Chinese cooking. It tastes spicy—some cooks say like both ginger and cinnamon—but there is really nothing else like it. The plant is pretty, rather like a coleus with single-colored leaves, and can be nestled in among your flowers as well as your vegetables.

Growing Instructions Perilla is an annual grown from seed sown either indoors or in place. The seeds need light to germinate, so just press them into the surface of a well-prepared seedbed, then tamp the soil

Main Dish Risotto

Authentic Italian risotto is made with white rice and just a bit of Parmesan cheese, but this heartier version is a great vegetarian main dish and a showcase for the rich flavor of rosemary. True saffron is expensive, so I use American saffron, which is quite reasonable. You can find American saffron in stores that sell herbs and spices in bulk. Please use the suggested type of rice—others will not work well in this dish. Serves four.

- 2 tablespoons oil
- 1 medium onion, chopped finely
- 1 cup short grain brown rice
- 1 teaspoon minced fresh rosemary or ½ teaspoon crushed dried leaves
- Salt, to taste
- 3 tablespoons minced fresh parsley leaves
- ½ teaspoon dried American saffron (safflower)
- 2 cups water or stock
- 1½ cup (or more) grated Monterey Jack cheese, or substitute part-skim mozzarella

Heat the oil and sauté the onion until soft but not brown. Add the brown rice and sauté, stirring constantly until the grains become translucent, only a couple of minutes. Stir in the rosemary, salt, parsley, and American saffron. Add the water (one of the world's noisiest cooking procedures) and stir once or twice. Turn the heat down and let the rice simmer, covered, until the water is absorbed and the rice tender. This should take about 30 minutes. Spread grated cheese over the top and put the lid back on for a couple of minutes to let it melt. Cut and serve.

down around them. They germinate in a week to 10 days, and are ready to plant out in 6 to 8 weeks. In the garden, plant perilla in any good, well draining garden soil. While it is tolerant of various types of soils, it may not do well in unamended clay. Plant it in the sun or in partial shade and keep it moist. Sidedress perilla lightly with manure tea or other fertilizer during the season, if you are harvesting heavily.

While perilla is generally considered a summer annual, it is tolerant of our colder temperatures and may actually do better in our colder months than in our summer, and in cooler locations rather than warmer areas. Try sowing a few seeds every couple of months from February on to see what works best in your location. Transplant or thin perilla to stand 6 inches apart.

The Harvest You can begin to harvest by using your thinnings, then pick leaves and stem tips from the time the plants are only a foot high. They can reach 2 to 3 feet high at maturity, but probably won't get that high if you are harvesting from them. You should be able to pick leaves for at least a month, before the plants go to seed, at around 3½ months.

A word of caution: Perilla, like many herbs, is OK in small amounts, but should not be eaten in large quantities like a vegetable, as it contains potentially harmful chemicals called ketones. These substances are naturally produced in the body during the digestion of some foods, but they are harmful in large quantities, so are one of the by-products the body eliminates. Too much perilla could introduce too much of them all at once.

Varieties There are red-leaved and green-leaved perilla varieties. These are grown the same way but used a little differently. The red ones are more pungent and contain more ketones. They are used medicinally, as a garnish, and also (sparingly) as a seasoning. On the plant, the leaves are a very dark red-purple. When used as a pickling spice, they add a red color. In fact, they provide the red color of umeboshi plums. Try a little red-leaved perilla chopped into black bean sauce or to season stir fried or steamed crab or shrimp. Red perilla is also pretty enough to appear in the ornamental border; it was a favorite of Victorian gardeners.

Green-leaved perilla can be eaten in larger amounts, has a milder flavor, and is more tender than red perilla, so it makes a nice addition to salads. When it is used as a seasoning, more is needed to make up for the mild flavor. Try two tablespoons of chopped green perilla in a pound of ground beef for meat loaf or patties. You can also use the stem tips with flowers as an edible garnish.

Sources

Red and green perilla: BCS, BI, EE, GS, JG, JSS, KIT, NGN, PGS, RH, SESE, SOC

Rosemary

Rosmarinus officinalis

Mint Family ❖ *Lamiaceae (Labiatae)*

Rosemary is a woody shrub with deep green, leathery, needlelike leaves, ½ to 1½ inches long. The small flowers are most commonly blue. The plant usually grows 2 to 4 feet high, but may reach 6 feet. There are also prostrate types that creep along the ground or hang picturesquely over rocks and retaining walls. This is a good ornamental plant for all parts of the region, being tough and evergreen and requiring little water. While it thrives in full sun, it seems not to mind the fog. Once you learn to recognize it, you will notice it often in both private and public gardens.

Growing Instructions One plant of rosemary is generally enough, or maybe more than enough, since some varieties grow vigorously to a large size. It's best to buy a plant, because it grows so slowly from seed.

Rosemary is native to dry places along both the European and African shores of the Mediterranean. In your garden it will also grow best in light, sandy soil that is on the dry side. Though it appreciates occasional water in summer, overwatering may cause the roots to rot. If your soil tends to heavy clay, amend it well to ensure good drainage before you plant this perennial herb.

The Harvest Break off stem tips or branches when you need rosemary, as well as to shape the plant and control its size. An untended upright plant will send out ungainly branches and age to a large, oddly shaped shrub, fine on a windswept hill in Spain or in a large garden, but maybe not what you had in mind for your small, tame herb garden. Prostrate types will be more attractive if you pinch them to keep the draping branches from completely covering the embankment. Stagger the ends, rather than cutting them all off in a straight line. Prune rosemary plants frequently if they are threatening to get too big. The best way to do it is through thinning cuts, ones that remove a too-long branch to the joint it forms with another, shorter, branch. When you are pruning, remember that rosemary is one of those plants that do not leaf out from bare wood. That is, if you prune a branch so that you have removed all of the part that has leaves growing on it, the leafless part of the branch left on the plant will die.

Whole fresh rosemary stem tips can be cooked in foods to lend flavor, then plucked out and discarded. Fresh leaves, stripped from the stems, can be chopped; dried ones need to be ground. (Use a mortar and pestle or an electric appliance to grind dry rosemary leaves.) The leaves are so leathery that they dry easily at room temperature. The best time to harvest for drying is midsummer, although you can dry rosemary whenever you pinch or prune your plant.

Rosemary is a common ingredient in Italian cuisine. It is used more subtly in the cuisines of France, Greece, and Spain. It's good with lamb—in fact, with most meats—and with fish and shellfish. It is also used in soups, spaghetti sauce, rice dishes, and breads, and to season vegetables. One of my favorite uses is on the Italian flat bread known as focaccia. Just before baking, the dough is brushed with olive oil, then sprinkled with rosemary. Don't add too much rosemary to any dish, though, as the flavor, reminiscent of pine, can be overpowering. Some flavors that hold their own against it well are onion, garlic, parsley, and wine.

Varieties Check nurseries for different rosemary cultivars, all of which are fine for culinary purposes. Among full-sized ones, two attractive ones are majorca rosemary, with pink flowers, and 'Collingwood Ingram', with graceful branches and blue-violet flowers.

The creepers include 'Prostratus' and 'Lockwood de Forest'. The latter has deeper blue flowers and brighter green leaves than most rosemary varieties.

Sources

Rosemary plants: JG, NGN, PS, RH, TERR

Sage

Garden Sage

Salvia officinalis

Variegated Sage (or Tricolor Sage)

Salvia tricolor

Pineapple Sage

Salvia elegans (*S. rutilans*)

Clary Sage

Salvia sclarea

Mint Family ❖ *Lamiaceae* (*Labiatae*)

While there are hundreds of sages, only a few are used in cooking. The sage commonly sold as a culinary herb is *Salvia officinalis*, garden sage. This is a perennial plant, a foot or two high, which bears stems of bright violet, pink, or white flowers in the late spring. The leaves are oblong, 1 to 2½ inches, grayish-green, with a roughly textured surface.

Garden sage is another of the Mediterranean herbs, a native of lands along the northern and down the eastern side of the Mediterranean Sea, and therefore well suited to our similar climate. *Salvia tricolor* is a very similar species, with leaves mottled white, purple, and pink. It is so similar, in fact, that some sage sold as *S. tricolor* may actually be a similar-looking cultivar of *S. officinalis*.

Two other species of sage are used less commonly in cooking. The fruity flavor of *Salvia elegans* reminds some people of pineapple. This Mexican native is often grown for its vivid red blooms, which attract hummingbirds and bees. The perennial plant grows 3 or more feet high and almost as wide.

Salvia sclarea, or clary sage, is the traditional flavoring, together with elder flowers, for muscatel wine. It's a biennial, but it is usually grown from seed in spring and kept only one year. Three or more feet tall, it has strongly—some would say overpoweringly—scented leaves and, in the second year, pale blue or white flowers in large lavender bracts.

Growing Instructions Although perennial sages are not difficult to start from seed, seedlings are so slow to mature that most gardeners buy plants in pots. Sages are adaptable to varied local conditions. They will grow in rock garden conditions of poor and dry soil. They will also grow in good vegetable garden soil as long as the drainage is adequate. They thrive in full sun, but will also do all right in foggy areas. In short, they are not very fussy. The only conditions they will not tolerate, and which will lead to early death, are poorly drained soil or soil kept constantly wet.

The Harvest Gather sage leaves whenever you need them. They are best used fresh. If you do pick for drying, do it either just before the plant blooms or later in summer when the leaves are fully grown. Dry leaves quickly with ventilation, to prevent blackening.

Trim back your garden sage plant, or plants of *S. tricolor*, every spring, removing woody growth to stimulate more tender shoots. Replace these plants every three or four years when they get too woody. Buy new plants or try layering to propagate new plants from your old ones (see page 59). Also, look under the plants, as seedlings may sprout there from fallen seed.

Garden sage, like rosemary, is an herb of hearty flavor. Although it is said to taste even stronger in hot climates, locally grown sage is very flavorful. Sage is a traditional ingredient in poultry stuffing and in sausages. In fact, you can make a nice low-fat sausage for breakfast patties by working finely chopped sage, garlic powder, salt, and pepper into fresh, lean (uncured) ground pork. Sage is also used in various meat, fish, and cheese dishes, as well as with peas and beans.

Harvest pineapple sage by pinching off leafy stem tips, shaping the plant as you harvest. Use the leaves to make tea or to flavor fruit dishes. The brilliant red flowers are striking in fruit salads, decorating a dessert, or in an autumn bouquet. Clary sage leaves have a strong scent; they can be used to make tea.

Varieties and Related Species 'Berggarten' is a large-leaved cultivar of *S. officinalis*, great for big sage users. The variety 'Dwarf' is good for small gardens or for those who want just an occasional bit of sage. 'Icteria' has two-tone gold-and-green leaves; 'Purpurescens' has purple ones.

If you are shopping for clary sage, don't confuse it with *Salvia horminium* 'Claryssa', a pretty annual plant grown as an ornamental.

Sources

Garden sage seed: Widely available
Berggarten garden sage seed: RH
Dwarf garden sage seed: RH
Garden sage plants: JG, NGN, RH, TERR

Pineapple sage plants: NGN, RH, TERR
Clary sage seeds: BI, JLH, NGN, PGS, RH, SOC, SS
Clary sage plants: AA, RH

Summer Savory

Satureja hortensis

Winter Savory

Satureja montana (*S. illyrica*, *S. intricata*)
Mint Family ❖ *Lamiaceae* (*Labiatae*)

Summer and winter savory are herbs with small, bright green leaves and a peppery flavor. Summer savory, the annual, is milder in flavor than winter savory. Both are used in soups and stuffings as well as to season snap beans and, because of this use, are sometimes called "bean herbs." Summer savory is mild enough to also be good as a seasoning for salads.

Growing Instructions Summer savory grows easily from seed. Plant it in the spring, ⅛ inch deep. Choose a sunny part of your garden with moderately rich, well-draining soil. Give the plants moderate water and thin them to stand 6 inches apart. They will grow rapidly to a maximum of 18 inches high. Even though savory is so easy to grow from seed, gardeners sometimes buy plants, because one plant is often enough.

Winter savory is a perennial, somewhat woody, plant, 6 to 12 inches high, spreading to 2 feet wide. It is most commonly started from small plants, though it can be started from seed in the same way you start summer savory. It doesn't need as rich a soil or as much water; in fact, it will probably live longer in leaner, drier soil.

The Harvest Begin to harvest summer savory by tip pinching when the plants are 6 inches high. Continue to harvest stem tips all summer, thus preventing the plant from blooming for as long as possible. When it finally is impossible to prevent blooming, wait for the lavender or white flowers to open; then it is time to make a cutting for drying or, if you wish, to pull the whole plant and hang it in a well-ventilated place to dry.

Our mild winters allow us to harvest fresh winter savory all year, making lighter pickings in the winter months when growth is slower. Keep the plants well-shaped by trimming back any branches that become ungainly. Replace the plants every few years or whenever they become unproductive. Use winter savory leaves fresh or dried. When dry, they are hard and, except for use in a bouquet garni, must, like rosemary leaves, be ground before they are used.

Varieties Winter savory, with its preference for dryish soil, is nice spilling over the rocks of a rock garden.

Sources
Summer savory seed: Widely available
Winter savory seed: Widely available
Winter savory plants: JG, NGN, RH

Stevia

Stevia rebaudiana
Sunflower Family ❖ *Asteraceae* (*Compositae*)

In recent years this plant has attracted attention because of the noncaloric super-sweet compound it contains. It is dried and used as a tea in its native South America, and an extract from the plant has been used to sweeten some processed foods in Japan. Stevia is a perennial, but the one I grew didn't survive a San Francisco winter. It can be grown from seed or from a purchased plant and will grow from stem cuttings. It has no special needs beyond good drainage, moderate irrigation and fertilization, and a sunny or mostly sunny spot. The plant I grew in the San Francisco Mission District was only about 10 inches high, making me suspect it wanted more warmth, since it is reported to grow to 2 feet high. The leaves were certainly sweet, but I was challenged to find ways to use them in cooking. There are books containing recipes for doing just that, should you want to try it out.

Medicinal uses of herbs are beyond the scope of this book, but stevia extract is said to lower blood sugar and blood pressure. This could be a good thing, but I bring it up as a caution. Learn more about this herb before you eat a lot of it if you already have a tendency toward low blood sugar, or if you are taking medications to lower your blood pressure.

Sources
Stevia seed: BG, JSS, NGN, RH, SSE, TERR
Stevia plants: BUR, NGN, RH, TERR

Sweet Woodruff (or Woodruff)

Gallium odoratum (*Asperula odorata*)
Madder Family ❖ *Rubiaceae*

Although sweet woodruff doesn't have many uses, the fact that it is very pretty and has the ability to grow well in shady places adds considerably to its appeal. This perennial plant grows low to the ground, never over a foot high, and usually quite a bit less. Whorls of six to eight leaves surround the stems at intervals, and small, four-petalled white flowers bloom at the tops of the stems in late spring. The leaves have little scent when fresh, but surprisingly, when dry they release a subtle, sweet scent that has been described as a combination of sweet hay and vanilla.

Growing Instructions Purchase woodruff plants, as seeding is not easy. (The seed may take 200 days to germinate.) Woodruff grows wild in European forests, particularly under beech trees. The soil there is moist, shaded, and rich with humus. You should imitate these conditions with well-amended garden soil, kept moist. Deep shade isn't necessary in foggy microclimates, but at least partial shade is a good idea in all but the foggiest. (And if you do have a shady problem spot in your garden, woodruff will grow there nicely.) Woodruff will spread, though the spreading plants are relatively easy to control by pulling them out where you don't want them. Still, do watch where woodruff is spreading, as it can be a bit of a problem if it gets mixed up with another perennial.

Sweet woodruff

The Harvest Pick small sprigs as needed, but make any major harvest just before the plants bloom. The leaves will dry quickly in warm shade. In Germany, a sprig of dried woodruff is traditionally added to sweet white wine to make May wine. You can make your own May wine by adding woodruff to a white wine, then restoppering and refrigerating it for a couple of days. The French add woodruff to champagne too, but I suspect this has to be done in the bottling process to avoid losing the bubbles. You can give apple juice a woodruff flavor by steeping the herb in it for a couple of days. Or you might like woodruff tea. Finally, woodruff sachets will scent a linen closet pleasantly.

Sources
Sweet woodruff plants: JG, RH

Tarragon, French

Artemesia dracunculus var. *sativa*
Sunflower Family ❖ *Asteraceae* (*Compositae*)

Many herbs have large variations in flavor within a single species. This is especially true of tarragon. One variety has an exquisite flavor; the others are quite unremarkable. I learned this difference the hard way. Someone planted tarragon seed in the herb bed of my community garden. After it grew into a typically ungainly Russian tarragon plant, I harvested some and tried to learn to love it. But try as I might, I couldn't develop any enthusiasm for its rather nondescript flavor.

If I had read up on tarragon first, though, I would have been suspicious as soon as I learned ours was grown from seed. True French tarragon, *A. dracunculus* var. *sativa*, rarely even blooms, let alone sets seed. It is propagated almost entirely by cuttings. So if you want to grow delicious tarragon, start with a French tarragon plant.

French tarragon has linear leaves, 1 to 3 inches long. The plant is quite variable in size. Most that I have seen locally are 6 to 8 inches high, but plants 3 inches to 3 feet high are possible. The stem bases lie on the ground, then turn upright. They also seem to vary considerably in vigor, some barely growing, others spreading rapidly. So if your plant seems very weak, you might try one from another source, or look for a friend with a vigorous one who will give you a start.

Growing Instructions Transplant French tarragon into moderately rich soil, well amended so it can be kept moist without waterlogging. Plant in full sun or partial shade.

In its native range from Southern Europe to Asia, tarragon gets yearly periods of winter dormancy during which it disappears aboveground. Our milder winters do not provide sufficient chill, so the plant is likely to decline from year to year. It may grow back for a few years, but return less vigorously each spring. You can mark your plant's location in winter, so you won't plant over it, and hope for a good return, or you can get a new plant each spring.

Plants may be reproduced by digging rooted stems or with root cuttings. To take root cuttings, separate the roots with care, cut several 1-inch root tip sections, and transplant them.

The Harvest Pick tarragon stem tips and use fresh leaves as needed, being sure not to take more than half of the plant at once. Drying often damages tarragon's flavor, but it can be done if you do it carefully. Harvest leaves for drying in June, being careful not to bruise them, and dry them in a single layer in a warm room. Tarragon also makes a classic herb vinegar. Gather fresh leafy stems in June and stuff them into a bottle. Fill the bottle with white wine vinegar and cover it tightly. It will be ready to use after two months, when you can remove the herb if you wish. Try tarragon in salads and cream soups, and in dishes with chicken, fish, eggs, or cheese.

Sources
French tarragon plants: JG, NGN, PGS, RH, TERR, VBS

Tarragon, Winter (or Mexican Tarragon or Sweet Mace)

Tagetes lucida

Sunflower Family ❖ *Asteraceae* (*Compositae*)

Winter tarragon, a type of marigold, makes a credible substitute for true French tarragon. Its flavor is quite similar, although it lacks some of the subtle undertones of true tarragon. It will generally provide more to harvest in a year than will French tarragon, partly by being a bit taller and partly by being green for more of the year (though it does have a short late-winter dormancy). And it doesn't need more chill than we get, so it grows back vigorously each spring. It's classified as a half-hardy perennial, which will probably recover from temperatures into the teens, though it may not regrow as soon after that degree of cold.

Winter tarragon leaves are narrow, slightly toothed, medium green, and up to 3 inches long. The plant grows a foot or so high, bearing a few small yellow marigold-type flowers in the fall.

Growing Instructions Plants are sometimes available in local nurseries. You may find seed, but starting with plants gives you the advantage of checking the scent before you buy. Seed or transplant it in the spring, in a sunny spot that has good garden soil with adequate drainage. Check the plant each spring for winter damage, and remove any dead leaves or branches. After a few years the clump will become crowded. You can dig it up in early spring and divide it into 3- or 4-inch-wide clumps—a nice time to share this wonderful discovery with another gardener.

The Harvest Harvest leaves as needed, especially in the fall and winter, but also in the rest of the year, to use any way you would use true tarragon (see French Tarragon). They are especially nice chopped very finely and sprinkled on salads. This herb is far better used fresh, but does retain scent if dried carefully and stored in a closed jar as soon as it is dry. Follow instructions for drying French tarragon.

This plant has a bit of an identity problem. In addition to the names just listed, you may find it called sweet marigold or Mexican sweet marigold, or even Spanish tarragon! Just look for the scientific name.

Winter tarragon

Sources

Winter tarragon seed: ABL, JLH, JSS, SOC, SSE

Thyme

Common Thyme (or English Thyme)

Thymus vulgaris

Lemon Thyme

Thymus × citrodorus

Caraway Thyme

Thymus herba-barona

Mint Family ❖ *Lamiaceae* (*Labiatae*)

Gardeners grow several species of thyme, some for culinary purposes, others as ornamental ground covers. If it is a cooking herb you want, these three are your best bets. All are low-growing perennial plants that thrive in dry conditions—good candidates for a rock garden.

Common or English thyme, *T. vulgaris*, is the thyme you buy from a spice rack. It's a small plant, 6 to 15 inches high, with very small leaves. Whorls of tiny white or lavender flowers bloom along the upper stems in spring and summer. Lemon thyme, *T.* × *citrodorus*, is a cross between *T. vulgaris* and a thyme known as *T. pulegioides*. It has a lemony scent and can be used in the same ways as common thyme. Caraway thyme, *Thymus herba-barona*, grows only 2 to 5 inches high, forming a flat mat of leaves. It is valued for its caraway scent.

Growing Instructions While thyme can be grown from seed, starting with plants is much easier and faster. Plant them in soil that is sandy, or well amended to make it very light. Keep established plants on the dry side to avoid root rot.

The Harvest Harvest thyme as needed, while allowing the plant to grow. You can shape the plant as you harvest, pinching off stem tips that are growing in ungainly directions. For drying, harvest most of the plant in the early summer, just before it blooms. Let the plant grow back, and don't harvest so heavily again until the same time the following year. The plants become woody with age and may die out in the center after three or four years. When this happens, replace them with a newly purchased plant or try layering the plant (see page 59).

The various culinary thymes are strongly flavored herbs and withstand cooking without losing their flavors. This trait has made thyme one of the classic ingredients of a bouquet garni. Try thyme with any meat, fowl, fish, or with shrimp, and in soups or salads.

Varieties and Related Species Common thyme has several varieties, with somewhat different scents, including one known as French thyme—the one most often used in French cooking. Other cultivars, with silver and golden leaves and two-tone green and gold, are not as predictably useful for cooking. Like common thyme, *T.* × *citrodorus* has golden and silver variegated cultivars, but these are good cooking herbs. A variety sold locally as "lime thyme" is a handsome, bright green plant often used to edge an ornamental border. It does have a scent, but one not as mellow as that of common thyme, and not citrusy at all.

If a thyme is listed as "creeping thyme," it is not likely to be much of a cooking herb. There is some confusion in names here, but creeping thyme is likely to be *T. serphyllum* or one of several similar species sold under this name. They make nice ground covers, but have little flavor.

Sources
Thyme seed: Widely available
Thyme plants: AA, JG, NGN, PS, RH, TERR

Yerba Buena

Clinopodium douglasii (*Satureja douglasii*)
Mint Family ❖ *Lamiaceae* (*Labiatae*)

Yerba buena, which means "the good herb," is the Spanish name for a plant that was known and used by California Indians long before the Spanish came. Indians brewed it into a tea to calm the stomach. It was also one of the herbs that they rubbed on their bodies before a deer hunt, to disguise their human scent. Early European settlers used the plant for tea also, and Yerba Buena became the name of the Spanish colonial village located on the present site of San Francisco.

Yerba buena is a low, trailing plant. Its arching stems lace through other plants along the ground in coastal redwood country, especially in small meadowy clearings. Its leaves are arranged on the stems in opposite pairs, rounded in shape, ½ to 1 inch long, and wavy on the edges. Its small flowers are typical two-lipped, mint family blossoms, white or lavender. The scent of the plant is minty, with a touch of lime.

In the wild, yerba buena thrives in moderately fertile, sandy soil. If it is not watered by seepage from a natural spring, it declines in the summer. It will look much fuller and prettier in a garden, where you can give it rich soil that's kept moist in the dry season. In sunnier parts of our region yerba buena can take some shade, but in foggier microclimates, plant it in full sun.

Harvest by clipping the stems partway back. Use leaves fresh or dried to make tea. As it is a New World herb, yerba buena isn't used in the Old World cuisines that are the basis of most of our cooking, but do try substituting it for other mints in your recipes.

Sources
Yerba Buena Plants: AA, RH, or local nurseries or at plant sales of the California Native Plant Society (see Appendix VI, Seed and Starter Plant Sources)

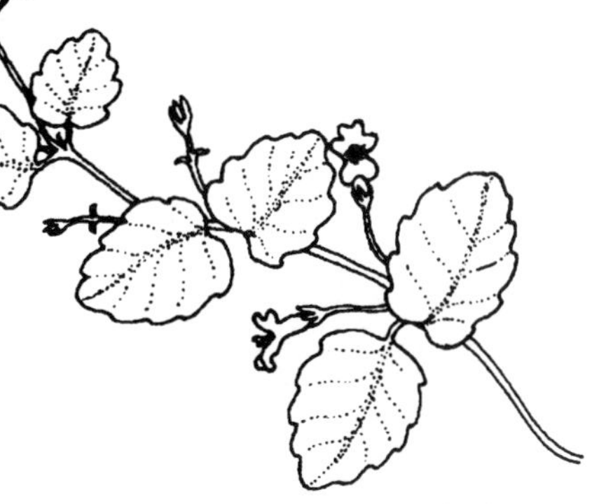

Yerba buena

THIRTEEN

Eating the Flowers

FLOWERS ARE NOT ONLY beautiful in your garden and on your dining table; they can also go right into your dinner. Edible flowers can lift your meals out of the ordinary, and the very best way to get them is to grow them yourself. The edible flowers in markets tend to be expensive and are not necessarily fresh. Also, they are sold in standard-sized packages rather than in the variable quantities in which you are likely to need them. If you grow your own edible flowers, you can pick them as you need them, they cost very little to grow, and, as a bonus, they brighten your yard before they appear on your plate.

USING EDIBLE FLOWERS

Form and color are the unique strengths of edible flowers. Sometimes these features are the main use of edible flowers in a meal. Flowers may appear only as a garnish on the side of the plate. As such, they may not actually be eaten, but it is best if they are an edible kind of flower, in case someone tries to eat them. Flowers also sometimes appear in a mainly ornamental role on top of a dish. For example, arugula blossoms can be floated on a soup, or violas and borage flowers arranged face up on top of a green or fruit salad or meat dish. Some flowers, such as calendula petals or lilac blossoms, can be sprinkled like confetti.

In addition to decorative uses, some flowers are an integral part of a dish. Squash blossoms are the basis for a Mexican soup and can also be fried alone (see page 370) or stuffed with meat or other fillings. Daylilies and tulips are also sometimes stuffed. Tulips have been used as cups for luncheon salads. Nasturtiums make nice hors d'ouevres when stuffed with flavored cream cheese or can flavor a salad dressing (see page 321). Carnations and roses serve as the basis for jellies and preserves, and carnations can be used to make a dessert sauce. Violas, borage, and calendula petals can be mixed into soft cheese. And of course all kinds of flowers can be chopped and added to omelets or rice dishes to add their color and flavor.

The flavor of edible flowers ranges from intense to bland, sweet to bitter. You will need to experiment to see which flowers you like and how you like to prepare them. Herb flowers usually share the flavor of the leaves. Onion and chive flowers taste mildly of onion. Nasturtiums are pungent and peppery. Carnations are spicy, borage cucumbery, and bean flowers taste beany. Many marigold blossoms have unpleasant flavors, but some, such as 'Lemon Gem,' are pleasant-tasting. Bland-flavored flowers, such as pansies, often make up for their lack of flavor with wonderful shapes and colors.

Many whole flowers are edible—for example, herb flowers, nasturtiums, or squash blossoms. Sometimes only the petals are eaten, as is the case with marigolds, calendulas, or carnations. In at least one case, that of daylily, you must remove the stamens and pistils from the flowers before you eat them. When a part of a flower is not eaten, it is usually because it is bitter or otherwise unpalatable.

It is best to pick edible flowers just before you use them. Being able to have them in absolutely fresh, prime condition is one of the advantages of growing them yourself. Usually, to save a step in the kitchen, they are picked without stems. However, if you must pick them in advance of using them, you can leave the stems on and put the flowers in a vase.

Safety for Flower Connoisseurs

Never eat flowers bought from a florist, since they are likely to have been sprayed with chemicals unsafe for human consumption. Because they are not intended to be eaten, these flowers are often treated against pests with systemic poisons—poisons that are absorbed into the sap of the plants and are impossible to wash off. If you buy a plant from a nursery, don't eat flowers from it for the first several months, to allow any pesticide to work its way out of the plant.

Beware too of flowers from parks or other people's yards, as these may have been sprayed. Roses and fuchsias are among the ornamentals that gardeners commonly put on a regular spray regimen.

Always be sure that the particular species of flower you are about to eat is an edible one. If you aren't absolutely sure of its identity, or have not seen it listed in a trustworthy list of edible flowers, don't eat it!

And, as with other new foods, consider the possibility of allergies to edible flowers. If a person has previously eaten other parts of the flowering plant, like beans, squash, or herb leaves, an allergy just to the flowers is highly unlikely. If however, the flower is the first part of the plant ever tasted, as is likely to be the case with pansies or day lilies, there is some question. While I have never heard of an allergy to an edible flower, they are possible. (One signal might be allergy to the flower's pollen.)

Here are some common POISONOUS flowers. Remember, DON'T eat these flowers!

Azalea, calla lily, crocus, daffodil, delphinium, foxglove, hyacinth, hydrangea, iris, lantana, larkspur, lobelia, lupine, oleander, poinsettia, ranunculus, rhododendron, sweet pea (*Lathyrus*), wisteria, tomato, potato, pepper, eggplant. This is not a complete list, only a list of some of the most common poisonous flowers. Contact your local poison control center for more information.

Or, if you have unused flowers that you picked stemless, put them in the refrigerator in a plastic bag. In either case, use within a day.

Always examine edible flowers carefully for insects, including looking down between the petals. Flowers are an unfamiliar food to many people, and you especially don't want their first edible flower experience to be a crawly one! If you garden without chemicals, and your garden is away from the street and not dusty, you may choose not to wash your flowers. If you do wash them, do it quickly in cool water, shake them out, and dry them on paper towels.

GROWING FLOWERS FOR EATING

It doesn't take much space to grow enough flowers to bring forth many ooohs and aaahs at the table. With very little space and effort, you could go out on a whim and get, say, borage flowers and nasturtiums for the occasional salad, or to decorate an iced cake so dramatically that few would forget it. With only a little more space and time, you could have many different edible flowers awaiting your creative impulse.

And you should be able to grow a wide variety of attractive and tasty flowers no matter how foggy your garden. Many of the most choice edibles are flowers that bloom best in cool weather. Refer to the chart that begins on page 322 for more information on growing and using some of them. In this chart, I have included the most popular edible flowers. Notice that many are also valuable as cut flowers. A second list on page 324 includes plants with edible flowers that are discussed elsewhere in this book—as vegetables, herbs, or even weeds.

Some mail-order seed catalogs now indicate in flower listings whether a particular flower is edible. A few seed sources give you a little more help. Johnny's Selected Seeds uses a pictorial symbol to indicate which flowers you can eat. The Cook's Garden and the Botanical Interests websites group edible flowers together.

Following are a few details about growing three annual edible flower mainstays:

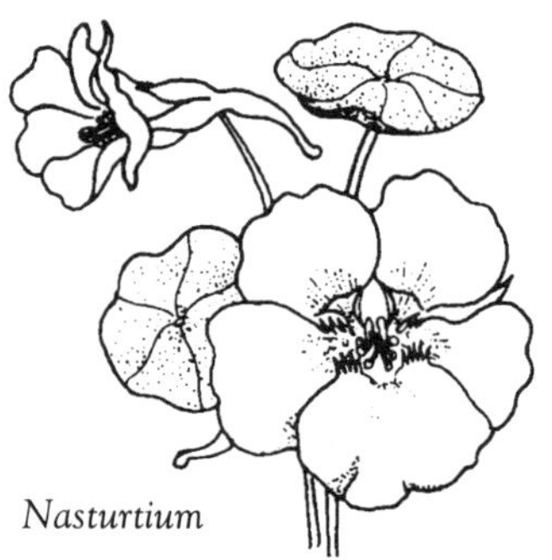

Nasturtium

Nasturtium Flower Salad Dressing

Only the essence of the flowers will remain, but it flavors this salad dressing nicely. For this recipe, thanks to my friend Nick Latham.

2 cups nasturtium blossoms
¼ cup virgin olive oil
½ cup red wine vinegar
½ teaspoon salt
¼ teaspoon pepper
1 tablespoon chopped onion
1½-inch piece red chile pepper (optional)
1 whole clove garlic

Wash the blossoms and check them carefully for insects. Put the blossoms in a quart jar, add all the other ingredients, and shake well. Let stand two weeks at room temperature. Strain to remove the garlic, onions, flowers, and pepper. This dressing is good in simple tossed green salads. Leftover dressing can be stored in the refrigerator.

Nasturtiums with Curried Cream Cheese

Try this surprise at a picnic or a party. The flower is peppery and the cheese is spicy, but when you bite into the blossom's nectary, it releases a burst of sweetness. Thanks to Caroline Morrison for the recipe for these tasty tidbits.

20 nasturtium blossoms
½ cup cream cheese (or low fat cream cheese substitute)
1 teaspoon curry powder

Wash the blossoms and check them over for insects. Set them on paper towels to dry. In a small bowl, mix the cream cheese and curry powder well.

Spoon a heaping teaspoon of cheese into each flower, and arrange the blossoms on a platter. If they can't be served immediately, cover them with a damp paper towel and refrigerate.

- Calendula is now available in a range of colors beyond plain orange, from pale cream to pink to scarlet. The plants bear flowers longer if you remove all flowerheads before they can make seeds. They are prone to powdery mildew, getting both the type peas get and the type squash gets. Cut plants back when they get leggy and have mildew, and fresh growth at the bottom will produce a new crop of flowers.
- Nasturtium also blooms in a wide range of flower colors, from pale yellow through deep maroon. Some varieties trail or climb, while others form neat mounds. Two varieties are notable for foliage as well: 'Empress of India' has blue-green leaves and scarlet blossoms; 'Alaska' has white-variegated leaves and mixed orange and yellow flowers. The leaves are useful in salads or on sandwiches.

Edible Flowers

ANNUALS

Plant Name	When to Plant	When to Harvest	How to Propagate	Color(s)	How to Use	Miscellaneous
Borage *Borago officinalis* (*Boraginaceae*)	Early spring through fall	All year	Seed	Blue or white	Pick flowers with or without hairy calyx.	Attracts bees, which help pollinate crops. Cucumber flavor. Self sows freely.
Calendula (or spring, pot marigold) *Calendula officinalis* (*Compositae*)	Summer, fall	Summer, fall, spring, some-times winter	Seed	Cream to orange	Use petals only, in salads, soups, rice dishes. Little flavor.	Very easy and dependable. Self sows readily.
Johnny-jump-up *Viola tricolor* (*Violaceae*)	Fall or spring	Spring, summer, fall	Seed	Yellow with purple and white	Use whole flower to decorate salads or dessert. Slight winter-green flavor.	Blooms profusely with little attention. Self sows.
Marigold, signet *Tagetes tenuifolia* (*Compositae*)	Spring, early summer	Summer to fall	Seed	Yellow, orange, red, white	Use petals only, in salads. Many have unpleasant taste. 'Lemon Gem' tastes lemony.	Other than signet marigolds, sample first. Also try 'Tangerine Gem' and 'Paprika'.
Nasturtium *Tropaeolum majus* (*Tropaeolaceae*)	Early spring through fall	Summer, fall, spring, sometimes winter	Seed	Yellow, red, orange, peach	Use whole flowers to decorate a salad, or stuff as appetizers. Chop flowers in omelets. Flavor is sweet and spicy.	Easy, dependable, one of the best-flavored and most useful of edible flowers. Self sows.
Pansy *Viola* × *wittrockiana* (*Violaceae*)	Fall or spring	Spring, summer, fall, sometimes winter	Seed	Many: both single color and bicolor	Use whole to decorate salads or desserts. Chop flowers in omelets. Little flavor.	Don't try to grow where snails, slugs, and earwigs are not controlled.

PERENNIALS

Plant Name	When to Plant	When to Harvest	How to Propagate	Color(s)	How to Use	Miscellaneous
Carnation *Dianthus caryophyllus* (*Caryophyllaceae*)	Spring	Summer, spring	Plant, seed	Red, orange, yellow, white, pink	Use petals only; trim away white bases. Try in salad, dessert sauces. Flavor is sweet.	Border types are easier to grow than florist types.
Chrysanthemum *Chrysanthemum morifolium* (*Compositae*)	Early spring	Summer, fall	Plant, cutting, seed	Yellow, rust, wine, white, etc.	Use petals only; trim away white bases. Use in soups, salads, cream cheese spreads. Subtle, aromatic flavor.	Pinch young plants to prolong bloom. Pick off smaller flower buds so the ones that open will make larger flowers.
Citrus flowers *Citrus* species (*Rhamnaceae*)	Late winter	Most of the year	Plant	White	Use whole blossoms as a garnish or in fruit salad, citrus desserts and sauces. Flavor is tangy.	Lemon and lime bloom most freely, but you can eat flowers of any citrus.

Edible Flowers

PERENNIALS (continued)

Plant Name	When to Plant	When to Harvest	How to Propagate	Color(s)	How to Use	Miscellaneous
Cottage pink (*Dianthus plumarius*) (*Caryophyllaceae*)	Fall or spring	Midspring	Seed, plant	White, pink, bicolor	Use petals only, in salads, desserts, sauces. Sweet flavor.	An heirloom dianthus, gray-green leaves. Other kinds of dianthus are also edible.
Day lily *Hemerocallis* hybrids (*Liliaceae*)	Early spring, late fall	Spring, summer	Division	Yellow, red, orange, pink, etc.	Remove stamens and pistils. Use on the day they open. Use in soup, tempura, stir-fries, egg dishes, salads. Flavor nutty, a bit sweet.	Dried day lilies are the "golden needles" of Chinese cooking. They are soaked in water 90 minutes before they're used.
Fuchsia *Fuchsia* hybrids (*Onagraceae*)	Any time	Early summer to fall	Plant	Red, pink, white, purple	Use whole flowers as a garnish or in salads. Flavor is acidic.	Don't eat flowers of plants that have been sprayed for fuchsia mites. Grow mite-resistant varieties.
Geraniums, scented; e.g., rose scented: *Pelargonium graveolens*; peppermint scented: *Pelargonium tomentosum* (*Geraniaceae*)	Fall or spring	Spring to fall	Plant or cutting	Various	Line a cake pan with whole flowers to scent a cake, or use petals in fruit salads. Flavor is like the plant's scent.	Other pelargoniums are also edible, but their flavor is often not very good. Still, the brightly colored flowers are dramatic as garnishes.
Lilac *Syringa vulgaris* (*Oleaceae*)	Spring or fall	Spring	Plant	Lavender, pink, white	Use individual blossoms in fruit salads or desserts.	Some varieties do not bloom every year because they need colder winters. Other varieties are adapted to our climate.
Pineapple guava *Feijoa sellowiana* (*Myrtaceae*)	Spring or when available	May or June	Plant	Red and white	Use only the petals, in salads, on ice cream, or as a garnish. The flavor is sweet.	If you remove the petals with care, the fruit will still ripen.
Rose *Rosa* species (*Rosaceae*)	All year	Spring into winter	Plant	Red, pink white, yellow, etc.	Use petals in meat dishes, fruit salads, desserts. Flavor varies. Roses with the most scent have the most flavor.	In our climate, roses get rust, mildew—choose resistant cultivars; polyanthas are usually safe. Plant bare-root in winter, or from containers all year.
Tulip *Tulipa* hybrids (*Liliaceae*)	Nov–Dec	Mar–Apr	Bulb	Red, yellow, pink, white, lavender, etc.	Remove pistils and stamens. Use as a container for dips or salads or chop petals into green salad. Vegetable flavor.	Tulips need colder weather to bloom well year after year. Here, gardeners usually plant new bulbs each year.

- Beyond the classic Johnny-jump-up (*Viola tricolor*), all kinds of violas are edible and bloom in a wide range of colors: white, yellow, orange, lavenders and purples, and deep red, often with mixed colors in each flower. While pansies are also edible, they are so big that they are less useful in a salad, for example, whereas violas can punctuate the dish with their cheery little faces (place them face up).

Johnny-jump-up

The three annual edible flowers just listed are all self-sowers (although too-assiduous removal of spent calendula flowers will reduce the amount of seeds it can form). The offspring of the plants will show mixing of the different flower colors and plant forms that were growing in your garden (or in nearby gardens). You can let some of the resulting seedlings grow up, transplanting them when they are small to a more convenient location, planting new seed only when you wish to introduce a new color of flower or leaf. Nasturtium, left to its own, will self sow a bit too much, so when you take out a spent plant, you may want to scoop up most of the large seeds from the soil surface.

ADDITIONAL EDIBLE FLOWERS

Vegetables: Amaranth, arugula, mustard, beans, okra, peas, quinoa, squash, or pumpkin. (Each immature baby corn kernel is really a corn flower. Also, artichoke, broccoli, and cauliflower are flower buds.)

Herbs: Anise hyssop, bee balm, borage, chamomile, chives, coriander, dill, fennel, garlic chives, hops, lavender, mint, rosemary, sage, pineapple sage, clary sage, or winter tarragon. Some herbs, such as thyme or savory, have flowers too small to use by themselves, though they often get eaten along with the leaves.

Weeds: Wild radish, onion lily (*A. triquetrum*), dandelion (buds), oxalis, or mallow.

FOURTEEN

The Backyard Florist

IF YOU BUY CUT FLOWERS OFTEN, you may find you can save more money by growing bouquets than by growing vegetables. Besides, growing your own flowers allows you to create delightfully serendipitous bouquets. If you go to a florist's with a few dollars in hand, you are most likely to emerge with six or a dozen of the same kind of flower, or with a standard mixed bouquet. But you can easily grow enough flowers to make armsful of bouquets, featuring combinations for which you would have to pay dearly, assuming you could even find them to buy.

Imagine a vaseful of crimson red ranunculus and red sweet peas, combined with rose-red and pale yellow columbines, pale yellow nasturtiums, and white freesias—all set amidst airy, lacy columbine leaves. Pure fantasy! Every time I looked at my bouquet I thought of those French tapestries where unicorns pose in fields of flowers. Or imagine filling a vase with yellow marguerite daisies or garland chrysanthemums, together with blue cornflowers and wild grass seed stalks—you'd be creating a piece of summer meadow in a vase. Or try combining some of the small flowers of early spring—Johnny-jump-ups, sweet alyssum, forget-me-nots, and grape hyacinths—for a small, tender nosegay. Or picture the dramatic accent in your fall kitchen of a single stem of the small, bright yellow "sunflowers" from a sunchoke plant.

The chart at the end of this chapter lists many annual and perennial flowers I've found to be both beautiful and reliable in local gardens. Of course, the possibilities for cut flowers are endless, including the flowers of many shrubs, such as roses and fuchsias, not covered in this book. This list, however, will provide you with a more than ample start. (For more detailed information about many of the easiest regional cut flower choices, see my book *Wildly Successful Plants: Northern California*, listed in Appendix VIII, Suggested Reading.)

Besides the flowers you plant especially for cutting, many vegetables, herbs, and even weeds produce flowers, seed heads, and foliage that you may find useful in bouquets. (See the Other Bouquet Possibilities sidebar on page 327.) But do be careful not to overcut foliage of crop plants, such as asparagus or artichoke, so as not to stunt their growth. And be sure not to let weeds take over your garden just because you are using them in bouquets. Nutsedge, for example, may be pretty, and you may as well use it if you have it, but it is too aggressive to tolerate in your garden.

GROWING FLOWERS FOR CUTTING

Many flowers grown for cutting thrive in the same full sunlight and rich garden soil, and with the same regular watering, that garden vegetables prefer. In fact, one way to grow them is simply scattered among the vegetables. There they can brighten your food garden as well as your home.

If your yard includes ornamental beds, you may choose to plant flowers for cutting there instead. If you do, you will need to consider their place in your decorative scheme, keeping in mind their height, color, and season of bloom. In addition to appearance, you will need to consider if they share growing requirements with the other plants in the beds.

For example, a shady ornamental bed is suitable only for cutting flowers that bloom well in shade.

A third approach to cut flower growing is to plant flowers for cutting in their own production beds, without particular attention to the aesthetics of their arrangement. This allows easier attention to their special needs. For example, tall forms can be staked to produce straight stems, without concern for the attractiveness of the staking material. This is the way to get the most flowers from the least space. Larger gardens often have several hundred square feet devoted to cut flower production, but even a tiny urban cutting bed, just few square feet in area, can produce many bouquets.

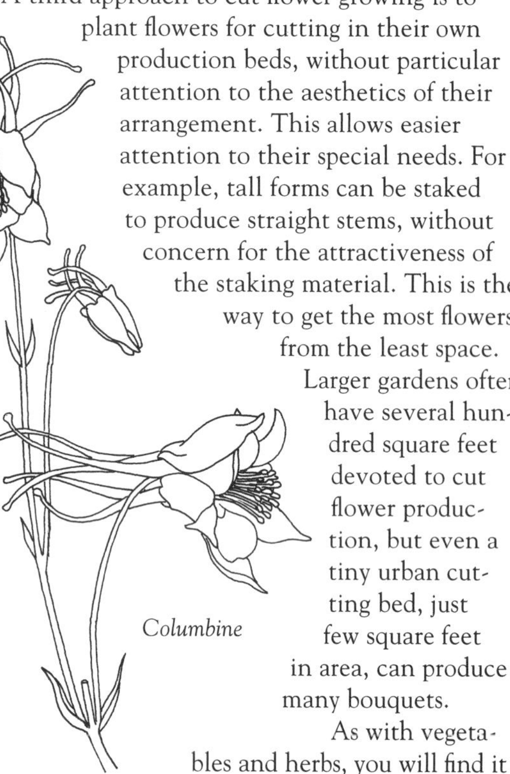
Columbine

As with vegetables and herbs, you will find it easier to keep annuals together, and to plant perennials where they won't be disturbed when you plant successive annual crops. Also, as with vegetables and herbs, you will find that some resow themselves. When the volunteers come up, you get to decide whether to weed them out, let them stay where they are, or transplant them to other sites.

Three techniques can improve the bloom of particular cutting flowers. The first is pinching, which means removing growing tips so that the plant will become bushier. This is often done when a plant is young, so that it will make more flowering stems. Among the plants that will respond well to this treatment are stock, snapdragons, and painted-tongue.

A second technique is disbudding. If a plant makes several buds in one place, you can remove all but one of them. The fewer flowers left will be larger. Common flowers you might disbud are the dahlia and the chrysanthemum.

Third, many flowering plants will bloom longer if you remove the spent flowers every week or so. Just picking the flowers for bouquets stimulates more flowers to form, but you should also prevent as many as possible of the remaining flowers from going to seed. Use this technique, sometimes called deadheading, to prolong bloom of marigolds, all kinds of daisies, pansies, sweet peas, and many other kinds of flowers.

Flowers grown from bulbs are some of the most dramatic of cutting flowers, from spring-blooming daffodils and tulips to summer's watsonias and lilies. Just remember to find out, before you grow a particular bulb, whether the bulb can remain in the ground from year to year, or whether it must be dug and stored—or even discarded—each year.

Many bulbs can stay in the ground from year to year, only needing to be divided when they get crowded. That is to say they will "naturalize." However, others cannot survive if they spend the whole year in the ground. Gladiolus and ranunculus are usually watered less after they bloom. They are then dug and stored in a cool, dry place until winter or spring, although both may come back the next year even if they are not dug. Tulip and hyacinth need much more winter chill than our climate provides. If left in the ground, they will decline rapidly, blooming poorly or not at all after the first year. Local gardeners sometimes dig and store them, but the more common tactic is to discard them, buying new tulip and hyacinth bulbs each autumn.

Often the bulbs that will naturalize here are dormant for much of the summer. If a bulb has a dormancy period, and you want to it to bloom next year, heed this warning: never cut back green leaves. Water the plants lightly until the leaves die back. Do not tie leaves in knots or knock them over. Just remove any that turn brown, and be patient.

Bulb plants in the process of going dormant can be a bit unsightly. Plan for this problem by planting summer-blooming flowers in front of them, to screen the foliage from view when the bloom is gone, or by blanketing the ground around the bulb plants with a small flowering plant like Johnny-jump-ups or alyssum.

Love-in-a-mist

CREATING A SIMPLE BOUQUET

If you are unfamiliar with flower arranging, a good beginning is a simple, but effective bouquet you build as you pick—the hand-held bouquet. Cut a few of a kind of flower you like and hold them as if your hand were the neck of a vase. Choose a stem length you can match with several kinds of flowers. Hold the first flowers you cut next to another kind of flower in your garden. If they look good together, cut a few stems of the second flower, too. Keep adding flowers until your arrangement pleases you and you have enough to fill a vase.

As you hold your expanding bouquet against each new flower, and before you cut it, move the bouquet up and down a bit. The stems don't have to be exactly the same length, and you will find that some flowers need to stand a bit above the others to look their best. Also, it often helps an informal bouquet to have several of one kind of flower, in the same color, in little groups throughout the arrangement, rather than having all of the kinds of flowers mixed evenly. And stems of foliage—such as fennel, columbine, or spearmint—often look best around the outside, a bit lower than the flowers they are framing.

When making a hand-held bouquet, you don't need to cut all of each kind of flower at the same time. Take some time to wander about, comparing and visualizing, until a bouquet emerges in your mind's eye. Sometimes you will find that a certain color or shape is, after all, wrong for your bouquet. If that happens, don't be afraid to take it out. Chances are that flower will look fine in a small vase by itself.

Your color scheme choices will be limited to what is blooming, but within that, here are some possibilities to consider. You may have all one kind of flower, but in several colors, or all one color, with several kinds of flowers. You might try analogous color schemes, like blue/purple/pink or yellow/orange/rust. A multicolor bouquet, with contrasting colors, can be either pastel (pink, pale blue, lavender) or bright (red, blue, gold, purple). A few stems of something white, or some greenery, will often show off your colors to better advantage.

A miniature handheld bouquet

This informal bouquet will be looser or tighter depending not only on the number of stems, but also on the proportions of the vase you choose to hold it. A tall vase (or a small-mouthed one) will hold the stems closer together. A short vase (or a wide-mouthed one) will let them stand farther apart. So as you are designing your bouquet, keep the proportions of your possible vases in mind too.

Other Bouquet Possibilities

Flowers from Vegetables: Artichoke, cardoon, garland chrysanthemum, mustard, scarlet runner bean, sunchoke.
From Herbs: African blue basil, anise hyssop, borage, chamomile (German), chives, comfrey, coriander, garlic chive, lavender, pineapple sage, garden sage, sorrel.
From Weeds: Dock, fennel, onion lily.

Seed Stalks from Weeds: Wild grasses, nutsedge, fennel.

Leaves from Vegetables: Artichoke, asparagus, beet, carrot, celery or celeriac, ground cherry, Swiss chard (white, green, red, or yellow stemmed).
From Herbs: Lemon balm, mint, parsley, rosemary, garden sage, sweet woodruff.
From Weeds: Horsetail, wild fennel.
From Flowers: Columbine, nasturtium, feverfew, calla lily.

Cut Flowers

PERENNIALS

Name	Bloom Size and Plant Height*	Color*	Fragrance	When to Plant
Calla lily *Zantedeschia aethiopica* (*Araceae*)	4–6" 1½–4'	White	Slight	Rhizomes: Fall Plants: As available
Chasmanthe *Chasmanthe floribunda* (*Iridaceae*)	3" 5–7'	Orange, pale yellow	None	Late summer or fall
Chrysanthemum *Chrysanthemum* × *morifolium* (*Compositae*)	2–4"+ 1–3'	White, yellow, bronze, maroon, lavender, pink	None or pungent	Early spring
Columbine *Aquilegia* species and hybrids (*Ranunculaceae*)	1½–2½" 1–3'	Blue, pink, yellow, lavender red, white (often bicolors)	None	Seed: Early spring Plants: Spring, summer
Coreopsis *Coreopsis lanceolata* (*Compositae*)	3" 2'	Yellow	Slight	Spring, summer
Crocosmia *Crocosmia* × *crocosmiiflora* *C. masoniorum* (*Iridaceae*)	1–2" 2½–4'	Yellow, orange, scarlet	None	Early spring
Daffodil *Narcissus* hybrids (*Amarylidaceae*)	1–3" 1–1½'	Yellow, white, orange, apricot (some are bicolors)	Sweet	Fall
Dahlia *Dahlia* hybrids (*Compositae*)	1–10" 1–6'	Many colors, but not blue (some are bicolors)	None	Spring, early summer
Feverfew, matricaria *Chrysanthemum parthenium* (*Compositae*)	¾" 1½–3'	White, yellow, white with yellow centers	Leaves are pungent	Fall, spring
Freesia *Freesia* species and hybrids (*Iridaceae*)	2" 1–1½'	White, yellow, red, lavender, pink, purple (many are bicolors)	Some are very sweet	Fall
Gaillardia *Gaillardia* × *grandiflora* (*Compositae*)	3–4" 2–4'	Red, yellow, orange, bronze (many bicolors)	None	Spring
Geraniums *Pelargonium* species and hybrids (*Pelargoniaceae*)	1–2" 1–3'	Red, pink, lavender, peach, maroon, some bicolors	Little unless scented varieties	Spring or fall
Gladiolus *Gladiolus hortulanus* (*Iridaceae*)	1½–4" 1½–4'	White, yellow, red, orange, pink, lavender, purple, green (many bicolors)	None	January to March
Iris *Iris* species and hybrids (*Iridaceae*)	2–4" 6"–4'	Blue, purple, yellow, white, wine, etc. (many are bicolors)	None	Midsummer, fall, spring

*See notes, page 334.

Cut Flowers

PERENNIALS

When to Pick	Propagate By?*	Growing and Cutting Tips	Miscellaneous
Spring, summer	Rhizomes	Sun or part shade. Most soils. Ample water.	Frequently grows wild. Species with colored flowers less invasive, but more difficult to grow
Winter	Corm; cut when lower flowers open.	Summer dormant, needs no water.	Attracts hummingbirds. *C.f. duckettii* is pale yellow. Avoid *C. aethiopica*, which is more invasive.
Late summer, fall	Cuttings, divisions	Sun. Soil with good drainage, well-amended and fertilized. Keep moist during growth and bloom.	Pinch plants often until midsummer to encourage branching. Stake plants. Fertilize 2–3 times in summer.
Spring, early summer	Seed	Sun, part shade. Soil with good drainage. Moderate water.	May self-sow. Sometimes attacked by leafminer, but this doesn't hinder bloom.
Summer, fall	Seed division	Sun. Soil with good drainage.	Pick flowers to prolong bloom. Divide plants when crowded.
Summer	Corm	Sun. Soil with good drainage, moderate fertility. Keep moist during growth and bloom.	Naturalize well. Some kinds are invasive. Look for heirloom varieties.
Spring	Bulb	Sun, part shade. Well-amended soil. If rains fail, water while growing and blooming. Leave drier when leaves begin to die and during summer, dormancy.	Bulbs are poisonous. Gophers don't eat them. Let leaves die back naturally; don't tie them in knots.
Summer into fall	Seed or tuberous root	Sun. Well-amended soil with good drainage. Moderate water; small-flowered types more.	Easy from seed. Tuberous roots can be dug and replanted the next spring, but it isn't required except to divide them. Snails and slugs eat the petals.
Spring, summer	Seed, division, cuttings	Sun or part shade. Most soils, good drainage, moderate water.	Cut back for rebloom. May reseed, be weedy. 'Golden Feather' has chartreuse leaves. Nice background flower in bouquets.
Spring	Corm	Sun. Soil with good drainage, moderate fertility. Let dry in summer months.	Freesias may naturalize. Many hybrid varieties have little scent.
Summer, fall	Seed, division	Sun. Soil with good drainage, poor or moderate fertility. Tolerates some drought.	Start from seed in May or from nursery plants in summer. Divide overgrown plants in early spring to maintain their vigor.
Spring to fall	Cuttings	Full sun, moderate water. Cut just as flowers open.	Several species, many hybrids, varied preferences for heat or cool weather.
March to May	Corm	Sun. Fertile, preferable sandy soil. Water while actively growing. Long-lasting if cut, stored dry to ensure winter survival. Thrips may attack plants.	Corms may be dug when leaves yellow and flower.
Spring, early summer	Bulb, rhizome	Sun. Some require rich soil, others are less particular. Moderate water while growing. Some should be drier after bloom.	Many kinds, some from bulbs, others from rhizomes.

Cut Flowers

PERENNIALS (continued)

Name	Bloom Size and Plant Height*	Color*	Fragrance	When to Plant
Lily *Lilium* species and hybrids (*Liliaceae*)	4–6" 2–5'	White, orange, yellow, red, pink, etc. (many are bicolors)	Some are sweet	Late fall, early spring
Marguerite *Chrysanthemum frutescens* (*Compositae*)	1½–2½" 3–4'	White, yellow, pink (some with yellow centers)	Slight	Spring
Naked lady *Amaryllis belladonna* (*Amaryllidaceae*)	4–6" 2–3'	Pink	Strong, sweet	Late summer, after bloom
Peruvian lily *Alstroemeria* hybrids (*Liliaceae*)	1½–2" 2–5'	Pink, red, yellow, peach, salmon, white, mauve, bicolors	None	Spring or as available
Purple toadflax *Linaria purpurea* (*Scrophulariaceae*)	½" 2-3'	Medium purple, pink, white	None	Spring
Ranunculus (Persian) *Ranunculus asiaticus* (*Ranunclaceae*)	2–4" 1–2'	White, yellow, gold, orange, red, pink (many are bicolors)	None	September to November or mid-February
Shasta daisy *Chrysanthemum maximum* (*Compositae*)	2–6" 2–4'	White, pale yellow	None	Spring, fall
Tulip *Tulipa* species and hybrids (*Liliaceae*)	2–6" 6"–2½'	Red, yellow, white, lavender, near-black, etc. (many are bicolors)	Slight or none	Fall, early winter
Watsonia *Watsonia borbonica* (*Iridaceae*)	2½" 4–6'	Species is pink to rose-red; hybrids pink, white, lilac, red	None	Late summer, early fall

ANNUALS

Name	Bloom Size and Plant Height*	Color*	Fragrance	When to Plant
Calendula (or pot marigold) *Calendula officinalis* (*Compositae*)	2–4" 1–2'	Yellow, orange, cream, peach, pink	Slightly pungent	Spring, summer, fall
Cornflower (or bachelor's button) *Centaurea cyanis* (*Compositae*)	1½" 1–2½'	Blue, pink, purple, white	None	Late summer, fall, or spring
Cosmos *Cosmos bipinnatus* (*Compositae*)	2–3" 3–6'	White to magenta, some bicolored, pale yellow	None	Spring to summer

*See notes, page 334.

Cut Flowers

PERENNIALS (continued)

When to Pick	Propagate By?*	Growing and Cutting Tips	Miscellaneous
Late spring, summer	Bulb	Sun, part shade. Fertile, well-amended soil. Keep moist during growth and bloom, drier when leaves yellow. Never let dry out completely.	Mulch soil to keep roots cool. Gophers eat the bulbs. There are many kinds. Most naturalize.
Summer, fall, spring, sometimes winter	Plants	Sun. Well-amended or sandy soil. Moderate water. Replace overgrown plants every 2–3 years.	Succeeds very near the ocean. Dependable perennial daisies.
Late summer	Bulb, seed	Full sun best, no summer water needed. Cut when first bud in cluster opens.	Straplike winter leaves die back in summer. Flowers are on naked stems.
Spring, summer, light fall/ winter bloom possible	Divisions, tuberous roots, seed	Provide afternoon shade in hot locations. Cut when first flowers in cluster are open. Cut out stem with flowers to reduce vigor of planting.	Taller types tend to be easier than short ones. Some kinds can be a bit invasive.
Spring, summer	Seed	Needs only moderate water. Spires of small snapdragon-like flowers.	Deadhead to reduce resowing. Cut out spent stems to keep plants tidy.
February to April	Tuber	Sun. Well-amended, preferably sandy soil. Regular water. After bloom, water less.	Tubers may overwinter successfully in the ground. For more certainty, dig and store till spring or buy fresh tubers each year.
Spring, summer, early fall	Seeds, division	Sun, part shade. Well-amended soil. Regular water.	Start seed late winter/early spring. Plant divisions fall or spring. Plant from containers any time.
Spring	Bulb	Sun. Fertile, well-amended soil. Regular water while growing and blooming.	Hybrid tulips do not naturalize here. Discard bulbs and buy new ones each year. Some species tulips do naturalize. Gophers eat the bulbs.
Spring	Corm	Sun. Well-drained soil. Can grow without supplemental water, better with water until bloom is past.	These naturalize. Dig only to thin or replant crowded plantings. Do this in summer.

ANNUALS

When to Pick	Propagate By?*	Growing and Cutting Tips	Miscellaneous
Summer, fall, spring, sometimes winter	Seed	Sun. Very easy to grow. Cut spent blooms to prolong bloom period.	Self-sows freely. Gets powdery mildew, but generally blooms anyway.
Spring to late summer (sometimes fall/winter)	Seed	Sun. Fertile soil. Moderate water.	Tall varieties may require staking. Deadhead to keep looking tidy.
Summer to fall	Seed	Sun. Best in lean soil with little water. Easy to grow.	Self-sows lightly. May break in strong winds.

Cut Flowers

ANNUALS (continued)

Name	Bloom Size and Plant Height*	Color*	Fragrance	When to Plant
Cosmos, yellow *Cosmos sulphureus* (*Compositae*)	1½–2½" 1–6'	Yellow to orange-red	None	Spring to summer
Flowering tobacco *Nicotiana alata* (*Solanaceae*)	1" 1–4'	White, greenish, red, mauve	Some are very sweet	Spring
Forget-me-not *Myosotis sylvatica* (*Boraginaceae*)	¼" 6"–1'	Most are blue. Some are pink or white.	None	Late summer or fall, spring
Foxglove *Digitalis purpurea* (*Scrophulariaceae*)	2" 1–4'	Lavender, rose, yellow, white	None	Fall or early spring
Godetia *Clarkia amoena* (*Onagraceae*)	1–3" 10"–3'	Pink, red, lavender, peach (some are bicolors)	Slight, sweet	Fall or spring
Johnny-jump up *Viola tricolor* (*Violaceae*)	½–¾" 6–8"	Purple/yellow/white (tricolor)	None	Early spring, early summer, or fall
Larkspur, annual delphinium *Consolida ambigua* (*Ranunculaceae*)	1½" 1–4'	Blue, pink, white, lilac, salmon	None	Fall or spring
Lavatera, Annual *Lavatera trimestris* (*Malvaceae*)	3–4" 2–5'	White, pink	None	Spring
Love-in-a-mist *Nigella damascena* (*Ranunculaceae*)	1½" 1–2'	Blue, white, rose	None	Early spring, fall
Marigold *Tagetes* (various species) (*Compositae*)	½–3" 6"–3'	Yellow, orange, white, rust, crimson (some bicolors)	None or pungent	Spring, early summer
Nasturtium *Tropaeolum majus* & *T. minus* (*Tropeolaceae*)	1½–2" 6"–6'	Orange, yellow, red, cream, pink (some bicolors)	Slight	Early spring through fall
Painted Tongue *Salpiglossis sinuata* (*Solanaceae*)	2–2½" 2–3'	Purple, crimson, lavender, yellow (contrasting veins)	None	Late winter, early spring
Pansy *Viola* × *wittrockiana* (*Violaceae*)	2–4" 6–8"	Purple, red, yellow, blue, white (some bicolors)	None	Fall or spring

*See notes, page 334.

Cut Flowers

ANNUALS (continued)

When to Pick	Propagate By?*	Growing and Cutting Tips	Miscellaneous
Summer to fall	Seed	Full sun. Best in lean soil with little water. Easy to grow.	Self-sows lightly. Look unkempt late in season.
Summer	Seed	Sun or part shade. Fertile, well-amended soil, kept moist. For reliable fragrance, try *N. alata* 'Grandiflora'.	Some self-sow readily. Some open only at night or on cloudy days. Some may overwinter to become short-lived perennials.
Late winter, spring, or summer	Seed	Part shade. Fertile soil; keep moist. Use in small bouquets.	Self-sows freely. Nice under spring bulbs. May get powdery mildew.
Spring, early summer	Seed	Light shade to full shade. Well-amended soil, keep moist.	May self-sow. Entire plant is poisonous.
Spring, summer	Seed	Sun. Grows well in poor, sandy soil.	May self-sow. Better for cutting than related clarkias, because flowers are at top of stem rather than on sides.
Spring, summer	Seed	Sun or shade. Fertile soil. Keep moist. Pick stems with leaves for small bouquets.	Self-sows freely. Sold as an edible flower more often than as an ornamental.
Spring, summer	Seed	Sun. Fertile soil. Moderate moisture.	Protect from strong winds.
Summer, early fall	Seed	Can be easily started indoors, planted out when weather warms. Easy and showy in the garden.	Flowers fade and new ones open in the vase. Remove spent lower flowers and leaves and recut stem for a second show. If reddish rust spots or black anthracnose spots appear, remove plants and don't compost.
Spring	Seed	Sun or part shade. Soil with very good drainage.	Dies in summer. May self-sow. Lacy seedpods also nice in arrangements.
Spring to fall	Seed	Sun. Most soils. Moderate water. Easy to grow.	Taller kinds may need staking. Deadhead to prolong bloom.
Spring, summer, fall, sometimes winter	Seed	Sun. Sandy soil best. Moderate water. Rich soil inhibits bloom. Easy to grow.	Succeeds very near the ocean. Self sows freely. Some varieties trail or climb, others form tidy mounds. 'Alaska' has variegated leaves.
Late spring to mid-summer	Seed	Sun. Fertile soil. Moderate water. Pinch when young to encourage branching.	Best to seed inside and transplant. If site is too damp and shady, blooms get gray mold.
Spring, summer, fall, sometimes winter	Seed	Sun. Fertile soil. Ample water. Pick stem with some leaves for bouquets.	Snails, slugs, earwigs eat blossoms. Deadhead to prolong bloom.

Cut Flowers

ANNUALS (continued)

Name	Bloom Size and Plant Height*	Color*	Fragrance	When to Plant
Pincushion Flower *Scabiosa atropurpurea* (*Dipsacaceae*)	1½" 2½–3'	Lilac, pink, maroon, white	May have sweet scent	Spring
Shirley Poppy *Papaver rhoeas* (*Papaveraceae*)	2–8" 2–5"	Red, pink, white, salmon, yellow (some bicolors)	None	Early to late spring
Sunflower *Helianthus annus* (*Compositae*)	4–15" 1–14'	Yellow, orange, red, burgundy (some bicolors)	None	Mid-spring
Statice *Limonium sinuatum* (*Plumbaginaceae*)	¼" 1–2½'	Blue, lavender, rose, white, yellow	None	Early to late spring
Stock *Matthiola incana* (*Cruciferae*)	1" 1–2½"	Pink, lavender, purple, cream, white, red	Very sweet	Fall or spring
Strawflower *Helichrysum bracteatum* (*Compositae*)	2–2½" 2–4'	Yellow, orange, wine, rust, pink, white	None	Late spring
Sweet alyssum *Lobularia maritima* (*Cruciferae*)	¼" 4–8"	White, rose, lavender	Sweet	Late winter through fall
Sweet pea *Lathyrus odoratus* (*Leguminosae*)	1–1½" 1–6'	Pink, lavender, purple, red, white, blue, salmon	Most are very sweet	Fall, winter, spring, summer
Sweet William *Dianthus barbatus* (*Caryophyllaceae*)	½" 6"–1½'	Red, pink, rose-violet, white (often bicolored)	Slight clove scent	Summer
Viola *Viola cornuta* (*Violaceae*)	1½" 6–8"	Blue, purple, yellow, white, apricot (some bicolors)	None	Late summer or early spring
Zinnia *Zinnia* hybrids (*Compositae*)	1½–6" 3"–2½'	Red, pink, yellow, orange, white, greenish	None	Spring

***Notes to the Cut Flower Chart**

Bloom Size/Plant Height: When there is a wide range of measurements, these refer to the range of cultivars of the flower. For example, there are dwarf marigolds, to only 6 inches tall, with ½-inch flowers, as well as varieties that grow to 3 feet, with huge, 3-inch pompoms. Consult references such as the *Sunset Western Garden Book* or seed catalogs to learn the names of different-sized varieties.

Colors(s): Refer to catalogs or seed packets for colors of specific offerings. Some will contain flowers of all one color, others will be mixtures.

Propagate By?: Most kinds of flowers grown from seed are also available as nursery transplants or can be started indoors and transplanted. Check seed packets for information about indoor seeding.

Cut Flowers

ANNUALS (continued)

When to Pick	Propagate By?*	Growing and Cutting Tips	Miscellaneous
Summer, fall, sometimes winter	Seed	Sun. Fertile soil. Moderate water. Can grow in alkaline soil.	Taller varieties need staking. Deadheading prolongs bloom period.
Spring, summer	Seed	Sun. Well amended soil. Moderate water. Cut just as color shows on buds.	Red ones sold as Flanders poppies. Last longer in the vase if you dip end of stem first in boiling water, then ice water.
Summer, early fall	Seed	Average to rich soil, ample water. Cut flowers that have just opened; use a knife.	Protect seedlings from slugs, snails, and earwigs. Leave seed heads uncut—birds enjoy the seeds.
Spring, summer	Seed	Sun. Best in lean sandy soil. Moderate water. Use either fresh or dried.	Succeeds very near the ocean. All plants may not come into bloom together.
Late winter, spring, summer	Seed	Sun. Well-amended soil. Moderate water.	Scent is stronger on overcast days and in the evening.
Summer	Seed	Sun. Well-amended soil. Moderate water. Use fresh or dried.	Tall forms may need staking. To dry, cut before center opens, hang upside down.
Almost all year	Seed	Sun. Most soils. Moderate water. Good in small bouquets.	Self sows. Cut back, to prolong bloom period.
Winter, spring, summer	Seed	Sun. Fertile, well-amended soil. Keep moist. Easy to grow.	Different varieties bloom in different day lengths. If a variety is fragrant, description will say so. Tall varieties need trellis.
Spring, summer	Seed	Sun. Fairly fertile soil. Moderate water. Long lasting cut flower.	Old varieties take nearly a year from seed. Some new ones bloom in as little as 10 weeks from spring sowing—check listings.
Winter, summer, spring, fall	Seed	Sun, part shade. Fertile soil. Ample water.	Like pansies, violas are really perennials, but treated as annuals.
Summer, fall	Seed	Sun. Fertile, well-amended soil. Ample water.	Zinnias prefer a warm microclimate. Near the coast, look for varieties bred to withstand cool days. Avoid wetting leaves to prevent mildew.

MAKING CUT FLOWERS LAST

The vase life of flowers is much improved by getting them into water as soon as possible. If your garden is far from home (true for many community gardeners), or if you are taking the bouquet to a friend, wrap the stems in a wet paper towel and put the stems or the whole bouquet in a plastic bag. Keep them out of the direct sun while in transport. When you are ready to put your flowers in a vase, always remove the lower leaves, so they won't decay in the water. If it has been more than a few minutes between cutting and putting your flowers in a vase, recut the stems, using clippers or a sharp knife to remove another ½ to 1 inch. For very delicate flowers, cut the stems while holding them under water in a bowl, then put the flowers immediately into a water-filled vase. If your cut flowers wilt despite these precautions, try this: as soon as you make an arrangement, put the vase in a cool room, away from direct sunlight. Keep a plastic bag over the flowers for a few hours or overnight, then remove the bag and move them to the place where you want them to be.

And don't forget your flowers after the first day. Changing the water every day or two and keeping your vases well filled with water will make your creations last longer.

FIFTEEN

Fruit from Fog or Sunshine

EMON TREES PRODUCE A steady supply of their tangy, bright yellow fruits in many a foggy local backyard, and plum trees droop under their sweet burden every summer. These are among the most reliable fruit trees for cool summer parts of our region. With attention paid to choice of variety and location, regional gardeners can also grow many other kinds of fruit—from the deciduous fruit trees such as apples and pears, to subtropical evergreen trees such as avocado, figs, and tangerines, as well as bush and vine crops such as blackberry and kiwi.

When you are choosing fruits for your garden, take your time to do some research before you purchase any plants. Don't just happen to see a fruit tree at a store and bring it home.

Your first step is to understand the microclimate of your garden and what kinds of fruit are likely to succeed in it. (Use earlier chapters in this book and Appendix I, The Climate of Our Region, to gain an understanding of your microclimate.) The Limiting Factors (page 339) explains the climatic factors that limit plants from surviving, fruiting, or making sweet fruit. This will help you to zoom in on the best bets for the place where you garden.

The next question to answer is which varieties of each fruit you should grow. Of course, as with any kind of fruit, personal choice is important. If your favorite kind of apple or pear is adapted to your microclimate, by all means grow it. But in some cases, only particular varieties will survive and bear fruit. Lists at the end of each fruit entry in this chapter give selections of some good variety choices, though they can't include every possibility—there are hundreds of apple varieties, for example. Do not be dogged in pursuit of fruit varieties listed in this book if you find a knowledgeable nursery with the experience to suggest others.

Because little fruit is grown commercially in the most coastal parts of our region, exactly what will succeed here isn't completely known. My species and variety recommendations are based on those of the University of California Cooperative Extension Service, Sunset Books, several experienced fruit growers and nursery owners, my own experience, and reports from other gardeners. The more inland parts of the region have grown, and sometimes still do grow, more fruits commercially. Large areas of Santa Clara County were once thriving orchards, and wine grapes are an increasing presence in several counties. Where this is true, more is known. Ideally, though, we'd have a census of successful home garden fruit trees, vines, and shrubs for each of the different parts of our region, and these would inform our choices.

As with vegetable crops, the particular location of your yard, and of the fruit plant in it, can make a significant difference. No matter what I write, some gardeners will experience disappointment and other gardeners will find unexpected success in growing a particular fruit.

You can do a little on-the-ground research to see what is happening near where you live. Start by looking around to see what kind of fruit is growing in your neighbors' yards and in community gardens or school gardens. Ask around to see if you can find any successful fruit growers in your neighborhood who might be able to give you advice. Taste fruit when you can (maybe offering flowers or vegetables in exchange). You may be able to find nearby fruit growers through www.craigslist.org or other websites

Strategies for Fruit-Growing Success

Buy deciduous fruit trees bare-root if at all possible. They are sold without soil on the roots during the winter and early spring, when they have no leaves. Bare-root trees are likely to establish themselves better and get off to a healthier start.

If you are buying a fruit tree or shrub in a container, ease it out and look at the roots. Reject plants with visibly circling roots, dead or damaged roots, or insects visible among the roots. If all the potting mix falls off of the roots, the plant may be a recently potted-up bare-root tree. Better to buy a bare-root tree earlier, when the selection is better and the tree won't have to adjust first to the container and then again to your garden.

Plan for pollination. Some kinds of fruit are self-fruitful, meaning no other trees of that species need be nearby to produce fruit. Others need cross-pollination from another variety of the same species. In many cases, some varieties of a fruit species are self-fruitful, while others need a mate, which is called a "pollinizer." Read about the fruit and varieties you plan to buy. I touch on these matters in the "Compendium of Fruits," but books, fruit nursery catalogs, and websites offer exhaustive charts. Bear in mind, however, that trees in someone else's yard, up to a half-mile away, can pollinize your trees.

Plan for annual pruning. Fruit trees are pruned to increase fruitful wood, open the crown to light and air, and keep the fruit within reach. Exact techniques vary, depending on the fruit; fruit growing resources can tell you how. You keep fruit within reach by pruning early to encourage low branches, and by making sure not to remove those low branches later. (What good is a fruit tree if you can't reach the fruit?)

Plan for preventative measures for pests and diseases. When a type of fruit is said to be susceptible to a pest, this doesn't mean it will get it, but it does mean you should learn the symptoms and the preventative measures you should take. These often include steps such as raking up any fallen fruit or spraying with dormant oils or biorational pesticides. Learn the measures to prevent particular problems, and you may never see them.

Don't plant your tree too deeply. It is important not to bury the lower part of the trunk—the part just above where roots begin. This is easy when a plant is in a container—you just plant at the same height. Bare-root trees are less obvious, but look for a slight flare at the trunk base and make sure it's above the ground—probably very near where the roots start. If there is a graft union, you will see it as a diagonal scar or a jog in the trunk, and it should remain well above ground. Books listed in Appendix VIII, Suggested Reading, as well as nursery catalogs and websites listed in Appendix VII, Resources for Gardeners, include illustrated guides to planting fruit trees.

Beware of growth coming from below the graft union. Rootstock may provide dwarfing, disease resistance, or other benefits, but the fruit it makes will be inferior. Remove any growth, called suckers, that originates below the graft union or from underground.

Don't let fruit go to waste. Maybe your tree had an especially large crop. Maybe your garden contains large trees planted before you lived there, or your family is smaller than it once was. If you have way more fruit than you can eat, find a way to share it. Share it with friends, pass it out at work, or find a way to get it to those who need food. Food banks may know of organizations that will harvest your fruit, leaving some for you and taking some to charities. Make it your responsibility to get the fruit to people who will eat it.

that help with local connections. You will also find plenty of advice on growing both rare and common fruits through the California Rare Fruit Growers (see listing in Appendix VII), and they have fruit tastings at their meetings.

Three related concerns, as you make your choices, are the eventual size of the plants you are choosing, how much fruit they are likely to bear, and when they will bear it. Full-sized fruit trees can bear immense crops and take up large areas. Dwarf or semidwarf trees may fit your space better, or you may be able to plan for special pruning to limit the size of your trees. For more on these issues, see Growing Fruit Trees in Small Spaces on page 340, and information in the Compendium of Fruits.

You will also want to have some idea of the amount of care your fruit plant will require. People often put fruit plants into the ground and then ignore them except to look for fruit. Most fruits need pruning, watering, mulching, and some attention to pest management. They may survive neglect, but they won't necessarily bear good fruit. Complete details are beyond the scope of this book, but I have given an overview for each crop in the Compendium of Fruits. Resources on page 407 and books in Appendix VIII, Suggested Reading, will help you plan the care of the fruit you choose to grow.

THE LIMITING FACTORS

When a frost destroys all of a lime tree's half-ripe fruit, resulting in no crop at all that year, the tree has just encountered a *limiting factor*. Frost is one of several factors that can limit fruit production in local gardens. These factors affect some crops more than others. Some, such as certain plum varieties, can live pretty comfortably within all of our region's limits. Others, including oranges or peaches, tend to bump into one or more of these limiting factors fairly regularly, so they don't produce good crops every year or throughout the region.

Winters That Are Too Cold

While some parts of our region may stay entirely above 32°F during some winters, it is more likely that a garden will dip slightly below freezing at least once a winter. Tropical and subtropical plants are sensitive to frost; some can't survive temperatures below freezing even briefly. Among fruit crop plants, the entire plant may be damaged, or it may survive but bear no fruit. The mango is a tropical tree we can't grow because the slightest frost will kill it. Banana plants may survive light frosts, but they cannot be counted on to ripen fruit here. Avocado trees and some kinds of citrus will lose their fruit for the year if frost hits them at the wrong time. Deciduous fruit trees don't mind the cold at all, being natives of cold-winter areas.

When a plant is borderline in your location—hardy enough for all but the lowest likely temperatures—you may not want to waste space on it. But if you still want to try it, use the same principles you would for placing vegetables to avoid winter frost. Put the fruit plants where they will get the most winter sunlight and radiated heat, as well as the best protection from cold winds. One good place for them is under an overhang—an arbor or a wider upper floor or eave of your house. It is best if the location is open to the sun on the south side, with west- or east-facing locations second and third best. Placement next to a heated building takes advantage of heat lost from the building. The shelter above the plant provides some protection from falling cold air. An enclosed patio or an atrium are other good places to try frost-sensitive fruits.

Sometimes a deciduous fruit tree, like apple or plum, may be quite able to withstand frost while it is dormant but not while it is blooming. It may be stimulated to bloom early by mild winter temperatures, only to lose its blossoms to a late frost. If you know a fruit variety may bloom very early, plant it where it will grow in a winter shadow, as this will cause it to bud out later; ideally after the chance of frost is over. However, choose early-ripening varieties for this, so the return of the shadow in late summer or fall won't cut short the ripening of the fruit.

Winters That Are Too Warm

A second limiting factor for fruit growing in our area is a lack of winter chill. Far from resenting an occasional frost, deciduous fruit trees such as apples, pears, peaches, nectarines, plums, and cherries require a minimum amount of winter cold to produce a good crop.

To calculate the amount of winter chill in an area, horticulturists add together all the hours in an entire winter during which the temperature is between 32 and 45°F. The total number of such hours is known as the *chill factor* for that year. Hours below 32° don't count, and hours over 60° get subtracted from the total chill hours. The chill factor in our central California coastal region ranges from fewer than 100 to 900 hours. Most coastal areas have up to 400 chilling hours. Areas more than a few miles from the ocean have 400 to 900 hours. If your location is blocked from the ocean influence by hills, or is shaded in winter, or is in a cold pocket, it will get more winter chill. Areas that get more winter tule fog may get additional chilling hours from the resulting cooler days, though not if warmer nights balance them out.

Some apple varieties need as many as 1,800 hours! Fortunately, researchers have found or developed varieties that can produce well with less chill. Thus some apples succeed with a chill factor of 400 hours or even less. Of the deciduous fruit trees mentioned previously, all have low-chill varieties, although in the case of peaches and nectarines, disease may still thwart our efforts. Figs, a deciduous tree from the Mediterranean, have a relatively low chill requirement—only 100 hours. Subtropical evergreen trees, such as avocado and citrus, have no chill requirement at all.

When a plant doesn't get enough winter chill, it does not end its dormant period in an orderly manner. It typically blooms late. Then the blossoms tend to open sporadically over a long period, rather than all at once. This reduces the chances of pollination because there are fewer blooms at a time. It also lessens the chance of cross-pollination, because the other trees that would have provided pollen may have already bloomed. In addition, the long bloom time weakens the tree, often leading to its early demise.

Although this is an important factor, it can be difficult to be exact in dealing with it. One uncertainty is that the chill factor rating for a fruit variety tends to be approximate—you will find published figures that vary by as much as 300 hours for the same variety. Also, you aren't likely to be able to find out the exact chilling hours for your garden's location. Experts assure me that predicting winter chill with statistical methods is more difficult nearer the coast than it is inland.

And since there is little commercial fruit-growing in the near-coastal region, there aren't likely to be efforts to record actual chilling hours here. Because of these uncertainties, local gardeners often find that taking risks pays off in successful harvests. Despite the uncertainties, you should make an effort to guess your level of winter chill, and try to choose plants that require less, or only a little more, winter chill than the average you are likely to get.

Increase winter chill for borderline crops by planting them in spots where they will be in the shade much of the winter (on the north sides of structures or evergreen trees, or on north slopes of hills), or in low spots, but make sure the plants will be in sun from bloom time to leaf drop. Avoid planting them against heated buildings.

Summers That Are Not Warm Enough

Many kinds of fruits require summers warmer than ours to ripen fruit that is sweet. Fruit growers calculate summer warmth in terms of *degree days*. While the meaning of the term varies depending on the fruit you are growing, the principle is that degree days accumulate when the mean temperature for a day is above a certain minimum. For grapes, the minimum is 50°F. So, for example, if the mean temperature of a day is 70°F, you would say it contributed 20 degree days toward the ripening of grapes.

As with the chilling hours, degree days are harder to predict for sites nearer the coast. But this factor is easier for us to guess at than the winter chill factor. When we feel chilly in the summer, chances are that heat-requiring fruit will not be getting enough heat. And we can pretty well assume that the degree day total is low in areas where the delay of the maximum temperature is great (see map on page 13). Cool summers will limit success with grapes, oranges, grapefruits, peaches, and pomegranates, among other fruits.

Sometimes we can find a variety of a particular fruit that can develop sweeter fruit than other varieties in a cool summer. But even then, it's a good idea to locate the plant in a favorable garden site to maximize warmth, using all the tricks you would use in locating a heat-requiring vegetable crop.

Too Much Humidity

Humid air fosters plant diseases such as apple scab, fireblight, peach leaf curl, and brown rot of apricot. In foggier regions, peach leaf curl may be hard to control even with repeated treatments. To prevent these diseases, choose resistant varieties whenever possible and plant where the trees will get as much sun as possible. When you prune to reduce dense foliage, let in light and air while taking care not to thin the foliage so much that the tree will be opened to sunburn where summer sun will be harsh. Also avoid leaving a garden sprinkler set where it will spray water into tree branches.

GROWING FRUIT TREES IN SMALL SPACES

Fruit trees used to require considerable garden space, as most grew to 25 to 40 feet high, with similar spreads. Now we are fortunate in having smaller versions of these trees, so that we can have several kinds of fruit in even a small yard. And if we choose varieties that ripen at different times, we can avoid having the glut of fruit that a full-sized tree can produce. Some backyard orchardists are also experimenting with planting several trees close together and controlling their growth through pruning. And formal pruning options, such as espalier, allow fruit to grow even in narrow spaces.

Growing Smaller Trees

Many dwarf and semidwarf trees have been created by grafting a full-sized variety onto a rootstock that stunts the tree. These can be highly satisfactory, bearing early and well. You can also often find dwarfs on rootstocks that offer resistance to local diseases and are particularly well adapted to local soils. However, the grafting process does tend to shorten the life of the tree somewhat, and you must take care to prune out any suckers that sprout near the ground from below the graft union, as these shoots will bear different fruit that is rarely desirable to eat.

More recently, a few natural, genetically dwarf trees have been discovered and developed. You may see them listed as either genetic dwarfs or miniature trees. These often bear even sooner than the dwarfs created by using dwarfing rootstock, and they seem to have considerably longer lives. Genetic dwarfs do not exist for all kinds of fruit trees, and the quality of fruit they bear is not always as high as that of the best rootstock-formed dwarfs, but breeding continues, resulting in new and better varieties every year.

Aside from using dwarf trees, many kinds of full-sized trees can be pruned and otherwise treated in ways that control their size somewhat. When your deciduous tree, such as apple or plum, is approaching the size you want, you can slow its growth by shifting your major pruning from winter to summer. If it is a fig tree you wish to control, prune it while it is dormant. Evergreens, such as avocado and citrus, can also be pruned to keep them in bounds; this is best done when they are most dormant, neither sprouting new shoots nor flowering. Judicious pinching and reduction of large limbs can keep even the usually huge avocado tree from reaching its normally Olympian heights.

Dwarf trees can be grown in containers. Half-barrels are a good container choice. These will last longer if they are spar varnished and have had their metal hoops bolted to the wood. Sometimes you can buy them already prepared in these ways. Drill two or three holes in the bottoms for drainage. Put each empty barrel on a small platform with wheels of the sort sold for houseplants, so you will be able to move it about. Then plant the tree in a good potting mix. Water and fertilize your container trees often, keeping the mix at the right moisture level for the kind of fruit you are growing—get a moisture meter. Flush the container with water periodically to remove excess salts. Every couple of years, while they are dormant, remove them from their containers. Trim out circling roots and the fattest of the rest of the roots, leaving thinner, fibrous roots. Repot, using fresh potting mix.

Training Trees to Fit Small Spaces

A number of kinds of fruit trees can be trained and maintained in very small forms, such as espaliers, cordons, or Belgian fences. These are all two-dimensional trees, trained and pruned so that all of the limbs lie in one plane. They are generally grown against a fence or wall. These pruning techniques not only save space but also provide a warm environment for the trees, because walls and fences radiate heat.

Espaliers may be pruned into very formal patterns, such as fans or candelabra forms, or they may be allowed to develop into a less formal but still two-dimensional pattern. A cordon is even more restrained than an espalier, being limited to a single stem, growing diagonally from the ground, with only very short side branches. Several cordons, grown in a row along a fence, allow the gardener to sample just a bit of several varieties or kinds of fruit while using minimum space. A Belgian fence is a row of several fruit trees espaliered to single V shapes, with their limbs overlapping, and maybe actually growing together, to form a "living fence."

Fruits vary in their ability to adapt to formal pruning and training such as the styles just described. Apples, pears, figs, persimmons, and citrus are among those that can be successfully treated this way. And among the varieties of a fruit, some will adjust better than others. Some fruits, or varieties of a particular fruit, will take to an informal espalier but not a formal one, or to a fan but not to candelabra tiers. Ask an experienced grower about the adaptability of a particular plant variety before you try to create your own espaliered tree.

All of these formally trained trees require careful pruning each year to create and maintain their form. A cordon is probably the simplest to do, then an informal espalier, with the more formal patterns taking more attention and work. You can buy trees already trained, several years old, ready to be set in front of your fence, saving yourself much of the trouble. Still, if you have never pruned fruit trees before and plan to do it yourself, get a guidebook and study it well in advance of your first pruning season.

START WITH PLANTS, NOT SEED

Notice that I have been talking about buying plants rather than starting your own fruit trees or shrubs from seed. This is with good reason, as most kinds of fruit do not come true from seed. That is, a seed from a plant with good fruit often will produce a plant with inferior fruit. It can be interesting to start fruit from seed, and some seedlings may turn out well, but after you wait several years for seedling fruit trees to reach bearing age, you will not want to find that a low proportion of your trees have high-quality fruit. For this reason, most fruits are grown by grafting a twig of a known variety onto a carefully chosen rootstock, or by rooting cuttings.

Probably the most common homegrown fruit seedling is the avocado, because it is such fun to germinate the large seeds. All of the foregoing cautions apply to avocados. While the chance of avocado seedlings maturing to trees with good fruit could be as high as 50 percent, if you have room for only one or two trees, those aren't very good odds. And if they do not bear well, you will have on your hands some large, heavily shading trees that are expensive to remove. So enjoy sprouting avocado or other fruit seeds as house plants, but invest in selected varieties for your yard.

While buying already-grafted trees is clearly the most practical route to good fruit trees, grafting your own, or grafting other varieties onto the trees you already have, is a pleasant exploration. Look for workshops where you can learn the basics. If you have a healthy seedling, you can use it as rootstock, grafting onto it a twig (scion) of a variety that produces reliably good fruit. Some gardeners even graft branches of several varieties, or even different fruits, onto the same mature tree. This can work, though it tends to exhaust a tree, especially when the different varieties develop fruit at different times. The California Rare Fruit Growers Society (listed in Appendix VII, Resources for Gardeners) has scion exchanges that are open to the public.

When you are ready to buy plants, try to purchase ones that have been grown as near as possible to our region, as these are more likely to be on rootstocks well suited to our climate and soils. Younger plants are often a better buy than older ones, as they frequently become established faster and so bear sooner. Inquire carefully about the mature size of the trees you are purchasing.

Compendium of Fruits

The following entries will give you a general idea of how to grow each fruit—soil, watering, pruning, and so on. When you have decided on the kind of fruit and the variety you want to grow, use references in this book for sources and detailed information about caring for them. In Appendix VII, see page 407, and in Appendix VIII, see page 421.

Almond

Prunus dulcis var. *dulcis*
Rose Family ❖ *Rosaceae*

Almonds bloom in February in the many Central Valley orchards that have made them California's largest agricultural export. The flowers, blooming at this time, are at some risk for frost or rain damage, but once nuts set they develop well in the summer heat. The nuts require six months to develop. A chill requirement in the 250- to 500-hour range suggests they could succeed near the coast, but cool, foggy summers work against success. They can succeed in hot summer parts of our region; they are borderline where summers are less hot and not recommended in the foggiest microclimates. Still, there are bearing trees of the varieties 'Nonpareil' and 'All in One' growing in a very warm part of San Francisco, so I won't say never. Give almonds a deep soil with excellent drainage and water deeply but not often. Almonds are a stone crop, in the same plant genus as peaches and plums, so they are susceptible to some of the same pests, including shot hole fungus, brown rot, and peach twig borer. They can also be damaged by mites, bacterial canker, and navel orangeworm. Squirrels will eat the nuts.

Almond Varieties

All-in-One: 400 to 500 hours. Late blooming and late maturing. Self-fruitful and can pollinize other almond varieties. Best variety for home orchards.

Ne Plus Ultra: 250 to 300 hours. Late blooming. Needs a pollinizer.

Nonpareil: 400 hours. Late maturing. Needs a pollinizer.

Apple

Malus species
Rose Family ❖ *Rosaceae*

Many apple varieties, including some of the most familiar, require 900 or more hours of winter chill. However, a substantial and increasing number of available varieties can produce well with only 300 to 400 chilling hours. A few even do well with as little as 100 hours, but those with the lowest chill requirements don't necessarily produce fruit of the highest quality.

Luckily, even nearest the coast in our Central California region, we can grow apple varieties with only moderately low chill requirements. Types needing 400 hours, and even ones rated as high as 750 hours, are known to thrive in San Francisco.

Apples require soil with reasonably good drainage, moderate fertilization, and infrequent deep watering in summer. They also need some annual pruning and need thinning of young fruit to allow the remaining fruit to grow larger. Apples are available as full-sized trees, which grow 25 to 40 feet tall, as semidwarfs to 12 to 14 feet tall, and as dwarf trees only 4 to 8 feet tall. Apple trees are good subjects for espaliers, cordons, or Belgian fences. Most varieties of apples need cross pollination.

Apples may get fireblight, scab, mildew, woolly apple and rosy apple aphids, codling moth "worms," or various other insect pests, and they may need treatments to combat these—most commonly with dormant oil or sulfur. While your apple trees may have any of these pest problems, they may also turn out to be relatively pest-free, depending on the variety, your preventative care, the weather of a particular year, and chance. San Francisco trees seem not to have codling moth damage, probably because the insect needs more warmth. Rootstocks not only determine the size of a mature fruit tree but also sometimes confer resistance to pests. For apples, M11 and M106 rootstocks reportedly resist woolly apple aphid.

Among the hundreds of apple varieties, the following are a few that should succeed in all or part of our region, though there are many others to discover. I have given required chill hours if they are available. Hot inland climates keep most red-skinned varieties from developing good color. Some very good varieties are heirlooms, not widely grown commercially, but with great potential for home gardens.

Apple Varieties

Recommendations: *not at coast **not inland

Anna: 200 to 300 hours. Very early, and may have 2 to 3 crops a year. Yellow with red blush, sweet, crisp. Stores well. Needs pollinizer.

***Beverly Hills:* 300 or fewer hours. Early. Pale yellow, red-striped, tender, juicy, tart, keeper. High heat spoils the fruit. Self-fruitful.

**Braeburn:* 600 or fewer hours. Late. Red blush over yellow-green ground. Crisp and tart, good fresh or for pie. Best somewhat inland, but drops fruit in high heat. Good keeper. Self-fruitful.

Beni Shogun Fuji: 400 hours. Better for cool summers than standard Fuji. Late. Redder in cool summer. Very sweet and crisp. Moderate scab resistance. Needs pollinizer.

Gala: 500 hours. Early. Red, juicy, crisp, aromatic. Keeps well. Self-fruitful. Pollinizes other varieties, but not Golden Delicious.

**Golden Delicious:* 600 to 700 hours. Midseason. Yellow to green, crisp, sweet, high quality. Stores well. Usually self-fruitful. Pollinizes other varieties well.

Gordon: 400 hours. Early to midseason—long ripening period. Red over green, sweet-tart, keeper. Self-fruitful.

**Granny Smith:* 400 hours, but chancy in foggier areas or areas with early frost, because of late ripening. Can be picked green and tart or later when yellow and sweet. Self-fruitful.

***Gravenstein:* 700 or fewer hours. Not suited to high heat. Early. Red over deep yellow, crisp, juicy, aromatic. Poor keeper. Needs pollinizer.

Grimes Golden: Similar but superior to 'Golden Delicious'. Late. Yellow, tender, sweet, spicy, fair keeper. Resists scab, mildew, fireblight. Self-fruitful and good pollinizer.

Hauer Pippin: The original Martinelli cider apple. Very late. Orange-blushed green, crisp, hard, juicy, tart, excellent keeper. Resists scab. Needs pollinizer.

**Hudson's Golden Gem:* 600 or less hours. Late. Yellow with brown russeting. Crisp, sweet, distinctive pear-like flavor. Stores well. Resists scab, powdery mildew; partially resists fireblight. Needs pollinizer.

**Liberty:* 800 hours. Midseason. Red, crisp, sweet-tart, good keeper. Immune to scab, resists powdery mildew. Self-fruitful.

Mollie's Delicious: 400 to 500 hours. Early. Red blush over yellow, firm, juicy, sweet, good keeper. Needs pollinizer.

**Pink Lady (Cripps Pink):* 400 to 500 hours. Late. Best flavor with hot summers. Pink blush over green, sweet-tart, cut flesh resists browning, storage improves flavor. Self-fertile.

**Pink Pearl:* 600 or less hours. Early. Pink bloom and flesh, pale green to pink skin. Firm, rich flavor. Stores well. Needs pollinizer.

Snow (Fameuse): Early. Yellow, blushed red, tender, sweet-spicy, snow-white flesh, fair keeper. Resists fireblight and powdery mildew. Partially self-fruitful.

Suntan: Late. Orange-red, crisp, sweet-sharp, aromatic, keeps well. Similar to 'Cox Orange Pippin' but resists scab and powdery mildew. Self-fruitful.

White Winter Pearmain: 400 hours or fewer. Late. Green, usually red-blushed, mildly sweet, firm, aromatic, keeper. Self-fruitful.

Yellow Newtown Pippin: 700 hours. Late. Green to yellow, aromatic, tart, good for cooking, good keeper. Resists scab. Self-fruitful.

Apricot

Prunus armeniaca
Rose Family ❖ *Rosaceae*

Apricots are considered risky in the areas of this region with cooler summers. Even when you choose low-chill varieties, pollination may be inhibited by cold, rainy, or windy weather during their bloom time, and fruit will not ripen properly if a site is too cool in the summer. In addition, humid weather encourages the fungus disease brown rot, which spoils the fruit and weakens the tree. In some coastal sites, fruit may develop purple blemishes known as "fog spots." Nevertheless, I have been told of three successfully bearing apricot trees in warmer parts of San Francisco, and these trees reportedly do not suffer from brown rot.

Soil, water, and fertilizer needs are similar to those of apples. Apricots need annual pruning to stimulate new growth, and they may be espaliered. Keep full-sized trees at 10 to 14 feet for ease of harvest. Some are self-fruitful; some need a pollinizer. Unless you are extremely lucky, they will need dormant spraying to try to prevent brown rot. (See Peach and Nectarine, page 353.)

The varieties I have listed are low-chill, but for the reasons just given, do best in areas with warm summers and minimal spring frost.

Apricot Varieties

Gold Kist: 300 hours. Ripens in May. Large, tart-sweet. Self-fruitful.

Flora Gold: 500 hours. Ripens in June. Good quality. Self-fruitful.

Harcot: 700 hours. Blooms late. Ripens early to mid-June. Sweet, juicy rich flavor. Resists brown rot and perennial canker. Self-fruitful.

Katy: 300 hours. Ripens in May. Excellent flavor. Self-fruitful.

Moorpark: 600 to 700 hours. Large, exceptional flavor. Fruit ripens over a long period, which is good for home gardeners. Self-fruitful.

Avocado

Persea americana
Laurel Family ❖ *Lauraceae*

Some avocados are too frost sensitive for our region; others fare pretty well. In all cases, leafy growth is more frost-hardy than the flowers or fruit, so varieties that bloom and begin to ripen fruit in warmer months are more likely to bear full crops here. Varieties with Mexican avocado parentage are hardier than those from Guatemalan avocado stock.

Avocados are very sensitive to waterlogged soil. Plant where drainage is very good, and don't overwater. Once established, irrigation every 4 weeks in the dry season is sufficient. Trees will grow best where soil has a pH of 5.5 to 6.5. They may require treatment with iron chelate to check iron-deficiency chlorosis. Don't rake fallen leaves from under an avocado tree, as they form a thick natural mulch that moderates soil temperature and probably adds just the fertility the tree needs.

Full-sized avocado trees are 30 to 60 feet high and 20 to 40 feet wide. While avocados don't need pruning for their health and well-being, you'd be wise to start, when your tree is small, pinching off terminal buds to encourage branching and limit the size of the plant. It's best if you can keep it no taller than 15 feet and no wider. Topping is an option when the tree is still small, but pinching is preferable. Leave lower branches on the tree, almost to the ground. One variety—known as 'Wurtz', 'Littlecado', or 'Minicado'—has a weeping, dwarf form. It is tantalizing for Bay Area gardeners with small spaces, but its ancestry is Guatemalan, so it is a risk this far north. I am also listing 'Don Gillogly', which is claimed to be dwarf, but it is too recently introduced for gardeners to be sure of its traits.

Most avocados are self-fruitful; however, if you plant an "A" type plant near a "B" type plant, both may produce better. Some varieties tend to produce larger crops in alternate years, but even the lighter crop is often sufficient for a home gardener.

Avocado Varieties

Bacon (A): Blooms in the spring and fruit matures in 18 months. It ripens around July, then hangs on the tree for six months longer. Good-quality fruit. Medium-large tree. Alternate year bearing. 'Jim Bacon' is more cold-hardy.

Don Gillogly (A): A Mexican or mixed-parentage variety claimed to bear 2 crops a year. Black when ripe. Claimed to reach only 10 feet high. Hardy to 27°F.

Hass (A): Black-skinned, excellent flavor. Blooms in winter and ripens the next December–January. Hardy to 30°F.

Mexicola (A): Heavy producer of small purple fruits with excellent flavor. Ripens August to October. Medium-sized, spreading tree. Hardy to 18°F.

Stewart (B): Small to medium fruits with excellent flavor ripen in fall and winter. Tree to 25 feet, compact form. Hardy to 18°F.

Wurtz (A): Dwarf tree of Guatemalan ancestry. Bears medium-sized green fruit in the summer. Tree can reach 10–12 feet. Bears in alternate years.

Zutano (B): Heavy producer of medium-sized green fruits with good flavor. Ripens December to January. Medium-sized, upright tree. Hardy to 26°F.

Blackberry

Rubus species, varieties, and hybrids
Rose Family ❖ *Rosaceae*

Blackberry varieties are either erect or trailing. The varieties that do best in our part of California are either trailing kinds or hybrids between uprights and trailers called "semi-erect." Blackberries require a deep soil, moderate fertilization, and plenty of water.

A good supply of organic matter in the soil is ideal. Trailing blackberries must be trained on a trellis or on wires, and if they are not pruned and trained with care, they will become a miserable tangle. See page 166 for a description of the pruning routine as modified for the very vigorous Himalayas, and Appendix VIII, Suggested Reading, for books with a more complete explanation of the process. Many modern blackberry varieties are thornless—a definite improvement over the painful experience that picking 'Himalaya' can be for the unwary. Two varieties, Boysenberries and Loganberries, are hybrids with red raspberries that offer uniquely flavored fruit. Red-berry mites sometimes attack, keeping fruit from ripening. Treatment is dormant spray with lime-sulfur. Some varieties get verticillium wilt.

Blackberry Varieties

Apache: Thornless, upright plants with large, firm, good-flavored fruit.

Himalaya: Our local weedy blackberry. Soft, sweet fruit. Few plant it, but it is common. See page 166 for more on this plant. One virtue is its long season—mid-July to October with summer water.

Olallieberry: Thorny, trailing plants. Good production of large, firm, sweet berries.

Triple Crown: Thornless. Semi-erect plants are very productive. Large, flavorful berries.

Thornless Boysen: Trailing. Fruit is deep maroon, sweet-tart, aromatic. Plants are very productive.

Thornless Logan: Trailing. Large fruits are tarter than Boysen, lighter in color. Needs less chill than Boysen.

Blueberry

Vaccinium corymbosum and hybrids
Heath Family ❖ *Ericaceae*

These wonderful berries are borne on long-lived and attractive shrubs. The plants bear small pink bell-shaped flowers in the spring, and berries in the summer, and often provide brilliant red or yellow fall color. New low-chill varieties of southern highbush are the best adapted for our region. They need full sun (part shade where summers are hot), ample water, and a soil similar to that needed by rhododendrons; that is, pH 4 to 5.2 with good drainage. To create this soil, you must add organic matter, and perhaps soil sulfur, until you have reached this pH, and then continue to add acidic mulch, acid-reaction fertilizer, and sulfur over the years to keep the soil from reverting to the pH of the surroundings. A pH meter is a big help in keeping track of this matter. Cottonseed meal is a good organic fertilizer with an acid reaction. Nitrate fertilizers are toxic to the plants—read labels.

To avoid this rigorous routine, some advise growing your blueberries in containers. For a 4-inch to 1 gallon plant, use a 2- to 5-gallon container; for a 2- to 5-gallon plant, use a 16- to 20-inch container. Dave Wilson Nursery (see Appendix VII, Resources for Gardeners) recommends mixing ⅓ pathway bark (quarter-inch), ⅓ shredded peat moss, ⅓ azalea mix, and a handful of soil sulfur, per plant.

I'd think full-sized plants would outgrow these containers rather fast though, since a full-sized plant is usually 5 to 6 feet high and nearly as wide. They are very bushy, not good subjects for espalier. Pollination will be better if you plant at least two varieties. Two full-sized plants per person are recommended for an adequate supply. (Berries are borne in large clusters, only a few of which will be ripe at any given time.)

Strip blossoms for the first two years, so plants will put more energy into growth.

Don't prune blueberries at all for the first four years. Then they need only light pruning, which may include some tip-pruning to prevent the plants from setting more fruit then they will be able to ripen. You may need to put netting over the plants when fruit is ripening to foil birds.

Blueberry Varieties

Earliblue: 400 hours. Northern highbush. Large berries with good flavor.

Misty: 150 to 300 hours. Southern highbush. Very early, large, good-flavored fruit, bears heavily. Tolerant of higher than usual soil pH.

O'Neil: 400 to 500 hours. Southern highbush. Very early, large, good-flavored fruit.

Sharpblue: Fewer than 500 hours. Southern highbush. Early to midseason. Very adaptable to low-chill areas. Nearly evergreen. Large, sweet-tart fruit.

Southmoon: 500 hours. Southern highbush. Midseason. Large fruit with excellent flavor. Good near coast or inland.

Sunshine Blue: 150 hours. Southern highbush. Midseason. Large fruit with tangy flavor. Dwarf—to only 3 feet. Tolerant of higher than usual soil pH.

Top Hat: Needs more chill than at the coast. Midseason. Small fruit with mild flavor. Dwarf to 1½ feet.

Cherry

Prunus species
Rose Family ❖ *Rosaceae*

The cherries most often sold in California are sweet varieties, like Bing. These generally require at least 700 to 900 hours of chill, so they can be grown only in parts of this region with the most winter chill. To ensure cross-pollination, they need careful attention to compatibility. They do not tolerate extreme heat, and the crop can be damaged by spring frosts or rain. One variety, 'Stella', and its semidwarf version, 'Compact Stella', are particularly recommended for home gardens in most inland parts of our region and intermediate areas. However, two new varieties, 'Minnie Royal' and 'Royal Lee', are the first with lower chilling requirements. Conveniently, they also pollinize each other. They should be adaptable in much of our region, even to sunny pockets in more coastal parts, though they are not going to like foggy summers.

Sour, or pie, cherries are somewhat more adaptable. They can take colder winters, but tend to require less chill to fruit. They can tolerate a bit more fog than the sweets. Still, none are recommended for the chilliest, foggiest parts of our region. Nevertheless, I do hear occasional reports of success with cherries relatively near the coast, and I have seen one bearing cherry tree, of an unknown variety, in San Francisco's sunny Mission District. Its location had winter shade, which perhaps increased its chilling hours.

Cherries are often available on dwarfing rootstock. They need pruning only to produce good structure and shape. Good drainage is important for both kinds, but particularly for sweet cherries. They can be struck by brown rot, blossom blight, scale, or mites. Birds are notoriously fond of the fruit.

Sweet Cherry Varieties

Minnie Royal: 400 to 500 hours. Medium-sized firm, red cherry with good flavor. Pollinized by 'Royal Lee'.

Royal Lee: 400 to 500 hours. Large, firm, red cherry, with excellent flavor. Pollinized by 'Minnie Royal'.

Stella: 700 hours. Good choice for intermediate and inland areas of our region. Firm, dark red cherry that is less prone to cracking if rain falls near harvest time than other cherries. Bears at a young age. Self-fertile. 'Compact Stella' is semidwarf version, 10 to 12 feet high.

Sour Cherry Varieties

English Morello: 400 to 700 hours. A tart cooking cherry. Dark red to nearly black. Small tree. Self-fruitful.

Montmorency: 700 or more hours. Red, sweet-tart when it ripens on the tree. Reliable. Self-fruitful.

Currant and Gooseberry

Ribes species
Gooseberry Family ❖ *Grossulariaceae*

The varieties of *Ribes* grown for fruit do best where summers are cool and humid, and in partial shade, and this makes them sound promising to near-coastal gardeners. However, in general they are rated with a chill requirement of 800 to 1,500 hours, so are not recommended for low-chill areas. Gardeners with less ocean influence may be able to ripen these fruits. Cooperative Extension research, just now beginning, will reveal, I hope, more about the adaptability of currant and gooseberry varieties to lower-chill areas. Preliminary findings suggest that 'Red Lake' currants may actually have a chill requirement of only 400 hours. California natives, such as *R. sanguineum*, are attractive garden plants, but their fruit is not as succulent as that of varieties bred for fruit.

Fig

Ficus carica
Mulberry Family ❖ *Moraceae*

A producing fig tree is a possibility throughout our region, given at least 8 hours of sunlight a day and at least moderate heat. Fig trees have a chill requirement of 100 or so hours and are hardy to 15 or 20°F. The limiting factor, near the coast, is lack of summer heat to ripen the fruit well. Fortunately, some varieties can produce sweet fruit in cooler summers; still, near the coast much depends on having a favorable location in which to grow a fig. It needs full sun, preferably on the south side of a light-colored wall or surrounded by paving, and good protection from wind. Inland, protect figs from the hottest sun—orchardists whitewash the trunks and limbs.

Figs tolerate various types of soil but grow best with good drainage. They need light to moderate applications of fertilizer, mainly a nitrogen source. They respond well to heavy applications of compost or manure. Although we think of them as a drought-tolerant tree, they require regular summer water to ripen good fruit.

Full-sized trees grow 15 to 30 feet high, dwarfs to 10 feet. After initial shaping, prune mature fig trees, while they are dormant, to remove deadwood, to thin overgrown limbs, and to keep the tree in bounds. Figs are fairly amenable to severe size control. (In areas with moderately cold winters, they freeze to the ground and grow back each year as a shrub.) Full-sized trees can be held to 10 or even 6 feet high or trained into an espalier. With meticulous attention to fertilization and watering, a fig can be grown in a container.

Figs typically make two crops a year, the *breba* crop, in late spring, and the larger, midsummer-to-fall main crop. Heavily pruned trees may not bear a *breba* crop, but you may consider this an acceptable price to pay for the pleasure of having a fig tree small enough for a very small yard or a large container. The commonly grown figs are self-fruitful.

Figs are relatively pest-free, but their roots are a favorite of gophers, and birds enjoy the fruit if they find it.

Fig Varieties

Black Mission (Mission): Purplish black skin, reddish flesh. Good fresh, dry, or canned. Produces best if not heavily pruned. Fruit often not sweet enough near the coast.

Brown Turkey: Purplish brown skin, pinkish flesh. Best if eaten fresh. Grows in cooler areas than Black Mission. Bigger main crop if pruned heavily.

Desert King: Green skin, strawberry red interior. Excellent flavor fresh or dried. Ripens one crop, in July. Good in cool areas.

Osborne Prolific: Purplish-brown skin, amber flesh. Very sweet. Best eaten fresh. Modest *breba*, good main crop. Low heat requirement, so good for cool coastal locations. Does less well with summer heat.

White Genoa (Genoa): Yellow-green skin, yellow-amber flesh. Good fresh or dried. Very sweet. Good for cooler regions. Modest *breba*, good main crop.

Ventura: Green skin, deep red flesh. Flavor excellent fresh or dried. Good *breba* crop. Ripens well in cool areas. Compact tree.

Grape

Vitis species and hybrids
Grape Family ❖ *Vitaceae*

The limiting factor for grape growing in our coastal area is lack of summer heat. When summers are too cool, fruit ripens slowly and may not ripen properly at all. Most grapes require at least 1,700 degree days, and summers of the most coastal parts of the region do not provide this. However, the minimum is reached fairly quickly as you move inland, so if your summers are warm to hot, you may wish to try very early grape varieties. Note that no grape varieties are recommended for exposed locations near the coast.

Grapes do best in a soil rich in organic matter. They may need a little nitrogen fertilizer, added early in the season. They need excellent drainage and require very little summer water. Most are self-fertile.

Training and careful annual pruning are necessary to keep grapes bearing well. And part of the purpose of pruning is to thin the crop, as a grape vine with too heavy a crop will not produce sweet fruit. Grapes are best grown on a trellis or fence.

A grape variety may be European in origin, American in origin, or a hybrid of the two. In general, American varieties have lower heat requirements. Also, European grapes are susceptible to mildew, while most American grapes are not. (I suspect that American/European hybrids vary in resistance.) If mildew strikes, it may be controlled by several dustings of sulfur. Without treatment, the mildew will often render a plant incapable of bearing fruit.

Table Grape Varieties

Campbell Early: Early. A deep purple grape that resembles Concord but is better for cool areas. American or hybrid.

Canadice: Early. Medium-sized, seedless, firm red fruit. Good fresh or as juice. One of the better for cool climates. American.

Concord: Midseason. Blue-black fruit with a distinctive, rich flavor. Used mainly for juice, jelly, baking. American.

Interlaken: Early. Firm, seedless green fruit. Ripens in NW cool summer areas. Fresh eating or raisins. American hybrid.

Vanessa: Early. Red, firm, seedless grape that will do better than 'Flame' in cool areas. Fresh eating or raisins. American.

Grapefruit

Citrus × *paradisi*
Citrus Family ❖ *Rutaceae*

Grapefruit is generally not recommended for the region nearest the coast because there isn't enough summer heat to produce fruit with good flavor. Your best bet for sweet fruit in cool summer areas is 'Oroblanco', a variety that resulted from crosses between grapefruit and a similar fruit called a pummelo (*C. maxima*). The fruit is sweet and juicy, though it may take as long as 18 months to ripen where summers are cool, so trees will still have ripening fruit while new fruits are setting. I have seen ripe fruit in the southeast corner of San Francisco. 'Oroblanco' is also among the good choices for more inland gardens, with attention to frost protection, since temperatures below 28°F will damage grapefruit trees. (See Citrus Fruit Trees, page 351.)

Guava (see Pineapple Guava)

Huckleberry, Evergreen

Vaccinium ovatum
Heath Family ❖ *Ericaceae*

If you've walked in the coastal redwoods in late summer, you may have tasted these small, almost black berries that grow on decorative evergreen shrubs. (The plants are so attractive that the florist industry grows them for the shiny sprays of foliage.)

Huckleberries are adapted to the coastal climate; they need much the same soil as rhododendrons, camellias, and blueberries. They will do better with some shade in less foggy parts of the region, but may take full sun in the foggiest places.

Little attention has been paid to selecting and breeding these plants for fruit production. There are more and less productive strains, but finding a productive one still involves an element of chance. (Maybe you will discover a particularly fruitful strain and propagate it for others.) You will find plants at plant sales of the California Native Plant Society as well as in nursery catalogs (see Appendix VI, Seed and Starter Plant Sources).

Kiwi Fruit

Actinidia deliciosa (*A. chinensis*), *A. arguta*, *A. kolomikta*
Actinidia Family ❖ *Actinidiaceae*

The kiwi sold commercially is fuzzy kiwi (*Actinidia deliciosa* or *A. chinensis*). It is borne on woody vines that will reach 30 feet if allowed. It can tolerate 10°F when it is fully dormant, but needs gradual cooling first, and needs weather to be above freezing in early autumn and late winter. The most common varieties require 600 to 800 chilling hours. Success has been reported even in warmer near-coastal microclimates, but fruit will not ripen without sufficient heat, so plants need placement that protects them from wind and maximizes sunlight and warmth.

Two other species of kiwis, sold as "hardy kiwis," may succeed in local gardens. *A. arguta* has 1- to 1½-inch smooth fruit that is generally sweeter than that of fuzzy kiwi. It is hardy to –25°F, given gradual cooling. *A. kolomikta*, with similar fruit, is also hardier in colder places than ours. It may have pink-white-green variegated leaves and prefers part shade. Hardy kiwis do need some winter chill, but how much has not been determined for the various cultivars.

All kiwis require a very sturdy trellis or fence for support. Commercial growers of fuzzy kiwi suggest starting with a 2-year-old bare-root plant in preference to container plants.

Plant kiwis in rich garden soil with good drainage, and don't let the soil completely dry out. You will probably have to water at least once a week. After the third year you can water them less frequently. They must be pruned twice a year to keep them under control and encourage fruiting.

To have fruit, you must plant at least two kiwi plants, one male and one female. These must have the same chilling requirements so they will bloom at the same time. The supplier selling you the female kiwi should be able to provide the correct male variety to pollinize it. Commercial growers report that pollination isn't so certain, since bees tend to prefer a number of other flowers to those of kiwi. They plant 1 male to 8 female kiwis, an efficiency not possible in a small garden, but at least, since male plants won't produce fruit, you can save space by cutting them back somewhat after they bloom.

Not many pests bother kiwi, though snails can seriously harm small plants, and gophers damage the roots. The California Rare Fruit Growers report that *A. arguta* attracts cats like catnip. Their rubbing can harm young spring shoots.

Fuzzy Kiwi Varieties

Chico male: Pollinizer for 'Hayward', 'Saanichton', or 'Vincent'.

Hayward: 600 to 800 hours. Common commercial variety.

Saanichton: Ripens a couple of weeks before 'Hayward'.

Vincent: 100 to 200 hours. Worth a try due to its low chill requirement.

Kumquat and Hybrids

Fortunella species and hybrids
Citrus Family ❖ *Rutaceae*

Kumquats owe the fact they are the hardiest of common citrus fruits to their origins in Northern China. They bear small orange fruit with a sweet, edible rind and more or less sour pulp. These can be eaten out of hand or used candied, in marmalade, or in sauces. Kumquats are hardy to at least 18°F, and require warm or hot summers with cool fall and winter nights to bloom and bear, so they are a better choice inland than near the coast. Kumquats are decorative plants, often with fruit and flowers at the same time. Full-sized plants can be 15 to 25 feet high; dwarfs, 3 to 6 feet high.

Also decorative, and better adapted to areas with moderately cool summers, is the calamondin, a kumquat/tangerine hybrid that requires less heat. The fruit looks like a miniature tangerine. It has sour pulp, with a rind that tends to be too sour to eat, and is used like a kumquat or for its sour juice. You can tell them apart because calamondin peels easily, kumquat doesn't; kumquat has 3 to 7 segments, while calamondin has 9 or 10.

Kumquat Varieties

Meiwa (F. margarita × F. japonica)*:* Neither the fruit nor the plant are as common as 'Nagami'. Fruit larger, round, pulp a bit sweeter. Often thornless.

Nagami (F. margarita)*:* The one more commonly sold. Oval fruit, to 1 inch long. Thornless.

Calamondin (F. margarita × Citrus reticulata): Narrow plants 8 to 10 feet tall. There is a yellow variegated variety.

Lemon

Citrus limon and *Citrus × meyeri*
Citrus Family ❖ *Rutaceae*

All four common varieties of lemon—'Eureka', 'Lisbon', 'Ponderosa', and 'Improved Meyer'—will grow and produce well throughout our region. While most citrus needs little or no pruning, lemon trees require occasional thinning of small branches and twigs to keep them from becoming too much of a tangle. They respond well to being cut back to keep the fruit within reach. Of the four varieties, I recommend any but 'Ponderosa', as the fruit of that variety, though quite large, is very thick-skinned, with little juice.

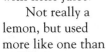

Not really a lemon, but used more like one than like any other fruit, is the yuzu. It is among the hardiest of citrus fruits, bringing a lemon-like fruit far inland. Considered a hybrid between a sour mandarin and the Chinese native species *Citrus ichangensis*, the peel and juice is used in Asian cuisines and can also be used to make marmalade.

Lemon Varieties

Eureka: The common grocery store lemon. Bears all year. Plant is somewhat thorny, sensitive to cold, and susceptible to insects, but should do well with reasonable care. It reaches 20 feet if full-sized and is available as a dwarf. Easy to espalier.

Lisbon: Fruit similar to 'Eureka', but heaviest crop is in the fall. Doesn't hold flavor well if left on the tree too long. More productive and frost-hardy than 'Eureka', but thornier. Full-sized tree grows to 25 feet. Available as a dwarf.

Improved Meyer: Larger, rounder, and thinner skinned than 'Eureka' or 'Lisbon', and still more frost-hardy than either of them. Has a unique, slightly sweet, taste that some think is superior to 'Eureka' or 'Lisbon', while others perceive it as "wrong" for a lemon. Bears all year and from a very early age. If full-sized, it reaches 12 to 15 feet. Available as a dwarf.

Variegated Pink: A sport of 'Eureka' that has white variegated leaves and green stripes on the immature fruit. Flesh is light pink.

Yuzu: Medium-sized yellow to orange fruit. Thorny plant is fast-growing, to 20 feet at maturity.

Lime and Hybrids

Citrus aurantifolia
Citrus Family ❖ *Rutaceae*

If you can grow a lemon in your area, you can also grow a lime. The ones you buy are most likely 'Bearss', which is a good choice for your garden as well. Though limes are sold green, they ripen to yellow. They are juicier when ripe, and some like the flavor better, but they do not hold well on the tree once they are ripe. Rangpur lime, a lime-mandarin hybrid, has the color of the mandarin but a unique flavor. Limequat, a lime-kumquat hybrid, is a result of a cross between 'Mexican' lime, which is too tropical for our region, and kumquat. Thai lime, or 'Kieffer' lime (*Citrus hystrix*), is grown mostly for its leaves, which impart a unique flavor to Thai cooking. The peel and scant, sour juice are also used, but fruit needs warmth to set, so cool microclimate gardeners may have to rely on the leaves alone. Thai lime plants are usually grafted onto less tropical roots, to help them survive our subtropical conditions.

Lime Varieties

Bearss: Best true lime for the region, though it may not do well in locations that are both very foggy and windy. It has larger fruit than the 'Mexican' lime, and is hardier. Most of its crop is ready in late winter and spring. Tree reaches 15 to 20 feet tall. Dwarfs are available.

Eustis Limequat: Small oval fruits that ripen to yellow. Rind is edible, like that of kumquat.

Rangpur Lime: The orange fruit of Rangpur lime hangs on the tree most of the year, giving it ornamental value. The flavor is interesting, different from both lemon and lime. Grows to a bushy 15 feet tall, dwarf to 8 feet.

Tavares Limequat: Similar to 'Eustis', fruit more elongated, form of plant more attractive.

Thai Lime: Leaves have a "waist," a narrowing between two broad areas. Fruit has lumpy skin. Tree is thorny, to 8 to 10 feet. Prune to harvest.

Loquat

Eriobotrya japonica
Rose Family ❖ *Rosaceae*

Loquat is a subtropical evergreen tree native to Southern China. Its large leaves have whitish, woolly undersides. Its fruit is oval, an inch or two long, yellow to orange, and varies from bland to sweet. Loquat is hardy to 20°F, but it blooms in winter, and if temperatures drop below 28°F while it is blooming, the flowers will drop without setting fruit. It prefers cool days to hot, but our Central California coastal summers may be too cool for some varieties. (Loquat bears very well near the coast in Southern California, where summers are a bit warmer and winters a bit milder than here.)

The plants are adaptable to various moisture conditions. They will grow through a drought if they are well established, though they will grow better if they get some water. They can take constantly moist soil, as long as the soil has good drainage, but too much water may make the fruit less flavorful. A moderate amount of fertilizer each year will encourage fruit production. For best flavor, let the fruits ripen completely on the tree. Loquats grow 15 to 30 feet tall. Prune them to shape the trees and to let in more light, as they can make a rather thick canopy. They can be espaliered.

Be especially careful when selecting a loquat tree. Fruitless varieties have been bred for use in ornamental settings where fruit drop isn't wanted, and you wouldn't want to wait a few years to discover you have one of those. Also, because the fruit is fairly low-key in flavor at best, you'll want to seek a variety that has been selected for good-flavored fruit. Look for named, grafted varieties.

Loquats are said to get fireblight and be more likely to get it when there are late spring rains. Some experts would not plant them near apples and pears, for fear of spreading the disease.

Loquat Varieties

Benlehr: White-fleshed, sweet fruit. Excellent flavor in southern California and recommended for central coastal regions.

Champagne: White-fleshed, sweet fruit. Probably needs more heat than foggier neighborhoods can provide. Needs pollinizer.

Gold Nugget: Flesh is deep orange, sweet if fully ripe. Sweet fruit in May and June. Best for coast and commonly available.

Grant Road: An improved 'Gold Nugget' that may be hard to find.

Mandarin (or Tangerine)

Citrus spp.
Citrus Family ❖ *Rutaceae*

Mandarins, or tangerines, represent several citrus species and their hybrids. They are, in general, sweet, orange, and easy to peel. They vary in flavor, size, and frost tolerance. Most require summer heat to produce sweet fruit, but a few varieties may succeed near the coast in sunny spots protected from cold wind. Inland or intermediate climate gardeners have more choices of variety and more leeway in choosing sites for mandarins.

Mandarin Varieties

Gold Nugget: Late winter to spring. Worth a try in a moderately warm location.

Kara: Winter to spring. Larger than 'Pixie'; reports vary on which is better in cool weather.

Owari Satsuma: Early fall to December. This variety has the best chance of producing in relatively foggy areas, such as protected, warmer parts of San Francisco. It has ripened sweet fruit even in Half Moon Bay. Full-sized tree 10 to 15 feet; dwarf, to 6 feet.

Pixie: Winter into spring. Relatively sweet where summers are cool.

Mulberry

Morus species
Mulberry Family ❖ *Moraceae*

Fruiting mulberries are a little-known and easy-to-grow option for home fruit gardeners. If you are familiar with mulberry trees, you probably know fruitless types—trees that grow rapidly to as high as 50 feet and create deep shade. However, there are fruiting varieties bred for large, good-flavored berries. These are well adapted throughout our region—coastal to inland, hardy to winter temperatures we experience, and require only 400 to 450 chilling hours. They also grow tall if allowed to, but for home fruit production they should be kept very small by early training and annual pruning.

The plants sold for fruit are female. Without a male tree nearby, they set seedless fruit. Some varieties fruit all summer long. Black-fruited varieties stain pavement if the fruit falls, but if the plants are kept small, they can more easily be sited away from

Citrus Fruit Trees

Citrus trees are evergreens of primarily subtropical origin. They have no chill requirements, but their success in different parts of our region is limited by frost or by a lack of summer heat. Most citrus is damaged by even light frost, needing protection at 28 to 32°F, though some kinds, such as kumquat, can survive temperatures in the low 20s, possibly even less. Inland gardeners need to select the hardiest varieties and site them where they get the best frost protection. Near the coast, cool summers limit choices and necessitate careful siting. The sour-fruited crops—lemon and some kinds of lime, and the less familiar Rangpur lime, calamondin, and kumquat—will ripen properly, but tangerines and oranges are borderline; grapefruits definitely need more heat. Most tangerines, oranges, and grapefruits do not develop full sweetness unless the summers can provide consistent temperatures in the 70s and 80s.

While citrus types may differ in hardiness and need for summer heat, they otherwise have very similar needs. They will tolerate a pH of 5.5 to 8, but if soil is not acidic, all citrus is likely to develop iron or zinc deficiency. The surest cure is application of iron or zinc chelates (see page 81), but for a longer-term cure you can use acidifying fertilizers and/or amendments to reduce the soil pH.

All citrus need a soil with good drainage and regular but not-too-frequent irrigation. If too dry, citrus will drop leaves—a problem especially common in container-grown trees. Even if leaf drop is severe, however, trees can usually be returned to health by beginning to water more frequently. All citrus trees respond to ample fertilization, divided into several applications a year, and to a compost mulch applied once or twice a year.

As to pruning, most citrus do not require it to improve fruit bearing, though you may want to prune them for shape and to let in a bit more light and air. They can be pruned to trees, but are easiest to harvest if you leave the limbs near the ground on and let the plants become big shrubs. Most citrus can also be made into sheared hedges or informal espaliers and still bear some fruit. They may also need pruning to remove dead twigs. Full-sized citrus trees range from 12 to 30 feet high, while grafted dwarfs, at 4 to 10 feet, are available for most of the fruits. Most citrus is self-fertile.

If citrus is growing well, it may escape pests, but it can become infested with mites, scale, whiteflies, or thrips. You can reduce the chance of infestation by occasionally washing the foliage with a vigorous spray of water. When you do this, spray both sides of the leaves, but do it briefly. Never leave a sprinkler on, drenching the tree for a long time, or you will encourage various diseases of the trunk or roots. Scale, aphids, and whiteflies all produce honeydew, which attracts ants and supports growth of the fungus sooty mold. Treatment for the insect pests will also control these secondary problems.

A disease that is fostered by cool, wet conditions is botrytis. If the plant is blooming during a rainy spell, blossoms may fall prey to this decaying fungus. Lemons and limes bloom several times a year, so a rain at the wrong time may cause only a short break in production. However, oranges, which bloom in the spring, could lose a year's crop.

Snails sometimes climb into citrus trees, where they rasp the leaves and fruit. You can stop snails by placing copper bands around the trunk if there are no low-hanging branches that snails can use as bridges to bypass the trunk. Otherwise, pick them out of your trees periodically and control them in the garden at large.

Gophers will eat the bark of citrus roots and the trunk near the soil. Rats or squirrels will damage or eat fruit, and rats will sometimes strip bark higher on the tree.

surfaces you don't want stained. Or you can choose a white-fruited, nonstaining cultivar. Another possible drawback is that the plants have shallow, aggressive roots. Site away from underground water pipes or foundations.

To make a mulberry into a manageable shrub, start as you would for a deciduous fruit tree, by cutting the new plant back to stimulate low branching. Then you can keep it in bounds with pruning in winter and summer to shape it and control its size. Commercial growers in Oregon plant mulberries only 7 feet apart and grow them into shrubs that are small enough to reach for picking. Plants this size can also be netted to save the crop from birds if needs be.

Mulberry Varieties

Illinois Everbearing (Morus alba × M. rubra): Fruit is black when ripe, sweet, highly flavored, 1½ inches long, and ripens continuously in July through September.

Pakistan (Morus alba)*:* Maroon colored berries, 3½ inches or longer, are very sweet and flavorful. Particularly good for hot summers. Bears in early summer.

White Fruiting (Morus alba)*:* Large, very sweet, blackberry-shaped fruit with slight red blush. Early summer.

Nectarine (see Peach and Nectarine)

Olive

Olea europea
Olive Family ❖ *Oleaceae*

The gray-green-leaved, picturesquely formed olive tree is practically the symbol of a Mediterranean climate. Considering only chill needs (100 to 200 hours) and hardiness (typically to 15°F), it should succeed in our Mediterranean region, but it is most productive in locations that have hot, sunny summers. Production is irregular in this area's cooler, foggier microclimates.

Olive trees survive in poor, stony soil, but rich, deep soil improves their appearance. And though they tolerate drought when established, they need moderate irrigation to bear a good crop. The trees are wind pollinated. Planting more than one variety is likely to increase fruit set. Falling olives stain pavement, so be careful about placement.

Olive trees grow 25 to 30 feet high. They should be allowed to grow untouched for 4 to 5 years, then trained for attractive form (open vase form, either single or multiple trunk) and for ease of harvest. Later they are pruned to keep them in bounds and let in some light and air. Plants bloom in May; olives are harvested for table use in September and October before they begin to turn color. They need to be cured to be edible; this can be done at home using one of several available processes. For oil, fruit is typically taken to a press. (One tree won't make much oil.)

In recent years, a relatively new pest, the olive fruit fly, has rendered many commercial and home olives inedible by laying eggs that hatch into maggots in the fruit. To avoid this pest or reduce damage, remove any fruit clinging after harvest and clean up all fallen fruit. Remove the fruit from the garden or bury it four inches deep. Cultivate the soil under the tree to four inches deep to kill overwintering pupae and again in mid to late summer. A new biorational pesticide with a fruit fly bait, GF-120 NF Naturalyte Fruit Fly Bait, can be sprayed, once before bloom and several times as fruit enlarges, to attract and kill adult flies. Tests are ongoing to find a predator that will prey on the fruit fly, but until then we have to live with it.

Home garden olives that aren't harvested serve as a reservoir for the fruit fly, so commercial growers would prefer you clean up your tree even if you don't use the fruit. Some home gardeners, frustrated by the pest, are spraying their trees with a hormone to prevent fruit set. (Ornamental olive varieties, bred to be fruitless, sometimes set fruit anyway, and the hormone is sold to prevent this.)

Olive Varieties

Manzanillo: Early. Large fruit with medium oil content. Common commercial variety. Tree more spreading than most. Least cold hardy of these three varieties.

Mission: Medium fruit, high oil content. Common commercial variety. Tree taller than others listed.

Sevillano: Largest fruit. Low oil content. Best choice for curing. Common commercial variety.

Orange

Citrus sinensis
Citrus Family ❖ *Rutaceae*

Most orange varieties require high heat to ripen well and need, on average, higher temperatures than mandarins. The following varieties are the ones with the widest adaptability in our region, though even these are not likely to make good fruit in foggy gardens.

Orange Varieties

Trovita: Known to produce fruit with good flavor in this area. Relatively dependable in, for example, Oakland. Large tree when full-sized. Dwarf is available.

Washington Navel and Robertson Navel: Borderline, but worth a try in a favorable San Francisco microclimate in warmer, inland locations.

Passion Fruit

Passiflora spp.
Passion Flower Family ❖ *Passifloraceae*

Passion fruit is produced by large evergreen or semi-evergreen vines that are native to South America. The plants were given their name by Spanish missionaries who were impressed with their spectacular flowers and saw in them religious symbolism. Most are tender to frost, though there are cultivars that can survive dips into the 20s. They do better where not exposed to high heat, but do appreciate some warmth. They need full sun, protection from wind, strong support, and plenty of room.

Passion fruits have an inedible shell filled with seed-studded pulp. They are most often used to make preserves or juice—often blended with other juices to add that certain tropical something to the flavor. The type most commonly grown for edible fruit, purple passion fruit (*Passiflora edulis*), is self-fruitful, bee pollinated. (Orchard bees are more effective for all passion fruit pollination than honey bees.) Yellow passion fruits, which can be several species or hybrids, tend to be sour, but still add the characteristic tropical-tasting passion fruit flavor, just with more sugar necessary. One species, banana passion fruit (*Passiflora mollisima*), is common in San Francisco as an ornamental. It's rather rampant, galloping along fences and up over trees if allowed. The flowers are maraschino cherry red, the fruit long, yellow, and sour.

Plant a passion fruit vine in soil that is rich in organic matter and has very good drainage. Keep the soil constantly moist during active growth, or fruit production will suffer. Fertilize regularly with a fertilizer that provides less nitrogen than phosphorus. Starting in the third year, prune plants annually just after the harvest, to keep them in bounds and to stimulate fruiting. Cut out dead inner branches and weak growth, then cut vigorous growth back by one third or more.

Pests are less common here than in the plants' native habitats, but they can be laid low by nematodes or fusarium wilt. Snails can strip leaves and bark from plants, which can be lethal if a plant is still small. When you choose a location for a passion fruit, give thought to how you will reach it to harvest, to prune, and to hunt snails.

Peach and Nectarine

Prunus persica (Nectarine is *P. persica nucipersica*)
Rose Family ❖ *Rosaceae*

Peaches and nectarines, which are the same species of plant, have very similar needs and problems. Their chill requirement varies between 100 and 1,200 hours. While there are low- and moderate-chill varieties that can fruit in our region, both kinds of fruit require so much summer heat to ripen well that the fruit is likely to be a disappointment in all but inland locations with the hottest, sunniest summers. Even there, if spring is cold and wet, diseases will be encouraged, and because the trees bloom early, rain often damages the flowers.

Peaches and nectarines require deep soil with good drainage and will not grow well in heavy, poorly drained soil. They need regular water, especially as the fruit is developing, and moderate fertilization. They are available as full-sized trees reaching 25 feet, as semidwarfs to 14 feet, as grafted dwarfs to 5 feet, or as 6-foot genetic dwarfs. All but genetic dwarfs need careful pruning each year. They require more attention to pruning than other fruit-bearing trees, because they fruit on newly grown wood. If you don't prune them back and force them to grow new, shorter branches, they will bear out at the end of long ones. All need fruit-thinning if the fruit set is heavy. Most varieties are self-fruitful.

Peaches and nectarines are susceptible to the disease peach leaf curl. By curling the leaves and causing them to drop off, this disease drastically weakens the tree. This disease and another, brown rot, which damages both fruits and twigs, are more common in areas with cool, wet springs. Preventative treatment for peach leaf curl is to apply a micronized copper or lime sulfur or fixed copper spray once around November 15th (after leaves have fallen), and again around February 1, just as the beds swell but before flowers open. Some would suggest a third spray at about the end of the year. (Spring or summer treatments will have no effect.) To prevent brown rot, copper fungicide can also be sprayed as flowers open. However, if springs and summers are cool and damp, these diseases may not be stoppable.

Peaches are well adapted to only the most inland parts of our region, borderline in areas with moderately cool summers. Though I know the temptation is great to try to grow a luscious peach, gardeners in cool, often foggy microclimates should select other kinds of fruits to grow. In borderline areas, gardeners sometimes try pruning peaches or nectarines as espaliers, under an overhang and against a south- or west-facing wall, or growing dwarfs in large containers put on wheels, so they can be moved out of rain.

As in the case of apples, there are hundreds of peach and nectarine varieties, so the following list can include only a few possible good choices. While there are low-chill peach varieties, in parts of our region with the lowest chill, any peach or nectarine is likely to be laid low by disease. And though some varieties resist peach leaf curl, none of these bear well with low chill. Of the resistant varieties I have identified, 'Frost', 'Muir', and 'Indian Free' are listed below. Of others not listed here but available for sale, 'Q-1-8' is estimated to require 700 to 800 hours, and while I don't have exact hours for

'Avalon Pride', 'Charlotte', and 'Oregon Curl-Free', these were all developed in the Northwest, where sufficient chill is not a problem. The only nectarine variety that resists peach leaf curl, 'Kreibich', originated in Washington state, and information on its chill requirement is unavailable.

Peach Varieties

Babcock: 250 to 400 hours. Early to midseason. A favorite low-chill, white-fleshed freestone with a sweet, rich flavor. Not early blooming. Self-fruitful.

Frost: 700 hours. Midseason to late. Red-blushed yellow skin with yellow flesh. Freestone with excellent sweet flavor. Resistant to peach leaf curl, but needs protection from it for the first few years. Self-fruitful.

Indian Free: 700 hours. Late midseason. Red flesh. Must be fully ripe for good flavor. Some ability to resist peach leaf curl. Needs another peach or nectarine for pollination.

Midpride: 250 hours. Midseason. Yellow freestone that is excellent for mild winter areas. Exceptional, some say "orangy" flavor. Self-fruitful.

Muir: 600 to 700 hours. Late midseason. A yellow freestone with dense, sweet, rich flavor. Found on John Muir's property around 1880. Strongly resistant to peach leaf curl. Self-fruitful.

Strawberry Free: 400-500 hours. Early midseason. An old favorite in the Bay Area for sweet, juicy, white-fleshed fruit. Excellent for home orchards. Self-fruitful.

Suncrest: 700 hours. Late midseason. Firm, large, and fine-flavored yellow freestone. Immortalized in the book *Epitaph for a Peach* by David Mas Masumoto. Self-fruitful.

Nectarine Varieties

Arctic Fantasy: 400 hours. Late midseason. Large, red with white flesh, sweet with the slight acidity of a yellow-fleshed nectarine. Freestone. Self-fruitful. Considered to be an improved form of another good selection, Gold Mine, but with better flavor.

Arctic Star: 300 hours. Early. A low-acid, very sweet, semi-freestone nectarine. Red skin and white flesh. Self-fruitful.

Desert Dawn: 250 hours. Very early. Red skin, yellow flesh, rich flavored, semi-freestone. Needs much pruning and fruit thinning. Self-fruitful.

Fantasia: 500 hours. Early. Large, yellow-fleshed freestone. Early fruit firm-ripe and tangy, later fruit sweet and rich-flavored. Self-fruitful.

Kreibich: Midseason. A white-fleshed, semi-freestone nectarine with a sweet flavor. Resists peach leaf curl. Discovered in Washington state.

Liz's Late: 600 to 700 hours. Late. Unusual, spicy, intense, sprightly sweet flavor in a yellow freestone. Self-fruitful.

Panamint: 250 hours. Late midseason. An intensely flavored, yellow-fleshed freestone with a nice acid-sugar balance. Self-fruitful.

Snow Queen: 250 to 300 hours. Early. A sweet and juicy white-fleshed freestone. Self-fruitful.

Pear, European

Pyrus communis
Rose Family ❖ *Rosaceae*

Pears require, on average, less winter chill than do apples, about 600 hours. Thus most should succeed in parts of our coastal region with the greatest winter chill. A few are rated at 500 hours, and one, 'Comice', requires only 200 to 300 hours. Several sources recommend against growing pears in foggier parts of our region, yet I know there are productive Bartlett and Comice pear trees in the Richmond District of San Francisco, a couple of miles from the ocean. Even if they get enough chill, in areas with the coolest summers, nearest the coast in Sonoma or Mendocino counties, pears may need protected sites if they are to get enough warmth in summer to ripen well.

Pears are mainly available as full-sized trees, which can reach 30 feet high, although there are a few semidwarf or dwarf varieties. One variety, 'Seckel', is naturally somewhat smaller than most other pear varieties.

Pears can take wetter and heavier soil than most fruit trees, but they do not need more than monthly deep watering in the dry season. Give them moderate amounts of fertilizer. After initial training, pears need only minimal annual pruning. Because they have a tendency to upright growth, and horizontal or diagonal growth on a fruit tree is generally more fruitful, gardeners sometimes use weights or spreaders (sticks from trunk to branch) to force young pear limbs into a wider angle, but this must be done with great care to avoid injuring the tree. They generally need cross-pollination, and the pollen of some varieties is not compatible with that of others.

Pears require special thought concerning the harvest, since most need to be picked at full size but while still hard and green (as soon as the stem separates when you lift the fruit), then ripened off of the tree. Be sure you understand what is required for the variety you plan to purchase. Some, such as 'd'Anjou' and 'Comice', need a month or more of cold storage, best if in a refrigerator. Others, such as 'Winter Nelis' and 'Seckel', will ripen if stored in a cool place, such as a basement or garage. Colder temperatures, below 40°F or even down to 32°F, will prolong shelf life. Fruit can be brought out of storage as needed and allowed to soften a couple of days. Pears that would be gritty and bland without this practice are soft and sweet with it.

If you have a mature tree, you will not have enough room in your refrigerator to store the harvest. Some fruit growers have a second "fruit storage refrigerator," but more energy-efficient solutions are a host of friends lined up to receive the excess or a food bank that can provide the necessary storage in a corner of a walk-in cooler.

Though pears are said to be prone to many diseases, including fireblight and a scab specific to pears, I know of one in a foggy San Francisco neighborhood that, though completely neglected, seems pest-free. Some pear varieties are fireblight resistant.

Pear Varieties

Bartlett: 800 hours. Early midseason. Sweet and tender. Pick green and ripen off the tree. May require pollinator in cool coastal areas; any but 'Seckel' will do. Better with summer heat.

Comice: 200 to 300 hours. Late. Excellent flavor and texture. (Ripens best after cold storage at 30 to 36°F for 2 to 3 months.) Self-fruitful, or plant with 'Bartlett' to be safe. May bear more some years than others.

D'Anjou: 800 hours. Late. Rounded, yellow with brown russeting when ripe. Pick green and store in a refrigerator one month for soft, sweet fruit. Moderate resistance to fireblight. Self-fruitful.

Moonglow: 500 to 700 hours. Early midseason. Large fruit, good flavor, juicy, soft. The most fireblight-resistant of the available pears. Needs a pollinizer. Pollinizes other pears. Not specifically recommended for this region, but widely adaptable.

Seckel: 500 hours. More fruit with 800 hours. Early midseason. Small but good dessert pear. Resists fireblight. Self-fruitful.

Winter Nelis: 700 hours. Late. Small, fine flavor. Requires pollinator.

Pear, Asian

Pyrus pyrifolia
Rose Family ❖ *Rosaceae*

Asian pears are sometimes called apple-pears, as they are round and have a crisper flesh than many European or American pears. They are different from both pears and apples in texture and flavor. They also differ from pears in having a somewhat lower chill requirement, low enough for success just about anywhere in the region. Most require 450 hours of winter chill, though some need only 350 hours. However, like pears, they may not ripen well nearest the coast in the northern part of this region because of insufficient summer warmth.

Asian pears have the same soil, water, fertilizer, and pruning requirements as European pears. Some are self-fruitful, while others are pollinized by other Asian pear varieties or by European pears—check carefully for compatibility before you buy. Most reach 40 feet if unpruned, although you can prune them to control size. Thin fruit in May or June, so the remaining fruits can become larger. Unlike European pears, Asian pears ripen well on the tree. They have good resistance to fireblight.

Asian Pear Varieties

20th Century: 450 hours. Early August. Sweet, juicy, crisp. Self-fertile or pollinized by 'Shinseiki', 'Bartlett', others.

Hosui: 450 hours. Mid-August. One of the tastiest of Asian pears, crisp, sweet, and juicy. Pollinized by 'Shinko', '20th Century', or 'Bartlett'.

Shinseiki: 450 hours. Late July/Early August. Sweet, juicy, crisp. Self-fruitful.

Shinko: 500 hours. September. Very good flavor, crisp and juicy. Tree small and also available as grafted dwarf. Pollinized by 'Bartlett', others.

Tsu Li and Ya Li: 300 hours. September. Both are juicy, crisp; 'Ya Li' is sweeter. They pollinize each other. Not specifically recommended for this region, but will probably do well here.

Persimmon, Asian

Diospyros kaki
Ebony Family ❖ *Ebenaceae*

Asian persimmons are a good home fruit tree in much of this region. They are hardy to 0°F, require under 400 hours of winter chill, do not need a pollinizer, and, once their basic form has been set, need little pruning to bear well. Their handsome, large leaves turn yellow or orange before falling. The most likely limiting factor is lack of summer warmth near the coast. Of the two common varieties, 'Fuyu' is slightly better able to ripen in cool summers than 'Hachiya'.

I do have reports of two bearing 'Hachiya' trees in San Francisco, one in a warm part of the city, one in a moderately warm spot. All I know about their fruit quality is that the one in the warmer site had a successful first crop, but in the second year the fruit stayed unpleasantly astringent even when ripe.

For persimmons, a loamy soil is best, but good drainage is more important than soil type. When they are established, they need infrequent but regular deep irrigation. Fertilize them lightly. Trees reach 30 feet high, though they can be kept at 10 feet using summer pruning. They are usually self-fruitful and are almost pest-free.

Persimmon Varieties

Chocolate: 100 to 200 hours. Very sweet when fully ripe; astringent (bitter) until ripe. Seedless and orange-fleshed without a pollinizer, brown-fleshed and seeded with a pollinizer.

Fuyu: 100 to 200 hours. Flattened fruit is sweet even when firm. Takes less heat to ripen than 'Hachiya'. Self-fruitful.

Hachiya: 100 to 200 hours. Dome-shaped fruit is usually picked while firm and ripened off the tree. Fruit loses astringency as it ripens. Needs warm summer to ripen fruit, so may not succeed in foggiest areas. Self-fruitful.

Izu: A 'Fuyu' type that ripens about three weeks before 'Fuyu'. Because it is a relatively small tree, it's a good choice for a home garden.

Pineapple Guava

Feijoa sellowiana
Myrtle Family ❖ *Myrtaceae*

The pineapple guava is a shrub or small tree that produces fruit as well as edible flowers. The red-and-white petals can be removed with care without preventing fruit set; they are tasty in salads or on ice cream. The ¾- to 3½-inch green fruit will fall to the ground when ripe, but will also ripen off the plant if picked while still firm. It is typically cut in half and the pale yellow, pineapple-flavored interior is eaten with a spoon. High pectin content also makes this a good fruit to add to jams and jellies.

This is not a true guava; those are more sensitive to cold. Pineapple guava is a subtropical plant that can survive cold to 15°F. It can also take high temperatures, so it should do well anywhere in our region. Cool weather seems to improve the fruit's flavor.

Here is a plant that survives many situations, such as poor soil, little water, and low fertility. However, if you want good harvests, give it well-drained soil with a neutral to slightly acidic pH, an organic mulch, regular water, and light fertilization. Lack of water will cause fruit to fall without maturing.

While new varieties are often self-fertile, cross-pollination with another variety will result in a better crop.

Left to their own, pineapple guava plants grow slowly into multistemmed shrubs 18 to 25 feet high. However, they can take all sorts of pruning, including as a low hedge or an espalier. The heaviest shearing and shaping will reduce fruiting, but shaping after the harvest will increase yields.

Pineapple Guava Varieties

Nazemetz: Large fruit with a thin skin and sweet pulp. Self-fruitful, but produces better if cross-pollinated by another variety.

Trask: Medium-sized fruit of fairly good quality. Requires cross-pollination.

Plum (Japanese)

Prunus salicina

Plum (European)

Prunus domestica
Rose Family ❖ *Rosaceae*

Plum trees are good choices for most of the region, with adapted varieties usually bearing large crops of good-quality fruit. The ones that do best here are low-chill types, mostly Japanese plums. The chill requirement of Japanese plums generally ranges from 500 to 1,600 hours, but that of our low-chill types is as low as 250 hours. Most European plums require 700 to 1,800 hours, but still, some can get by with little enough chill to produce well in the right location.

Plums grow best in soil with ample organic matter and good drainage. They need moderate to high amounts of fertilizer and occasional deep watering in the dry season. Standard varieties grow to 20 feet, dwarf to 8 to 10 feet high. After initial training, European plums need some annual pruning; Japanese plums need, on the average, heavier pruning to keep vigorous shoots thinned out. Dwarf varieties can be espaliered. Some kinds of plums are self-fertile. When a pollinizer is needed, check compatibility carefully—Japanese and European plums do not pollinize each other, although Japanese varieties can serve as pollinizers for hybrids between American and Japanese plums. While plums can get various pests, they don't seem to be seriously plagued by any particular pest in our region. Many varieties will succeed here, so this is only a selection.

Japanese Plum Varieties

Beauty: 250 hours. Red over yellow skin with red-streaked, amber flesh. More productive in coastal climates than 'Santa Rosa'. Self-fruitful.

Elephant Heart: 500 hours. Mid to late season. Large, dark red freestone fruit with a rich flavor. Use 'Santa Rosa' as a pollinizer.

Howard's Miracle: 300 hours. Midseason. Yellow with red blush, flesh yellow with spicy flavor. Can be eaten while green, when it has an apple-like flavor. Use 'Santa Rosa' as a pollinizer.

Mariposa: 250 hours. Midseason. Nearly freestone, large, sweet, juicy. Use 'Santa Rosa', 'Nubiana' as pollinizers.

Nubiana: 400-500 hours. Midseason. Dark purple skin, amber flesh, sweet, firm. Self-fertile.

Santa Rosa: 300 hours. Early. Red-purple skin, flesh yellow and red, juicy, with a pleasant tangy flavor. Self-fruitful. Pollinizes 'Satsuma', 'Mariposa', and many other plums.

Satsuma: 300 hours. Early midseason. Maroon skin, red flesh, mild, sweet flavor. Use 'Santa Rosa' as a pollinizer.

Weeping Santa Rosa: 400 hours. Early. Fruit similar to 'Santa Rosa'. Weeping habit is useful in landscapes. Can be grown on trellis or espaliered. Height can be controlled at 8 feet. Self-fruitful.

European Plum Varieties

Green Gage: 500 hours. Midseason. Green-and-yellow fruit with amber flesh. Rich flavor, juicy. Self-fruitful.

Sugar Prune: 500 hours. Small fruit is reddish purple with very sweet, greenish yellow flesh. Self-fruitful.

Plum Interspecies Hybrids

Prunus hybrids
Rose Family ❖ *Rosaceae*

Breeders have experimented by cross-pollinating plums and other stone fruits in the plant genus *Prunus*, in hopes of creating new and interesting fruits. When a cross between a plum and an apricot is 50-50, the result is called a plumcot. If it is three-quarters plum, it's a pluot. A three-quarter apricot is an aprium. Cherries have been crossed with Japanese plums, and the resulting fruit is named a cherry-plum. (Note that these are not the same as the old cherry plum trees with small yellow fruit that come up wild in our region.)

Plum Interspecies Hybrid Varieties

Dapple Dandy Pluot: 400-500 hours. Skin ripens to a maroon and yellow dapple, white and red flesh, flavor of both plum and apricot. Marginal at the coast. Needs pollinizer. 'Santa Rosa' plum will work.

Delight Cherry-Plum: 400 hours. Blue-black fruit with yellow interior. Tangy-flavored clingstone. Very productive, even under adverse conditions. Interfruitful with 'Sprite' cherry-plum.

Flaverella Plumcot: 250 hours. Translucent golden fruit with a light red blush and slight pubescence. Excellent flavor, firm and juicy. Pollinize with a Japanese plum such as 'Santa Rosa' or another plumcot.

Sprite Cherry-Plum: 400 hours. Blue-black fruit with yellow interior. Sweet and freestone. Adapted to most climates. Interfruitful with 'Delight' cherry-plum.

Pomegranate

Punica granatum
Pomegranate Family ❖ *Punicaceae*

Pomegranates are small deciduous subtropical trees that can reach 15 to 20 feet, but can be kept at 10 feet high. They are hardy to 18 or 20°F and need only 100 to 200 chilling hours. Hot summers will produce the sweetest pomegranates. In slightly cooler microclimates fruit can form, but it isn't as sweet. In the coolest, near-coastal microclimates fruit may not set, or you might get only sparse fruit that doesn't ripen properly. Some varieties are said to ripen better than others in cool weather, but I'm not at all sure that applies to foggy and windswept coastal locations.

Soils too basic for most plants will support a pomegranate, but the plant will do better in neutral or slightly acidic loam. Good drainage with an occasional deep watering, light fertilization, and light pruning will keep the plant in good shape. It is relatively pest-free in this region.

Pomegranate is often grown as an ornamental, for its small shiny leaves and bright red summer flowers. If you are purchasing a plant for fruit, be sure you aren't getting one of the ornamental varieties that don't produce palatable fruit in any microclimate. Among these are miniature varieties, such as 'Nana'.

Pomegranate Varieties

Eversweet: 150 hours. Very sweet, almost seedless. Better adapted than some to cooler areas. Self-fruitful.

Kashmir: 150 to 200 hours. A good choice because it has a good blend of complex flavors. Self-fruitful.

Sweet: 100 hours. Sweeter than 'Wonderful' and better quality in cool-summer climate. Compact plant that is suitable for container or espalier. Self-fruitful.

Wonderful: 150 hours. Good quality, large fruit, with best quality in hot inland climates. Self-fruitful.

Quince

Cydonia oblonga
Rose Family ❖ *Rosaceae*

You probably know the ornamental "flowering quince," with its thorny branches and bright red, or pink, late winter flowers. Flowering quinces are plants of Asian origin, members of the genus *Chaenomeles*. Some of these plants do bear fruit, and can be eaten in preserves, but the quince more likely intended when cooks discuss the matter is a plant of the genus *Cydonia*. This is a shrub or small tree, to 25 feet high, with thornless branches and white to pink flowers. (It can be pruned to keep it smaller.) Like *Chaenomeles*, it is handsome enough to be an ornamental, but the fruit is more useful. It has traditionally been used in cooking, either alone or with apple or other fruit. (There are some who say that if a dish calls for cooked apples, it is usually better with quince.) Quince adds a distinctive flavor to jams and jellies and is used in Spanish cuisine to make a thick, sliceable paste. Some new varieties are sweet enough to eat fresh.

Quince is recommended even for the foggy areas of this region. It needs only 100 to 300 hours of chill and is hardy enough for inland areas. It is best grown in clayey soil with good drainage, but it is relatively tolerant of wet soil. It needs only light fertilization. Pruning back about one-half of new growth of long, weeping branches will strengthen the tree, and you need to thin out bushy growth as well. Quince is self-fertile. It can get fireblight, especially if overfertilized.

Quince Varieties

Aromatnaya: Sweet yellow flesh with a pineapple flavor. Fruit can be sliced thinly and eaten fresh. Pick and let soften indoors until soft. Disease resistant. Self-fruitful.

Havran: White-fleshed variety that is sweet enough for fresh eating. Self-fruitful.

Orange: Bright yellow fruits often exceed 1 pound. Good flavor, aromatic, good for cooking. Self-fruitful.

Pineapple: Soft flesh, not the best flavor, but a pineapple taste. Self-fruitful.

Smyrna: Light yellow flesh, well-flavored fruit. Self-fruitful.

Raspberry

Rubus ideaus and hybrids
Rose Family ❖ *Rosaceae*

The fruit of blackberries and black forms of raspberries look very much alike; however, most raspberries are red. But even if they were the same color, you could tell the difference by this: When you pick a raspberry, the core of the fruit remains on the stem, while the core of a blackberry comes off with the fruit. Raspberries have the same basic cultural needs as blackberries—that is, deep soil, moderate fertility with ample organic matter, and even moisture. They range in chill needs from 200 to 800 hours and do best where springs are cool and warm up slowly. They can be grown throughout our area, but are marginal where it is foggiest.

There are two kinds of raspberries. One kind, called summer bearing, has one crop in early summer. The other, called fall or everbearing, has a main crop in fall (or late summer) and a smaller one in early summer. Pruning is different for the two. For a large crop in both periods, plant some of each kind. The plants are most often grown on wire trellises. Expect to remove some suckers near your plants, or dig and transplant them to acquire new plants. Raspberries are self-fruitful.

Raspberry Varieties

Summer bearing:

Canby: Small to medium, bright red, moderately firm fruit, robust flavor.

Sumner: Medium, firm, sweet berries. The best variety for heavy, poorly drained soils.

Fall bearing:

Autumn Bliss: Large, medium to dark red berries. A pleasant, mild flavor. Two weeks earlier than 'Heritage', and with higher yields.

Caroline: Largest of the fall-bearing varieties. Variety highest in vitamins and antioxidants.

Heritage: Old variety with large, good-flavored fruit. Sturdy plants need little support.

Yellow Raspberry:

Anne: Large pale yellow fruits in late summer into fall. Good, sweet flavor.

Strawberry

Fragaria × ananassa
Rose Family ❖ *Rosaceae*

It turns out that most of what I once knew about growing strawberries is wrong for our subtropical area. I used to plant them in the middle of spring, mulch thickly with straw or pine needles, discard all fruit until the middle of summer during the first year, keep the plants for several years, and then get new plants by rooting runners. Wrong! This style of growing strawberries is more suited to colder climates.

I was right about some things. I chose a sunny spot, added plenty of organic matter, made sure that the bed was weed-free, and never let the soil get too dry. I added a nitrogen fertilizer in fall and pruned off dead leaves in spring. My bed of everbearing strawberries produced small fruit, lightly, from March into November. However, for the largest crop of luscious berries, we would do well to listen to the advice given by local Cooperative Extension agents.

The most common strawberry planting time in Central California is November. Short-day varieties may also be planted from late summer to November. Planted at these times, short-day plants

Day Length and Strawberries

There are two main kinds of strawberry varieties. "June bearing" or "short day" types have a short, early season. In California, these begin to bear long before June and can even produce in fall, winter, and early spring where winters are mildest, mostly in Southern California. "Day neutral" types produce continuously as long as the temperatures are not too high. (A third category, "Everbearers," is for all intents and purposes synonymous with "day neutral" in California.) Though the day-neutral varieties bear longer, the harvest from short-day types is likely to be larger and possibly higher quality.

will bear the following spring and day-neutral ones will bear the next summer and fall. Cold improves the ability of strawberry plants to bear a heavy crop of fruit, and the plants sold in the nurseries during November were raised in areas with chilly early autumns.

The best time to prepare soil for a strawberry bed is fall of the previous year. This gives you a year to get weeds under control. It also allows you to amend the soil early enough so that any harmful salts from animal manure, mushroom compost, or other materials can leach out before the salt-sensitive strawberry plants go in. If you are planting an ongoing garden, you can plan a rotation that puts strawberries in a bed one year after the last manuring.

Strawberries need good drainage. Sandy loam is best, but other soils are acceptable if they are well amended. If you have clay soil, add plenty of organic matter the year before and plant in a raised bed. Although the crop can grow in soil with a pH as low as 5, it will grow much better in pH 7 or even a bit higher. This probably comes as a surprise to most gardeners, who may have thought, as I did, that an acidifying mulch was just the ticket for this crop.

You may find strawberry plants sold in containers or bare-root. Container plants are easier to transplant, since you have only to set them at the same depth they were in the container. If you plant bare-root plants, be careful not to bury the base of the shoot, called the crown, or to expose the roots. Many nurseries supply a pamphlet showing the right way to plant. If there is no handout, ask the nurseryperson to show you how it is done. Spread the roots of bare-root plants in the planting hole so that they will grow out and down, rather than back toward the plants.

Whether you start with containers or bare roots, space the strawberry plants 10 inches apart. Don't set the plants in depressions or on individual mounds, but rather keep the soil level around them. If the plants are in depressions, soil often falls in and buries the crowns, encouraging decay. If the plants are on small mounds, they will dry out too easily. When you use a raised bed to improve drainage in heavy soil, make it wide enough so that the plants are at least 8 inches from the edges of an unframed bed, or 6 inches from the edges of a framed bed.

When you plant, apply a nitrogen fertilizer. Put some under each plant, making sure to keep it at least 1 inch from the roots. Either use a slow-release fertilizer that will last nine to twelve months or side-dress four to five times a year with a faster-acting nitrogen source.

Commercial growers have found that using a clear plastic mulch greatly improves the yield and quality of strawberry crops. They apply it to the November planting right away, since it can stimulate runners instead of fruit if it is applied later. The plastic warms the soil, helping the plants to grow in cool weather and allowing the fruit to ripen better. It also protects the fruit from decay. The catch is that weeds will grow under clear plastic. Commercial (nonorganic) growers fumigate the soil before they plant, killing every living thing. I don't recommend you do that, so it's probably a better idea to use black plastic, which blocks light to the weeds, than the clear. (That is, unless you live where summer is hot and you have solarized your soil earlier in the year. See page 149.) Cut very small planting holes in the black plastic, to keep weeds from popping up near the strawberry plants. Tuck the edges of the black plastic into the soil to prevent snails and slugs from living under it. If you don't intend to use black plastic, it is best to either not mulch or use only a thin cocoa bean hull or other dark-colored mulch.

You can also use floating row cover over plants in winter, but remove it when fruiting is about to begin. I almost said when flowering begins, but you should remove flowers that form in winter on day-neutral plants, so the cover can stay on until spring.

Drip irrigation is ideal for strawberries, especially if it is used under a clear plastic mulch. It keeps moisture off the berries so they are less likely to decay, and it reduces weeds in areas that are not near an emitter. Water enough so that the plants don't dry out, but don't keep the soil soggy. If you don't have a drip system, you can water carefully at soil level. If you are using a plastic mulch, water through holes in the plastic.

Most strawberries make at least a few runners—that is, arching stems that root to form new plants. You may have read about many styles of growing strawberries that include rooting these runners to make new plants. In our mild-winter area the hill system, in which all runners are removed, is your best bet. By removing the runners, you are encouraging the crown on the mother plant to develop, thereby increasing fruit production. Just go over the plants once a week and pick off any runners that form.

It is tempting to grow new plants from the ones that form on the runners, but their quality isn't likely to be as high as that of strawberry starts you buy from a nursery. The ones you buy will be virus-free, while the ones in gardens tend to pick up viruses. Also, purchased plants have been chilled the right amount before you buy them. I will describe the closest you can come to preparing your plantlets at home, but I really think it best that you just buy more plants. Start new plants in mid- to late summer, aiming for rooted plants in the middle of October. Don't let the parent plants make too many plantlets—cut off all but one or two. To root a plantlet, sink a small pot into the soil between strawberry plants and weight a runner so that a plantlet is resting on the soil in the pot. Sometimes a runner keeps growing to make another plantlet even further from the parent plant. If this happens, cut the extension off to keep energy directed toward rooting the first plantlet. When that plantlet has roots, sever the runner from the mother plant and lift the pot.

In the middle of October, remove the plants from the pots and gently shake off the soil. Store the bare-root plants in plastic bags at 34°F for two weeks. That sounds easy, but it isn't, since your refrigerator is probably between 38° and 42°F, and your freezer is well below freezing. Perhaps you can tolerate your refrigerator a bit colder for a couple of weeks, or you may have access to a second refrigerator. Put a small thermometer in the refrigerator you will use and experiment with the temperature dial until it registers 34°F. You don't ever want it to dip below 32°F, since neither the strawberry plants nor your other stored produce should freeze. Plant the strawberries in early November.

Don't prune November-planted strawberries at all the first year. If you keep them over for another winter, remove all the old or dead leaves in the middle of the second February. Commercial growers usually keep their plantings only one year, since production and fruit size tend to decline the second year. However, you can keep your plants for several years if you are satisfied with your production. Day-neutral varieties may decline in one or two years, while short-day plants may bear well for three or four years. If you have let runners root until the bed has become overgrown, thin the planting. Either pull out plants and discard them, leaving healthy plants no less than 10 inches apart, or dig up and move healthy plants to another bed.

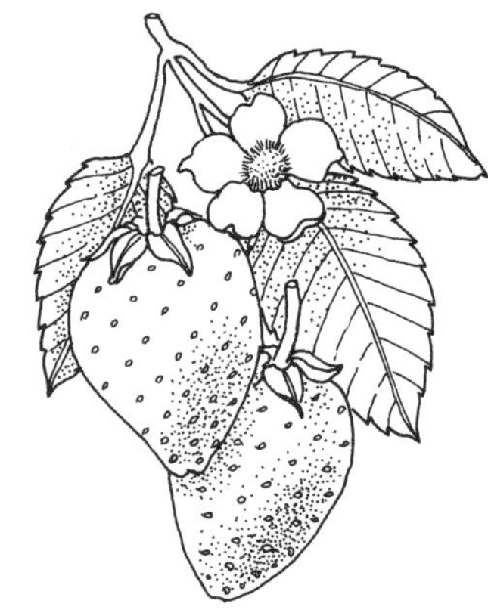

Begin to harvest as soon as the first fruit ripens. Unless you are going to pop the berries into your mouth right away (not a bad idea), pick them so that the green caps and a little bit of stem stay attached. Then refrigerate them unwashed until you are ready to serve them. Only then should you remove the caps and wash the berries.

A number of pests enjoy strawberries as much as we do. Birds, earwigs, slugs, snails, and sow bugs may nibble ripe fruit. If birds are a problem, cover the planting with a net. Control the other pests as best you can and discourage them by lifting ripening fruit onto dry mulch or pieces of wood. (One gardener protected her small planting from slugs by using clean old socks to cover the nearly ripe berries.)

Strawberry plants are also susceptible to aphids and spider mites, especially when they are under stress, such as weed competition or inconsistent watering. Try to avoid aphids, which spread incurable and often fatal viruses to strawberry plants.

The crop is also susceptible to verticillium wilt, an incurable fungus disease. Infected plants wilt during warm weather, and their outer leaves turn brown starting at the tips and moving down between the veins. The plants may make a partial recovery during cool weather, but they seldom recover completely. Remove any plants that are infected by viruses or verticillium wilt.

Strawberry plants are vulnerable to powdery mildew. They may also get fungal leaf spots, which appear early in the season and can be recognized by spots with gray or white centers and purple edges.

Strawberry Varieties

There are many strawberry cultivars, most of them not adapted to climates throughout the nation, so you want to be sure to choose ones that will grow well here in central California. Bare-root or container plants you find at local nurseries are highly likely to be varieties that will produce well where you garden. Mail order sources also carry varieties adapted to central California, but probably also carry ones that are not, and the catalog probably won't specify which are which. I change variety lists with each edition of this book, and breeding for better flavor, productivity, and/or disease resistance means my lists change dramatically as time goes by. If this edition is more than a few years old (check the copyright page), check with your county Master Gardeners for a current list.

Short-day varieties:

Aromas: Late for a short-day variety. Large fruit with good flavor. More upright plant helps with harvest and avoiding disease.

Camarosa: Early. Huge berries, conical shape. Well-adapted to California, especially to Southern California.

Chandler: Semi-early. Medium large, juicy, flattened berries with good flavor. Good in Santa Barbara and south, or as an annual elsewhere. Shuts down in summer heat.

Sequoia: Earliest. Developed for coastal climate. Widely adapted. Excellent flavor, resistance, and productivity.

Day-neutral varieties:

Albion: Good red color outside and in, excellent flavor. Good "weather tolerance."

Seascape: Large fruit is very sweet, good fresh or in preserves. Good at the coast and widely adaptable; OK in hot, dry climate. Resists viruses and fungal diseases.

Tri-star: Large fruits with excellent flavor, widely adapted, but plant is smaller in warmer weather.

Strawberry, Alpine

Fragaria vesca 'Alpine'
Rose Family ❖ *Rosaceae*

These wild European strawberries bear very flavorful small, pointy fruit. They tolerate more shade than ordinary garden strawberries and won't mind the fog as much. Give them partial shade in the sunnier parts of the region and as much sun as possible in the foggier areas. They bear from spring to fall.

Alpine strawberries are most commonly grown from seeds, which are sold by a number of the vegetable seed sources listed in this book. They are also sold as starter plants by fruit nurseries. Seeds take two to three weeks to germinate at 60° to 75°F. Sow the seeds indoors from February to April, and set the plants out whenever they are sturdy enough to transplant and the soil is sufficiently warm. Space them 8 to 12 inches apart. Alpines are less invasive than other strawberries, since they form few or no runners, but they will self-sow. Try them as a border or at the edge of an ornamental planting.

You may be able to pick some fruit from alpines the first fall, and you will definitely get a full crop the following spring. They produce fruit for several years, as long as they don't succumb to virus diseases. Save seedlings, or use divisions of healthy overgrown plants, to replace old plants.

Watch your alpine planting for aphid infestations and for the virus infection that aphids can spread. Control aphids, and remove any stunted or malformed plants.

Alpine Strawberry Varieties

There are a number of similar red-ripening varieties of alpines, some of which promise larger fruit. For an unusual treat, try an alpine variety that ripens to white—really pale yellow. The berries are very tasty, and their color may fool birds.

Strawberry Pots

I have never seen a healthy, productive planting of strawberries in strawberry pots—those large pots with holes in the sides. I suspect that the plants need more root space (they need at least 4 inches in all directions) and that the plantings I have seen were not being given adequate water or fertilizer. If you decide to plant in one of these containers, get the largest you can afford, provide the best growing conditions, and don't try to keep them there for more than one season.

Tangerine (see Mandarin Orange)

Wintergreen (Teaberry)

Gaultheria procumbens
Heath Family ❖ *Ericaceae*

If you like the flavor of wintergreen, you might like to try this pretty little plant. Both the leaves and the red berries of this eastern U.S. native have the familiar wintergreen flavor. You can make tea from the leaves and eat the berries. This plant used to be the main source for oil of wintergreen, but now most of this flavoring is extracted from, of all things, a birch tree! (It's the cherry birch, *Betula lenta*, another eastern U.S. native.)

Wintergreen is a creeping groundcover, to 6 inches high. It will thrive in soil prepared as for rhododendrons, with moderate summer water. Give it partial shade in sunnier microclimates. 'Red Baron' has larger fruits than the species.

I offer wintergreen in preference to the California native *Gaultheria shallon*, known as salal. Salal does have edible, black berries, but they haven't much flavor.

SIXTEEN

A Garden-Based Cuisine

WHEN I GROW MY OWN FOOD, I become involved in an ongoing conversation between my garden and my kitchen. I plant what I think I will want to eat; I then try to eat everything I have grown. I find that the second goal is its own challenge. It involves timely harvesting and then coping with crops offered in the seasons and quantities a garden can offer. It also offers the challenge of learning to prepare, deliciously, the food I grow; to combine foods I hadn't thought of combining before, and to use unique opportunities the garden provides.

I've learned ways to prepare all the crops I have grown. Since I have gardened in mostly foggy places, this has meant learning about using the many cool-preferring crops that I can grow year-round. In other words, as tomatoes can never be my main crop, I have had to consider: What else is there? What are some good ways to prepare such ingredients as Florence fennel, collards, or Swiss chard? These are questions that are useful area-wide, not only for coastal California gardeners but for inland gardeners, too. Inland, the winters can be mild enough that these cool-preferring crops can be grown fall to spring.

My explorations in making the most of the foods I grow have led to a larger one: determining what a local garden cuisine can be. All cuisines began in gardens, fields, orchards, and pastures. They developed over centuries with the foods people knew, could grow, and could preserve. What cuisine choices, if any, does a garden in this region suggest?

Because the climate is mediterranean, with dry summers and mild, wet winters, our interest is directed toward diets that originated around the Mediterranean Sea. But what does this mean in terms of our cuisine? One discovery I've made is that it means eating considerably more vegetables, many of which originated in that Mediterranean region, thriving through their similar winters. Artichoke, cabbage, chard, collards, fennel, lettuce, onion, peas, cilantro, parsley, and chervil are among the crops that descended from wild Mediterranean plants.

I have also learned that there is a band of earth at latitudes similar to that of the Mediterranean extending across into Asia, where vegetables grown from seed are similarly favored in gardens and cuisines. These Asian climates are not mediterranean, in that they have widely varying rain patterns, but they share a cool to mild temperate winter and a reasonably long growing season, so, with appropriate irrigation, they can produce many of the same crops. There has been much exchange of crops across this band of earth since ancient times, with origins sometimes obscured by early trade.

Because we can grow many temperate Asian crops, we should also look to these Asian regions for cuisine inspiration. Interestingly, a recent study of the cuisine of Americans (which didn't separate out those with Mediterranean roots) found that Asian Americans eat far more fresh vegetables than do many other Americans, having retained that part of their culture.

These days, I'm not alone in such explorations. Many people are exploring what it means to be a "locavore," to eat mostly food grown nearby. A garden is about as nearby as it gets, but our region is so rich in produce all year long, if you add what else can be had locally, the list is truly amazing.

Stuffed Zucchini

One year a group of gardeners from my San Francisco community garden made a harvest feast. It featured big plates of sliced tomatoes vinaigrette, garlic bread, and stuffed zucchini. Delicious! (But don't ever let your zucchini get this big unless you are planning to stuff them.) Serves four.

1 zucchini, 14 to 16 inches long
1 egg
1 cup lowfat or nonfat cottage cheese
½ cup diced mild cheese
½ teaspoon crushed dried rosemary (or ¾ teaspoon chopped fresh rosemary leaves)
1 tablespoon chopped fresh parsley
½ cup chopped chard leaves (or other greens)
¾ cup cooked rice (brown or white), or substitute ¼ cup cooked soy grits for ¼ cup of the rice
Grated Parmesan cheese

Sauce

½ cup finely diced onion
1 clove garlic, minced
1 tablespoon olive oil or other oil
One 15-ounce can tomato sauce (or 2 cups Quick Homemade Tomato Sauce, page 365)
2 tablespoons minced fresh basil (or 1 teaspoon dried basil)
⅛ teaspoon crushed red chili pepper

Halve the zucchini lengthwise, being sure any curve goes to the side, so the halves will lay flat. Scoop out the center rather deeply, leaving about a ⅝-inch to ½-inch shell. Steam or parboil the zucchini shells for 5 to 10 minutes. Do not overcook; they should be slightly cooked but *not* fork tender. (If you have no pot large enough, cut the halves into 4-inch pieces.)

Chop the removed zucchini centers into bite-sized pieces. Mix these with the egg, cottage cheese, cheese, rosemary, parsley, and chard. Mix in the rice in increments, stopping when you have enough filling. (Put any extra rice in the sauce instead.) If you have added all of the rice and it looks like too little filling, add more cottage cheese.

Stuff the zucchini shells, mounding the filling high and smoothing and forming it with your hands or a spoon. Arrange the stuffed shells on a baking sheet. Top with a sprinkling of Parmesan cheese. Bake in a 350°F oven until tender and the cheese is browned—about 30 minutes.

To prepare the sauce, sauté the onion and garlic in oil over medium-low heat until cooked but not browned. Stir in the tomato sauce and add the basil and red pepper. Simmer for 20 minutes.

To serve, cut the stuffed zucchini into 4-inch sections, put them on plates, and pour some sauce over each.

We are in a geographic location that inspires people in the rest of the nation to roll their eyes and say: "Oh well, that's fine for *you* to be a locavore. You're in California." And yet, in the midst of this plenty, many of us still eat comparatively few fresh vegetables and fruits, and we also eat many foods trucked or flown in from far away.

FARM COOKING

My interest in gardening, nutrition, and cuisines began when I was growing up. As a child, I lived in a household that sent mixed messages about food and cuisine. My father's parents were farmers, as were many of our ancestors. The first of his ancestors to arrive in America were Quakers who came to Pennsylvania in 1684. Others came from Ireland or Germany. Most, if not all of them, were links in unbroken lines of farming families that went back many more centuries.

A farmer might be able to produce a very good diet. Especially before modern transportation allowed fresh foods to be supplied from afar to the cities, prosperous farmers often enjoyed a diet fresher than that of many city dwellers. However, it is also true that because farm families depended on the land, even successful farmers could always see the lurking shadow of a failed crop or a bad year. And food might run short seasonally. In cold winter regions, late winter and early spring often represented a "hunger gap," a period when stores might run short before warm weather brought new food sources.

My grandparents, Frank Peirce and Pearl Fullheart Peirce, farming and raising six children in Indiana from roughly 1890 to 1940, had a basically Northern European cuisine that had adapted itself to the crops of the New World and lost some of the crops, especially herbs, of the Old. In talks with my father, I have reconstructed what they grew and ate.

My grandparents were farming at a time when new technology was beginning to improve the diets of many Americans. By the first years of the twentieth century, refrigerated railroad cars were transporting fresh meats and produce. Commercial canning allowed many to buy ready-to-eat food and store it even without the aid of an icebox. By the 1920s, mechanical refrigerators were becoming common in middle-class homes. These advances in transportation and preservation permitted a relatively varied and dependable year-round food supply.

But my grandparents' subsistence living in the first decades of the last century had much in common with an earlier time in American history. For the most part, the family ate only what they could grow. The stores they could reach in their horse and buggy had little or no meat or produce for sale, let alone ready-to-eat or commercially prepared food. And few in the area would have bought such foods in any case. As my father told me, "farmers had no money, only a living."

Still, they had a wholesome and varied diet including beef and pork in winter, and sausage or cured pork into the spring and summer; fresh produce, starting with the earliest wild spring greens, then summer's garden vegetables; wild walnuts and hickory nuts; fruit, including wild and domestic berries, apples, pears, peaches, plums, and grapes. There were enough potatoes to last almost all year, wheat to have milled into flour, hard corn for cornmeal, popcorn, sorghum cane grown for a little molasses, and dried beans, harvested by the whole plant, to be shelled out of the pods by the whole family on winter evenings.

The food eaten had to be balanced against some cash crops. For example, many of the eggs had to go to the grocery, "to be applied to the bill, past, present, or future." Butter, and later, cream, were sold to a creamery, and eventually milk went to a cheese factory.

And the diet also had to be planned to cope with natural seasonal shortages. Meat was butchered when weather was cold enough to keep it. Then beef would be traded with neighbors, by the quarter, so that no one had more than they could deal with at once. Pork sausage was preserved under lard in stoneware crocks, and other pork sugar-cured. When the pork ran out, there would be little meat until the next fall butchering, except a few chickens (young roosters or old hens), young rabbits turned up during the haying, and a bit of other wild game, turtle, or fish caught nearby.

Quick Homemade Tomato Sauce

There are fancier ways to make tomato sauce, but if you have an abundance of tomatoes and are in a hurry, this will do the trick. If you would rather not have seeds in your sauce, scoop them out before you put the fruit in the blender.

Wash ripe tomatoes and cut out the stem end and any blemished parts. Cut large tomatoes into several pieces, and halve the smaller ones. Purée the tomatoes in a blender, about 2 cups at a time. Pour the puréed tomatoes into a stainless steel or glass saucepan, bring to a boil, and simmer at least 15 minutes. Cool, then use in recipes or freeze in plastic freezer containers. The sauce will be rather thin for most uses, so if you have time, simmer it longer, until some of the water has evaporated, leaving a thicker sauce. If you don't have time, freeze it as is and cook it down longer, if necessary, when you pull it from the freezer. Season as you desire.

Southwest Chili Vegetable Soup

This soup is quick to make and very satisfying—great for lunch after a morning in the garden. You can vary the vegetables with the season, substituting other summer squash, chayote, leek, green beans, bok choy, sunchokes—whatever is available, but always include either leek or onion. Add the vegetables to the broth in order of the amount of cooking time they require. I like to make this with my own Homemade Chicken Stock (page 373). Serves two to three.

- 4 cups chicken or vegetable stock (or broth made with instant powdered mix; if you don't have that either, just plain water will do)
- ¼ medium head cabbage, thinly sliced
- 1 large unpeeled boiling potato, cut into ¾-inch dice
- 1 small onion, cut into 1-inch chunks
- One 5- to 6-inch zucchini, cut into ¼-inch slices
- One 8-ounce can tomato sauce (or 1 cup Quick Homemade Tomato Sauce, page 365)
- 2 tablespoons prepared chili powder

Bring the stock or water to a boil. Turn the heat down to maintain a simmer and add the cabbage, potato, and onion to the soup. When the simmering vegetables are almost tender, add the zucchini and cook 5 minutes longer. Add the tomato sauce and chili powder. Stir well and cook a few more minutes to heat through.

Fresh vegetables and fruits were mostly unavailable when not in season. A few could be stored or preserved. Potatoes, pumpkins, and root crops kept over winter in a root cellar, and sweet corn was scraped off the cob and dried. Apples could be stored for a while, or would keep longer if sliced and dried, and drying made prunes and raisins of some of the plums and grapes. Jellies and jams could be preserved under paraffin in stoneware crocks. Even with the best planning, however, winter could bring periods of mostly bread, gravy, and potatoes.

Cooking was without the benefit of most herbal flavorings. Flavoring agents included home-produced salt pork, onion, molasses, and cider vinegar, as well as purchased sugar, salt, and pepper. Prepared dishes were mainly soups, stews, or fried foods. Bread was sourdough at first, as yeast was not readily available. There were rolls, biscuits, corn bread, fruit pies, and, occasionally, doughnuts.

By the time of World War I, the family had enough cash to buy canning jars. At first, they could can only tomatoes, fruits, and fruit juices, but later, as they learned cold pack and pressure cooker methods, they could safely can less-acidic vegetables and have canned meat in any season.

Examples of recipes from the cuisine of Midwestern farmers such as my grandparents are Wilted Lettuce (page 233), Fried Green Tomatoes (page 275), and Fried Squash Blossoms (page 370)—although the tomatoes and squash blossoms would have been fried in lard rather than olive oil.

BRINGING FARM CUISINE TO THE CITY

When I was a child, we had a large garden, created by my father. Though we lived in a city, he still had the habit of producing and collecting fresh, whole foods in season. The garden grew a profusion of fresh vegetables every summer. I loved helping my Dad prepare the garden. I also liked to eat the vegetables raw, standing in the garden, imagining I was foraging in a bounteous wild. Besides the garden, we had four apple trees, several kinds of berries, and grape vines. Food, as my father understood it, was made up mainly of unprocessed plant and animal products, cooked at home. We ate a salad at every dinner, served first to be sure we ate it all. In winter, when the garden was under snow and lettuce was pricey, our salads were mainly cabbage, but they still came first. Bread, as Dad understood it, was not soft and squishy. We discovered a bakery owned by Latvian Americans where one could buy a rye bread of great and satisfying solidity, and also salt-rising bread, which was white, but solid and almost cheesy in flavor from the particular starter used in the baking.

In spring, we went to a place along the railroad tracks where Dad had discovered wild strawberries, and we picked them for shortcakes and jam. In the fall, after the first frost, we drove to an American persimmon tree growing in a wild place and picked up the fruit that frost had turned sweet, to use in persimmon pudding. Dad fished, often bringing home sunfish or catfish. My brother and I put our foot down, though, when he brought home a turtle, so I can't tell you the flavor of the turtle soup he made.

The diet of my father's family had depended on home cooking and preserving, and he saw no reason we shouldn't continue to preserve whatever excess we could grow. I loved the homegrown fresh fruits and vegetables, but was less charmed by my father's insistence that we preserve food for winter. Among our stored foods were applesauce, jellies and jams, tomatoes, and green beans. My mom, who was not employed outside the home, did most of the canning, and of course I was called upon to help prepare the produce. Mom hated this work; I put up with it. We would sit on the back steps peeling and coring apples for what seemed like hours. (The upside was time for long mother-daughter talks.) At the end of the session, Mom would boil a vast amount of apple chunks for sauce and use a few to make an apple pie. When I grew up, I decided to make an apple pie. After I prepared enough apples to make it, I realized that, unconsciously, I had expected the job to take hours, conditioned as I was by those early apple-peeling marathons.

By winter, we had rows and rows of jars on shelves in the basement. My least favorite of the preserves was home-canned green beans. When I scanned the jars of olive-drab pods, far from feeling satisfaction in our wisdom in putting food by, I felt approaching doom as I pictured one-fourth of a jar on my dinner plate.

A BATTLE OF CUISINES

My childhood aversion to the idea of preserving our own food stemmed from my mother's influence. Unlike my father and his parents, my mother grew up in a city, far from the sources of her food. When she was young, her family employed a cook who didn't want children in the kitchen. The family was from urban New England, the cuisine strongly English in nature. Seasonings other than salt or sugar were restrained and vegetables were most often served boiled and in cream sauce. Plum pudding—a steamed sweet bread made with beef fat and topped with a confectioners' sugar and butter "hard sauce"—was the favorite holiday dessert. Then, in her teenage years, Mom found herself in an orphanage eating their institutional food (another story,

Trying Something New

Are you looking through this book and noticing a number of foods you've never tried before? Wondering if you'd like them? I've included many less common vegetables in this book, including quite a few that can be grown in foggier microclimates. Here are some tips for seeing if you can fit a garden-produced ingredient into your menus.

Whenever possible, start by buying some of a new food first or by asking a friend who is growing it to let you taste some that they have grown. If neither is possible, just plant a little of it and see what you get.

If a new crop requires preparation, start collecting recipes for it as soon as you start considering whether you would like it. Ask other gardeners, and check for recipes in this book, cookbooks, specialty seed catalogs, magazines and newspapers, and on the Internet. Look for recipes with flavorings and secondary ingredients you know you will like. To widen the possibilities for finding ways to use new crops, think of which unfamiliar vegetable your new one resembles, and try substituting it in recipes. For example, try chayote in recipes for summer squash, garlic chives for ordinary chives, or Bolivian sunroot for jicama. The recipe for Mexican Vegetables (page 376) works just as well if purslane is substituted for the Swiss chard.

Chocolate Beet Cake (or Carrot or Zucchini Cake)

I learned the recipe for this moist, rich-tasting cake from Elaine Affronti, who brought it to a potluck in one of my City College vegetable gardening classes. It is a favorite of her grandchildren Roan and Fiona.

- 1 cup unbleached flour
- 1 cup granulated sugar
- 2 tablespoons plus 2 teaspoons unsweetened cocoa powder
- ½ teaspoon salt
- ½ teaspoon baking powder
- ½ teaspoon baking soda
- 2 large eggs, at room temperature
- ¾ cup vegetable oil
- ½ teaspoon vanilla (optional)
- 1 cups coarsely shredded beets (about two 3-inch beets) or carrots (about 3 or 4) or zucchini (about 3 or 4).

Preheat oven to 350°F. Grease and flour a 9-inch cake pan. (The ones with a metal scraper built in to help remove the cake are very nice.) Use a coarse cheese grater to shred the beets or other vegetable. If you are using zucchini, put the shredded squash in a colander and gently press out excess moisture. Use a paper towel on top to absorb some of the moisture.

In a medium bowl, combine the flour, sugar, cocoa powder, salt, baking powder, and baking soda. In a larger bowl, using an electric mixer or by hand, beat together the eggs, oil, and vanilla until well blended.

Add the flour mixture to the liquid, about a cup at a time, and beat after each addition until just combined. Add the shredded beets and mix well.

Pour the batter into the prepared cake pan. This will be stiffer than most cake batters, so you need to gently push it to the sides of the pan and smooth out the top.

Bake for 50 to 60 minutes, until a cake tester comes out clean. Cool on a rack for 10 minutes, then remove the cake from the pan and let it cool completely. This cake is delicious without any icing, but could be iced for a special occasion.

Note: For a larger, more elegant cake, double the recipe and use a tube pan or springform pan at least 2 inches deep. (Baking time is the same.)

to be told elsewhere). She didn't learn much about cooking, didn't like to cook, and embraced with open arms all the "convenience foods" that were being introduced in the mid-twentieth century.

This was a time when the supermarkets of America were offering an ever-increasing selection of easy-to-prepare options. This included frozen pot pies, soup mixes, and macaroni and cheese in a box. Processed cheese melted nicely and was never stringy. Cake came out of one box, frosting out of another, and "whipped cream" out of a spray can nozzle. Jell-O was the wonder ingredient that could make salad or dessert, and instant pudding and pie filling could be added to the cake from the box to improve its texture. It became difficult to talk about food without using brand names. Mom loved it all.

My Mom was not alone in embracing the new convenience foods. Many Americans did so. In fact, it was often the choice of people who formerly ate a farm-based diet like my dad's. To them, and often to recent immigrants, it represented modernity and escape from the hard labor of growing all that one ate, from periodic dietary boredom, and from the fear of want. It was thought of as the American way of eating, pulling many away from traditional food cultures.

In the 1970s, my dad's sister, Aunt Helen—who, mind you, grew up on the same farm as my Dad—wrote me a letter asking if I would like to submit a recipe for the volunteer fire department cookbook of Losantville, Indiana, the town near where my grandparents had farmed. I sent her a variation on a Mexican dish that contained eggs, a bit of oil, onion, Anaheim or bell peppers, and Monterey Jack cheese. Without consulting me, she decided that the ingredients were too weird (she had never heard of Anaheim peppers or Monterey Jack cheese) and entered, over my name in the book, a recipe I had never seen. It is "Casserole Bread," containing "1 package hot roll mix, ½ cup warm water, 2 eggs, separated, ¾ cup cream style cottage cheese, 1 envelope dry onion soup mix, and onion salt." Besides introducing a certain doubt in my mind about the authenticity of the other recipes attributed to my relatives and the townswomen of Losantville, this event illustrated to me their preference for prepared foods, as well as their reluctance to investigate unfamiliar ingredients.

In my childhood years, I felt the pull of commercial, prepared foods, which my mother embraced, and the pull of whole foods, led by my father. What I didn't eat as a child was "fast food." At the time, fast-food restaurants in their current guise were just getting under way. The techniques of appealing to children with high-profit foods that are high in fat, salt, and calories were still being developed. In any case, had they been fully developed, I would not have been allowed to eat such food. We rarely ate out, and when we did it would be a cafeteria-style place that included salad and vegetables.

In the end, when I left home, whole foods had mostly won in the cuisine battle, which is not to say I ate a perfect whole-foods diet. I still ate salads and never developed a soda habit, but I didn't eat all that many whole grains, and I ate rather a lot of sugar. I also had a strong interest in nutrition and continued to learn more about it. In retrospect, I appreciate the fact that my father modeled and taught a curiosity about all kinds of new foods. This has meant that the more I learn, the more I can try, and the more I find that is nutritious and tasty.

WHOLE FOODS MOVEMENT

By the 1960s, convenience foods, engineered foods, fast foods, and junk foods were winning in most American households. Children were being raised on fast food and junk food, seeing in this fare as much of a cuisine as one based on what a farm could provide. Then there arose, out of the developing mainstream culture and convenience food cuisine, a movement to return to whole and minimally processed foods. Maybe some of the advocates had grown up with more traditional diets or with mixed signals, as I had. Or maybe they were heeding the words of some nutritionists who warned that we were swimming in dangerous waters. Maybe the movement was a rejection of other aspects of the mainstream culture as well.

There were four major aspects to this trend. One was an interest in returning to farm or even peasant food. For example, the simple, hearty breads of this period might contain soy flour or soy grits, harking back to breads fed to medieval European

Garden Planning Tips

Learning to eat from a garden requires thought and practice. Here are some tips that will help you.

- At first, grow mostly crops that you would buy and eat even if you weren't gardening.
- Be aware of the yield and duration of harvest of the crops you want to grow.
- Be realistic: Don't plant more of a crop than you would normally eat.
- Look at your garden with recipes in mind. Are there recipes that use two or more crops you plan to grow? Maybe these crops can be planted so that they can be harvested together.
- Stay on the lookout for recipes that use your most successful crops.
- Check your garden, just as you check your refrigerator, before you go grocery shopping. Leave a note on the fridge, if others will be shopping, to let them know what *not* to buy.
- If you go on vacation, leave instructions not only for watering, but also for harvesting. That way you won't return to find that some crops, such as summer squash and beans, have matured fruit and so stopped producing in your absence.

Fried Squash Blossoms

There are many recipes for stuffed squash blossoms, and I'm sure they're very good, but I am always too impatient to get these tender morsels fried and onto the plate to take time to stuff them.

3 to 8 squash blossoms per serving (leave small squashes on any female blossoms)
Whole wheat flour
Oil for frying
Freshly ground pepper to taste
Salt or soy sauce

Check the blossoms over for insects. Sort out the male and female blossoms. If the young squash behind the female blossoms is over ½ inch in diameter, halve the squash and blossom lengthwise. Dip the blossoms in water, then in whole wheat flour. Fry in a thin layer of oil until they are light brown and a bit crispy. Pepper to taste. Add a light shake of salt or serve with soy sauce.

peasants, especially in times of famine, which often contained "peas and vetches."

A second source of culinary inspiration was the austere diets of spiritual practitioners, such as the Zen macrobiotic diet. This diet, which encouraged eating whole grains and seasonal vegetables, consists of ten progressively restrictive stages. The final stage, which is not nutritionally sound, consists of 100 percent whole grains, with brown rice considered the most perfect food and therefore the whole grain of choice. Many followers prepared simple, seasonal meals based on the principles of this diet, though (fortunately for their survival) few attained the brown-rice-only level.

A third trend was an interest in eating organically produced food. Organic farming and gardening originated around the time of World War II, when synthetic fertilizers were becoming popular and synthetic pesticides were being introduced. It was a reaction by those who felt it was unwise or dangerous to use such chemicals. The 1960s and 1970s saw a burst of interest in the method and its foods.

The fourth and final motivating factor was vegetarianism, often embraced because people were concerned about overpopulation and world hunger. Frances Moore Lappé's book *Diet for a Small Planet* led the way, explaining how many more resources were required to produce meat than to produce vegetable protein and how to combine vegetable proteins to make a sustaining diet. (Later research showed that her dictates were more rigid than need be, in that various plant proteins eaten on the same day can be combined by our bodies, rather than their having to be in the same meal; that said, her contributions are still of great value.)

The new whole foods movement didn't have to reach back very far to find historical continuity. Both organic food and vegetarian meals were part of my dad's farm experience. Synthetic fertilizers and pesticides didn't exist yet or were not affordable to my grandfather, so his farm was essentially organic. Also, vegetarian meals make up a part of many farm cuisines. Even when a family was not intentionally vegetarian, meat often was available only seasonally or only in small amounts combined with larger amounts of legumes, grain, and vegetables.

The whole foods movement of the 1960s introduced or popularized some foods and ideas previously uncommon in American cuisine. People learned to make and eat tofu, sprouts, yogurt, and granola. They learned to stir-fry vegetables and eat them with rice. They drank herbal teas. In some cases, the desire to create healthful meals trumped a delight in delicious food. However, it also resulted in some very good recipes. Recipes in this book that reflect this new cuisine include Main Dish Risotto (page 311) and Stuffed Zucchini (page 364).

TOWARD A REGIONAL CUISINE

A new whole foods cuisine began to emerge in the 1980s that was more sophisticated than that of the 1960s and 1970s. It drew its inspiration from world cuisines and adapted them in a more authentic manner. The ingredients were still whole and healthful, but there was greater emphasis on flavor and presentation. There had been a shift from a desire to eat like a peasant to a desire to adapt the best ideas from world cuisines for using fresh, whole foods. It recognized the place we live, and the foods we produce nearby, and looked to inspiration from cuisines developed by farmers and gardeners who grow food in similar climates (for us, this would be the Mediterranean Basin or in Asia at similar latitudes).

Because this new cuisine began in California, it was often called "California cuisine." The ideas it embraced have spread beyond our borders, enlivening and nutritionally improving diets elsewhere, but it began and continues as a regional cuisine. Because of the emphasis on fresh, local produce, the development of this cuisine has been a boon to local gardeners. It has meant that if we want to try an unfamiliar crop, to see if we like it well enough to grow it, we can first go out and buy it. And once we have it, we can look for cookbooks filled with lively, delicious ways to prepare it. In this book, some example recipes of this more recent regional cuisine are Bolivian Sunroot and Blood Orange Salad (page 195) and Roasted Root Vegetables (page 378).

But while a regional cuisine continues to develop, it is still not quite the same thing as a regional *garden cuisine*. California cuisine is based on what is available for purchase in our region seasonally, not necessarily on the particular rhythms of what one can grow in a garden. And while there is overlap between the two, it is worth considering the differences.

WHAT IS A GARDEN CUISINE?

A garden cuisine, whatever its details, is dependent on the climate, irrigation, pests, and other factors that affect a garden. A particular garden can produce some crops easily, others with more difficulty. It can produce some crops all year, others only part of a year. The very crop we desire most may be the hardest to grow—or the easiest. Some crops have a long season, others very a short one. Some are easy to preserve, while others require time and skill. For example, my father's garden produced green beans in such abundance in mid to late summer that we couldn't eat them all fresh. On the other hand, his garden grew only a few kohlrabies, which we sliced to eat raw, as a delicacy.

Our Bay Area gardens, with their mediterranean climate, allow us to harvest a wider variety of crops, over wider seasons, than gardens in climates with colder winters. We can harvest many kinds of herbs all year. Thus fresh herbs can become staples—always available for our kitchens. At any time we can have fresh parsley, cilantro, oregano, thyme, sage, marjoram, rosemary, tarragon (or winter tarragon), and mint. And we can have fresh vegetables all year as well. Our winter garden may provide more leeks, chard, and cole crops, while our summer garden is bountiful in beans, squash, and, where warmth is sufficient, tomatoes and peppers, but there can always be *something* available to serve fresh.

A nice surprise when you have a garden is that traditional recipes that contain many ingredients—several vegetables and a list of fresh herbs—do not require a trip to the store with a long shopping list, but simply a trip to the garden in a particular season with a harvest basket or bag. It is while harvesting for such recipes that I am most aware how all of our cuisines began in a garden. In our region, we can have this experience with some recipe or other most any day of the year.

Despite the mild climate that gives us something to harvest all year, we, like all gardeners, are generally dealing with an overabundance of some crops and a scarcity of others. In a market economy, abundance is reflected in a lower price, scarcity in a higher one. You can easily avoid having an oversupply of an item that is plentiful in the market, simply by not buying too much, no matter how cheap it is, and those with a larger budget can obtain more of a scarce food if they are willing to pay more.

The ruling factors in a supply of garden food are different than those of a market economy. Abundance and scarcity are affected by what a climate will let you grow, the size of your garden, your gardening skill, and a certain amount of chance. When you find yourself harvesting an unexpected bounty, you can't refuse it, because you already have it. If you stop picking a crop, it will still be there. Letting it go to waste will probably leave you with an uneasiness that will reduce your pleasure in gardening—I know it does for me.

And ease of production doesn't correlate particularly with price in the market. Crops that struggle in your garden may be cheap to purchase. Others that are always pricey to buy may be among the easiest to grow. Price in the store may reflect such factors as time required to harvest the crop and care required to keep it in good shape. This is certainly

Making Soup Stock

Soup stocks, or broths, serve as the basis for many delicious homemade soups and sauces. They are made by boiling vegetables, herbs, and, if meat is in your diet, some bony meat, for several hours. Then the fat, bones, and vegetables are discarded. Only the liquid and sometimes any lean meat are saved.

Modern soup stock recipes call for freshly purchased ingredients, but cooks used to make soup stocks out of their scraps. If you include bones, you may still purchase those just for the stock. They could be beef, pork, or lamb soup bones, or the bony parts of chickens. You can also use bones from a cooked roast or the carcass of a roast chicken after you eat the meat. The vegetables you use can be ones that got a bit old in the refrigerator, but as a gardener, you have access to many of the plant parts that cooks who garden have traditionally put into their stock—parts that aren't usually eaten, but that have plenty of flavor to release.

Many kinds of vegetables can be used, although cabbage family crops are usually excluded because long cooking gives them an unpleasant flavor. Favorite choices for stock are crops in the onion and carrot family. Use at least one crop from each family. You can use not only the parts we usually eat, but the green tops of leeks and carrots, or the leaves of celery, cutting celery, or celeriac. You can also use onion, leek, or parsley plants that have tough stalks because they are about to flower. You can even use carrots that the carrot rust fly has damaged a bit, cutting away the damage and using the undamaged parts.

Use fresh herbs if you have them, dried if you don't. Bay leaf, thyme, and garlic are usually included; oregano or marjoram optional.

Making soup stock sounds time-consuming, but it takes little of your attention most of its cooking time. You can simmer it while you eat dinner, turn it off at bedtime, and let it cool overnight in a cool room. In the morning, put the pot in the refrigerator. That evening, skim off and discard any fat that has hardened on the surface, then strain out all the vegetables, herbs, and bones. You will find many uses for your stock, including Southwest Chili Vegetable Soup (page 366). The recipe for Minestrone (page 189) includes a beef soup stock.

the case with edible flowers, which must be picked one by one, washed, and kept from being crushed. With all of that care, edible flowers still have a short shelf-life. However, in other cases the price reflects cachet—the perception that a food is extra special—when in fact it may be practically a garden weed. Arugula, for example, considered by some the pricey food of elitists, will reseed itself readily in gardens.

One answer to overabundance in the garden is to pick crops as baby vegetables, a tactic that limits their total production. Zucchinis picked with the flowers still attached, slender green bean pods, and young lettuce plants are all delicious. There are special carrot varieties meant to be pulled while still small. By harvesting baby vegetables, you are eating something that would be pricier to buy than if it grew bigger. A warning, though: getting yourself to pick vegetables young may be difficult. You may find yourself thinking, "Maybe it should get just a bit larger," or "Seems a pity to pull that when I just put it in." Baby vegetables can cost you extra determination and planning, rather than extra cash.

Because a garden is a different kind of food source from a grocery, a cookbook for a gardener should likewise be different from an ordinary cookbook. It should have seasonal recipes, combining several crops that can be harvested together. It should index the garden ingredients, so one can look up what there is to do with the crops one has ready. And it should give amounts a gardener can relate to—such as how many cups of a crop to use, rather than pounds of it or the size of the can to open. Finally, it should feature garden specialties, such as squash blossoms or shell beans, which are not often found in the grocery.

A garden in one place is a different source of food from a garden in another place. The crops that can be harvested together will be different. What is easy or hard to grow will be different. Gardens in this region can be immensely productive all year long. The subset of crops and planting times is a bit different near the coast, but it is equally as varied as the possible crops and planting times inland. And the proximity of different microclimates is such that we can supplement what we grow with purchased produce from a different microclimate and still be buying locally.

Homemade Chicken Stock

You can buy whole chickens when they are on sale and cut them up, saving the backs and necks for soup, or you can just buy the bony parts for this soup stock.

3 pounds of bony chicken parts (backs, necks, wings)
2 medium onions, coarsely chopped (or the equivalent in other onion crop plant parts)
2 medium carrots and 2 stalks of celery (or the equivalent in other carrot family plant parts)
1 handful parsley leaves
2 bay leaves, fresh or dry
½ teaspoon whole black peppercorns
4 quarts water
Several sprigs fresh thyme (or 1 teaspoon of dried thyme)
1 or 2 sprigs fresh marjoram and/or oregano (or 1 teaspoon dried of either)

Cut any large leaves or stems into pieces a couple of inches long. Combine all the ingredients in a large pot. Bring to a boil. Skim off foam that forms on top. Lower heat, partially cover, and simmer for 2 or 3 hours. It should bubble very gently. Taste the stock and decide if it needs to cook down a bit more, uncovered, to concentrate the flavor. Cool the stock and then refrigerate or, if it is in a cool room, refrigerate it in the morning.

When the stock is chilled, skim off any hardened fat from the top and discard it. If the liquid has jelled, heat it until it liquefies, stirring to distribute the heat. (It will be liquid when it is just a little warm.) Discard all of the vegetables, herbs, bones, and other waste solids. (You may want to return any lean meat to the broth later.) Strain the broth through a fine strainer or a colander lined with a paper towel.

If you plan to make the soup in the same pot, scrub it before returning the stock to it. If you don't plan to use the soup stock right away, freeze measured amounts for future use. Label and date the containers.

DEPENDING ON A GARDEN

When I garden, I connect to the lives of all humans who are living, or have lived, directly from the earth. I call it "emotional archaeology." On a small scale, without the risk of starvation, I experience the demands and the generosity of the plants, the joys and frustrations of trying to harness them to my needs. I appreciate the concern that motivated the Navajo people to walk in their cornfields at specified times, from seeding to harvest, singing songs that coaxed the plants to produce a bountiful crop. I understand the frustration that led my grandfather to plant the watermelons in the middle of the cornfield, where they would be shielded from the eyes of would-be watermelon rustlers.

And when I eat from a garden, I experience the emotions that others before me have felt when trying to match what the plants provide with what I want to eat. When I thaw a container of last summer's pesto on a stormy winter day, I can appreciate the pleasure my father must have felt when he first tasted home-canned green beans in a snowbound farm house. And when I pick a few wild and tame greens for a late winter salad, even though my garden is active all winter, I still can imagine the pleasure of the first spring greens gathered in late March after a winter of snow and ice—and after weeks of mostly potatoes, biscuits, and gravy.

To intensify these feelings and the understanding they generated, I tried, for several years, to avoid buying anything that I could grow. I found I could eat fairly well, if a little oddly at times, from a few hundred square feet of garden. I did still buy a little produce, including apples and oranges, fresh mushrooms, and supplementary potatoes, carrots, and onions.

Backyard Omelet

Here's an omelet made with the backyard gleanings of a chilly December morning. (If you feel nervous about making a proper omelet, you can scramble the eggs instead, and they will taste just as good.) Serves two.

4 eggs
4 medium sage leaves, finely minced
One 2-inch sprig rosemary (tender parts only), finely minced
6 nasturtium flowers, chopped
6 nasturtium leaves, chopped
6 garlic chive leaves (or onion lily or garlic leaves), chopped
2 tablespoons butter or margarine
¾ cup grated Monterey Jack cheese (or other mild cheese)

Beat the eggs in a bowl and stir in the minced herbs, nasturtiums, and garlic chives.

Melt the butter in a frying pan and pour in the eggs. Shake the pan back and forth to prevent sticking. As the eggs begin to cook, slip a spatula under the edges and tilt the pan so that the uncooked egg can run under the cooked part to the center of the skillet. When the omelet is almost set, sprinkle the cheese over half of it. Fold the omelet in half over the cheese and slide it out of the pan onto a plate.

Note: For scrambled eggs, beat the eggs and stir in all the ingredients except the butter. Melt the butter in a frying pan and cook the eggs, mixing and turning until the eggs are set to your liking.

I enjoyed late winter's glut of artichokes—and I had enough of them that I also enjoyed the lull in production that followed. I loved the profusion of cucumbers, from midsummer to midfall. I liked the fresh cabbage, so sweet and crisp that I cut large wedges of it to eat raw. I also enjoyed my efforts to achieve year-round self-sufficiency in such crops as garlic and lettuce. Though of course I could never be self-sufficient overall, my limited successes gave me a feeling of satisfaction that was well worth the effort. They also gave me a stronger sense of connection with those who live from the land.

If you want to try self-sufficiency in some crops, or even a single crop, choose ones you can either produce year round or store easily. Some good candidates are garlic, carrots, leeks, green onions, lettuce, and parsley. Don't worry too much about perfection. If you grow too little of a crop, buy some; if too much, give some away.

I may preserve some excess, though I make it a point not to preserve any food unless the result is truly delicious. If I can make dried tomatoes that are as good as the ones I can buy, then I will do that. If they turn out to be inferior, I will not try that again unless I learn a different technique. If I haven't picked a crop when it's small, can't give it away, and it doesn't preserve well, then I must look for more recipes for that crop and grow less next time.

Because of the fluctuations in the supply of garden crops, there are two kinds of recipes that gardeners love: (1) ones that find yet another way to use up lots of whatever you have too much of, and (2) ones that use a little of this and a little of that, whatever you have around. In the first category are recipes such as Zucchini Fritters (page 377), Wilted Lettuce (page 233), or Southeast Asian Cucumber Salad (page 220). Look for salads or soups that are based on a single vegetable. Then look for unusual ways to prepare a crop, in dishes in which you wouldn't expect to find it, or with seasoning unlike that of dishes you already make—anything that will dispel the impression that you are eating the same thing every day.

If, instead of too much, you find yourself with only a little of this and that crop, you will find the second kind of recipe useful. Times you are likely to find yourself with these "wee bits" of any one item are when a crop hasn't done well, or at the beginning and end of a harvest. When you have only a little of several crops, make mixed soups or salads, omelets, casseroles, stir-fries, or vegetable curries. One day in early summer you will go out and find that you have ready for harvest seven green bean pods, one baby zucchini, a few small side heads of broccoli, and a few leaves regrown from a cut cabbage head. These slim pickings can serve as the basis for a very nice Year-Round Vegetable Curry (page 210). Other such recipes in this book are Backyard Omelet (page 374) and Southwest Chili Vegetable Soup (page 366).

In many cases, you will have, for a given planting of a given crop, a cycle of scarcity as it begins to bear, then bounty, then scarcity again. This cycle will be most intense with crops such as corn, lettuce, or cilantro that do not last long once they are ready and do not keep very well in storage either. With these crops, you can reduce the production bulge by making a series of small plantings, rather than only one.

And sometimes you will find that you waited a bit too long, so a crop has become too mature, or has begun to go to seed. Soup stock is a handy use for any members of the carrot or onion family that are past their prime. Soup stock relies on vegetables for flavoring, then the vegetables themselves are discarded. For this purpose, it matters little if the vegetables are too tough to eat. (See Making Soup Stock on page 372.)

DEVELOPING A REGIONAL GARDEN CUISINE

Unlike many parts of the world, California does not have a long history of eating from local gardens and farms. What we call our local—our California—cuisine is in fact an amalgam of many different foods and ways of preparing them that arrived from many parts of the world. We are not eating a local traditional garden cuisine, but began creating one from scratch rather recently.

Native American Californians didn't grow crops, living instead on the abundance of foods they could hunt or gather, including acorns and other wild seeds and the plentiful shellfish of the area. However, this abundance was relative. It supported a small population nicely, but would not support the larger population that currently lives here. Agriculture was introduced to California by Spanish missionaries only in 1769, the year that Father Junipero Serra walked through the state, beginning the founding of missions.

The Spanish explorers who arrived with Christopher Columbus on an island in the Caribbean, and the soldiers and colonists who soon followed, had little interest in eating what the people already living in these places were eating. They wanted to duplicate the diet of Spain. Ironically, because the Spanish did not understand the world's climates, it took them a long time to find places their Mediterranean crops would thrive. In their first settlements, on tropical Caribbean islands and coastal Mexico, they were unable to grow wheat, barley, grapes, olives, or many of their cool-season vegetables. They eventually learned that wheat could be grown inland Mexico, and olives and grapes in Chile's mediterranean climate. But they didn't begin to farm or garden in California, or what was then called "Alto California," until Father Serra's journeys. He carried with him seeds of wheat, olives, grapes, and castor bean. The missionaries who followed brought fruit trees and vegetables.

Native American Californians offered the missionaries gifts of acorns and pine nuts. Spanish missionaries introduced the native peoples to European fruits and vegetables. It was also the first time the peoples of California had seen corn, squash, and beans, though these crops had been grown for many centuries by people living to the east and south, and, more recently, had been gradually accepted as food by the Spanish. There were eventually twenty-one missions, farmed in the Spanish colonial fashion by the labor of the native people. There were few other Europeans in the state. The Mexican Californios followed after the missionaries, bringing a Mexican-Spanish agriculture and cuisine, but they were never numerous.

With the Gold Rush of 1849, a large population of Americans began to arrive, bringing with them a cuisine that was more influenced by England and Northern Europe than by the crop possibilities California presented. Their crops were ones that had been grown by Northern European farmers and gardeners who came to America, and that they then grew on farms and in gardens in (mostly) colder regions of America. So there were no artichokes, no broccoli, and no olive oil. And their recipes reflected these more Northern European cuisines.

For the next century or so, many Californians ate pretty much like the rest of the country. While I was eating fish sticks, Jell-O, and boxed macaroni and cheese in Indiana, California kids probably were too; after all, fast-food restaurant concepts were incubated in Southern California.

But there were factors that set the stage for change. One was our availability of fresh produce all year. Another was the great diversity in California. People from many non–Northern European nations started arriving early on; many

Mexican Vegetables

In summer, substitute purslane for Swiss chard in this delicious Mexican dish. This can be served as a main dish or a side dish.

- 6 to 8 leaves Swiss chard, stems included (or 2 cups chopped young purslane)
- 1 tablespoon oil
- 1 small onion, chopped
- 1 clove garlic, minced
- One 15-ounce can tomato purée (or 2 cups Quick Homemade Tomato Sauce, page 365)
- 2 medium potatoes, diced
- 1 cup cooked garbanzo beans
- ½ to 1 jalapeño pepper, pickled or fresh, finely chopped

Cut the stem sections from the chard and chop them into ½-inch pieces; set aside. Chop the chard leaves and keep separate.

Heat the oil in a medium skillet and sauté the onion and garlic until just tender, but not browned, about 5 minutes. Add the tomato purée, potatoes, and chard stems. Simmer until tender, 10 to 15 minutes.

Add the chopped chard leaves (or all of the purslane if that's the green of choice), garbanzos, and jalapeño. Simmer another 5 minutes.

others came as time passed. Italians who became farmers in California introduced artichokes and broccoli to California and the rest of America in the early twentieth century. Many other groups ate their traditional cuisines. Pretty soon we began sharing our ingredients and cuisines with each other. (The food section of *Sunset* magazine, from the middle of the twentieth century onward, shows this trend and probably influenced it greatly.)

Because of this sharing, our diets began to reflect a wider range of what we can grow. Snow peas and bok choy are stir-fried by many who aren't Asian in heritage; jalapeños and cilantro go into the guacamole of many whose families are not of Latin American origin. Mediterranen pestos are made in kitchens of Californians whose ancestors did not live in Europe. It has become obvious that our gardens can be used to reproduce a number of particular garden cuisines from elsewhere, but we can, more interestingly, continue the development of a regional garden cuisine that is uniquely of our time and place.

THE "GREENING" OF OUR DIETS

When I wrote the first edition of this book in 1993, I had been gardening in California for twenty years. I had learned to use the whole year to grow some kinds of food in my garden and could match my crops to seasonal recipes. But I was still not hearing the full message from my garden about what I could be eating. My diet, while it included more vegetables and fruits than that of the average American, was still meat-centered, not plant-centered.

But as I studied the cuisines of those who live near the Mediterranean, I realized that the Mediterranean diet has been, and is, much higher in vegetables in general, and particularly in leafy green ones, than the recent American interpretation of those cuisines would suggest. Mainstream American cuisine now features Italian dishes such as veal parmesan, spaghetti with meatballs, pizza with pepperoni, and eggplant parmesan. All well and good, but where are the Mediterranean recipes using greens? Where is the Italian kale soup? The Greek mixed greens steamed and dressed with olive oil and a few drops of lemon? The dolmas made with chard leaves? The pizza topped with cooked broccoli raab? The tabouli made with lots of parsley? You can certainly find such recipes, but it seems that most often Americans have pulled out just the parts that feature lots of meat and cheese and pretty much left out the greens. Because adding greens would improve many American diets most effectively, I became particularly interested in the connection between the climates that so resemble ours and their greater use of greens.

You can often tell how plentiful or easy a crop is to grow in a region by the variety and number of recipes that use it. A rare or difficult crop, or one

Zucchini Fritters

A delicious answer to the summer zucchini glut, these fritters are also good when they are made with any other type of summer squash, with chayote, sunchoke, or potato, or with combinations of any two of these vegetables. They can be served for breakfast, lunch, or dinner. Serves two or three.

- 1 cup grated zucchini (or other summer squash, chayote, sunchoke, or potato)
- 1 cup lowfat or nonfat cottage cheese
- 2 eggs
- 1 cup whole wheat or unbleached flour
- 2 teaspoons oil plus extra for frying

Mix the zucchini, cottage cheese, eggs, flour, and 2 teaspoons oil in the order given. Heat oil in a skillet. When water drops sprinkled on the skillet jump, spoon in the fritter batter. Make fritters about 4 inches in diameter and ½ inch or so thick. When the first side is browned, turn and brown the second side. Serve plain or with butter and, if desired, plum jam, applesauce, or syrup. Serves two or three.

with a rather short season, may be featured in only a few recipes in a cuisine, while one that is plentiful or easy or has a long season will be in many more. Greens are not the forte of northern European cuisine, but are plentiful in Mediterranean cuisines as well as in many cuisines at similar latitudes across the globe into Asia.

In cold-winter places, people often crave greens after the long winter of stored fruits, seeds, and roots. They seek them out as a "spring tonic." My father spoke of collecting wild greens in spring as soon as they leafed out. Curly dock was the family's favorite, and his list of spring greens always ended with "even the young raspberry leaves." But the mediterranean garden is green all winter; in fact, fall and winter are its greenest times. And, with irrigation, summer can produce greens too.

In her book *Animal, Vegetable, Miracle*, Barbara Kingsolver imagines a "vegetannual," a composite vegetable plant meant to give new gardeners a rough idea of the sequence of crops in a spring to fall garden. A "vegetannual" gives leaves in spring, then flower buds (broccoli) and immature fruits (snap beans and summer squash), then mature fruits (tomato and pumpkin), and by fall has fleshy roots (carrots and beets) to store in the soil into cold weather. However, this doesn't accurately describe a yearly cycle in our region's vegetable gardens. Here, along with all those other crops, this imaginary plant would keep on putting out fresh leaves all year. It would have them in our long cool spring, and on into summer. In late summer there would be more, and there'd be yet more in fall. It would offer more all winter, and they would become especially tender and succulent in late winter.

Not only can our gardens produce greens all year, but they can produce them in large quantities. A plant makes leaves fast, and it makes more of them than, say, fruits. Whether you grow lettuce and other salad greens, bok choy, gai lan (Chinese broccoli), parsley, cilantro, chard, or collards, greens are quick and productive.

All parts of mediterranean California can produce greens all year long. The cool summer parts of our region can grow cool-preferring, or cool season, greens all year, and hot summer parts of the region can grow them fall to spring. If you live in a hot-summer microclimate, you can grow greens in summer, too. In the Midwest, we thought summer was too hot for greens. But I have since learned that greens we hadn't heard of there are grown in parts of the world with hot summers. Greens like amaranth, fenugreek greens, and Malabar spinach, unknown to my European ancestors, grow best with summer heat.

Because I grew up eating a cuisine in which greens other than lettuce and cabbage were not plentiful, my range of ideas for preparing them was narrow. Most commonly, we boiled or steamed them and served them with either butter or vinegar. Their

Roasted Root Vegetables

Oven roasting is one of the tastiest ways to prepare many kinds of root vegetables. In addition to the ones listed, you can use turnip or rutabaga. Try all of these, even ones you think you don't like, at least once, because you may find you like them this way. Then you can settle on a selection and proportion of vegetables that you like best. Serves two or three.

1 celeriac
2 medium boiling type potatoes
1 parsnip
1 carrot
1 small fennel bulb, or ½ large bulb
1 small onion, thinly sliced
2 tablespoons olive oil
5 cloves garlic, peeled and halved
2 tablespoons finely chopped fresh oregano
1 teaspoon finely chopped fresh rosemary (or 1 teaspoon dried Italian seasoning in place of oregano and rosemary)
Salt and freshly ground pepper

Trim and peel the celeriac, being careful to cut deeply enough to remove the tough fibers under the surface. Cut the celeriac, potato, parsnip, and carrot into ½-inch slices, then cut the slices so that none is wider than 1 inch. Trim roots and leaf stems from the fennel bulb, then cut it into wedges, each with a bit of core and about ½ inch at the wide side.

Preheat the oven to 400°F.

Put the olive oil in a 9- by 13-inch baking pan. Add the celeriac, potato, parsnip, carrot, fennel, onion, garlic, and herbs to the pan. Turn the vegetables to coat with oil and herbs. Add salt and pepper to taste, and turn a bit more to distribute seasoning.

Cover the pan with aluminum foil and roast for 50 minutes. Stir once or twice during baking.

season was short and ended before you really got tired of them, though a reason you might still was that there was so little creativity in preparing them.

In the years since the first edition of *Golden Gate Gardening* was published, I have challenged myself to better match my cuisine to the strengths of my garden and at the same time improve my diet, by learning more interesting ways to prepare greens and eating more of them. For some examples of this, see To Grow and Make a Green Salad (page 379), Italian-Style Swiss Chard (page 269), and Couve Mineira (Sautéed Collard Greens) (page 216).

AMERICA'S CUISINE BATTLE CONTINUES

As we continue to eat our way into the twenty-first century, we see the division in American cuisines that was illustrated in my childhood still flourishing, with some repeated themes and some new ones. The whole-foods trend is expanding; supermarkets offer organic foods, and even fast food restaurants offer salads. Vegetarianism continues to gain interest, with a new motivator being conditions on factory farms and in slaughterhouses that are both cruel to the animals and sometimes dangerous to the health of those who eat the meat. The idea of eating locally is new and spreading rapidly, with farmers markets multiplying, and many people making an effort to be "locavores." The international "slow food" movement has come to California, stressing, among other things, local produce grown sustainably. Meanwhile, convenience food has continued its advance and merged with fast food/junk food; together, they still represent the diet of a majority of Americans.

In the face of increasing childhood obesity and rising rates of diet-related metabolic disorders, you would think that the idea of eating differently would

To Grow and Make a Green Salad

With only a little space in your garden, you can enliven your salads with garden-fresh ingredients such as sprouts, microgreens, or cut-and-come-again mixed greens (mesclun). To learn more about all of these small-space options, see page 236. In a few pots or a small garden bed, you can let leafy lettuce mature and pick it leaf by leaf. Add some arugula, mizuna, 'Ruby Streaks' mustard, a plant or two of frisée, and a few edible flowers, and you have the basic makings for weeks of green salad. By replanting every few weeks, you can have these most of the year.

If you have more garden space, you will have seasonal treats to add to your salad. In winter you can enjoy sliced and lightly steamed brussels sprouts, broccoli, and baby fava beans. In spring, snap peas and slices of Bolivian sunroot. In summer, steamed snap beans, zucchini, and, if your garden is warm enough, cucumbers, peppers, and tomatoes. In fall, sliced kohlrabi, pickled beets, grated carrots, and lightly steamed broccoli florets.

But the joy of the garden is also in the garnishes and herbs you can grow. There are edible flowers all year round, and herbs that can be snipped to sprinkle on top or flavor your dressing. And there is usually some edible weed to collect. In winter and spring, chickweed, onion lily (wild onion), and miner's lettuce are delicious additions. (In fact, during its season, miner's lettuce can substitute for domestic lettuce.) In spring and summer, use wild radish pods or purslane.

Here's how to harvest most efficiently for green salads. Use separate containers for different kinds of ingredients. Mild-flavored leafy greens can go into one, spicy or strong-flavored greens in another, herbs and edible flowers in a third, and any solid, nonleafy crops like beans or peas in a fourth. I have always divided them so, because this makes it easier in the kitchen to assemble the salad. I was charmed to read in Paula Wolfort's cookbook *Mediterranean Grains and Greens* that this is just how Greek women gather their wild greens. They call them "apron greens" for the pocketed aprons women wear while gathering them. One pocket is for mild greens, one for spicy, and, in their case, one for wild mushrooms (wish I found those in my garden).

Harvest in ways that reduce later trimming and cutting. I always pick the round leaves of miner's lettuce with only about a half-inch of stem. Placed in a closed container in the refrigerator right away, they stay crisp and fresh. When I have pulled the whole plants, I found they wilted immediately, and I also ended up with some leaves that were tiny or had holes in them. By picking the best leaves individually, without the stems, I have just what I want when I am ready to use them. Harvesting chickweed or purslane? Just pinch off two-inch tips. They will be tender and will not require any further cutting to prepare them. Pick edible flowers without stems as well, unless you plan to put the stems in a cup of water and use the flowers the next day.

In the kitchen, start by tearing the leafy greens, domestic or wild, into pieces. Tear the spicier leaves into smaller pieces than the mild ones to avoid too heavy a presence. (If you are making individual salads, you can customize them to accommodate different preferences for mild/spicy balance.) To add chives or onion lily leaves, cut them into 2- to 4-inch pieces, because smaller bits of these linear greens tend to fall to the bottom of the bowl when you toss. If any of your greens are particularly pretty—like variegated 'Alaska' nasturtium leaves or curled cress—reserve a few of them for the top of the salad. Toss the greens well to mix them up. Next add any solids, such as cut-up snap peas, steamed and cut-up snap beans, or tomatoes. Last, add edible flowers and any reserved pretty leaves, placed nicely over the top of the salad with their best sides facing up. Don't overdo the top decoration; let some of the regular leafy greens show through. For a fancy finish, make a vegetable confetti by chopping a couple of brightly colored Swiss chard stems into tiny bits and scattering them on top.

be obvious, but of course it isn't so simple. Start with the fact that what you ate as a child is your food culture, no matter how unhealthy. Add to that the fact that each fast or junk food is tested carefully to appeal to our senses as it is being formulated (and often marketed to children with the express intention of creating new customers). And finally, consider that, ironically, perceptions have done a flip-flop, so that whole foods advocates, the ones who eat more like food-rich but cash-challenged farmers, are now considered by the mainstream eaters to be "elite."

You don't have to eat fancy or expensively to eat well. All you need is whole, real food. Cutting through the endless talk about what we should eat,

Two Homemade Salad Dressings

Balsamic Vinaigrette

3 parts olive oil, 1 part balsamic vinegar, salt, pepper, garlic powder or freshly minced garlic, other freshly minced herbs if desired. Shake well and immediately pour over the salad. For a large single-serving salad, use about 2 tablespoons of oil and 2 teaspoons of vinegar.

Creamy Dressing

2 parts light mayonnaise, 1 part nonfat yogurt, a little lemon juice, salt, pepper, herbs to taste. Mix ingredients well. Best used immediately.

Michael Pollan, in his book *In Defense of Food: An Eater's Manifesto*, proposes seven words to guide us: "Eat food. Not too much. Mostly plants." Even if we don't grow enough to eat only from a garden, the experiences it generates pull us in the right direction.

A garden can help us in showing us plants to eat at their best, and in making them less of a luxury. In garden cuisine, luxury and poverty shake hands. It is how you prepare the food that makes it luxurious, and sometimes the easiest food to grow can create the most luxurious of meals. You may have only some wild miner's lettuce, some arugula, and some edible flowers, but your salad will be a fresh delicacy (see the previous page). The garden gleanings that create a Backyard Omelet (page 374) will make your eggs a gourmet meal.

Mainstream eaters say that organic food is too expensive. The food we grow in our gardens can be organic if we choose, eliminating the premium price organic food commands. Shopping at farmers markets will help also, allowing access to organic produce at lower prices because there are fewer middlepersons involved. Different governmental farm policy could also help, by providing more assistance to farmers who are exploring more productive organic farming systems. But in truth, while I'd like to see everyone eating organically, simply eating more vegetables and fruits is probably more critical to improving the average American diet than eating organic food.

Another change that would greatly improve many diets is preparing and eating food at home. Studies show that just eating at home, even given that many will choose some convenience foods, generally means eating more healthfully. The kind of restaurant that serves whole, fresh foods, not too much of them, mostly plants, is uncommon, and certainly costs more than the average fast-food joint. And it seems we got into the habit of wanting a restaurant to give us meats and deep-fried stuff, and not so much salad or vegetables. Maybe it is because the latter need to be prepared with love and care and served as soon as they are prepared, or salads wilt and cooked vegetables become the stuff of steam tables, overcooked and unappealing.

Cooking is an art, like gardening, that is central to being human. It can be one of our most rewarding activities, resulting in delicious food prepared just as we want it. Does it take a long time to cook? It varies greatly, and the deliciousness of a dish is not necessarily related to how long it took to prepare. I, like most busy people, often put together fast meals. Simple combinations are sometimes just as good as ones that take time and care to prepare. But there are times when I indulge in the luxury of preparing something time-consuming but wonderful, like minestrone soup or a vegetarian Indian meal, and enjoy both the process and the results.

My mom would rather watch TV. We got one when I was twelve, and from then on, she cooked the evening meals mainly during the commercials. Our menu would have become considerably less interesting at that point had I not learned to cook myself.

I hope your garden inspires you to cook well and healthfully. And I hope you enjoy a long life eating, as Pollan suggests, "food, not too much, mostly plants."

APPENDIX I

The Climate of Our Region

Why do parts of our region get so much fog in the summer?

Summer fog is common because we are located between a very cold ocean and a very hot inland area. As the Central Valley warms, the heated air above it rises. Air from the west rushes in to fill the vacuum, creating an onshore wind.

Since the air carried by this wind has just passed over great expanses of cool ocean water, it is cool and humid. It is made even colder by the fact that there is a band of especially cold ocean water just off our coast. As the air passes over this cold water, it is cooled precipitously. The moisture it contains is condensed, becoming visible as fog. The pull of air from ocean to valley is often called the "fog pump."

Why is the ocean near our coast so cold?

The California Current flows parallel to the California coast, carrying cold water from the north and west. Then, deflected by the rotation of the earth, this water turns away from the California shore. It is replaced by an upwelling of deep ocean water that is 10 to 15°F colder than the already chilly surface water.

The band of cold coastal ocean reaches from Oregon to Point Conception (just below Lompoc, California), centering on the stretch between Cape Mendocino and Monterey Bay. It begins to appear in May, peaks in August, and then tapers off. Ocean temperatures equalize by the following March.

Why does the summer fog build up for a few days and then go away for a few days?

After cold ocean air has been rushing into the Central Valley for a few days, the valley becomes cooler. When this happens, the fog pump stops, letting the onshore wind die down until the Valley warms up again. This process often takes a few days, but may take several weeks.

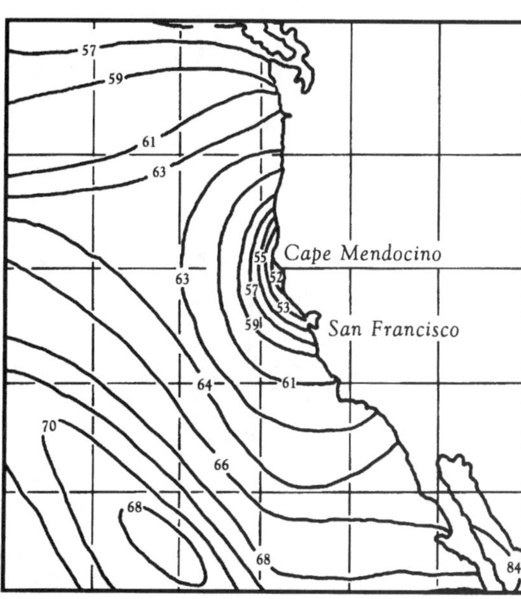

Surface water temperatures in August (Univ. of California Publications in Geography, vol. 3, 1931)

Which areas get the most summer fog and why?

Areas nearest the ocean and those located along fog gaps get the most fog. The map on page 385 shows areas most likely to be foggy. Fog often covers a substantial swath of ocean off the coast and blankets the coast to the first hills. In the midsummer months, Point Reyes, on a long spit of land extending into the cold current, has the coldest summer temperatures in the contiguous 48 states.

A fog gap is any place low enough for the fog to be able to flow through. The two main places through which fog can move inland are the San Francisco and Monterey Bays. The Golden Gate itself is narrow, but the whole distance between Mount Tamalpais and Mount Montara (just south of Pacifica) is lower than 500 feet. Marine air, often carrying fog, blows through this mega-gap, covering San Francisco, the San Francisco Bay, the southern tip of Marin and the central Bay coast of Alameda County (Albany, Berkeley, Alameda). On days when the fog is extensive, it continues to flow up the Carquinez Strait toward Stockton and also flows through gaps in the East Bay hills.

Monterey Bay has a wide mouth, but there are high mountains to the north and south. The

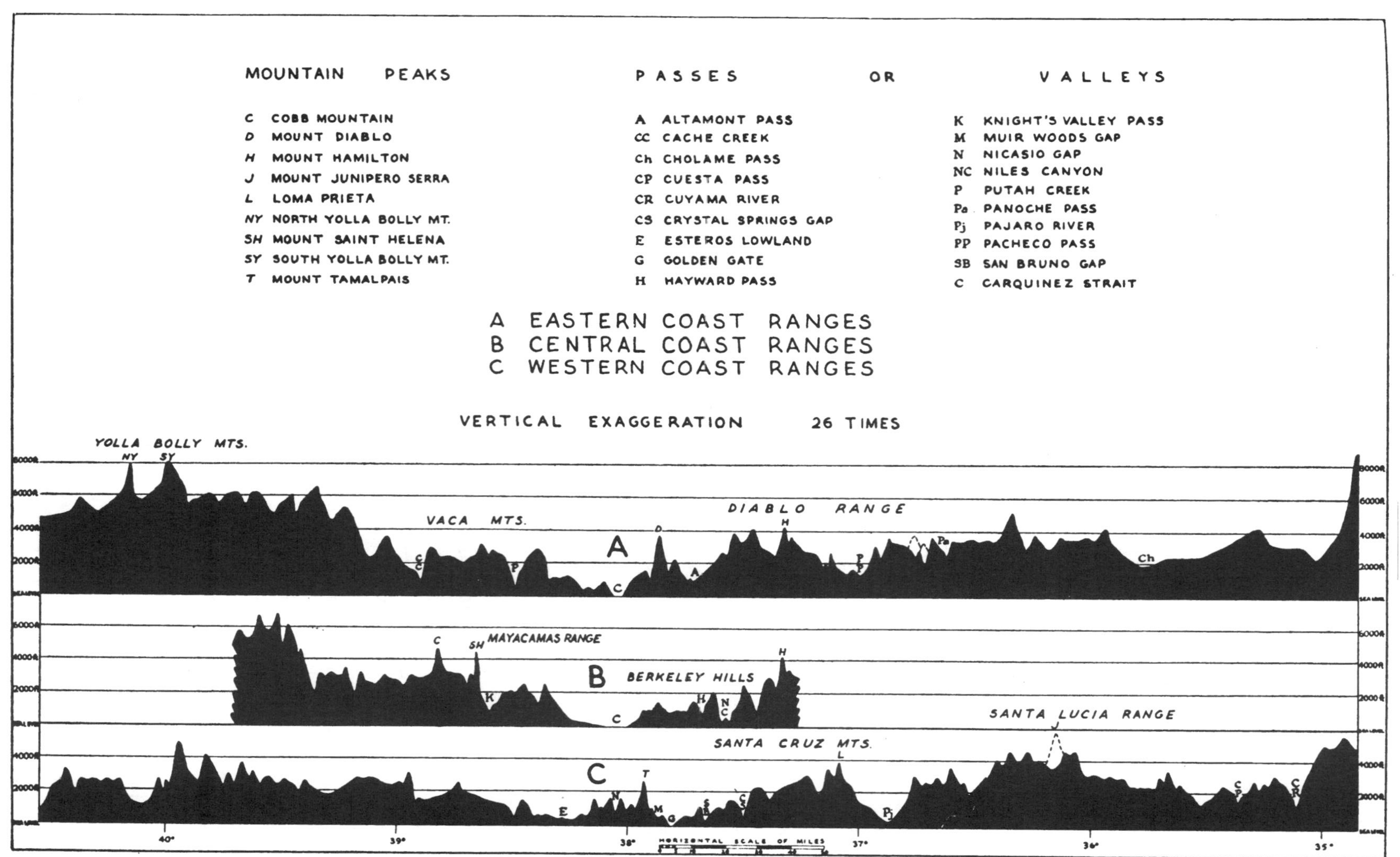

Crestline profiles of Coast Ranges in central California with names of passes and valleys. (Univ. of California Publications in Geography, vol. 7, 1951)

fog moves inland against the hills, with Chittendon Pass serving as a fog gap to let air into the Santa Clara Valley and the San Benito Valley. Fog sometimes spreads up the Salinas Valley, and Monterey Bay fog occasionally meets that from the San Francisco Bay at San Jose.

Outside of these two main entry points, there are also areas with narrower and/or higher gaps, and there are areas that are foggy at the coast with high hills blocking inland fog. (See map on this page for locations of main fog gaps and graph on the opposite page for a view of the coastal mountains that block the flow of fog.) If a fog gap is parallel to the prevailing northwesterly summer wind, more fog will be able to enter it. Also, on the inland end of the gap, areas to the south and southeast will get more fog than ones to the north, since the wind will still be a more or less northwesterly one.

When the fog does get over a hill, why does it stop flowing and just hang there on the top of the hill?

The air does not stop flowing, but as it passes the peak of the hill it begins to fall. Falling air warms, a process called adiabatic warming. As the air warms, the fog evaporates. Sometimes you will see fog on the coast and at the peaks of the coastal hills, then more fog on the west side of hills on the east side of the San Francisco Bay. The ocean breeze carrying the fog has to rise to get over the East Bay hills, thereby cooling, so the fog condenses out again. This effect creates protected sites on the downwind sides of even relatively low coastal hills. Hills over 500 feet tall block much of the fog.

Is the summer near the coast so cold because of the fog?

No. The main reason for the cold is that the ocean breeze is cold. True, the fog blocks some sun, but on days when the breeze is not carrying fog, it is still a cold breeze.

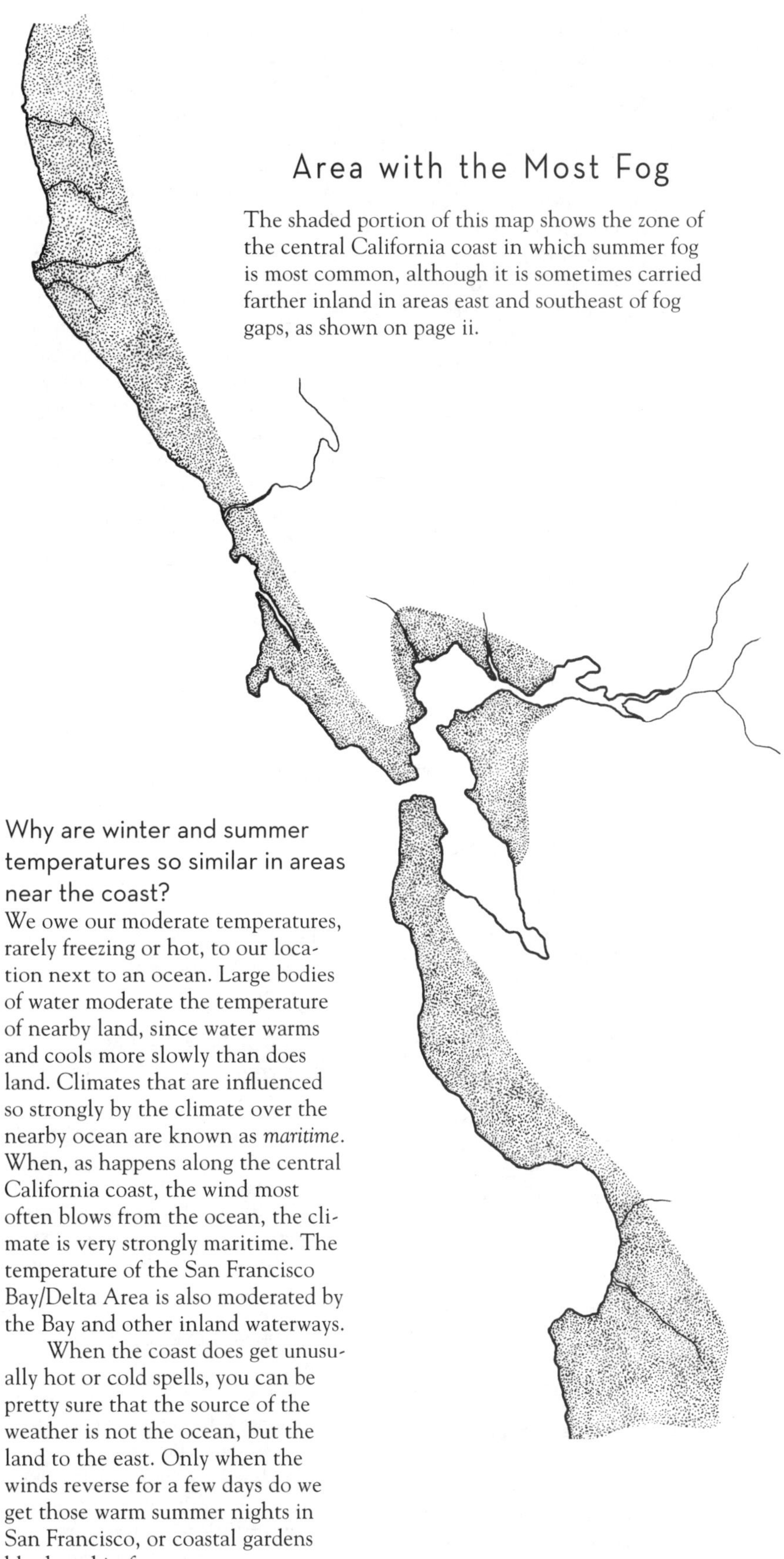

Area with the Most Fog

The shaded portion of this map shows the zone of the central California coast in which summer fog is most common, although it is sometimes carried farther inland in areas east and southeast of fog gaps, as shown on page ii.

Why are winter and summer temperatures so similar in areas near the coast?

We owe our moderate temperatures, rarely freezing or hot, to our location next to an ocean. Large bodies of water moderate the temperature of nearby land, since water warms and cools more slowly than does land. Climates that are influenced so strongly by the climate over the nearby ocean are known as *maritime*. When, as happens along the central California coast, the wind most often blows from the ocean, the climate is very strongly maritime. The temperature of the San Francisco Bay/Delta Area is also moderated by the Bay and other inland waterways.

When the coast does get unusually hot or cold spells, you can be pretty sure that the source of the weather is not the ocean, but the land to the east. Only when the winds reverse for a few days do we get those warm summer nights in San Francisco, or coastal gardens blanketed in frost.

Why is the coastal region warmest in September and October?

Even though the most sun shines on the northern hemisphere on June 21 (the longest day of the year), there is a lag time before the warmest days occur, while the earth itself warms up. In the center of a continent, this takes about 30 days. But when winds blow from an ocean, especially cold, foggy winds like ours, the days of maximum temperature are delayed. The land can't warm up until the water temperature rises.

The longest delay of the maximum along the Central California Coast is 90 days—all the way to September 21! The warmest part of San Francisco has a delay of 75 days, which is the first week of September. The area in which the delay of the maximum is significant to gardeners is where the maximum temperature is delayed 45 days or longer. You can see a map of this factor on page 13.

You can judge the degree of marine influence in a particular location by seeing how long the maximum is delayed. San Francisco's warmest month is usually September, San Rafael's is August, and Walnut Creek shows a more continental July maximum. The warmest weather in more inland locations is also usually warmer than the warmest weather near the coast.

Incidentally, the warm days of late summer are not, strictly speaking, an "Indian Summer." This term is used in the central and eastern parts of the country to refer to a continuation of summer's warmth after continental cold fronts have brought fall's first frost. Our climate has quite different sources, and our stormy fall weather usually hasn't yet begun when we finally get our warm days.

Why does it rain mainly in the winter?

We alternate between wet winters and dry summers because we are located between two large climate zones. One, centered off the coast of the Pacific Northwest, is stormy. The other, centered off the southern California coast, is calm. The stormy zone brings rain to Seattle most of the year, but it dips far enough south to soak us only in winter. The fair weather zone brings a semi-arid climate to San Diego, and gives us our dry summers.

A climate like ours, subtropical with summer drought and winter storms, is known as *mediterranean*. It is named after the Mediterranean Sea, but climatologists now know that it is a climate typical of a zone 30 to 40° from the equator on the west coasts of continents. We share this climate not only with lands bordering *the* Mediterranean, but also with parts of the coast of Chile, of the southwestern tip of Africa and of southwestern Australia.

Why does the amount of rain vary so much from year to year?

Our rainfall varies because we are on the southern edge of the rainy climate zone. Many storms hit in the center of the zone, in Washington and Oregon, but the storms at the edge are fewer and less regular. The normal annual rainfall in San Francisco is 19 to 21 inches, but there has been as much as 49.27 inches of rain and as little as 7.16 inches.

Why do different locations in this region get different amounts of rain?

Topography affects rainfall. Most of our storms originate over the ocean. The windward north or west sides of coastal hills get the most rain from these storms. Hills create rain shadows, with less rain falling south and east of them.

Why do we have fog in the winter?

Winter fog—called tule fog, after the tule reeds found in marshes—forms over damp land on clear, calm nights. It is the fog that makes Interstate 5 so difficult to drive in the winter. Tule fog forms in the Central Valley and slides down to the Delta on a weak wind that moves west from Carquinez. It forms up to 500 feet deep over the San Francisco Bay, and reaches onto the San Francisco peninsula and Marin. Winter days may see the reverse of summer—the coast clear, while inland areas are deep in tule fog.

Rarely, a marine fog forms in winter. It usually precedes a storm approaching the coast, unlike summer marine fogs that come with calm weather.

Why are some days so smoggy and others so clear?

The atmosphere farther from the earth is ordinarily colder than that near the surface. A reversal of this normal condition is called a temperature inversion. When the cold ocean breeze blows onto the central California coast in summer, it passes under a layer of warm air, creating a temperature inversion. Inversions may also form in the winter, when the air is cooled by the cold land. These winter inversions usually last less than 24 hours, but summer inversions may last for days at a time. It is during summer inversions that we most often see smog increase for many days, filling the basin of air above the Bay and spilling into the valleys that open onto it.

When there is no inversion, pollution rises unhindered into the air, becoming more dilute as it spreads vertically into a larger volume of air. During an inversion, smog circulates within the cold air, but the cold air, being heavier than the warm air above it, does not rise. When the sun warms the land, the cold lower air is warmed, and only then can it break the inversion and rise, carrying away the smog.

Which are the smoggiest parts of the region?

The most urban areas are smoggiest, since the auto is the main polluter of the area's air. But urban areas closest to the ocean have fewer smoggy days than those inland, since the ocean breeze blows the pollution eastward.

What will air pollution do to a vegetable garden?

When you see a brown haze in the air, you are looking at nitrogen dioxide, which is mostly from auto exhausts. Some crops, including beans and tomatoes, are sensitive and will be weakened by exposure to this gas.

When smog builds for several days under an inversion and clear sky, the energy from sunlight causes chemical reactions in the smog, creating new chemicals that are often more damaging to both plants and humans. This is called "photochemical smog." It is particularly likely to harm lettuce.

Lead used to be a much worse air pollutant when all cars used leaded gas. Now all cars use lead-free gas, but soil near roads can still be contaminated. (For more on soil lead, see page 75.)

While some of your crops may be somewhat harmed by air pollution, the current pollution level is not usually high enough for serious damage, and diagnosis is usually difficult.

Gardeners have a special interest in reducing particulate air pollution, since more of it could mean more fog, not less. Particulate pollution is any floating solid matter, like smoke, dust, lead, and cadmium. While the heaviest of these don't float much, smoke and dust rise into the air. Such floating particles, as well as the salt that is in the ocean spray, serve as nuclei for the condensing water droplets that make up fog. While we can't prevent ocean spray, we can support efforts to stop any smoky polluters.

What will be the effect of global warming on our gardens?

As we humans continue to burn more and more fossil fuel and cut down forests, the amount of carbon dioxide gas (CO_2) in the atmosphere has risen dramatically. This has led to a rise in the earth's temperatures. While this may sound appealing, especially to those who garden near the coast, many of the effects of this trend will be far from pleasant.

First, there is no guarantee that coastal gardens will become less foggy. In fact, higher temperatures inland could pull fog over the coastal area more often. In addition, we are seeing a global trend toward less predictable rainfall. There is an increase in extremely heavy rains that can cause flooding (over 2 inches in 24 hours) at the same time that other areas are suffering prolonged drought. And the overall warming trend is causing polar ice caps to melt. If these glaciers were to melt completely, the oceans would rise to a level that puts much of the Bay Area underwater. Already, low lying islands off the coast of India are noticing losses of their coastal land.

The effect on plants is varied, and not always good. Some tender perennial plants will survive longer if winters are milder, while other plants, ones that need winter chill to flower or bear fruit, will suffer. Plants that require winter chill include most of the deciduous fruit trees, as well as grapes. Warmer summers near the coast would improve the performance of summer crops like tomatoes, however even heat-loving crops have limits. As inland gardeners sometimes discover, heat over 95°F will slow production of tomatoes, beans, and strawberries.

Plants can also be killed by prolonged periods of very hot weather. This is because respiration continues to increase with rising temperatures, but photosynthesis does not. Photosynthesis must exceed respiration so that the plant will have enough stored food reserves to continue respiration and growth. The metabolic imbalance created by high temperatures was responsible for $10 billion in agricultural losses in the European heat wave of 2003, and that heat wave was probably only an opening salvo of the coming global climate change.

Because of these observed effects and predictions, many informed people have been working, on a personal and political level, to reduce the "carbon footprint," meaning the amount of CO_2 produced by individual habits and by practices of world economic systems. At the present, the United States is adding the most CO_2 to the atmosphere per person, and China, while adding far less per person, is increasing the amount it adds at the fastest rate. Personal, corporate, national, and international efforts to slow the process of climate change are starting, however much more change is needed if we are to prevent the worst effects.

Resources:

- To learn more about global warming and actions you can take to help combat it, see the website of the Union of Concerned Scientists (www.uscusa.org/global_warming)
- To take part in a citizen project to study how plants are reacting to climate change, as expressed by their bloom times, see Project BudBurst (www.windows.ucar.edu/citizen_science/budburst)
- For a record of rising CO_2 levels in the atmosphere that are causing the warming trend, see the CRCHandbook of Chemistry and Physics (look for it in the reference room of a library).

APPENDIX II

Using Scientific Plant Names

In each heading for a plant discussed in this book, you will find a scientific name. After the scientific name, you will find the common and Latin names of the plant family to which it belongs. For example, for potato (page 251), the scientific name *Solanum tuberosum* is given. On the following line, you see: Nightshade Family ❖ *Solanaceae*.

The scientific name of a plant species contains two words. The first word is the name of the genus it belongs to; the second identifies the particular species within the genus. The two words of the scientific name are always written in italics. If the plant species has a naturally occurring variety or a subspecies, that name is also written in italics. (See, for example, celeriac on page 208.) The genus name is capitalized, but the species and variety names are not.

If a species has a cultivar, or human-created variety, that name is also written after the species name. It is not in italics, but it is capitalized and in single quotes. For example, *Solanum tuberosum* 'Yellow Finn', commonly known as 'Yellow Finn' potato. (For more on cultivars, see pages 42–44.)

Sometimes a scientific name will be followed by another one, the second in parentheses. This means that the international body that decides plant names has changed the name. This can happen for several reasons, a very common one today being the use of genetic analysis, which shows plant relationships more clearly and reveals a plant to be misclassified. The name in parentheses is the former name.

When many cultivars have been developed from the same species, the cultivars are sometimes informally divided into groups of similar cultivars, such as "Sugar snap type peas" or "Beefsteak type tomatoes."

Sometimes the cultivars are even divided into semiformal groups. For example, the onion species, *Allium cepa*, has been divided into the groups *Cepa* (common onion), *Aggregatum* (potato onion and shallot), *Fistulosum* (bunching onion) and *Proliferum* (top onion). When this is the case, you will find these semiformal group names in the heading under the species name (see the various onion listings).

Knowing plant scientific names sometimes helps you to find the plant you want, as each plant has only one scientific name. It can also help you understand the relationships among plants. There are often similarities in the flavors of related edible plants, in how you grow them, and in the pests that plague them.

Plant Families Mentioned in This Book That Have New Scientific Names

Common Names	Traditional Family Name	Modern Family Name
Carrot Family	*Umbelliferae*	*Apiaceae*
Grass Family	*Graminae*	*Poaceae*
Mint Family	*Labiatae*	*Laminaceae*
Mustard Family	*Cruciferae*	*Brassicaceae*
Pea Family	*Leguminosae*	*Fabaceae*
Sunflower Family	*Compositae*	*Asteraceae*

The names of some plant families have been changed. This was done because botanists wanted all plant family names to end in the letters "aceae," and this ending was not proper Latin spelling for the old names. Though these names have been changed, the older names are still widely used and more familiar to many. In plant headings throughout this book, I have given the new family name first, followed by the older name in parentheses.

APPENDIX III

Inland Planting Calendars

The calendars in this appendix show suggested planting dates for two inland locations: San Jose and Walnut Creek. Both of these locations have warmer, less foggy summers than near-Bay or near-ocean locations, and the period during which winter frost can happen in these places is a bit longer. The two cities represent two slightly different inland microclimates.

San Jose, in Santa Clara County, at the south end of San Francisco Bay, is representative of Zone 16 in the well-known climate zone system published by *Sunset* magazines and books. Here, summers are warm to hot, and although winter here can drop to lower temperatures than near the coast, the winter temperature of San Jose is often higher than in San Francisco. Strips of this favored climate exist from Marin County (Fairfax) southward through the state as far as Point Conception.

Walnut Creek, in central Contra Costa County, represents a climate with hot summers and winter lows a bit lower than in Zone 16. It is representative of the climate *Sunset* calls Zone 15. This climate forms relatively wide bands from Klamath County in the north into Marin County, through much of Sonoma and Napa counties, the Central San Francisco Peninsula, inland areas of Santa Cruz and Monterey counties, and a strip from San Simeon to Santa Maria.

I compiled both of these calendars using data provided by Master Gardeners and other volunteers with long vegetable gardening experience in the counties represented, and to some extent from existing planting calendars for the two regions. As with the calendars in Chapter 3, I urge you to experiment and test limits. Our terrain is so complex that you may be in a microclimatic pocket quite different from the surrounding area, or it may be that the gardeners who advised on these calendars didn't try a particular crop in a particular month. (Feedback is welcome if you can contribute new information for these calendars.)

In some ways, these calendars are quite similar to the near-Bay and near-ocean calendars in Chapter 3. October and November are good months to plant garlic throughout the region. Gardeners in all of our microclimates will be planting bush beans and tomatoes in May and June. And fava beans will be going into the ground both inland and coast-side in late winter and then again in the fall.

However, there are some significant differences. In these more inland climates, you will find the warmth-preferring crops grow bigger and faster, while fewer cool-preferring crops can grow in summer. These inland calendars have summer breaks in planting dates for a number of cool-preferring crops, like carrots and broccoli. And note that the break often ends a bit earlier in San Jose than in the hotter Walnut Creek. But notice that there are still plenty of planting dates for cool-preferring crops in fall through late winter. These crops are far hardier than many of us expect. The root crops will be fine underground as long as they have matured before winter cold strikes. And broccoli, chard, and many others tolerate a surprising amount of frost. As I mention earlier, Binda Colebrook's *Winter Gardening in the Maritime Northwest* originally inspired me to write this book. If she could enjoy winter harvests in Washington State, so can you!

Planting Times for San Jose Region—Santa Clara County

	January	February	March	April	May	June	July	August	September	October	November	December
Artichoke (bareroot)	■	■	■									■
Bean, fava		■	■						■	■		
Bean, scarlet runner				░	■	■						
Bean, snap (bush)				░	■	■						
Bean, snap (pole)				░	■	■						
Beet		■	■	■	■	■	■	■	░			
Broccoli (plants)		■	■	■				■	■	■		
Brussels sprouts (plants)							■	■				
*Cabbage (plants)		■	■	■			■	■				
Carrot		■	■	■					■			
*Cauliflower (plants)		■	■	■					■			
Celery (plants)		■	■					■	■			
*Chinese cabbage		■	■					■	■			
Collards			■	■				■	■			
Corn, sweet				?	░	■	■					
Cucumber				■	■	■						
Eggplant (plants)				░■	■	■						
Garlic (sets)										■	■	
Kale			■	■				■	■			
Kohlrabi (plants)		■	■	?				■	■			
*Leek		■	■	■	■	?						
Lettuce	■	■	■	■				░	■	■	■	
Melon				■	■	■						
Mustard	░	■	■	?				?	■	■		
Okra					░	■						
*Onion, bulb (seeds)								■	■			
Onion, bulb (sets)											■	■
Parsnip		■	■					░	■	░		
Pea (any kind)								░	■	░		
Pepper (plants)				░	■	■						
Potato (sets)		■	■	■								
Radish (small)	░	■	■	■	■	■	■	■	■	■	░	
*Radish (winter)									■	■		
Rhubarb (bareroot)	■	■	■									░
Shallot (sets)								■	■			
*Spinach		■	■	■					■	■		
Squash, summer			░	■	■	■	■					
Squash, winter				■	■	■						
Sunflower				■	■	■	■	■				
Swiss chard		■	■	■	■				■	■		
Tomato (plants)				░■	■	■						
Turnip		■	■	■				■	■			

KEY: ■ A heavily shaded area means it is okay to plant this crop at these times.

░ A lightly shaded area means that these times will work for some varieties, in some locations, and/or in some years.

Planting Times for Walnut Creek Region—Central Contra Costa County

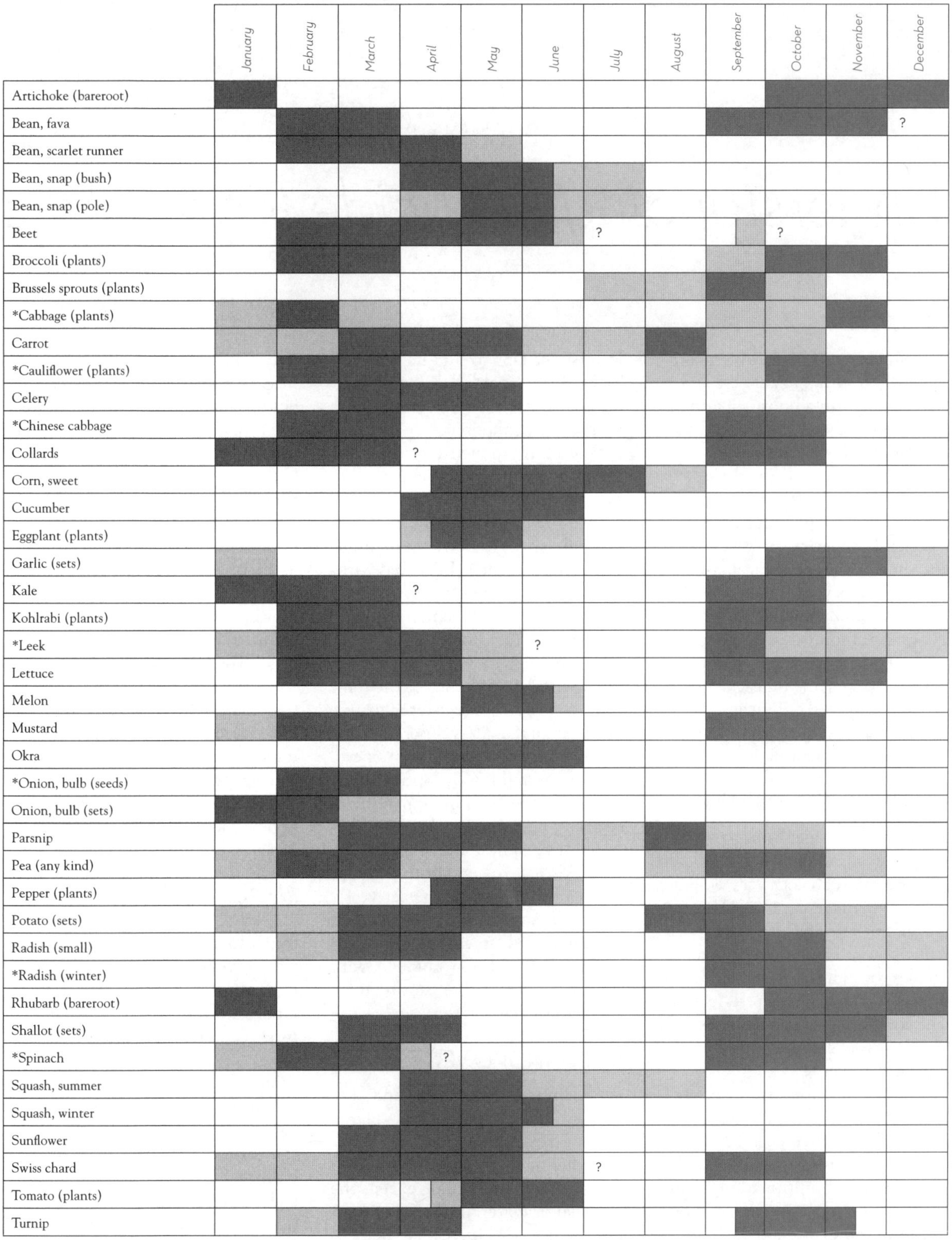

	January	*February*	*March*	*April*	*May*	*June*	*July*	*August*	*September*	*October*	*November*	*December*
Artichoke (bareroot)												
Bean, fava												?
Bean, scarlet runner												
Bean, snap (bush)												
Bean, snap (pole)												
Beet							?			?		
Broccoli (plants)												
Brussels sprouts (plants)												
*Cabbage (plants)												
Carrot												
*Cauliflower (plants)												
Celery												
*Chinese cabbage												
Collards				?								
Corn, sweet												
Cucumber												
Eggplant (plants)												
Garlic (sets)												
Kale				?								
Kohlrabi (plants)												
*Leek						?						
Lettuce												
Melon												
Mustard												
Okra												
*Onion, bulb (seeds)												
Onion, bulb (sets)												
Parsnip												
Pea (any kind)												
Pepper (plants)												
Potato (sets)												
Radish (small)												
*Radish (winter)												
Rhubarb (bareroot)												
Shallot (sets)												
*Spinach				?								
Squash, summer												
Squash, winter												
Sunflower												
Swiss chard							?					
Tomato (plants)												
Turnip												

KEY (cont.):

? — A question mark (?) means that you may sometimes be able to extend planting times even beyond the end of the lightly shaded area, though not commonly.

* — An asterisk before the name of a crop (*) means that varieties of the crop have widely differing preferred planting times. For example, most winter radishes should be planted from midsummer into fall, but some varieties can be planted in the spring.

APPENDIX IV

Understanding Pesticide Ingredients

Throughout this book, I've encouraged you to think about pest management in a holistic manner, considering the entire web of living creatures and forming a management strategy that disrupts the environment as little as possible, which often means stopping short of chemical tactics. However, there are times when a chemical, used judiciously, is your best option. For example, sulfur, applied at the right times, can limit tomato russet mite damage while sparing predatory mites. Or, spraying oil each winter when a fruit tree is dormant can reduce a host of problems when the tree leafs out in spring.

ACTIVE INGREDIENTS

When you consider using a pesticide, the first thing you should learn about it is which active ingredient, or ingredients, it contains. This is printed on the label, and when you know the active ingredient of a pesticide, you can research it to find out how it works against a pest, its acute and long-term toxicity, its effects on the environment, and how long it remains active.

You can learn a little about the active ingredient by reading the label. (See page 109 for more on reading labels.) You will also find much information at the website of the National Pesticide Information Center, or you can call and ask them questions (see Appendix VII, Resources for Gardeners). Or conduct a web search for a product along with the letters "MSDS" to find its Material Safety Data Sheet. While you can do this yourself, I've researched a number of common active ingredients used in products registered for use on food crops and have made recommendations on usage.

In the time since this book was first published, the Environmental Protection Agency (EPA) has withdrawn some of the more toxic and environmentally disruptive active ingredients from home gardener use, or manufacturers have voluntarily withdrawn them. At the same time, the EPA has registered many newly available active ingredients, adding choices that are less toxic to humans and less disruptive to the environment. This appendix reflects some of these changes. I've added several new active ingredients. Also, at the end of this appendix is a list of some of the active ingredients mentioned (though not recommended) in earlier editions of this book, but now not sold, with short notes about their status and the hazards they present.

INERT INGREDIENTS

Between previous editions and this one, the EPA also took some actions concerning pesticide inert ingredients. Inert ingredients are everything in a pesticide except the material or materials intended to kill the pest. An inert ingredient may help an active one dissolve in water, make a product easier to apply, spread a product over leaves or soil and make it stick there, move the active ingredient into insects' bodies, stabilize the product for a longer shelf life, or make the product more effective in some other way. Inerts have historically been considered trade secrets, so they have not been revealed by pesticide manufacturers or listed on labels. To communicate at least a hint that "inert ingredients" may have negative aspects, the EPA is now encouraging pesticide manufacturers to use the word "other" rather than "inert."

The EPA decided that, though they may be inert as far as the target pests were concerned, some inert ingredients were significant poisons. The agency has been reviewing these ingredients, and after their review they have forbidden the use of several in any pesticides and classified others they have studied into four Reassessment Status Lists.

Inert ingredients of highest toxicological concern, grouped on the EPA's first Reassessment Status List, must now be listed on the label, and their toxicity is taken into account when determining the Signal Word for a label. Materials on their fourth list, those of minimal toxicological concern, and a very few of those on the third list are permitted by the National Organic Program. While these changes do not completely take the mystery out of inert ingredients, we now know that if a product is approved for organic farmers—for example if it bears the "OMRI Listed" logo—there are no inerts in it that the EPA deems seriously harmful.

If you really need to know everything that is in a pesticide besides the active ingredient, you may be able to find out through the manufacturer or by filing a Freedom of Information Act request. The National Pesticide Information Center (see Appendix VII) says that it is standard procedure for the government to send a denial letter for such a Freedom of Information Act request, but that you should challenge the denial and persist.

MINIMAL RISK PESTICIDES

Another development in pesticide regulation is that in 1996 the EPA created a new class of products known as "minimum risk pesticides." These don't need to have an EPA registration number on their labels. The EPA's goal was to let manufacturers create pesticides that present little or no risk without having to go through an expensive and time-consuming registration process. These are also often called "exempt" pesticides. Another EPA goal in creating this category is to free resources for the study and regulation of higher-risk pesticides.

To be exempt, a pesticide's active and inert ingredients must come from lists of materials judged to be "demonstrably safe for the intended use." There are thirty-one exempt active ingredients, including clove oil, citric acid, and thyme oil. There is a longer list of permissible, or exempt, inert ingredients, such as glycerine, mineral oil, and vitamin E.

There are specific rules for the labels of exempt products. For these products, all of the ingredients, active or not, must be listed on the label. Materials from the exempted inerts list can't be listed as active ingredients unless they are also on the exempt active ingredient list, and then they can't be listed as both. Note that these are federal laws, but state regulatory agencies may have more stringent registration requirements, so it's possible that a federally approved minimal risk pesticide might not be available in a particular state unless it also meets state requirements.

NOTES AND EXPLANATIONS ABOUT THE FOLLOWING LISTING OF PESTICIDE ACTIVE INGREDIENTS

Material Name: The name of the active ingredient. If the active ingredient is an organism, such as a bacterium, I have given the scientific name of that organism.

Brand Name(s): These are sample brand names used for pesticides that contain the particular active ingredient. These are the names you will see written large on the label, such as Sluggo or Garden Defense Spray. Sometimes the brand name includes the name of the active ingredient, but often you have to read the fine print to find out the active ingredient(s) in a pesticide.

Material Type: The chemically simplest active ingredients are chemical elements and simple compounds containing them. Some elements used as pesticides, such as sulfur, iron, or copper, are actually plant nutrients, though it is possible to use too much copper in pesticide applications, making the soil toxic to plants. Poisonous elements such as arsenic or mercury were once used as pesticides, but when we understood that we were also poisoning ourselves, their use was discontinued.

Many active ingredients are not simple inorganic compounds but complex organic ones. Plants contain organic chemicals that help protect them against pests, and some pesticides, known as botanicals, consist of extracts of these chemicals. Examples are pyrethrum and neem. The main trait that botanicals share is that they break down quickly into simpler compounds and don't remain to pollute our environment. Contrary to common belief, they are not necessarily low in toxicity to life forms you didn't intend to kill, such as yourself or a honeybee. Nicotine has been used as a pesticide in the past, but its use was discontinued because it is extremely toxic to humans. And rotenone, which has long been approved for use on organic crops, lost its EPA registration for farm and garden use in 2006.

The mid-twentieth century saw the first of the human-created synthetic organic pesticides. These active ingredients are *organic compounds*, complex compounds containing carbon, but they are not compounds that normally exist in living creatures. They enter a living creature masquerading as a normal life-created chemical, but they don't work in living systems, so they injure or kill the creature. The first of these, DDT, was withdrawn because it bioaccumulated in animals. Later synthetics didn't, but a number have been withdrawn from the market or restricted, to limit their ill effects on our health and on the environment.

Research has shifted to less problematic materials. Soaps, oils, and pesticides based on a living microbe or a toxin it produces are all represented. The development of microbial pesticides is particularly promising. Bt, an early microbial pesticide, consists of a living bacterium that infects and kills its host. *Bacillis subtilis* is a living organism, while spinosad is a toxin produced by a bacterium.

Category of Pesticide: Here I have listed the words used to describe what kind(s) of pest the active ingredient will kill. These terms include the type of pest, followed by the suffix *-icide*, meaning "to kill." In some cases the ingredient doesn't kill but repels, deters feeding, deters egg laying, or regulates growth (meaning it doesn't let a pest reach maturity).

Some Registered Uses: Samples of the pests of food crops for which the active ingredient is registered. Read labels to determine a full list of pests a particular pesticide is registered to control.

Acute Toxicity: Here I have reported the LD50s for the active ingredients, and often some further comments about acute effects on mammals. As discussed on page 109, the LD50 represents the amount that killed 50 percent of test animals, usually rats, mice, or rabbits. (You can learn what animals were used by reading MSDS forms or other summaries of information about an active ingredient.) The oral LD50 (from eating the active ingredient) and the dermal LD50 (from skin exposure) are expressed in milligrams per kilogram of body weight, so a lower LD50 means it takes less of an ingredient to kill a creature.

The "signal words" to be displayed on a label are determined by a summary of what is known of LD50s. It may include information on dermal or inhalation LD50, but if the oral LD50 alone is considered, the relationship is as follows: LD50 up to 50 mg/kg = Danger (I; restricted to professional use); LD50 50 to 500 mg/kg = Warning (II); LD50 500 to 5,000 mg/kg = Caution (III); LD50 > 5,000 mg/kg = Caution (IV). (Take into account that the LD50 of the active ingredient may not be the same as that of the finished pesticide product, if the active ingredient is only a small percentage of the final product.)

Fortunately, many of the currently available pesticides have a relatively high LD50, but this doesn't mean there are not hazards to being exposed to them. Because of this, it is important to follow safety precautions that are on the label and treat every pesticide as a poison.

Long-Term Health Hazards: Toxicity is a complex matter. The LD50 may sound like a relatively tidy summation, but it is not. Look further than the acute symptoms to see what other hazards the chemical might create. Ideally, a pesticide would affect only the target organism, but often it can interfere with mammalian, and therefore human, systems in ways that cause lasting damage. For example, ingesting a sublethal amount of metaldehyde, once the main active ingredient available to kill snails, can result in mental deficiencies and memory loss for up to a year. And exposure to malathion—one of the last of the synthetic organic group called organophosphates left on the market—causes damage to the central nervous system, immune system, adrenal glands, liver, and blood.

Environmental Hazards: In addition to mammalian toxicity, the EPA studies the effect of active ingredients on various components of the living environment: birds, fish, the aquatic invertebrates on which fish feed, earthworms, and beneficial insects. Honeybees are often the only beneficial insect tested, but if these insects are killed, you know that other beneficial bees and wasps will also be killed.

Breakdown: Chemicals we use in the garden go into the soil, water, and air, where they do or do not break down into simpler compounds. Elements like copper and sulfur remain what they are or enter into living systems. Vegetable oils or soaps are digested by microbes. Natural or synthetic organic toxins have the capacity to continue to poison until they break down into simpler compounds, and their breakdown products may also be toxic. They may break down faster in certain conditions, such as sunlight, sandy soil, or in warm temperatures. It used to be felt that long-lasting toxins were a boon, since they killed pests longer, but now we know that it is better to use short-lasting toxins, to spare beneficial creatures. When a material breaks down over time, the term "half-life" is used to mean the period it takes for half of it to break up into simpler compounds.

Recommendation: Brief comments on which active ingredients are preferable or should be avoided.

PESTICIDE ACTIVE INGREDIENTS

Bacillus Subtilis (QST 713 strain)

Brand Name(s): Rhapsody, Serenade
Material Type: Living bacterium
Category of Pesticide: Fungicide
Registered Uses for Food Crops: Botrytis, downy mildews, fire blight, tomato late blight, powdery mildews, others
Acute Toxicity:
LD50 (oral): >5,000 mg/kg
LD50 (dermal): >5,000 mg/kg
The bacterium is not known to cause human disease. Prolonged skin exposure may elicit an allergic response. No toxic effects were reported for oral or inhalation trials with laboratory animals.
Long-Term Health Hazards: None known.
Environmental Hazards: Ubiquitous in the environment. Practically nontoxic to mammals, birds, or insects.
Breakdown: Living organism, may die in dry conditions. Remnants aren't hazardous to environment.
Recommendations: Use nonchemical pest management methods in preference. Consider use of this material when these aren't practical.

Bacillus Thuringiensis (Bt) subspecies Kurstaki (Btk)

Brand Name(s): Dipel, Bt Worm Killer, Caterpillar Killer
Material Type: Living bacterium and a toxin it produces
Category of Pesticide: Insecticide
Registered Uses for Food Crops: The subspecies *kurstaki* kills caterpillars, other subspecies kill beetles, still others kill fly larvae.
Acute Toxicity:
LD50 (oral): >8,100 mg/kg
LD50 (dermal): >7,200 mg/kg
LD50 (inhalation): >5,000 mg/kg
Avoid getting Bt in your eyes or in open wounds, as it is irritating and could cause a treatable eye ulcer.
Long-Term Health Hazards: Rarely, humans develop allergic reaction after exposure to high doses of Bt.
Environmental Hazards: Proved nontoxic to birds and fish. May be toxic to aquatic invertebrates.
Breakdown: The toxin produced by Bt breaks down rapidly in sunlight. Remnants aren't hazardous to environment.
Recommendations: Use nonchemical pest management methods in preference. Consider use of Bt when

those aren't practical or appropriate. Freshly mixed wettable powders will be most effective.

Capsaicin

Brand Name(s): Hot Pepper Wax Insect Repellent, Deer Off, Squirrel Away
Material Type: Botanical extract (from hot peppers)
Category of Pesticide: Pest mammal repellent, insecticide, miticide, feeding depressant
Registered Uses for Food Crops: Aphids, spider mites, whiteflies, pest mammal repellent
Acute Toxicity:
LD50 (oral): The oral LD50 for humans has been estimated at 0.5 to 5 g/kg.
Capsaicin can cause skin irritation but little is absorbed through the skin. Spray in the eyes can cause temporary blindness. Inhalation temporarily causes coughing, bronchoconstriction, nausea, and upper body incoordination.
Long-Term Health Hazards: Workers chronically exposed to capsaicin may develop a low cough threshold or contact dermatitis. People who consume 90 to 250 mg of capsaicin per day (in jalapeño peppers) had a greater risk of stomach cancer than people who ate 0 to 29.9 mg of capsaicin a day.
Environmental Hazards: Birds do not detect capsaicin, and I found no bird or fish toxicity studies. The EPA waived the requirement for study of aquatic species, feeling that restrictive labeling would protect them. Capsaicin is toxic to honeybees and other beneficial insects.
Breakdown: Capsaicin has an estimated half-life in soil of 2 to 8 days. Soil bacteria digest it into simpler compounds.
Recommendations: Used as directed, capsaicin products are minimally environmentally disruptive. Don't spray flowers that bees may be using as a pollen source.

Captan

Brand Name(s): None found.
Material Type: Synthetic Organic Compound (Phthalate)
Category of Pesticide: Fungicide
Registered Uses for Food Crops: Mainly used to treat seed to prevent decay
Acute Toxicity:
LD50 (oral): 9,000–15,000 mg/kg
Captan is toxic to eyes and permanently damaged eyes of rabbits exposed.
Long-Term Health Hazards: Over time, captan has been shown to cause cancer in rats and mice and is considered a probable human carcinogen. The EPA has suspended a number of food crop uses and continues to evaluate this chemical.
Environmental Hazards: Highly toxic to fish, moderately toxic to aquatic invertebrates. Relatively nontoxic to honeybees.
Breakdown: Half-life in soil is 1 to 10 days. Half-life on plants is 3 to 13 days.
Recommendations: This is less commonly sold than it once was. Avoid it by not using treated seed.

Carbaryl

Brand Name(s): Sevin
Material Type: Synthetic Organic Compound (Carbamate)
Category of Pesticide: Insecticide
Registered Uses for Food Crops: Flea beetle, imported cabbageworm, corn earworm, cutworm, earwig, tomato hornworm, pill bug, sow bug
Acute Toxicity:
LD50 (oral): 300 to 700 mg/kg
LD50 (dermal): >2,000 mg/kg
Cats were the most sensitive mammal tested, with an oral LD50 of 125 to 250 mg/kg.
Long-Term Health Hazards: Considered likely to cause cancer in humans, but animal testing is inadequate.
Environmental Hazards: Practically nontoxic to birds, moderately toxic to fish, but highly toxic to honeybees and other helpful insects on treated crops. When applied to soil, it kills earthworms, ground beetles, and other helpful creatures. Mite outbreaks often follow applications of carbaryl, since predator mites are more sensitive to the spray than pest mites.
Breakdown: Half-life in water with neutral pH is 12 days, in acidic water (pH 5) it is 1,600 days. In soil with air, the half-life is 4 days; without air, 72 days.
Recommendations: Depend on nonchemical pest management methods. Use other substances, such as oils, soaps, Bt, neem, or spinosad if they are registered for the pest. The EPA has withdrawn a number of uses of this chemical, and many products have also been voluntarily withdrawn, so it is less commonly found in home garden products.

Chlorothalonil

Brand Name(s): Fung-onil, Bravo, Daconil
Material Type: Synthetic organic compound (chloronitrile)
Category of Pesticide: Fungicide
Registered Uses for Food Crops: Botrytis, celery late blight, onion downy mildew, peach leaf curl, others
Acute Toxicity:
LD50 (oral): >5,000 mg/kg
LD50 (dermal): >5,000 mg/kg
Irritating to the respiratory tract if inhaled; harmful to eyes; skin allergic reactions are possible. Skin and eye hazards are severe enough to give some formulations of this ingredient a Danger (I) rating.
Long-Term Health Hazards: This substance is toxic to the kidneys and is suspected of causing kidney tumors.
Environmental Hazards: Practically nontoxic to birds and mammals, relatively nontoxic to honeybees, very toxic to fish and to aquatic invertebrates.
Breakdown: Half-life is one to two months. One of its breakdown products is moderately toxic to birds and highly toxic to fish.
Recommendations: Use nonchemical methods of pest management in preference. As a fungicide, use *Bacillus subtilis*, sulfur, superior oils, or neem oil in preference when they are registered for the pest you have.

Copper Sulfate (Tribasic Copper Sulfate)

Brand Name(s): Microcop
Material Type: Inorganic mineral compound

Category of Pesticide: Fungicide
Registered Uses for Food Crops: Celery late blight, peach leaf curl, fireblight
Acute Toxicity:
LD50 (oral): 472 mg/kg (for copper, in rats)
Acute poisoning causes burning internal pain, intense nausea, diarrhea, headache, and stoppage of urination. Acute copper poisoning damages the spleen, liver, and kidneys and may also injure the brain and gastrointestinal tract. It is readily absorbed through the skin, producing the same symptoms as if ingested. Skin contact can also cause itching and eczema.
Long-Term Health Hazards: Chronic poisoning causes anemia and lack of appetite, and studies in animals show testes and endocrine gland are affected. Liver disease has been documented in vineyard sprayers after 3 to 15 years of exposure.
Environmental Hazards: Relatively nontoxic to birds. Highly toxic to fish and to aquatic invertebrates. Its use in orchards kills most animal soil life, including large earthworms. Copper is a micronutrient, but it can build up to toxic levels if used repeatedly, so its usefulness as a pesticide is limited.
Breakdown: Some is bound to the soil, some leaches down through the soil, some reacts with oxygen to form other compounds.
Recommendations: Concentrate on preventive methods to avoid fungus disease. Use other substances, such as *Bacillus subtilis*, sulfur, superior oils, and neem oil, in preference when they are registered for the disease you are combating.

Glyphosate

Brand Name(s): Buccaneer, Roundup, Total Kill Brand
Material Type: Synthetic chemical (category unavailable)
Category of Pesticide: Non-selective herbicide
Registered Uses for Food Crops: A non-specific weed killer that is not registered for use near food crops.
Acute Toxicity:
LD50 (oral): 750 to >5,000 mg/kg
LD50 (dermal): >5,000 mg/kg
Exposure can result in burning or itching skin; swollen eyes, face, or joints; chest pain; coughing; high heart rate and blood pressure; headache; and nausea.
Long-Term Health Hazards: Glyphosate has been shown to be associated with late spontaneous abortions, possibly due to damage to placental cells. Recent studies suggest a relationship between use of glyphosate and non-Hodgkin lymphoma. Roundup appears to be more toxic than glyphosate alone.
Environmental Hazards: Binds to soil and was once thought not to enter groundwater, but so much is being used in agriculture that it is contaminating water. Thought to be relatively low in toxicity to fish, birds, aquatic invertebrates, and earthworms, but reassessments are probably needed in view of continuing toxicity studies.
Breakdown: Half-life of up to 19 weeks in sandy soil, or as little as 3 weeks in loam. Most of the breakdown is due to bacterial action. Herbicidal action in soil lasts 1 to 2 weeks.
Recommendations: Use nonchemical weed control methods in preference to chemical, and less-toxic herbicides such as ones based on clove oil, citric acid, or soaps, in preference to glyphosate.

Iron Phosphate

Brand Name(s): Slug Magic, Escar-go!, Sluggo (Escar-go! Supreme and Sluggo Plus also contain spinosad—see information on it on page 397)
Material Type: Inorganic mineral compound
Category of Pesticide: Molluscicide
Registered Uses for Food Crops: Snails and slugs
Acute Toxicity:
LD50 (oral): >5,000 mg/kg
LD50 (dermal): >5,000 mg/kg
Long-Term Health Hazards: None known.
Environmental Hazards: None known.
Breakdown: Fairly common in the environment. The ions in the compound act as plant nutrients.
Recommendations: Always use cultural and mechanical methods of controlling snails and slugs, with chemical methods as backup. Use iron phosphate baits in preference to metaldehyde baits.

Lime Sulfur (Calcium Polysulfide)

Brand Name(s): Mostly sold just as lime sulfur
Material Type: Inorganic mineral compound
Category of Pesticide: Fungicide, insecticide, miticide
Registered Uses for Food Crops: Overwintering insect eggs, mites, peach leaf curl, brown rot
Acute Toxicity:
LD50 (oral): 512 to 712 mg/kg
LD50 (dermal): 2,000 mg/kg
Some people are particularly sensitive to sulfur-based materials, so protective clothing and gear is needed to avoid possible irritation of eyes, ears, nose, and skin. Direct contact with this chemical will cause skin irritation and eye damage.
Long-Term Health Hazards: Only from exposure to near-lethal doses of the gas H_2S (see Breakdown).
Environmental Hazards: In mammals, causes eye damage and skin irritation.
Breakdown: Leaves a sulfur residue, which continues to have a pesticidal action. If it comes into contact with acids, lime sulfur yields the gas H_2S, which is quite toxic, though high concentrations of this gas are unlikely during ordinary use as a pesticide in well-ventilated areas.
Recommendations: Check to see whether the pest you seek to control can be managed by sulfur alone or by an oil spray before you use the more caustic lime sulfur.

Malathion

Brand Name(s): Malathion is usually part of the name.
Material Type: Synthetic organic compound (organophosphate)
Category of Pesticide: Insecticide
Registered Uses for Food Crops: Aphid, imported cabbageworm, cabbage looper, grasshopper, leafminer, red spider mite, onion maggot (fly), whitefly, pill bug, and sow bug

Acute Toxicity:
LD50 (oral): 5,400 to 5,700 mg/kg
LD50 (dermal): 2,000 mg/kg
Toxicity depends in part on sex, with female mammals being more susceptible, and low protein intake increasing susceptibility. A single dose may affect future immune system response.
Long-Term Health Hazards: Reproductive toxicity. Damage to central nervous system, immune system, adrenal glands, liver, and blood.
Environmental Hazards: Very toxic to honeybees, to aquatic stages of amphibians, and to aquatic invertebrates. Varies in toxicity to fish, depending on the species, from slightly (goldfish) to highly (brown trout) toxic. Moderately toxic to birds. May contain manufacturing contaminants that are more toxic than the malathion itself. With continued use, pests are likely to develop resistance to this chemical.
Breakdown: Half-life of 1 to 25 days in soil.
Recommendations: Use nonchemical methods of pest management in preference. If you use a chemical, use others in preference to malathion.

Metaldehyde

Brand Name(s): Bug-Geta Slug & Snail Bait, Deadline, Slug & Snail Death
Material Type: Synthetic chemical. This is the same material used as a fuel for camp stoves under the brand name Sterno.
Category of Pesticide: Molluscicide
Registered Uses for Food Crops: Snails, slugs
Acute Toxicity:
LD50 (oral): as little as 75 to 100 mg/kg has killed a child
LD50 (dermal): 2,275 to >5,000 mg/kg (rats)
Irritates skin, eye membranes, and upper airways. When metaldehyde is ingested, the kidney and liver are damaged; mental deficiencies and memory loss may persist for a year or longer.
Long-Term Health Hazards: Reproductive toxicity. Metaldehyde or its breakdown by-products may cause central nervous system problems and lesions in kidneys and liver. Repeated skin exposure may cause dermatitis and inflammation of eyes, airways, and digestive tract.
Environmental Hazards: Very toxic, and attractive, to dogs. Death of birds feeding where metaldehyde is used have been reported, with symptoms that strongly suggest metaldehyde poisoning, though no precise LD50 values are available. Toxic to domestic and wild mammals. Extremely toxic to aquatic invertebrates. Reportedly not toxic to honeybees when used as directed.
Breakdown: Half-life is on the order of several days.
Recommendations: Always use cultural and mechanical methods of controlling snails and slugs, with chemical methods as backup. Use iron phosphate baits in preference to metaldehyde baits.

Neem or Azadirachtin

Brand Name(s): Agroneem, Bioneem
Material Type: Botanical extract. A leaf extract is sold as neem, a seed extract as neem oil, and some products contain neem oil that has been made into a soap. They have different uses.
Category of Pesticide: Insecticide, insect growth regulator, egg-laying deterrent. Neem oil is a fungicide.
Registered Uses for Food Crops: Aphid, corn earworm, hornworm, imported cabbage worm, leaf miner, looper, scale, weevil, whiteflies, others. Neem oil is effective against aphids, mites, and other soft-bodied pests that other oils control and is labeled to combat botrytis and fungal diseases (in general).
Acute Toxicity:
LD50 (oral): >5,000 mg/kg
LD50 (dermal): 2,000 mg/kg
Moderately irritating to skin and eyes. Gloves recommended during use.
Long-Term Health Hazards: Reversible reproductive disruption in male rats and mice.
Environmental Hazards: No significant effects on other wildlife reported. Could harm aquatic invertebrates or fish if it polluted water. Insects that don't feed on plants aren't likely to eat enough to cause harm. Bee larvae fed heavily with pollen contaminated with neem could become unable to mature, so don't spray bee-pollinated plants when they are in flower. Earthworms fed neem leaves and ground neem seeds grew faster and survived better than ones fed a normal diet.
Breakdown: Breaks down in light or water after 100 hours. In most soil or aquatic environments, microbes would readily digest neem.
Recommendations: Use nonchemical pest management methods in preference. If you do use a chemical, choose superior oils, soap, Bt, or *Bacillis subtilis* in preference when they are registered for the pest you are combating. Use neem in preference to synthetic organic pesticides.

Oil, Superior (Petroleum) (Summer Oil, Narrow-Range Oil)

Brand Name(s): Ultra-Fine Spray Oil (most names include "spray oil")
Material Type: Petroleum Product (unsulfonated residue of paraffinic oil)
Category of Pesticide: Insecticide, miticide, fungicide
Registered Uses for Food Crops: Aphids (eggs), leafrollers, scale, mites, whiteflies, some fungi, more
Acute Toxicity:
LD50 (oral): >15,000 mg/kg
LD50 (dermal): >5,000 mg/kg
Long-Term Health Hazards: None found
Environmental Hazards: Low, in general. Toxic to fish.
Breakdown: They tend to evaporate rather than contaminating soils or groundwater. Unclear what happens to evaporates.
Recommendations: Concentrate on nonchemical means of managing pests. Use vegetable oil-based pesticides in preference to petroleum-based products.

Oil, Superior (Vegetable Oils) (Summer Oil, Narrow-Range Oil)

Brand Name(s): None in particular.
Material Type: Emulsifiable Vegetable Oil. These are products based on oils such as canola or soy oil. (See also neem oil within the Neem entry.)

Category of Pesticide: Insecticide, miticide
Registered Uses for Food Crops: Aphids (eggs), corn earworm, leafrollers, scale, whitefly, more
Acute Toxicity: Most are basically nontoxic.
Environmental Hazards: They are unlikely to have any effect on untargeted wildlife.
Breakdown: Digested quickly by microbes.
Recommendations: If you are choosing an oil spray, choose a vegetable oil spray over one made of petroleum products. (You will probably have to read the fine print to identify which spray oils are vegetable oils.)

Permethrin

Brand Name(s): Ambush, Pounce
Material Type: Synthetic organic compound (pyrethroid). Pyrethroids such as permethrin are synthetic compounds similar to naturally occurring pyrethrins.
Category of Pesticide: Insecticide
Registered Uses for Food Crops: Asparagus beetle, caterpillars, leaftiers, weevils (adult)
Acute Toxicity:
LD50 (oral): Varies widely among pyrethroids
Like pyrethrins, pyrethroids are neurotoxins. Many also produce skin irritation that may last for about two days.
Long-Term Health Hazards: Permethrin is considered likely to be carcinogenic to humans.
Environmental Hazards: Pyrethrins are highly toxic to fish and aquatic invertebrates and to honeybees. They are slightly toxic to birds, and become more so with increasing temperature. Causes deformities in tadpoles and is particularly toxic to cats.
Breakdown: Has a half-life of 1 to 3 weeks on plants, but can remain active in the sediment under a body of water for up to a year.
Recommendations: Use nonchemical methods of pest management when possible. If you do use a chemical, use oils, Bt, soaps, or neem in preference to pyrethrins, and use pyrethrins in preference to a pyrethroid such as permethrin.

Potassium Bicarbonate

Brand Name(s): Kaligreen, Greencure
Material Type: Inorganic mineral compound (KHCO4)
Category of Pesticide: Fungicide
Registered Uses for Food Crops: Offers at least partial control of powdery mildew.
Acute Toxicity:
LD50 (oral): 3,358 mg/kg (for Kaligreen, which is 82.5% potassium bicarbonate)
Long-Term Health Hazards: None reported
Environmental Hazards: Do not apply directly to bodies of water or allow it to contaminate water.
Breakdown: Relatively stable in the environment, but the ions of this compound (potassium and bicarbonate or carbonate ions) are very common in nature and don't have toxic effects.
Recommendations: Use nonchemical methods of preventing powdery mildew when possible. Use potassium carbonate in preference to sodium bicarbonate, since sodium is toxic to plants.

Potassium Salts of Fatty Acids

Brand Name(s): Insect Killing Soap, Insecticidal Soap, Fast Acting Weed and Grass Killer
Material Type: Soap
Category of Pesticide: Insecticide, miticide, herbicide. (The formulations for different purposes have different proportions of various fatty acids.)
Registered Uses for Food Crops: Aphid, whitefly, spider mites, earwig, others (see labels)
Other Registered Uses: Nonselective weed killer, effective against annual weeds
Acute Toxicity:
Extremely low toxicity for humans
Long-Term Health Hazards: None found
Environmental Hazards: When high concentrations of soaps contaminate waterways, algae grow rapidly and are considered pollutants. The soaps are also slightly toxic to fish and highly toxic to aquatic invertebrates. However, as commonly used by home gardeners, pesticidal soaps are much less likely to enter waterways than are soaps used in cleaning.
Breakdown: Half-life in soil is less than one day. Microbes digest them.
Recommendations: Consider nonchemical tactics first. Soap sprays are a minimally toxic pesticide. Oil sprays may work better when insect reproduction is rapid, since oils kill insect and mite eggs.

Pyrethrum and Pyretherins

Brand Name(s): Pyganic Crop Protection (pyrethrins), Pyola (pyrethrins with canola oil), Sure Fire Tomato and Vegetable Insect Killer (pyrethrins with soap)
Material Type: Botanical. Pyrethrum is the ground-up flowers of pyrethrum, a white daisy called *Tanacetum cinerarifolium*. Most pyrethrum pesticides contain active compounds extracted from it, called pyrethrins.
Category of Pesticide: Insecticide
Registered Uses for Food Crops: Aphids, cucumber beetle, whiteflies
Acute Toxicity:
LD50 (oral): Varies among pyrethrins from 200 to 2,600 mg/kg
LD50 (dermal): >1,800 mg/kg
Pyrethrum exposure is more dangerous for infants and children, who are not able to break it down efficiently, than for older humans. Inhalation of high levels of pyrethrum may cause asthmatic wheezing, sneezing, nasal stuffiness, headache, nausea, tremors, and convulsions.
Long-Term Health Hazards: As usually used, pyrethrum is considered one of the least toxic to mammals among pesticides. At high doses, it can damage the central nervous system and the immune system. Liquid formulations of pyrethrins often contain piperonyl butoxide, which reduces an insect's ability to detoxify pyrethrum, but is prohibited to organic farmers.
Environmental Hazards: Toxic to earthworms, fish, aquatic invertebrates, and honeybees.

Breakdown: Pyrethrum and pyrethrins break down quickly in light and air.
Recommendations: Use nonchemical pest management tactics in preference. Choose Bt, oils, or soaps, in preference to pyrethrum products.

Spinosad

Brand Name(s): Bull's Eye, Escar-Go! Supreme, Sluggo Plus
Material Type: Metabolic product of the actinomycete *Saccharopolysora spinosa*
Category of Pesticide: Insecticide
Registered Uses for Food Crops: Asparagus beetles, imported cabbageworms, leafminers, leafrollers, thrips, earwigs, sow and pill bugs, cutworms
Acute Toxicity:
LD50 (oral, rat): 3,738 (male), >5,000 mg/kg (female)
LD50 (dermal, rabbit): >5,000 mg/kg
If product gets in your eye, it hurts, but probably is only an irritant. Prolonged contact with skin may cause slight irritation and redness.
Long-Term Health Hazards: None found
Environmental Hazards: Practically nontoxic to birds; slightly toxic to aquatic invertebrates; slightly to moderately toxic to fish; highly toxic to marine mollusks. Highly toxic to honeybees in the first three hours after spraying. Once plant surfaces are dry, spinosad is generally safe for nonplant-feeding insects.
Breakdown: Half-life is 1.6 to 16 days (shorter in sunlight). In water, breaks down very quickly if sunlight reaches it; half-life can be up to 200 days in sunless water.
Recommendations: Use nonchemical methods in preference. Choose soaps, oils, or Bt in preference when they are registered for the pest in question. Choose spinosad over synthetic organic pesticides.

Sulfur

Brand Name(s): Product names usually include sulfur
Material Type: Mineral element
Category of Pesticide: Fungicide, Miticide
Registered Uses for Food Crops: Powdery mildew, leaf spot, rust, peach brown rot, apple scab, most mites
Acute Toxicity:
LD50 (oral): >5,000 mg/kg
LD50 (dermal): >5,000 mg/kg
Sulfur is considered to pose little if any risk to human and animal health. Some people are sensitive to sulfur-based materials, so a respirator mask and protective clothing are needed when you are using them. They can cause irritation to eyes, ears, nose, and skin. Water-soluble, sprayable formulations are easiest to apply.
Long-Term Health Hazards: Generally recognized as safe, though mine workers exposed to sulfur dioxide for many years often had eye and respiratory disturbances.
Environmental Hazards: Very low in toxicity to fish and honeybees, considered nontoxic to birds.
Breakdown: Sulfur is an element, so it does not break down. It enters biological compounds due to metabolic action of microbes. Some enter the air as sulfur dioxide.
Recommendations: Use nonchemical methods to control pests when possible, supplementing them, if necessary, with carefully timed applications of sulfur to manage diseases and mites for which it is labeled.

WHAT HAPPENED TO . . . ?

The following pesticide active ingredients—which were described, but not recommended, in earlier editions of *Golden Gate Gardening*—are no longer available for home garden use.

Diazinon

An organophosphate insecticide that was phased out of residential uses in 2004. It has become much less common in drinking water since then. It is so toxic to birds that they may fall over dead if they walk on treated areas.

Methoxychlor

An organochlorine insecticide that the EPA denied registration in 2004. It causes liver and kidney damage.

Nicotine Sulfate

Voluntarily withdrawn from production, with an EPA registration to be cancelled in 2013. This botanical insecticide has an LD50 of 83 mg/kg and is extremely toxic to birds and other wildlife.

PCNB

An organochlorine fungicide no longer registered by the EPA for residential use since 2006. It causes liver damage and is suspected of causing cancer and prenatal damage. Toxic to fish and other aquatic organisms.

Rotenone

In 2006, the EPA declined to reregister rotenone for any use but that of killing unwanted fish species. Despite being permitted to organic farmers for many years, the botanical insecticide rotenone is highly toxic. It has a rat acute oral LD50 of only 102 mg/kg (males) and 39.5 mg/kg (females), and high exposure has recently been shown to produce Parkinson's disease–like symptoms. While it breaks down in about a week in sunlight, recent assessments have suggested that degradation products may be more toxic than the rotenone itself.

APPENDIX V

San Francisco Tomato Variety Trial Methods and Results: 1987–89

Saladette or Standard-Sized Varieties

Variety	Det or Ind	DTH	Earliness[1]	Production[2]	Size[3]	Flavor[4]
Celebrity VFFNTASt F_1	Det	70	Poor	Poor	Large	Poor
Early Girl VFF F_1	Ind	52–60	Good	Good	Small	Very Good
Early Pick F_1	Ind	62	Fair	Fair	Large	Good
Fantastic VF F_1	Ind	65–85	Poor	Poor	Small	Good
Floramerica VFF-NTStAsc F_1	Det	70	Poor	Poor	Med	Fair
Marmande (or Super Marmande)	Det	70–75	Good	Fair	Large	Good
Nepal	Ind	78	Fair	Poor	Large	Very Good
Oregon Spring	Det	55–70	Very Good	Poor	Large	Good
Quick Pick VNTMV F_1	Ind	68–79	Fair	Fair	Small	Poor
San Francisco Fog	Ind	70	Fair	Fair	Small	Fair
Santiam	Det	55–60	Good	Fair	Fair	Poor
Siberia	Det	55	Good	Fair	Fair	Fair
Stupice	Ind	52	Very Good	Very Good	Small	Very Good
Visitacion Valley	Ind	Unkn.	Very Good	Very Good	Med	Good

[1]Each year, seeds were sown indoors all on the same day and six-week old plants were set out all on the same day in early May. The first ripe fruit on the earliest bearing plants appeared by July 30. Most plants were bearing fruit by the end of August, though some varieties took until the end of October when they were growing in the chilliest sites.
[2]Total production by weight ranged from about 3 pounds to 22 pounds per plant.
[3]The largest size was just under three inches in diameter. Fruit this size weighs about 4 ounces. All the plants were unpruned.
[4]Based on public and private tastings.

Paste Varieties

Variety	Det or Ind	DTH	Earliness[1]	Production[2]	Fresh Flavor[3]	Paste Flavor[3]
La Roma F_1	Det	62	Fair	Fair	Good	Good
Nova	Det	Unkn.	Good	Fair	Fair	Fair
Roma VFA	Det	75	Poor	Poor	Fair	Fair
Ropreco	Det	70–75	Good	Good	Good	Good
Sprinter	Det	Unkn.	Good	Good	Very Good	Very Good

[1]The paste tomato trial took place during one year: 1989. Seeds were started indoors, and six-week-old plants were set out late, in the middle of June. (Although seeds were sown in the middle of March, they grew very slowly, due to overcast, cool conditions.) They all produced at about the same time, mostly throughout October, with some starting a bit earlier than others.
[2]Total production by weight ranged from about 12 to 29 pounds per plant.
[3]Based on a private tasting by food professionals.

Note: In all of the trials, we grew four to six of each variety in each site, and arranged them randomly so that position vis a vis sun, wind, or other factors wouldn't be an issue. We drew names from a hat to make the map showing the random arrangement we would use. We weighed the fruit from each plant and used standard USDA tomato sizing rings to size the fruit.

2009 SOURCES FOR ORIGINAL TRIAL TOMATOES

Celebrity: Widely available
Early Girl: BUR, GS, NGN, PGS, TERR, TGS, TT, VBS, WCS
Early Pick: BUR
Fantastic: TERR, TGS, TT
Floramerica: All-America Seed Selections, which awarded this variety its top award in 1978, says it is considered to be replaced by 'Celebrity'. None of the sources selected for the seed appendix of this book carry it, but is offered by Reimer Seeds (www.reimerseeds.com).
Marmande (Super Marmande): BCS, BG, GS, IST, JG, SOC, T&M, TGS, TT
Nepal: JSS, TGS
Oregon Spring: ABL, JSS, NGN, PGS, SOC, TERR, TGS, TT, WCS
Quick Pick: TERR
San Francisco Fog: TGS
Santiam: SOC, TERR
Siberian: ABL, BI, SSE, TGS, TT
Stupice: ABL, BG, CG, NGN, PGS, SESE, SOC, SSE, T&M, TERR, TGS, TT, WCS
Visitacion Valley: Sweetwater Organics sells plants only. They are a wholesale nursery in Sebastopol, CA, at (707) 823-1577, info@sweetwaterorganic.com.
La Roma F_1: TGS
Roma: TT
Nova: Unavailable
Ropreco: SOC
Sprinter: Unavailable

APPENDIX VI

Seed and Starter Plant Sources

In the following pages you will find contact information for the mail order seed and starter plant companies I've found useful over the years, plus a few I've recently discovered, with the codes I've used for them in source lists elsewhere in this book. I've also included some definitions of terms and concepts that will help you understand what a company is offering and how they do business.

TERMS AND CONCEPTS USEFUL WHEN YOU ARE BUYING SEEDS OR STARTER PLANTS

I wrote Chapter 5, Obtaining Seeds and Other Starts, to help you choose among the sources and varieties available. Following is a supplemental list of terms and concepts that provides more help in understanding information provided by seed and starter sources.

Days to Maturity (DTM)

In most cases, the "days to maturity" (DTM) or "days to harvest" means the time between planting the seed and beginning to harvest the crop. However, the custom for tomatoes and cole crops is to subtract the days it takes to grow a seedling big enough to plant out in the ground—4 to 6 weeks for tomatoes, 5 to 7 weeks for cole crops. Therefore, for example, a 70 DTM tomato plant is already 30 to 42 days old when you begin the count to 70 days.

Be aware that the DTM a seed company lists may refer to the place they are located and test seeds. Times could be somewhat different in say, Western Oregon and South Carolina. And of course in a Bay Area cool summer, or when overwintered, a variety may take longer than listed in a catalog.

Safe Seed Pledge

This pledge states that a company will not knowingly buy or sell genetically engineered seeds or plants. Most companies now print it on their websites and in their catalogs. In truth, it is unlikely that any home gardening seed company would be selling such seed, for two reasons: (1) it is so unpopular, and (2) besides a few sweet corn varieties and a virus-resistant squash, genetically engineered crops are not commonly created for sale to home gardeners.

If a company hasn't signed the pledge, you can certainly ask them their policy, but for the preceding reasons, it is unlikely that what they offer will be genetically engineered. In the unlikely eventuality that such seed ever becomes commonly offered, it will not be organic seed or heirloom seed.

Organic Seed

Certified organic seed has been harvested from plants that were raised according to the standards of the National Organic Program and have been legally certified as organic. Organic farmers are required to seek seed of a particular variety that was raised organically before they buy conventional seed. Home gardeners are not. Practically speaking, a seed is such a tiny part of a mature plant that if you garden organically, you can consider the crop organically grown. However, some gardeners favor organic seed because they want to encourage organic farming on land that grows seeds.

Biodynamic Seed

Certified biodynamic seed has been harvested from plants that were grown according to biodynamic principles. An organization known as the Demeter Association, Inc., certifies that seed has been produced in this way. There is no legal definition of biodynamic certification in this country, so these seeds are not "legally organic," unless they have also been through the organic certification process as well, though they may have been grown according to organic principles in addition to those of biodynamic farming.

Seed Trials

When a retailer buys seed from a seed wholesaler, sometimes the retailer germinates it to be sure that the germination rate is good, or grows it out to see if it is what it is claimed to be. If it is grown out, this can also reveal details such as flavor or tenderness that may not be in the general description received with the seed.

Variety Trials

In addition to the basic seed trial, some retailers have plots in which they can plant several varieties of a crop at the same time and compare the growth, production, flavor, and other traits, and then choose the best ones to sell. Some companies carry only tried-and-true varieties; others use variety trials to expand their knowledge and find new varieties or newly available heirlooms to sell.

Plant Breeding

Occasionally a retail seed company will also breed some new varieties. Burpee is famous for its vegetable and flower breeding programs. And Rob Johnston, founder of Johnny's Selected Seeds, created at least two new selections: 'Baby Bear' pumpkin, a small pumpkin with a proportional, narrow stem, and the multicolored Swiss chard mix 'Bright Lights'.

Large wholesale seed companies develop new plant varieties and offer them for sale to seed retailers. Plant breeding also goes on in universities as well as by freelance breeders. You may read about the sources of some seeds in variety descriptions. For example, Oregon State University's Dr. James Baggett developed early tomato and snap pea cultivars, and freelance plant breeder Dr. Alan Kapular develops various open-pollinated cultivars. In this region, freelance plant breeder Fred Hempel of Baia Nicchia is working to develop new tomato varieties.

Disease Resistance

Some crop varieties, open pollinated or hybrid, have the ability to stand up to particular diseases. In some cases, codes after the cultivar name will tell you which diseases they stand up to. For example, PM or PMR stands for "powdery mildew resistance." (There is a standardized code list, usually explained somewhere in a catalog. For information on some codes that relate to tomatoes, see page 275.)

The description "resists disease" is too general. Look in different catalogs to try to learn what such varieties resist, or contact a seed company to ask.

A variety said to "tolerate" a disease may show symptoms if the disease strikes, and could produce a crop anyway. A resistant plant is less likely to get the disease but could if it is grown poorly or if a new disease strain appears. A plant listed as immune will never get the disease.

Hybrid Seed

When a seed catalog lists a variety as a hybrid, they generally mean it is an F_1 hybrid (see page 43).

Heirloom Seed

An heirloom variety is one that has been passed down for a long time, generally from early in the twentieth century or before that. These varieties may have been selected from plants growing on a farm or in a garden, grown and passed from generation to generation, and then "discovered" for wider distribution. Or they may be very old commercial varieties.

An heirloom will always be an open-pollinated variety, since they have been grown from seed saved and passed on, whereas an F_1 hybrid seed will not breed true, so it couldn't have been passed on.

The word *heirloom* has an aura of treasure, but like the word *antique*, it basically means "old." While an old variety may well have been replaced by one that is better, many old varieties are truly treasures. Using heirloom seed, when it meets your preferences for the crop it produces, helps preserve genetic diversity and keep it in diverse hands, rather than letting hybrid seed producers have a monopoly.

Treated Seed

Seed, typically large seed like corn or beans, is sometimes treated with fungicides to prevent soil fungi from rotting it in cold, wet soil. Such seed is dyed a bright color, such as hot pink, so you won't handle it with bare hands. Conventional farmers use it to avoid costly seed losses, but it is not approved for organic farmers. Seed companies tell you when seed is treated, and usually you can request seed of the same variety untreated.

MAIL-ORDER SEED AND STARTER PLANT SOURCES

Following is updated contact information for many companies that offer seeds and small plants of vegetables, herbs, and flowers through the mail. While you can often find just what you need in a local store, having access to mail-order sources dramatically expands your options. I have included some information about each source and why you might want to shop there.

Since the last edition of *Golden Gate Gardening*, many of the following companies have created websites that go beyond the basics of seed or plant lists and order forms. I have seen videos of bluegrass (www.rareseeds.com); looked at antique catalog covers (www.burpee.com); read essays on the hoax of citronella pelargonium (www.richters.com); and found a detailed, illustrated guide to saving and cleaning seeds (www.seedsofchange.com). Another advantage of websites is that because they are less expensive to produce and change than print catalogs, a company often lists more seed varieties and other items on its website than are in the print catalog. In addition, a number of companies offer email newsletters or blogs to share more information.

Still, print catalogs are valuable resources. They often contain important growing tips. They are available for study wherever you are. And if you have the catalogs of several seed companies you can quickly compare the varieties offered by each. When different companies offer the same variety, you can learn more about it by reading blurbs in different catalogs. I also find it easier to compare prices, amounts, and shipping costs when I can flip through several print catalogs at once.

Catalog Codes

The source codes given elsewhere in this book stand for various seed and plant sources. Here's a list of the codes I've used:

- Abundant Life Seeds: ABL
- Annie's Annuals & Perennials: AA
- Baker Creek Heirloom Seeds: BCS
- Botanical Interests: BI
- Bountiful Gardens: BG
- Burpee Gardens: BUR
- The Cook's Garden: CG
- Evergreen Y.H. Enterprises: EE
- Gourmet Seed International: GS
- Italian Seed and Tool Company: IST
- J. L. Hudson, Seedsman: JLH
- Johnny's Selected Seeds: JSS
- Kitazawa Seed Company: KIT
- Le Jardin du Gourmet: JG
- Native Seeds/SEARCH: NSS
- Nichols Garden Nursery: NGN
- Park Seed Company: PS
- Pinetree Garden Seeds: PGS
- Redwood City Seed Company: RCS
- Renee's Garden: RG
- Richters Herb Specialists: RH
- Ronniger Potato Farm: RPF
- Seed Savers Exchange: SSE
- Seeds from Italy: SI
- Seeds of Change: SOC
- Select Seeds Company: SS
- Southern Exposure Seed Exchange: SESE
- Territorial Seed Company: TERR
- Thompson & Morgan: T&M
- Tomato Growers Supply Company: TGS
- Totally Tomatoes: TT
- Vermont Bean Seed Company: VBS
- West Coast Seeds: WCS

Abundant Life Seeds (ABL)
P.O. Box 279
Cottage Grove, OR 97424-0010
Phone: (541) 767-9606
Fax: (866) 514-7333
Customer service/gardening questions: (541) 767-9606
www.abundantlifeseeds.com
info@ abundantlifeseeds.com
Abundant Life Seed Foundation was founded in 1975 as a nonprofit to preserve heirloom varieties, many of them grown by a seed growers' network. After a disastrous fire in 2003, the foundation decided to focus on other aspects of variety preservation and let selling the seeds become a sister business of Territorial Seed Company. Seeds and starts offered are certified organic or biodynamic. Includes a selection of garlic and organically certified mushroom kits. Free catalog.

Annie's Annuals & Perennials (AA)
Nursery: 740 Market Avenue
Office: 801 Chesley Avenue
Richmond, CA 94801
Phone: (888) 266-4370
Fax: (800) 819-5319
www.anniesannuals.com
contact@anniesannuals.com
Annie's offers only plants, at their nursery and in other local nurseries, through their website, and in a free print catalog. Annie's started out selling annual flower species that were "rare in the trade" and has now expanded to offer perennials. Most are ornamental only, but they do carry some that can be used as herbs, as well as rocoto pepper plants. Check their website or catalog to learn the dates of four garden parties at the nursery each year.

Baker Creek Heirloom Seeds (BCS)
2278 Baker Creek Road
Mansfield, MO 65704
Phone: (417) 924-8917
Fax: (417) 924-8887
www.rareseeds.com
seeds@rareseeds.com
This company, founded just as the second edition of *Golden Gate Gardening* was being released, carries a big list of heirloom, nonhybrid seeds—mostly vegetables, but some old-fashioned flowers, too. They look for new heirlooms in far corners of the world and celebrate farming in festivals on their farm. In 2009 the website was alphabetized better than the free print catalog.

Botanical Interests, Inc. (BI)
660 Compton Street
Broomfield, CO 80020
Phone: (303) 410-1677
Fax: (303) 464-6468
www.botanicalinterests.com
You will find Botanical Interests seeds on seed racks in some local nurseries as well as for mail order on their website. Their seed packets are unique for the amount of information they contain, on both the outside and inside. Part of their seed list is a line of organic vegetable, herb, and flower seed. No print catalog.

Bountiful Gardens (BG)
18001 Shafer Ranch Road
Willits, CA 95490
Phone: (707) 459-6410
Fax: (707) 459-1925
www.bountifulgardens.org
bountiful@sonic.net
John Jeavons, who also founded Common Ground Garden Supply in Palo Alto, created this business to sell open-pollinated seeds. In addition to vegetables, there are crops for grain and fiber and for producing organic matter for compost. Also offered are books and pamphlets about Jeavons' biointensive growing methods and announcements of

tours and workshops at his Research Mini-Farm in Willits. The online seed list includes some items that are not in the free print catalog.

Burpee Gardens (BUR)
300 Park Avenue
Warminster, PA 18974
Phone orders: (800) 888-1447
Fax orders: (800) 487-5530
Customer service: (800) 333-5808
www.burpee.com
W. Atlee Burpee began to sell seeds mail order in 1876, when he was 18. After many permutations, Burpee Gardens still offers flowers and vegetables, both hybrid and open-pollinated. Through breeding programs over the years Burpee is responsible for many vegetable cultivars with "Burpee" or "Fordhook" in their names and for white marigolds. Free print catalog.

The Cook's Garden (CG)
P.O. Box C5030
Warminster, PA 18974-0574
Phone: (800) 457-9703
Fax: (800) 457-9705
www.cooksgarden.com
Gardener@cooksgarden.com
A company founded by Shepherd and Ellen Ogden, farmers and garden writers, The Cook's Garden is now a division of Burpee. They still specialize in lettuce and salad greens, along with other gourmet vegetables and a few flowers. Free print catalog.

Evergreen Y.H. Enterprises (EE)
Oriental Vegetable Seeds
P.O. Box 17538
Anaheim, CA 92817
Phone/fax: (714) 637-5769
www.evergreenseeds.com
eeseedsyh@aol.com
Evergreen offers only Chinese and other Asian vegetable varieties and books on growing or cooking them. Their website includes a useful reference that gives the names of the vegetables in several Asian languages. No print catalog.

Gourmet Seed International LLC (GS)
HC12 Box 510
Tatum, NM 88267-9700
Phone: (575) 398-6111
www.gourmetseed.com
A company that offers seeds from around the world. They are a good source for European heirloom vegetable cultivars, such as French and Italian snap and shelling beans and eight kinds of broccoli raab, and also offer herb and flower seed. Some seed is organic, some is hybrid, and notations identify these. Free print catalog.

Italian Seed and Tool Company (IST)
HC12 Box 510
Tatum, NM 88267-9700
Phone: (505) 398-6111
Fax: (505) 398-6151
www.italianseedandtool.com
customerservice@italianseedandtool.com
catalog@italianseedandtool.com
A sister company to Gourmet Seeds International, Italian Seed and Tool offers a different but overlapping seed list. They are a distributor for Bavicchi of Italy seeds and also offer gardening tools imported from Italy. No print catalog.

J. L. Hudson, Seedsman (JLH)
P.O. Box 337
La Honda, CA 94020-0337
www.jlhudsonseeds.net
J. L. Hudson offers a large, quirky seed list including many unexpected offerings. In addition to a short list of common vegetables, you will find rarities such as sea kale (*Crambe maritima*), yellow alpine strawberries, and culantro (*Eryngium foetidum*), as well as flowers, herbs, woody ornamentals, trees, wild edibles, and native plants. Save for common vegetables, plants are listed by scientific name. There is no telephone number (Hudson says: "If your phone doesn't ring, it's me."). Free print catalog, which you can request by mail or through the website.

Johnny's Selected Seeds (JSS)
955 Benton Avenue
Winslow, ME 04901
Phone: (877) 564-6697
Fax: (800) 738-6314
www.johnnyseeds.com
service@johnnyseeds.com
Johnny's offers many particularly useful vegetable varieties for cool microclimate gardeners, including a wide selection of cool-season vegetable varieties. Their big, informative catalog includes some organically certified seed, many heirlooms, and hybrids. There are more varieties on their website than in the free print catalog.

Kitazawa Seed Company (KIT)
P.O. Box 13220
Oakland, CA 94661-3220
Phone: (510) 595-1188
Fax: (510) 595-1860
www.kitazawaseed.com
seeds@kitazawaseed.com
Kitazawa carries a large selection of vegetables used in Japanese and Chinese cuisine, sold in generous packets. There are both heirloom and hybrid varieties, most of which are well-suited to our microclimates. Kitazawa seeds are also sold in some retail stores. Free print catalog.

Le Jardin du Gourmet (JG)
P.O. Box 75
St. Johnsbury Center, VT 05863-0075
Phone: (802) 748-1446
Fax: (802) 748-1446
www.artisticgardens.com
infodesk@artisticgardens.com
This is the home of the 35-cent seed packet. The list is limited, and there are only brief descriptions of the vegetable, herb, and flower varieties, but if they have what you want, they are a budget source of it. They also offer (but not at 35 cents) garlic and shallot bulbs and herb and perennial flower plants. The brief print catalog is downloadable on their website.

Native Seeds/SEARCH (NSS)
526 North Fourth Avenue
Tucson, AZ 85705
Phone: (866) 622-5561
Fax: (520) 622-5591
www.nativeseeds.org
info@nativeseeds.org
A nonprofit organization that seeks to conserve the traditional crops, seeds, and farming methods of the Native peoples of the U.S. Southwest and northern Mexico. They offer seeds of traditional vegetables and herbs, many of

which (but not all) are better for warm summer climates. Look on their website for Native American craft items and baking mixes, such as blue corn–amaranth. Free print catalog.

Nichols Garden Nursery (NGN)
1190 Old Salem Road NE
Albany, OR 97321-4580
Phone: (800) 422-3985
Fax: (800) 231-5306
www.nicholsgardennursery.com
customersupport@nicholsgarden nursery.com
This was the first place I found some of the vegetable varieties that are still among my favorites. Many of the ones they carry are adapted to the Northwest climate, which is similar to ours. They also carry herb and flower seeds; herb plants; starts of oca, yacon, garlic, top onions; hops plants and brewing equipment; and more. Free print catalog.

Park Seed Company (PS)
1 Parkton Avenue
Greenwood, SC 29647-0001
Phone: (800) 213-0076
www.parkseed.com
info@parkscs.com
Park Seed has been offering its products since 1868. Like Burpee, they are a large company that has bred hybrid vegetables bearing their name. Their website offers some internet-only offerings as well as web specials on other products. Free print catalog.

Pinetree Garden Seeds (PGS)
P.O. Box 300
New Gloucester, ME 04260
Phone: (207) 926-3400
Fax: (888) 527-3337
www.superseeds.com
pinetree@superseeds.com
A large, well-selected list of vegetable, herb, and flower seeds at very low prices—most packets are under $1.50. They may not have all you want to grow, but they do have heirlooms and hybrids, as well as ethnic specialties. They also carry bulbs, perennial flower plants, mushroom kits, papermaking kits, and books. Free print catalog.

Redwood City Seed Company (RCS)
Box 361
Redwood City, CA 94064
Phone: (650) 325-7333
www.ecoseeds.com
The company is now heavily focused on peppers, from mild to hot, including one touted as "the world's hottest pepper." There is also a collection of open-pollinated vegetable seeds. In the print catalog there is a hotness scale for pepper varieties offered. Among books and pamphlets offered, notable is a report on proprietor Craig Dremann's iconoclastic trials of traditional companion planting: "Carrots *really detest* tomatoes." Free print catalog.

Renee's Garden (RG)
Phone: (888) 880-7228
Fax: (831) 335-7227
www.reneesgarden.com
renee@reneesgarden.com
You will find Renee's Garden seeds on garden center seed racks, and you can call the toll-free number to locate a local source. Or order from her website. She offers a nice vegetable list, herbs, and flowers. Look here for a wide selection of such cool-season flowers as sweet pea, California poppy, and nasturtium. No print catalog.

Richters Herb Specialists (RH)
357 Highway 47
Goodwood, ON LOC 1AO
Canada
Phone: (905) 640-6677
Fax: (905) 640-6641
www.richters.com
orderdesk@richters.com
This Canadian company sells a huge list of herbs as seeds or plants, whichever is most appropriate. If you have heard of an herb, and it is practical to grow it, Richters probably sells it, listed by its common name and accompanied by the correct scientific name. They also carry a short list of vegetables and a nice list of books on herbs. Free print catalog.

Ronniger Potato Farm LLC (RPF)
12101 2135 Road
Austin, CO 81410
Phone: (877) 204-8704
Fax: (877) 204-8704
www.ronnigers.com
info@ronnigers.com
Ronniger's carries the widest selection of potato varieties that I know of. They also offer Jerusalem artichoke and garlic starts and onion specialties such as potato onions. Free print catalog, which can also be downloaded from their website.

Seed Savers Exchange (SSE)
3094 North Winn Road
Decorah, IA 52101
Phone: (563) 382-5990
Fax: (563) 382-6511
www.seedsavers.org
A nonprofit membership organization dedicated to preserving heirloom varieties of vegetables and fruits and rare breeds of livestock and poultry. They offer a large selection of heirloom vegetable, herb, and flower seeds, organically grown, with a 10-percent discount for members. Membership allows them to continue to preserve and promote heirlooms and teach people about them. Free print catalog.

Seeds Blüm
They have gone out of business. Those who remember their hugely informative catalog of heirloom vegetables and herbs, with its many whimsical drawings, understand why I keep mine, though I will never be able to order from it again. Thanks, Jan Blüm.

Seeds from Italy (SI)
P.O. Box 149
Winchester, MA 01890
Phone: (781) 721-5904
Fax: (612) 435-4020
seeds@growitalian.com
www.growitalian.com
Seeds from Italy is a distributor through the internet for the Italian seed company Franchi. Franchi seeds are also available on some local seed racks. Free print catalog.

Seeds of Change (SOC)
P.O. Box 15700
Santa Fe, NM 87592
Phone: (888) 762-7333
www.seedsofchange.com
seedsofchange@marketingconcepts.com
Seeds of Change started out as a small independent seed company with a commitment to organic farming and heirloom preservation. They were sold to a major food corporation, but have managed to keep their focus on organic and heirloom plants and education. They have a nice selection of vegetable, herb, and flower seeds, and garlic and potato starts. Free print catalog and separate professional catalog aimed at farmers.

Select Seeds Company (SS)
180 Stickney Hill Road
Union, CT 06076
Phone: (800) 684-0395
Fax: (800) 653-3304
www.selectseeds.com
This is a company that sells flower seeds and plants only. I've included it because of its focus on heirloom cottage garden annuals, many of which vegetable gardeners will love growing from seed. Free print catalog.

Southern Exposure Seed Exchange (SESE)
P.O. Box 460
Mineral, VA 23117
Phone: (540) 894-9480
Fax: (540) 894-9481
www.southernexposure.com
gardens@southernexposure.com
While this seedlist is aimed at those in the Mid-Atlantic region, there are plenty of choices for even our coolest microclimates. Plenty of greens, early corn and tomato varieties, and an heirloom Cherokee popcorn, for example. Seeds are open-pollinated, and many are organically grown. Catalog can be downloaded from the website or is available as a free print catalog.

Territorial Seed Company (TERR)
P.O. Box 158
Cottage Grove, OR 97424
Phone: (800) 626-0866
Fax: (888) 657-3131
Customer service/gardening questions: (541) 942-9547
www.territorialseed.com
info@territorialseed.com
"Seeds that grow West of the Cascades" is their motto. They test vegetable varieties near the Oregon Coast, in a maritime climate that is wetter and somewhat colder than ours. It is a fat catalog, with many useful varieties and much useful growing information. They also issue a separate catalog exclusively for crops and varieties suitable for a fall to spring garden. Free print catalogs.

Thompson & Morgan (T&M)
220 Faraday Avenue
Jackson, NJ 08527-5073
Phone: (800) 274-7333
Fax: (888) 466-4769
www.tmseeds.com
service@tmseeds.com
This American branch of a British Company offers vegetable seed, including many fava and scarlet runner bean varieties. A long list of flower seed is coded from easy to "challenging." Free print catalog.

Tomato Growers Supply Company (TGS)
P.O. Box 60015
Fort Myers, FL 33906
Phone: (888) 478-7333
Customer service: (239) 768-1119
Fax: (888) 768-3476
www.tomatogrowers.com
There are thousands of tomato varieties. Tomato Growers Supply doesn't sell even close to all of them, but they have an impressive frontlist of both heirlooms and hybrids. The backlist plants get only a name and number in the catalog, but they do get a photo on the TGS website. They also sell peppers, tomatillos, and eggplants. Free print catalog.

Totally Tomatoes (TT)
334 West Stroud Street
Randolph, WI 53956
Phone: (800) 345-5977
Fax: (888) 477-7333
www.totallytomato.com
Another catalog that amazes with its multitude and diversity of tomato cultivars, both heirloom and hybrid. They also carry a wide variety of peppers, as well as a short list of other kinds of vegetable seeds. Free print catalog.

Vermont Bean Seed Company (VBS)
334 West Stroud Street
Randolph, WI 53956
Phone: (800) 349-1071
Fax: (888) 500-7333
www.vermontbean.com
A full range of vegetable seeds and flower seeds, including a wide selection of beans for eating at the snap, shelling, or dry stage. Free print catalog, but they print a limited run, so order early.

West Coast Seeds (WCS)
3925 64th Street, RR #1
Delta, BC V4K 3N2
Canada
Phone: (888) 804-8820
Fax: (877) 482-8822
www.westcoastseeds.com
A Vancouver, BC, company with many vegetable varieties we can love in our own milder maritime climate. Quite a few of their seeds are open-pollinated varieties, though their list does include a few hybrids. Some seeds, garlic, and potato sets are certified organic in Canada. Free print catalog in Canada only, so U.S. customers have to order from their website.

APPENDIX VII

Resources for Gardeners

USE THIS APPENDIX TO FIND

- Book and gardening supply sources
- Fruit sources and information
- Education and advocacy groups
- Organic farming and gardening information
- Cooperative Extension contact information
- Community garden information
- Working and model farms with educational programs
- Urban food security programs
- Gardening for schools
- Demonstration gardens with edible plants
- Herbariums
- Horticulture libraries
- Nearby colleges with departments of agriculture or horticulture
- Bee and other insect information
- Pest identification and IPM information
- Pesticide information
- Underground Service Alert (USA)

BOOK AND GARDENING SUPPLY SOURCES

Acres USA
P. O. Box 91299
Austin, TX 78709
Phone: (800) 355-5313
Fax: (512) 892-4448
www.acresusa.com
info@acresusa.com
A mail-order book catalog from the company that publishes the magazine *Acres USA: The Voices of Eco-Agriculture*. While the magazine is about commercial scale organic farming, the catalog includes books on both commercial agriculture and home gardening.

American Soil and Stone
565A Jacoby Street
San Rafael, CA 94901
Phone: (415) 456-1381
Fax: (415) 456-1754
www.americansoilandstone.com
2121 San Joaquin
Richmond, CA 94804
Phone: (510) 292-3000
Fax: (510) 526-3175
www.americansoil.com
Carries a full line of blended soil mixes, organic amendments, and mulches. Wholesale and retail. Will make custom blends. Soil tests and personal consultation available.

Bell's Bookstore
536 Emerson Street
Palo Alto, CA 94301
Phone: (650) 323-8822
www.bellsbooks.com
A bookstore with a large and excellent selection of new and used books on horticulture and gardening.

Builders Booksource
1817 Fourth Street (near Hearst)
Berkeley, CA 94710
Phone: (510) 845-6874
Fax: (510) 845-7051
www.buildersbooksource.com
This store caters to building professionals, including those in the building trades, architects, urban designers, and landscape architects. They carry a wide selection of gardening books.

Common Ground Organic Supply Store
See Educational and Advocacy Groups, page 408.

Garden Bookstore
San Francisco Botanical Garden
Ninth Avenue and Lincoln Way
Golden Gate Park
San Francisco, CA 94122
Phone: (415) 661-1316 Ext. 409
Located just inside the main gate of the Botanical Garden, this tiny bookstore is packed with books on plants and gardening. Although its collection on food gardening is relatively small, it is a wonderful overall resource for gardeners. Open 10 a.m. to 4 p.m. every day.

Gardener's Supply
128 Intervale Road
Burlington, VT 05401
Phone: (800) 863-1700
Fax: (800) 551-6712
www.gardeners.com
Mail-order gardening supply company that does a good job of

selecting products for usefulness and quality. Among the products they carry are quality tools, the Accelerated Propagation System (APS), floating row covers, bird netting, self-watering planters, a prefab wire compost bin, and a soaker hose irrigation system. They issue four seasonal catalogs a year.

General Feed and Seed
1900 B Commercial Way
Santa Cruz, CA 95065
Phone: (831) 476-5344
Fax: (831) 476-1953
www.generalfeedandseed.com
Carries a wide selection of organic fertilizers, soil amendments, and organic pest control supplies. Also sells open-pollinated seed, including seed for green manure crops.

Harmony Farm Supply
Warehouse Store
3244 Highway 116 North
Sebastopol, CA 95472
Phone: (707) 823-9125
Fax: (707) 823-1734
www.harmonyfarm.com
Sprinkler and drip irrigation systems, organic fertilizers, organic soil amendments, ecologically safe pest controls, solar electric systems, gopher wire and root cages, beneficial insects, bare-root fruit trees, gardening books, vegetable and cover crop seeds. Soil tests, with recommendations for organic fertilization. Free educational workshops. Catalog upon request.

Mrs. Dalloway's
2904 College Avenue
Berkeley, CA 94705
Phone: (510) 704-8222
Fax: (510) 704-8228
www.mrsdalloways.com
Primarily a bookstore, specializing in gardening books and literature, Mrs. Dalloway's also carries small garden tools and some plants.

Peaceful Valley Farm Supply
125 Clydesdale Court
Grass Valley, CA 95945
Mailing address: P.O. Box 2209
Grass Valley, CA 95945
Phone: (888) 784-1722
www.groworganic.com
A mail-order source of organic fertilizers and soil amendments, ecologically safe pest controls, (including gopher-proof root cages), cover crop seeds, quality tools, floating row covers, watering equipment, and books. Free print catalog.

Smith and Hawken
P.O. Box 8690
Pueblo, CO 81008-9998
Phone: (800) 940-1170
www.smithandhawken.com
This company began as a purveyor of fine English tools. They still sell tools, as well as plants and garden apparel, but have become more and more a place to buy fine garden furniture and décor. You can buy online or request a print catalog; there are also seven Bay Area stores. You can locate the store nearest you through the website.

University of California
ANR Communication Services
6701 San Pablo Avenue, 2nd Floor
Oakland, CA 94608-1239
Phone: (510) 642-2431
Toll-free: (800) 994-8849
Fax: (510) 643-5470
http://anrcatalog.ucdavis.edu
The UC Cooperative Extension (see separate listing on page 410) publishes many books and pamphlets of great use to farmers and gardeners. Their *Master Gardener Handbook* has large sections on vegetable and fruit growing along with basic horticulture. Other topics include the home orchard, garden pests, weeds, and soil improvement. Some are listed in Appendix VIII, Suggested Reading. These books do not often appear in bookstores, but you can order them through the online catalog or the free print catalog.

Urban Farmer Store
2833 Vicente Street
San Francisco, CA 94116
(415) 661-2204
653 East Blithedale
Mill Valley, CA 94941
(415) 380-3840
2121 San Joaquin Street
Richmond, CA 94804
Phone: (510) 524-1604
www.urbanfarmerstore.com
Urban Farmer stores carry drip irrigation, sprinkler system supplies, weather-based self-adjusting irrigation controllers, quality tools, and low-wattage outdoor LED lighting. Free classes. Free print catalog.

SOURCES OF FRUIT-BEARING TREES, VINES, AND SHRUBS

Bay Flora
1563 Solano Avenue #428
Berkeley, CA 94707
Fax: (888) 549-2969
www.bayflora.com
A retail mail-order nursery that specializes in a list of subtropical and Mediterranean fruits, including citrus, olives, mulberries, and figs. Purchases are through the website only and come with complete growing instructions, and Bay Flora has a policy of donating up to 15 percent of your purchase price to a nonprofit group of your choice.

California Rare Fruit Growers
The Fullerton Arboretum—CSUF
P.O. Box 6850
Fullerton, CA 92834-6850
www.crfg.org
This organization promotes growing of subtropical fruit, but also has information on well-known fruits and some unusual vegetables. The statewide membership organization has a very informative website; publishes a bimonthly magazine, *The Fruit Gardener*; and maintains a seed bank and a book service. There are local chapters throughout the state; in the Bay Area there are two: the Golden Gate Chapter for the northern part, and the Santa Clara Valley Chapter for the southern part. Both have meetings open to the public, a newsletter, scion exchanges, and an opportunity to learn from experienced gardeners and orchardists. You can join at the local or state level or both.

Dave Wilson Nursery
Phone: (800) 654-5854
www.davewilson.com
Dave Wilson is a wholesale nursery only, selling fruit trees, vines, and bushes in many of the region's retail garden centers. Through their website you can find out what they carry and which nearby retail outlets carry it. The website also includes many

useful topics, such as: planting fruit trees, the chill factor, and keeping deer out. At the retail sources, ask for useful pamphlets about their trees or call the 800 number, which is a hotline for tree questions.

Four Winds Growers
www.fourwindsgrowers.com
A wholesale and retail source of dwarf citrus plants. You can order directly through their website or look for the plants in regional retail nurseries. The website includes much useful information on growing citrus.

Fruit and Nut Research and Information Center
Department of Plant Sciences
Mail Stop 2
University of California
One Shields Avenue
Davis, CA 95616-8780
Phone: (530) 754-9708
Fax: (530) 754-8523
http://fruitsandnuts.ucdavis.edu
Here is a wealth of information for California fruit growers, both large scale and in home gardens. It includes chilling hour and degree day records for many counties, though not for San Francisco, San Mateo, or Humboldt counties. In a separate section home orchardists can learn basic care and pest management. Another has links to many other websites with fruit and nut information.

Harmony Farm Supply
(See listing under Book and Gardening Supply Sources.) Call or send for their winter catalog, showing their offerings of bare-root fruit trees and shrubs. While they will ship if absolutely necessary, they prefer that you pick up plants in person.

One Green World
28696 South Cramer Road
Molalla, OR 97038-8576
Phone: (877) 353-4028
Fax: (800) 418-9983
www.onegreenworld.com
A retail nursery with a garden center in Oregon, One Green World sells fruit trees, shrubs, and vines. They offer a wide variety of crops, but put the emphasis on cold hardiness and do not provide much information on adaptability to mild winter regions, so do your climate research elsewhere. Free print catalog.

Raintree Nursery
391 Butts Road
Morton, WA 98356
Phone: (360) 496-6400
Fax: (888) 770-8358
www.raintree.com
A retail nursery with a garden center in Washington State, Raintree is known for its bare-root fruit and nut trees and berries of all kinds. You can order from their website or free print catalog. The website is full of useful information such as pollination and ripening order charts and a section on fruit types and varieties for Northern California, divided into climate zones.

Trees of Antiquity
20 Wellsona Road
Paso Robles, CA 93446
Phone: (805) 467-9909
Fax: (805) 467-9909
www.treesofantiquty.com
A mail-order retail nursery that specializes in organically grown bare-root fruit trees, they also carry berries, table grapes, and olives. They have a wide selection of apples, many of them heirlooms. Their website offers help selecting varieties by keywords, and there are several informational articles on choosing and growing fruit trees. They call themselves "a sport of Sonoma Antique Apple Nursery." Free print catalog.

EDUCATIONAL AND ADVOCACY GROUPS

California Certified Organic Farmers (CCOF)
2155 Delaware Avenue, Suite 150
Santa Cruz, CA 95060
Phone: (831) 423-2263
Fax: (831) 423-4528
www.ccof.org
Formed in 1973, even before California's Organic Food Act created a California organics program, the CCOF continues to serve the state's organic farmers. It offers a certification program, acts as a trade association, and also provides education and political advocacy. Here is a portal through which you can learn about the history of organic farming in California and about the current laws and issues.

California Native Plant Society (CNPS)
2707 K Street, Suite 1
Sacramento, CA 95816-5113
Phone: (916) 447-2677
Fax: (916) 447-2727
www.cnps.org
CNPS works to increase understanding and appreciation of California's native plants and to conserve them and their natural habitats through education, science, advocacy, horticulture, and land stewardship. It provides education, outreach, and conservation-related services to botanists, land planners, government agencies, gardeners, and the general public. Many chapters hold native plant sales in the spring and fall seasons. Members receive the quarterly journal *Fremontia* and a quarterly *CNPS Bulletin* along with discounts at nurseries and garden supply stores.

Center for Urban Education about Sustainable Agriculture (CUESA)
One Ferry Building, Suite 50
San Francisco, CA 94111
www.cuesa.org
CUESA operates the Ferry Plaza Farmers Market in San Francisco and seeks to educate urban consumers about sustainable agriculture. They sponsor educational displays and workshops, farm tours, and lectures. They also schedule visits to the market by children's classes. Their website includes a schedule of upcoming events, curriculum aids, and links to other sources of curriculum on farming and food production.

Committee for Sustainable Agriculture
406 Main Street, Suite 313
Watsonville, CA 95076
Phone: (408) 763-2111
Fax: (831) 763-2112
www.eco-farm.org
This organization promotes ecological farming. The annual Hoes Down

Harvest Fair held at Full Belly Farm in Yolo County provides family fun. You can also learn the latest information on sustainable agriculture techniques at the annual Ecological Farming Conference, held in January, and at regional workshops held throughout the year.

Common Ground Organic Garden Supply and Education Center
559 College Avenue
Palo Alto, CA 94306
Phone: (650) 493-6072
www.commongroundinpaloalto.org
Common Ground Garden Supply and Education Center offers hands-on classes and events in organic gardening, edible gardening, complete-diet mini-farming, school garden basics, and other gardening and sustainable living topics. The center also sells specialty supplies to help gardeners: seeds and plant starts, organic composts, fertilizers and mulches, tools, and natural disease and pest control products, books, and magazines.

Ecology Center
2530 San Pablo Avenue
Berkeley, CA 94702
Phone: (510) 548-2220
Fax: (510) 548-2240
www.ecologycenter.org
Promotes efforts toward a healthy environment. Garden-related information is available through their newsletter, library, bookstore, and classes. They sell organic fertilizers and compost and sponsor a seed exchange. The center serves as a clearinghouse for Bay Area gardening resources.

Garden for the Environment
Mailing Address:
780 Frederick Street
San Francisco, CA 94117
Garden Address:
7th Avenue and Lawton Street
Phone: (415) 731-5627
Fax: (415) 731-5607
www.gardenfortheenvironment.org
A demonstration garden and education center offering both informal learning experiences and formal classes in organic gardening and urban compost systems. The Gardening & Composting Educator Training Program (GCETP), a three-month-long certificate program in organic gardening, prepares adults to teach home composting and gardening. Summer youth programs teach environmental and other skills to youth ages eleven through thirteen, and school-year programs reach younger children. The garden is open for viewing in daylight hours and for volunteering on Wednesdays and Saturdays. Call for details and with general gardening and composting questions. The website lists local gardening and composting resources. They also offer online listings of their schedule of classes and other garden-related local events; subscribe through the website.

National Gardening Association (NGA)
1100 Dorset Street
South Burlington, VT 05403
Phone: (802) 863-5251
www.garden.org
The National Gardening Association seeks to assist as many Americans as possible in the enjoyment of gardening. Their website is full of information, including regular articles by regional editors, how-to videos, pest and weed ID and management libraries, and lists of ideas for readers to build community through gardening. They promote and sponsor school gardening programs through their "Kids Gardening" division (see listing under Gardening for Schools, page 414). The NGA Garden Shop offers "Products with a Mission," including composting equipment, greenhouse and shed kits, equipment, and tools for children's and school gardens.

National Sustainable Agriculture Information Service (ATTRA)
P.O. Box 3657
Fayetteville, AR 72702
Phone: (800) 346-9140, 7 a.m.–7 p.m. Central Time (English)
Phone: (800) 411-3222, 8 a.m.–5 p.m. Pacific Time (Spanish)
attra.ncat.org
This organization's goals are to help "farmers, ranchers, market gardeners, Extension agents, educators, farm organizations, and others involved in commercial agriculture, especially those who are economically disadvantaged or traditionally underserved." Their website offers many online publications on both sustainable agriculture and organic agriculture. You can learn anything from the details of becoming and practicing as a certified organic farmer, to resources for teachers planning farm visits, to an explanation of transgenic crops and their implications for sustainable agriculture. For farmers, they offer help researching solutions to problems. A page in Spanish links to many resources in Spanish and a separate Spanish phone line.

Occidental Arts & Ecology Center
15290 Coleman Valley Road
Occidental, CA 95465
Phone: (707) 874-1557
www.oaec.org
This multifaceted institute maintains a large organic garden and orchard dedicated to preserving a collection of heirloom crops and distributing seeds to other nonprofit gardening programs. In addition, they offer classes and consultations on subjects that include ecological agriculture, permaculture and ecological design, landscape painting, applied carpentry, intentional communities, and operation of a school gardening program. They say much of their work is "in response to the challenge of how to create ecologically, economically and culturally sustainable communities that are democratic and serve as a counterpoint to privatized and corporatized society."

Regenerative Design Institute & Permaculture Institute of Northern California
P. O. Box 923
Bolinas, CA 94924
Phone: (415) 868-9681
www.regenerativedesign.org
Permaculture endeavors to design living environments to provide as many needs as possible, including food, shelter, energy, and waste recycling. The Regenerative Design Institute offers permaculture classes, including two-week intensives and yearlong classes that meet once a

month. They also offer courses in nature awareness.

San Francisco Botanical Garden Society
Ninth Avenue and Lincoln Way
Golden Gate Park
San Francisco, CA 94122
Phone: (415) 661-1316 Ext. 303
www.sfbotanicalgarden.org
This society is the private nonprofit organization created to support San Francisco's public botanical garden. The society runs the Helen Crocker Russell Library (see Horticultural Libraries), a small bookstore (see Book and Gardening Supply Sources), and classes, workshops, and tours on gardening for adults and youth, including some on food gardening and permaculture.

StopWaste.org
1537 Webster Street
Oakland, CA 94612
Phone: (510) 891-6500
Fax: (510) 893-2308
www.stopwaste.org
A program of the Alameda County Waste Management Authority, StopWaste.org is set up to encourage composting, water conservation, less-toxic pest management, green building, and other "Bay Friendly" methods. They offer classes for county residents, but the wealth of information on the website, including a downloadable book on *Bay Friendly Gardening*, is accessible to all.

UNIVERSITY OF CALIFORNIA COOPERATIVE EXTENSION SERVICE

http://ucanr.org/ce.cfm
The University of California, Davis, is a Federal Land Grant College. When the federal government gave land to the states for agricultural colleges, it stipulated that these colleges had to provide public education on agricultural matters. The state organization that does this is UC Agriculture and Natural Resources, which sponsors projects such as publications (see UC ANR Communication Services, page 407) and the UC IPM program (see page 417), as well as county Cooperative Extension offices.

County Extension offices employ experts who conduct research, such as vegetable and fruit variety trials, and answer questions from the public. They are valuable sources of current and local information.

Many counties also have Master Gardener programs, which offer training in gardening to members of the public in exchange for volunteer help from graduates. Master Gardeners answer questions from the public and may carry out variety trials, sponsor gardening clinics or symposia, and pursue other activities.

Another project of County Extension offices is the 4-H program, which offers classes for children on subjects ranging from raising livestock to plant propagation. Since 1999 there has been a 4-H Junior Master Gardener Program—see listing at end of county offices.

The website listed here provides a clickable map. When you click on a county, the website of its Cooperative Extension program will appear, offering useful gardening information including whether your county has a Master Gardener or 4-H program. Following are street addresses and phone numbers for the County Cooperative Extension offices of the greater Bay Area and Central Coast region of California.

County Cooperative Extension Offices

Alameda County
Cooperative Extension Alameda County
1131 Harbor Bay Parkway, Suite 131
Alameda, CA 94502
Phone: (510) 567-6812
Fax: (510) 748-9644

Contra Costa County
Cooperative Extension Contra Costa County
75 Santa Barbara Road, 2nd Floor
Pleasant Hill, CA 94523-4215
Phone: (925) 646-6540
Fax: (925) 646-6708

Marin County
Cooperative Extension Marin County
1682 Novato Boulevard, Suite 150-B
Novato, CA 94947
Phone: (415) 499-4204
Fax: (415) 499-4209

Mendocino County
UCCE-Mendocino County
890 N. Bush Street
Ukiah, CA 95482
Phone: (707) 463-4495
Fax: (707) 463-4477

Monterey County
Cooperative Extension Monterey County
1432 Abbott Street
Salinas, CA 93901
Phone: (831) 759-7350
Fax: (831) 758-3018

Napa County
Cooperative Extension Napa County
1710 Soscol Avenue, Suite 4
Napa, CA 94559-1315
Phone: (707) 253-4221
Fax: (707) 253-4434

San Mateo-San Francisco Counties
Cooperative Extension San Mateo–San Francisco Counties
80 Stone Pine Road, #100
Half Moon Bay, CA 94019
Phone: (650) 726-9059
Fax: (650) 726-9267

Santa Clara County
UCCE Santa Clara County
1553 Berger Drive, Building 1
San Jose, CA 95112
Phone: (408) 282-3110
Fax: (408) 298-5160

Santa Cruz County
Cooperative Extension Santa Cruz County
1432 Freedom Boulevard
Watsonville, CA 95076-2796
Phone: (831) 763-8040
Fax: (831) 763-8006

Sonoma County
Cooperative Extension Sonoma County
133 Aviation Boulevard, Suite 109
Santa Rosa, CA 95403-2894
Phone: (707) 565-2621
Fax: (707) 565-2623

California Junior Master Gardener Program

University of California Agriculture and Natural Resources
669 County Square Drive, #100
Ventura, CA 93003
Phone: (805) 662-6943
Fax: (805) 645-1474
ca4h.org/projresource/jrmaster gardener/index.asp
The 4-H Youth Development Program, run by the Cooperative Extension, has since 1999 offered a Junior Master Gardener Program, which combines hands-on learning with a program to strengthen math, science, language, and social studies skills.

COMMUNITY GARDENING INFORMATION

American Community Gardening Association
1777 East Broad Street
Columbus, OH 43203
Phone: (877) 275-2242
Fax: (614) 645-5921
www.communitygarden.org
An organization of professional community garden organizers, neighborhood leaders, and others who share an interest in community gardening in the United States and Canada. Their primary function is to provide help and information to people interested in starting community gardens, including locating nearby programs. They publish a journal, *Review*, and sponsor an annual conference.

Ecology Center (see full listing on page 409)
Check out the Ecodirectory of the Ecology Center in Berkeley for a list of contact information of Bay Area community garden programs.

San Francisco Gardeners Resource Organization (SFGRO)
www.sfgro.org
Formed to support community gardeners in San Francisco, SFGRO is a fledgling organization with a website that provides information and links for community and other San Francisco gardeners.

San Francisco League of Urban Gardeners (SLUG)
This organization, which supported community, school, and home gardening in San Francisco and employed at-risk youths and adults, has folded. The Garden for the Environment (see page 409), once a project of SLUG, carries on some of their good work.

San Francisco Recreation and Parks Department Community Gardens Program
Mr. Marvin Yee
Community Gardens Program Manager
Recreation and Park Department
Tel: (415) 581-2541
Fax: (415) 581-2540
recpark.gardens@sfgov.org
www.sfgov.org
Since the demise of SLUG, San Francisco's community gardens have been managed by the Recreation and Park Department. Find their community garden program on their website under "Activities." A garden list includes most, though not all, gardens, with contact information.

WORKING AND MODEL FARMS OFFERING EDUCATIONAL PROGRAMS

Ardenwood Historic Farm
34600 Ardenwood Boulevard
Fremont, CA 94555
Phone: (510) 796-0199
www.ebparks.org/parks/ardenwood
This demonstration Victorian farm is run jointly by the East Bay Regional Park District and the City of Fremont. It is open to the public and to school classes for day visits. Reduced public entrance fees on Tuesday and Wednesday, when the grounds only are open. On Thursday through Sunday, admission includes demonstrations and workshops teaching old-fashioned farm skills, and in April through October, hayrides and train rides.

Camp Joy
131 Camp Joy Road
Boulder Creek, CA 95006
Phone: (831) 338-3651
www.campjoygardens.org
Camp Joy is a small working French Intensive Biodynamic farm that offers tours and adult classes as well as an apprenticeship program.

Center for Agroecology and Sustainable Food Systems (CASFS)
1156 High Street
Santa Cruz, CA 95064
Phone: (831) 459-4140
Fax: (831) 459-2799
http://casfs.ucsc.edu
There are three programs at this center: an apprenticeship program, public tours and workshops, and membership. Contact each through this address and through the following phone numbers and website:

CASFS Apprenticeship Program
Phone: (831) 459-3695
This six-month hands-on apprenticeship is offered through the University of California Extension (not through U.C. Santa Cruz). Students gain experience on the 25-acre farm and 4-acre gardens. College credit is possible, but must be negotiated with the college you attend.

CASFS Workshops and Tours
Phone: (831) 459-3240
CASFS offers workshops, events, and group tours for the public. Call, write, or check the CASFS website to obtain a current schedule. School field trips are available through Lifelab Science Program (see listing under Gardening for Schools). They also hold annual spring and fall plant sales and a fall Harvest Festival, which includes activities for children.

CASFS Membership in Friends of the Farm and Garden
Phone: (831) 459-3376
Membership in CASFS helps to support its programs, and members receive a quarterly newsletter, *The Cultivar*, that lists workshops, events, and resources, and includes articles useful to gardeners.

Ecology Action
5798 Ridgewood Road
Willits, CA 95490
Phone: (707) 459-0150
Fax: (707) 459-5409
www.growbiointensive.org
This is the headquarters and research farm of Ecology Action, run by John Jeavons. They sponsor six-hour tours, three-day introductory workshops and five-day teachers workshops in biointensive gardening. Write or check out the website for current dates and fees. See also Common Ground Store, in Nonprofit Groups and the Ecology Action seed catalog "Bountiful Gardens" in Appendix VI, Seed and Starter Plant Sources.

Elkus Youth Ranch
1500 Purisma Creek Road
Half Moon Bay, CA 94019
Phone: (650) 712-3158
Fax: (650) 712-3153
cesanmateo.ucdavis.edu
This working ranch can be visited by any of a wide variety of children's groups, from preschoolers up. Visits may range from a couple of hours to overnight stays. The ranch is equipped for visits by persons with disabilities.

Green Gulch Farm Zen Center
1601 Shoreline Highway
Sausalito, CA 94965
Phone: (415) 383-3134
www.sfzc.org/ggf
This working farm associated with the Zen Center supplies restaurants and natural food stores and sells at farmers markets. It also serves as a Zen Buddhist retreat. Green Gulch Farm offers gardening workshops and apprenticeships, as well as workshops on topics relating to Zen.

Hidden Villa
26870 Moody Road
Los Altos Hills, CA 94022
Phone: (650) 949-8650
Fax: (650) 948-4159
www.hiddenvilla.org
Frank and Josephine Duveneck, who donated this land, began a tradition of good works here that is continued by a nonprofit organization. In the winter, it is the site of a hostel; in the summer, there are multiracial day and residential camps. The summer camps include involvement in a large garden and the care of farm animals along with traditional camping activities. Hidden Villa also offers environmental field experiences for school classes. In addition to the educational garden, they run a community supported agriculture (CSA) project that provides food to members and a farming internship for high school students. Visitors are often welcome at Hidden Villa—check days and hours on their website.

Prusch Park
San Jose Recreation and Parks
647 South King Road
San Jose, CA 95116
Phone: (408) 926-5555
www.pruschfarmpark.org
Prusch Park, run by the city of San Jose, is a demonstration farm including farm animals and a series of demonstration orchards including rare fruit trees, a high-density fruit orchard, a deciduous fruit orchard, and a citrus orchard. It is available for school tours and hosts gardening workshops. You can learn about their history and upcoming events on their website. The site also includes some of the city-run community gardens.

Slide Ranch
2025 Shoreline Highway
Muir Beach, CA 94965
Phone: (415) 381-6155
Fax: (415) 381-5762
www.slideranch.org
Children and teenagers can participate in programs at this working farm, exploring both the farm and the surrounding wild area. For children, there are one-, two-, or three-day programs; for teens, "farmhand weekends," summer camp, and Teacher-in-Residence internships. There are also spring, summer, and fall "family days." The garden, chicken coop, and farm animals are all wheelchair accessible.

URBAN FOOD SECURITY PROJECTS

Gardening projects with a social goal—whether to donate food to charities, help low-income people grow their own food, provide job skills to at-risk youth, or increase the amount of knowledge about food gardening in the community, have been multiplying and evolving. Harvesting unpicked fruit to share with those who need it is often part of such programs or a freestanding program. The following are a sampling of such projects.

City Slicker Farms
1625 16th Street
Oakland, CA 94607
Phone: (510) 763-4241
www.cityslickerfarms.org
Getting good food to West Oakland residents is the central theme in the several City Slicker Farm projects. There are several large garden sites, with regular volunteer hours; "neighbors, volunteers, and kids are welcome." In addition, there is a Backyard Garden Program, which helps would-be gardeners set up gardens and learn to grow food.

Homeless Garden Project
P.O. Box 617
Santa Cruz, CA 95061
Phone: (831) 426-3609
The mission of this project is to employ and train homeless people in Santa Cruz County within a community-supported organic garden enterprise. They run a CSA that supplies subscribers with deliveries of food from the garden and also produces garden-source craft items that they sell in a store in downtown Santa Cruz. The goal is to teach gardening as well as other marketable skills that can help people "lift themselves out of their homeless or marginalized situation."

Pie Ranch
P.O. Box 138
Davenport, CA 95017
Phone: (650) 879-0995
This is a working farm, located near Ano Nuevo, between San Francisco and Santa Cruz, with an educational mission. Products of

the farm include popcorn, wheat, berries, honey, goat's milk, and eggs. An active youth education program gives priority to links to particular schools that provide multiple, regular visits by teenage participants, but visits for other age groups and onetime visits are also offered as time permits. The ranch is linked to a store in San Francisco—Mission Pie, at 2801 Mission Street, (415) 282-4743—which employs teenagers and provides an urban link to the farm programs.

San Francisco Victory Gardens
c/o Garden for the Environment
7th Avenue and Lawton
San Francisco
Phone: (415) 731-5627
www.sfvictorygardens.org
This project, inspired by the Victory Gardens of World War II, redefines victory "in the pressing context of urban sustainability, food security, and reducing the food miles associated with the average American meal." The project, cosponsored by the City of San Francisco, is responsible for the food garden that was built in front of City Hall in 2008 and featured in the 2008 Slow Food International event held in San Francisco. Fifteen San Francisco residents were selected in 2008 to get materials, seeds, and help learning to garden. A demonstration garden at the Garden for the Environment (see page 409) shows residents what is possible, and a registry allows City residents to "become part of a network of urban food producers."

Spiral Gardens
2830 Sacramento Street
Berkeley, CA 94702
Phone: (510) 843-1307
www.spiralgardens.org
On two blocks of public land in southwest Berkeley, this nonprofit runs a community farm, nursery, produce stand, and outdoor community classroom. The food from the community farm is shared among the volunteers who grow it and low-income seniors in the adjacent housing complex. The produce stand sells mostly organic produce from nearby farms, at cost, and the nursery sells plants, including edibles, at affordable prices. A community harvest project organizes volunteers to pick extra fruit from residential garden fruit trees and distribute it to organizations that feed the homeless.

Sustainable Agriculture Education (SAGE)
1625 Shattuck Avenue, Suite 210
Phone: (510) 526-1793
Fax: (510) 524-7153
www.sagecenter.org
SAGE developed Sunol Ag Park on 18 acres of SF Public Utilities Company land, 25 miles southeast of Oakland. The land hosts several projects, including a large garden tended by Southeast Asian refugee women, a plot sponsored by People's Grocery in West Oakland, and several for-profit endeavors. It is meant to be a model, showing integration of "community benefit agriculture, natural resource stewardship, and public education." The project includes agricultural education for tenants and internships for youth and college students. Volunteers are welcome.

GARDENING FOR SCHOOLS

California Department of Education
Nutrition Services Division
Healthy Eating and Nutrition Education.
A Garden in Every School
1430 N Street
Sacramento, CA 95814-5901
Phone: (800) 952-5609
www.cde.ca.gov/ls/nu/he/garden.asp
The policy of the California Department of Education is to encourage and support a garden in every school, to help children learn better food choices, and to integrate gardening activities into other coursework. Their book, *A Child's Garden of Standards: A: Linking School Gardens to California Education Standards, Grades Two Through Six*, is downloadable from the website.

California Junior Master Gardener Program
See listing under University of California Cooperative Extension on page 411.

California School Garden Network
www.csgn.org
This nonprofit organization was created to facilitate the connection between resource organizations and educators dedicated to creating and sustaining school gardens. On their website, you will find free print resources on starting and running a school garden, as well as on curriculum. There are also links to help you search for grants or develop fundraising ideas.

Edible Schoolyard
Martin Luther King Jr. Middle School
1781 Rose Street, Berkeley
Phone: (510) 558-1335
Fax: (510) 558-1334
www.edibleschoolyard.org
One of the most successful of school gardens, this one-acre garden is coordinated with instruction in kitchen "classrooms." Monthly tours of both are available and must be scheduled well in advance. The garden is closed to the public during school hours except for these tours, but the garden is open for public viewing after school and on weekends. Check to see if summer workshops for educators are scheduled. The website offers links to many organizations that offer assistance to school gardens.

Life Lab Science Program
1156 High Street
Santa Cruz, CA 95064
Phone: (831)459-2001
Fax: (831) 459-3483
www.lifelab.ucsc.edu
This organization publishes curriculum guides for grades K through 6 that teach science and nutrition through gardening. Adaptable to a single planter or to an acre of flowers and vegetables. Life Lab will work directly in some schools. They offer educator workshops in garden-based learning. They also

publish a more comprehensive book of curricula: *The Growing Classroom*.

National Gardening Association
Kids Gardening Program
1100 Dorset Street
South Burlington, VT 05403
Phone: (800) 538-7476
Fax: (802) 864-6889
www.kidsgardening.org
This program of the National Gardening Association (see their other listing on page 409) provides curriculum, materials, and support for school garden programs. The K through 8 curriculum, called GrowLab, was developed with support from the National Science Foundation to use plants and gardens to teach about science and the environment. They sell curriculum guides on gardening, nutrition, and cooking, as well as GrowLab light gardens that provide indoor learning tools. They also sponsor Youth Garden Grants and awards.

Occidental Arts & Ecology Center
See listing on page 409.

San Francisco Green Schoolyard Alliance (SFGSA)
135 Van Ness, Room 408
San Francisco, CA 94102
Phone: (415) 355-6923
www.sfgreenschools.org
The SFGSA was created to promote community-based efforts to create schoolyards that contain "green" elements such as gardens, water elements, outdoor classrooms, small farm animals, and trees. It is a coalition of schools, civic organizations, and government agencies. On the website, you can download a self-guided tour of some San Francisco school gardens. The organization sponsors workshops for educators, parents, and garden coordinators; hosts an annual Growing Greener Grounds conference; and publishes a monthly SFGSA Resource Digest, to which you can subscribe through the website.

Slide Ranch
See listing on page 412.

DEMONSTRATION GARDENS AND BOTANICAL GARDENS WITH EDIBLE PLANTINGS

Arboretum at U.C. Santa Cruz
1156 High Street
University of California at Santa Cruz
Santa Cruz, CA 95064
Phone: (831) 427-2998
Arboretum.ucsc.edu
This arboretum is focused on plants of mediterranean climates around the world, but it also features plantings of rare fruits and a small library.

Gamble Garden Center
1431 Waverly Street
Palo Alto, CA 94301
Phone: (415) 329-1356
www.gamblegarden.org
A historic home with gardens that include ornamental plantings, fruit trees (good examples of espaliers), vegetables, and herbs. The center also offers gardening workshops. The garden is open during daylight hours. The office and library are open 9 a.m. to noon on weekday mornings.

Garden for the Environment
7th Avenue and Lawton Street
San Francisco, CA
Phone: (415) 731-5627
www.gardenfortheenvironment.org
Garden for the Environment is a half-acre demonstration garden that includes a drought-tolerant ornamental garden, a compost demonstration area, and demonstration edible plantings. For more on their educational programs, see listing on page 409. It offers weekly organic gardening classes and The Gardening & Composting Educator Training Program (GCETP), a three-month certificate program in organic gardening. Call or see the website for upcoming classes.

Lakeside Park Demonstration Garden
Inside Lakeside Park (by Lake Merritt)
666 Bellevue Avenue
Oakland, CA 9461
Phone: (510) 238-2197
gardensatlakemerritt.com
This garden, located in a city park, shows East Bay gardeners the many possibilities for growing vegetable and fruit crops. Within the community garden area are fruit tree and vegetable demonstration gardens, and a trials garden in which different varieties of the same plant are grown. It is gardened by a variety of local groups and is open to the public daily from 8 a.m. to 5 p.m.

Mendocino Coast Botanical Gardens
18220 North Highway One
Fort Bragg, CA 95437
Phone: (707) 964-4352
www.gardenbythesea.org
This coastal garden and nursery includes an herb garden, an organic vegetable garden, and an old orchard as well as fine ornamental plantings. Classes on a wide variety of topics are offered throughout the year, including mushroom identification and ornamental and edible plants.

U.C. Botanical Garden
200 Centennial Drive
Berkeley, CA 94720-5045
Phone: (510) 643-2755
http://botanicalgarden.berkeley.edu
In addition to extensive and excellent ornamental plantings, included are "Crops of the World," a collection of economically important species from around the world; "Chinese Medicinal Herb Garden," containing traditional Chinese herbs; and "Herb Garden," containing western herbs and a vegetable garden. These areas are most interesting in spring and summer. The entrance planting is a demonstration garden of plants that do well with low water use.

HERBARIUMS

An herbarium is a library of pressed plant specimens. If you are trying to identify a plant and having no luck elsewhere, the botanists who work at an herbarium should be able to tell you what it is. Always call first.

California Academy of Sciences Naturalist Center
55 Music Concourse Drive
Golden Gate Park

San Francisco, CA 94118
Phone: (415) 379-5494
www.calacademy.org/academy/exhibits/naturalist_center

College of the Redwoods Mendocino Coast Herbarium
Science Division
College of the Redwoods
1211 Del Mar Drive
Fort Bragg, CA 95437
Phone: (707) 962-2656
www.redwoods.edu
Specializes in unusual plants of Mendocino County.

Humboldt State University Vascular Plant Herbarium
1 Harpst Street
Arcata, CA 95521
Phone: (707) 826-4801
www.humboldt.edu/~hcrb
Regional herbarium, centering on plant communities of Northwest California and Southern Oregon.

Sonoma State North Coast Herbarium
Biology Department
1801 East Cotati Avenue
Rohnert Park, CA 94928-3609
Phone: (707) 664-2303
Fax: (707) 664-3012

U.C. Davis Center for Plant Diversity
University of California, Davis
1026 Sciences Laboratory Building
Davis, CA 95616
Phone: (530) 752-1091
http://herbarium.ucdavis.edu
One of their specialties is agricultural weeds.

U.C. Santa Cruz Herbarium
Museum of Natural History
239 Natural Sciences 2
University of California at Santa Cruz
Santa Cruz, CA 95064
Phone: (831) 459-4763
www2.ucsc.edu/mnhc

University and Jepson Herbarium
University of California
1001 Valley Life Science Building, #2465
Berkeley, CA 94720-2465
Phone: (510) 642-2465
Fax: (510) 643-5390
ucjeps.berkeley.edu
Specializes in California native plants.

HORTICULTURE LIBRARIES

San Francisco Botanical Garden
Helen Crocker Russell Library of Horticulture
Golden Gate Park
1199 9th Avenue
San Francisco, CA 94122
Phone: (415) 661-1316, Ext. 403
www.sfbotanicalgarden.org/library
A small but wonderful horticulture library with helpful librarians, located within the Arboretum. In addition to a large collection of books and magazines on gardening and botany, it includes videotapes (viewable in the library), seed and nursery catalogs, and children's picture books. An online catalog lets you browse or search for a specific item through their website. Open 10 a.m. to 4 p.m. every day except major holidays.

U.C. Berkeley Bioscience and Natural Resources Library
University of California, Berkeley
2101 Valley Life Sciences Building, #6500
Berkeley, CA 94720-6500
Phone: (510) 642-2531
www.lib.berkeley.edu/BIOS
This is a branch of the campus library. All of the library's extensive print and electronic sources are open to the public. However, one can check out materials only after paying an annual fee. This library has all of the research journals on horticulture and agriculture, in case you want to look up an article reviewed in, for example, the magazine *HortIdeas*.

NEARBY COMMUNITY COLLEGES WITH PROGRAMS IN AGRICULTURE OR HORTICULTURE

In most cases, classes at these colleges are open to the public without prior enrollment in a degree program. Fees are low, and classes are often offered in the evening or on weekends.

Cabrillo College (Horticulture)
6500 Soquel Drive
Aptos, CA 95003
Phone: (831) 479-6241
www.cabrillo.edu/academics/horticulture

City College of San Francisco (Environmental Horticulture)
50 Phelan Avenue
San Francisco, CA 94112
Phone: (415) 239-3236
www.ccsf.edu/Departments/Environmental_Horticulture_and_Floristry

College of Marin (Environmental Landscaping)
835 College Avenue
Kentfield, CA 94904
Phone: (415) 457-8811, Ext. 8200
www.marin.edu

College of San Mateo (Horticulture)
Building 20
College of San Mateo
1700 West Hillsdale Boulevard
San Mateo, CA 94402
Phone: (650) 574-6170
http://collegeofsanmateo.edu/horticulture

Diablo Valley College (Horticulture)
321 Golf Club Road
Pleasant Hill, CA 94523
Phone: (925) 685-1230, Ext. 2443
www.dvc.edu/org/departments/biology/horticulture

Foothill College (Environmental Horticulture & Design)
12345 El Monte Road
Los Altos Hills, CA 94022
Phone: (650) 949-7402
www.foothill.edu/bio/programs/hort

Mendocino College (Horticulture)
1000 Hensley Creek Road
Ukiah, CA 95482
Phone: (707) 468-3148
www.mendocino.edu/tc/program/1/detail.html

Merritt College (Landscape Horticulture)
12500 Campus Drive
Oakland, CA 94619
Phone: (510) 436-2418
www.merrittlandhort.com

Monterey Peninsula College (Ornamental Horticulture)
980 Fremont Street
Monterey, CA 93940
Phone: (831) 646-4123
www.mpc.edu/academics/lifescience/ornamentalhorticulture

Santa Rosa Junior College (Environmental Horticulture)
1501 Mendocino Avenue
Santa Rosa, CA 95401
Phone: (707) 527-4408
www.santarosa.edu/instruction/instructional_departments/agriculture/environmental_horticulture/index.shtml
The horticulture department is difficult to locate on the website. The preceding address works. Apologies for its length. Maybe the website will be easier to navigate by the time you read this.

Solano Community College (Horticulture)
4000 Suisun Valley Road
Fairfield, CA 94534
Phone: (707) 864-7155
www.scc-careertech.com

West Valley College (Landscape Architecture)
14000 Fruitvale Avenue
Saratoga, CA 95070
Phone: (408) 741-4097
www.westvalley.edu/careers/arch/landscape.html

FOUR-YEAR COLLEGES AND UNIVERSITIES WITH PROGRAMS IN HORTICULTURE OR AGRICULTURE

California Polytechnic State University
1 Grand Avenue
San Luis Obispo, CA 93407
Phone: (805) 756-2279
http://crops.calpoly.edu
Cal Poly offers undergraduate degrees in Horticulture and Crop Science, Plant Protection Science, Fruit Science, Wine and Viticulture, and Landscape Architecture.

University of California at Davis
Department of Plant Sciences
One Shields Avenue
Davis, CA 95616
Phone: (530) 752-1703
www.plantsciences.ucdavis.edu
Offers undergraduate degrees in Environmental Horticulture as well as many areas of agriculture, including Agricultural Systems and Environment (sustainable agriculture). Also offers graduate degrees in Horticulture and Agriculture. There is a summer course, "Introduction to Sustainable Agricultural Systems" (6 units), offered at the Student Experimental Farm.

University of California at Santa Cruz
Environmental Studies
405 ISB
1156 High Street
Santa Cruz, CA 95064
Phone: (831) 459-2634
http://envs.ucsc.edu
This department offers BA and PhD degrees in Environmental Studies, with an emphasis on agroecology and sustainable agriculture. (See also the Center for Agroecology and Sustainable Food Systems, listed under Working and Model Farms Offering Educational Programs.)

BEE AND OTHER INSECT INFORMATION

citybugs
www.cnr.berkeley.edu/citybugs/index.html
This is a website created at the UC Berkeley College of Natural Resources to help you learn about common insects of the San Francisco Bay Region. It offers a search feature by common name, starting with large groups, such as beetles, and then showing common species. There are also links to many other insect resources.

San Francisco Beekeepers Association
c/o The Randall Museum
199 Museum Way
San Francisco, CA 94114
www.sfbee.org
This organization provides support for those who want to keep bees in San Francisco, and education about bees for the general public. Volunteers bring a demonstration hive to schools and other interested groups. They meet at the Randall Museum on the second Wednesday of each month. Meetings are open to the public. The "Resources" page of their website offers links to beekeeping organizations all around the Bay Area.

Urban Bee Gardens
http://nature.berkeley.edu/urbanbeegardens
Dr. Gordon Frankie of the University of California studies bees. This website, developed through his "bee lab," provides information about attracting honey bees and the many species of California native bees to your garden, including gardens in urban locations.

PEST IDENTIFICATION AND IPM INFORMATION

Bio-Integral Resource Center (BIRC)
Phone: (510) 524-2567
Fax: (510) 524-1758
www.birc.org
A membership organization promoting integrated pest management. They offer practical advice on least-toxic methods for solving pest problems. Their web feature, "Ask the Expert," allows people to submit questions on how to control a pest in the least toxic or nontoxic way. You can usually receive a reply in one working day. They publish two journals: *Commonsense Pest Control Quarterly*, offering how-to approaches for solving pest problems in the garden and home, and *IPM Practitioner*, which deals with larger structural and agricultural settings. Members receive a subscription to one or both of their journals (you pay extra to get both). A free catalog of materials published by BIRC, including reprints of articles from the journals, is available, and you can also view all of the materials online.

California Department of Food and Agriculture
Plant Health and Pest Prevention Services Division
Integrated Pest Control
1220 N Street
Sacramento, CA 95814-5607
www.cdfa.ca.gov/PHPPS/ipc
This website page is that of Integrated Pest Control, within the Plant Health and Pest Prevention Services section of the website of the CDFA. From this page you can enter the Encycloweedia, a marvelous searchable list to help identify and manage all the weeds defined as noxious by California law. Also of interest is the *Noxious Times*, a quarterly newsletter on weed management that you can read online.

California Invasive Plant Council
1442-A Walnut Street, #462
Berkeley, CA 94709
Phone: (510) 843-3902
Fax: (510) 217-3500
www.cal-ipc.org
The goal of this organization is to protect California wildlands from invasive plants, through restoration, research, and education. They keep a list of the worst wildland invaders and lists of plants to watch. Through material they publish, you can learn which plants require caution or are best not planted in gardens, and the best IPM methods for dealing with weeds, especially ones that have taken over a piece of untended land. Two of their books, *Invasive Plants of California's Wildlands* and *The Weed Workers Handbook*, appear (illustrations and all) on their website.

UC IPM Online
Statewide Integrated Pest Management Program
http://ipm.ucdavis.edu
This site serves as a clearinghouse for online UC IPM resources and provides links to some other useful sites. You will find UC pest notes about insects, mites, diseases, nematodes, weeds, and vertebrate pests for both home gardeners and agriculturalists, as well as information on managing nonnative plant and animal invaders in California's natural environments. Under "Educational Resources" you will find training material used to teach retail nursery workers about pesticides and IPM methods that reduce their use.

PESTICIDE INFORMATION RESOURCES

California Poison Control System
Phone: (800) 222-1222
www.calpoison.org
This office provides phone advice and assistance in case of pesticide or other poisoning. The phone is manned 24 hours a day, every day. Over 100 languages spoken.

National Pesticide Information Center
Phone: (800) 858-7378
http://npic.orst.edu
The mission of this organization is to provide unbiased, science-based information about the use and safety of pesticides. View their website or call (available every day, with over 100 languages spoken) for help in reading a label or for all kinds of information about particular pesticides. There is much emergency information on this site, though if you have a human poisoning emergency, they advise you to call 911 or the California Poison Control Center (see previous listing).

Pesticide Action Network of North America (PANNA)
49 Powell Street, Suite 500
San Francisco, CA 94102
Phone: (415) 981-1771
Fax: (415) 981-1991
www.panna.org
PANNA is part of a worldwide network of organizations working to stop misuse of pesticides and to support reliance on safe, ecologically sound alternatives. They publish a magazine, *PAN North America*, three times a year, which keeps you up-to-date on global pesticide issues and campaigns. You can also subscribe to a weekly internet update called PANUPS.

UC IPM Pesticide Information Resources
www.ipm.ucdavis.edu/GENERAL/pesticides.html
This page of the UC IPM Online website provides links to many sources of information on pesticides and their safe and effective use, both ones sponsored by UC and external sites.

HOUSEHOLD HAZARDOUS WASTE COLLECTION FACILITIES

In San Francisco

San Francisco Household Hazardous Waste Program
Phone: (415) 330-1405
www.sfhazwaste.com
This free service is for San Francisco residents only. They accept most kinds of toxic household waste, including leftover pesticides. You may bring products to their facility at 501 Tunnel Avenue, Thursday through Saturday, from 8 a.m. to 4 p.m., or call the phone number to arrange for pickup. Call or view the website for more information.

In Other Counties

There is a statewide mandate to develop hazardous waste facilities. To see what exists in your county, call your county Health Department.

BEFORE YOU DIG

USA (Underground Service Alert)
(800) 227-2600
Our basic services are often supplied by underground pipes or cables, and it is entirely possible to damage these when you are digging a garden. Be prudent, and avoid this hazard, by calling the USA number two working days before you plan to dig in any unfamiliar area. Ask for the free "mark and locate service" for underground pipelines and cables.

APPENDIX VIII

Suggested Reading

§ means a book is out of print but is still worth looking for in libraries or for purchase.

FOOD GARDENING IN GENERAL

The Bountiful Container
Rose Marie Nichols McGee and Maggie Stuckey
Workman Publishing
New York, NY, 2002
A cheerful and informative book about growing all kinds of edibles in containers. Includes crop-by-crop advice, theme garden suggestions, and basic container gardening information.

Fresh Food from Small Spaces
R. J. Ruppenthal
Chelsea Green Publishing
White River Junction, VT, 2008
The author shares his experiences with gardening on a balcony in containers and offers carefully thought-through advice on using tiny spaces well, including information on sprouting, fermenting, mushrooms, bees, chickens, and composting in small spaces.

Gardening at the Dragon's Gate: At Work in the Wild and Cultivated World
Wendy Johnson
Bantam Books
New York, NY, 2008
The experiences of Zen Practice and gardening at the Green Gulch Farm Zen Center in Marin County led to the writing of this book. All gardening is a spiritual practice, and Johnson's wisdom and humor teaches us to see this more clearly as we garden.

Gardening When It Counts: Growing Food in Hard Times
Steve Solomon
New Society Publishers
Gabriola Island, BC, Canada, 2005
The founder and former owner of Territorial Seed Company is now gardening in Tasmania, in a climate similar to the one he left behind in Oregon. He has written a valuable book about serious food gardening done frugally. Read what he has to say about seed sources, least expensive fertilizers, and making good compost. Best read after reading a basic gardening book or two.

How to Grow More Vegetables (and Fruits, Nuts, Berries, Grains, and Other Crops) Than You Ever Thought Possible on Less Land Than You Can Imagine
John Jeavons
Ten Speed Press
Berkeley, CA, 2006
An explanation of the methods of biodynamic/French intensive gardening with an emphasis on mini-farming to produce as much as possible of your food needs.

How to Have a Green Thumb Without an Aching Back §
Ruth Stout
Exposition-Phoenix Press, Inc.
Fort Lauderdale, FL, 1955
Gardening under a permanent mulch allowed Ruth Stout to garden after disabilities of age confined her to a wheelchair. A wise, witty, and informative book.

The Organic Salad Garden
Joy Larkcom
Frances Lincoln Limited
London, England, 2004
How to grow salad ingredients, including Asian greens, herbs, flowers, and wild plants. Includes useful and inspiring color photographs of each crop and of finished recipes.

REGIONAL GARDENING BOOKS

Backyard Farmer §
Lee Foster
Chronicle Books
San Francisco, CA, 1995
A small, personal book about using a city lot in Oakland to grow food crops.

California Master Gardener Handbook
Dennis R. Pittenger, Editor
University of California
Agriculture and Natural Resources
Communication Services
Publication 3382
Oakland, CA, 2004
A gardening primer used in Master Gardener training programs, this book covers basic topics and has considerable information on vegetable and fruit gardening. (For Home Fruit Gardening in particular, see also *The Home Orchard*, Publication 3285.)

The City People's Book of Raising Food §
Helga and William Olkowski
Rodale Press, Book Division
Emmaus, PA, 1975
Not ostensibly a local book, but this thoughtful introductory gardening book was written from East Bay experience.

Grow Your Own §
Jeanie Darlington
Random House, Inc.
New York, NY, 1983
A small, charming, personal book on vegetable gardening in Albany, California, just north of Berkeley. A historical treasure first published in 1970.

Growing Vegetables West of the Cascades
Steve Soloman
Sasquatch Books
Seattle, WA, 2007
The coastal region of Oregon has colder winters than we do, and seems to be about a month behind us in the spring, and the pests are somewhat different, but conditions are similar enough that this book makes very interesting reading.

Northern California Gardening: A Month-by-Month Guide
Katherine Grace Endicott
Chronicle Books
San Francisco, CA, 2005
Key garden tasks, month by month, with separate listings for coastal gardeners. Helps you to integrate your edible and ornamental gardening calendars.

Sunset Western Garden Book
Kathleen N. Brenzel, Editor
Sunset Publishing Co.
Menlo Park, CA, 2007
An important reference for all gardeners west of the Rocky Mountains. Lists hundreds of kinds of ornamental and food-bearing plants and describes their growing requirements. Sunset divides the West into twenty-four climatic regions and rates each plant for these regions.

Winter Gardening in the Maritime Northwest, 3rd Edition §
Binda Colebrook
Sasquatch Books
Seattle, WA, 2002
The winter weather of Seattle is enough wetter and colder than ours that some of the advice in this book will not apply here. Still, the book is very inspiring for those who want to garden through the colder months, and it shows that many of our winter crops can take considerably more severe conditions than those of our area.

LESS COMMON FOOD CROPS

Amaranth—Modern Prospects for an Ancient Crop §
National Research Council Staff
Rodale Press
Emmaus, PA, 1987
The history of amaranth, methods of cultivation, and over 80 recipes.

Cornucopia II: A Source Book of Edible Plants
Steven Facciola
Kampong Books
Vista, CA, 1998
A unique reference containing descriptions and sources for hundreds of edible flowering plants, fungi, algae, and bacteria.

Lost Crops of the Incas: Little-Known Plants of the Andes with Promise for Worldwide Cultivation §
National Research Council Staff
Books for Business
Washington, D.C., 2002
Includes the history, methods of cultivation, nutritional value, and potential for wider use of many crops, including yacon (Bolivian sunroot), oca, quinoa, amaranth, goldenberry, and different types of potato and pepper.

Microgreens: A Guide to Growing Nutrient-Packed Greens
Eric Franks and Jasmine Richardson
Gibbs Smith
Layton, UT, 2009
Everything you need to know to produce these greens that are barely older than sprouts.

Oriental Vegetables: The Complete Guide for the Gardening Cook
Joy Larkcom
Kodansha International
New York, NY, 1991
Explicit cultivation instructions based on the author's experience and observations in Asia. Traditional recipes and ideas for using these crops in Western-style cooking. Includes Chinese and Japanese characters for each plant, as well as English alphabet transliterations of the names in Mandarin, Cantonese, and Japanese.

Perennial Vegetables: From Artichokes to Zuiki Taro, A Gardener's Guide to Over 100 Delicious and Easy to Grow Edibles
Eric Toensmeier
Chelsea Green Publishing
White River Junction, VT, 2007
This book will help you evaluate, select, and grow crops that return year after year.

The Random House Book of Vegetables
Roger Phillips and Martyn Rix
Random House
New York, NY, 1993
Over 650 vegetable varieties and species, common and uncommon, described and discussed. Wonderful photos from around the world, histories of crops, cultivation information.

Unusual Vegetables: Something New for This Year's Garden §
Anne Moyer Halpin and the Editors of Organic Gardening and Farming
Rodale Press, Inc.
Emmaus, PA, 1978
A really useful compendium of cultural and culinary information for some of the less familiar crops.

HERBS

Herbal Renaissance: Growing, Using, and Understanding Herbs in the Modern World
Stephen Foster
DIANE Publishing Company
Layton, UT, 2003
Full information on how to grow and use herbs.

Tyler's Honest Herbal: A Sensible Guide to the Use of Herbs and Related Remedies
Steven Foster and Varro E. Tyler, PhD
Routledge
Philadelphia, PA, 2007
A modern, myth-free look at herbal remedies. Explains how active ingredients work and what they can and cannot be expected to do.

Your Backyard Herb Garden: A Gardener's Guide to Growing over 50 Herbs Plus How to Use Them in Cooking, Crafts, Companion Planting, and More
Miranda Smith
Rodale Press
Emmaus, PA, 1999
Whether you want to design an herb garden or integrate herbs into a flower garden, learn to make dried arrangements and potpourri or learn culinary uses of lavender, this illustrated book will guide you.

FLOWERS

Complete Garden Guide to Native California Perennials §
Glenn Keator
Chronicle Books
San Francisco, CA, 1990
Information to help you grow over 500 species of native perennial flowers. Includes advice for using them in your garden plan.

Cutting Gardens §
Anne Halpin and Betty Mackey
Simon and Schuster
New York, NY, 1993
Good information on how to lay out a cutting garden, choose plants to grow, plant, and maintain the garden, and tips for creating arrangements.

The Flower Arranger's Garden §
Rosemary Verey
Little, Brown and Co.
New York, NY, 1989
Guidance in designing a garden that produces cutting flowers. Includes many inspiring photos of flower arrangements.

Growing California Native Plants
Marjorie Schmidt
University of California Press
Berkeley, CA, 1981
Detailed techniques of propagation and culture for more than 350 annuals, perennials, bulbs, shrubs, and trees.

Landscaping with Perennials §
Emily Brown
Timber Press
Portland, OR, 1986
A wealth of detail about growing perennial flowers in our region from a gardener who gardened for many years at Filoli, the great public garden on the Peninsula.

Successful Perennials for the Peninsula: A Selection by Members of the Western Horticultural Society §
Keith Bickford, Editor
Western Horticultural Society
Palo Alto, CA, 1989
Here is information on growing some of the best perennial flowers for our region, chosen by some of our best horticulturists. (The list is different from the classic perennial list for eastern gardens.)

When Does It Bloom? A Guide to Planning Seasonal Garden Color §
Matthew J. Leddy
275 D Street
Redwood City, CA, 1996
This book gives the sequence of bloom in Sunset Zone 15. While it refers precisely to the area from Redwood City to Mountain View, bloom sequence will be very similar to that of other nearby areas. Lists flowers by plant type, color, height, and whether they need sun or shade.

Wildly Successful Plants: Northern California
Pam Peirce
Sasquatch Books
Seattle, WA, 2004
An ornamental gardening primer for Northern California and information on gardening with 50 easy and historic California plants. Most are drought-tolerant, many are deer tolerant and good as cut flowers and/or for attracting hummingbirds.

EDIBLE LANDSCAPING

The Complete Book of Edible Landscaping
Rosalind Creasy
Sierra Club Books
San Francisco, CA, 2010
This book will help you design a beautiful garden containing a high proportion of edible plants. Includes an encyclopedia of food-bearing plants, with growing and harvesting information as it relates to their use in the landscape.

Designing and Maintaining Your Edible Landscape Naturally
Robert Kourick
Metamorphic Press
Santa Rosa, CA, 1986
A book packed with information on the nitty-gritty of planning and constructing an edible landscape. Includes extensive information on choosing and growing fruit trees and a chart of flowers to attract beneficial insects.

Landscaping with Fruit
Lee Reich
Storey Publishing
North Adams, MA, 2009
Combines basics of garden design and a few sample plans with information on designing with and growing fruit plants. It contains much useful information, but assumes subtropical fruit will be grown in containers.

FRUIT GROWING

(see also Food Gardening in General, Regional Gardening Books, Less Common Food Crops, Edible Landscaping, and Pruning)

All About Citrus and Subtropical Fruits §
Maggie Klein, Paul Moore, and Claude Sweet
Ortho Books
San Ramon, CA, 1985
Information on growing and using all kinds of citrus and other subtropical and tropical fruits.

Citrus: Complete Guide to Selecting, Growing, and Using More Than 100 Varieties in California, Arizona, Texas, and Florida
Lance Walheim
Ironwood Press
Tucson, AZ, 1996
A book on growing citrus by someone with extensive experience growing it in the ground in California.

The Home Orchard: Growing Your Own Deciduous Fruit and Nut Trees
Chuck A. Ingels, Pamela M. Geisel, and Maxwell V. Norton, Technical Editors
University of California
Division of Agriculture and Natural Resources Publication 3485
Berkeley, CA, 2007
An immensely helpful publication that will guide you in selecting, planting, pruning, and maintaining deciduous fruit trees.

URBAN LIVESTOCK

The Backyard Beekeeper: An Absolute Beginner's Guide to Keeping Bees in Your Yard and Garden
Kim Flottum
Quarry Books
Beverly, MA, 2005
Beekeeping societies in many localities can help you get started, but this book provides a valuable orientation in bee biology, techniques for beekeeping, and bee maladies. Includes color photographs.

Keep Chickens: Tending Small Flocks in Cities, Suburbs, and Other Small Spaces
Barbara Kilarski
Storey Publishing
North Adams, MA, 2003
A book for urban fowl keepers. All the basic topics and special city considerations (such as permits and clearing your plans with your neighbors first).

Storey's Guide to Raising Chickens
Gail Damerow
Storey Publishing
North Adams, MA, 1995
This thorough book on chicken keeping isn't specially aimed at urban farmers, but you will appreciate the detailed information, including how to deal with problems that can occur.

See also *The Integral Urban House*, under Ecology/Ecosystem Complexity

SEEDS

(see also Ecology/Ecosystem Complexity)

Garden Seed Inventory
Kent Whealy
Seed Savers Exchange
Decorah, IA, 2005
An inventory of seed catalogs listing all nonhybrid vegetable seeds offered in the U.S. and Canada. New editions are issued every couple of years. See also Seed Savers Exchange in Appendix VI.

The New Seed Starters Handbook
Nancy Bubel
Rodale Press, Inc.
Emmaus, PA, 1989
Detailed instructions for starting crops from seed.

Saving Seeds: The Gardener's Guide to Growing and Storing Vegetable and Flower Seeds
Marc Rogers
Storey Publishing, L.L.C.
North Adams, MA, 1991
Crop-by-crop descriptions of how to avoid cross-pollination, collect the seed of vegetables and ornamentals, and clean it for storage.

Seed to Seed: Seed Saving Techniques for the Vegetable Gardener
Suzanne Ashworth
Seed Savers Exchange, Inc.
Decorah, IA, 2004
From personal experience, the tried and true details for successful small scale-seed production of 160 vegetable crops.

WATERING AND WATER CONSERVATION

Create an Oasis with Greywater: Choosing, Building, and Using Greywater Systems, Revised and Expanded 5th Edition
Art Ludwig
Oasis Design
Santa Barbara, CA, 2007
Teaches how to assess your site, design a system, and avoid common errors. A separate, shorter supplement, *Builder's Greywater Guide*, by the same author and press, includes California, Arizona, and New Mexico laws on gray water and specific information on meeting building codes.

Drip Irrigation for Every Landscape and All Climates, 2nd Edition
Robert Kourik
Metamorphic Press
Occidental, CA, 2009
Good introduction to drip irrigation and information on how to place emitters for best plant growth. Includes information on gray water and rainwater systems.

Rainwater Harvesting for Drylands and Beyond: (Vol. 1) Guiding Principles; (Vol. 2) Water-Harvesting Earthworks
Brad Lancaster
Rainsource Press
Tucson, AZ, 2008
Two books covering everything you could wish to know about trapping the water from rain, either in storage containers or in your soil.

SOIL AND SOIL FERTILITY

Gypsum and Other Chemical Amendments for Soil Improvement
University of California
Division of Agriculture and Natural Resources Publication 2149
Revised Edition, 1980
Some clay soils benefit from the addition of gypsum. Don't buy gypsum before you use the test in this pamphlet to find out if your soil will benefit from it.

Hunger Signs in Crops: A Symposium §
Howard B. Sprague
Longman Publishing Group
New York, NY, 1964
Recognizing nutrient deficiencies is not always easy, since symptoms overlap with each other and with disease symptoms. That's why soil tests are so helpful. However, books such as this are good guides if you have a problem and want to try to identify the cause.

Let It Rot! The Gardener's Guide to Composting
Stu Campbell
Storey Publishing, L.L.C
Pownal, VT, 1990
Humorous but effective introduction to composting.

Roots Demystified
Robert Kourik
Metamorphic Press
P.O. Box 412
Occidental, CA, 2008
Whether you are growing vegetables or fruit trees, this book will help you imagine their roots and tells you the latest information on growing healthy ones. Many illustrations of root patterns.

The Soul of Soil: A Soil-Building Guide for Master Gardeners and Farmers, 4th Edition
Grace Gershuny and Joe Smillie
Chelsea Green Publishing Company
White River Junction, VT, 1999
An excellent way to dig deeper into the whys and hows of soil improvement that includes much practical information.

Start with the Soil: The Organic Gardener's Guide to Improving Soil for Higher Yields, More Beautiful Flowers, and a Healthy, Easy-Care Garden
Grace Gershuny
Rodale Press
Emmaus, PA, 1993
Thorough guide to soil improvement for many different kinds of plants, including those growing in containers.

Worms Eat My Garbage
Mary Appelhof
Flowerfield Press
Kalamazoo, MI, 1997
How to set up and maintain a worm composting system.

See also *Life in the Soil,* in the Insect and Other Wildlife Appreciation section.

PRUNING

American Horticultural Society: Pruning and Training
Christopher Brickell (ed.), David Joyce
Dorling-Kindersley
New York, NY, 1996
Great before-and-after photos and illustrations will aid you in learning how to prune over 800 kinds of ornamental and fruiting plants.

Espalier Fruit Trees: Their History and Culture §
Alan Edmunds
Pomona Books
Rockton, Ontario, Canada, 1986
Espalier, from basic to fanciful. History, how-to, and many amazing drawings and photos.

How to Prune Fruit Trees, 21st Edition
R. Sanford Martin
Martin Bio-Products
147 North Ontario Street
Burbank, CA 91505, 2006
A small book that contains brief but clear directions for pruning deciduous and subtropical fruit trees, berries, and grapes. Includes useful drawings.

The Pruning Book
Lee Reich
Taunton Press
Newtown, CT, 1999
Good advice, well-illustrated, on pruning many kinds of plants, including fruit trees, shrubs, and vines.

VEGETATIVE PROPAGATION AND GRAFTING

Creative Propagation, 2nd Edition
Peter Thompson
Timber Press
Portland, OR, 2005
This book covers seeding, cuttings, and division. It gives all the information you need to use these methods for all types of plants, and includes "propagations summaries" for hundreds of species.

Plant Propagation, Principles and Practices, 7th Edition
Hudson Hartman, Dale Kester, Fred Davies, Jr., and Robert Geneve
Simon and Schuster
Upper Saddle River, NY, 2001
The standard textbook on plant propagation. It describes the techniques and explains why and how they work.

Secrets of Plant Propagation: Starting Your Own Flowers, Vegetables, Fruits, Berries, Shrubs, Trees, and Houseplants
Lewis Hill
Storey Communications
Pownal, VT, 1985
Overview of propagation including seeds, cuttings, and grafting. Specific methods for many kinds of plants, including fruits and nuts.

WEED APPRECIATION

The Flavors of Home: A Guide to Wild Edible Plants of the San Francisco Bay Area
Margit Roos-Collins
Heyday Books
Berkeley, CA, 1990
Help locating, identifying, and using weeds, escaped domestic plants, and native plants that grow in the Bay Area.

My Weeds: A Gardener's Botany
Sarah Stein
University of Florida Press
Gainesville, FL, 2000
Reading this book will give you an understanding of weeds, and a painless introduction to many aspects of botany—from plant anatomy to evolution.

Plants, Man, and Life
Edgar Anderson
Dover Publications, Inc.
Mineola, NY, 2005
A delightful exploration of the relationship humans have maintained with weeds and crop plants.

Weeds, Guardians of the Soil §
Joseph A. Cocannouer
Greenwich, Devin-Adair Publishers, Inc.
New York, NY, 1980
The other side of the weed story: the value of weeds to the soil and as food and animal fodder.

WEED IDENTIFICATION AND MANAGEMENT

Invasive Plants of California's Wildlands
Carla C. Bossard, John M. Randall, and Marc C. Hoshovsky
University of California Press
Berkeley, CA, 2000
Learn to recognize and manage California's wildland invasives. Home gardeners can also learn much from the logical way that a wildland weeder thinks through a management program for a weed.

Weeds of the West
Tom Whitson
Western Society of Weed Science
University of Wyoming
Laramie, WY, 2000
Full-color photos (three for each weed) and descriptive text will help you identify over 350 weeds. Also available as UC Publication 3350 (see University of California Cooperative Extension Service in Appendix VII, Resources for Gardeners).

Also, refer to local libraries for regional "floras"—lists of plants found in your particular region—to help you identify uncommon weeds.

INSECT AND OTHER WILDLIFE APPRECIATION

California Insects
Jerry A. Powell, Charles L. Hogue
University of California Press
Berkeley, CA, 1989
Pictures and descriptions of most of the insects you are likely to encounter, including color photos of 128 of them. Includes good introductory material about insects.

Insects, A Golden Guide
Herbert S. Zim, Ph.D., and Clarence Cottam, Ph.D.
St. Martin's Press
New York, NY, 2001
A guide to common North American insects, with illustrations. Introduction is helpful for those beginning to study insects.

Life in the Soil: A Guide for Naturalists and Gardeners
James B. Nardi
University of Chicago Press
Chicago, IL, 2007
Learn about all the creatures that live in soil, their relationships with each other, and how we can work in partnership with them to make the soil a good place for our plants to grow. Plenty of illustrations.

Natural Enemies Handbook: The Illustrated Guide to Biological Pest Control
Mary Louise Flint, Steve Dreistadt
University of California
Division of Agriculture and Natural Resources Publication 3386
Berkeley, CA, 1998
A thorough and readable explanation of biological control of pests, weeds, nematodes, and diseases, both the naturally occurring natural enemies and ones that are introduced.

PEST MANAGEMENT

The Gardener's Bug Book, 4th Edition §
Cynthia Westcott
Doubleday and Company
New York, NY, 1973
Like her *Plant Disease Handbook*, this Cynthia Westcott book has a checklist of pests by plant damaged in the back, individual pests described in the front. Invaluable for help with identification and learning life cycles of pests. Advice is way out of date—though DDT, which had just been banned as of the printing of this book, was eliminated from this last edition.

The Gardener's Guide to Common-Sense Pest Control
William Olkowski, Sheila Daar, Helga Olkowski
Taunton Press
Newtown, CT, 1996
A selection from the larger *Common-Sense Pest Control* of information of particular interest to gardeners. Thorough and precise integrated pest management techniques from some of the pioneers in the field.

The Ortho Problem Solver, 7th Edition
Edited by Michael D. Smith
Ortho Information Services
San Ramon, CA, 2008
Over 1,000 pages of pest control information. Each entry includes a photo of the symptom you are most likely to see, a description of the problem, an analysis, and some solutions. The book lists mainly chemical controls, so you will usually need another reference to plan a control strategy. Look for reference copies in libraries and nurseries.

Pests of the Garden and Small Farm: A Grower's Guide to Using Less Pesticide, 2nd Edition
Mary Louise Flint
University of California
Division of Agriculture and Natural Resources Publication 3332
Berkeley, CA, 1998
Here are excellent descriptions of problems and plans for integrated pest management of the pests of California vegetable and fruit crops. Includes great color photos and a troubleshooting table for each crop.

Pests of the West: Prevention and Control for Today's Garden and Small Farm
Whitney Cranshaw
Fulcrum Publishing
Golden, CO, 1998

Clear, thorough, easy to find information on insects, diseases, weeds, and pesticides. Appendix on attracting insectivorous birds to your garden.

Rodale's Pest and Disease Problem Solver: A Chemical-Free Guide to Keeping Your Garden Healthy
Linda Gilkeson, Pam Peirce, Miranda Smith
Rodale Press, Emmaus, PA, 1996
Includes entries for common plants and for common animal pests and diseases, listing organic methods of pest control. A section on "the healthy garden" describes garden methods that prevent problems.

Snails: From Garden to Table §
Frances Herb
Illuminations Press
St. Helena, CA, 1990
This little book tells you how to become a predator of *Helix aspersa*, the brown garden snail that so plagues us. Here are directions for catching, cleaning, and preparing snails, as well as many savory recipes.

Westcott's Plant Disease Handbook, 7th Edition
Revised by R. Kenneth Horst
Springer
New York, NY, 1990
This classic plant disease reference, originally by Cynthia Westcott, is being kept up to date. It is invaluable for the listings by plant in the rear that refer you to diseases in the main text. While the current edition will have latest information, it is worth picking up any older edition you come across.

Wildlife Pest Control Around Gardens and Homes, 2nd Edition
Terrell P. Salmon, et al.
University of California
Division of Agriculture and Natural Resources Publication 21385
Berkeley, CA, 2006
Uses an IPM approach to prevention and management of damage by vertebrate pests from woodpeckers to deer.

COMPANION PLANTING

Companion Planting: Rodale's Successful Organic Gardening §
Susan McClure, Sally Roth
Rodale Press
Emmaus, PA, 1994
Mentions traditional lore, adds comments on scientific proof when available, and includes new information on growing companion plants that attract beneficial insects.

Companion Plants: Carrots *Really Detest* Tomatoes
Craig Dremann
Redwood City Seed Co., 1992
P.O. Box 361
Redwood City, CA 94064
A pamphlet reporting the author's experiments with traditional and other plant companion combinations. In most cases, the traditional combinations did not prove beneficial. He did find some one-sided companion pairs—that is, only one of the pair benefited.

Good Neighbors: Companion Planting for Gardeners §
Anna Carr
Rodale Press, Inc.
Emmaus, PA, 1985
Reviews traditional companion pairs in the light of current research.

PESTICIDES

The Safe and Effective Use of Pesticides, 2nd Edition
Patrick J. Marer
University of California
Division of Agriculture and Natural Resources Publication 3324
Berkeley, CA, 2000
The best practical reference, covering every phase of pesticide use, emphasizing personal and environmental safety at every step.

GARDEN RESEARCH/ GARDEN SCIENCE

Botany for Gardeners: An Introduction and Guide
Brian Capon
Timber Press, Inc.
Portland, OR, 1990
Illustrated with photos and line drawings, this small book explains the basics of plant structure and function. This information will help you learn to identify plants and understand how best to care for them.

Breed Your Own Vegetable Varieties: Popbeans, Purple Peas, and Other Innovations from the Backyard Garden
Carol Deppe
Chelsea Green Publishing
White River Junction, VT, 2000
Deppe sets forth the information you need to breed your own, new varieties, including genetic information for 801 edible plant species. As she states, "Crop varieties incorporate the values of their creators." This new, expanded edition challenges you to put your values into your crops.

Improve Your Gardening with Backyard Research §
Lois Levitan
Rodale Press
Emmaus, PA, 1980
You can find out what really works in your garden and what does not if you use logical methods to test your theories. This book will help you set up sound experiments.

The Informed Gardener
Linda Chalker-Scott
University of Washington Press
Seattle, WA, 2008
The author is a plant physiologist who takes on a number of horticulture and gardening myths, such as putting pot shards in the bottom of containers or using compost tea to fight disease. In so doing, she teaches how scientists test and retest theories to discover what's true.

Living With Plants: A Guide to the Practical Application of Botany
Donna N. Schumann
Mad River Press
Eureka, CA, 1992
Presents botany—including plant structure and function, soils, propagation, and climatic adaptation as needed to understand horticulture.

Includes chapters on indoor plants, pruning, and garden design.

GARDENING WITH CHILDREN

A Garden for Children §
Felicity Bryan
Michael Joseph Ltd
London, England, 1986
How to create an attractive garden that children will also enjoy. Lots of great ideas for sharing a garden with children, including safety tips. The watercolor illustrations are an inspiration in themselves.

Grow Lab: Activities for Growing Minds
Eve Pranis, Joy Cohen
National Gardening Association
Burlington, VT, 1990
Contains forty-five lesson plans for hands-on indoor plant-based K–8 science lessons. Also includes activities for using indoor gardens to teach math, language arts, and environmental topics.

Grow Lab: A Complete Guide to Gardening in the Classroom
Eve Pranis, Jack Hale
National Gardening Association
Burlington, VT, 1988
A teacher's guide for using indoor gardening setups. Complete plans for a grow lab garden, planning and planting, pest control, and special garden projects.

Nourishing Choices
National Gardening Association
Burlington, VT, 2008
A road map for educators, parents, and others who want to develop a food education program and excite children about healthy eating. (See also National Gardening Association in Appendix VII, Resources for Gardeners.)

Worms Eat Our Garbage: Classroom Activities for a Better Environment
Mary Appelhoff, Mary Frances Fenton, Barbara Loss Harris
Flowerfield Press
Kalamazoo, MI, 2004
A worm compost bin lets children learn composting lessons indoors.

GARDENING FOR PEOPLE WITH SPECIAL NEEDS

Accessible Gardening for People with Physical Disabilities: A Guide to Methods, Tools, and Plants
Janeen R. Adil
Woodbine House
Bethesda, MD, 1994
How to adapt an existing garden for use by persons with physical disabilities, set up container gardens, choose tools and plants. Resource list.

The Enabling Garden: Creating Barrier-Free Gardens
Gene Rothert, HTR
Taylor Publishing Co.
Dallas, TX, 1994
Designing and constructing a garden for persons with special physical needs, choosing and adapting tools, tips for choosing and maintaining plants. Helpful illustrations, plans, and resource list.

ECOLOGY/ECOSYSTEM COMPLEXITY

Forgotten Pollinators
Stephen L. Buchman, Gary Paul Nabham, Edward O. Wilson
Island Press
Washington, D.C., 1996
Essays on the plight of pollinators in the modern world. Teaches us to appreciate the importance and the diversity of pollinating insects and other creatures.

Gaia's Garden: A Guide to Home-Scale Permaculture
Toby Hemenway
Chelsea Green Publishing Company
White River Junction, VT, 2001
Applying principles of permaculture to create an "ecological garden."

Integral Urban House §
Helga Olkowski, Bill Olkowski, Tom Javits, and the Farallones Institute Staff
Sierra Club Books
San Francisco, CA, 1979
The Integral Urban House was a demonstration project in Berkeley showing how to maximize food production and energy conservation in an urban residence. This book explains it all—from vegetable and small livestock production, to solar heating and composting toilets.

Noah's Garden: Restoring the Ecology of Our Own Backyards
Sarah Stein
Houghton Mifflin Co.
New York, NY, 1995
As delightful as her first book, *My Weeds*, this one describes her efforts to recreate her ornamental garden into one that the native wildlife could inhabit. It's an Eastern garden, but these are lessons we can apply to California gardens.

Plant Life in Mediterranean Climates
Peter R. Dallman
University of California Press
Berkeley, CA, 1998
Globally, there are five places with mediterranean climates. This book explains how their climates are the same and how they vary, then explores the native plants and plant communities of each.

Shattering: Food, Politics, and the Loss of Genetic Diversity
Cary Fowler, Pat Mooney
University of Arizona Press
Tucson, AZ, 1990
Reviews the development of genetically diverse food crop plants over 10,000 years and exposes the loss of diversity in the past 100 years. Lays out what will be needed to stop the losses, including worldwide individual seed saving.

Weather of the San Francisco Bay Region
Harold Gilliam
University of California Press
Berkeley, CA, 1962
A unique illustrated handbook about our weather patterns.

FOOD IN AMERICA

Animal, Vegetable, Miracle: A Year of Food Life
Barbara Kingsolver with Steven L. Hopp and Camille Kingsolver
HarperCollins Publishers
New York, NY, 2007
A fine tale, by an author who also writes fiction and poetry, about a

year as locavores (people who eat as much as possible from nearby sources). From the chronicle of the family's gardening and poultry-raising year to a story of a local farm cooperative whose tomatoes rotted unsold because a California supplier wholesaled tomatoes at a few pennies less, you will learn the joys and pains of, and the many reasons for, learning to eat more locally.

The Earth Knows My Name: Food, Culture, and Sustainability in the Gardens of Ethnic Americans
Patricia Klindienst
Beacon Press
Boston, MA, 2006
From the Native American garden in a New Mexico Pueblo to the gardens of Italian Americans who fled Mussolini's tyranny, this book beautifully chronicles tradition and change, spiritual values, and the understanding that the earth is our life.

Fast Food Nation: The Dark Side of the All-American Meal
Eric Schlosser
HarperCollins
New York, NY, 2002
Valuable history of fast food and what it has done to farmers, slaughterhouse workers, restaurant workers, and our nation's health.

In Defense of Food: An Eater's Manifesto
Michael Pollan
Penguin Group
New York, NY, 2009
Written as a companion to his book *The Omnivore's Dilemma*, this book proposes a simple, liberating approach to making choices about healthful and pleasurable eating.

The Omnivore's Dilemma: A Natural History of Four Meals
Michael Pollan
Penguin Press
New York, NY, 2006
The four meals Pollan explores are industrial (fast food), big business organic, small farm organic, and home produced (grown, hunted, and foraged). We learn about the sources of these meals, and their hidden costs, and explore how we choose the food we eat.

Parsnips in the Snow: Talks with Midwestern Gardeners
Jane Anne Staw and Mary Swander
University of Iowa Press
Iowa City, IA, 1990
In a series of interviews with farmers and gardeners, this book chronicles the place of food growing in the culture of America's heartland. We learn the details of the farms and gardens and about the many lives enriched by them.

RECIPE BOOKS

Chez Panisse Vegetables
Alice Waters
Harper Collins
New York, NY, 2002
From a cook with a passionate desire to share her appreciation of fresh vegetables. The recipes for each vegetable are arranged from the simplest to the more complicated. Look for the unexpected combinations, such as butternut squash pizza or asparagus with blood orange. Includes information on the basics of handling each crop in the kitchen.

Classic Indian Vegetarian and Grain Cookery
Julie Sahni
William Morrow and Company, Inc.
New York, NY, 1985
Relatively easy recipes for everything from curry to dahl, with explanations of less familiar ingredients and spices. Vegans can substitute soy products for the dairy in this cuisine.

The Complete Book of Mexican Cooking
Elizabeth Lambert Ortiz
Xlibris Corporation
Philadelphia, PA, 1998
Includes great recipes for using tomatillos, cactus pads, cilantro, epazote, chayote, and other garden produce.

Cooking Fresh from the Bay Area
Fran McManus and Wendy Rickard, editors
Eating Fresh Publications
Hopwell, NJ, 2000
Recipes based on seasonably available foods that are sold in the Bay Area by small farmers give home gardeners plenty of ideas for using home-grown produce in delicious seasonal meals.

Edible Flowers from Garden to Palate
Cathy Wilkinson Barash
Fulcrum Publishing
Golden, CO, 1995
Recipes that use flowers. Includes color photos of the food and of the flowers in the garden as well as tips for growing each kind of flower.

The Essential Reference: Vegetables from Amaranth to Zucchini
Elizabeth Schneider
HarperCollins (William Morrow)
New York, NY, 2001
On just about every page of this thick book you will find an inspiring new way to prepare a familiar or less common crop. There are 500 recipes, and additional descriptions of ways foods are used in many cultures. Between the A and Z are such crops as chayote, fenugreek greens, and various wild greens.

Flowers in the Kitchen: A Bouquet of Tasty Recipes
Susan Belsinger
Interweave Press
Loveland, CO, 1993
Recipes; large, inspiring photos of finished dishes; an edible flower garden plan; and a chart listing 50 kinds of edible flowers.

Fresh from the Garden: Cooking and Gardening Through the Seasons
Perla Meyers
Clarkson N. Potter, Inc
New York, NY, 1996
Lively, delicious recipes arranged by crop. They are excellent gardener's choices, mostly from European Mediterranean cuisines.

From the Earth: Chinese Vegetarian Cooking
Eileen Yin-Fei Lo
MacMillan Publishing Co
New York, NY, 1995
The author includes traditional recipes learned in her grandmother's

kitchen in China as well as fresh personal creations. Included are a glossary of ingredients and explanations of basic techniques and tools.

Kwanzaa: An African-American Celebration of Culture and Cooking
Eric V. Copage
William Morrow and Company, Inc.
New York, NY, 1991
Here you will find both traditional and updated recipes from Africa and the African diaspora in America, along with African-American history and information on celebrating Kwanzaa.

Lorna Sass' Complete Vegetarian Kitchen: Where Good Flavors and Good Health Meet
Lorna Sass
Harper Collins Publishers
New York, NY, 2002
One of the best vegan recipe writers around. Her dishes are creative and taste good.

Mediterranean Grains and Greens: A Book of Savory, Sun-Drenched Recipes
Paula Wolfort
HarperCollins Publishers
New York, NY, 1998
Recipes from all around the Mediterranean, from Spain to Turkey to Egypt and back around to Morocco. This book is valuable for its documentation of the use of greens, including wild greens, in these cuisines. You will find inspiration and revelations.

Potager: Fresh Garden Cooking in the French Style
Georgeanne Brennen
Chronicle Books
San Francisco, CA, 2000
Recipes for fresh garden vegetables and photos of gardens in the French potager style.

Recipes from a Kitchen Garden and More Recipes from a Kitchen Garden
Renee Shepherd
Shepherd's Garden Publishers
7389 West Zayante Road, Felton, CA 95018
Two collections of garden-based recipes that were developed to appear in a seed catalog. The second book has more recipes using herbs and chilies.

Rosalind Creasy's Recipes from the Garden
Rosalind Creasy
Tuttle Publishing
North Clarendon, VT, 2008
Two hundred exciting garden-inspired recipes from the author of *Edible Landscaping*.

Silk Road Cooking: A Vegetarian Journey
Najmieh Bathmanglij
Image Publishers
Washington, D.C., 2004
A lavishly illustrated book that takes you from the Mediterranean Basin to China, with recipes that feature regional ingredients and show the influences of exchanges along the ancient trade route.

The Victory Garden Cookbook
Marian Morash
Knopf
New York, NY, 1982
Lots of recipes for all kinds of garden produce. Includes information on translating pounds into cup measurements, ways to store and preserve, and many simple ideas for using up crops that you have grown.

The Yogi Cookbook §
Yogi Vithaldas and Susan Roberts
Pyramid Communications, Inc.
New York, NY, 1968
A small, charming introduction to Indian vegetarian cooking, including curries, pilao rice, Indian breads, raitas, and chutneys.

GARDENING MAGAZINES

Fine Gardening
The Taunton Press, Inc.
63 South Main St., PO Box 5506
Newtown, CT 06470-5506
Phone: (203) 426-8171
Fax: (203) 426-3434
www.finegardening.com
Taunton used to also publish *Kitchen Garden*, which has folded. They still maintain the website www.vegetablegarden.com, which contains some articles from that magazine and some new ones. *Fine Gardening*, which is primarily about ornamental gardening, publishes six times a year.

HortIdeas
750 Black Lick Road
Gravel Switch, KY 40328
users.microtek.com/~gwill/hi-index.htm
Bimonthly summaries of horticultural research and news. Reports new ideas, new products, new plants, and includes book reviews. Sample articles appear on their website.

Organic Gardening Magazine
33 East Minor
Emmaus, PA 18098
www.organicgardening.com
The oldest magazine for food gardeners, and still a good one. Twelve issues a year.

Pacific Horticulture
P.O. Box 680
Berkeley, CA 94701
Phone: (510) 849-1627
Fax: (510) 883-1181
www.pacifichorticulture.com
A nonprofit magazine for West Coast gardeners. Chronicles plants, gardens, and techniques for the region. Has an excellent series on beneficial insects. Four issues a year.

Sunset: The Magazine of Western Living
80 Willow Road
Menlo Park, CA 94025
www.sunset.com/magazine
Though the total pages devoted to gardening are few, the information is local (there are regional editions) and is very good. Twelve issues a year.

Index

Page numbers in **bold** refer to main Compendium entries.

D

E

F

Q

R